BUSINESS BASIC

FOR THE

IBM PC®

·WITH CASES·

THE TIMES MIRROR/MOSBY
DATA PROCESSING AND INFORMATION SYSTEMS SERIES

BUSINESS BASIC

FOR THE

IBM PC®

·WITH CASES·

Eli B. Cohen
Jeff Alger
Elizabeth C. Boyd

TIMES MIRROR/MOSBY COLLEGE PUBLISHING

ST. LOUIS   TORONTO   SANTA CLARA
1987

Dedication

To the future generation: Ben, Chuck, Kathy, Nicholas, Rob and Sarah.

Editor	Susan A. Solomon
Developmental Editor	Rebecca A. Reece
Editorial Assistant	Pamela Lanam
Text Designer	Paula Schlosser
Cover Designer	Nancy Benedict
Production Coordinator	Hal Lockwood, Bookman Productions
Illustrator	Reese Thornton

FIRST EDITION

Copyright © 1987 by Times Mirror/Mosby College Publishing
A division of The C.V. Mosby Company
11830 Westline Industrial Drive, St. Louis, MO 63146

Library of Congress Cataloging-in-Publication Data

Cohen, Eli,
  Business BASIC for the IBM PC with cases.

  Includes index.
  1. BASIC (Computer program language) 2. IBM
Personal Computer. 3. Business—Data processing.
I. Alger, Jeff. II. Boyd, Elizabeth. III. Title.
HF5548.5.B3C64 1987   005.2'165   86–23100
ISBN 0-8016-1244-6

PR/VH/VH   9 8 7 6 5 4 3 2 1   02/B/217

Brief Contents

PART I
FUNDAMENTALS OF BASIC 1

PART II
MORE ABOUT BASIC 251

PART III
SOLVING BUSINESS PROBLEMS WITH BASIC 521

CONTENTS FOR PARABLES FOR PROGRAMMERS

This feature encapsulates programming wisdom that students so often discover only accidentally through discouraging hard work.

CONTENTS

Each chapter concludes with "The Story's End"—the complete solution to the opening business scenario—and Chapter Exercises.

PART I

FUNDAMENTALS OF BASIC 1

CHAPTER **2** · **YOUR FIRST BASIC PROGRAM** 45

CHAPTER **3** · **INTRODUCTION TO STRUCTURED PROGRAMMING: PLANNING AND DESIGN** 78

PART II

MORE ABOUT BASIC 251

CHAPTER 7 · SEQUENTIAL FILES 253

CHAPTER **8** · **STORING LISTS IN ARRAYS**   298

PART III

SOLVING BUSINESS PROBLEMS WITH BASIC 521

Each case includes Problem Specification, Functions to be Performed, Structure Charts, Data Dictionary, Pseudocode, Program Listing, Program Output, and Exercises.

PREFACE

THE INTENDED AUDIENCE

We wrote *Business BASIC for the IBM PC with Cases* for computer courses that teach BASIC or include a component of BASIC. The flexible organization makes this text ideal for short as well as in-depth courses in BASIC and structured programming. No prior knowledge of business, computers, or programming is required. The book can be used for any introductory course in BASIC in either the DPMA, ACM, or independent computer science or computer information systems curriculum.

OUR PURPOSE

We wrote this book because we could not find a suitable BASIC text for the course we teach. In our opinion, all available texts suffer from one or more of the following problems.

Failure to Teach Good Programming Practice

- They do not reinforce structured programming concepts. Most texts show students only program segments, not whole programs. But the ideas of structured programming are more relevant for large programs than for

xvii

program fragments. As a result, students leave their BASIC class with the impression that structured methods are a waste of time.

▪ They miss an opportunity to teach problem-solving skills. Programming requires logical thinking and exactitude, skills that students need in their future jobs.

▪ They teach syntax without teaching grammar, that is, they teach how to construct BASIC statements without teaching how statements fit together to express a thought. This makes programming appear to be "magical." The students learn BASIC without learning to program.

No Orientation to Business

▪ Programming is taught without a sense of purpose. Students ask, and rightfully so, "What does this have to do with my major?" Such texts conceal the central role programming plays in business environments. A good text will show students how important the information systems department is to the welfare of the firm.

▪ They miss the opportunity to reinforce other business courses. Increasingly, instructors are called upon to integrate into their courses the skills and knowledge taught in the business school as a whole. Students can apply general business knowledge when writing BASIC programs to solve other business problems.

Not Specific to the IBM PC

▪ The instructor must take precious class time to cover keyboard placement, booting the computer, screen editing, and so on.

▪ These texts, therefore, do not teach file handling, since different versions of BASIC use different syntax. Students come away from the text thinking that file handling is not important or is too complex.

▪ These texts often use single-letter variable names, thereby undermining the importance of using descriptive variable names.

▪ Important IBM PC BASIC enhancements such as SWAP, LINE, and BEEP are omitted.

Unreadable Style

▪ Texts that appeal to instructors are rejected by students because they are too technical and have too few real-life examples to reinforce content. As a result, students are left feeling that BASIC is too obscure or too difficult for them to understand.

▪ These texts waste the instructor's time, since he or she must explain the text rather than supplement it.

Programming Errors

▪ Students try out the examples and are chagrined to discover that the examples—as printed—are faulty. Sometimes the problem is merely a typographical error. Often, however, the error is a more fundamental problem, indicating that the program probably was not tested properly.

REASONS TO CONSIDER THIS BOOK

Our text teaches students sound programming practice. We teach good style as well as syntax. Our comprehensive coverage includes structured program development, structured testing, debugging, data dictionary creation and maintenance, and documentation. Flowcharts are used as documentation and teaching tools. Programs are developed using pseudocode, data dictionaries, and structure charts. Moreover, we give students "the whole picture" by showing complete programs, not fragments, and thereby pedagogically reinforce the value of structured programming.

Our text is business oriented. Through the use of easy-to-understand, realistic business scenarios, we reinforce how BASIC programming is used in practice.

Our text is written expressly for use with IBM PC compatible computers. We begin by discussing the IBM PC disk operating system and physical layout, including the keyboard. Throughout the text we address all important features specific to IBM PC BASIC, such as on-screen editing and file handling.

Our book is student friendly. We understand that students may be intimidated by computers. That's why we geared our presentation to motivate all students in the course—those who have to "unlearn" bad programming habits learned in high school, those who are business majors but have a limited knowledge of business, and those who haven't yet declared a computer science or MIS major. Our writing style, business scenarios, and other pedagogical features discussed below are further evidence of our efforts to reach a wide student audience.

Our book provides unparalleled flexibility in teaching BASIC. Part I covers BASIC fundamentals, Part II contains more advanced BASIC coverage, and Part III features six cases that present common business problems. Instructors can select the chapters and cases that best suit their needs.

Our book and its programs have been thoroughly tested. We have tried to ensure an error-free book by class testing our manuscript and testing each program. Furthermore, several publishing professionals have individually proofread the manuscript.

Our text has a wealth of effective teaching and learning aids:

1. *Business scenarios, chapter lessons, and Story's End.* Each chapter opens with a "business scenario" in which a character encounters a business problem. The solution requires more knowledge of BASIC than

the student currently possesses. The "chapter lesson" takes the student step by step through the problem-solving process. Then "The Story's End" contains the *complete* solution to the business scenario. By seeing how to solve these problems, students learn programming and also to appreciate more the important role data processing plays in business.

2. *Parables for programmers.* Each chapter contains a parable. These encapsulate some of the wisdom so often learned only in the school of hard knocks.

3. *Key boxes.* Boxes with a "key" logo highlight important concepts and contain key commands and statements.

4. *Quick reference section.* Summaries of BASIC syntax covered in the chapter lesson occur in these sections at the end of each chapter. These can also serve as a reference manual for BASIC after the completion of the course.

5. *Boldface terms and commands.* All terms are boldfaced on first mention, and BASIC reserved words are in caps throughout, providing a useful student review and study aid.

6. *End-of-chapter exercises.* Each chapter ends with a series of exercises that are graded in level of difficulty. The student progresses from giving short answers to questions to analyzing code and, finally, to creating statements and programs.

How to Use This Book

For a Brief Introduction to BASIC

This text is ideal for introductory classes that teach BASIC as but one component of the course. Instructors should assign Part I, which covers the fundamentals of BASIC and programming. Chapters from Part II can be assigned as desired, along with the first or second case. Students can skim the rest of the text to get a feel for the complete capabilities of BASIC.

For an In-Depth Study of BASIC

The depth of coverage in this text makes it ideal for a thorough BASIC course. Instructors can assign all of Part I and as much of Parts II and III as they desire.

Additional Options

BASIC programming is often taught in combination with fundamental computer concepts and/or microcomputer applications. Thus this text may be used with:

- A computer concepts text
- A microcomputer applications text

Times Mirror/Mosby's four offerings in these areas are Floyd, *Essentials of Data Processing* (1987); Dravillas-Stilwell-Williams, *Power Pack for the IBM PC* (1986); Spence-Windsor, *Microcomputers in Business: WordStar, dBASE II and III, and Lotus*

1-2-3 (1987); and Spence-Windsor, *Using Microcomputers: Applications for Business* (1987).

SUPPLEMENTS

Instructor's Guide

The Instructor's Guide is designed to be an effective teaching resource; it contains:

- An overview of the text
- Suggestions for pacing and chapter selection for a variety of teaching situations
- Ideas for presentation of cases
- Answers to end-of-chapter exercises
- 40 transparency masters
- An additional case for more advanced students
- Cauzin SoftStrips® for all programs

Data Diskette

A diskette with all programs and selected examples is available at no charge to all instructors who adopt our text. They may duplicate this diskette so that students who use our text can work with the programs without manually keying them in.

ACKNOWLEDGMENTS

We wish to thank the many individuals who contributed to our work as reviewers and market research respondents:

Reviewers

Dave Allen
San Antonio College

Bonnie Bailey
Morehead State University

Lonnie Bentley
Purdue University

Jim Blaisdell
Humboldt State University

Marilyn Bohl
IBM

Barry Brosch
Miami-Dade Community College

James Cox
Lane Community College

Steve Deam
Milwaukee Area Technical College

Daria Harry
Miami University-Ohio

C. Brian Honess
University of South Carolina

Peter Irwin
Richland College

Margaret Jones
Longview Community College

Riki Kuchek
Orange Coast Community College

Jack McLaughlin
Catonsville Community College

Micki Miller
Skyline College

Rick Stearns
Parkland College

Kathleen Priem
Cuyahoga Community College

James Teng
University of Pittsburgh

John Rooney
Hartwick College

Glenn Thomas
Kent State University

Gerald Saunders
Virginia Commonwealth University

Market Research Respondents

Alabama: Bill Allman, David Feinstein, Muhammad Ghanbari, Joyce Vann. **Arizona:** Robert Autrey, Burton Bartram, Michael Blicharz, Chuy Carreor, C.D. Carruth, M. Frieband, Lyle Langlois, Barbara Miller, Sharon McFall. **Arkansas:** Don Roberts, Gene Weber, Gloria Wigley. **California:** Amberse Banks, Hossein Bidgoli, D.L. Blakley, Beverly Blaylock, Charles Bonini, Gary Brown, James Buchan, Barbara Buhr, Michael Capsuto, A. Carlan, Allan Cruse, Rosemary Damon, Glenn Davidson, Roger Debelak, Robert Dependahl, Paul Dilger, Paul Duchow, Annalee Elman, Arthur Engbritson, George Evinger, C.E. Falbo, Abi Fattahi, M. Fraser, Vivian Frederick, Gunther Freehill, S. Ganeshalingam, John Gelles, Wayne Gibson, Ken Gorham, Thomas Green, Walter Harcos, David Harris, Norman Helsel, Norman Jacobson, Henry James, Gene Kennon, James Kho, Steven Lawlor, Anita Millspaugh, James Montalbano, M.J. Montiel, Aminai Motro, Thomas McCullough, Wesley Nance, Jeff Nash, Robert Norton, Allan Orler, Barbara Pence, Gordon Peterson, Joe Scherrei, James Southern, James Stanton, Tom Tuttle, John Van Zandt, Robert Verkler, G.A. Waggoner, Clark Williams. **Colorado:** Kerry Bailey, Boyd Baldauf, Gregory Bell, John Brown, J. Cole, Steven Janke, Thomas Laase, Linda Lujan, Michael Milligan, Thomas Mourey, C.N. Podraza, Harris Robnett, Lee Shannon, Robert Tolar. **Connecticut:** Art Adolfson, Frank Grella, Sharon Huxley, L. Van der Haplen. **Delaware:** Arthur Bragg, James Klingerman, Lizzie Waller-Townsend. **District of Columbia:** J.H. Carson, Basil Jackson. **Florida:** Robert Cameron, Franklin Chinn, Marilyn Correa, Wanda Heller, David Huey, Darlene Long, Gene Medlin, Wendell Motter, Jack Munyan, L.R. Penegor, M. Repsher, Wiley Russell, Mae Smith, T.J. Surynt, Michael Weston. **Georgia:** Paul Caylor, P.S. Chiang, Edward Domaleski, George Evans, J.W. Inman, R. Jensen, Merle King, M. Lewin. **Hawaii:** Emilio Alcon. **Idaho:** Shelby Freeman, Fred Humphrey, Milan Kaldenberg, Kay Nelson, E.A. Richardson. **Illinois:** Kerry Adams, Robert Aker, James Anderson, Carol Asplund, Reginald Bishop, Jim Burkhart, Sam Carter, James Corcoran, Dennis Dudek, Raymond Einig, Wayne Gallenberger, Mordechai Goodman, James Gron, Barbara Harris, Donald Harris, J.M. Hynes, Sue Isermann, R.L. Johnson, Christine Kay, Stephen Mansfield, Judd Miller, James Moore, Herbert Morris, Arthur Moser, V. Nahgasser, Gary Phillips, Bonnie Simmons, Bruce Sisko, Eugene Wagner. **Indiana:** Hyun Ahn, James Caristi, Robert Miller, James Moore, J.B.

Orris, D.L. Stroup, George Tschumakow. **Iowa:** Brian Buhrman, Kerry Frampton, Dale Grosnevor, Doug Meyers, Sheila McCartney, Hollis O'Hare, Yon-Bong Wan-Yoon. **Kansas:** Jeffrey Barnett, Larry Blamberg, L. Jay Brinkmeyer, Constanza Castro, Laurence Friedman, Katharine Goombi, J.R. Lossing, Mary Ann Miklich, Dale Miller, Kae Phillips, Lawrence Sanders. **Kentucky:** Bonnie Bailey, Philip Brashear, Richard DiSilvestro, Elizabeth Galloway, Richard Gray, William Rafaill. **Louisiana:** Billy Bagwell, James Calloway, Anand Katiyar, James Hu, Margaret Killen, L.E. Scheuermann. **Maine:** James Westfall. **Maryland:** Don Cathcart, Bernadine Esposito, Penny Fanzone, R. Sabin, Preston Shellenberger, Terry Snider, George Waggoner. **Massachusetts:** P.J. Amaria, Howard Aucoin, Gerry Bates, Russell Birchall, Tony Castro, Charles Glassbenner, John Gorgone, Laurie Kovijanic, Robert Kowalczyk, Normand Lavigne, Brenda Miccio, M. Noonan, Alex Prengel, Thomas Rourke, C.E. Sandifur, Robert Schilling. **Michigan:** Joyce Abler, Dennis Benincasa, Janis Bitely, Ron Boelema, Dwayne Channell, Bill Courter, Herbert Dershem, Harry Edwards, Charles Finkbeiner, T. Greff, Nancy Hansen, Greg Hodge, Ron Jacobson, Eugene Kozminski, Fred Lovgren, Richard Matson, Lawrence McNitt, Charles Meiser, J. Smith, Homa Tinadall, Tim Trainor, Kenneth Wright. **Minnesota:** Robert Bateson, Kenneth Becker, Lowell Fitzgerald, B. Folz, Patrick Holmay, George Mitchell, Suzanne Molnar, Gerald Rowell, Joseph Van Wie. **Mississippi:** Billy Denton, Thomas Goeller, John Jamison, Patricia Mapp, Joe Sallis, Jonathan Turner. **Missouri:** William Boothby, Margaret Heard, Carrie Johnson, Peggy Jones, Susumu Kasai, Markita Price. **Montana:** Jack Goebel. **Nebraska:** Cecilia Daly, J. Max Hoffmann, Jack Imdieke, Donna Kizzier, Tom White, James Wright. **New Hampshire:** Paul Kenison, Robert Mitchell, Martha Villenueve. **New Jersey:** Roanne Angiello, Fred Cleveland, Joseph Colasante, James Cosmos, Charles Drocea, Irvin Feldman, Lewis Hofmann, Jean Lane, Professor Leung, Margaret Westhead. **New Mexico:** James Nelson. **New York:** W. James Abbott, John Baldwin, Bruce Bosworth, Larry Clark, R. Coen, Dallas DeFee, Donald Fama, Robert Frascatore, G. Gordon, Gireesh Gupta, Richard Hubbard, Winston Hyman, Kimyong Kim, John Klein, Arnold Kleinstein, Stephen Klotz, Carl Kohls, William Link, A. Lytton, Elizabeth McMahon, Bill Mein, Ganesh Nankoo, John Rooney, Erik Rosenthal, Angelo Scordato, H. Laverne Thomas, Roger Tiede, A. Vasilopoulos. **North Carolina:** Wilna Ates, Sarah Britt, Yvonne Brown, Aubrey Calton, Leo Edwards, Nancy Floyd, Pamela Gobel, Earl Hassett, William Johnson, R. Johnston, Hattie Jones, Benjamin Klein, H. Ledbetter, R.W. McClellan, Steven Miller, James Parks, Robert Ralph, Maxine Romney, Robert Tesch, Michael Tucker, Hugh Walker, Don Williams. **North Dakota:** John Deering, Curtis Lechner, David Melgaard, Mike Schiwal, Donald Varvel. **Ohio:** John Berton, Richard Brown, James Case, John Chappelear, Barbara Denison, Bob Dressel, Raghava Gowda, Benjamin Heard, Anthony Malone, Don Mittleman, Judy Murray, D.M. Pudloski, Kendall Rogers, Leo Schneider, W.R. Smith, Leonard Sweet, Jim Swingle, Ronald Walker. **Oklahoma:** P.C. Almes, Gayle Austin, Vernon Cline, C.M. Flynn, Robert Lanctot, Gene Laughrey, Dennis Middlemist, Steve St. John, Delana Worrell. **Oregon:** Fran Beisse, Dale Bryson, George Chou, Margaret Chou, James Cox, Samuel Ellis,

George Farrimond, David Gillette, Robert McCoy, E. Gladys Norman, Don Phillips, J. Van Curk. **Pennsylvania:** John Beyer, Donald Caputo, William Charlton, Samuel Davis, J.R. Haudt, Ralph Hoffman, Nancy Houston, Harvey Koch, John Koch, Kenneth Krauss, Irvin Lichtenstein, Charles Loch, David Lott, K.A. Nair, J.M. Peck, D. Platte, Mary Rasley, Gustav Stangline, Susan Traynor, Edward Troyan, June Trudnak, Michael Woltermann. **Rhode Island:** Anthony Basilico, Paul Dane, Louise Perl. **South Carolina:** Albert Atkins, Thomas Brewer, Alan Broyles, Nancy Goettel, Greg Huseth, Alice Markwalder, Stanley Ricketts. **South Dakota:** David Ballew, Robert Broschat, John Roberts, Miles Smart. **Tennessee:** Bill Austin, Leonard Bailey, Mark Ciampa, B.C. Dam, Dana Harville, Don Irwin, Gary Pickett. **Texas:** Cherry Baker, Rayford Ball, Albert Barnes, Josephine Brunner, Joseph Dean, Richard Diller, George Dubay, Craig Elders, Bill Glover, M.T. Harkrider, Jim Ingram, George Katz, James King, Barry Kunkle, D.P. Maddox, Alvin McGaugh, Roy McKenzie, Don Mershawn, Edward Pfister, Larry Pickens, Herbert Rebhun, R.M. Richards, Greg Taylor, Steven Thoede. **Utah:** Russell Anderson, Thomas Doyle, David Hanscow, Val Stauffer, A.M. Thomas. **Vermont:** William Anderson, Michael Bethel, Bernard Byrne, Paul Novak. **Virginia:** Charles Bamford, Raymond Brogan, Ben Burrell, Barbara Comfort, Larry Davis, Nancy Hammersky, Gary Jessee, Willard Keeling, Steve Lemery, John Schwalje. **Washington:** James Brink, Ron Burke, Kent Burnham, Alan Hale, Alan Howard, David Murphy, Carole Peterson, James Richardson, Douglas Underwood, E.J. Wells. **West Virginia:** Lloyd Cowling, Theodore Erickson, William Grimsley, **Wisconsin:** Paul Almquist, Pierre Bettelli, John Cage, John Castek, T.P. Comer, Robert Dahlin, Robert Germer, James Haine, Michael Hall, Dennis Hill, G.K. Hutchinson, Gary Klott, Kent Magnuson, Eugene Maurer, Richard Nagle, Ronald Osantowski, Roger Pick, Pete Ramberg, C. Regner, Charles Rhyner, John Roush, Susan Shepanek. **Wyoming:** E.R. Bailey, Claude Dotson. **Puerto Rico:** J.F. Colon.

The work of Donna Goldberg and our students, Tracy Mears, David Truzinski, and Vicki Zuppan, in helping to develop this text demand special note. We further wish to thank particularly Susan Solomon, acquisitions editor; Rebecca Reece, developmental editor; Pam Lanam, editorial assistant; Hal Lockwood, production editor; Reese Thornton, artist; Jonas Weisel, copy editor; and James Donohue, marketing manager. We also gratefully acknowledge the work and patience of our spouses — which too often goes unacknowledged.

Eli B. Cohen
Jeff Alger
Elizabeth C. Boyd

BUSINESS BASIC

FOR THE

IBM PC®

·WITH CASES·

FUNDAMENTALS OF BASIC

INTRODUCTION TO PART I

THE TEXT IS divided into three parts. In this first part you will learn the fundamentals of BASIC and structured programming. It is written for readers with no prior knowledge of the IBM PC or programming. With this in mind we've taken a special effort to make this part not only clear but interesting. We've tried to weave for you the fabric of business programming from threads of IBM PC specifics, the BASIC language, structured programming philosophies, and business applications.

Chapter 1 introduces the features of the IBM PC, reviews the keyboard, and begins to present some of the vocabulary of BASIC. In Chapter 2 we explain what a program is and we look at several simple commands. Chapter 3 describes how to plan programs that do what you want them to do.

Since programs are not "written in stone," Chapter 4 explores the methods and tools for editing. In Chapter 5 we see how the processes of selection and repetition can be built into programs. Finally, Chapter 6 describes how to create modules.

GETTING STARTED WITH YOUR IBM PC AND BASIC

MEET THE IBM PERSONAL COMPUTER

Sandy knew something was up the moment The Boss walked in. This was not the usual Friday afternoon grin; the last time The Boss looked so smug was minutes after pulling into the parking lot with a new Porsche.

This afternoon the beaming face shone fully on Sandy. Instinct alone foretold that Sandy's job was about to be permanently changed—for better or worse there was no way of telling.

"Come out to the car and give me a hand," The Boss's voice jovially boomed. "Help me carry in XYZ Records' newest asset. Sandy, I bought it with you in mind."

"Uh-oh, here it comes," thought Sandy, spying boxes piled in the back of the car. The Boss was known for impulse buying. A month ago it was a third coffee machine ("we can always use another one, can't we?"). Before that a ceiling fan, several old mechanical calculators ("a great buy!"), a huge wall clock that chimed "When Irish Eyes Are Smiling" every hour . . . what now?

With relief Sandy spotted the familiar IBM logo and realized what the boxes contained—a new IBM Personal Computer! The Boss started lifting boxes out of the car and piling them into Sandy's outstretched arms, talking all the while. "Sandy, you've finally convinced me: it's high time XYZ Records entered the

3

twentieth century. All other record chains in town already have computers, why not us? Besides, you're perfectly right when you say we've been growing too fast to keep up with the paperwork by hand."

Arms full, Sandy tried hard to suppress an "I told you so." Ever since joining XYZ after college, Sandy had waged a one-person campaign to see the business automated. There was too much duplication in the paperwork done by hand, and many things simply didn't get done in time. "The Boss sure is stubborn," thought Sandy while struggling up the steps, "but maybe not so unreasonable after all."

"What changed your mind?" Sandy asked.

"You did," answered The Boss, wiping off a light sweat. "I may be stubborn, but I'm not unreasonable." Feeling a twinge of guilt, Sandy quickly looked away. "I've been giving a lot of thought to your suggestions that we get a computer," continued The Boss, "and it seems to me that the time is right. We've been growing 30 percent annually for three years. I can either add more staff or spend some money on a computer. Well, having added people before I'm not anxious to do it again unless I have to. Besides," said The Boss, pausing to stare straight at Sandy, "I now have someone on my staff who believes in this stuff. As far as I'm concerned, Sandy, this is your project. Learn to use this computer and you'll be moving up fast."

It took a moment for this to sink in, then Sandy felt a surge of pride and, at the same time, fear. After all, Sandy knew little about how to actually program and use computers. A little fast learning was clearly in order.

"Take your time to get used to it, Sandy," The Boss said, climbing into the Porsche. "Let me know when you're ready to put the computer to use. The computer store is tossing in a few hours of instruction; I told them you'd be in tomorrow." With that, The Boss drove into the weekend sunset, leaving Sandy plotting how to put the IBM PC to quick use.

This is *not* the way to acquire a business computer system!

Introduction to the IBM PC

Early Saturday morning Sandy walked into the nearby computer store where The Boss had purchased the computer. Explaining the situation, Sandy quickly enlisted the aid of a trainer in learning the basics of using an IBM PC. The trainer outlined the three topics they would cover:

1. The components of the computer (the **hardware**)
2. The **disk operating system (DOS),** a collection of programs that controls many of the details of communication between the hardware components
3. **BASIC,** the programming language that Sandy will be using to write programs for the computer

The trainer then pointed to a huge drawing on the wall (see Figure 1.1) above the sign:

COMPUTER = KEYBOARD + MONITOR + SYSTEM UNIT (+ PRINTER)

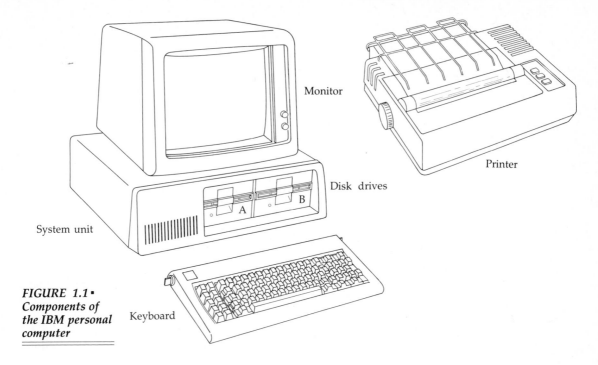

Monitor

Printer

Disk drives

System unit

FIGURE 1.1 •
Components of
the IBM personal
computer

Keyboard

"The basic IBM PC consists of three boxes," the trainer explained. "If you think about what a computer does, which is to manage data, there are three steps involved: putting data into the computer, letting the computer do something with the data, then getting data back out. These functions are frequently called input, process, and output, respectively. The three boxes correspond to these functions."

Keyboard Is for Data Entry
"The bottom box in the diagram is the keyboard," the trainer continued. "This is your primary means of putting data into the computer, or **input.** You will notice that it is very similar to a standard typewriter keyboard, but it has some extra keys. We'll talk more about the keyboard in a minute."

Monitor Displays Data
"The top box is called the monitor. It's the one with the televisionlike display. This display is the PC's primary way of showing you data, or **output.**"

System Unit (Processor) Is the Brains and Short-Term Memory
"The middle box is the system unit. This is where the processing of data takes place. It is also where data are stored. The 'brain' of the computer is on circuit cards housed in this box. (A circuit card is a flat, rigid board that holds the

computer's electronic circuitry.) These circuit cards control the operation of the components."

Magnetic Disk Drives Store Data Long Term

"The system unit also contains the disk drives, if the system has any. Most IBM PCs use magnetic disks to store data permanently. Magnetic disks have a surface that is analogous to the surface of magnetic recording tapes, like those you use to record music, and a shape that resembles the shape of a phonograph record. Like a tape, the disk allows data to be both recorded and played back — called writing and reading, respectively — but like a phonograph record, the disk doesn't have to be wound through in order to get to data in the middle. The computer's equivalent to the phonograph needle, the **read/write** head, can position itself directly over any part of the disk."

Printer Prints Data onto Paper

"There are many times when a monitor is not the best way to output data," explained the trainer. "The display on a monitor is temporary; if a permanent copy of output is needed, a printer is often used."

Sandy interrupted, "Is a printer just a typewriter that can obey a computer?"

"That's a good analogy," replied the trainer. "However, there are some differences. For one thing, most printers, including the standard printer for the IBM PC, do not have a keyboard. They cannot do anything without explicit instructions from a computer."

"Do you have to have a printer in order to use an IBM PC?" asked Sandy.

"No, you can do everything without a printer that you can do with one, except create printed copies of output. By the way, because printed output is permanent and monitor displays temporary, it is common to call printed output **hardcopy** and monitor output **softcopy.** My advice to you is to learn a little about the PC before you start using the printer. Let's talk more about disks."

Using Floppy Disks to Store Long-Term Data

"Are those the disk drives in front?" asked Sandy, pointing to the two slotted black panels on the front of the system unit.

"Yes, they are," the trainer replied. "This particular kind of magnetic disk is called a **floppy disk** because it is flexible. They are sometimes called diskettes, or just disks." The trainer steered Sandy away from the diagram and over to a real PC, then picked up a floppy disk (see Figure 1.2).

Floppy Disks Fit in the Disk Drives

"Floppy disks are flexible, round disks housed in square jackets made of a cardboardlike material. You put the floppy disks into the slots of the **disk drives.** Disk drives are to floppy disks as a record player is to records. This particular PC has two disk drives. The one on the left is called drive A and the one on the right is

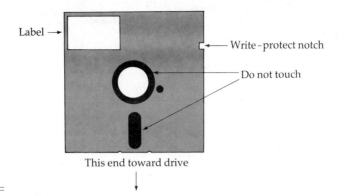

Label →

Write-protect notch

Do not touch

FIGURE 1.2 •
The floppy disk

This end toward drive

called drive B, as you can see on the drawing (see Figure 1.1). You can also order a PC with only one floppy disk drive, or with none at all."

"Hmm, I'm quite sure our PC also has two disk drives. How do I go about putting a floppy disk in the drive?" asked Sandy.

Floppy Disks Need Special Handling

"Before you handle your floppy disks you need to know something about how to care for them. They should not be exposed to extreme temperatures (most manufacturers recommend the range of 50 to 125 degrees Fahrenheit). When not in the machine, they should be kept in their protective sleeve and away from cigarette or other smoke and from any magnetic fields. You will see there is an oval opening about a centimeter wide in the jacket. This is the one place where the surface of the disk is exposed and you must be careful not to touch it or let it come in contact with anything that might scratch it. Get into the habit of always putting the disk into the sleeve with the opening protected as soon as you remove the disk from the drive. It is also a good idea to have some sort of case or box in which to store the diskettes."

There Is Only One Right Way to Insert a Disk in a Drive

"First you must line up the disk properly (see Figure 1.3). Take a careful look at the disk. The oval opening must be pointing toward the back of the system unit when the disk is put into the drive. Also, the label on the disk should be facing up, not down, and the notch cut out of the edge should be on your left as you face the drive."

"What happens if I don't orient the disk properly?"

"Hopefully, it just won't work. You won't hurt the disk drive, but you may accidentally touch the exposed portion of the disk and destroy the data that are written there."

"Once you have the disk oriented the way I have it now, with the oval openings pointing toward the drive and the label on top, the next step is to insert it into the slot in the drive. You will notice that there is a latch that, when closed, covers

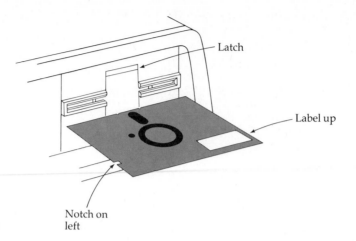

FIGURE 1.3 •
Inserting a floppy disk into a disk drive. Position the disk as shown, being careful not to touch the shiny parts, then push into the drive gently until you feel a click. Then flip the latch closed (down).

Latch

Label up

Notch on left

the middle of the slot. This latch must be open to insert or remove a floppy disk. If the one on your computer is closed, flip it open by pulling gently on the unattached edge.

"When the latch is open, carefully push the disk into the slot until you feel it catch against the back of the drive. You don't need to push very hard, but make sure you feel it click. When the disk is in place, flip the latch closed and you're ready to go. To remove the disk, simply flip the latch open, then pull out the disk."

"That seems pretty straightforward," Sandy contentedly observed, "but what is the notch on the edge of the disk for?"

Write-Protect Notch Prevents Erasure

"That notch is called the write-protect notch. When the notch is covered by the write-protect paper tab, the disk drive will not alter any data on the disk. This prevents valuable data from being accidentally changed or erased. The adhesive tabs that cover write-protect notches come with each box of floppy disks."

Hard Disks Store More Data

So far, so good, thought Sandy. "One final question about disks. Are floppy disks the only kind of disks available on the PC?"

"No, there is a second kind of disk called a **hard** or **Winchester disk.** These are more expensive than floppy disks, but they are faster and hold many times more data than floppy disks. Hard disk drives have the disk itself permanently sealed inside; the disks cannot be removed, except by service personnel.

"The model of the IBM Personal Computer that has a hard disk drive is called the IBM Personal Computer XT. It functions almost identically to a PC with floppy disks, so almost everything you learn about programming a PC with floppy disks will apply to the standard PC XT as well. Typically there is only one floppy disk on the PC XT called drive A, and the hard disk is called drive C.

"The IBM AT is a third member of the IBM PC family. Its disk drives (both floppy and hard) have higher capacities than the XT. It also operates faster."

Each Keyboard Key Has Its Own Function

"OK, I understand disk drives," Sandy said with rising confidence. "Now, could you explain the keyboard?"

"Sure," replied the trainer. "Take a look at this diagram (see Figure 1.4). You will notice that the keyboard is divided into three parts: function keys, typewriter keys, and the numeric keypad. Let's start with the typewriter keys.

"The unshaded keys are almost identical to the keys you would find on a typewriter. When you press the A key, the keyboard transmits a letter *a* (lowercase) to the processor, and the processor will normally cause an *a* to be printed on the monitor.

"There is an important difference between using a typewriter and using a computer keyboard. When typing, you can usually use a lowercase letter *l* ("el") to indicate the number one and the letter *O* ("Oh") to indicate a zero. To a computer, however, the digit 1 (one) and the letter *l* (el) are two different characters, as are the letter *O* (Oh) and the digit 0 (zero). One of the most common mistakes beginners make, especially those used to typewriters, is to confuse these letters and digits. If you get errors that you didn't expect, check your ones and zeros carefully."

Shift Keys

"If you want an uppercase *A*, press and hold down either of the **shift keys** as you press the A key. The shift keys are the ones on either side of the typewriter keys with fat arrows pointing up. The shift keys work pretty much the same way as the shift keys on a typewriter, although we'll talk about some exceptions in a moment."

Caps Lock Key

"As on a typewriter, there is also a **Caps Lock** key, which locks the letter keys into uppercase. The Caps Lock key is the one just beneath the right-hand shift key. Press it once and the letter keys lock into uppercase. Press it again and the letters

FIGURE 1.4 ▪
The IBM PC
keyboard

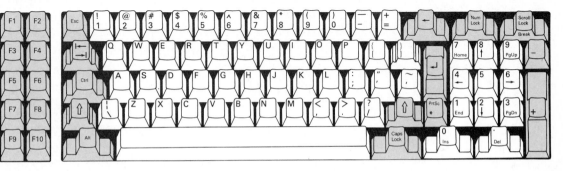

Function keys   Typewriter keyboard   Numeric keypad

return to lowercase. One of the features that often frustrates users is that you cannot tell by looking at the keyboard whether the Caps Lock key is on or off. If you do not remember whether you have turned it off or on, you type a letter and see if it displays in upper- or lowercase."

"You said only the letter keys get locked into uppercase," observed Sandy. "Does that mean the keys with nonletters are not affected by the Caps Lock key?"

"Right you are," exclaimed the trainer. "That is one of the differences between the keyboard of an IBM PC and that of a typewriter. The Caps Lock key affects only letters. The keys for numbers and special characters other than letters are not affected. To control those keys, you must still use the shift keys, regardless of whether Caps Lock is currently locked in.

"Another difference that frequently confuses people is that a typewriter with its Caps Lock (or Shift Lock) key on allows you to only get uppercase letters. On the IBM PC keyboard, when the Caps Lock key is locked into uppercase letters, you can get lowercase letters by using the shift keys! This is seldom useful, but you should be aware of it so you won't be confused should you get lowercase letters by accidentally pressing the shift key while the Caps Lock key is on.

"The best way to get used to the shift and Caps Lock keys is to practice with them."

Control and Alternate Keys

"There are two keys to the left of the space bar, immediately above and below the shift key, labeled **Ctrl** and **Alt.** They are the Control and Alternate keys, respectively. Each works like the shift key in that either key pressed by itself does nothing. It is only when you press another key at the same time that either the Control or Alternate key has any effect. For the moment, don't worry further about what the Control and Alternate keys do; you'll learn more about them later."

Tab Key

"Immediately above the Control key is a key with two horizontal arrows pointing in opposite directions. This is the **tab** key, which acts somewhat like the tab key on a typewriter. The **cursor** is a blinking underline, which shows where the next keystroke will be displayed. When you press the tab key, the cursor moves to the next tab setting on the line. In BASIC, as we will learn, the tabs are preset to every eight spaces."

Escape Key

"Above the tab key is a key labeled **Esc** for Escape. Its use depends on what program is currently running in the computer. Many computer programs use Escape as a way of canceling whatever the program is currently doing."

Enter (or Return) Key

"Moving to the right side of the typewriter keyboard, above the key labeled PrtSc, we see a key with a crooked arrow on it. This is called the **Enter** or **Return** key. It's called Return because it is much like the carriage Return key on a typewriter; when you press this key, it generally advances the cursor to the beginning of the next line. It's called Enter because it is used to signal the system unit that you have completed an entry. In general, the computer will ignore anything that you type until you hit the Enter key."

Backspace Key

"Above the Enter key is a key with a left-pointing arrow. This is the **backspace** key. When you are using BASIC, it will delete the character immediately to the left of where you are and shift the remainder of the line one place to the left, filling in the place of the deleted character."

Print Screen Key

"Next to the right-hand shift key is a key with an asterisk (*) in lowercase and **PrtSc** in uppercase. This key represents a simple asterisk in lowercase, but when you press shift and this key at the same time, the current screen display is printed out on the printer, if a printer is attached to your computer. This is useful when you wish to make a printed copy of what is shown on the monitor. However, do not try to use this key to print the screen if you don't have a printer attached to your computer. If you do, the computer may **hang up,** which is to say, it will not respond to anything."

Numeric Keypad

(See Figure 1.4.) "The numeric keypad looks somewhat like a ten-key adding machine keypad, but don't be fooled; there are some important differences. Unlike the adding machine, the meaning of the keys on the numeric keypad can be changed by use of the shift key. You will notice that there are arrows or words as well as numbers on some of the keys. These represent the 'lowercase' values of these keys and are used to move around the monitor display. To get the corresponding numbers, you must use the shift key. The Caps Lock key does not affect the keys of the numeric keypad, but there is a separate key labeled **Num Lock** at the top of the numeric keypad. Num Lock functions for the numeric keypad the way Caps Lock does for letters. If Num Lock is pressed once, all the keys will have their 'uppercase' or numeric values; if it is pressed a second time, they will return to their 'lowercase' values. Using the Num Lock key will allow you to lock the keypad into its numeric mode. Just as with the Caps Lock key, you cannot tell whether the **Num Lock** key is on or off by looking at the keyboard; you need to press one of the keys to find out."

Turning the Computer On and Off: the Power Switches

At this point Sandy was anxious to see a PC running, so the trainer leaned over to point out the power switches on the PC. "There are either one or two power switches, depending on your particular equipment," the trainer continued, "the one on the system unit and one on the monitor. The one on the system unit is

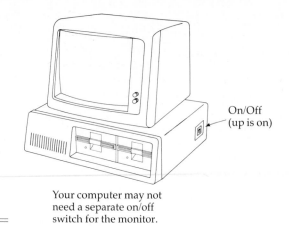

On/Off
(up is on)

FIGURE 1.5 •
Location of
power switches

Your computer may not
need a separate on/off
switch for the monitor.

bright red and is on the right side toward the back (see Figure 1.5). The down
position is off, the up position on.

"The location of the on/off switch for the monitor depends on which monitor
you have, but most are on the lower right front of the monitor case. On some
systems the monitor plugs directly into the system unit. If this is the case, you can
leave the monitor on all the time and just use the system unit switch to turn the
system on and off.

"Oh, yes, if you have a printer, it will probably have a separate on/off switch
as well. The location depends on what kind of printer you have.

"When you unpack the computer, there will be a master floppy disk called the
Operating System disk. It will probably be labeled ''PC-DOS 2.10,'' ''PC-DOS
3.0,'' or ''PC-DOS 3.10.'' PC-DOS is the name of the operating system, or control
program, for the IBM PC (DOS stands for Disk Operating System). The designa-
tions 2.10, 3.0, and 3.10 are the versions of PC-DOS. For the standard PC or XT,
any of these versions is suitable. The AT requires DOS 3.0 or above.

"To turn on the computer, first place the operating system disk in drive A (the
one on the left), turn on the monitor, then flip up the power switch on the system
unit. The computer will beep, then appear to just sit there for a few moments.
During this time the computer takes a look at itself to make sure all the components are working properly. If there is a problem, you will see a message on the
monitor.

"If you get an error, try removing all disks and turning the power off. Check
that you put the disk in properly and that all plugs and cables are not loose.
Reinsert the operating system disk and turn the power back on. If you continue to
get an error, you may need technical assistance.

"If everything goes OK, when these tests are done, you will see the little red
light on drive A go on and hear the drive buzzing. Soon after, the monitor will
display a message asking you for the correct date." The trainer demonstrated by
firing up the PC. Sandy saw this on the monitor as it waited for the correct date.

```
Current date is Tue 1-01-1980
Enter new date:_
```

"When you get this display, type the current date with either hyphens or slashes between the numbers and press the Enter key. Do not type the day of the week; the system will calculate that for you. For example, if the date is October 7, 1987, you can respond by typing either 10-7-87 or 10/7/87 and pressing Enter.

"After you have entered the date, the computer will ask you for the time."

```
Current time is 0:00:00.00
Enter new time:_
```

"There is a clock maintained automatically by the computer from the time you turn the power on to the time you turn it off. The system started its internal clock when you turned the computer on so the actual time displayed will be different than all zeros, depending on how long it took you to get to this point. The system keeps time down to the seconds and hundredths of seconds, which are the two figures that display after the hours and minutes. To set the clock to the correct time, type in the hour, a colon, and the minutes and press Enter. The system uses a 24-hour clock, so 8:18 A.M. would be entered as 8:18, while 8:18 P.M. would be entered as 20:18.

"If the date and time displayed are acceptable, you may select them by just pressing the Enter key in response to each message.

"After you have entered the time, the monitor display looks like this."

```
The IBM Personal Computer DOS
Version 2.10 (C)Copyright IBM Corp 1981, 1982, 1983
A>
```

"This process is known as starting or **booting** the computer. Booting the computer brings it under the control of PC-DOS. The greater than sign (>) means PC-DOS is waiting for you to enter a command. The letter A in front of the greater than sign refers to drive A, meaning that drive A is the one currently considered active—more on that later.

"You now know how to turn the computer on. Before you turn it off you need to remove all floppy disks. Although the IBM has built-in protection so that data on disks will not be harmed if the system is turned off with the disks still in the drive, it is good to get in the habit of always removing the disks before turning the system off.

"When the red light on the drive is on, the system is accessing the disk, and the drive door should not be opened until the light goes off. Once the disks are removed, turn off the power switches for the monitor (if this applies to your system) and the system unit.

"Just one thing to be wary of when turning on the computer. If you put the operating system disk into the wrong drive (it belongs in drive A) or put it into drive A improperly, the computer will display a different message than the one you just saw."

While talking, the trainer demonstrated by putting the disk in upside down.

```
The IBM Personal Computer Basic
Version C1.00 Copyright IBM Corp 1981
xxxxxx Bytes free
Ok
```

"The message indicates that the computer thinks that there are no disk drives available. In this case it brings up the program that is permanently stored in the computer. This program is referred to as Cassette BASIC, because it uses a cassette tape recorder instead of a disk drive for storage. The C that appears after *Version* identifies this as Cassette BASIC. You can use Cassette BASIC to play around or to learn BASIC, but it has little practical use for most of us.

"If you get this message, you need to take the disk out of the drive and replace it correctly, then restart the operating system by pressing the Control, Alternate, and Delete keys at the same time (hold down Control and Alternate first, then, while holding them down, press the Del key on the numeric keypad and then release all three). This is a shortcut way of restarting the computer and can be done any time you wish to return to the operating system. Note that since this action returns the computer to its initial state, it *erases all data you had entered* from the computer's memory. This process is known as **rebooting.**"

The Cursor Is the Computer's Pointing Finger

"Tell me more about the cursor," asked Sandy.

"Think of the cursor as the point of the computer's electronic pencil and the monitor as a piece of paper being written on by the pencil. A pencil can write onto a piece of paper at only one location at a time — wherever its point happens to be. Similarly, the computer always prints characters on the monitor at the current location of the cursor.

"There are ways to move the cursor around on the screen. For example, the Enter key acts like the carriage return key on a typewriter, moving the cursor to the beginning of the next line. The lowercase 2, 4, 6, and 8 keys on the numeric keypad are used to move the cursor in the direction indicated by the arrow. Not all programs allow these keys to be used. For example, you cannot move the cursor up in PC-DOS. You can use them when programming in BASIC, which will be very important to you.

"While we're back on the subject of the numeric keypad, notice that there are lowercase functions for the 0, '.', 1, 3, 7, and 9 keys. **Ins** allows you to insert text into the middle of a line. **Del** deletes the character immediately above the cursor. **Home** moves the cursor to the upper left corner of the screen. **End** is used in BASIC to move the cursor to the end of a line of text. These same keys are used for other purposes by other programs, but your interest is in programming in BASIC. The **Pg Up** and **Pg Dn** keys are used by other programs for special purposes defined by the program. They are not used by BASIC.

"There are also + and − keys to the right of the numeric keypad. These are the same as the + and − keys at the top right of the typewriter keypad.

"The only key on the numeric keypad we haven't talked about is the one labeled **Scroll Lock** on its top and **Break** on its front surface. This key is used by some programs, but is only used by BASIC in combination with the Control key to interrupt the operation of a running program and for stopping certain other activities. You will learn about these uses as you learn BASIC."

Introduction to PC-DOS

"I think I've got a good understanding of the components of the IBM PC and how to turn it on and off," Sandy said. "Now, how about a little more information about PC-DOS?"

"PC-DOS is an **operating system,** as I mentioned earlier. An operating system is a computer program that is always in the computer, even when other programs are running. The operating system makes it easy to write other programs by taking care of the details of communications between the different components of the computer. In particular, the operating system makes it easy to store data onto disks, read data from disks, and use the monitor and keyboard."

Pointing to the monitor of the PC, with its A> on display, the trainer continued. "Most of the time when you are programming in BASIC, you will not need to know or worry about PC-DOS. BASIC is pretty much an island unto itself. However, a few essentials about PC-DOS might be helpful to know.

"When you turn on the computer, PC-DOS is in control, just as it is now. You can tell this by the A>, which is on display just in front of the cursor. The A>, known as the **system prompt,** means that PC-DOS is waiting for you to enter a command."

DIR

"Let's try a simple PC-DOS command, **DIR.** PC-DOS, like most operating systems, stores data on floppy disks in **files.** A file can be a collection of data put there by some program, such as a list of names and addresses, or it can be a program. PC-DOS maintains a directory of files on each disk. The directory lists the file name and its size. DIR is the command that lists a directory. To use DIR, just type in DIR after the A> and then press Enter. You will learn much more about files after you have used BASIC a while."

Changing Default Disk Drive

"You said earlier that the A> referred to disk drive A," observed Sandy. "What exactly does that mean?"

"Good question," replied the trainer. "When we typed in the DIR command, it automatically gave us a list of files on drive A. How did it know to use drive A, not drive B?

"The answer is that PC-DOS always assumes, unless you tell it otherwise, that you want to work with the currently selected **default** drive. The default drive is always indicated by the letter in front of the greater than sign (>), in this case drive

A. To change the default drive, type in the drive letter that is to become the new default drive followed by a colon and then press Enter.''

```
A> B: (Press Enter)
B>
```

''I see,'' said Sandy. ''If we used DIR right now, it would list the directory of the disk in drive B, right?''

''Right.''

''Is there a way to get a directory of a drive without changing default drives?'' asked Sandy.

''Yes, by following the command DIR with a space and the drive you wish to list, followed by a colon.''

```
B> DIR A:
```

''Even though B is the currently selected default drive, the directory listing you see is of drive A. In general in PC-DOS, you can specify a disk drive by using the drive letter followed by a colon. Before we go further, let's switch back to drive A.''

```
B> A:
```

DISKCOPY Makes a Duplicate Disk

The trainer continued, ''PC-DOS contains a great many commands, but you will only need to know a few of them in order to program in BASIC. One of the most important is DISKCOPY, which is used to make copies of floppy disks. It is important to make copies of all valuable disks. Disks are not 100 percent reliable; besides normal malfunctions, you might twist one or spill coffee on it. Don't laugh; it has happened!

''Let's assume that you have two floppy disk drives on your PC. To copy one of them, with the operating system disk in drive A, type the command

```
A> DISKCOPY A: B:
```

''This tells the computer to execute the program called DISKCOPY, which copies the first disk you list to the second one; in this case copy disk A to disk B. After you have entered the command, remember to press Enter. The computer does not do anything until you press Enter.

''After you press Enter, the computer displays a message telling you to put the source disk in drive A and the destination disk in drive B. The **source disk** is the one you want to copy, the **destination disk** the blank one onto which you wish to copy. Make sure you get the right one in the right drive! Any data previously stored on the destination disk will be erased and replaced by the data from the source disk. The easiest way to destroy the data on a good disk is to make a backup copy the wrong way! A good safeguard against this is to put a tab over the write-protect notch of the original disk before attempting to copy it. This prevents an inadvertent mistake.

"If you wish to copy the operating system disk, you do not need to change disks at this point. However, if the disk you want to copy is not the operating system disk, remove the operating system disk from drive A and insert the disk you wish to copy. Put the disk you wish to copy onto in drive B. When you are ready, press any key (such as the space bar) and the computer will make a copy of your disk. When the copy is done, remove the original and the copy, label the copy, and put the operating system disk back into drive A." (Copyrighted material should be copied only for archival or backup purposes.)

FORMAT *Prepares a Disk for Use*

"If you want a blank disk to be ready for use by a BASIC program, but do not wish to copy another disk onto the new disk, use the FORMAT command. Floppy disks are not ready to use as they come new. They must be set up by either DISKCOPY or FORMAT first. To format a disk, place your disk containing DOS in drive A, type in the command FORMAT and the drive letter followed by a colon."

```
A> FORMAT B:
```

"The computer will then ask you to put the destination disk, which is to say, the new one to be formatted, into drive B. When you have done so, press any key, such as the space bar, and the computer will format the disk.

"Formatting erases all data on a disk, so be sure you do not FORMAT a disk that has data you wish to keep.

"You will learn other PC-DOS commands later on. For now, remember DIR, DISKCOPY, FORMAT, and how to change the default drive."

Getting Started in BASIC

"How do I get started programming in BASIC?" Sandy asked.

"First I should explain about the different IBM PC BASIC programs. The PC, even if is has no disk drives, has a BASIC program built into its memory. This is Cassette BASIC, the BASIC program that we encountered when we put the diskette in upside down. This version of BASIC is stored entirely in Read-Only Memory, or ROM."

·THREE KEY PC-DOS COMMANDS·

DIR displays a list of files.
DISKCOPY copies one disk to another.
FORMAT prepares a disk for use.

RAM and ROM: Two Types of Internal Memory

"Before you go any further," interrupted Sandy, "will you please explain the difference between ROM and RAM?"

"Certainly," the trainer replied. "ROM and RAM are similar in that both are components of the system unit and are used to store data. The difference is that ROM (Read-Only Memory) has data permanently stored on it. You can read this data, but you cannot change it. ROM is not available for the user's own programs or data.

"In contrast, RAM (Random Access Memory) can be written to as well as read from.

"There is one more important difference. When the power is turned off (or when the system is rebooted with CRTL-ALT-DEL), all data in RAM memory disappears; it is transient or temporary. Data stored in ROM, however, is permanent."

Versions and Releases of BASIC

"Let's return now to the different versions of BASIC. In addition to Cassette BASIC, which is permanently in ROM, there are two BASIC programs stored on your operating disk. These are Standard BASIC and Advanced BASIC (or BASICA). Both these programs reside on the operating disk and add some extensions to Cassette BASIC. Mainly, they let you use disk storage. Advanced BASIC has

· VERSIONS OF BASIC ·

Cassette BASIC
Permanently stored in memory.
Accessed by booting with no disk or with disk not in drive properly.
Message is: Version C1.00 Copyright . . .

Standard Disk BASIC
Stored on disk.
Invoked by typing: BASIC.
Adds capabilities to Cassette BASIC.
Message is: Version D2.10 Copyright IBM . . .

Advanced BASIC
Stored on disk.
Invoked by typing: BASICA.
Adds still more capabilities—particularly graphics—but leaves less room
   for programs.
Message is: Version A2.10 Copyright IBM . . .

many more graphic and music features. Because of this, it uses more memory, leaving less for your programs. Some large programs, which do not need the features of Advanced BASIC, may require that you use the nonadvanced BASIC in order to have enough space."

"What do the letter and numbers mean that appear after the word *version?*" asked Sandy.

"The letter indicates the version of BASIC," replied the trainer. "The letter *C* indicates Cassette BASIC; the letter *D* indicates nonadvanced Disk BASIC; the letter *A* indicates Advanced BASIC. The release number following the letter indicates how many different times this version has been revised. Version 1.0 of BASICA was released before 2.0, which was released before 3.0. In the future there may be a 4.0. In between version numbers, minor changes are sometimes made, perhaps to fix a minor error. For this reason, you will also see versions such as 2.10, which is a minor revision of 2.0. Most systems are currently using either version 2.10 or 3.1. The XT requires DOS version 2.0 or above. The AT requires DOS version 3.0 or above. Each DOS version has its own corresponding version of BASIC. The DOS 3.1 disk contains BASIC version 3.1, and BASICA version 3.1.

"Most of the time you will use the Advanced BASIC. When you wish to use it, start the system as I have explained with your operating system disk in drive A. When the A> is on the screen, type in BASICA and press the Enter key. You should get a message similar to the one shown in Figure 1.6."

FIGURE 1.6 • *What BASICA displays on startup. This display tells you that BASICA is ready for you to start writing programs in BASIC. The number shown may be different on your computer. Other versions of BASIC are available.*

```
The IBM Personal Computer BASIC
Version A2.10 Copyright IBM Corp. 1981, 1982, 1983
60891 Bytes free
Ok
```

FIGURE 1.7 ▪
*Steps for starting
up BASICA*

Step 1. Turn on the power with the operating system disk in drive A.

Step 2. When PC-DOS displays the A> prompt, type BASICA and press Enter.

Step 3. To return to PC-DOS from BASIC, type *system*.

Prompts Say "I Await Your Command"
"Where is the A> and what does Ok mean?" asked Sandy.

"You are no longer in the control of PC-DOS but of BASIC. BASIC has no A> prompt. Instead BASIC displays the prompt "Ok" to indicate that it is waiting for your next action. If you are in BASIC and wish to return to DOS, type the word *system* and then press the Enter key. You will then see the DOS prompt A>.

"We have used up most of our time. Rather than teach you BASIC here, I will give you a copy of *The ABCs of BASIC on the IBM Personal Computer* by Cohen, Alger, and Boyd. Follow the book and you should have no trouble learning how to program in BASIC."

"As a reminder, here's a card with the steps for starting up BASICA" (see Figure 1.7).

Sandy picked up a copy of the ABCs book and, thanking the trainer profusely, left to practice with the PC at the office.

▪*THE ABC OF BASIC ON THE IBM PERSONAL COMPUTER*▪

LESSON 1: HOW TO DISPLAY VALUES AND PERFORM CALCULATIONS

Welcome to the world of the IBM Personal Computer and the BASIC programming language. This book presents a series of lessons designed to teach you most of what you need to know to solve business problems using BASIC and the IBM PC. Each lesson covers a group of useful and related BASIC instructions.

Before starting in with the first lesson, let's examine some of the conventions used in this book:

1. You will find it helpful to enter the examples in the text. Turn on the computer and invoke the BASIC language by typing *BASICA* before starting any of these lessons.

2. Throughout the text, dialogues between you and the computer will be shown to illustrate the various BASIC commands or statements and their use. These dialogues are indented from the rest of the text so that you can easily tell what is and is not part of the dialogue.

3. You will be typing on the keyboard text that will be displayed on the computer's monitor, and the computer will be displaying responses on the monitor as well. To distinguish between the two, the lessons list text that you are expected to enter as underlined text, while text that the computer generates in response is not underlined. Do not attempt to underline what you enter; the underlining is only to clarify the dialogues in this book.
4. At the end of each line that you type on the keyboard, you are to press the Enter key once. This is the signal to BASIC that you have completed your entry. For the first one or two examples the text will remind you to do this by printing (Press Enter). After these examples, the reminder will be omitted.
5. Unless otherwise indicated, assume that *all* characters listed in the dialogues with the computer are significant. For example, in the dialogue

```
PRINT "hello"
hello
Ok
```

the quote marks around the word *hello* are part of what you are expected to type. The preceding dialogue means that you are to type the text

```
PRINT "hello"
```

then press Enter, to which the computer responds by printing the word

```
hello
```

on the next line and the word *Ok* on the following line. Remember: the underlines are not to be typed; they are only to show what you are typing on the keyboard.
6. Do not try to learn BASIC purely from reading the lessons. Any competent computer programmer can tell you that there is no substitute for hands-on experience. Follow the dialogues on your computer and experiment with the BASIC statements. Don't be afraid to experiment with BASIC and the computer.

Computers are very good at mathematics. In this lesson you will learn how to use the IBM PC and the BASIC language as a powerful calculator. Two BASIC instructions are explained: PRINT and LET.

PRINT Displays Information

Let's start with a dialogue to introduce PRINT.

```
PRINT 17    (Press ENTER)
 17
Ok
```

What happened? You typed in the word *PRINT,* a space, and the number 17, and then pressed Enter, and the computer displayed the value of the number 17 on the next line. BASIC then printed the message *Ok* to let you know that it is ready for more operations. This works for any number.

```
PRINT 123
 123
Ok
PRINT 12.5
 12.5
Ok
print 12.5000
 12.5
Ok
PRINT 1.00
 1
Ok
Print -34.56
-34.56
Ok
```

These examples show a few more capabilities of PRINT. Numbers do not have to be integers; they can have fractional parts to the right of the decimal point as well, as in 12.5 and −34.56. Such numbers are called "real" numbers. In general, you can use real numbers and integers interchangeably with PRINT. In the lessons most of the example dialogues will use only integers for simplicity, but you should experiment with real numbers as you learn each new instruction.

Notice what happened to the trailing zeros in the examples. When PRINT evaluates a number, it does not print trailing zeros to the right of the decimal point.

Numbers Are Printed with Extra Spaces

Look carefully at the spacing in the preceding PRINT examples. Do you notice the space before the numbers in the first four examples? With the PRINT statement, positive numbers will be printed or displayed with a leading space. Negative numbers will be preceded by a minus sign instead of the space as in the preceding example. Although you cannot see it in these examples, both positive and negative numbers also print with a space following them.

Uppercase and Lowercase Are Both Allowed

Notice also the statement itself. It doesn't matter whether you type the instruction in lowercase, as in *print*, or in uppercase, as in *PRINT*, or even in a combination of lower- and uppercase, as in *Print*. BASIC translates anything that is not in quotes into uppercase. You will probably find it easier to type in lowercase.

Error Messages in BASIC: Syntax Errors

If you have been entering the preceding examples, you may have already run into another feature of BASIC, the error message. When you make a mistake, it is likely that BASIC will let you know by printing a message. Suppose you mistype the word *PRINT*.

```
PINT 17
Syntax error
Ok
```

"Syntax error" is one of many error messages that BASIC may print, depending on the particular error you make. A syntax error indicates that what you have entered does not make any sense to BASIC. If you get an error message, don't panic; just retype the line.

```
PRINT 17
 17
Ok
```

Pressing ESC Erases the Line

Should you get partway through typing a line and realize that you have made a mistake, you can either backspace to the start of the line, or you can erase the entire current line by pressing the Esc key (on the top left corner of the keyboard).

PRINT Prints Characters, Too: Strings

In addition to printing numbers, PRINT can be used to print text such as "Hello" or "This is an example of the PRINT statement". These are called **character strings,** or simply **strings.** A string is a series of characters, which can be numbers, letters, or special characters. A string is enclosed in quotes to signal to BASIC where the string starts and ends, but the quotes are not part of the string.

```
PRINT "Hello"
Hello
Ok
PRINT "This is an example of the PRINT statement."
This is an example of the PRINT statement.
Ok
```

Some other examples of strings are:

```
"California"
"Sacramento, CA 95831"
"JANUARY 1, 1986"
"01/01/86"
"The TOTAL is: "
"DEPRECIATION SCHEDULE"
```

A string will print exactly as it appears between the quotes, but the quotes themselves will not be printed. Also, in contrast to the printing of numbers, no space is placed before or after a string; if spaces are desired, they must be part of the string. For example, if you wish three spaces to appear before the words *REPORT TITLE*, you can use the following statement:

```
PRINT "   REPORT TITLE"
   REPORT TITLE
Ok
```

One PRINT Statement Can Print Multiple Values

You can print more than one value — whether numbers, strings, or both — with one PRINT statement. There are 80 character positions in one line on the monitor (and on most printers), and you can control where the items print in several ways.

PRINT with a Comma Skips to the Next Print Zone
By separating the values with commas, as in the following examples, PRINT inserts spaces between them:

```
PRINT "The cost is:", 5
The cost is:    5
Ok
print 1,2,3,4,5,6,7,8,9
 1             2             3             4             5
 6             7             8             9
Ok
```

BASIC divides the 80-character print or display line into 5 print "zones," starting in positions 1, 15, 29, 43, and 57 — fourteen spaces apart. Using a comma between values will cause BASIC to go to the next print zone and start printing the next value there. If you list more than five values separated by commas, the printing will overflow the current line and continue on the next line.

PRINT with a Semicolon Suppresses Skipping
If you don't want the spacing caused by the commas, use a semicolon instead.

```
PRINT "Pat Smith"
Pat Smith
Ok
PRINT "Pat Smith is ",19," years old."
Pat Smith is    19            years old.
Ok
PRINT "Pat Smith is ";19;" years old."
Pat Smith is  19  years old.
Ok
```

The only difference between using semicolons and commas is that a semicolon suppresses moving to the next print zone before printing the next value; therefore, one value prints immediately after the other. In the preceding example, showing the use of the semicolons, there are two spaces before and after the 19. One of these is due to the space that is included in the text within the quotes. The second appears because positive numbers PRINT with a space in front and after the number.

Study the following four examples. Why did they print as they did?

```
PRINT 1, 2, 3
 1               2               3
Ok
PRINT 1; 2; 3
 1  2  3
Ok
PRINT -1; -2; -3
-1 -2 -3
Ok
PRINT "ONE"; "TWO"; "THREE"
ONETWOTHREE
Ok
```

Remember that with the PRINT statement numbers print with a space after them and are preceded by a space if they are positive and a minus sign if they are negative. Strings print exactly as they appear between the quotes.

Adding Spaces Makes Lines More Readable

Adding spaces in BASIC lines make the lines more readable. Only a few BASIC features prohibit placing spaces between items. We will note these exceptions as we come to them. It is good practice, when you start writing programs, to use spaces for clarity. Experiment with the use of spaces and PRINT; you will find that there are only a few limits. One is that you must have at least one space following the word *PRINT*.

Remember that spaces within a string are a part of that string, and adding spaces within the quotes of a string will cause those spaces to be printed.

```
PRINT "EXAMPLE OF SPACES ";"ADDED TO STRINGS"
EXAMPLE OF SPACES ADDED TO STRINGS
Ok
PRINT "EXAMPLE   OF   SPACES ";"ADDED   TO   STRINGS"
EXAMPLE   OF   SPACES ADDED   TO   STRINGS
Ok
PRINT "EXAMPLE OF SPACES ";   "ADDED TO STRINGS"
EXAMPLE OF SPACES ADDED TO STRINGS
Ok
```

The additional spaces within the quotes were printed as part of the string, but the additional spaces outside of the quotes were ignored.

TAB Skips to Specified Column

```
PRINT 1 TAB(20) 2
 1                  2
Ok
```

The TAB(20) tells BASIC to move (or tab) to the twentieth character position before printing the next value. Notice that in the preceding example there is no punctuation (commas or semicolons) before or after the TAB(20). Since TAB is controlling where to move the cursor, punctuation is not necessary. If you wish to use punctuation, semicolons may be placed between the items without affecting the results.

```
PRINT 1; TAB(20) 2
 1                    2
Ok
```

Commas will cause the cursor to move to the next print zone and, therefore, should not be used with TABs.

TAB is one of BASIC's features that has restrictions on the use of extra spaces. No space may be placed between TAB and the beginning parentheses. Spaces may be placed after the opening parentheses or before the ending parentheses, just not before the opening one. The following are examples of valid and invalid formats for TAB:

Valid
```
PRINT TAB(20) "This is OK"
PRINT TAB( 20) "This is OK"
PRINT TAB( 20 ) "This is OK"
```
Invalid
```
PRINT TAB (20) "This is not OK"
```

You can put as many tabs into a PRINT line as you wish; you can even put mathematical expressions inside the parentheses of the tab statement to compute the column number to which to tab.

```
PRINT 11 TAB(5) 22 TAB(5 + 5) 33 TAB(5 + 10) 44
 11  22  33  44
Ok
```

In this example, the TAB told BASIC to move to the fifth column, the tenth column and the fifteenth column as it printed the numbers.

BASIC cannot tab backward. If a TAB tells BASIC to move backward on the line, it will cause BASIC to display the line as it stands at that point, then skip to the next line and move to the indicated tab stop on the next line.

```
PRINT TAB(30) 123 TAB(10) 555
                             123
         555
```

BASIC printed 123 starting in position 30, then went to the next line and printed 555 starting in position 10.

PRINT by Itself Prints a Blank Line
One feature of PRINT that can be used to improve the readability of reports is the use of PRINT all by itself. This will cause a blank line to be printed, which is often useful in separating segments of a report.

·THE PRINT STATEMENT·

PRINT 123.4
    Prints the numeric value 123.4.
PRINT "TEST MESSAGE"
    Prints the characters within the quotes.
PRINT value, value, . . .
    Comma causes values to print in next print zone.
PRINT value; value; . . .
    Semicolon causes values to print next to each other.
PRINT TAB(x) value
    TAB to position x before printing the value.
PRINT
    Prints a blank line.

```
PRINT

Ok
```

Arithmetic Expressions: +, −, *, /

PRINT can also be used with arithmetic expressions.

```
PRINT 17 + 13
 30
Ok
PRINT 8/4
 2
Ok
PRINT 17 - 13
 4
Ok
PRINT 4 * 8
 32
Ok
```

As you can see, BASIC uses the following notation for the four basic arithmetic operations:

+   indicates addition
−   indicates subtraction
/   indicates division
*   indicates multiplication

The asterisk is used instead of an "x" with computers to indicate multiplication. The expression 4x8 does not have the same meaning as 4 * 8; 4x8 will cause the computer to give you incorrect results (try it.)

```
PRINT 4x8
 4   0
Ok
```

Arithmetical expressions can be as complex as you wish.

```
PRINT 1 + 2 + 3 + 4 + 5
 15
Ok
PRINT 4 * 8 + 3 * 5
 47
Ok
```

The expression (4 * 8 + 3 * 5) could be interpreted in several different ways: as (4 * 8) + (3 * 5), or as 4 * (8 + 3) * 5, or even as 4 * (8 + (3 * 5)). In high school algebra you learned that such an expression is to be interpreted as (4 * 8) + (3 * 5); BASIC interprets it the same way. Whenever there is a mixture of addition, subtraction, multiplication, and division in the same statement, BASIC always does the multiplication and division first, then the addition and subtraction.

Here are some sample expressions and the way in which BASIC evaluates them:

Expression	BASIC's Interpretation
$1 + 2 * 3$	$1 + (2 * 3)$
$1 * 2 + 3$	$(1 * 2) + 3$
$1 + 2/3$	$1 + (2/3)$
$1/2 + 3$	$(1/2) + 3$
$1 * 2/3$	$(1 * 2)/3$
$1 * 2 + 3/4$	$(1 * 2) + (3/4)$
$1/2 * 3$	$(1/2) * 3$

The last example is interesting because multiplication and division receive equal priority. It could logically be argued that 1/2 * 3 should be either (1/2) * 3 or 1/(2 * 3). BASIC always resolves such problems by proceeding from left to right; in this case, the expression is evaluated by first dividing 1 by 2 and then by multiplying the result by 3.

As in algebra, the order of execution can be changed by the use of parentheses. BASIC evaluates expressions inside the parentheses first.

```
PRINT 1 + 15 * 3
 46
Ok
PRINT (1 + 15) * 3
 48
Ok
```

In the first example the multiplication was performed first, yielding the result of 45, to which 1 was added for the final result of 46. In the second example, the operation within the parentheses is performed first, giving 16 times 3, or 48.

```
PRINT ((1 + 15) * 3)/(3 + 3)
 8
Ok
PRINT (1 + 3)/(16/4), (7 + 3) * 5
 1               50
Ok
```

As you can see, parentheses can be nested, one set inside another, to any level of complexity. You may use parentheses at any time to improve the clarity of a line or to make sure the expression is evaluated exactly in the order you intend, even if they are not required.

More Arithmetic Operators: Exponentiation, Integer Division, Modulo

So far, you have seen only four arithmetic operators: $+$, $-$, $*$, and $/$, for addition, subtraction, multiplication, and division, respectively. Although these are all you will need for most programs, BASIC also provides a few more operators for special purposes.

Exponentiation: The carat operator ($\wedge$) raises a number to some power. The expression 4 $\wedge$ 3 means four raised to the third power, or 4^3, or $4 \times 4 \times 4$, or 64.

Integer Division: The backslash operator ($\backslash$) means integer division. Before the division is performed, the numbers are rounded to integers. After the division, the quotient is truncated to an integer (i.e., the fractional part of the result is dropped); thus, the answer is always an integer. 8 $\backslash$ 3 will yield the answer 2 (2.6666 . . . with the fractional part dropped off.) Note that the result is not rounded; the remainder is simply truncated or cut off.

MOD (Modulus Arithmetic): The MOD operator yields the remainder after integer division. The expression 7 MOD 2 is 1, since 7 divided by 2 yields a remainder of 1. The notation 9 MOD 3 is 0, since 9 divided by 3 yields no remainder. The representation 10 MOD 3 is 1, 11 MOD 3 is 2, and 12 MOD 3 is 0.

Negation: Another operator is the unary minus, or negation, operator, such as -3. It is used to indicate a negative number.

```
PRINT 5 - (-3)
 8
Ok
```

The first minus sign means subtraction and the second a negative value.

Order of Precedence Determines How Expressions Are Evaluated

As stated earlier, BASIC does multiplication and division before addition and subtraction. BASIC also follows strict rules with all of the other arithmetic operators. The order in which operations are performed is called the **order of precedence.** Table 1.1 lists the arithmetic operators in their order of precedence.

LET Stores Values in Variables

Very often you will want to use one number—say, the wholesale cost of an item—over and over. Wouldn't it be convenient if you could give that number a name, such as COST, and have the computer remember the number by that name? In BASIC, the LET statement does just that.

```
LET COST = 8
Ok
LET PRICE = 10
Ok
PRINT COST, PRICE
 8              10
Ok
```

What happened here? Think of a set of index cards. The statement LET COST = 8 caused BASIC to take an imaginary card, label it COST, and put the value 8 on that card (see Figure 1.8). Similarly, LET PRICE = 10 created another card labeled PRICE and put the value 10 on that card.

In the line PRINT COST, PRICE, BASIC recognized that COST and PRICE were not themselves values, but rather the names of the cards that hold values. It looked up the cards with those names in BASIC's card box of variables, then substituted the values on those cards for the names COST and PRICE in the PRINT statement. BASIC can handle many, many variables; a typical business program might contain over a hundred.

TABLE 1.1 · *Order of Precedence for Arithmetic Operators*

OPERATOR	MEANING	EXAMPLE
$\wedge$	Exponentiation	$3 \wedge 2 = 9$
$-$	Negation	-3
*, /	Multiplication, Division	$3 * 2 = 6$ $6/2 = 3$
\	Integer division	$7 \backslash 3 = 2$
MOD	Remainder	$7 \text{ MOD } 3 = 1$
+, −	Addition Subtraction	$3 + 2 = 5$ $3 − 2 = 1$

NOTE: Expressions in parentheses are evaluated first. When ties in precedence occur, expressions are evaluated from left to right.

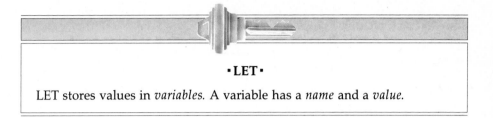

·LET·

LET stores values in *variables.* A variable has a *name* and a *value.*

In this example the index cards are called variables, and COST and PRICE are called variable names. A variable has two attributes: a name and a value. COST is the name, 8 the value; PRICE the name and 10 the value.

Once a variable has been assigned a value, that value can be retrieved any number of times by simply using the name of the variable anywhere you would normally use a number. BASIC makes the substitution automatically.

```
PRINT PRICE - COST
 2
Ok
PRINT (PRICE - COST)/PRICE
 .2
Ok
```

Suppose COST is the wholesale cost of a good and PRICE is the retail price. Then PRICE − COST is the gross margin as a flat amount, while (PRICE − COST)/PRICE is the margin as a fraction of the retail price. Instead of having to remember and retype the cost and price over and over for different calculations, you can just store the values once via LET statements, then refer to the values by name. As you can see, the combination of PRINT and LET makes BASIC a very powerful calculator.

Values stored in a variable can be changed at any time by using another LET statement.

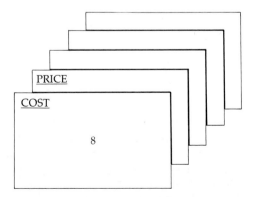

FIGURE 1.8 ▪
LET assigns a
VALUE to a
variable

LET COST = 8

Think of variables as index cards.

Each card has a label (or name) and a value written on it.

LET "looks up" the card named in the statement and places a value on that card.

```
LET COST = 9
Ok
PRINT PRICE, COST, PRICE - COST, (PRICE - COST)/PRICE
 10          9             1               .1
Ok
```

In this example the value stored under the name COST was changed from 8, its original value, to 9, the value in the most recent LET statement. When BASIC encounters a LET statement, it looks first to see whether the variable already exists. If it does, the value currently in that variable (our imaginary index card) is changed to the new value. If it does not, a variable (new card) is created with the given name, and the value is assigned to that variable. Thus, when we initially typed LET COST = 8, BASIC found that there was no variable named COST, created one, and gave it the value 8. When we subsequently typed LET COST = 9, BASIC found that a variable named COST already existed, so it merely changed its value from its old value, 8, to its new value, 9.

LET Evaluates Arithmetic Expressions

You can also put mathematical expressions into a LET statement.

```
LET MARGIN = PRICE - COST
Ok
PRINT PRICE, COST, MARGIN
 10          9               1
Ok
```

When LET is used in this way, the variable you are defining must appear to the left of the equal sign, and the variables used to calculate it must appear to the right. The statement LET PRICE − COST = MARGIN is an invalid statement in BASIC and will produce an error message.

The computations in a LET statement can be as simple or as complex as you desire. As you can see, a LET statement can include references to other variables as part of the computations.

Using an Undefined Variable Name

Suppose you refer to a variable that has never been assigned a value by a LET statement. What does BASIC do? The answer is that, for numeric variables such as we have been discussing, BASIC creates a variable of that name and gives it the initial value zero.

```
PRINT A.NEW.NUMBER
 0
Ok
```

In this example we have not previously assigned a value to the name A.NEW.NUMBER with a LET statement. Nevertheless, BASIC lets us use that name in a PRINT statement, substituting a value of zero for the name. Remember this habit of BASIC's! One of the most common errors in BASIC programs is to misspell a variable name. When you do, BASIC will happily go along with you, assigning the initial, and probably erroneous, value zero to the variable!

```
LET ANSWER = 10
Ok
PRINT ASNSWER
 0
Ok
```

LET Is Optional

The word LET may be omitted. For example, COST = 10 is the same as LET COST = 10. It is a good idea to use LET explicitly while you are learning; all of the examples in this book do. Once you are familiar with its use, you may omit the word LET if you wish.

String Variables Hold Text as Values

Remember the discussion of strings earlier in this lesson? We said then that a string is a sequence of characters enclosed in quotes, such as "Hello". BASIC allows you to store not only numbers, but also strings in variables.

```
LET MYNAME$ = "Terry Smith"
Ok
PRINT MYNAME$
Terry Smith
Ok
```

Remember the imaginary card box? BASIC created a card named MYNAME$ and put on that card the value Terry Smith. When BASIC interpreted the statement, PRINT MYNAME$, it saw that MYNAME$ was a variable and replaced it by the value stored under MYNAME$ in BASIC's card box.

In order to store a string in a variable, that variable must have a name ending with a dollar sign ($). Here's an example to illustrate the importance of that trailing dollar sign.

```
LET MYNAME$ = "Terry Smith"
Ok
LET MYNAME = 17
Ok
PRINT MYNAME$,MYNAME
Terry Smith    17
Ok
```

In this example BASIC created two variables, one named MYNAME$ and one named MYNAME. They are not the same variable! The one with the dollar sign can contain only characters, while the one without the dollar sign can contain only numbers!

Notice from the examples that values assigned to string variables must always be entered in quotes in the LET statements but are displayed without the quotes when you use a PRINT statement. The quotes are just the way of telling BASIC that what you typed is a string, not the name of a variable. There is a big difference between the next two examples, even though they differ only in the quotation marks.

```
PRINT MYNAME
 17
Ok
PRINT "MYNAME"
MYNAME
Ok
```

In the first case BASIC knew that MYNAME was a variable name. In the second case, BASIC knew that "MYNAME" was a literal string, not a variable name. The quotes distinguish between the two cases, but BASIC does not actually store the quote marks in string variables in LET statements anymore than it actually prints them in a PRINT statement.

Using a numeric variable that has not been initialized to a value (for example, using LET) causes BASIC to create the variable with a value of zero, but what about string variables? BASIC also creates string variables as needed with an initial value of the null string. This is a string of zero length with no characters, and is usually indicated by ''''. A null is not the same as a space or a zero.

```
LET ZERO = 0
Ok
LET BLANK$ = " "
Ok
LET NULL$ = ""
Ok
```

The first defined the numeric variable ZERO and assigned it the value of zero; the second defined the string variable BLANK$ and placed a space into it (note that there is a space between the two quotes); the third defined the string variable NULL$ and assigned it a null value (note that there is no space between the quotes).

Not All Variable Names Are Legal

So far, most of the variable names we have used have consisted of all letters. However, BASIC allows you a lot of flexibility in naming variables. Here are the rules that apply to naming variables:

1. A variable name must begin with a letter, but after that first letter you may use any letters, digits, or one or more periods (.). A dollar sign is only legal as the last character in the name of a string variable.
2. Variable names may be up to 40 characters long.
3. You may not embed spaces in a variable name. To separate words that together make up a name, use periods, such as FIRST.NAME$.
4. Certain words are not allowed by themselves as variable names. These are words like PRINT and LET, which have special meanings to BASIC. They are called reserved words. If you attempt to use a reserved word as a variable name, BASIC will give you an error message. Appendix B gives a complete list of BASIC reserved words. You may use a reserved

---

┌─────────────────────────┐
│ • *PARABLES FOR*   │
│ *PROGRAMMERS* •   │
└─────────────────────────┘

Impractical Jokes

Once upon a time there lived a programmer who loved practical jokes. This programmer thought it especially funny to make variable names out of ohs and zeros: names like OO000OO and O000OOO. What a great joke! Nobody could tell the difference between the variables because they all looked almost identical.

It was funny, that is, until one day when the programmer's supervisor found out and carried on for almost half an hour. "These programs are too valuable to be the subject of pranks," the furious supervisor bellowed. "It's too easy for one of our people to make a mistake which could cost the company thousands of dollars. Either you change your ways or look for another job!"

MORAL: Make your variable names helpful to others.

---

word within a variable name but not as the entire name. PRINT.FIRST is a valid variable name. The only exception is that you may not begin a variable with the letters *FN*; these are reserved for functions, a topic that will be discussed in a later chapter.

These are the rules that BASIC enforces. However, there are some other rules you should follow to make your programs more readable.

5. Use names that make sense to someone not familiar with the details of your programs. Names like S2 are obscure and confusing; names like COST.OF.SALES have meaning.
6. Don't be "cute" with variable names.

Here are a few examples of acceptable variable names.

```
COST
PRICE
COST.OF.SALES
HOURLY.PAY.RATE
COST.ON.DEC31.1986
```

Here are some variable names that are not allowed.

```
1ABC                    (begins with a number)
COST OF SALES           (contains embedded spaces)
NUMBER.OF.#S            (contains an illegal character, #)
MARGIN.AS.%.OF.SALES    (contains an illegal character, %)
```

Numbers and Strings Are Like Apples and Oranges

In true arithmetical operations all variables must be numeric. Although a string variable may contain a number, it is considered text and no arithmetical operations may be done on it.

```
LET LOTUS$ = "123"
Ok
```

This is a valid statement; the characters 1, 2, and 3 have been placed in the string variable called LOTUS$.

```
PRINT LOTUS$ + 5
Type mismatch
Ok
```

BASIC displayed an error message, indicating that you were trying to perform an operation that is not allowed on that type of variable. BASIC stores strings and numbers in the computer in different ways, and even though LOTUS$ contains the characters 123, you cannot add a number to it anymore than you can add 5 to R2D2$ or to GEORGE.LUCAS$.

One way to correct this is the following:

```
LET LOTUS = 123
Ok
PRINT LOTUS + 5
 128
Ok
```

Here LOTUS is defined as a numeric variable, and you can perform addition with another number.

Strings and Numbers Are Even Printed Differently

In addition to not being able to perform arithmetic on a string variable even if it contains numbers, the strings consisting of numbers will follow the rules for printing that apply to strings, not those that apply to numeric variables.

```
PRINT "TEST";123;"PRINT"
TEST 123 PRINT
Ok
```

·NUMBERS AND STRINGS·

Numbers and strings are not stored the same way by BASIC. "123" is *not* the same as 123. You cannot do arithmetic on strings.

In this case 123 is a positive numeric variable; therefore, it is preceded and followed by a space.

```
PRINT "TEST";"123";"PRINT"
TEST123PRINT
Ok
```

In the second example, 123 is a string variable; therefore, it has no space either in front or after it.

Concatenation

There is one nonmathematical operation that can be performed on strings called *concatenation*. Concatenation is shown by a plus sign between two strings, but the effect is to join one after the other:

```
LET FIRSTNAME$ = "Chris"
Ok
LET LASTNAME$ = "Jones"
Ok
PRINT FIRSTNAME$ + LASTNAME$
ChrisJones
Ok
LET AMOUNT1$ = "123"
Ok
LET AMOUNT2$ = "456"
Ok
PRINT AMOUNT1$ + AMOUNT2$
123456
Ok
```

AMOUNT1$ and AMOUNT2$ were defined as strings; therefore, even though they contained numbers when they were concatenated, the result was a longer string, not addition.

As you will discover later, concatenation is a useful tool in combining string variables. It should be noted that subtraction, multiplication, and division have no meaning with strings.

THE STORY'S END

Sandy practiced all weekend using the PRINT and LET statements and by Monday morning was ready for The Boss.

"Well, Sandy, what can you do with this new addition to our company?"

"Just give me any calculation," Sandy replied, "no matter how complicated, and I can figure it out on the computer."

Over the next hour they computed margins, inventory turnover rates, and labor factors. Everything The Boss could dream up, Sandy was able to calculate. The Boss was particularly impressed that Sandy didn't have to keep typing the same numbers over and over. By assigning them names, Sandy could easily go through a complicated series of calculations without making a mistake. This was a vast improvement over normal calculators.

"Sandy," said The Boss when they finished, "I am impressed. In a short time, you've already learned how to use the computer as a calculator. I expect to see you writing full programs before long." Sandy smiled, vowing inwardly to learn more about programming in BASIC on the IBM PC. If one lesson made the PC this useful, just think of the difference a few more lessons could make!

·QUICK REFERENCE FOR LESSON 1·

In this lesson you learned the PRINT and LET statements and how to use variables in BASIC.

PRINT Sends Display to Screen

PRINT a single item

> PRINT 123.456
> PRINT "Message"
> PRINT X where X is a numeric variable
> PRINT A$ where A$ is a string variable
> Numbers print with a space following them.
>> Positive numbers are preceded by a space.
>> Negative numbers are preceded by a minus sign.
> Strings print exactly as they appear within the quotes.

PRINT more than one item (a, b, c, and d represent any of the items in the preceding PRINT statement)

> PRINT a, b, c, d
>> Print each item in the next available print zone.
>> Print zones begin in columns 1, 15, 29, 43, and 57.
> PRINT a; b; c; d
>> Print one item immediately after the other.
>> No spaces will appear between strings.
>> Numbers will have one space after them and either a space or a minus sign in front.

PRINT TAB(X). Move to column X before printing next item. May not put space between TAB and beginning parentheses.

PRINT. Print statement by itself will print a blank line.

Arithmetic Operators

BASIC provides the following arithmetic operators.

When one or more appear in the same expression, they are executed in the order of precedence shown in the following table. Those higher on the list precede those lower on the list. If two or more operators with the same precedence occur together, they are evaluated from left to right.

The order of precedence may be changed by the use of parentheses. Operators within parentheses are evaluated first.

Exponentiation	^	4 ^ 5	four raised to the fifth power
Negation	—	−7	negative 7
Multiplication	*	A * 3	the value of A times 3
and Division	/	A / 3	the value of A divided by 3
Integer Division	\	Y \ Z	Round the values of Y and Z to integers. Divide Y by Z. Truncate the quotient to an integer.
Modulo	MOD	8 MOD 3	the integer that is the remainder after integer division of 8 divided by 3
Addition	+	4 + B	4 plus the value of B
and Subtraction	—	C − 18	the value of C minus 18

LET Assigns a Number or String to a Variable

LET X = 123.45. Assign numeric value of 123.45 to the numeric variable named X.
LET A$ = "string". Assign the characters *string* to the string variable named A$.
LET X = expression (where expression is a valid mathematical expression)
  Evaluate the expression and assign the result to the variable named X.

Variable Names

Must start with a letter.
May be up to 40 characters long.
Valid characters are letters, numbers, or period.
Spaces are not valid in variable names.
All letters will be converted to uppercase.
Reserved words are not allowed as variable names (with or without $).
May not start with letters *FN*.

Numeric Variables

May hold only numbers.
Name does not end with $.
Value is not enclosed in quotes.

String Variables

May hold any combination of characters, including only numbers.
Name ends with a $. The $ is not counted in the 40-character limit for name.
Value must be enclosed in quotes.

• EXERCISES •

Short Answer

1. Which of the following are acceptable variable names?

a. RENT	d. FLIGHT. NUMBER	g. N
b. NAME$	e. ACCOUNT#.CUST	h. P$
c. INTEREST RATE	f. $AMOUNT	i. 1040.FORM

2. Correct the following variable names:
a. `1099.FORM`
b. `ZIP CODE`
c. `%.INTEREST`
d. `PRINT`
e. `LAST NAME$`

3. Variable name check: Tell whether each of the following is a valid string variable name, valid numeric variable name, or an invalid variable name.
a. `NUMBER`
b. `AMOUNT.OF.PAY`
c. `FIRST.NAME$`
d. `1ST.NAME$`
e. `PRINT`
f. `FICA.*`
g. `TOTAL.NUMBER.1`
h. `TOTAL.#.1`
i. `THIS.VARIABLE.IS.PERCENT.OF.GROSS`
j. `PAY-AFTER-DEDUCTIONS`
k. `COLUMN.1.HEADING$`
l. `AMOUNT.LEFT.OVER.AFTER.SUBTRACTING.ALL.DEDUCTIONS`
m. `XJQW$`
n. `NET.PAY$`
o. `LAST.NAME`
p. `LET$`
q. `LET.$`

4. Correct the following:
a. `LET FIRST.NAME$ = JACK`
b. `LET AMOUNT = "241.23"`
c. `PRINT TAB$(10) "HELLO"`
d. `PRINT TAB (15) "GOODBYE"`

5. Calculate the following expressions as BASIC would:
a. `10 + 2/4 - 3`
b. `5 + 6 * 2 ^ 3`
c. `1 + 2 + 3 + 4 * 5`
d. `4 * 4 - 5/2`

6. Matching: Match each item in the left-hand column with one item in the right-hand column.
(1) keyboard
(2) monitor
(3) system unit
(4) disk drive
(5) printer
(6) floppy disk
(7) hard disk
(8) shift key
(9) PC-DOS
(10) DOS
(11) cursor
(12) DIR
(13) DISKCOPY

a. uppercase
b. file directory
c. computer "brain"
d. output device
e. input device
f. CRT
g. prepare disk for data
h. advanced BASIC
i. Winchester
j. copies of floppy disks
k. data storage
l. disk operating system
m. flexible storage medium

(14) format	n. Read-Only Memory
(15) RAM	o. position indicator on screen
(16) ROM	p. IBM operating system
(17) BASICA	q. Random Access Memory

7. Name the four components of a basic IBM PC configuration:

   _____

8. A device used to permanently store data is called _____ .

9. The two keys that work like the shift keys do nothing unless pressed at the same time as another key are the _____ and _____ keys.

10. The blinking line on the monitor that shows you where on the screen the next character you enter will appear is called the _____ .

11. If the write-protect notch of a floppy disk is covered, data cannot be written onto the disk. (T/F)

12. RAM has data permanently stored on it. (T/F)

13. To use the DOS command, DISKCOPY, two floppy disk drives are required. (T/F)

14. The disk operating system is a software program. (T/F)

15. In order to use a new disk, it is necessary to FORMAT the disk first. (T/F)

16. Describe the difference between the three types of BASIC available on the IBM PC.

17. Briefly explain the differences between a floppy disk and a hard disk.

18. Explain what is meant by the "default drive."

19. a. You boot your IBM PC, but do not see anything on the screen. List three things that could be wrong.
    b. You boot your IBM PC with a disk, but get Cassette BASIC. List three things that could be wrong.

Analyzing Code

20. PRINT: What will be printed by each of these statements? Try it. Why did BASIC print these lines as it did?
    a. `PRINT 1,000; 2,000; TAB (30) 3,000`
    b. `PRINT 1, 2, 3, 1 + 2 + 3`
    c. `LET SUM = 6`
       `PRINT "The sum is"; SUM`
    d. `PRINT "SOMETHING", IS, WRONG`
    e. `PRINT "SOMETHING IS"; "ALMOST RIGHT"`
    f. `PRINT SOMETHING IS AMISS`

21. Numeric constants: What is wrong with each of the following?
    a. `PRINT 5 1/4`
    b. `PRINT 99%`
    c. `PRINT $5.09`
    d. `PRINT 9,999,999`

22. Arithmetic expressions: How does BASIC evaluate each of these expressions? Test your understanding by first answering and then testing your answer by typing "PRINT" and then the expression. For example, type PRINT 1 + 1 to see how BASIC evaluates 1 + 1

    a. 13 + 2
    b. 13 * 2
    c. 13/2
    d. 13 - 2
    e. 13 ^ 2
    f. 13\2
    g. 13 MOD 2
    h. 13 * 2 + 13 * 2
    i. 13 + 2 * 13 ^ 2
    j. 13 MOD 3 - 2

23. Type the following. Pay careful attention to the results. Experiment with some statements of your own.

    a. PRINT 1, 500, 52.7, 777777
    b. PRINT 1; 500; 52.7; 777777
    c. PRINT 1; 500, 52.7; 777777
    d. PRINT "MY NAME IS ", "Jane", "THANK YOU"
    e. PRINT "MY NAME IS" TAB(15) "Jane" TAB(30) "THANK YOU"
    f. PRINT "MY NAME IS" TAB(50) "Jane" TAB(30) "THANK YOU"

24. Type the following series of statements and notice the results.

    a. LET POSITION = 10
       PRINT 5 TAB(POSITION) 10 TAB(POSITION + 10) 20
       TAB(POSITION + 20) 30
    b. LET MESSAGE$ = "MY NAME IS"
       PRINT MESSAGE$, "Frank"
       PRINT MESSAGE$; "Elsie"

    (How did that look? Try this instead.)

       LET MESSAGE$ = "MY NAME IS "
       PRINT MESSAGE$; "Elsie"
       PRINT MESSAGE$; "Frank", MESSAGE$; "Elsie"
       PRINT MESSAGE$ TAB(15) "Frank", MESSAGE$ TAB(30) "Elsie"

    (What happened when the tab was to the left of the cursor?)

    c. LET CITY$ = "SACRAMENTO"
       LET STATE$ = "CA"
       LET ZIP$ = 95813

    (What happened and why?)

       LET ZIP = 95813
       PRINT CITY$ + STATE$
       PRINT CITY$ + ", " + STATE$
       LET ADDRESS$ = CITY$ + ", " + STATE$
       PRINT ADDRESS$
       PRINT ADDRESS$ + " " + ZIP

    (What happened and why?)

       LET ZIP$ = "95813"
       PRINT ADDRESS$ + " " + ZIP$
    d. LET A = 15
       LET AMOUNT = 75

```
      PRINT AMOUNT/A
      LET RESULT = AMOUNT/A
      PRINT RESULT
   e. PRINT 10 + 30 + 40
      PRINT (10 + 30 + 40)/4
      PRINT 10 + 30 + 40/4
      PRINT (10 + 30) + 40/4
      LET FIRST.ANSWER = (10 + 30) * 5 + (20/(3 + 2))
      PRINT FIRST.ANSWER
   f. LET AMT1 = 10
      LET AMT2 = 30
      LET AMT3 = 40
      LET RESULT = AMT1 + AMT2 + AMT3
      PRINT RESULT
```

Writing Statements

25. a. Write a statement that will print your name, age, and birthdate on one line in separate print zones.
   b. Now rewrite the preceding to print the same information on one line but with name beginning in column 4, age beginning in column 35, and birthdate in column 60.
   c. Now rewrite the preceding to print the same information on three separate lines.

26. A house measures 100 feet by 25 feet and costs $4.85 per square foot to build. Write a series of statements that
   a. calculates and prints the total number of square feet.
   b. calculates and prints the total cost.

27. The formula for calculating the area of a circle is pi times the radius squared. Write a series of statements that will calculate and print the area of a circle with a radius of 15 (pi = 3.145926).

28. The formula for calculating the future value is:

$$FV = PV \left(1 + \frac{R}{C}\right)^{(CY)}$$

   where: PV = initial principal
   R = annual interest rate (as a decimal)
   C = number of conversion periods per year
   Y = number of years

   Write a series of statements in BASIC to calculate this. Use as many lines as you need to do this. Use the values PV = 1000, R = .10, C = 4, Y = 5

29. Write the following as a line(s) of BASIC:
   a. $3b + 2(c + 3a)$
   b. $x^2 + 3(c + 10)/z$
   c. $a + 1/2(3a + (b)(c) + 2b/c)$
   d. $\dfrac{a^2 + b^2}{ab} - \dfrac{b - a}{2}$
   e. $3 \dfrac{(2x^2 + y/z + 100)}{(a + b)}$

30. Write the following in conventional mathematical notation:
   a. a + b * (d + c)/e
   b. 2 * b + a + c/e
   c. a ^ 2 + (b - c * (a - b))/c

31. Your gross pay is $300.00. From this the following is withheld:

Social Security tax, which is .0715 of the gross
Federal withholding tax, which is $45.00
Disability insurance, which is .009 of the gross
This results in a net pay of $232.00.

Write a series of statements that will calculate and print the net pay.
   a. Do each calculation separately and print each deduction with a description.
   b. Do the calculation with one line of code and print just the net pay.

YOUR FIRST
BASIC PROGRAM

BUGS BREED IN BOREDOM

As vice president for finance for ACME Brothers, Inc., TJ was comfortable around numbers. It was a running joke in the office that you could always tell how much money was involved in a corporate deal by the amount of smoke rising from TJ's calculator keypad.

Recently, ACME Brothers had been aggressively buying other companies, management feeling that the time was ripe for diversification. In each case TJ had spent lots of time cranking out the financial ratios that indicated the relative health and wealth of the various candidates for takeover, both before and after the proposed acquisitions.

Taking figures like total sales, current assets, and accounts receivable from the financial statements of a company, TJ was able to determine the company's inventory levels, the average collection period for accounts receivable, and many other facts that affected its value as a takeover candidate.

During the third acquisition project TJ started taking a fresh look at the process of computing all those business ratios. Each of the calculations was simple enough; one number was divided by another. Unfortunately, there were so many that TJ was prone to making mistakes while punching in the numbers by hand.

The calculations were pretty much the same each time around; TJ wondered if he could just store the calculations in a computer for use over and over?

The idea seemed so logical that the next day TJ put in a request to Data Processing for a program to meet these needs. In return, Data Processing sent back so much paperwork that TJ decided it would be less trouble to continue doing the calculations by hand. Besides, Data Processing said it had a backlog of two and a half years on new program requests, while the acquisitions were going on now!

A few months earlier, the Finance office made an acquisition of its own: an IBM Personal Computer. It was used mainly for budgeting, but a lot of the time it was unused. Angry at the inability of ACME's own Data Processing shop to handle such a simple request, TJ decided to tackle it alone using the PC.

Next to the PC was a copy of *The ABCs of BASIC for the IBM Personal Computer*. TJ read Lesson 1 and experimented with PRINT and LET; already the ratios became easier to calculate. Variables could be set to the basic values from the financial statements using the LET statement and the ratios could be computed and displayed by the PRINT statement.

However, every time TJ turned off the computer, the variables were lost. What was needed was a way of storing the values so they didn't have to be reentered each time the computer was turned on.

Also, it seemed to TJ that there should be a way to store the sequence of LETs and PRINTs in the computer, so that TJ need only enter the new values and the LETs and PRINTs would execute in sequence automatically. Hoping to find a way to do this, TJ turned to Lesson 2.

·THE ABCS OF BASIC ON THE IBM PERSONAL COMPUTER·

LESSON 2: YOUR FIRST BASIC PROGRAM

In the first lesson you learned how to use LET and PRINT to perform calculations and to display information. In this lesson you will first learn how to store a sequence of statements as a "program" so they can be executed any number of times without retyping. Because programs in memory are erased when the computer is turned off or rebooted, you will learn how to make permanent copies of the programs on disk using "SAVE". To do this, we will cover the following commands and statements: STOP, RUN, LIST, DELETE, REM, FILES, KILL, and NAME.

We will also introduce pseudocode, one of several tools used by programmers to design and document programs.

A Program Is a Numbered Sequence of BASIC Statements

Programs are sets of numbered statements that can be saved for reuse and can be easily modified (compared to retyping each statement in sequence).

• PROGRAMS •

A program is a numbered sequence of BASIC statements.
Programs can be stored on disks.
Programs can be changed, or edited.

Here is an example of a simple BASIC program that prints the word *hello* on the monitor.

```
10 PRINT "hello"
20 END
RUN
hello
Ok
```

Let's go through this example line by line.

```
10 PRINT "hello"
```

This is the same as the PRINT statement you learned in Lesson 1, except that it has a number 10 in front of it. Without the number, BASIC would have immediately printed *hello* on the monitor. With the number in front of the line, BASIC does nothing with the PRINT statement immediately; it stores it as the first line in your program.

END Finishes the Program

```
20 END
```

This is line 20 of the program. It contains a new BASIC statement called END. END, appropriately enough, marks the end of processing. It tells BASIC that the program is through and returns control to the user. Remember that BASIC hasn't

• LINE NUMBERS •

A BASIC statement preceded by a line number is stored for later use.
A BASIC statement not preceded by a line number is executed immediately and is not stored.

done anything with either the PRINT or the END statements yet; it has simply stored them by their line numbers.

RUN Tells BASIC to Execute the Program

```
RUN
hello
Ok
```

Another BASIC command is RUN. The RUN command tells BASIC, "OK, I'm done entering my list of statements (program). Now I want you to execute the statements I entered." BASIC responds by executing the program starting with the first line, which is line 10, the PRINT statement. This causes *hello* to be displayed on the monitor. BASIC then executes the next line (line 20), which contains the END statement. This stops the program execution and returns control to the screen. The "Ok" message is displayed to show that the program has been finished.

Pseudocode Is Programmers' Shorthand

A computer program is a pretty simple concept. If you have ever followed a cooking recipe, the instructions for assembling a toy, or even a corporate procedure manual, you have "executed" a program of sorts. BASIC programs are also numbered sequences of steps, using BASIC statements instead of English to describe the actions to be taken.

This analogy is so strong that many experienced programmers design their programs by starting with an English-like description of the steps they wish the program to follow. For example, when designing a program to compute the gross margin of an item, one might start with the following outline:

1. Set variables GROSS and COST to the sales price and cost of the item, respectively.
2. Compute the gross margin in dollars by subtracting COST from GROSS.
3. Compute the gross margin as a percentage of sales price by dividing the gross margin in dollars by GROSS, then multiplying by 100 to convert to a percentage.
4. Print out the results.

·END AND RUN: THE STOP AND GO OF BASIC·

END stops execution of a program.
RUN starts execution of a program.

An outline such as this can be readily translated into specific BASIC statements, and it provides a better starting point for programming than plunging into LETs and PRINTs directly. For a program as simple as this, it may seem a waste of time to start with an outline, but as you will soon learn, programs are rarely this simple. As humans, we have trouble thinking "in BASIC." Using outlines is one tool you will learn to help bridge the gap between the way humans think and read and the instructions a computer must have to operate.

Code is commonly used to describe collectively the statements in a computer program. Because outlines of programs are usually written in half-English, half-BASIC, such outlines are called **pseudocode.** You will learn this and other methods of designing programs, such as techniques for visualizing a program by drawing boxes, arrows, and other symbols to describe the intended action. The use of pseudocode and/or visual design tools is the hallmark of the professional programmer.

Questions and Answers about Line Numbers

Here are the answers to some common questions about line numbers in BASIC.

1. *Q: How many lines can I have in a program?*
   A: This depends on how much temporary memory (RAM) your IBM PC has, but it's in the thousands.
2. *Q: What are legal line numbers?*
   A: Line numbers can be any integer from 0 through 65529. No matter what numbers you give the lines, BASIC will sort them into ascending numeric sequence. Most programmers use multiples of 10 for their line numbers. As you will see in later examples, this allows new lines to be inserted easily into the program.
3. *Q: How long can a BASIC program line be?*
   A: A line in a BASIC program can be up to 254 characters long. This may be a little confusing, since the monitor can only display 80 characters on one line of the display. If a BASIC program line is more than 80 characters long, it is split on the monitor into more than one line for display purposes only; BASIC still considers it to be one line in your program. For example, the following is one line in a BASIC program, even though it is displayed on two lines on the monitor.

```
10 PRINT "This is a very long message.  It is all part of one big PRINT statement
, even though it appears on more than one display line"
```

4. *Q: What happens if I enter more than 254 characters?*
   A: BASIC will let you type it in but will ignore all characters beyond the 254th character. Since three 80-column display lines total 240 characters, it is convenient to remember that BASIC program lines that exceed three displayed lines should be checked carefully to make sure they do not exceed the 254 character maximum.
5. *Q: Can I put more than one statement on a line?*
   A: Yes. Separate them by colons (:). This will be discussed later.

Direct Mode Versus Indirect Mode: Do It Now or Later?

Most BASIC statements can be either directly typed in without a line number, as you did with PRINT and LET in Lesson 1, or be used in one or more lines of a program. If you enter a statement without a line number, BASIC executes it as soon as you press Enter. This is the **direct mode** of operation (sometimes called command mode). If you type a statement with a number in front of it, BASIC assumes that it is a line to be stored in the current program. In this case, the statement is stored for later use, not executed immediately. This is called BASIC's **indirect mode.** The program can be executed at a later time by using the RUN command.

NEW Clears Memory for New Program

BASIC can only hold one program at a time in its temporary memory. Before you start typing in a new program, you should clear out the current program by using the NEW command. Otherwise, the new lines you type will be merged with lines from the old program.

Remember that NEW erases your current program from temporary memory. If you want to save a copy of your program first, use the SAVE command (explained later in this lesson) to store a copy permanently onto a floppy disk before using NEW.

```
NEW
Ok
```

Programs Can Be Run Again and Again

Here is a short program that computes and prints the gross margin.

```
NEW
Ok
10 LET COST = 8
20 LET PRICE = 10
30 LET MARGIN.IN.DOLLARS = PRICE - COST
40 LET MARGIN.IN.PERCENT = MARGIN.IN.DOLLARS / PRICE * 100
50 PRINT "Cost =";COST,"Selling price =";PRICE
60 PRINT "Gross margin in dollars ="; MARGIN.IN.DOLLARS
70 PRINT "Gross margin as % of price ="; MARGIN.IN.PERCENT
80 END
RUN
Cost = 8  Selling price = 10
Gross margin in dollars = 2
Gross margin as % of price = 20
Ok
```

You could have accomplished the same thing by typing the PRINTs and LETs for immediate execution. In fact, it probably would have taken less time without all those line numbers. However, once a program is in the computer's memory, it can be executed over and over by typing and retyping RUN.

•THE NEW COMMAND•

NEW clears the current program out of memory so that a NEW one can
be entered.
NEW does not save a copy!

```
RUN
Cost = 8  Selling price = 10
Gross margin in dollars = 2
Gross margin as % of price = 20
Ok
```

You didn't have to retype the PRINTs and LETs since the program is retained in
memory. You can execute it any number of times.

Why Edit a Program?

It has been said that there are three things that are certain in life: death, taxes, and
changes to your computer programs. Changes need to be made for a variety of
reasons:

1. The programmer made a mistake.
2. The person telling the programmer what the program is supposed to do
   made a mistake or was not clear enough.

•EDITING•

Editing Commands
LIST displays all or part of the current program.
DELETE deletes one or more lines.

Editing Techniques

ADDING A LINE
Select a line number that places the new line in the correct sequence in the
program, then type in the new line using that line number.

CHANGING A LINE
Retype the line using the old line number.

3. The needs of the business have changed, and the program must be changed to match.
4. Extra features are to be added to a working program.

The process of changing a program is called **editing.** Some typical editing tasks might involve:

1. Changing one or more lines in a program
2. Adding one or more new lines to a program
3. Deleting one or more lines from a program,
4. Renumbering the lines in a program

BASIC provides a variety of ways to do editing. In this chapter we will discuss two commands, LIST and DELETE, plus a few techniques that will allow you to get by for the moment. Lesson 4 examines editing in much more detail.

LIST Displays Lines in a Program

It is difficult to change something you can't see, so the first editing command you should learn in BASIC is LIST. The LIST command displays all or some of the current program's lines on the monitor. The lines are always listed in order of increasing line numbers.

LIST Displays All the Lines

```
LIST
10 LET COST = 8
20 LET PRICE = 10
30 LET MARGIN.IN.DOLLARS = PRICE - COST
40 LET MARGIN.IN.PERCENT = MARGIN.IN.DOLLARS/PRICE * 100
50 PRINT "Cost =";COST,"Price =";PRICE
60 PRINT "Gross margin in dollars =";MARGIN.IN.DOLLARS
70 PRINT "Gross margin as % of price =";MARGIN.IN.PERCENT
80 END
Ok
```

LIST n Displays Just One Line

As you can see, all of the lines typed in earlier are displayed in line number order on the monitor by the LIST command. If you want to list only one line of the program, put the number of that line after the LIST command:

```
LIST 10
10 LET COST = 8
Ok
```

LIST n-z Displays a Group of Lines

By putting a single line number after the LIST command, you have told BASIC to list only that one line. If you wish to list a range of line numbers, type LIST followed by the lowest line number to be listed, a hyphen or minus sign (-), and the highest line number to be listed.

```
LIST 10-30
10 LET COST = 8
20 LET PRICE = 10
30 LET MARGIN.IN.DOLLARS = PRICE - COST
Ok
```

The command "LIST 10-30" caused lines 10 through 30, inclusive, to be listed.

LIST -z Displays From First Line to Line z
If you want to list from the first line in your program up to, and including, a particular line, follow the LIST command with a hyphen and the ending line number:

```
LIST -30
10 LET COST = 8
20 LET PRICE = 10
30 LET MARGIN.IN.DOLLARS = PRICE - COST
Ok
```

LIST n- Displays Lines From n to End
If you want to list from a particular line to the end of the program, follow the LIST command with the beginning line number and a hyphen:

```
LIST 60-
60 PRINT "Gross margin in dollars =";MARGIN.IN.DOLLARS
70 PRINT "Gross margin as % of price =";MARGIN.IN.PERCENT
80 END
Ok
```

LLIST and LPRINT Send a List to the Printer
If your computer has a printer, you may want to use these two additional statements, LLIST and LPRINT. LLIST is the same as LIST except that the listing is sent to the printer instead of the monitor. LPRINT is the same as PRINT except that the output appears on the printer instead of the monitor.

Adding Lines to Programs

To add a new line to a program, select a line number that indicates where in the program the line is to be placed and type in the line.

```
5 PRINT "Gross Margin Report"
RUN
Gross Margin Report
Cost = 8  Selling price = 10
Gross margin in dollars = 2
Gross margin as % of price = 20
Ok
LIST 5-10
5 PRINT "Gross Margin Report"
10 LET COST = 8
Ok
```

As you can see, BASIC automatically puts the new line, numbered 5, in its proper place in the program.

Suppose you now want to add a line that prints a blank line between the title of the report and the body. You could use any number between 5 and 50 that is not already being used in the program.

```
6 PRINT
LIST 5-10
5 PRINT "Gross Margin Report"
6 PRINT
10 LET COST = 8
Ok
RUN
Gross Margin Report

Cost = 8  Selling price = 10
Gross margin in dollars = 2
Gross margin as % of price = 20
Ok
```

Numbering Lines by 10s Is Good Programming Practice

Because it is common to have to add new lines to a program, most experienced BASIC programmers number their lines in multiples of 10. This gives nine intermediate numbers to use for adding lines later.

In large programs, it is common to assign a block of line numbers to particular sections or modules of the program. For example, all the introductory lines might use numbers 100 through 199, the main processing module might use numbers 1000 through 1999, another section might use numbers 2000 through 2999, and so on. This practice makes a long program easier to read.

To Change a Program Line, Retype It

To change a line, type in the line as you wish it to be using its current line number. If you enter a line with the same line number as a line currently in the program, BASIC deletes the old line and substitutes the new one. In the preceding program, if you wish to change the value of COST from 8 to 9, simply type the following:

```
10 LET COST = 9
LIST 5-20
5 PRINT "Gross Margin Report"
6 PRINT
10 LET COST = 9
20 LET PRICE = 10
Ok
RUN
Gross Margin Report
```

```
Cost = 9  Selling price = 10
Gross margin in dollars = 1
Gross margin as % of price = 10
Ok
```

Line 10 has been changed to the line you typed in.

DELETE Deletes Lines from a Program

To delete one or more lines from a program, use the DELETE command. As with LIST, if you want to delete one line, place the number of that line after the word DELETE. If you want to delete a range of line numbers, put the lower and upper numbers after DELETE, separated by a hyphen.

DELETE n

```
DELETE 5
LIST
6 PRINT
10 LET COST = 9
20 LET PRICE = 10
30 LET MARGIN.IN.DOLLARS = PRICE - COST
40 LET MARGIN.IN.PERCENT = MARGIN.IN.DOLLARS/PRICE * 100
50 PRINT "Cost =";COST,"Selling price =";PRICE
60 PRINT "Gross margin in dollars ="; MARGIN.IN.DOLLARS
70 PRINT "Gross margin as % of price ="; MARGIN.IN.PERCENT
80 END
Ok
```

DELETE n-m

```
DELETE 30-70
LIST
6 PRINT
10 LET COST = 9
20 LET PRICE = 10
80 END
Ok
```

DELETE -n Where n Is Any Line Number

As with LIST, you can specify all lines from the beginning of the program through any line by using DELETE followed by a hyphen and the line through which you wish deleted.

DELETE n- Where n Is Any Line Number

To delete all lines from a given line to the end of the program, use the form shown in this heading.

Be Careful with DELETE; It's Easy to Make a Big Mistake!
DELETE used all by itself will erase all lines of your program from memory, as will DELETE followed by just a hyphen.

WARNING! A line number typed by itself will delete the line with that number from your program. For example, if you now type 10 without a statement following it, line 10 will be deleted.

```
10
LIST
6 PRINT
20 LET PRICE = 10
80 END
Ok
```

Typing a line number that is not in the current program has no effect on the program and will produce the message "Undefined line number."

```
25
Undefined line number
Ok
LIST
6 PRINT
20 LET PRICE = 10
80 END
Ok
```

Temporarily Halting a Program's Execution

STOP

STOP is similar to END: it causes the program to stop executing. However, END is intended to stop the program for the last time, while STOP is intended to halt the program temporarily. This allows you to PRINT the contents of variables or take other action to ensure that the program is working properly. While both will terminate the processing of a program and return control to the screen, there are two main differences between END and STOP.

1. STOP will cause the following message to appear: "BREAK in line nn" where nn is the number of the line in which STOP appears. END will not cause this message to appear.
2. END closes all open files; STOP does not close files. (Lesson 7 discusses files in detail.)

END is the preferred statement for indicating the end of a program. Technically, you could simply allow your BASIC program to run out of lines, without using an END statement at all. When BASIC has executed the last line in your program and finds that there are no higher-numbered lines, BASIC terminates processing and returns control to the screen. This, however, is poor programming practice. It is much better to tell BASIC (and any other programmer who must read your program) explicitly where the program is to end.

Use STOP to Find Errors: DEBUGGING with CONTinue

STOP is useful for finding programming errors. It can be inserted while looking for errors and removed later. If your program has STOPped, you can tell BASIC to resume where it left off by using the CONT (for "continue") command.

```
BREAK IN LINE 590
CONT
```

In this example, presumably line 590 contained a STOP statement, which caused BASIC, upon reaching that line, to print out the BREAK message. The CONT command would then cause the program to pick up where it left off — namely, with the statement following STOP.

BREAK Stops Program Execution without a STOP Statement

Pressing Ctrl-Break (holding down the Control key while pressing the Scroll Lock/Break key) while a program is executing also will STOP the program and print a BREAK AT LINE nn message.

As with STOP, processing can be continued using the CONT command.

Colon (:) Allows More Than One Statement on a Line

As mentioned earlier, it is possible to put more than one statement on a line in BASIC. To do so, place a colon (:) between the statements.

```
NEW
10 LET COST = 8: LET PRICE = 10: LET MARGIN = PRICE - COST
20 PRINT COST, PRICE, MARGIN
30 END
RUN
8               10              2
Ok
```

Line 10 has three LET statements connected by colons. This technique can be used with any BASIC statements to build complicated lines. In general, however,

---

•STOP, Ctrl-Break, AND CONT: THREE TOOLS FOR TESTING•

STOP is placed in a program to stop processing at a specific line. Displays message: "Break in line nn".

Ctrl-Break, when pressed at same time during processing, will cause stop at line currently being processed. Displays message: "Break in line nn".

CONT will continue processing at point where STOP or BREAK occurred.

you should try to avoid putting more than one statement on a line. This makes it easier to read and understand the program. It also makes it easier to change individual statements in the program. This said, there are cases where two or more statements so naturally group together that it actually improves the readability of the program to group them on one line. There are no absolute standards to follow; let your instincts guide you. If there is any doubt, put the statements on separate lines.

REM or ' Provides Remarks for Program Documentation

There is one BASIC statement that does absolutely nothing: REM (short for REMark). Having a REM statement does not cause a program to behave any differently than not having a REM statement, but REM is arguably one of the most important statements in BASIC.

REM is used to record your comments about a program in the program itself. It is one means of communicating your thoughts about the program to another programmer, or even to yourself at a later date. REM does not change the program's behavior, but it does change the behavior of people who create and maintain the program.

```
NEW
Ok
10 REM This is a comment about the program
20 PRINT "FIRST LINE"
30 END
LIST
10 REM This is a comment about the program
20 PRINT "FIRST LINE"
30 END
Ok
RUN
FIRST LINE
Ok
```

As you can see, the REM statement appeared in the listing but had no effect on the operation of the program.

·THE REM STATEMENT·

REM allows you to record comments in a program. This makes the program easier to read and understand. The symbol ' may be used in place of REM.

BASIC allows you to use an apostrophe (') instead of REM for convenience. We could have written line 10 as follows:

```
10 ' This is a comment about the program
```

REMarks and Documentation Are Vital to Good Programming

In large, complex programs REM is not only convenient; it is vital. Computer programs get complicated very easily and are soon too complicated for the human mind to follow without help. For this reason, experienced programmers insert REM statements into their programs to explain that program to others, or even to themselves! This is called **internal documentation.** "Documentation" here means that it explains the program; "internal" means it is embedded in the program as opposed to a separate document.

It is tempting for the inexperienced programmer to write computer programs with few or no REMs, but there are several good reasons to put explanatory REMs in every computer program, no matter how small:

1. Good documentation is usually taken as a sign of competence.
2. Good documentation is required by most employers.
3. Good documentation allows someone else to maintain your programs, freeing you up for promotions and new assignments. Without good documentation, you are married to your programs.
4. Good documentation can actually speed up the process of writing and testing a computer program.

The word *good* is used in each of these reasons, but unfortunately there is no universally accepted definition of "good documentation." Everyone agrees that "good" documentation:

1. Is easy to read.
2. Can be understood by someone who knows BASIC but who doesn't know anything about the problem the program tries to solve.
3. Does not use technical terminology except where unavoidable.
4. Does not use any abbreviations or acronyms that are not clearly defined.
5. Adds to, rather than mimics, the program itself.

This is an example of good documentation:

```
1050 REM Add the accumulated interest (INTEREST) to the principal (PRINCIPAL)
1060 LET PRINCIPAL = PRINCIPAL + INTEREST
```

This is an example of bad documentation:

```
1050 REM Increment P by I
1060 LET P = P + I
```

See the difference? The first example adds to the meaning of the BASIC program; the comment in the second example just gets in the way. To borrow a phrase, "Good documentation is something that no one can define but that everyone can recognize." Remember that the idea is to explain your program to someone who probably knows little about the problem at hand and the techniques you used to solve that problem. With this in mind, you will not go too far wrong. When in doubt, put in extra REMarks to make the program understandable.

Although REM statements are not executed, they still must be analyzed by BASIC. For this reason they slightly slow processing speed. However, they make programs easier to maintain. Therefore, business programs should be well documented since processing speed is generally not a problem. One of the authors of this book once spent several weeks trying to comprehend a three-year-old BASIC program so that certain changes could be made. The program had been written by a brash young programmer who, lacking experience, used very few REMs. At the time the programmer felt that since his programming style was impeccable, the program was "self-explanatory." Three years later it proved to be anything but obvious; the program, although well written, was almost unmaintainable. This, of course, was frustrating to your author, but he was doubly frustrated because it was he who had written the program three years earlier!

Documenting Program Lines Using Apostrophe
One frequent use of the colon is to put a REM at the end of a line.

```
10 PRINT GROSS.PAY - DEDUCTIONS: REM Print net pay
```

Instead of typing (: REM), you may simply type an apostrophe (').

```
NEW
10 REM This program prints two lines
20 ' and demonstrates the Remark Statement
30 PRINT "LINE ONE": REM First Line
40 PRINT "LINE TWO" ' Second Line
50 END
RUN
LINE ONE
LINE TWO
Ok
```

Notice that when ' is used, the colon (:) after the previous statement is not needed.

When a remark is placed on the same line with other statements, everything after the :REM or ' is considered part of the remark.

```
NEW
10 LET A = 10: LET B = 20: REM Set Variables: LET C = 30
20 PRINT A; B; C
30 END
RUN
 10  20  0
Ok
```

The statement LET C = 30 was considered part of the remark and not executed by BASIC.

•PARABLES FOR PROGRAMMERS•

No Comment

Once upon a time there lived two programmers, Fanny and Alexander. Both were clever programmers who could write the most difficult of programs, but they disagreed over the use of comments in their programs.

Alexander used few comments. He felt that his programs were "obvious" and therefore didn't need comments. Besides, it took a lot of time and energy to write comments, time which could be spent writing more and better programs. Alexander also claimed that comments took up valuable space in memory and slowed down programs.

Fanny believed in using comments throughout her programs. She wrote the comments in such a way that any person with a knowledge of BASIC, but without any knowledge of the problem at hand, could understand and change her programs. Because she took the time to write lots of comments, Fanny did not program as quickly as Alexander, but when a management position opened, Fanny got the promotion.

"Alexander," the boss said, "you have all the qualifications for promotion but one: I can't replace you! Because your programs don't have comments, you are the only one who can fix them.

MORAL: A program without comments is an albatross about your neck.

Using REM to Break Up a Program into Sections, or Where to Draw the Line
In large programs it is frequently useful to put blank lines into a program to break up the program into smaller sections, called modules. It is a lot easier to read ten modules of five lines each than one 50-line program. If you want a blank line, put a REM statement (or a ') after the line number but with no comment following the word REM. (If you enter just a line number without a REM, BASIC will simply DELETE the line with that line number.)

Some programmers like to draw lines between modules of a program by using a REM followed by 60 or 80 minus signs, equals signs, or asterisks. This is also good practice and breaks up a program even better than blank lines.

The following is the program we used earlier to compute gross margin with REMarks added to it. We have used a number of different styles to demonstrate the flexibility of REM. When writing a program for production, it is good practice to adopt one style and use it throughout the program. Even though this is a short program, notice how the three "modules" of initialization, calculation, and output are separated by the REM statements.

```
10 REM * This Program Calculates and Prints Gross Margin *
20 REM ***
30 ' *** Written by T. J. Carlson, 05/17/87
40 '
50 ' ===========================================================
60 REM
70 '        ***      Initialize Values   ***
80 LET COST = 8:     REM COST is the wholesale cost
90 LET PRICE = 10   '     PRICE is the selling price
100 '
110 ' ------------ Compute Margin -------------------------
120 '
130 LET MARGIN.IN.DOLLARS = PRICE - COST
140 LET MARGIN.IN.PERCENT = MARGIN.IN.DOLLARS/PRICE * 100
150 REM
160 REM ===========================================================
170 REM         PRINT MARGIN
180 REM ===========================================================
190 PRINT "Cost ="; COST, "Selling price ="; PRICE
200 PRINT "Gross margin in dollars ="; MARGIN.IN.DOLLARS
210 PRINT "Gross margin as % of price ="; MARGIN.IN.PERCENT
220 END
230 '    ######    END OF PROGRAM ##########
```

How to Store Programs Permanently on Magnetic Disks

You now know that only one program at a time can be held in temporary memory and that the program disappears when you turn off the power or use the NEW command. Obviously, there must be some way of permanently storing a program or BASIC would not be a very useful programming language.

BASIC allows you to store copies of your programs on floppy disks. Floppy disks are organized into **files,** making each floppy disk a filing cabinet of sorts (see Figure 2.1).

FIGURE 2.1 · Programs and files. Think of each floppy disk as a filing cabinet. Each folder in the cabinet is a "file." Some files contain BASIC programs, while others may contain data or other types of files. Each file is identified by its name.

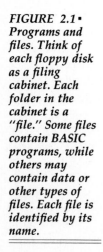
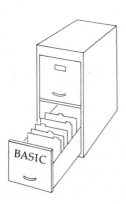

BASIC provides several commands that allow you to manipulate programs and floppy disks.

SAVE Puts a Copy of Your Program on the Disk

The SAVE command makes a copy on disk of the program in temporary memory. Before you SAVE a program, you must have a formatted diskette in your disk drive.

```
NEW
Ok
10 LET DEBT = 100
20 LET EQUITY = 50
30 PRINT "debt/equity = ";DEBT/EQUITY
40 END
RUN
debt/equity = 2
Ok
SAVE "DEBTEQU"
Ok
```

Each Program Can Be Named

Your program is now stored (saved) on the floppy disk. The SAVE command told BASIC to store the program as a file on the disk under the name "DEBTEQU". In BASIC each separate file must be uniquely identified by the combination of a name and an extension. The name may be up to eight characters, the extension three. The characters allowed are all letters and digits and the following special characters

( ) { } @ # $ % ^ & ! - _ ` ' / ~

Characters you may not use are

* [ ] , + : ; = < > \

•COMMANDS RELATED TO FILES•

SAVE "filename.ext" stores the current program on a disk.
FILES displays a list of files on a disk.
LOAD "filename.ext" brings a file from disk into memory.
KILL "filename.ext" removes a file from a disk.
NAME "oldfile.ext" as "newfile.ext" changes the name of a file on a disk.

(The symbols <, >, and \ were allowed in early releases of BASIC but cannot be used in filenames in version 2.0 and later.) The name may have fewer than eight characters but should have no embedded spaces. The preceding file "DEBTEQU" has a seven-letter name. It could have been named "DEBT-EQU" or "DEBT_EQU" but should not be named "DEBT EQU".

The extension is a period followed by up to three characters. If you do not specify the extension in a SAVE command, BASIC will automatically append ".BAS" as the extension. Thus, as stored by the SAVE command, your program will be in filename "DEBTEQU.BAS". Programmers often use the extension to categorize their programs. For example, all accounts payable programs might have the extension ".AP", and all marketing programs might have the extension ".MKT". Later in this lesson you will learn how to get a listing of all programs sharing a common extension. The use of extensions other than ".BAS" to categorize programs has both advantages and drawbacks. As long as your usage is consistent with that of others who must share your programs, the use of extensions is a matter of style.

In the SAVE command we entered the filename with quotes around it. Filenames are string constants and therefore must have quotes around them. If you attempt to use a filename without quotes, BASIC will assume that the name given is that of a variable, not a file. This is true for all BASIC commands and statements in which filenames are specified.

It is possible to use string variables to hold filenames.

```
LET A$ = "DEBTEQU"
Ok
SAVE A$
Ok
```

What Happens If You Specify More Than Eight Characters?

If you inadvertently make your filename longer than eight characters and do not specify an extension, BASIC will insert a period after the first eight and use the extra characters (up to three) for the extension. The rest will be ignored. If you make your filename longer than eight characters and also specify an extension, BASIC will give you an error message.

```
SAVE "ALONGNAME"
```

results in a file named "ALONGNAM.E". Beware of this "feature" of BASIC.

SAVE Copies Over Existing Files with the Same Name

WARNING! If you use SAVE with a file name that is currently used for another file on the disk, the old file is replaced with the current program! Don't panic; this can be an advantage when you have made corrections to a program and want to replace the old copy with a corrected version. However, you can easily wipe out a good program by using the wrong filename by mistake. For this reason it is vital that you keep track of all the filenames currently in use. If you do not know or have forgotten what filenames have been used, use the FILES command.

FILES Lists the Files on the Disk

In Lesson 1 you learned about DIR, the DOS command that displays the names of the files that are on the disk. There is a similar command in BASIC called FILES. To get a list of the files on your disk, type FILES as shown in the following example:

```
FILES
COMMAND .COM    FORMAT  .COM    CHKDSK  .COM    SYS     .COM
RATIOS  .BAS    CKWRITE .AP     INVEST  .BAS    CKRECON .AP
TESTPROG.BAS    FORCAST .MKT    DEBTEQU .BAS
Ok
```

When you use FILES on your disk, the listing produced will probably be longer than this list. We are simplifying things a little here. Notice that on the listing there are always eight spaces reserved for the file name and three characters after the period as the extension. Try FILES on your disk and see what files are there.

Most of the time you will not be interested in files with any extension other than ".BAS". To list only those files, use this form of the FILES command:

```
FILES "*.BAS"
RATIOS  .BAS    INVEST  .BAS    TESTPROG.BAS    DEBTEQU .BAS
Ok
```

The files actually listed will, of course, depend on the contents of your disk, but notice that on the author's sample disk, only programs with an extension of ".BAS" were listed. The asterisk (*) in this case means "I don't care what the name is, just the extension." The asterisk acts as a "wild card."

The asterisk can be used in a number of combinations to select names of files. When the asterisk is used, BASIC will match on all the characters that appear to the left of the asterisk in either the filename or the extension. The following are examples using the files listed earlier.

```
FILES "DE*.BAS"
DEBTEQU .BAS
Ok
```

Only files with the ".BAS" extension, and whose names begin with the letters "DE", were listed.

```
FILES "FOR*.*"
FORMAT  .COM    FORCAST .MKT
Ok
```

Files that began with FOR were listed; the extension does not matter. Remember that to get a listing of the files use the FILES command from the BASIC prompt (Ok) and use the DIR command from the DOS prompt (A>).

LOAD Reads in from Disk a Previously Stored Program

If you want to retrieve a program from disk, use the LOAD command.

```
NEW
LIST
Ok
```

This shows you that there is now no program in memory.

```
LOAD "DEBTEQU"
Ok
LIST
10 LET DEBT = 100
20 LET EQUITY = 50
30 PRINT "debt/equity = ";DEBT/EQUITY
40 END
Ok
RUN
debt/equity = 2
Ok
```

The LOAD command brought our file from the disk into memory. As with SAVE, BASIC assumes that the extension is ".BAS" if you do not supply a different extension. If the extension is something other than ".BAS", it must be specified when using the LOAD command.

If you want to LOAD a file and immediately RUN it, you can use a variation on the RUN command to both load and run a program stored on disk. The command RUN "DEBTEQU" is equivalent to the command LOAD "DEBTEQU" followed by RUN. Beware: this version of RUN wipes out any program currently in memory in order to load the requested program.

KILL Deletes Unwanted Files from Disk

If you decide that you want to get rid of a disk file, use the KILL command.

```
KILL "DEBTEQU.BAS"
Ok
```

The file "DEBTEQU.BAS" is now gone. Notice that you must type in the entire name, including the ".BAS" extension, with the KILL command. BASIC doesn't want you to make a casual mistake by confusing two files with the same name but different extensions. KILL is obviously capable of wreaking a lot of unintended havoc, so be very careful to think before you use it and, above all, spell correctly!

NAME Renames Files on Disk

Rounding out the file commands is NAME, which allows you to rename a file on a floppy disk.

```
NEW
Ok
10 PRINT "Hello"
20 END
SAVE "TEST"
FILES "TE*.BAS"
TEST .BAS
Ok
NAME "TEST.BAS" AS "TEST2.BAS"
Ok
FILES "TE*.BAS"
TEST2 .BAS
Ok
```

The NAME command changed the name of this program from "TEST.BAS" to "TEST2.BAS". Notice that the entire filename, including the extension, is needed with NAME.

NAME changes only the name of a file; it does not alter the contents nor does it make an extra copy. Before executing NAME, BASIC will check to see if a file with the old name currently exists on the disk. If none does, the message "File not found" will be displayed. BASIC will also check that no file with the new name is already on the disk. If there is one, the message "File already exists" will be displayed.

But My Computer Has Two Disk Drives!

If your IBM PC has two disk drives, they will be referred to as drive A and drive B. At all times one of the two is the "default" drive. We talked a little about drive names and default drives in Lesson 1 as regards using PC-DOS before getting to BASIC. Let's see how having two drives affects BASIC.

Whenever you use a file name in a BASIC command such as SAVE without explicitly telling BASIC to which drive it should refer, BASIC assumes that the file is to apply to the disk in the default drive. Drive A is generally the default drive. Therefore, as long as you are working on files that are on drive A, you need not specify the drive. If, however, you wish to use drive B, you must put a "B:" in front of the filenames in all BASIC commands. For example:

SAVE "DEBTEQU" saves the file on the current drive, drive A, in this case.
SAVE "B:DEBTEQU" saves the file on the disk in drive B regardless of
    which drive is current.

This rule holds for all commands that use filenames, including SAVE, LOAD, FILES, KILL, and NAME.

Commands Versus Statements

You may have noticed that two terms have been used in explaining BASIC: command and statement. For example, we described PRINT as a statement and

SAVE as a command. The distinction between the two has lost much of its original importance today but is in wide use in BASIC documentation and books nonetheless.

In the early days of BASIC certain features of the language could only be used in direct mode (i.e., directly typed in for immediate execution, not as part of a program). These features included, for example, RUN, which at that time had no meaning as part of a program. These were called **commands.** Other features were primarily used as parts of programs, such as LET and PRINT. These were called **statements.**

Today's versions of BASIC allow most commands to be used in programs, and most statements to be executed directly. Thus, the terminology has lost much of its original meaning. However, when reading reference materials on BASIC, you should understand what is meant by these terms:

- **Commands** are features that are almost always entered in direct (immediate) mode. RUN, LIST, SAVE, and NEW are examples of commands.
- **Statements** generally are used in programs (i.e., indirect mode). LET and PRINT are examples of statements.

Knowing the distinction between the two is not all that important, as long as you know what can be used in a program and what cannot. In this book the terms *statement* and *command* have been used in the same context as the standard IBM BASIC manual for the PC.

When Your Disk Isn't "Big" Enough

Disks are a fixed size and therefore can fill up to the point where there is no more room for files. Try to avoid keeping copies of worthless programs on your disks by using the KILL command wisely. If your disk is full and you attempt to SAVE a program, you will get an error message. When this happens, you have three options:

1. KILL one or more files to make room.
2. SAVE the program on a different disk.
3. Forget about saving the program.

Techniques for Readability

We discussed earlier the importance of using the REM statement to make programs easier for people to read and understand. Likewise, spacing can frequently improve the readability of a line of code without affecting the outcome. For example, these lines:

```
70 PRINT "Current Ratio: " TAB(16) CURRENT.ASSETS/CURRENT.LIABILITIES,
         "Debit Ratio: "   TAB(42) TOTAL.DEBT/TOTAL.ASSETS,
         "Inv. Turnover"   TAB(75) SALES/INVENTORY
```

are easier to read than:

```
80 PRINT "Current Ratio: " TAB(16) CURRENT.ASSETS/CURRENT.LIABILITIES, "Debit Ra
tio: " TAB(42) TOTAL.DEBT/TOTAL.ASSETS, "Inv. Turnover" TAB(75) SALES/INVENTORY
```

Extra spaces between variables, as shown in line 70, will not affect processing; however spaces *within* the quotes, as in the following example, will.

```
90 PRINT "Current Ratio: " TAB(16) CURRENT.ASSETS/CURRENT.LIABILITIES, "Debit
        Ratio: " TAB(42) TOTAL.DEBT/TOTAL.ASSETS, "Inv. Turnover" TAB(75)
        SALES/INVENTORY
```

Assuming that the variables have been defined earlier in the program, here is the result when each of the three lines is run:

```
Current Ratio:  2       Debit Ratio:  .3              Inv. Turnover      10
Current Ratio:  2       Debit Ratio:  .3              Inv. Turnover      10
Current Ratio:  2       Debit            Ratio:
                                  .3              Inv. Turnover      10
```

As we expected, the first two lines of output are exactly the same. However, the extra spaces that were inserted with the string "Debit Ratio: " in line 90 appear on the output line as well.

To get the extra spaces at the end of the physical lines as we did in line 70, you can press the space bar the desired number of times. After BASIC displays the cursor in column 80, it wraps around to column 1 on the next line on the screen. But BASIC also gives you a shortcut that you can use to space down to the next line when you are entering a long line of code. Holding down the Ctrl key as you press Enter will insert enough spaces to take you to the beginning of the next line. This Ctrl/Enter acts as a pseudo-linefeed.

It is good programming practice to make your lines of code as easy to read as possible. Just remember that all spaces you insert are counted in the 254 character maximum line length.

THE STORY'S END

TJ now knew the program could be saved to be used over and over. All those tiresome calculations, once saved, could be recalculated easily. Each time there was a new company being considered for acquisition, the program could be LOADed into memory, edited to change the values of particular variables, and RUN. No more piles of adding machine tapes! No more going through 20 calculations only to discover an error was made on the first and they all had to be done again! Now different acquisitions could be considered quickly and accurately.

It was even possible to change one or two of the variables slightly and see how the results changed. Because of the hours and hours it used to take, TJ never had been able to do this before.

TJ solved his problem by writing a program in BASIC. First TJ wrote pseudo-code as a shorthand for what the program was to do. TJ's program is shown, followed by the output from the program.

Program Design: Pseudocode

1. Initialize variables to desired values
2. Print report headings
3. Calculate ratios and print
   a. Calculate Liquidity Ratios
      Current Ratio = Current Assets/Current Liabilities
      Quick Ratio = (Current Assets/Inventory)/Current Liab
   b. Calculate Leverage Ratios
      Debt Ratio = Total Debt/Total Assets
      Times Interest Earned = (Profit before Tax + Interest)/Interest
      Fixed Charge Coverage = (Profit before Tax + Interest + Lease
         Oblig)/(Interest + Lease Oblig)
   c. Calculate Activity
      Inventory Turnover = Sales/Inventory
      Avg Coll Period = Receivables/(Sales/365)
      Fixed Asset Turnover = Sales/Net Fixed Assets
      Total Asset Turnover = Sales/Total Assets
   d. Calculate Profitability
      Profit Marg on Sales = Net Profit after Tax/Sales
      Total Return on Asset = Net Profit after Tax/Total Assets
      Return on Net Worth = Net Profit after Tax/Net Worth

Program to Analyze Financial Ratios

```
10 ' PROGRAM TO ANALYZE RATIOS 'RATIOS'
20 ' BY T.J. CARLSON
30 ' MARCH 1, 1987
40 '
50 '........................ Initialize Variables
60 LET CURRENT.ASSETS = 700
70 LET CURRENT.LIABILITIES = 300
80 LET INVENTORY = 300
90 LET TOTAL.DEBT = 1000
100 LET TOTAL.ASSETS = 2000
110 LET PROFIT.BEFORE.TAXES = 200
120 LET INTEREST.CHARGES = 70
130 LET LEASE.OBLIGATIONS = 20
140 LET SALES = 3000
150 LET RECEIVABLES = 200
```

```
160 LET NET.FIXED.ASSETS = 1300
170 LET NET.PROFIT.AFTER.TAXES = 120
180 LET NET.WORTH = 1200
190 '
200 ' ................................. Print Ratios
210 'Print Title
220 PRINT TAB(25) "Financial Ratios for the ABC Co.": PRINT: PRINT
230 PRINT TAB(40) "Liquidity Ratios"
240 PRINT "Current Ratio",,CURRENT.ASSETS/CURRENT.LIABILITIES
250 PRINT "Quick Ratio",,(CURRENT.ASSETS-INVENTORY)/CURRENT.LIABILITIES
260 PRINT
270 PRINT TAB(40) "Leverage Ratios"
280 PRINT "Debt Ratio",,TOTAL.DEBT/TOTAL.ASSETS
290 PRINT "Times Interest Earned", (PROFIT.BEFORE.TAXES +
    INTEREST.CHARGES)/INTEREST.CHARGES
300 PRINT "Fixed Charge Coverage", (PROFIT.BEFORE.TAXES + INTEREST.CHARGES
    + LEASE.OBLIGATIONS)/(INTEREST.CHARGES + LEASE.OBLIGATIONS)
310 PRINT TAB(40) "Activity"
320 PRINT "Inventory Turnover", SALES/INVENTORY
330 PRINT "Average Collection Period", RECEIVABLES/(SALES/365)
340 PRINT "Fixed Asset Turnover", SALES/NET.FIXED.ASSETS
350 PRINT "Total Asset Turnover", SALES/TOTAL.ASSETS
360 PRINT TAB(40) "Profitability"
370 PRINT "Profit Margin on Sales", NET.PROFIT.AFTER.TAXES/SALES
380 PRINT "Total Return on Assets", NET.PROFIT.AFTER.TAXES/TOTAL.ASSETS
390 PRINT "Return on Net Worth", NET.PROFIT.AFTER.TAXES/NET.WORTH
400 END ' of ratios program
RUN
```

Financial Ratios for the ABC Co.

		Liquidity Ratios
Current Ratio	2.333333	
Quick Ratio	1.333333	
		Leverage Ratios
Debt Ratio	.5	
Times Interest Earned	3.857143	
Fixed Charge Coverage	3.222222	
		Activity
Inventory Turnover	10	
Average Collection Period	24.33333	
Fixed Asset Turnover	2.307692	
Total Asset Turnover	1.5	
		Profitability
Profit Margin on Sales	.04	
Total Return on Assets	.06	
Return on Net Worth	.1	

·QUICK REFERENCE FOR LESSON 2·

Programs and Lines

A program is a sequence of BASIC statements preceded by integer line numbers. More than one statement can be placed on a single line by separating statements with colons (:). Any single line can contain up to 254 characters. A line in a BASIC program that is more than 80 characters will be displayed on the monitor in successive lines.

RUN Executes a Program

RUN executes the program currently in memory.
RUN "FILENAME" loads from disk the program with name of FILENAME and executes it.

END

Terminates execution of program and returns to immediate mode.
Closes all open files.
No special message is displayed.

STOP

Terminates execution of program and returns to immediate mode.
Does not close files.
Displays message "BREAK in line nn," where nn is the line number containing the STOP statement.

CONT

Resumes execution with the statement following STOP or at statement following pressing of Ctrl-Break.

NEW

Clears current program from memory.
Clears all values assigned to variables.
Closes all open files.

LIST Displays Line(s) of a Program Currently in Memory

LIST   List all lines.
LIST n   List only line number n.
LIST n-z   List lines n through z.
LIST n-   List all lines starting with line number n through the end of the program.
LIST -z   List all lines from the beginning of the program through line number z.

DELETE Erases Lines from the Program Currently in Memory

DELETE n   Delete line number n.
DELETE n-z   Delete lines n through z, including n and z.
DELETE n-   Delete all lines from and including n to the end of the program.

DELETE -z   Delete all lines from the beginning of the program through z.
DELETE -   Delete entire program.
or DELETE

REM or '

Places a nonexecutable REMark or comment in the program.

A REMark appears on the listing of a program but does not appear when the
program is run.

If a REMark is placed on the same line as other statements, ' may be used in place
of :REM.

Everything following the REMark statement on a line will be considered part of the
REMark and not executed.

SAVE "FILENAME.EXT"

Writes program currently in memory onto disk.

If a file already exists by this name, it will be replaced by the file currently in memory.

Files are identified by:

Filename (up to eight characters), plus

Extension (period followed by up to three characters)

Valid characters in file names and extensions are:

All letters (lowercase will be converted to upper)

All digits (0–9)

Special characters ! @ # $ % ^ & ( ) _ -` ' ~ { }

If an extension is not specified, BASIC will automatically add ".BAS."

LOAD "FILENAME.EXT"

Erases program currently in memory.

Brings a program file from disk into memory.

If the extension is not specified, BASIC will assume it is ".BAS" and look for a file
with that extension.

FILES Lists the Names of Files Currently on the Disk

FILES. List all the files on the disk.

FILES. Use * to list a group of files. The asterisk (*) is used as a wild card. FILES
followed by one or more characters ending in an asterisk lists all files whose
names match the given characters up to the asterisk, regardless of the remaining
characters in the filename. The same applies to an asterisk in the extension.

FILES "A*.BAS". List all files whose names begin with A and whose extension is
".BAS."

FILES "A*.*". List all file names beginning with A regardless of the extension.

FILES "*.*". Same as FILES; lists all files.

KILL "FILENAME.EXT"

Removes one or more files from the disk.

The full name of the file, including the extension, must be specified.

Nothing in memory is affected by the KILL command.

NAME "OLDNAME.EXT" as "NEWNAME.EXT"

Changes the name of the file identified by the first filename and extension to the
  second filename and extension.
Extension must be specified.
The old file must already exist on the disk.
No file with the new name may currently exist on the disk.
The file is merely being renamed; no extra copy is made.

· EXERCISES ·

Short Answer

1. The last line of a program should always be the statement _____ ..

2. In order to execute a program, the command _____ must be entered.

3. What command sends the listing of code to the printer?

4. What is the command to erase one or more lines of code?

5. BASIC allows you to store permanent copies of your program with what command?

6. The statements in a program are called code. (T/F)

7. The maximum number of characters that will fit in a line of code is 240. (T/F)

8. A semicolon separates more than one statement on the same line. (T/F)

9. LIST 60- displays all the lines of the program from line 0 to line 60. (T/F)

10. STOP temporarily halts a program while END permanently halts it. (T/F)

11. Explain the different results from running a BASIC program that is numbered and one
    that is not.

12. Explain what pseudocode is.

13. What does a REM statement do?

14. Explain the difference between BASIC commands and statements. Give three exam-
    ples of each.

15. If you save a program with a name that already exists, which of the following occurs?
    a. The new file replaces the old.
    b. The computer displays a warning message.
    c. The computer prompts you to enter a different name.

16. Which of the following are valid characters for file names?
    a. letters *a-z*   e. all of the above
    b. letters *A-Z*   f. a, c, d
    c. all numbers   g. b, c, d
    d. special characters (@ & ! #)

17. If an extension is not specified for a file name, which of the following occurs?
    a. None is added to the filename.
    b. BASIC automatically adds ".BAS".
    c. BASIC automatically adds ".EXT".

18. The command "FILES C*.BAS" will do which of the following?
    a. list all files on the disk
    b. list only those files whose names begin with C and whose extension is "BAS"
    c. list only those files whose extension is "BAS"

19. The command LOAD "filename" does which of the following?
    a. erases the program currently in memory
    b. brings a program file from disk into memory
    c. prompts you for the filename extension if none was entered
    d. all of the above
    e. a and b

20. The BASIC statement "STOP" does which of the following?
    a. closes the files
    b. terminates execution of program and returns to immediate mode
    c. a and b

21. You have just finished entering a program into BASIC and type "RUN 'filename'".
    BASIC will do which of the following?
    a. execute the program currently in memory
    b. load the program from disk into memory and execute it
    c. prompt you to first save the program

22. Matching: Match each item in the left-hand column with one item in the right-hand
    column.

    (1) NEW   a. renames a file
    (2) END   b. displays lines in a program
    (3) STOP   c. statements in a computer program
    (4) RUN   d. clears out the current program
    (5) LIST   e. temporarily halts a program
    (6) DELETE   f. retrieves a program from disk
    (7) REM   g. removes one or more lines from a pro-
                                  gram
    (8) SAVE   h. outlines of program written in English
                                  and BASIC
    (9) LOAD   i. terminates program
    (10) FILES   j. numbered sequence of BASIC statements
    (11) KILL   k. executes a program
    (12) NAME   l. COMMAND.COM, CHKDSK.COM,
                                  INVEST.BAS
    (13) PROGRAM   m. stores a copy of a program on disk
    (14) PSEUDOCODE   n. destroys unwanted files
    (15) CODE   o. statement that does nothing but is used to
                                  record your comments about a program

Analyzing Code

23. Find and correct the errors in the following:

```
NEW
10 LET AMT$ = 100
20 PAYDAY$ - "FRIDAY"
30 PRINT "PAYDAY IS" PAYDAY$
40 PRINT "I WILL RECEIVE";AMT$ "ON PAYDAY"
50 END
```

24. Type in the following program:

```
NEW
10 PRINT "HELLO"
20 PRINT "THIS IS A COMPUTER PROGRAM"
30 PRINT "PROGRAMMING IS SUCH FUN!"
40 END
```

Now run it.
Now type in the following:

```
10 PRINT "THAT'S ALL FOR NOW - BYE"
20 END
```

Now run it.
What happened? What statement is needed in between programs?

25. What would happen if you ran this program:

```
10 NEW
```

Try it. List the program. What happened?

26. What's wrong with the following program?
a. LET A$ = B$ + 5
b. LET NAME$ = "MARY"
(*Hint:* NAME is a reserved word, so you may not have a variable called NAME$. You'll get a syntax error it you try. But MY.NAME$ and NAME.$ are allowed. Similarly, the following names are illegal: ON$, ERROR$, IF$.)
c. LET TYPE = "SMALL"
d. "Today is "; 2DAY

27. Here is a fun program:

```
10 LIST
```

Now LIST this program, which will display the following:

```
10 LIST
```

Now RUN this program. What happens?
This program has the same output when listed as when run. Can you come up with a similar program, which has the same output listed and run?

Writing Programs

28. The formula for calculating the value of an investment at the end of any given year is

$$V = A \left(1 + \frac{I}{100} \right)^Y,$$

where V = value of the investment at the end of the year
  A = amount invested
  I = interest percent specified as a whole number
  Y = years the amount has been invested

Write a BASIC program to calculate the value where: A = 10,000, R = 12 percent, Y = 5. Make sure the program prints out and defines all the values. Do the following:
a. Write pseudocode for the program.
b. Code the program.

    c. Change part b so that the interest rate is 16 percent rather than 12 percent.

    d. Make other changes in the Amt, Rate, or Years. Experiment with the LIST command.

    e. Add comment lines to the program.

29. Write a program to print out a monthly household expenses and calculate and print the total expenses. Use the following items:

Rent = $450.00
Car payment = $175.00
Food and misc. = $359.00
Credit card minimum = $40.00

Do the following:

a. Write pseudocode.

b. Code the program.

c. SAVE the program under the name "BUDGET".

d. LOAD "BUDGET" and run it again.

e. Rename "BUDGET" to "BILLS."

INTRODUCTION TO STRUCTURED PROGRAMMING: PLANNING AND DESIGN

PROGRAMMING REQUIRES PLANNING

"There must be a better way to spend a Tuesday evening than wading through paperwork," Pat muttered. Spreadsheets, scratchpads, broken pencils, and reams of tape from the calculator sprawled across the desk and much of the office floor. A cup of cold, stale coffee and crumbs from a vending machine candy bar testified to the lateness of the hour.

Pat was a junior accountant for Consolidated Glomerate, Inc., assigned to the Solid Waste Removal Division. As the junior member of the accounting staff, Pat was always assigned the work that no one else wanted; the depreciation calculations Pat slaved over this particular night were a prime example. The Solid Waste Removal Division owned a lot of equipment, such as trucks and trash bins, which had to be depreciated by a variety of methods, but no one in Accounting wanted to get stuck with cranking out all the computations.

Not that the actual calculations were very difficult. There were three methods with which Pat had to deal: "straight line," "sum of the digits," and "double declining balance." Each method wrote off the money spent on a piece of equipment over a period of years, but they differed in the schedule of write-offs. The

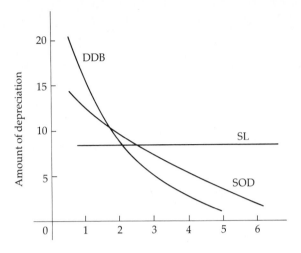

FIGURE 3.1 •
Three methods of
depreciation

SL — Straight Line
SOD — Sum Of Digits
DDB — Double Declining Balance

straight line method wrote off the same amount each year, while the other two methods wrote off more in the first few years than in the later years (see Figure 3.1).

"A piece of cake," Pat said initially when The Boss assigned the job of comparing these methods for specific pieces of equipment. What Pat did not count on was the boredom; these calculations had to be repeated over and over, year after year, for different numbers of years, different initial values, different salvage values, and different depreciation methods. The result was supposed to be a report for each piece of equipment listing the year-by-year depreciation allowances under each of the three methods. Since, there were so many calculations, it was impossible to completely avoid mistakes; the best Pat could hope for was to catch the errors before The Boss did.

This was certainly not the first time Pat had pounded out depreciation schedules using the calculator, but this night brought an inspiration: why not use the Accounting Department's new IBM personal computer? Pat's friend in Data Processing, Chris, owed Pat a favor; maybe Chris would write the program.

The next morning Pat called Chris and, after a little arm twisting, Chris agreed to write the program.

Specifications Make Sure You Solve the Right Problem

"All right, tell me all about your problems," Chris began, "and remember that I'm not an accountant like you, just a computer programmer who doesn't know anything about depreciation."

Pat explained, "Money spent to produce income is generally tax deductible. If a business buys something inexpensive or expendable, such as a box of paper clips, the entire cost can be deducted in the year in which the purchase is made. However, if a business buys a major item with a useful life of several years, the cost of the item must be apportioned piecemeal over a period of years according to one of the approved formulas. This is called 'depreciation', and the formulas are called 'depreciation schedules'. Because there are several methods available, we here in Accounting must choose which one to use every time Con. Glomerate buys an expensive piece of equipment. It's my job to compare the methods."

As Pat talked, Chris started typing at the computer terminal. "What is that program you are using?" Pat asked.

"It's a word processing program," Chris replied. "Before I start programming, I want to make sure that we both agree on exactly what the program is supposed to do. The document I'm typing, and which you will initial before I begin programming, is called 'specifications'."

"I don't think that will be necessary," Pat said. "After all, the calculations are pretty easy to describe. If you have any questions while you're programming you can just ask me."

· PARABLES FOR PROGRAMMERS ·

The Operation Succeeded But the Patient Died

"What a fool I was," the manager lamented. "I spent thousands of dollars on a computer program only to find out I'd wasted the money."

"Did the program have syntax errors, like misspelling a BASIC statement?" I asked.

"No," the manager replied, "nothing as simple as that."

"Were there errors in logic? An improper computation of formula perhaps?"

"No, there were no errors in logic."

"Was the program too slow? Did it use too much memory? Was it too difficult to use or to understand?"

"No, no, no. The program worked perfectly; it just solved the wrong problem," the manager snapped. "I thought the programmer understood my accounting needs perfectly, but when I tried to use the program, I found that it could handle accounting for only one company. I have *four* companies under one umbrella. In order to use that program I'd have to run it four times! The program would have worked fine for a single company, but for me it's useless."

MORAL: Make sure your program solves the right problem.

Chris looked a little annoyed at this response. "It may seem obvious to you as an accountant, but remember that computers aren't accountants and neither am I. You probably have heard horror stories about businesses that have purchased computer programs only to find that they won't work. Why do you suppose that's so common?" Pat shifted uneasily. "I'll tell you why," Chris continued. "Nine times out of ten, it's because someone thought that what the computer was supposed to do is 'obvious'. In all my years of programming, I've never yet found an 'obvious' computer application.

"People tend to think that the toughest part of programming computers is the actual writing of the program, but in the real world the toughest and most important step in writing a program is to first decide exactly what the program is supposed to do, and to write that down in the form of specifications. That's the only way to make sure that you and I are communicating properly, me from my technical perspective and you from your position pushing figures. I'll illustrate my point with this tale."

"You were describing the different methods of depreciation," Chris said. "Please continue."

As Pat talked, Chris typed in the details of how the various methods of depreciation worked. Chris asked a lot of pointed questions about the various calculations and the format of the output report. After about an hour, they agreed that the following document accurately described what the program was supposed to do.

Depreciation Program Specifications

General Purpose
This program is to prepare a report that compares side by side three methods of depreciation for a given item: straight line, sum of the digits, and double declining balance.

Output
The output of the program is a report in the following format:

```
            DEPRECIATION SCHEDULES


INITIAL VALUE: ##,###.##
SALVAGE VALUE: ##,###.##
NUMBER OF YEARS OVER WHICH TO DEPRECIATE: ##


YEAR        STRAIGHT        SUM OF          DOUBLE
              LINE          DIGITS         DECLINING
            _____        _____       _____

 ##        ##,###.##       ##,###.##       ##,###.##
 ##        ##,###.##       ##,###.##       ##,###.##
  .            .               .               .
  .            .               .               .
  .            .               .               .
            _____        _____       _____
TOTALS:    ##,###.##       ##,###.##       ##,###.##
```

Amounts on each line represent the amount of the write-off for the year number indicated at the beginning of the line and the method indicated by the column. One report represents a depreciation schedule for one item with specific initial and salvage values over a specific number of years, as indicated in the report heading.

Input

The program is to ask the user for three values:

1. The initial cost of the item
2. The number of years over which to depreciate
3. The salvage value at the end of that period

The initial cost and salvage values will never exceed $99,999.99. The number of years is always an integer larger than zero and will never exceed 99 years.

Definition of Depreciation Methods

The following define the computations the program is to use for each of the three depreciation methods. For ease of presentation, in these definitions the following variables are used:

COST the initial cost of the item

YEARS the number of years over which to depreciate

SALVAGE the salvage value at the end of the depreciation period

CURRENT.YEAR a single year in the depreciation schedule

1. *Straight Line Depreciation.* In a straight line depreciation the amount to write off in each year is the same. It is the difference between the initial cost (COST) and the salvage value (SALVAGE), divided by the number of years:

   WRITE.OFF = (COST − SALVAGE)/YEARS

2. *Sum of the Digits Method.* In a sum of the digits depreciation the amount to write off in each year depends on the year number (CURRENT.YEAR). The program must compute the "sum of the digits" by totaling the digits, which represent each year as follows:

   SUM.OF.DIGITS = 1 + 2 + · · · + YEARS

   This can also be calculated by the formula:

   SUM.OF.DIGITS = YEARS * (YEARS + 1)/2

   The amount to write off in year CURRENT.YEAR is:

   WRITE.OFF = (COST − SALVAGE) * (YEARS − CURRENT.YEAR + 1)/SUM.OF.DIGITS

3. *Double Declining Balance Method.* As with the sum of the digits method, the amount written off in early years using double declining balance is

greater than the amount written off in later years. The first year's write-off is calculated by first using the same formula as straight line but disregarding the salvage value. This amount is then doubled to give the amount to be written off that year. The write-off is subtracted from the original amount to give the remaining balance. The next year's write-off is calculated in the same way using the remaining balance as the base.

The program must keep track of the total not written off to date in order to calculate the current year's write-off. Call this value DDB.REMAINING. DDB.REMAINING must be set to COST at the start of the computations. As each year's write-off is computed, the program must subtract that amount from DDB.REMAINING. The amount to write off in a given year (CURRENT.YEAR) is WRITE.OFF = DDB.REMAINING * 2/YEARS.

Chris had Pat initial the specifications, then yawned and said, "Enough for today. Tomorrow I'll roll up my sleeves and start programming."

Pat asked, "Do you mind if I look over your shoulder?"

"Not at all," Chris said. "What BASIC statements do you know?"

"Just PRINT and LET."

"Why don't you read about FOR . . . NEXT, INPUT, PRINT USING, and CLS in your BASIC book this evening? I'll write the program with those four statements plus PRINT and LET."

• THE ABCS OF BASIC ON THE IBM PERSONAL COMPUTER •

LESSON 3: SCREEN MAGIC: STRUCTURED PROGRAMMING, INPUT, FOR . . . NEXT, AND PRINT USING

In addition to four new BASIC statements: INPUT, FOR . . . NEXT, PRINT USING, and CLS, this lesson will discuss two programming tools: structure charts and flowcharts.

Structure charts and flowcharts are to the programmer what blueprints are to the architect. They are means for designing and documenting programs.

You have learned about variables: what they are and how to assign them values using LET. A LET statement requires that you code the value of the variable into your program. Frequently, you will want to ask the person using a program (commonly called the **user**) to enter a value, then have your program set a variable to that value. That is the purpose of the INPUT statement.

The pair of statements FOR and NEXT allow blocks of statements to be repeated many times. Using LET and PRINT, you can write only programs that are executed one line at a time in line number order. Each line in the program is executed exactly once. Most business applications call for the computer to do something, not once, but repeatedly. That's why FOR and NEXT are so important.

The PRINT statement you have been using so far is adequate for many purposes but suffers from a drawback: you cannot round dollar amounts to the nearest cent nor can you insert commas into large numbers. This lesson shows you how to round to the desired number of decimal places and how to make formatting reports easier with the PRINT USING statement.

Finally, the lesson covers CLS, a simple statement which clears the display on the monitor.

Flowcharts and Structure Charts: Techniques for Structured Programming

Business treats its software as an asset, just like trucks and machines. These assets are similar in that they are costly to acquire, require maintenance, and are expensive to replace. Just like these other corporate assets, programs need maintenance. Program maintenance refers to changing the program to meet changing business needs.

For example, as the tax laws change each year, programmers must modify the payroll program to reflect these changes. Since business programs are typically used for ten years or so, business application programs must be easy to modify.

Structured programming meets these business needs. It aids the programmer in writing programs that are easy to understand, test, and modify. The term *structured programming* however, refers to a philosophy of programming rather than just to one technique. A programmer using structured programming gives up some artistic freedom and follows a set pattern in developing programs. In return, the programmer becomes much more productive in modifying his or her own programs and those of others. The programmer is also more confident that these programs are free of bugs and will be completed within the time schedule.

The guidelines called structured programming include techniques for design and programming, testing, and documentation. You have already learned about pseudocode, a design and programming technique. We will now present two other techniques for program design and documentation: flowcharts and structure charts.

Flowcharts Aid in Understanding Processing

A **flowchart** is a type of visual diagram. It shows the logical steps a program will perform and their order of execution. It also shows the conditions that affect that order.

A flowchart can describe any sequence of logical steps. For example, Figure 3.2 illustrates the process of preparing a homework assignment. Notice how flowcharting shows each step or task as a symbol. It indicates connections between tasks (the flow of processing) with arrows. Processing begins at the top of the page, and the main line of processing flows down the page, ending at the bottom.

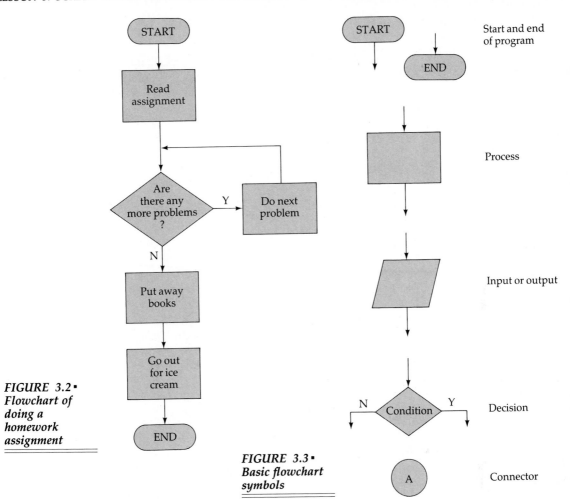

FIGURE 3.2 •
Flowchart of
doing a
homework
assignment

FIGURE 3.3 •
Basic flowchart
symbols

The basic symbols used in flowcharts are shown in Figure 3.3. (To assist in drawing, plastic templates with these symbols are available from bookstores.) These five basic symbols and what each represents are as follows:

1. Box—processing
2. Diamond—decision making
3. Parallelogram—input or output
4. Oval—processing start and end
5. Circle—connection of one part of a flowchart to another

Notice that the process and input/output boxes have one arrow entering and one arrow leaving. The start/stop ovals have only one arrow leaving or one arrow entering. The decision symbol (the diamond) has one arrow entering but two leaving. As the chart indicates, one arrow points to the next task if the answer to the decision is yes (or true), while the other points to the task performed if the decision is no (or false).

Examine Figure 3.2. Notice that the task to be performed, if there are more problems (Do Next Problem), is to the right side of the diamond. The "no" task is beneath the diamond.

Types of Modules

A structured program is made up of three types of **modules** or processes. Figure 3.4 shows these three basic structures.

1. **Sequence.** Each step is performed one after the other in the order in which they are written. The flowchart illustrates this with the symbols placed one under the other and the flow going straight from the top to the bottom.

2. **Repetition.** Based on the value of some condition, a particular step or sequence of steps is repeated a number of times. The condition is placed in a decision diamond. The steps that are repeated are placed to the side of the diamond so that the main line of the flow continues to go from top to bottom. At the end of each repetition the flow returns to the diamond and the condition is tested again.

3. **Selection.** Depending on the value of some condition, one of two series of steps is taken. Again the condition is placed in the decision diamond.

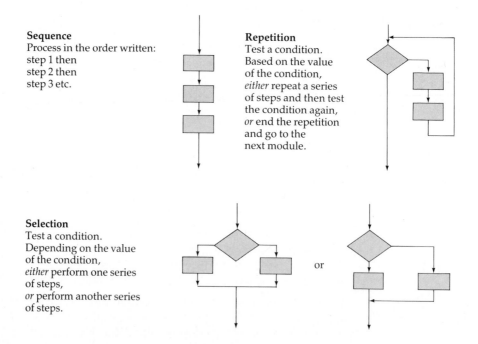

Sequence
Process in the order written:
step 1 then
step 2 then
step 3 etc.

Repetition
Test a condition.
Based on the value
of the condition,
either repeat a series
of steps and then test
the condition again,
or end the repetition
and go to the
next module.

Selection
Test a condition.
Depending on the value
of the condition,
either perform one series
of steps,
or perform another series
of steps.

or

**FIGURE 3.4 ·
The three
structures of
structured
programming**

Note: Each module has only one entrance and one exit.

The flow is to the right side or beneath the diamond based on the condition. After the selected steps are performed, the flow of processing returns to the main line.

(Some programmers show selection with one task to the left side of the diamond and one to the right. Others show selection as we described it earlier—with one task to the side and the other beneath the diamond. Figure 3.4 shows both of these styles. We feel both methods are useful.)

These three structures can be used to represent any process. Figure 3.5 charts the process for baking a cake. The first module, "preparation," is a simple sequence of steps, performed each time a cake is baked. The second module picks a selection depending on the number of cakes desired. Module three repeats the mixing process until the batter is smooth. The chart ends with another sequential module.

Figure 3.6 is another flowchart illustrating the process for dividing one number by another.

There are a number of accepted standards for flowcharts. For example, the flow should be from the top of the page to the bottom. However, the most important factor is that the diagram be easy to understand. Figure 3.7 illustrates the processing of payroll for various types of employees. There are a number of selections shown in this diagram. In all of them if the condition is no, the flow is to the left. If the condition is yes, the flow is to the right.

The Debate over Flowcharts

As structured programming has developed, newer tools, such as structure charts and pseudocode, are replacing or supplementing flowcharts in program design. There are several reasons for this switch:

1. Flowcharts do not inherently promote structured programming.
2. Usually a flowchart must be completely redrawn when modifications are made to it.
3. Flowcharts lose important design information, such as a program's logical structure.
4. Flowcharts are hard to "level." That is, since you see all the detail, you cannot easily see the big picture of what the program is doing.

Still, well-designed flowcharts are very helpful in program documentation. They can explain a process or **algorithm** (series of logical steps to produce a desired result) to the reader clearly and unambiguously. They are particularly helpful in diagramming complicated procedures. A complicated procedure may perform one of many actions depending on several different conditions.

We will be using some simple flowcharts in this chapter to illustrate or document how BASIC interprets a particular series of statements.

Structure Charts Are Another Programming Tool

Another technique for designing a program is the structure chart. A **structure chart** is a visual outline or table of contents of the processes the program will

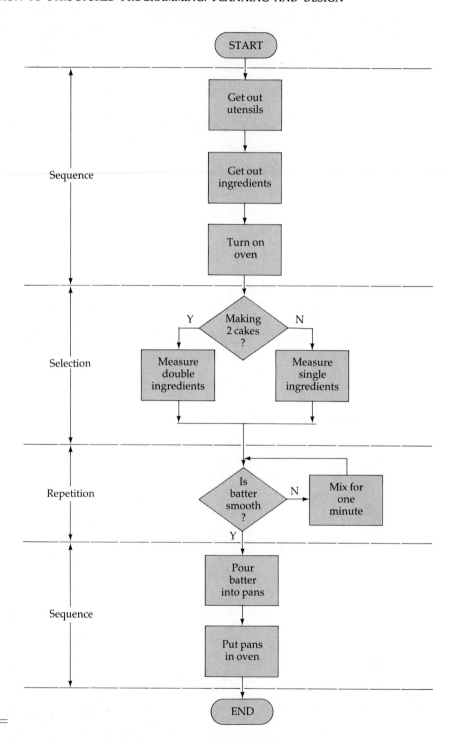

FIGURE 3.5 •
Baking a cake
using the three
structures

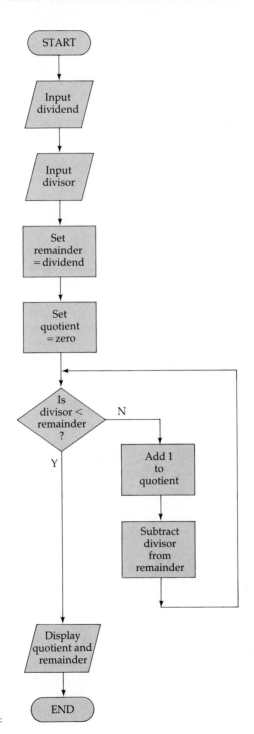

FIGURE 3.6 •
Flowchart of
division

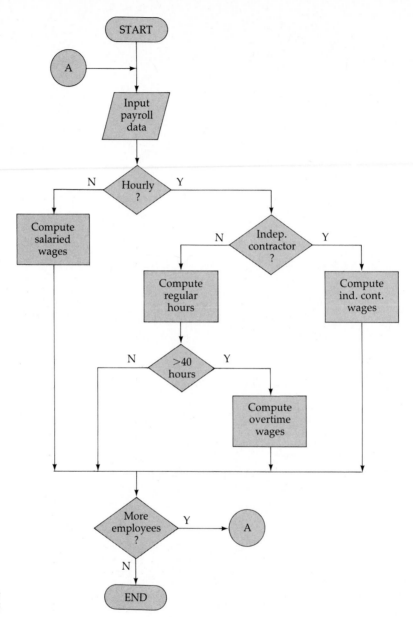

FIGURE 3.7 ▪
Payroll flowchart

perform. It uses boxes at different levels in much the same way that an outline uses roman numerals, letters, and numbers to indicate major categories, minor categories, and subcategories. A structure chart looks a little like the traditional organizational chart. It places the highest level at the top and positions each department and subdepartment at progressively lower levels.

The top box on a structure chart represents the entire program. For many business programs the next level can be represented by three boxes.

1. *Things Done Only Once at the Beginning (Initialization).* Activities done in this "chapter" of the program include printing a report heading, setting variables to their initial values, and so on.
2. *Processing of Transactions.* This is usually a series of steps done over and over for each transaction. This could include inputting information, printing a detail line on a report, and accumulating a total.
3. *Things Done Only Once at the End of the Program.* This could be the printing of final totals.

Figure 3.8 shows a structure chart for the process of baking a cake. Notice that the structure chart does not show the direction of flow. Nor does it show the decision factors. Instead it shows the major modules and the steps that are to be performed in each of them.

Figure 3.9 is a sample structure chart for a program that creates a sales report by doing the following.

1. Initialize totals and print headings.
2. Input data from the keyboard; perform a calculation on the data; add to totals; and print a report line.
3. Print totals.

One of the features of a structure chart is that it clearly defines each set of steps as a separate section or module. The programmer can write instructions for each module and test it as a separate miniprogram or subroutine. As the programs you write become more complex, you will appreciate this technique for program

FIGURE 3.8 •
Structure chart
for baking a cake

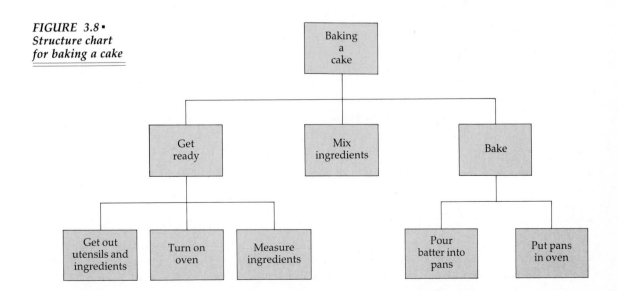

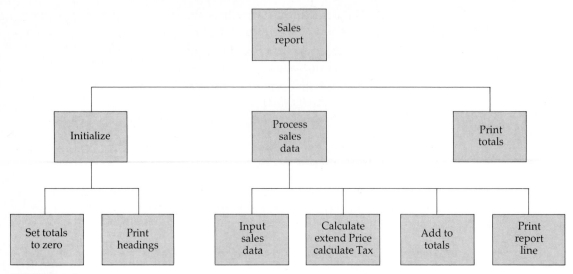

FIGURE 3.9 ·
Structure chart
for sales report

design. It breaks down a big program into sets of manageable steps. It allows you to defer thinking about details until later.

As we will see, for a structured program the structure chart modules follow the "One Rule." They have only one entry point and one exit point, and they perform only one task.

Flowcharts, Structure Charts, and Pseudocode Compared

We have examined three tools: flowcharts, structure charts, and pseudocode. Let's compare these tools and discover why we need all three.

The strong point of flowcharts is their ability to explain algorithms. Some critics look down upon flowcharts because historically these illustrations have so often been misused. For instance, data processing managers often require programmers to use flowcharts as design tools — that is, to create the flowcharts before they code. However, just to meet the requirements, many programmers draw their required flowcharts *after* they have developed their programs. These programmers are failing to appreciate flowcharting's assistance in checking the accuracy of a program's logic.

Studies have found flowcharts to be useful in explaining or documenting (for future users of the program) what sections of the program do. They are an alternative to pseudocode. Flowcharts show the flow of control: what the program does and when. And they show this flow spatially, which some people find helpful.

Structure charts are of primary use in program design, but they are also helpful as documentation tools. Their virtue is that they show the "big picture" and show how each module relates to all other modules. They are like an outline. They do not show the details of any module, nor do they show how processing is to work or when modules are called.

Pseudocode shows these features. It is very helpful in program design, but it is only marginally easier to understand than the code itself for documentation.

One good way to develop a program is to begin with a structure chart. Start with just the first module and write the pseudocode for it. If a module has complicated logical conditions, use a flowchart to illustrate the procedures. Continue this process for each module. Begin to write the code only when you are satisfied that the process is logically correct.

INPUT Puts Information Entered from Keyboard into Variables

The INPUT statement asks the user to enter one or more values, then assigns those values to the variables specified in the statement.

```
NEW
Ok
10 INPUT A
20 PRINT "A = ";A
30 END
RUN
?
```

The program is now waiting at the INPUT statement on line 10. The question mark displayed on the screen is a **prompt;** it signals to the user that he or she is expected to type a value and press Enter.

```
? 10
A = 10
Ok
RUN
? 175
A = 175
Ok
```

•THE INPUT STATEMENT•

INPUT Variable Name
Displays ? and space and pause for user to key data.

INPUT "Prompt"; Variable.name
Displays prompt followed by ? and space.

INPUT "Prompt", Variable.name
Displays prompt. The ? and space are suppressed.

As you can see, the value that you enter is assigned to the variable *A*, just as if there had been a LET statement in the program (see Figure 3.10).

INPUT Works with Strings, Too

```
NEW
Ok
10 INPUT CLIENT.NAME$
20 PRINT "The name is "; CLIENT.NAME$
30 END
RUN
? J. Doe
The name is J. Doe
Ok
```

Using INPUT with Prompts

Admittedly, a question mark is pretty cryptic. How is the user supposed to know what to enter? Fortunately, there are variations of INPUT that allow you to display a helpful message, called a prompt, which tells the user what is expected. To display a prompt, put the prompt in quotes after the word INPUT and before the variable name and put a semicolon or a comma after the quoted prompt.

```
NEW
Ok
10 INPUT "What is the customer balance"; BALANCE
20 PRINT "The balance is";BALANCE
30 END
RUN
What is the customer balance? 21
The balance is 21
Ok
```

The literal string in quotes is the prompt. You can put anything you want in a prompt, as long as the entire prompt is enclosed in quotes. There are two ways to use a prompt with INPUT. In the preceding example, the prompt string was separated from the variable name "BALANCE" by a semicolon (;). If a semicolon is used, BASIC automatically puts a question mark and a space after the prompt. If a comma is used, both the question mark and the space are suppressed.

```
10 INPUT "Please enter the customer balance:", BALANCE
20 PRINT "The Balance is";BALANCE
30 END
RUN
Please enter the customer balance:21
The balance is 21
Ok
```

Notice that when the comma is used, there is no space after the prompt. For easier reading, add a space to the prompt as follows.

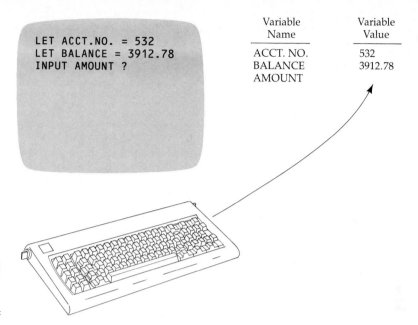

Variable Name	Variable Value
ACCT. NO.	532
BALANCE	3912.78
AMOUNT	

FIGURE 3.10 •
How INPUT
works. INPUT
takes the value
the user enters on
the keyboard and
assigns it to a
variable.

```
10 INPUT "Please enter the customer balance: ", BALANCE
RUN
Please enter the customer balance: 21
The balance is 21
Ok
```

INPUT Can Be Used with More Than One Variable at a Time

```
NEW
Ok
10 INPUT "What are the cost and retail price"; COST, PRICE
20 PRINT "The cost is "; COST
30 PRINT "The price is "; PRICE
40 PRINT "The margin is "; PRICE-COST
50 END
RUN
What are the cost and retail price? 20,25
The cost is 20
The price is 25
The margin is 5
Ok
```

Notice that the user must enter the values separated by commas and that the values entered are assigned in the order of the variables in the INPUT statement. The first value entered (20) was assigned to the variable COST, and the second value (25) was assigned to the variable PRICE.

If the user makes a mistake, BASIC displays an error message. Mistakes can include:

1. Entering a non-numeric value for a numeric variable
2. Entering too many values for the list of variables in the INPUT statement
3. Entering too few values for the list of variables in the INPUT statement

```
RUN
What are the cost and retail price? I don't know
?Redo from start
What are the cost and retail price? 1,2,3,4
?Redo from start
What are the cost and retail price? 1
?Redo from start
What are the cost and retail price? 1,2
The cost is 1
The price is 2
The margin is 1
Ok
```

"?Redo from start" is BASIC's standard error message to the user when the values entered are incorrect in any of these ways. BASIC will stick with the INPUT statement, repeating the prompt, until the user enters something valid.

Remember when writing your programs that the user may know very little about how the program works. Your prompts should be very explicit about what the user is to enter.

Some Additional Comments about INPUT

INPUT WITH NO KEYBOARD ENTRY.   If, in response to an INPUT statement, the Enter key is pressed without anything else having been typed, a zero will be placed into a numeric variable, and a null will be placed into a string variable. (Remember, a null means no character. It is not the same as a space.)

ENTERING STRING DATA CONTAINING COMMAS.   What happens if you want to enter a string such as *SACRAMENTO, CA 95831?* That string contains a comma; therefore, this is what will happen if you try to enter it as we have been doing with strings not containing commas:

```
10 INPUT "Enter City, State Zip ", CITY.STATE$
RUN
Enter City, State Zip SACRAMENTO, CA 95831
?Redo from start
```

The error message appeared because BASIC interpreted the commas as separators between two variables, rather than as part of the string. To indicate that commas are to be included as part of the string, you must place quotes around the string as follows:

```
RUN
Enter City, State Zip "SACRAMENTO, CA 95831"
Ok
```

SEMICOLON DIRECTLY AFTER INPUT INHIBITS CURSOR MOVEMENT. If a semicolon is placed immediately after INPUT and before any prompt or variables, the cursor will not move to the next line after Enter is pressed. This could be useful in displaying two different messages on the same line as in the example following:

```
NEW
Ok
10 INPUT; "Last Name"; LAST.NAME$
20 INPUT " First Name"; FIRST.NAME$
RUN
Last Name? JOHNSON First Name? BERTHA
Ok
```

When Enter was pressed after typing JOHNSON, the cursor did not move to the next line. Instead, the second prompt was displayed immediately after JOHNSON. Notice that a space was placed as the first character in the prompt for first name. If the space had not been placed in the prompt, there would have been no space between JOHNSON and First Name.

FOR . . . NEXT Causes BASIC to Process Statements Repeatedly

It is common to write programs that repeat one or more lines. This is called **iteration,** or, less formally, **looping.** BASIC has two pairs of statements designed for this purpose. In this lesson we will cover the first of these, FOR and its companion statement NEXT.

Here is an example of their use.

```
NEW
Ok
10 FOR YEAR = 1 TO 5              ' For
20    PRINT "The year is"; YEAR ' Loop Body
30 NEXT YEAR                     ' Next
40 END
RUN
The year is 1
The year is 2
The year is 3
The year is 4
The year is 5
Ok
```

In this example the PRINT statement is repeated five times, with the variable YEAR taking on the values 1, 2, 3, 4, and 5 in order. This program illustrates the three parts of all FOR . . . NEXT loops:

•THE FOR . . . NEXT STATEMENTS•

FOR COUNTER = X to Y STEP Z

.

.

.

NEXT

1. Initialize COUNTER to the value of X.
2. If COUNTER is greater than Y, go to step 6.
3. Execute the statements between FOR and NEXT.
4. Increment COUNTER by the value of Z. (If STEP Z is omitted, increment COUNTER by 1.)
5. Go back to step 2.
6. Continue with the statement following NEXT.

1. The FOR statement (line 10) names a variable that will be used as a counter to control the number of times the loop is repeated. The IBM reference manual calls this variable the **counter,** which is the term we will use. It is also sometimes referred to as the index, the control variable, or the loop variable. In this example the counter is named "YEAR."

   The FOR statement also specifies the starting and ending values of the counter, in this example 1 and 5, respectively. The starting and ending values may be a numeric variable or a mathematical expression as well as specified number. The starting and/or ending value can also be negative.
2. The NEXT statement (line 30) names the counter again and marks the end of the loop body.
3. All statements in between are collectively called the **loop body.** In this case the body is just one line (line 20), but we could just as easily have put dozens of statements on dozens of lines between the FOR and NEXT statements. All statements in the loop body are repeated for each value of the counter.

Figure 3.11 illustrates the flow of a FOR . . . NEXT loop.

The sample program demonstrates a convention common among experienced programmers: indenting all lines within a FOR . . . NEXT loop. This clearly sets those lines off from the rest of the program and makes the program easier to read.

Suppose that the starting value is greater than the ending value. Will the loop body execute at all? Let's see by changing line 10 of our sample program to the following:

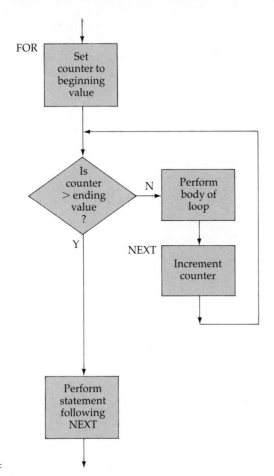

FIGURE 3.11 •
Flowchart of a
FOR . . . NEXT
loop (with
positive step)

```
10 FOR YEAR = 10 TO 5
RUN
Ok
```

The answer is no. The starting value of 10 is greater than the ending value of 5, so the loop never starts. Using this form of FOR . . . NEXT BASIC will never enter the loop if the starting value is greater than the ending value.

Using STEP with FOR . . . NEXT Gives You Control over Incrementing the Counter

In the form of FOR . . . NEXT you have used so far, the counter is always incremented by one each time through the loop. BASIC provides a way to increment the counter by any amount you desire by adding STEP to the FOR statement.

```
NEW
Ok
10 FOR I = 1 TO 10 STEP 2
20     PRINT I
30 NEXT I
40 END
RUN
 1
 3
 5
 7
 9
Ok
```

The number following the word *STEP* is called the **increment.** As with starting and ending values, this may be a number, a numeric variable, or a mathematical expression. It may also be negative, but when the increment is negative, the ground rules change a little. Here are the results of running the preceding program with line 10 changed to use a negative increment.

```
10 FOR I = 5 TO 1 STEP -1
20     PRINT I
30 NEXT I
40 END
RUN
 5
 4
 3
 2
 1
Ok
```

Since the increment is negative, BASIC counted backward from the starting value to the ending value. The rules that we stated earlier are all reversed.

1. If the increment is negative, the loop starts at the starting value and proceeds until the counter is less than the ending value. In the example the loop continues until I is less than one.
2. If the increment is negative and the starting value is less than the ending value, the loop never executes.

Both of these are the reverse of the logic used when the increment is positive but are perfectly logical if you remember that a negative STEP makes BASIC count backward.

If a FOR statement has no STEP clause, BASIC assumes that the increment is one.

Danger of STEP with Value of Zero
As a further note on using STEP, if the increment is set to zero, the program will be in an infinite loop!

Nested FOR . . . NEXT Loops Provide for Loops Inside Loops

One FOR . . . NEXT loop may be placed inside another FOR . . . NEXT loop; these are called **nested loops.**

Have you ever wondered just how many gifts were given in the song "The Twelve Days of Christmas"? We will write a program that uses nested FOR . . . NEXT loops to print the number of gifts.

First we will write pseudocode for the program:

```
LET TOTAL.GIFTS equal zero
FOR each DAY.OF.CHRISTMAS from 1 through 12
    PRINT Message with number of the day
    FOR each GIFT from this day to the first day
        PRINT number of GIFT
        ADD GIFT to TOTAL.GIFTS
    NEXT GIFT
NEXT DAY.OF.CHRISTMAS
PRINT TOTAL.GIFTS
```

Now we will write the code. (Note the use of a "dummy" input statement in line 90, which causes the program to pause until Enter is pressed, allowing the user time to read the display.)

```
1 'Days of Christmas
2 'Written by S. Claus
3 'Program calculates the number of gifts needed each of
4 'the 12 days of Christmas
5 '
10 LET TOTAL.GIFTS = 0 ' TOTAL.GIFTS will be the grand total
20 FOR DAY.OF.CHRISTMAS = 1 TO 12
30     PRINT "On the ";DAY.OF.CHRISTMAS;" day of Christmas"
40     PRINT "My true love gave to me:"
50     FOR GIFT = DAY.OF.CHRISTMAS TO 1 STEP -1
60         PRINT GIFT
70         LET TOTAL.GIFTS = TOTAL.GIFTS + GIFT
80     NEXT GIFT
90     INPUT "Press Enter to continue",ANYTHING$
100 NEXT DAY.OF.CHRISTMAS
110 PRINT "On the 13th day of Christmas I had ";TOTAL.GIFTS; "gifts."
120 END
```

In this program the counter for the outer loop is DAY.OF.CHRISTMAS; the body of this loop includes lines 30 through 90, and it concludes with the NEXT statement in line 100. The counter for the inner loop is GIFT; the body of this loop includes lines 60 and 70, and it concludes with the NEXT statement in line 80. These loops comply with the two restrictions on nested FOR . . . NEXT loops.

   1. Each FOR . . . NEXT loop must use a different counter than any other FOR . . . NEXT loop within the same nest.

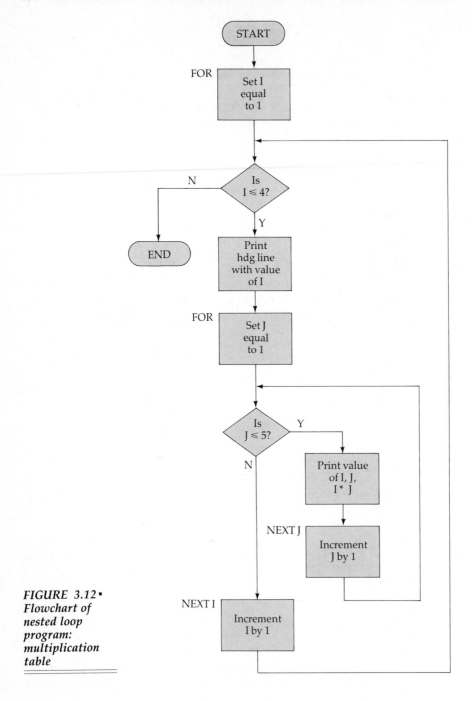

FIGURE 3.12 •
*Flowchart of
nested loop
program:
multiplication
table*

TABLE 3.1 ▪ How BASIC Matches FOR . . . NEXT Loops

YOU TYPE	BASIC MATCHES
10 FOR FIRST = 1 TO N	FOR FIRST = 1 TO N
20 FOR SECOND = 1 TO M	FOR SECOND = 1 TO M
30 FOR THIRD = 1 TO P	FOR THIRD = 1 TO P
.	.
.	.
.	.
80 NEXT	NEXT
90 NEXT	NEXT
100 NEXT	NEXT

2. The entire inner loop, including the FOR and NEXT and all statements in between, must lie wholly within the loop body of the outer loop.

BASIC matches each NEXT with the closest unmatched FOR (see Table 3.1). When writing a program, in order to make clear which NEXT is matched to which FOR, you indent each set of FOR . . . NEXT.

Following is an example of a program with a nested loop, which prints a short multiplication table for the numbers one through four. Figure 3.12 is a flowchart of this program.

```
NEW
Ok
10 FOR I = 1 TO 4
20     PRINT "** Table for the number: "; I
30     FOR J = 1 TO 5
40         PRINT I; " times "; J; " equals "; I * J
50     NEXT J
60 NEXT I
70 END
RUN
** Table for the number: 1
 1 times 1 equals 1
 1 times 2 equals 2
 1 times 3 equals 3
 1 times 4 equals 4
 1 times 5 equals 5
** Table for the number: 2
 2 times 1 equals 2
 2 times 2 equals 4
 2 times 3 equals 6
 2 times 4 equals 8
 2 times 5 equals 10
```

```
** Table for the number: 3
 3 times 1 equals 3
 3 times 2 equals 6
 3 times 3 equals 9
 3 times 4 equals 12
 3 times 5 equals 15
** Table for the number: 4
 4 times 1 equals 4
 4 times 2 equals 8
 4 times 3 equals 12
 4 times 4 equals 16
 4 times 5 equals 20
```

In all the examples so far we have named the counter in the NEXT statement. IBM PC BASIC does not require that you do this and will automatically match a NEXT to the most recent (innermost) unmatched FOR statement. For single, unnested loops you will probably find it more convenient to omit specifying the counter and just use NEXT by itself. (Your program will actually run slightly faster when you omit the variable.) However, for nested loops, we recommend specifying the counter since it helps both in preventing programming errors and in following the program logic by clearly indicating which NEXT goes with which FOR. You should also be aware that some non-IBM BASIC's require that the counter be specified in all NEXT statements. Figure 3.13 illustrates valid and invalid nested FOR . . . NEXT loops.

There is an alternate way of writing the NEXT statement when one or more nested loops conclude on adjacent lines. In the example in Figure 3.13 the K, J, and I loops conclude with the three NEXT statements written one line right after the other. These three lines could be combined into the single statement:

```
NEXT K, J, I
```

The order in which the variables are written is critical; since the K-loop is the innermost loop it must be written first, followed by J then I.

A final note on FOR . . . NEXT loops. BASIC will allow you to change the value of the counter while within the body of the loop. One possible use of this could be to test for a particular condition, and when it occurs, set the counter to the ending value to force an exit from the loop. Because changing the value of the counter in this way makes the loop behave in other than its normal way, do this only when necessary and clearly describe what you are doing with REM statements.

PRINT USING Displays Output in Formatted Form

PRINT USING is similar to PRINT, except that you show BASIC exactly where on the line to print data and how to format the data. It is especially useful when printing reports.

Here is an example.

```
NEW
Ok
10 PRINT USING "The number is ####.##"; 123.4567
20 END
RUN
The number is 123.46
Ok
```

The words "The number is " were printed as they would be with a PRINT statement, but the pound signs (#) were replaced with the number that followed the semicolon. This number was also rounded before it was printed.

The string following PRINT USING ("The number is ####.##") is called the **mask** or **format.** The mask contains formatting characters (the #s), which control how the values or variables following the semicolon will print. The mask may also contain text that will print just as it appears within the mask.

When numeric variables, are being printed, the pound signs to the left of the decimal represent the number of spaces to be reserved for the integer portion of the variable. If the number being printed is positive, each # will allocate space for

Inner loops must be wholly within outer loops:

VALID Loops:

```
10    ┌──→FOR I = 1 to 10
20    │      PRINT I
30    │  ┌──→FOR J = 5 to 25 STEP 5
40    │  │      PRINT J
50    │  │  ┌──→FOR K = 10 to 100 STEP 10
60    │  │  │      PRINT K
70    │  │  └──NEXT K
80    │  └──NEXT J
90    └──NEXT I
```

YES! FOR and NEXT are matched correctly. This is legal.

INVALID Loops

```
10    ┌──→FOR I = 1 to 10
20    │      PRINT I
30    │  ┌──→FOR J = 5 to 25 STEP 5
40    │  │      PRINT J
50    └──│──NEXT I
60       └──NEXT J
```

No! FOR . . . NEXT Loops cannot overlap. This is illegal.

FIGURE 3.13 • Valid and invalid nested FOR . . . NEXT loops

The invalid loop will not work because the entire inner loop (the J-loop) is not within the outer loop (the I-loop). Because NEXT I comes before NEXT J, BASIC cannot properly match the FORs and NEXTs. When it comes to line 60, BASIC will print the error message, "NEXT without FOR in 60."

·THE PRINT USING STATEMENT·

PRINT USING "Mask"; Variable, . . .
The mask may contain both text and special format characters that indicate how the values are to be printed.

one digit. If the number is negative, the first position will be taken up by the minus sign. For example, PRINT USING "###"; A will print correctly values of A from −99 to 999.

If you try to print a number with more digits than allowed by the mask, a % will print in front of the number as a signal that the number has overflowed the mask.

```
PRINT USING "###"; 7321
%7321
Ok
```

If the number has fewer digits than the number of pound signs in the mask, spaces will be placed to the left of the number.

```
PRINT USING "###"; 1
  1
Ok
```

Pound signs to the right of the decimal point indicate the number of digits to be printed following the decimal. If the value being printed has more digits than the mask, the printed result will automatically be rounded to the number of places indicated in the mask. If the value has fewer, the places are filled with zeros.

```
PRINT USING "##.##"; 12.456
12.46
Ok
PRINT USING "##.##"; 12.4
12.40
Ok
```

Notice that the space normally in front of a positive number does not appear. PRINT USING overrides the normal PRINT spacing.

PRINT USING will work with variables, as is shown in this simple program, which illustrates the operation of PRINT USING.

```
NEW
Ok
10 FOR I = 1 TO 5
20    INPUT "NEXT NUMBER "; TEST.NUMBER
30    PRINT USING "####.##"; TEST.NUMBER
```

```
40 NEXT
50 END
RUN
NEXT NUMBER ? 123.456
 123.46
NEXT NUMBER ? 7217
7217.00
NEXT NUMBER ? -6783.274
%-6783.27
NEXT NUMBER ? .2839
 0.28
NEXT NUMBER ? -12.5
 -12.50
Ok
```

Experiment with some values of your own.

Variations in Printing Numbers

Showing the Sign

The preceding examples did not print a sign if the number was positive and printed a leading minus sign if the number was negative. You can change when and where the sign prints with the following formats:

+####   means sign will always print and will appear in front of the number.

####+   means sign will always print and will appear at end of the number.

−   means sign will print only if negative and will appear at the end of the number.

Here is a demonstration:

```
NEW
Ok
10 INPUT "Enter a value:", A.VALUE
20 PRINT USING "+####.## "; A.VALUE ' Sign in front of number
30 PRINT USING " ####.##+"; A.VALUE ' Sign trailing number
40 PRINT USING " ####.##-"; A.VALUE ' Trailing negative only
50 END
RUN
Enter a value:1234.56
+1234.56
 1234.56+
 1234.56
Ok
RUN
Enter a value:-1234.56
-1234.56
 1234.56-
 1234.56-
Ok
```

This last format, which prints negative numbers with a trailing minus sign, is especially useful for accounting programs to indicate credit amounts.

Adding Commas for Thousands, Millions, and so on

Commas can be inserted following the standard notation of placing them between every three digits to the left of the decimal. To accomplish this simply place a comma in the mask to the left of the decimal.

```
PRINT USING "##,###.##"; 12345.67
12,345.67
Ok
PRINT USING "##,###.##"; 123.45
   123.45
Ok
```

As you can see, PRINT USING only inserts commas when the number is large enough to warrant them. Although a comma inserted anywhere in the mask left of the decimal will cause commas to be inserted in the standard places, it is good practice to put them in the mask in the places you expect to find them. PRINT USING "####,#.##" would give the same results, but it would be confusing to anyone looking at it. You can put more than one comma if you wish, but only one is necessary. Just remember to place enough #s in the mask to allow for each space in which a comma may print.

Dollar Signs and Asterisks

If you want dollar signs in front of the numbers, there are two options available in PRINT USING. A single dollar sign in front of the pound signs will cause a dollar sign to be printed in that position; two dollar signs in front of the pound signs will cause the dollar sign to "float" and be placed in front of the first digit printed. (If you put more than two dollar signs in the mask, you will get an overflow error indicator.)

```
PRINT USING "$#####,###.##"; 1234.56
$    1,234.56
Ok
PRINT USING "$$####,###.##"; 1234.56
    $1,234.56
Ok
PRINT USING "$$####,###.##"; -12.789
   -$12.79
Ok
```

The first dollar sign in the mask represents the dollar sign, and no digit will be printed in this position. The second dollar sign is used as a signal and a digit can be printed in this position. Both of the preceding masks will print values from 9,999,999.99 to −999,999.99 (remember the minus sign takes one of the positions).

Notice how the negative number printed. The minus sign is printed in front of the floating dollar sign. In most cases it would be more desirable for the minus sign to appear at the end of the number. To achieve this, use the format that prints negative signs at the end:

```
PRINT USING "$$####,###.##-"; -12.79
     $12.79-
```

The floating dollar sign is a way of protecting dollar amounts from easy alteration. An even better way is to use a format that inserts asterisks instead of spaces into the unused positions. To cause asterisks to be inserted, replace the first two pound signs with asterisks.

```
PRINT USING "**##,###.##"; 123.45
*****123.45
Ok
```

If you also want a dollar sign, you have two ways of doing it. If you want the dollar sign to always print at the beginning of the field and the remaining spaces to be filled with asterisks, place one dollar sign in front of the asterisks.

```
PRINT USING "$**##,###.##"; 123.45
$*****123.45
Ok
```

If you want the dollar sign to be placed immediately to the left of the uppermost digit, place the dollar sign after the two asterisks.

```
PRINT USING "**$##,###.##"; 123.45
*****$123.45
Ok
```

With this type of mask you may encounter a condition in which you cannot put the comma in its normal position in the mask. Consider the case in which you wish to print a numeric value of up to four digits left of the decimal, have a comma printed if the number is in the thousands, have a floating dollar sign, and fill spaces with asterisks.

```
PRINT USING "$**,##.##"; 123.45
$**123.45
Ok
PRINT USING "$**,##.##"; 9876.54
$9,876.54
Ok
```

Since we cannot put a comma between the two asterisks, we placed it immediately after them.

Multiple Variables in the Mask

As with PRINT, you can put more than one expression after the mask. If you wish the same mask to be used by all of the variables, you can write the mask once and follow it by the variables you wish to use.

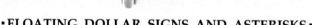

·FLOATING DOLLAR SIGNS AND ASTERISKS·

Floating $
Place two $ at beginning of mask.
Example: $$###.##

*Fill with ***
Place two * at beginning of mask.
Example: **###.##

*Leading $ and Fill with ***
Place single $ at beginning of mask followed by two *.
Example: $**##.##

*Floating $ and Fill with ***
Place two * at beginning of mask followed by $.
Example: **$##.##

```
PRINT USING "####.##"; 125.789, -34.7, 768.21, -.378
 125.79 -34.70 768.21 -0.38
Ok
```

Notice that PRINT USING overrides the spacing that is normally caused by commas separating variables in a PRINT statement. (In fact, it makes no difference whether you use commas or semicolons between the variables with the PRINT USING statement.) This mask has indicated that seven positions are to be used for each of the variables (four positions to the left of the decimal, the decimal, and two positions to the right of the decimal.) In the preceding line BASIC has allowed exactly that number of positions for each of the numbers.

You can also use a single mask into which you want several variables inserted at different places:

```
PRINT USING "DAY ## MONTH ## YEAR ####"; 27, 9, 1984
DAY 27 MONTH 9 YEAR 1984
Ok
```

Suppose you want to print three numeric variables in columns. Each variable will be no greater than 9999 and you wish each column to use five spaces. You could do it in either of these two ways (assume A has the value of 123, B has the value of 4, and C has the value 5678):

```
PRINT USING " #### #### ####"; A, B, C
     123    4 5678
Ok
PRINT USING " ####"; A, B, C
     123    4 5678
Ok
```

So far, the mask in the PRINT USING statement has always been a literal string in quotes. You may also use a string variable to hold the mask. This may be useful when you wish to use the same format in several places in a program and do not want to have to rewrite it each time.

```
NEW
Ok
10 LET MASK$ = "The value is #,###.##-"
20 INPUT "Please enter the value ", TEST.VALUE
30 PRINT USING MASK$; TEST.VALUE
40 LET NEW.VALUE = (TEST.VALUE + 450)/3
50 PRINT " calculating"
60 PRINT USING MASK$; NEW.VALUE
70 END
RUN
Please enter the value 600
The value is 600.00
   calculating
The value is 350.00
```

How Many Digits Will the Mask Hold?

When designing a report you need to know the largest value a variable may hold, and you must make the mask large enough to handle the largest value. There is no difficulty with the places to the right of the decimal, since there is no punctuation in this section. But with the possibility of commas, dollar signs, and asterisks, the places to the left of the decimal are not so simple. Remember these guidelines when planning your masks.

No Punctuation, Sign Position Not Specified

Put a # for each digit in the largest number to be printed. If the number will always be positive, no sign will print and all positions reserved by the # can be used to print a digit. If the number is negative, the minus sign will print preceding the number and will occupy one of the reserved positions.

```
    EXAMPLE:        MASK        "#####.##"
       999.99 will print as       999.99
      -999.99 will print as      -999.99
     99999.99 will print as     99999.99
    -99999.99 will give overflow error
```

No Punctuation, But with Sign Position Specified

If the sign is indicated in the mask, that position is reserved for the sign and no digit can print in that position.

```
EXAMPLES:          MASK      "+####.##"
    999.99 will print as       +999.99
   -999.99 will print as       -999.99
  99999.99 will give overflow error
                   MASK      "#####.##+"
    999.99 will print as        999.99+
   -999.99 will print as        999.99-
  99999.99 will print as      99999.99+
 -99999.99 will print as      99999.99-
                   MASK      "#####.##-"
    999.99 will print as        999.99
   -999.99 will print as        999.99-
  99999.99 will print as      99999.99
 -99999.99 will print as      99999.99-
```

With Commas

If commas are to be printed, each position in which a comma may print must be reserved; the comma in the mask will reserve one of these positions, the others must be reserved with #s or with additional commas.

```
    EXAMPLE: To print positive numbers through 9 million
with commas.
          MASK      "#####,###" (or "#,###,###")
    9999 will print as          9,999
  999999 will print as        999,999
 9999999 will print as      9,999,999
99999999 will give an overflow error
```

Fill with Asterisks ("**")

All of the positions reserved by the asterisks may be used by digits.

```
EXAMPLE:           MASK      "$$###.##"
    999.99 will print as      **999.99
   9999.99 will print as      *9999.99
  99999.99 will print as      99999.99
```

Floating Dollar Sign ("$$")

One position will always be reserved for the dollar sign. The second dollar sign is used as a signal to BASIC, and that position may be used by a digit.

```
EXAMPLE:           MASK      "$$###.##"
    999.99 will print as       $999.99
   9999.99 will print as      $9999.99
  99999.99 will give an overflow error
```

*Floating Dollar Sign and Fill with Asterisks ("**$")*

One position will always be reserved for the dollar sign. The positions reserved by the asterisks may be used by digits.

```
EXAMPLE:         MASK         "**$##.##"
   999.99 will print as    *$999.99
  9999.99 will print as    $9999.99
 99999.99 will give an overflow error
```

The best way to learn the spacing is to experiment. If you are not sure your mask will handle the values you expect, test it.

PRINT USING with Strings

While most of the time you will probably be using PRINT USING to format numeric output, there are some interesting things you can do with strings.

& Prints Entire String

If you wish the entire string to be displayed or printed, no matter what its length, you can use the ampersand (&) in a mask:

```
PRINT USING " & "; "Elizabeth", "Tony", "Robert"
 Elizabeth Tony Robert
Ok
```

! Prints First Character Only of String

If you wish only the first letter of the string to be displayed, use the exclamation point (!):

```
PRINT USING " ! "; "Elizabeth", "Tony", "Robert"
 E T R
Ok
```

\ \ Prints Specified Number of Characters

If you wish only a certain number of the first characters of the string to print, you can do this by using backslashes (\) to indicate the number of characters. The number of characters printed will be two (one for each backslash) plus the number of spaces between the backslashes. If there are fewer characters in the string than positions indicated by the mask, spaces will be added at the end of the string:

```
PRINT USING " \      \      "; "Elizabeth", "Tony", "Robert"
 Eliza Tony   Rober
Ok
```

Although it is hard to see on the printed page, there are three spaces between the backslashes, indicating that five characters in all are to be printed.

An example of the use of all three is in designing a formatted output of a list of names. Suppose you have three strings for each person: LAST.NAME$,

FIRST.NAME\$, and MIDDLE.NAME\$. You wish to print the list so that the first name will appear in the first eight spaces, followed by one space, the middle initial, a space, and the last name. The full last name will be printed, no matter how long. Here is a line that will do that:

```
PRINT USING "\        \ ! &"; FIRST.NAME$, MIDDLE.NAME&, LAST.NAME&
```

These names:

Christopher Patrick Jones
Tom Jacob McDonald
Catherine Marie Franklin
Jane Elizabeth Smith

will be printed as:

```
Christop P Jones
Tom       J McDonald
Catherin M Franklin
Jane      E Smith
```

There are a few more features available in PRINT USING, but they are rarely used. Table 3.2 gives a complete list of PRINT USING features.

Experiment with PRINT USING. It will be one of your most useful tools in designing reports.

LPRINT USING Allows Formatted Printed Reports

All of the features of PRINT USING also apply to LPRINT USING. Printed reports of columnar data can be formatted by LPRINT USING.

Inhibiting Cursor Movement After Printing

In all the examples that we have used thus far, after you printed a line, the cursor moved to the next line. It is possible to instruct BASIC to keep the cursor on the same line (the one just printed) by ending the PRINT or PRINT USING statement with a comma or a semicolon.

```
NEW
Ok
10 PRINT 1;
20 PRINT 2,
30 PRINT 3
40 PRINT 4
50 INPUT "Please enter your name: ", MY.NAME$
60 PRINT USING "The age of & is "; MY.NAME$;
70 INPUT AGE
80 INPUT "Please enter your monthly salary ", SALARY
90 PRINT "MONTHLY SALARY" TAB(50);
100 PRINT USING "$$#,###.##"; SALARY
```

TABLE 3.2 ▪ PRINT USING Options

MASK	VALUE	PRINTED AS	COMMENTS
####	123.4	123	Rounded to whole number
####	123.5	124	Rounded to whole number
####	−12	-12	Leading minus sign
###	1234	%1234	% indicates overflow
####.##	12.345	12.35	Rounded to two decimal places
####.##	−12.345	-12.35	Leading minus sign
####.##	12	12.00	Zero filled decimal places
+####	123	+123	Forces sign in front of number
+####	−123	-123	Forces sign in front of number
####+	123	123+	Forces sign after number
####+	−123	123-	Forces sign after number
####-	123	123	Sign after negative num. only
####-	−123	123-	Sign after negative num. only
##,###	12345	12,345	Insert comma
##,###	12	12	
$####	123	$ 123	Print $ in first position
$####	−12	$ -12	
$####-	−12	$ 12-	
$$####	123	$123	Floating $
$$####	−12	-$12	
$$####-	−12	$12-	
**####	12	****12	Fill with asterisks
**####	−12	***-12	
**####-	−12	****12-	
$**####	12	$****12	$ in first position, fill with *
**$####	12	****$12	Float $, fill with *
####^^^^	123	123E+00	Exponential notation
##.###^^^^	123	1.23E+02	
&	"Hello There"	Hello There	Print entire string
!	"Hello There"	H	Print first character only
\\	"Hello There"	He	Print first two characters
\ \	"Hello There"	Hel	Print first three characters
\ \	"Hello There"	Hello T	Print first six characters

```
run
 1 2        3
 4
Please enter your name: JANET
The age of JANET is ? 46
Please enter your monthly salary 3769.70
MONTHLY SALARY                              $3,769.70
Ok
```

In line 10, the semicolon at the end of the line supressed movement of the cursor to the next line; therefore, the PRINT statement in line 20 caused the 2 to print on the same line as the 1. The comma at the end of line 20 caused the cursor to move to the next print zone on that line but supressed the advance to the next line. There is neither a comma nor a semicolon at the end of line 30; therefore, the cursor advances to the next line after executing this line.

Line 60 demonstrates how you can display a formatted message on the same line that an INPUT is used by placing a semicolon at the end of a PRINT USING statement.

The semicolon at the end of line 90 causes the formatted dollar amount in line 100 to print on the same line as the TAB( ) statement.

You will find these features helpful in screen and report design.

These same conventions apply as well to LPRINT and LPRINT USING.

CLS Clears the Screen

CLS clears the display and puts the cursor in the upper left-hand corner of the screen. The format is:

```
CLS
```

If you plan to display a report on the monitor, it is usually wise to use a CLS first to clear extraneous data from the screen. CLS can also be used in command mode to clear the screen, but there is another way to use the keyboard to clear the screen: press Control-Home (the Ctrl and Home keys simultaneously).

THE STORY'S END

The next day Chris presented the finished program to Pat, and they sat down to go over it.

Structure Chart

Chris first described the structure chart (see Figure 3.14). "Even though this is a fairly short program, it still breaks down into the three major modules common to many business programs. These are represented by the three boxes on the second level of the chart.

"The first box represents the initialization module in which the user is asked to input the initial values, the report heading is printed, and other opening tasks are performed. Each of these tasks is represented by a box at the next level. I have also noted the program line numbers in these detail boxes so that I can quickly find the related section of the program.

"The second box represents the printing of the detail lines of the report. This process will be repeated again and again for each year over which the item is to be depreciated.

"The third box shows the printing of the totals that have been accumulated."

Flowchart

Next they looked at the flowchart (see Figure 3.15). Again the three major modules were easily identified. The flowchart showed the sequence in which each step would be done as well as points at which decisions needed to be made.

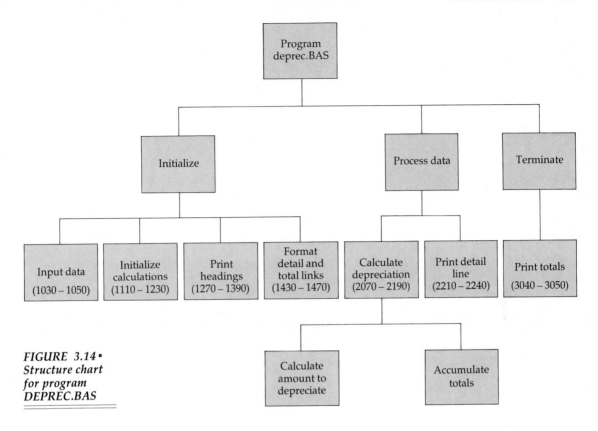

FIGURE 3.14 ▪
*Structure chart
for program
DEPREC.BAS*

Pseudocode

INITIALIZE
INPUT Parameters
  COST = Initial Value
  SALVAGE = Salvage Value
  YEARS = Number of Years for Depreciation
Do Initial Calculations
  SOD = Sum of Digits
  AMOUNT.TO.DEPRECIATE = COST − SALVAGE
  DDB.REMAINING = COST
  Set totals to zero
PRINT Headings
Set format for detail lines
PROCESS DATA
FOR CURRENT.YEAR = 1 TO YEARS
  Calculate depreciation
  Accumulate totals
  PRINT detail line

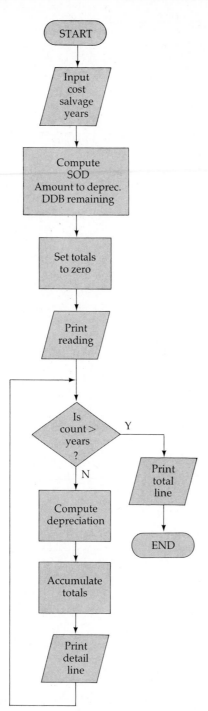

FIGURE 3.15 •
Flowchart for
program
DEPREC.BAS

       NEXT CURRENT.YEAR
       PRINT TOTALS

Program Code

Finally they wrote the program and ran it.

```
LIST
100 ' PROGRAM NAME: "DEPREC.BAS"
110 ' CREATED:   03-01-86
120 ' PROGRAMMER:   CHRIS JOHNSON , CON GLOMERATE
140 ' PROGRAM HISTORY:
150 '             NONE TO DATE
160 '
170 ' Program Prints Report Comparing 3 Methods of Depreciation
180 '      1) Straight Line (SL)
190 '      2) Sum of Digits (SOD)
200 '      3) Double Declining Balance (DDB)
210 '
220 ' Variables Entered by User
230 '    COST - Initial Value of Item
240 '    SALVAGE - Salvage Value
250 '    YEARS - # of Years over which to Depreciate
260 ' Formulas Used
270 '
280 '      Straight Line (SL)
290 '         Total Amount to Depreciate = COST - SALVAGE
300 '         Amount to Depreciate Each Year = (COST - SALVAGE)/YEARS
310 '
320 '      Sum of Digits (SOD)
330 '         Total Amount to Depreciate = COST - SALVAGE
340 '         Sum of Digits (SOD) = (YEARS * (YEARS + 1) )/2
350 '         Amount to be Depreciated the Current Year =
360 '            (COST - SALVAGE) * (YEARS - Current Year + 1)/SOD
370 '
380 '      Double Declining Balance (DDB)
390 '         Total Amount to Depreciate = COST
400 '         DOB.REMAINING = Previous Remaining Amount to Depreciate -
410 '               Amount Depreciated the Previous Year
420 '         Amount to be Depreciated the Current Year =
430 '               (DDB.REMAINING * 2)/YEARS
1000 '- - - - - - - - - - - - - - - - - - - - - - - - - - - - - - -
1010 CLS
1020 ' ** Ask User for Parameters **
1030 INPUT "ENTER INITIAL VALUE: ", COST
1040 INPUT "ENTER SALVAGE VALUE: ", SALVAGE
1050 INPUT "ENTER NUMBER OF YEARS OVER WHICH TO DEPRECIATE: ", YEARS
1060 '
1070 ' = =   =   =   =   = =   =   =
```

```
1080 '
1090 ' ** Calculate the Sum of Digits **
1100 '
1110 LET SOD = (YEARS * (YEARS + 1) )/2
1120 '
1130 ' ** Calculate the Amount to Depreciate for SL and SOD Methods
1140 '
1150 LET AMOUNT.TO.DEPRECIATE = COST - SALVAGE
1160 '
1170 ' ** Set the Undepreciated Balance for DDB Method to Initial Value
1180 '
1190 LET DDB.REMAINING = COST
1200 '
1210 ' ** Set Totals to Zero to Start **
1220 LET SL.TOTAL = 0: LET SOD.TOTAL = 0: LET DDB.TOTAL = 0
1230 '
1240 ' =     =     =     =     =     =     =     =
1250 '
1260 ' ** Clear the Screen. Then Print the Report Heading **
1270 '
1280 CLS
1290 PRINT TAB(10);"DEPRECIATION SCHEDULES"
1300 PRINT
1310 PRINT USING "INITIAL VALUE: ##,###.##";COST
1320 PRINT USING "SALVAGE VALUE: ##,###.##";SALVAGE
1330 PRINT USING "NUMBER OF YEARS OVER WHICH TO DEPRECIATE: ##" ;YEARS
1340 PRINT
1350 PRINT        "YEAR      STRAIGHT      SUM OF       DOUBLE"
1360 PRINT        "          LINE          DIGITS       DECLINING"
1370 LET LINES$ ="----      ---------      --------     ---------"
1380 PRINT LINES$     ' LINES$ will also be used at the footing
1390                              ' before Totals
1400 '
1410 ' =     =     =     =     =     =     =     =
1420 '
1430 LET MASK1$ = " ##      ##,###.##      ##,###.##      ##,###.##"
1440 LET MASK2$ = "TOTALS: ##,###.##      ##,###.##      ##,###.##"
1450 '
1460 ' * MASK1$ will be used as a PRINT USING Mask to PRINT Each Line
1470 ' * MASK2$ will be used as a PRINT USING Mask to PRINT Final Totals
2000 '-------------------------------------------------------------
2010 ' ** NOW LOOP THROUGH EACH YEAR **
2020 '
2030 FOR CURRENT.YEAR = 1 TO YEARS
2040 '
2050 ' ** Calculate Amounts to Depreciate this Year **
2060 '
2070     LET SL.AMOUNT = AMOUNT.TO.DEPRECIATE/YEARS
2080     LET SOD.AMOUNT = AMOUNT.TO.DEPRECIATE *
             (YEARS - CURRENT.YEAR + 1)/SOD
```

```
2090      LET DDB.AMOUNT = DDB.REMAINING * 2/YEARS
2100      '
2110      ' * Subtract Current Depreciation from DDB.REMAINING Value
2120      '
2130      LET DDB.REMAINING = DDB.REMAINING - DDB.AMOUNT
2140      '
2150      ' * Accumulate Totals
2160      '
2170      LET SL.TOTAL = SL.TOTAL + SL.AMOUNT
2180      LET SOD.TOTAL = SOD.TOTAL + SOD.AMOUNT
2190      LET DDB.TOTAL = DDB.TOTAL + DDB.AMOUNT
2200      '
2210      ' * PRINT Detail Line
2220      '
2230      PRINT USING MASK1$; CURRENT.YEAR, SL.AMOUNT, SOD.AMOUNT,
             DDB.AMOUNT
2240 NEXT CURRENT.YEAR
3000 '- - - - - - - - - - - - - - - - - - - - - - - - - - - - - - -
3010 '
3020 ' * PRINT TOTAL LINE *
3030 '
3040 PRINT LINES$
3050 PRINT USING MASK2$; SL.TOTAL, SOD.TOTAL, DDB.TOTAL
3060 END
Ok
RUN
```

(The screen cleared and the prompts appeared.)

```
ENTER INITIAL VALUE: 50000
ENTER SALVAGE VALUE: 5000
ENTER NUMBER OF YEARS OVER WHICH TO DEPRECIATE: 5
```

(The screen cleared again and the report printed on the screen.)

```
            DEPRECIATION SCHEDULES
INITIAL VALUE: 50,000.00
SALVAGE VALUE:  5,000.00
NUMBER OF YEARS OVER WHICH TO DEPRECIATE: 5
YEAR      STRAIGHT       SUM OF      DOUBLE
            LINE         DIGITS      DECLINING

----      ---------      --------    ---------
 1        9,000.00       15,000.00   20,000.00
 2        9,000.00       12,000.00   12,000.00
 3        9,000.00        9,000.00    7,200.00
 4        9,000.00        6,000.00    4,320.00
 5        9,000.00        3,000.00    2,592.00

----      ---------      --------    ---------
TOTALS:   45,000.00      45,000.00   46,112.00
Ok
```

"It certainly gives me the results I wanted," said Pat. "The calculations didn't take very many lines, but about half of the program seems to be comments. Isn't this a waste of time and space?"

"Not at all," replied Chris. "The comments serve two purposes. First, they give information about what the program is doing so that someone not familiar with the program can understand it easily. Second, they separate the modules so that each can be found quickly. Let's go through it and you'll see what I mean.

"The first few lines (100–150) identify the program. The name of the program is on the first line. This way, if you ever forget the name of the program, you can easily find it on the listing. This reminds me to tell you that a printed listing of a program should always be a part of the permanent documentation.

"The next section of lines (160–430) briefly describes what the program does. Notice how blank comment lines improve readability.

"Line 1000 begins the working part of the program. I have used a remark line of dashes to separate each of the three modules of this program. I have also used blocks of line numbers for each module. The 1000s are for initialization, the 2000s for processing, and 3000s for closing. This is a helpful programming practice.

"In the first module (1000–1470) the submodules that were noted on the structure chart are separated by lines with equal signs. Take a look at lines 1350 and 1360. See those extra spaces between PRINT and the text to be printed? Those spaces are ignored by BASIC, but they helped me to see that the text would line up correctly with that printed by lines 1310–1330 and by 1380.

"The second module (2000–2240) contains the FOR . . . NEXT loop in which each year's depreciation is calculated, printed, and added to the final totals. The final module (3000–3060) prints the totals."

"Now it makes more sense," said Pat. "The remarks clearly help me to see what is going on where. But does anyone really look at them?"

"They certainly do," exclaimed Chris. "A programmer depends on good comments any time a change needs to be made to the program."

"But there won't be any changes to this program," Pat said.

Chris guffawed, then said, "You'll learn."

"Thanks a lot for your help," Pat said as Chris walked out. "You accomplished in a day what would have taken me a week."

"That may be true today," Chris replied, "but with a little practice you'll be able to write your own programs in no time at all. I hope this program works well for you."

•QUICK REFERENCE FOR LESSON 3•

INPUT *Allows the User to Enter Data for Use by the Program*

INPUT A *or* INPUT A$, where A is a numeric variable and A$ is a string variable.
Causes the program to display a ? followed by a space on the screen and pause for user input. After the user has keyed the data and pressed Enter, the program

will continue. If the user has entered string data for a numeric variable, the error message "?Redo from start" will be displayed, and the user can enter the correct data.

INPUT "Message"; A or INPUT "Message"; A$. This causes the program to display the text between the quotes followed by a ? and a space and pause for user input.

INPUT "Message", A or INPUT "Message", A$. The comma after the message will suppress the display of the ? and the space after the text. (If a space is desired, it must be included in the text within the quotes.)

Multiple Items. More than one variable can be entered with a single INPUT statement using one of the following formats:

INPUT A, B$, . . . , Y, Z
INPUT "Message"; A, B$, . . . , Y, Z$
INPUT "Message", A, B$, . . . , Y, Z$

The variables must be entered with commas between each item, and Enter must be pressed after all the items have been keyed.

Entering the wrong type of data or more or less than the indicated number of variables will cause the error message "?Redo from start".

Special Format: INPUT; "Message", A. A semicolon immediately after INPUT (and before any message or variable) will prevent the cursor from moving to the next line after the item has been Entered.

FOR . . . NEXT Loops

FOR I = X TO Y STEP Z
.
.
.
NEXT

Causes the program to repeat the lines between the FOR and NEXT statements a specific number of times.

I is the variable controlling the number of times the loop is executed and is called the counter.

X is the initial value to which the counter is set.

Y is the limit for the counter.

Z is the amount by which I is to be incremented each pass through the loop.

I, X, Y, and Z must be numeric. (They may not be double precision. We'll discuss double precision in Chapter 4. Double precision is a way to have BASIC use more digits when doing its arithmetic.) They may be specific numbers, numeric variables, or expressions.

If the STEP is omitted, it is assumed to be 1.

For a Positive Step

If X is not greater than Y, the lines between FOR and NEXT will be executed at least once. When NEXT is encountered, the counter is incremented by the amount specified after the step. If I is not greater than Z, processing returns to the line immediately after the FOR. If I is greater than Z, processing continues with the line immediately after the NEXT.

For a Negative Step

If X is not less than Y, the lines between FOR and NEXT will be executed at least once. When NEXT is encountered, the counter is decremented by the amount specified after the step. If I is not less than Z, processing continues with the line immediately after the NEXT.

PRINT USING

Causes one or more items to be displayed according to a specified format, also called a mask.

PRINT USING MASK$; A, B$, . . .

In this case MASK$ contains text to be printed as well as the following format characters, which control the printing of the variables. Numeric variables will be rounded to the number of decimal places shown in the mask. A is any numeric constant, variable, or expression and B$ is any string.

Numeric Formatting Characters

Represents a digit position. The # indicates the number of positions reserved for printing the number. Unused digit positions to the left of a decimal are filled with spaces; unused positions to the right of the decimal are filled with zeros. Unless otherwise changed by the use of + or − in the format, positive numbers print with no sign and negative numbers print with a leading minus sign. The leading minus sign will take one of the reserved positions.

. *Indicates where the decimal is to be printed.*

+ *Forces printing of the sign.* The plus sign at the beginning of the #s causes the sign (+ or −) to be printed at the beginning of the number. The plus sign at the end causes the sign to be printed following the number.

− *Prints minus sign at end of number.* The minus sign at the end of the #s will cause the sign for a negative number to print following the number instead of in front of it. No sign will be printed for positive numbers.

** *Fills spaces with asterisks.* Two asterisks as the first format characters cause all unused positions to the left of the decimal to be filled with asterisks instead of spaces.

$$ *Floats the dollar sign.* Two dollar signs as the first format characters cause the dollar sign to be printed in the position immediately to the left of the first digit that is printed. Any remaining positions to the left of the dollar sign will be filled with spaces.

**$ *Floats dollar sign and fills spaces with asterisks.* The dollar sign will be printed immediately to the left of the first digit and any remaining positions to the left of the dollar sign will be filled with asterisks.

$** *Leading dollar sign and fills with asterisks.* The dollar sign will print in the first position and any spaces between it and the first digit will be filled with asterisks.

, *Inserts comma in standard places.* A comma to the left of the decimal causes a comma to be placed in every third position to the left of the decimal. Commas are not printed to the left of the last printed digit. Add extra #s for the comma position taken up for millions, trillions, and so on.

String Formatting Characters

! *Causes only the first character of the string to be printed.*

\n spaces\ *Prints specified number of characters.* The number of characters printed will be two (one for each backslash) plus the number of spaces between the backslashes. If the string has fewer characters than the number specified by the mask, the string will be left justified and any unused positions to the right will be filled with spaces.

& *Causes the entire string to be printed.*

CLS Clears the Display from the Screen

It also moves the cursor to the upper left corner.

═══════════════╣ **·EXERCISES·** ╠═══════════════

Short Answer

1. You are allowed only one variable at a time with each INPUT statement. (T/F)

2. If you enter too many values for the list of variables in the INPUT statement, BASIC drops the extra variables and proceeds. (T/F)

3. If you enter a non-numeric value for a numeric variable in the INPUT statement, BASIC issues an error message. (T/F)

4. The starting and ending values of a FOR . . . NEXT loop must be positive. (T/F)

5. The loop body of a FOR . . . NEXT statement won't execute if the starting value is greater than the ending value as in: FOR N = 5 to 1. (T/F)

6. The question mark or message that signals a user to enter a value is called a _____ .

7. When one or more lines of a program repeat, it is called _____ or _____ .

8. When you want to increment the counter in a FOR . . . NEXT statement by a value other than 1, what statement must be used? _____

9. Explain the two procedures that are encompassed within the INPUT statement.

10. Explain the differing results from separating a prompt string from the variable name with a comma or with a semicolon.

11. What happens if you press the Enter key (without anything else typed in) in response to an INPUT prompt?

12. Name the three parts of the FOR . . . NEXT statement and describe the function of each part.

13. Name the two types of values for the starting and ending values in the FOR statement.

14. What are the requirements for nested FOR . . . NEXT loops?

15. Explain the difference between using the PRINT statement and the PRINT USING statement.

16. The mask serves what purpose in a PRINT USING statement?

17. What does the statement CLS do?

Analyzing Code

18. What, if anything, is wrong with each of the following statements? What would be an appropriate correction?
    a. `INPUT A NUMBER`
    b. `INPUT A, NUMBER`
    c. `INPUT "A NUMBER"`
    d. `INPUT A.NUMBER`
    e. `LET INPUT = A.NUMBER`
    f. `LET A.NUMBER = INPUT`
    g. `PRINT INPUT`
    h. `FOR 1 TO 5`
    i. `FOR 1 = X TO 5`
    j. `FOR X = 1,2,3,4,5`
    k. `NEXT 10`
    l. `STEP 2`
    m. `FOR X$ = 1 TO 5`
    n. `FOR X = 1-5`

19. Which of the following are valid FOR statements:
    a. `FOR NUMBER = 1 TO 5 STEP -1`
    b. `FOR YEAR = 1900 TO 1985 STEP 5`
    c. `FOR COST = 1 TO LIMIT`
    d. `FOR INT.RATE = 5.5 TO 15.4 STEP .2`
    e. `FOR TIME = 12 TO 1 STEP 2`

20. How would the number 2345.678 appear in the following formats?
    a. `"##,###.##"`
    b. `"$$,###.#"`
    c. `"**#,###.###"`
    d. `"##,###+"`

21. Matching: Match each mask in the left-hand column with the correct sample of output in the right-hand column.

(1) `"#,###.##"`	a. `**1,234`
(2) `"&"`	b. `$1,234.56`
(3) `"###-"`	c. `PROGR`
(4) `"+####"`	d. `123-`
(5) `"$#,###.##"`	e. `1,234.56`
(6) `"$$#,###.##"`	f. `P`
(7) `"**#,###"`	g. `$**345.67`
(8) `"$**###.##"`	h. `$1,234.56`
(9) `"**$.##"`	i. `PROGRAMMING`
(10) `"!"`	j. `**$.34`
(11) `"\ \"`	k. `+123`

22. The following programs don't work. Figure out why and fix them.
    a.
    ```
    10 LET GROSS.PAY = HRS.WORKED * PAY.RATE
    20 INPUT HRS.WORKED, PAY.RATE
    30 PRINT GROSS.PAY, INPUT
    40 END
    ```

```
b. 10  PRINT "CUSTOMER LIST"
   20  PRINT
   30  FOR NBR.OF.CUSTOMERS = 1 TO 10
   40      INPUT "CUSTOMER NAME";CUSTOMER.NAME$
   50  NEXT
   60  PRINT CUSTOMER.NAME$
   70  END
c. 10  INPUT "THE CLASS SIZE IS "; CLASS.SIZE
   20  FOR SIZE = 1 TO CLASS.SIZE
   30      INPUT "STUDENT.NAME"; STUDENT.NAME$
   40  NEXT CLASS.SIZE
   50  END
d. 10  FOR COUNTER = 1 TO 20
   20      LET TOTAL = 0
   30      INPUT "AMOUNT OF SALE"; AMT.OF.SALE
   40      LET TOTAL = TOTAL + AMT.OF.SALE
   50  NEXT
   60  PRINT USING "TOTAL SALES $######.##"; TOTAL
e. 10  FOR HOURS = 1 TO 24
   20      PRINT "HOUR IS "; HOURS
   30      FOR MINUTES = 1 TO 60
   40          PRINT "MINUTE IS "; MINUTE
   50          FOR SECOND = 1 TO 60
   60              PRINT "SECOND IS "; SECOND
   70  NEXT
   80  END
f. 10  LET TOTAL.SALES = 0
   20  INPUT "HOW MANY CUSTOMERS";NBR.OF CUSTOMERS
   30  FOR I = 1 TO NBR.OF.CUSTOMERS
   40      INPUT "CUSTOMER NAME"; CUSTOMER.NAME$
   50      INPUT "AMOUNT OF SALE";CUSTOMER.AMOUNT
   60      LET TOTAL.SALES = TOTAL.SALES + CUSTOMER.AMOUNT
   70      PRINT CUSTOMER.NAME, CUSTOMER.AMOUNT
   80  NEXT
   90  PRINT "TOTAL SALES";TOTAL.SALES
   100 END
```

23. What's wrong with the following programs using FOR . . . NEXT?
   a. You run a program and get the message "NEXT without FOR".
   b. You run a program and get the message "FOR without NEXT".
   c. Find all of the errors in this program:

```
10  LET BIRTH = 0: LET DEATH = 100
20  FOR AGE = BIRTH TO DEATH
30      LET NUMBER.OF.TOYS = NUMBER.OF.TOYS + AGE
40  NEXT YEAR
50  PRINT The number of toys in lifetime is; "TOYS"
60  NEXT
70  END
```

24. PRINT USING:

a. Enter the following program:

```
10 FOR I = 1 TO 10
20     INPUT A
30     PRINT USING "####";A
40 NEXT
```

b. Run the program, experimenting with different values of value A.

c. Try some values with greater than four digits.

d. Change line 30 to:

```
30     PRINT USING "#,###.##";A
```

Programming

For the following programs:

a. Draw a structure chart

b. Draw a flowchart

c. Write pseudocode.

d. Code the program.

25. Practice with INPUT

a. Write a program that uses an INPUT statement to ask the user to enter a number, then prints the number. Use a prompt explaining to the user what to enter.

b. Write a program that uses a single INPUT statement to allow the user to enter two numbers, then prints their sum and product. Use a prompt.

c. Do (a) and (b) above, once with semicolons after each prompt and once with commas after each prompt.

26. Write a program that asks the user for an employee's name, gross monthly pay, and the percentage of the pay he or she wants withheld and deposited in a credit union. Then calculate and print for 12 months the monthly balance assuming an interest rate of 1 percent per month. The output should look as follows:

```
           Credit Union Withholding
Employee: Jane Doe        Gross:    $3,500      Percent: 5
Month                     Amt To Date
  1                            $175.00
  2                            $351.75
  3                            $530.27
  .                               .
  .                               .
  .                               .
```

27. The future value (*FV*) of an investment (*I*) compounded for *N* years at rate of interest *R* is given by the formula $FV = I(1 + R)$ raised to the *N*th power. Write a documented program that inputs the values for *I*, *R*, and *N*, and prints the computed value for *FV*.

28. Write a documented program that does the following:

a. For each whole number, 3 to 13, prints out the number, its square, and its cube.

b. Does the preceding first, and then prints out the sum of all the numbers, of all the squares, and of all the cubes.

29. WEATHER REPORT: Write a program that prompts the user to enter the high and low temperatures for each day of the week. The program should calculate the change in low and high temperatures for each successive day.

   Use the following format:

	LOW	CHANGE	HIGH	CHANGE
DAY 1	55	0	80	0
DAY 2	60	+5	88	+8
.	.	.	.	.
.	.	.	.	.
.	.	.	.	.
DAY 7	65	+2	90	-4

30. CARPET PURCHASE: You have three rooms to carpet, and you want a program that will allow you to enter the measurements of each room (in feet) and the cost per square yard of the carpet for that room. You also want to know the total cost for all three rooms.

31. SALES REPORT: Prompt the user to enter the number of customers (this will become your loop variable). For each customer, the user will input the account number (numeric, five digits), product code (alphanumeric, up to six characters), selling price (up to 999.99), and the number purchased (up to 9999). This program should calculate the total price for each customer and print the following report (if you have access to a printer, do the report on the printer).

   SALES REPORT

ACCOUNT NUMBER	PRODUCT NUMBER	UNIT PRICE	QUANTITY PURCHASED	TOTAL PURCHASE
99999	XXXXXX	$999.99	9999	$9,999,999.99
.	.	.	.	.
.	.	.	.	.
.	.	.	.	.

   TOTAL AMOUNT PURCHASED $99,999,999.99

32. SAVINGS ACCOUNT: Write a program that prints out a schedule of a savings account in which the interest is compounded monthly. The user will input the amount of the original deposit, the annual interest rate, and the number of months to be printed. The program will produce the following report (if you have access to a printer, print the report on it).

```
ORIGINAL INVESTMENT: $##,###.##
ANNUAL INTEREST RATE: ##.## %
NUMBER OF MONTHS:   ###
```

MONTH	INTEREST	NEW BALANCE
###	$##,###.##	$###,###.##
.	.	.
.	.	.
.	.	.

   TOTAL INTEREST EARNED $##,###.##

33. POWERS OF 2

a. Write a program that will calculate and print out a table of the powers of 2. The user will input the highest power he or she wishes to be printed (maximum allowed is 99). Display as follows:

```
2 raised to the power of 1 is 2
2 raised to the power of 2 is 4
                 .
                 .
                 .
```

b. Modify the preceding program, so that the user can generate the same table using any power less than 100.

34. SALARY REPORT: Prompt the user to enter the monthly gross and the amount of income tax to be withheld for each of 12 months. The program will calculate FICA (Social Security) withholding at 7.15 percent and Disability at .9 percent. For each month the gross, amounts withheld, and net are to be printed. At the end of each quarter, print the year-to-date totals. (Hint: you will need to use nested FOR . . . NEXT loops.)

MONTH	GROSS	INCOME TAX	FICA	DISABIL.	NET
1	##,###.##	####.##	####.##	###.##	##,###.##
.	.	.	.	.	.
.	.	.	.	.	.
3	.	.	.	.	.

QUARTERLY Y T D	###,###.##	#####.##	#####.##	####.##	###,###.##
4	.	.	.	.	.
	.	.	.	.	.

EDITING PROGRAMS

THE ONLY THING CONSTANT
IN BUSINESS IS CHANGE

Chris seldom wrote computer programs as a favor. Long experience had shown that the favor didn't stop when the program was done. Programs of any complexity tended to have "bugs," or errors, and it was a dead certainty that, whenever a bug occurred, Chris as the original author would get a call.

Even more frightening to Chris than the prospect of bugs was the knowledge that programs, even ones that worked perfectly, seldom stayed the same for very long. "Any business environment is dynamic," Chris often mused, "so any computer program which solves problems in that environment must also be dynamic. That means changing needs, which means changing programs, which means I get a phone call."

Little wonder that for months after finishing a program, especially one of which Data Processing would disavow any knowledge, Chris lived in fear of the telephone. In the case of Pat's depreciation program, the call came after just two weeks.

"Hi, Chris. Oh, say, Chris, I sure did appreciate your writing that depreciation program. It's already saved me a lot of time. Made me look really good in front of The Boss."

"Sure thing, Pat," Chris said, knowing that Pat had not called simply to pass the time. "What's the problem?"

"Problem? Oh, well, I wasn't going to bring that up, but now that you mention it, I have been having a few problems with the program."

"Here it comes," thought Chris.

"You remember that I said no piece of equipment would ever be worth more than a hundred thousand dollars?"

"Don't tell me," Chris broke in. "You tried to use it for something more expensive and it didn't work. It put percent signs in front of all the numbers on the report to let you know they were too big."

"Right," replied Pat. "So, what do I do about it?"

"I don't suppose you can just live with a funny-looking report?"

"No, The Boss insists on everything looking polished."

"Just how expensive is this piece of equipment?"

"About three million dollars."

"What! Three million dollars?! We spent all that time carefully going over all aspects of the program, drafting specifications that you agreed to, which said that nothing will cost over a hundred thousand dollars, and today you call to tell me that you're using it for something that costs three million dollars?"

"Settle down, Chris," cried Pat, who was able to hear every word even though the telephone receiver was held at arm's length. "I know I said that all our equipment cost less than a hundred thousand dollars, and I was right . . . at the time."

"You don't mean . . ."

"Exactly. The Boss liked your program so much, we're now using it for equipment in some of the other divisions, not just Solid Waste Removal. As you know, Con. Glomerate also owns a mining company, and it so happens that the mining company owns some very expensive earth-moving equipment. Why, one of them alone costs . . ."

"Let me guess, three million dollars."

"$3,174,562.95, to be exact," said Pat. "Chris, The Boss expects me to get this thing working. Can you help me out? Please? I'll really owe you one."

The request could be refused, but Chris realized that to do so would be indefensible. Once a programmer has finished a program, people become dependent on it. This automatically places a certain burden on the programmer to see to it that those who use a program have some way to get it fixed and changed, and Pat was not yet capable of handling the changes alone.

Had the program been developed through normal channels, it would have been turned over to others in Data Processing whose job it is to maintain programs; by violating normal procedures, Chris had to assume some responsibility for the fate of Pat's program.

"All right, Pat," Chris finally said with a sigh. "I'll fix your program but on one condition. I know that you know a little about BASIC. Because I wrote this program as a favor to you, I expect you to return the favor by learning how to maintain it yourself in the future. Start by learning about integer and double-precision variables in your BASIC book. That'll explain why the program isn't working the way you want and what needs to be changed.

"Then, study BASIC's advanced features for editing programs. If we had to retype every line that needed changing, we'd have to retype just about the entire program. Fortunately, BASIC provides some easy ways to make changes. See you tomorrow."

"Thanks three million," Pat said as Chris hung up.

• THE ABCS OF BASIC ON THE IBM PERSONAL COMPUTER •

LESSON 4: PRECISION OF VARIABLES AND PROGRAM EDITING

By now you have learned to manipulate numbers and variables with your IBM Personal Computer, but in today's lesson you will learn that not all numbers and variables are created equal!

BASIC has three different types of variables that hold numbers as values, called single precision, double precision, and integer. Each is capable of holding numbers of certain sizes and types. (A fourth type of variable is the string variable, which holds text, not numbers.) Single-precision variables are the ones you have been using so far, but, as you will see, single-precision variables have some important limitations.

This lesson also explains some advanced features of BASIC for changing, or editing, a program. Up to now you have learned only to retype any line that is in error. BASIC allows you to make changes much more simply than this. Built into BASIC is the **screen editor,** which allows you to position the cursor anywhere on the monitor and make changes directly where they are needed. The EDIT command is a companion to the screen editor.

The BASIC commands AUTO and RENUM are used in connection with line numbers in a BASIC program. AUTO saves a little typing time by automatically assigning line numbers in sequence as you type in a program. RENUM is used to renumber lines in a program. Both are useful when editing programs.

Finally, for those who don't like to type, we'll look at several shortcuts available in BASIC to make typing easier.

Precision of Variables: Integer, Single and Double Precision

You already know that a variable with a dollar sign at the end of its name holds text, such as "Jane Doe", while a variable without a dollar sign on the end holds

TABLE 4.1 ▪ Four Types of BASIC Variables

VARIABLE TYPE	SAMPLE NAME	VALUES ALLOWED	EXAMPLES
Single precision	A.VARIABLE or A.VARIABLE!	Real numbers, precise to 7 digits	53748 $-1.23456E2$
Double precision	A.VARIABLE#	Real numbers, precise to 17 digits	5432134565 $-1.23456789D2$
Integer	A.VARIABLE%	Whole number between $-32{,}768$ and $32{,}767$, inclusive	2 32032
String	A.VARIABLE$	Text up to 255 characters long	"This test" "Charles"

numbers. However, BASIC provides two additional types of variables, each designed to hold certain kinds of numbers. Like string variables, which have a $ at the end of their name, these two variable types also have type declaration characters placed at the end of their name (see Table 4.1).

Single Precision

The variables you have used so far have been **single-precision variables,** which can only hold up to seven digits. In the examples BASIC has automatically set variables with no type declaration character at the end to be single precision. The type declaration character of an exclamation point (!) can be used to indicate single precision. What happens when you try to use more than seven digits with a single-precision variable? Here's a simple program which illustrates the effects.

```
NEW
Ok
10 LET EQUIPMENT.COST = 123456.78
20 PRINT EQUIPMENT.COST
30 END
RUN
 123456.8
Ok
```

What happened? We set EQUIPMENT.COST to an eight-digit number, 123456.78, and got back a seven-digit number, 123456.8. This is a fundamental limitation on the kinds of numeric variables you have seen so far: they can only hold seven digits. It doesn't matter where the decimal is, as long as there are seven or fewer digits.

```
LET A.NUMBER = .12345678
PRINT A.NUMBER
 .1234568
Ok
LET A.NUMBER = 9876.5432
```

```
PRINT A.NUMBER
 9876.543
Ok
LET RATIO = -5.5555555
PRINT RATIO
-5.555556
Ok
```

As you can see, BASIC rounds a number with more than seven digits to exactly seven digits. If the eighth digit is five or more, the seventh digit is rounded up; if the eighth digit is four or less, the seventh digit is left alone.

```
LET X = 1.1111115
LET Y = 1.1111114
PRINT X,Y
 1.111112        1.111111
Ok
```

Exponential Notation for Single-Precision Variables

So far, all our examples of seven-digit numbers are numbers with at least one digit right of the decimal point. Put another way, they are all less than 10,000,000, since to represent 10,000,000 or more requires more than seven digits left of the decimal point. BASIC faces a dilemma when you assign a value to a single-precision numeric variable greater than ten million; it can't simply round it off, since that would leave a trailing zero, which still takes up a digit. For example, if 33,111,222 were rounded to seven digits, the result would be 33,111,220, which is still eight digits long, including the trailing zero.

BASIC solves this problem by using exponential notation.

```
LET COST = 33111222
PRINT COST
 3.311122E+07
Ok
```

This notation means "3.311122 times ten to the seventh power." Ten to the *n*th power means a one followed by *n* zeros, so ten to the seventh power is 10,000,000.

Exponential notation (using E as part of a number) can also be used in entering or storing numbers.

```
10 LET I = 3E+4 : LET J = .2123E+3: LET K = 1234E-4
20 PRINT I,J,K
run
 30000         212.3            .1234
Ok
new
Ok
10 INPUT I
20 PRINT I
```

```
run
? 9.876E+2
 987.6
Ok
run
? 123456.78E-8
 1.234568E-03      ⟵ | notice that the number is rounded |
Ok
```

Did you notice that BASIC had a similar solution to displaying a very small single-precision number with a significant digit in the eighth position to the right of the decimal point?

Another way of explaining exponential format is that the E indicates how many places to move the decimal point, and the sign indicates the direction to move the decimal point; a positive sign means move it to the right, and a negative sign means move it to the left.

When BASIC is asked to display a single-precision number, it will try to keep eight significant digits and display the number in the format x.xxxxxxxE+xx or x.xxxxxxxE−xx if required.

Here are some examples of exponential notation:

$1 = 1E+00$
$10 = 1E+01$
$1,000 = 1E+03$
$1,000,000 = 1E+06$
$0.1 = 1E-01$
$0.001 = 1E-03$
$1,234 = 1.234E+03 = 12.34E+02 = 123.4E+01 = 1234E+00$
$0.00123 = .123E-02 = 1.23E-03 = 12.3E-04 = 123E-05$

Double-Precision Variables Are Precise to 17 Digits

It is very common for a business program to deal with amounts larger than one hundred thousand dollars, so the variables you have been using so far are not adequate for all purposes. For this reason BASIC has another type of variable available, the **double-precision variable,** which stores up to 17 digits. (Although up to 17 digits are stored, only 16 digits will print.)

You will remember that string variables have the same kinds of names as single-precision variables but with a dollar sign on the end. Double-precision variables work much the same way but with a pound sign (#) on the end.

Putting a # at the end of a variable name signifies that this variable will contain double-precision numbers. In the same way you may put a ! at the end of a single-precision variable name to show that it is single precision. If you do not put any suffix at the end of a variable name, it is assumed to be single precision (unless you change the rules using DEF type, as we will explain later in this chapter.)

In the same way, you may put the # at the end of a number to show that it is significant to 17 digits.

```
LET COST# = 33111222#
PRINT COST#
 33111222
Ok
LET TOTAL.REVENUES# = 544375321.55#
PRINT TOTAL.REVENUES
 0
Ok
```

Wait a minute! We tried to print "TOTAL.REVENUES" and got a zero! The reason is that we forgot the pound sign, and BASIC had no way of knowing that "TOTAL.REVENUES" and "TOTAL.REVENUES#" were supposed to be the same. Instead BASIC created a new variable without the pound sign and initialized it to a value of zero. Be very careful with pound signs and dollar signs in your variable names; forgetting them is one of the most common errors in BASIC!

```
PRINT TOTAL.REVENUES#
 544375321.55
Ok
```

Exponential Notation and Double Precision Allow Very Large Numbers to Be Stored to 17 Digits Precision

Double-precision numbers do not use E to express the scientific notation. They use the letter D. In all other respects, D and E are used in the same way, as is seen in this example:

```
10 'Program to demonstrate D notation
20 FOR I = 35 TO 40
30    LET BIG# = I * 2D+21
40    PRINT BIG#
50 NEXT
60 END
run
 7D+22
 7.2D+22
 7.4D+22
 7.4D+22
 7.6D+22
 7.8D+22
 8D+22
Ok
```

Double-precision variables can accurately hold up to 17 digits. As with single-precision variables, double-precision variables can hold either integers or real numbers, and the total maximum of 17 digits does not depend on the location of the decimal point. For business uses, a double-precision variable can hold dollar amounts in the thousands of trillions of dollars accurately to the penny.

```
LET A.BIG.DOLLAR.AMOUNT# = 11222333444555.66
PRINT A.BIG.DOLLAR.AMOUNT#
 11222333444555.66
Ok
```

To appreciate more fully the size of this number, we will print it with a PRINT USING statement:

```
PRINT USING '###,###,###,###,###.##'; A.BIG.DOLLAR.AMOUNT#
 11,222,333,444,555.66
Ok
```

Integer Variables Store Whole Numbers Between −32,768 and 32,767 Only
The third type of numeric variable you can use in BASIC is the **integer variable.** An integer variable has a percent sign (%) at the end of its name. Integer variables, as the name implies, hold only integer values, such as 346 or 2 or 12345. If you attempt to assign a noninteger value to an integer variable, BASIC rounds it to an integer.

```
LET DAYS% = 432
PRINT DAYS%
 432
Ok
LET DAYS% = 123.45
PRINT DAYS%
 123
Ok
```

If the fraction is less than one-half, or 0.5, BASIC rounds down to the next smaller integer. If the fraction is greater or equal to one-half, BASIC rounds up to the next higher integer. A number such as 55.5 gets rounded up to 56, while 55.49 gets rounded down to 55.

Integer variables can hold whole numbers in the range −32,768 to +32,767. These strange-looking limits come from the way the computer stores integers. If you attempt to store a number outside this range in an integer variable, BASIC gives an error message. (For the curious, 32,767 is two to the fifteenth power, minus one.)

```
LET QUANTITY% = 45123
Overflow
Ok
```

Unlike single- and double-precision variables, there is no exponential notation for integer variables.

In a business environment we usually are concerned with the number of digits that can be stored accurately, so the question naturally arises, how many digits can you store in an integer variable? The answer is, "sometimes four, sometimes five, depending on the size of the number." For example, the five-digit number 31,555 will fit in an integer variable while the five-digit number 46,782 will not.

To keep things simple, many BASIC programmers adopt the rule that all numbers that may exceed four digits are always stored in single-precision or double-precision variables. That way, there is never a potential for overflow.

When to Use Double-Precision and Integer Variables

Since a single-precision variable holds 7 digits and an integer variable 4 to 5, a single-precision variable is capable of holding anything an integer variable can and then some. Double-precision variables, with their 17-digit capacity, hold much more than single-precision or integer variables.

If double-precision variables can hold everything that single-precision and integer variables can, why not always use double-precision variables? There are two major reasons: speed and space.

Integer variables are very fast in BASIC, single precision slow, and double precision very slow. To see the difference, try the following program.

```
NEW
10 LET X% = 0
20 PRINT "starting the loop"
30 FOR I% = 1 to 5000
40 LET X% = X% + 1
50 NEXT I%
60 PRINT "done"
70 END
RUN
starting the loop
done
Ok
10 LET X = 0
40 LET X = X + 1
RUN
starting the loop
done
Ok
10 LET X# = 0
40 LET X# = X# + 1
RUN
starting the loop
done
Ok
```

This nonsense program performs 5000 additions. The first time through, you used X%, an integer; the second time X, a single-precision variable; and finally X#, a double-precision variable. You will notice that there is a dramatic difference in speed between the integer version and the other two, but not much difference between single precision and double precision. This is typical of BASIC programs.

Speed is less of a concern than accuracy in business programs written in BASIC, so avoiding double-precision variables just to make a program run faster is generally bad practice. However, a good case can be made for using integer variables wherever you know (a) that the variable will only hold integer values and (b) all values will be in the range ± 32,767. This is almost always true of the counter in FOR . . . NEXT loops, such as I% in the preceding program. In fact, BASIC will not allow double-precision variables to be used as the counter in a FOR . . . NEXT loop.

As far as the amount of space used, integer variables take two bytes of memory, single precision four, and double precision eight. For most business applications this difference is seldom significant. The only time that it could become significant is if your program builds large tables within memory and so uses lots of variables; in that case, you will want to use integer or single precision if you can.

Since variables tend to be scattered throughout a program, changing a variable from one precision to another because you did not define it properly in the beginning is a time-consuming, frustrating task. Most of the time when a variable must be changed from one precision to another, it is from single to double precision. For this reason it is wise to follow this rule in selecting the precision of your variables: if the variable can safely be made an integer variable, do so; otherwise make it double precision. This rule is sometimes cumbersome, but it helps make sure your programs won't round values unexpectedly.

Don't Use Single-Precision Variables When You Need Double Precision

Errors can occur when arithmetic mixes single- and double-precision values. One cannot increase precision; if any variable or constant in an arithmetic expression is single precision, the answer can be counted on to be precise to at most seven digits. The error occurs when you store this value, which is precise only to seven digits, in a double-precision variable. What BASIC does is put "garbage" digits in the remaining less significant digits of precision.

An example may clarify this danger:

```
10 'Program to demonstrate the danger of using mixed (single and double)
20 'precision arithmetic when double precision is required
30 '
40 LET A# = 10000000#
50 PRINT "        How much is .1 times 10000000?"
60 PRINT "Mixing single and double precision -----> ";A# * .1
70 PRINT "Double precision with double precision -> ";A# * .1#
80 '
90 'Note that placing a pound sign # after a number makes it double precision
100 LET SINGLE! = A# * .1
110 LET DOUBLE# = A# * .1
120 PRINT "Single precision stores correct value --------> ";SINGLE!
130 PRINT "But double precision variable is not correct -> ";DOUBLE#
140 END
```

Before we look at the results of running this program, think a moment and consider what results we should expect. Here is the output:

```
        How much is .1 times 10000000?
Mixing single and double precision -----> 1000000.014901161
Double precision with double precision -> 1000000
Single precision stores correct value --------> 1000000
But double precision variable is not correct -> 1000000.014901161
Ok
```

The point is that one cannot increase precision by storing a value in a double-precision variable. To yield a double-precision value to be stored in a double-precision variable, all the variables and constants of an arithmetic expression must be double precision or integer. Constants can be made double precision by appending a pound sign to the numeric value.

DEFtype: Predefining Variables as Integer, or Double or Single Precision

There are actually two ways to tell BASIC that you want a variable to represent an integer, or a double- or single-precision number. The first way is what we have been doing up to this point—we explicitly put a type declaration character (#, %, !) at the end of each variable name. As you'll recall, % is used for integer; ! for single precision; # for double precision; $ for string variables. BASIC uses a default rule that any variable without a type indicator is single precision.

The second way is to change this default rule. We can tell BASIC that we want all variables that begin with a certain letter to be of a specified TYPE (integer, single precision, or double precision, or string) by using the DEFtype statement. Then all variables that begin with that letter and do not have a TYPE indicator will be of the DEFined type.

For example, to tell BASIC that we want all variables that begin with the letters A, B, and C (and that do not have type indicators) to be double precision, we use the following:

```
DEFDBL A-C
```

We include this statement early in the program before we define any variables that start with the letters A, B, or C.

After this statement is executed, the variables ADAM, BOOK.AMT, and CHOCOLATE would all be of type double precision.

There are similar statements for integers (DEFINT), single precision (DEFSNG), and string (DEFSTR).

This example illustrates the use of the DEF functions:

```
10 DEFINT A,D-F
20 DEFSNG B,G-K,O
30 DEFDBL C,L,M,N,P-Z
40 ' First let's look at how single and double precision handle large numbers
50 LET BELLOWS = 1234567890123456789
60 LET CHARLES = 1234567890123456789
```

```
70 PRINT BELLOWS,CHARLES
80 ' Now let's look at how integer precision handles large numbers
90 LET ANERROR = 1234567890123456789
100 PRINT ANERROR
run
 1.234568E+19                1.234567890123457D+19
Overflow in 90
```

In this sample program we used the DEFtype statement to tell BASIC that we were changing the rules of what precision to assign variables with no type indicator. We told it that all variables whose name begins with an A or D through F were to be stored as integer, those whose name begins with a B, O, or G through K were to be stored as single precision, and all the rest (C, L, M, N, P – Z) were to be stored as double precision.

The program assigned a very large number a single-precision variable (BELLOWS) and a double-precision variable (CHARLES) and printed the results. When we tried to assign this number (which is greater than 32767) to an integer variable (ANERROR), we got an overflow error.

The DEFtype statement in the preceding program defined the precision only for numeric variables in that program that had no type declaration character after the variable name. Placing a type declaration character after the variable name will override the precision set by the DEFtype statement for that variable. For example: ANERROR is integer, but ANERROR# is double precision because the type indicator for double precision (#) is appended as part of its name. ANERROR and ANERROR# are two different variables because they are of different precision, but ANERROR and ANERROR% are the same variable. It is good programming practice never to use variable names that are almost identical; therefore, you would not use both ANERROR and ANERROR# in the same program. However, if you get unexpected results from a program, you might check that you haven't accidentally created two variables when you intended only one.

· DEFTYPE STATEMENTS ·

DEFtype Statements make type declaration characters (#, !, %, and $) unnecessary.

DEFINT A, . . . define as integer
DEFSNG A, . . . define as single precision
DEFDBL A, . . . define as double precision
DEFSTR A, . . . define as string

The Screen Editor

So far, whenever you have made a change to a program, you have had to retype the line or lines to be changed. This is very time consuming and prone to errors, so BASIC provides an efficient alternative: the screen editor.

To use the screen editor, follow these steps:

1. Display the line to be changed on the monitor. It may already be on display anywhere on the monitor, or you may display it by using the LIST command.
2. Move the cursor to the spot at which the change is to be made. To do this, you use the arrow keys on the numeric keypad. (See Figure 4.1.)

    The arrow keys (lowercase 2, 4, 6, and 8) move the cursor in the indicated direction. In order for them to function as cursor-positioning keys, the Num Lock key must be off. The Num Lock is like the Caps Lock key, in that you cannot tell by looking at the keyboard whether it is on or off. However, as soon as you press one of the keys, you will discover the current setting. The "Home" key (lowercase 7) moves the cursor to the upper left-hand corner of the display. The "End" key (lowercase 1) moves the cursor to the end of whatever line the cursor is currently on.
3. If you want to replace the character over the cursor, just type in the correct character.
4. If you want to delete the character over the cursor, press the Del key (the period key on the numeric keypad). This deletes the character directly over the cursor and shifts all remaining characters on the line one space to the left. The Backspace key, which you learned to use in Lesson 1, is not the same as the Delete key. Pressing the Backspace key causes the character to the left of the cursor to be deleted and the remaining characters to be shifted one space to the left.

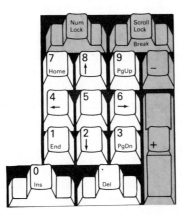

FIGURE 4.1·
The numeric
keypad

5. If you want to insert one or more characters, press the Ins key (the zero key on the numeric keypad) and then type the characters to be inserted. When you press the Ins key, the computer goes into "insert mode." As long as you are in insert mode, every character you type is inserted into the current line between the character over the cursor and the character immediately preceding the cursor.

   Insert mode is stopped whenever you press a special key, such as an arrow key, the Del key, or Enter or when you press Ins a second time. To let you know when you are in insert mode, the computer changes the shape of the cursor from the normal blinking underline character to a small, blinking square box, which is sometimes called a **fat cursor.** The square box is flashed only while you are in insert mode.

6. When you are all through with the changes on one line, press the Enter key. This is important! If you do not press Enter, the changes will not be recorded!

Here is an example of screen editing. First, type in the following short program. It should look familiar; it was the last example in the section on variable precision.

```
NEW
Ok
10 LET X% = 0
20 PRINT "starting the loop"
30 FOR I% = 1 TO 5000
40    LET X% = X% + 1
50 NEXT I%
60 PRINT "done"
70 END
```

Now, with this program currently on display, let's try to change all occurrences of X% to just X. There are only two lines on which X% appears, lines 10 and 40. To edit line 10, use the arrow keys on the numeric keypad to move the cursor to the % on line 10. When the cursor is blinking on line 10 directly under the %, press the Del key once. The % should disappear and the remaining characters should move over.

Now — and this is very important — press the Enter key. The cursor should now be under the 2 in the next line number, 20. Line 10 is now changed. Now for line 40. Move the cursor, using the arrow keys, to the first % on line 40, then press the Del key. Move the cursor to the next % on line 40 and press the Del key again. Both percent signs are now gone, so press Enter to record the change. Move the cursor down a few lines to a blank line and enter a LIST command to verify the changes.

(There is a quick way to get a blank line on the screen; simply press the Escape key. Doing so will only clear what is on the screen; it will not erase your program line from memory. Rather than moving the cursor to a blank line as was suggested, you can press Escape to clear the line and then type LIST.)

```
LIST
10 LET X = 0
20 PRINT "starting the loop"
30 FOR I% = 1 TO 5000
40    LET X = X + 1
50 NEXT I%
60 PRINT "done"
70 END
Ok
```

As you can see, the changes have been made. What if you hadn't pressed Enter after making the changes? Let's try it and see. Move the cursor to the *t* in the word *the* on line 20, then press the Del key four times. This deletes the letters *t*, *h*, and *e* and the space from the display. Now move the cursor down to a blank line without first pressing Enter and enter a LIST command.

```
LIST 20
20 PRINT "starting the loop"
Ok
```

The change you made to line 20 was not recorded because you didn't press Enter before leaving the line.

EDIT Command Displays a Line, Ready for Editing

The EDIT command is a shortcut for editing a line that may or may not be on display. To use the EDIT command, just type in the word *EDIT* followed by a space and the line number to be edited. BASIC displays the line and puts the cursor at the beginning of the line. Editing then proceeds as usual.

The screen editor is a very convenient, powerful way to change your programs, but it has other uses as well. If you want to use a command that is already on display somewhere on the screen, just move the cursor to that line and press Enter. BASIC will execute that command just as if you had typed it in again.

For example, suppose you really did want that change to line 20, deleting the word *the*. Try typing "EDIT 20", delete the word *the*, then press Enter. Now move the cursor up a few lines to the command "LIST 20" and press Enter. The

·THE EDIT COMMAND·

EDIT Line Number
Displays line and places cursor under first digit of the line number.

computer will execute the LIST command and list the new line 20. This technique can be used for any line on the screen.

The only way to become truly comfortable with the screen editor is to experiment with it. In a short time you will become a master of program editing.

AUTO Types Line Numbers for You

When you are typing in a new program, it is sometimes frustrating to have to type in all those line numbers. The AUTO command in BASIC saves some of the typing by having BASIC type the line numbers for you.

```
NEW
Ok
AUTO
10 _
```

The AUTO command told BASIC to assign the line numbers for you. BASIC displays line number 10 and waits for you to type in the statements that go on that line. When you are done with that line and press Enter, BASIC will display line number 20, and so forth until you press Control-Break (the Ctrl and Break keys simultaneously—in case you have forgotten, the Break key is found at the upper right corner of the numeric keypad). Be sure you press Control-Break when you are through entering program lines! Otherwise, everything you type in will become a part of your program.

The following is a common error when using AUTO. The user used AUTO to automatically type line numbers, then typed in the program (lines 10–50). However, the user never pressed Control-Break, so the LIST, RUN, and EDIT commands, which weren't supposed to be part of the program, ended up as lines 60, 70, and 80. The AUTO command is still working, and the cursor is sitting after line number 90 waiting for a new command. The correct action now is to press Control-Break, then delete lines 60–80.

·THE AUTO COMMAND·

AUTO Line Number, Increment
Automatically numbers program lines beginning with the line number
    specified and incrementing by the increment specified.
If line number is not specified, AUTO begins with line number 10.
If increment is not specified, AUTO increments by 10.

Press Control-Break to cancel AUTO.

```
NEW
Ok
AUTO
10 LET TOTAL% = 0
20 FOR I% = 1 TO 10
30 LET TOTAL% = TOTAL% + I%
40 NEXT I%
50 END
60 LIST
70 RUN
80 EDIT 30
90 _
```

ASTERISK Shows If AUTO Line Number Already Exists

If there is already a line in memory with the same line number AUTO tries to use, an asterisk appears beside the line number to let you know that you are changing an existing line. If you don't want to replace that line, press Control-Break. AUTO will stop and the old line will still be intact.

```
NEW
Ok
30 ' this line is already taken
AUTO
10 ' first
20 ' second
30*            ←⎯ press Control-Break here
Ok
list
10 ' first
20 ' second
30 ' this line is already taken
Ok
```

Changing the Default Start Line and Line Increment

By just typing in AUTO, you are telling BASIC to start numbering with line 10 and continue in increments of 10. If you want to start with another line number, type that line number after the AUTO command.

```
AUTO 300
300 _
```

If you want to change the increment from 10 to some other number, put a comma and the increment after the starting line number.

```
AUTO 300,20
300 LET X% = 3
320 _
```

In this example, BASIC starts with line number 300 and will continue with lines 320, 340, and so on every time you press Enter.

A word of warning about editing with AUTO on. Suppose that you are entering a program using AUTO to number your lines and you realize that three lines prior to where you currently are, you made an error. With AUTO still on, you move the cursor up to the line, make the correction and press Enter. Because AUTO is still on, instead of the old line being corrected, this line including the line number, will be added as the next line of your program. The following is an example:

```
NEW
Ok
AUTO
10 LET HOURS = 40
20 LET RITE = 5.75
30 LET GROSS = HOURS * RATE
40 PRINT USING "###,###.##"; GROSS
```

At this point you realize that you misspelled RATE in line 20. You move the cursor up to line 20, correct the spelling, and press Enter. Now press Ctrl and Break to end AUTO and LIST your program. This is what you will see:

```
LIST
10 LET HOURS = 40
20 LET RITE = 5.75
30 LET GROSS = HOURS * RATE
40 PRINT USING "##,###.##": GROSS
50 20 LET RATE = 5.75
```

Instead of correcting line 20 as you intended, you created a new line 50. To correct this you need to stop AUTO by using Ctrl and Break, delete line 50, then enter the correction for line 20.

Because you must turn off AUTO before you use the screen editor to change previous lines, you will have to decide for yourself whether AUTO makes your entry easier or not.

RENUM Renumbers Program Lines

It is very common to have to add lines to a program. Look at the following program.

```
NEW
Ok
AUTO
10 LET PRICE# = 50
20 LET COST# = 40
30 PRINT PRICE#, COST#, GROSS.MARGIN#
40 END
50
Ok
```

(If you enter this program, be sure to press Control-Break when line 50 shows on the monitor. Otherwise, AUTO will continue typing line numbers!)

There is something wrong with this program. Nowhere is GROSS.MARGIN# computed! We must add a line.

```
25 LET GROSS.MARGIN# = PRICE# - COST#
LIST
10 LET PRICE# = 50
20 LET COST# = 40
25 LET GROSS.MARGIN# = PRICE# - COST#
30 PRINT PRICE#, COST#, GROSS.MARGIN#
40 END
Ok
```

Now the program is fixed, but our line numbering sequence, in increments of 10, is destroyed. This example is not too bad, but with larger programs and major changes, line numbering can be messed up to the point where it is difficult to read the program. RENUM solves this problem.

```
RENUM
Ok
LIST
10 LET PRICE# = 50
20 LET COST# = 40
30 LET GROSS.MARGIN# = PRICE# - COST#
40 PRINT PRICE#, COST#, GROSS.MARGIN#
50 END
Ok
```

Changing the Default Start as Line Number, First Line Number, and Increment
RENUM, by itself, always renumbers the entire program, starts the new line numbering with 10, and proceeds in increments of 10. Sometimes you will want to renumber the entire program with some line number other than 10 as your beginning number. To do so, put the line number with which you wish to begin after the RENUM command.

```
RENUM 100
Ok
LIST
100 LET PRICE# = 50
110 LET COST# = 40
120 LET GROSS.MARGIN# = PRICE# - COST#
130 PRINT PRICE#, COST#, GROSS.MARGIN#
140 END
Ok
```

You may want to renumber only a part of your program. Suppose we want lines 130 and 140 of the example program to be renumbered, starting as line number 2000.

```
RENUM 2000,130
Ok
LIST
100 LET PRICE# = 50
110 LET COST# = 40
120 LET GROSS.MARGIN# = PRICE# - COST#
2000 PRINT PRICE#, COST#, GROSS.MARGIN#
2010 END
Ok
```

In this example, the command RENUM 2000,130 told BASIC to renumber all lines in the program from line 130 to the end, and to start renumbering with line number 2000.

The final option in the RENUM command is to specify the increment between line numbers, if it is to be other than 10.

```
RENUM 3000,120,50
Ok
LIST
100 LET PRICE# = 50
110 LET COST# = 40
3000 LET GROSS.MARGIN# = PRICE# - COST#
3050 PRINT PRICE#, COST#, GROSS.MARGIN#
3100 END
Ok
```

Warning: RENUM Will Ruin Neat Block Numbering

The most important thing to remember about RENUM is that it always renumbers all lines to the end of the program. You can tell it where to begin but not where to end. If you have blocks of BASIC code neatly numbered (such as all the lines in the 6000s doing one thing, 7000s another), renumbering will ruin your block numbering. RENUM will not renumber selectively.

Table 4.2 compares the options of RENUM.

RENUM and REMarks

Keep RENUM in mind when putting comments into your programs. If you reference specific line numbers in your comments, they may become obsolete when you do a RENUM. For this reason it is better to avoid comments that reference a specific line number. In later chapters you will learn about statements such as GOSUB and GOTO, which direct BASIC to change its normal flow of sequentially processing the lines and continue processing at a particular line number. RENUM will automatically take care of changing these references for you.

Alternate Key Generates BASIC Keywords

You may have wondered by now what the Alternate key (ALT) is used for. Like Control and Shift, it doesn't do anything by itself; it is only when you press Alternate in combination with other keys that Alternate has any effect. Try

TABLE 4.2 • Variations of RENUM

FORMAT: RENUM AS-NEW-#, START-WITH-OLD-#, INCREMENT

EXAMPLES	NEW STARTING LINE NUMBER	LINES AFFECTED	INCREMENT
RENUM	10	All	10
RENUM 500	500	All	10
RENUM 500,100	500	Line 100 to end	10
RENUM 500,100,50	500	Line 100 to end	50
RENUM ,,2	10	All	2
RENUM 500,,50	500	All	50

pressing Alt-A (the Alternate and A keys simultaneously). AUTO appears on the display. Instead of pressing five keys (A-U-T-O-space), you only had to press one. Each letter except J, Q, Y, and Z pressed in combination with Alternate displays some BASIC command or statement. You may use Alternate keys anytime as a shortcut to typing the entire statement. The following list shows all of the available Alternate keys. Notice that the letter used with Alternate is always the first letter of the BASIC command. This makes it easier to remember the more frequently used Alternate keys. Note also that BSAVE is not the same as SAVE. This command and some of the others shown here are beyond the scope of this book.

A	AUTO	B	BSAVE	C	COLOR
D	DELETE	E	ELSE	F	FOR
G	GOTO	H	HEX$	I	INPUT
J	(not used)	K	KEY	L	LOCATE
M	MOTOR	N	NEXT	O	OPEN
P	PRINT	Q	(not used)	R	RUN
S	SCREEN	T	THEN	U	USING
V	VAL	W	WIDTH	X	XOR
Y	(not used)	Z	(not used)		

To practice using the Alternate key, enter this simple program. The Alternate and letter you are to press are underlined; what you will see on the screen is within the parentheses.

```
NEW
Ok
ALT A (AUTO)
10 ALT P (PRINT) "This is an example of using Alternate"
20 ALT F (FOR) COUNTER = 100 TO 500, STEP 100
30 ALT P (PRINT) ALT U (USING) ; "The counter is ###"
40 ALT N (NEXT)
50 END
* Press Control-Break to end AUTO *
ALT R (RUN)
```

Function Keys also Generate Keywords

You may also have wondered what the Function keys on the left side of the keyboard are for. They, like the Alternate keys, are shortcuts. Function keys are labeled F1, F2, and so on through F10.

Press F1. The command LIST appears on the display. Each Function key has some sequence of keystrokes prestored for use when the key is pressed. The last line (row 25) of the monitor shows you the current definition of each Function key.

KEY LIST Lists the Function Key Definitions

Another way to see what definitions have been assigned to each of the Function keys is by using the command KEY LIST. KEY LIST will list the current Function key definitions to the monitor.

```
key list
F1 LIST
F2 RUN<--
F3 LOAD"
F4 SAVE"
F5 CONT<--
F6 ,"LPT1:"<--
F7 TRON<--
F8 TROFF<--
F9 KEY
F10 SCREEN 0,0,0<--
Ok
```

As you will shortly learn, you can change these meanings for a particular session or program. However, they will always be reinitialized to these settings whenever BASIC is loaded into the system. Some of these settings will not have much meaning to you at the moment, but others such as LIST, RUN, and PRINT are old friends by now.

Some of the keys show an arrow after the command. This means that the Enter is automatically generated for you. For example, F1 will generate LIST, but you must press Enter before it is acted upon. F2 shows RUN with an arrow after it.

•FUNCTION KEY STATEMENTS•

KEY LIST lists the values of the Function keys.
KEY OFF turns off display of Function keys on the twenty-fifth line.
KEY ON turns on display of Function keys.
KEY x, A$ assigns the string A$ to the Function key indicated by x.

Pressing F2 will do the same as if you typed in RUN and pressed Enter; you do not need to press Enter for the current program to be run.

Some of these statements are new to us. TRON and TROFF will be explained in Chapter 6. You will learn about SCREEN in Chapter 14. However, you may find it useful to press the F10 key should a BASIC program cause the screen display to be unreadable.

Also notice that the LOAD and SAVE generated by F3 and F4 already have the beginning quote; you do not need to type it.

We can use the Function keys to SAVE, LOAD, and RUN the program we entered earlier while practicing with the Alternate key. We will give this program the name "TESTALT".

```
F4 (SAVE") TESTALT"
Ok
F3 (LOAD") TESTALT"
Ok
F2 (RUN)
```

You did not have to press Enter after using F2, but you did after F4 and F3. Remember that Alternate R will also generate the command RUN, but you will need to press Enter after using it.

KEY ON and KEY OFF Display and Remove Display of Key Definition Line

Some people do not like having the Function key definitions displayed on line 25. You can use the KEY OFF statement to prevent the KEY definitions from being displayed.

```
KEY OFF
Ok
```

The last line is now blank. If you want the list back, use the KEY ON statement.

```
KEY ON
Ok
```

The list is now displayed.

KEY Redefines Function Key Settings

Unlike the Alternate keys, the Function keys can be defined at will. Suppose we wish to change Function key 6 so that it will generate the PRINT statement when it is pressed. To redefine a Function key, use this version of the KEY statement:

```
KEY 6,"PRINT"
Ok
```

The definition of Function key F6 is now changed to PRINT. (If you have done this, look at the last line on the display.)

The format of the KEY statement is KEY $x,x\$$, where x is a number from 1 to 10 corresponding to the key number and $x\$$ is the string that defines the key and may contain a maximum of 15 characters.

Here is another example of changing the setting of the Function keys to speed entry and reduce errors. Suppose you have several parts with long codes. It is critical that they be entered correctly, yet because of their length, errors are frequently made. You could set up some of the Function keys so that they would enter the number for you. In this example we will assign the part number XQZ 233P 7X to Function key 7 and the part number 34WWIJ 37 ZT to Function key 8.

```
KEY 7, "XQZ 233P 7X"
Ok
KEY 8, "34WWIJ 37 ZT"
Ok
```

Now enter this program:

```
NEW
Ok
10 INPUT "Part Number"; A$
20 PRINT A$
30 END
RUN
Part number?
```

At this point, press F7. The string XQZ 233P 7X will now appear on the screen. Press Enter and the program will continue. Try running again using F8.

KEY LIST Revisited

The string defining a Function key may be up to 15 characters long. If it is more than 5 characters, only the first 5 characters are displayed on the last line of the display. To see the full definition, use the KEY LIST statement.

```
KEY LIST
F1 LIST
F2 RUN <-
F3 LOAD"
F4 SAVE"
F5 CONT <-
F6 PRINT
F7 XQZ 233P 7X
F8 34WWIJ 37 ZT
F9 KEY
F10 SCREEN 0,0,0 <-
Ok
```

As shown here, it is possible to use Function keys to respond to INPUT statements. In fact, it is frequently useful to write programs that use KEY statements to set up a range of up to ten options for the user, who needs only push the right Function key to choose from the options. By combining use of these keys with the techniques you have learned so far, you are on your way to developing comprehensive programs.

Call It a "Feature"

Once upon a time Marian, a computer programmer, was approached by Edwin, who happened to use one of Marian's programs. "Marian, I need to have you fix a bug in this program," said Edwin. "The program calculates certain financial information from month to month, but it seems to assume that all months are thirty days long, with exactly twenty-one working days in each month. This clearly is incorrect for months such as February."

"I see," said Marian. "Well, not to worry—the program was designed that way intentionally. You see, taking into account all of those vagaries of the Roman calendar system is so distasteful that I decided to invent a better calendar. That's no bug; it's a feature!"

Aghast, Edwin argued that such decisions were not Marian's to make. Marian, for her part, countered that the specifications did not spell out *which* calendar system was to be used. She simply used her judgment in closing a loophole.

After much sometimes acrimonious discussion, Edwin and Marian were finally able to agree on two points: that the specifications could never be absolutely airtight, but that programmers must not use that as an excuse for solving the wrong problem. Marian, recognizing that her idea was still ahead of its time, fixed the program.

MORAL: A "feature" becomes a "bug" when it prevents a program from accomplishing its original purpose.

The Story's End

After reading Lesson 4 and experimenting with the screen editing features of BASIC, Pat felt confident enough to make the changes, and Chris was only too happy to let Pat try. First, Pat changed all variables that held dollar amounts to double-precision variables by adding a pound sign to the end.

This presented a bit of a problem, since the variables were scattered throughout the program. Pat figured out a very systematic way to make the changes. "LIST 0-200" displayed the first 20 or so lines on the monitor. Pat changed these as needed using the arrow and "Ins" keys. "LIST 210-400" listed the next 20 lines, "LIST 410-600" the next 20, and so forth until the entire program was changed.

Pat also changed some variables to integers, specifically those that held years as values. "Years," Pat correctly reasoned, "are always integer values, at least as far as this program is concerned. The program will never be used for a depreciation schedule of more than 32,767 years, so why not use integer variables?"

The PRINT USING statements also had to be changed to allow for larger dollar amounts. Pat chose to be conservative; the program, as changed, could now handle transactions up to $999,999,999.99. Even Con. Glomerate didn't buy equipment worth more than that!

Last, but not least, Pat made sure that any comments were changed appropriately and added a note of the changes to the "Program History" section of the comments. As the changes were made, Pat repeatedly ran the program to verify that it worked properly. On several attempts Pat discovered errors due to the editing. The most common error was forgetting to put a # or a % on the end of a variable on some obscure line in the program. Pat soon came to recognize this cause, since in such cases BASIC substituted a value of 0 for the intended value.

All told, the changes took less than 20 minutes, after which Pat felt a flush of pride and marched off to present the program to The Boss.

Program Listing

```
100 ' PROGRAM NAME: "DEPREC.BAS"
110 ' CREATED:        03-01-88
120 ' PROGRAMMER:    CHRIS JOHNSON, CON GLOMERATE
140 ' PROGRAM HISTORY:
150 '      3-15-86 Expanded to accept values up to 999 million
160 '
170 ' Program Prints Report Comparing 3 Methods of Depreciation
180 '      1) Straight Line (SL)
190 '      2) Sum of Digits (SOD)
200 '      3) Double Declining Balance   (DDB)
210 '
220 ' Variables Entered by User
230 '      COST     - Initial Value of Item
240 '      SALVAGE - Salvage Value
250 '      YEARS    - # of Years over Which to Depreciate
260 ' Formulas Used
270 '
280 '      Straight Line (SL)
290 '         Total Amount to Depreciate = COST - SALVAGE
300 '         Amount to Depreciate Each Year = (COST - SALVAGE)/YEARS
310 '
320 '      Sum of Digits (SOD)
330 '         Total Amount to Depreciate = COST - SALVAGE
340 '         Sum of Digits (SOD) = (YEARS * (YEARS + 1) )/2
350 '         Amount to be Depreciated the Current Year =
360 '            (COST - SALVAGE) * (YEARS - Current Year + 1)/SOD
370 '
380 '      Double Declining Balance (DDB)
390 '         Total Amount to Depreciate = COST
400 '         DOB.REMAINING = Previous Remaining Amount to Depreciate -
410 '            Amount Depreciated the Previous Year
```

```
420 '          Amount to be Depreciated the Current Year =
430 '              (DDB.REMAINING * 2)/YEARS
1000 '- - - - - - - - - - - - - - - - - - - - - - - - - - - - - - - - - - -
1010 CLS
1020 ' ** Ask User for Parameters **
1030 INPUT "ENTER INITIAL VALUE: ", COST#
1040 INPUT "ENTER SALVAGE VALUE: ", SALVAGE#
1050 INPUT "ENTER NUMBER OF YEARS OVER WHICH TO DEPRECIATE: ", YEARS%
1060 '
1070 '   =    =    =    =    =    =    =    =    =
1080 '
1090 ' ** Calculate the Sum of Digits **
1100 '
1110 LET SOD# = (YEARS% * (YEARS% + 1) )/2
1120 '
1130 ' ** Calculate the Amount to Depreciate for SL and SOD Methods
1140 '
1150 LET AMOUNT.TO.DEPRECIATE# = COST# - SALVAGE#
1160 '
1170 ' ** Set the Undepreciated Balance for DDB Method to Initial Value
1180 '
1190 LET DDB.REMAINING# = COST#
1200 '
1210 ' ** Set Totals to Zero to Start **
1220 LET SL.TOTAL# = 0: LET SOD.TOTAL# = 0: LET DDB.TOTAL# = 0
1230 '
1240     '   =    =    =    =    =    =    =    =
1250 '
1260 ' ** Clear the Screen. Then Print the Report Heading **
1270 '
1280 CLS
1290 PRINT TAB(10) "DEPRECIATION SCHEDULES"
1300 PRINT
1310 PRINT USING "INITIAL VALUE: ###,###,###.##";COST#
1320 PRINT USING "SALVAGE VALUE: ###,###,###.##";SALVAGE#
1330 PRINT USING "NUMBER OF YEARS OVER WHICH TO DEPRECIATE: ##";YEARS%
1340 PRINT
1350 PRINT          "YEAR          STRAIGHT           SUM OF          DOUBLE"
1360 PRINT          "              LINE               DIGITS          DECLINING"
1370 LET LINES$ ="----          -----------        -----------      -----------"
1380 PRINT LINES$    ' LINES$ will also be used at the footing
1390                 '   before Totals
1400     '
1410     '   =    =    =    =    =    =    =    =
1420 '
1430 LET MASK1$ =
               " ##        ##,###,###.##    ###,###,###.##    ###,###,###.##"
1440 LET MASK2$ =
               "TOTALS: ###,###,###.##    ###,###,###.##    ###,###,###.##"
```

```
1450     '
1460 ' * MASK1$ will be used as a PRINT USING Mask to PRINT Each Line
1470 ' * MASK2$ will be used as a PRINT USING Mask to PRINT Final Totals
2000 '- - - - - - - - - - - - - - - - - - - - - - - - - - - - - - - -
2010 ' **   NOW LOOP THROUGH EACH YEAR    **
2020 '
2030 FOR CURRENT.YEAR% = 1 TO YEARS%
2040 '
2050 ' ** Calculate Amounts to Depreciate this Year **
2060     '
2070     LET SL.AMOUNT# = AMOUNT.TO.DEPRECIATE#/YEARS%
2080     LET SOD.AMOUNT# = AMOUNT.TO.DEPRECIATE# *
             (YEARS% - CURRENT.YEAR% + 1)/SOD#
2090     LET DDB.AMOUNT# = DDB.REMAINING# * 2/YEARS%
2100     '
2110     ' * Subtract Current Depreciation from DDB.REMAINING Value
2120     '
2130     LET DDB.REMAINING# = DDB.REMAINING# - DDB.AMOUNT#
2140     '
2150     ' * Accumulate Totals
2160     '
2170     LET SL.TOTAL# = SL.TOTAL# + SL.AMOUNT#
2180     LET SOD.TOTAL# = SOD.TOTAL# + SOD.AMOUNT#
2190     LET DDB.TOTAL# = DDB.TOTAL# + DDB.AMOUNT#
2200     '
2210     ' * PRINT Detail Line
2220     '
2230     PRINT USING MASK1$; CURRENT.YEAR%, SL.AMOUNT#, SOD.AMOUNT#,
             DDB.AMOUNT#
2240 NEXT CURRENT.YEAR%
3000 '- - - - - - - - - - - - - - - - - - - - - - - - - - - - - - -
3010 '
3020 ' * PRINT TOTAL LINE *
3030 '
3040 PRINT LINES$
3050 PRINT USING MASK2$; SL.TOTAL#, SOD.TOTAL#, DDB.TOTAL#
3060 END
```

Program Output

```
        ENTER INITIAL VALUE: 3174562.95
        ENTER SALVAGE VALUE: 317456.30
        ENTER NUMBER OF YEARS OVER WHICH TO DEPRECIATE: 10

                DEPRECIATION SCHEDULES

        INITIAL VALUE:    3,174,562.95
        SALVAGE VALUE:      317,456.30
        NUMBER OF YEARS OVER WHICH TO DEPRECIATE: 10
```

YEAR	STRAIGHT LINE	SUM OF DIGITS	DOUBLE DECLINING
1	285,710.67	519,473.94	634,912.59
2	285,710.67	467,526.54	507,930.07
3	285,710.67	415,579.15	406,344.06
4	285,710.67	363,631.76	325,075.25
5	285,710.67	311,684.36	260,060.20
6	285,710.67	259,736.97	208,048.16
7	285,710.67	207,789.57	166,438.53
8	285,710.67	155,842.18	133,150.82
9	285,710.67	103,894.79	106,520.66
10	285,710.67	51,947.39	85,216.53
TOTALS:	2,857,106.65	2,857,106.65	2,833,696.85

·QUICK REFERENCE FOR LESSON 4·

Variable Precision

BASIC has three kinds of variables that hold numeric values.

A single-precision variable may have either no special character or an exclamation point (!) on the end of its name and can hold up to seven decimal digits.

A double-precision variable has a pound sign (#) on the end of its name and can hold up to 17 decimal digits.

An integer variable has a percent sign at the end of its name and can hold integer values between $-32,768$ and $+32,767$, inclusive.

DEFtype Defines Variables as the Type Indicated

DEFINT   Define as integer.
DEFSNG   Define as single precision.
DEFDBL   Define as double precision.
DEFSTR   Define as string.

The DEFtype statement may be followed by a single letter, several letters separated by commas, or a range of letters.

All variables beginning with the letter appearing in the DEFtype statement will be of that type.

The DEFtype statement must be encountered before any of the variables to be defined are used.

A type declaration character placed after a variable name will override the DEFtype statement.

Screen Editor

The screen editor allows you to simply move the cursor to any part of the screen and type in changes, then press Enter to record them.

The arrow keys move the cursor in the direction of the arrow.
The Home key moves the cursor to the upper left-hand corner of the screen.
The End key moves the cursor to the end of the current program or statement line.
The Insert key allows you to insert one or more characters in the middle of a line.
The Delete key deletes a character from a line.

EDIT Line Number

The EDIT command is a shortcut to display and change a line. EDIT displays a line and places the cursor under the first digit of the line number.

AUTO Automatically Numbers the Lines in a Program

AUTO. Start with line number 10 and increment by 10.
AUTO line number. Start with the line number specified and increment by 10.
AUTO line number, increment. Start with the line number specified and increment by the amount specified.
AUTO, increment. Start with line number 10 and increment by the amount specified.

To cancel AUTO press the Control and Break keys at the same time.

RENUM Renumber the Lines in the Current Program

RENUM will renumber all lines from where you tell it to start *to the end of the program.*

RENUM. Renumber all the lines. Give the first line the number 10 and increment the line numbers by 10.

RENUM number. Renumber all the lines. Give the first line the number specified and increment the line numbers by 10.

RENUM number, line number. Renumber the lines beginning with the line number specified. Give this line the number specified and increment the line numbers by 10.

RENUM number, line number, increment. Renumber the lines beginning with the line number specified. Give this line the number specified and increment the line numbers by the amount shown.

RENUM , , increment. Renumber all the lines. Give the first line the number 10 and increment by the amount shown.

RENUM number, , increment. Renumber all the lines. Give the first line the number specified and increment the line numbers by the amount shown.

Alternate Keys

The Alternate key pressed in conjunction with letter keys types various BASIC statements for you (see the complete list of Alternate Keys earlier in this chapter).

Function Keys

Each Function key F1–F10 may be defined to represent up to 15 characters. When a Function key is pressed, the characters it is defined to represent are automatically typed.

The first 5 characters of the definition of each key are listed on the bottom line of the display.

> KEY OFF   If you wish to turn off the display on the bottom line of the display use the KEY OFF statement.
>
> KEY ON   If you subsequently wish to turn the display back on, use the KEY ON statement.
>
> KEY LIST   Lists the full, up-to-15 character definitions of each key.
>
> KEY x,x$ Redefines key *x* (1 through 10, inclusive) to represent string x$ (up to 15 characters).

• EXERCISES •

Use the Alternate and Function keys as much as possible when doing these exercises.

Short Answer

1. A single-precision variable holds _____ digits, while a double-precision variable holds _____ digits.

2. The range of values that can be stored in integer variables is between _____ and _____.

3. The command AUTO causes BASIC to number lines automatically, beginning with _____ and incrementing by _____.

4. For what uses is exponential notation most applicable?

5. What happens if you try to enter a noninteger value into an integer variable?

6. Which precision numeric variable does BASIC process the fastest and which the slowest?

7. Explain what the statements DEFINT, DEFDBL, and DEFSNG do.

8. When would you use single-precision, double-precision, and integer variables, and why?

9. Name three ways to make changes in a line of code.

10. How do you turn off AUTO?

11. What is the function of the ALT key in BASIC? What is the use of the Function keys?

12. What statement is used to redefine a Function key?

13. Which type is each of the following variables?
    a. X%
    b. X#
    c. X
    d. X!
    e. X$

14. Matching: Match each item in the left-hand column with one item in the right-hand column.

(1) Single precision	a. changes program line numbers
(2) Double precision	b. stores sequence of keystrokes for shortcuts
(3) Integer	c. holds up to 7 digits
(4) Screen Editor	d. allows user to change program without retyping whole lines
(5) AUTO	e. whole numbers
(6) RENUM	f. automatically assigns line numbers
(7) Exponential notation	g. stores up to 17 digits
(8) Alternate key	h. pressed with other keys, displays a basic command
(9) Function keys	i. uses the letter E to express scientific notation

15. Practice with the screen editor. Type in the following program:

```
NEW
Ok
10 REM THIS IS A LONG PROGRAM
20 PRINT "IT CONTAINS ERRERS"
30 LETNUM.OF.ERZORS = NUMBER.OF.GRROR + 1
40 PRINT "GEE, WHAT A RIDICULOUS PROGRAM!"
50 END
```

Now use the screen editor, including the keys on the numeric keypad, to make the following changes:

Line 10: Change "LONG" to "SHORT"
Line 20: Correct the spelling of "ERRORS"
Line 30: Put a space between "LET" and "NUM";
    Change "NUM.OF.ERZORS" to "NUMBER.OF.ERRORS";
    Change "NUMBER.OF.GRROR" to "NUMBER.OF.ERRORS"
Line 40: Make a duplicate copy of this line as line number 50.
    To do this, move the cursor to the 4 in 40, then type a 5, then press Enter.

LIST, then RUN, the program to make sure the changes were made.

16. More practice with editing:
   a. Write a program that uses a single INPUT statement to ask the user to enter two numbers, then prints the sum and the product of the entered values. Make sure your program contains a prompt that explains to the user what to enter.
   b. Use the screen editor to change the program so that it uses two INPUT statements, one for each number, with separate prompts for each number.
   c. Change the program to clear the screen after the numbers have been entered and before the results are displayed.
   d. Have the program print the results in the following format:

```
x PLUS y EQUALS a
x TIMES y EQUALS b
```

where x and y are the values entered by the user, a is their sum, and b is their product.

e. Have the program round the input numbers and the results to two decimal digits and display the sign, if negative, to the right of the numbers.

f. Renumber your entire program to start at line 100.

g Renumber all lines after 100 to start at 1000 and increment by 50. In other words, your program should have a single line number 100, then line 1000, then 1050, and so on.

Programming

For the following programs:

a. Write a structure chart.

b. Write a flowchart.

c. Write pseudocode.

d. Code the program.

17. Practice with AUTO: You are a big-time investment house, handling millions of dollars in investments. Your investments pay a fixed rate of interest in each period. Write a program that prints a report for any given client showing how much interest the client will earn over a given number of periods for a given investment amount and interest rate.

Use AUTO to type in the line numbers for the new program, which will start at line number 100 and have lines numbered in multiples of 20. Ask the user to input the following information (be sure to use prompts):

First name
Last name
Middle initial
Street address
City
State
Zip code
Initial investment amount
Interest rate (be sure to tell the user whether to enter it as a percent or decimal)
Number of periods of investment
The investment amount should be a double-precision amount, the interest rate a single-precision amount, and the number of periods an integer amount. All other values are strings. Print a report that looks like the following:

```
<first name> <middle initial> <last name>
<street address>
<city> <state> <zip code>
INVESTMENT AMOUNT: ###,###,###.##
INTEREST RATE:             #.###
NUMBER OF PERIODS:         ###
PERIOD      INTEREST EARNED  BALANCE
------      ---------------  --------------
  ###         ###,###,###.##   ###,###,###.##
  ###         ###,###,###.##   ###,###,###.##
```

and so forth for the number of periods of the investment.

The "INTEREST EARNED" column is the cumulative interest, not just the interest earned in a given period. Remember to compound the interest at the end of each period—that is, calculate interest on the balance, not the initial investment. Make sure your program is well documented.

18. COMPOUNDING INTEREST: If you let your principal (P) compound N times yearly for Y years at a rate of interest (R), the future value (FV) of your investment after Y years is given by the formula

$$FV = P \left(1 + \frac{R}{N}\right)^{YN}$$

Write a program that asks the operator for values for P, Y, and N, and displays a chart showing what the future value would be had the interest rate been .08, .10, .12, .14, .16, .18, or .20. (HINT: use a FOR . . . NEXT loop.) Since the future value may be very large, use double-precision variables. Have FV print as $###,###,###.##.

19. PURCHASE REPORT: Your company purchased large quantities of an item that has a cost that fluctuates from day to day and from vendor to vendor. You want a weekly report which shows:
   a. For each day: the number of items purchased, the cost, and the average cost per item.
   b. For the week: the total number of items, the total cost for the week, and the average cost per item for the week.
   c. Number your program lines so that the introductory section begins with line number 100 and increments by 10.
   d. The section that inputs the week's data begins with line 1000 and increments by 20.
   e. Use comment lines to clearly separate each section.

```
              WEEKLY  PURCHASE  REPORT
        ITEMS PURCHASED          COSTS              AVERAGE COST/ITEM
DAY  1      ###,###          $###,###,###.##          $###,###.##
  .             .                   .                      .
  .             .                   .                      .
DAY  7          .                   .                      .
WEEK
TOTAL     #,###,###        $#,###,###,###.##        $#,###,###.##
```

20. SALE OF PROPERTY: The amount the seller receives from the sale of property can be calculated as follows:

amount seller receives = selling price less broker fees less expenses

The broker fee is a percent of the selling price.
   Write a program to input:
   a. Selling price (it can be over 9,999,999, so use double precision)
   b. Broker percentage (be sure to specify if it is to be entered as % or decimal)
   c. Expenses
   The output should resemble the following:

```
              SALE  OF  PROPERTY
SELLING PRICE              $###,###,###.##
BROKER FEE                  ##,###,###.##
EXPENSES                    ##,###,###.##
DUE SELLER          **     $###,###,###.##
```

21. ATTENDANCE REPORT: There are 12 weeks of instruction per quarter. Each day's attendance is recorded in a log. At the end of the quarter, these figures are entered into the computer to produce the following report:

```
                         ATTENDANCE REPORT
                  ATTENDANCE              INCREASE/DECREASE
                                          FROM PREVIOUS PERIOD
WEEK  1
      DAY  1            ####                  +/- ####
      DAY  2            ####                  +/- ####
        .                   .                     .
        .                   .                     .
        .                   .                     .
TOTALS FOR WEEK  1     ####                  +/- ####
        .                   .                     .
        .                   .                     .
        .                   .                     .
TOTALS FOR WEEK 12     ####                  +/- ####

TOTAL FOR QUARTER ## ####         AVERAGE DAILY ATTENDANCE ####
```

Write a program to produce this report.

SELECTION AND REPETITION

INVESTMENT DECISIONS FOR A TOY TYCOON

Terry firmly believed in the American Way, and why not? Where else on earth could one make a fortune from an idea as offbeat as the Pet Pineapple?

It took two years to bring the idea to market, but within three months after the lovable, furry fruits hit the stores, Terry had cleared over $300,000 in profits. The problem no longer was how to make the money but how to invest it.

Investing the money was a tedious, although pleasant, task. To help him evaluate the alternatives Terry bought an IBM personal computer.

Terry was interested primarily in "money market" types of investments, where interest was paid on the principal according to a variety of rules. One investment Terry looked at compounded interest daily by automatically reinvesting the interest earned each day into the fund. Another investment paid a higher interest rate than the first but didn't compound the interest. Yet a third fund offered higher rates than both the first two but paid interest quarterly and charged a commission on the initial investment as well as a commission every time you reinvested interest payments into the fund.

The more Terry delved, the more variations on these themes came up. Terry could have figured out the effective yields with a calculator by hand, but he concluded that a computer would make the job faster and easier. Hoping to find some new BASIC statements that would make the job easier, Terry turned to Lesson 5 of *The ABCs of BASIC*.

·THE ABCS OF BASIC ON THE IBM PERSONAL COMPUTER·

LESSON 5: STRUCTURED DECISION MAKING: IF, WHILE . . . WEND, LOGICAL OPERATORS

Computers are not only great for performing mathematical calculations but are also good for making decsions. One of the most powerful capabilities of a computer is the ability to choose between two alternative courses of action.

Called **selection,** this represents the third of three major structures used in constructing structured programs. The first, which you learned in Lesson 2, is sequence, or executing statements in line-number order only. The second is called repetition; the FOR . . . NEXT loops you used in Lesson 3 are examples of repetition.

In this lesson we will examine two sets of statements (IF and WHILE) used for decision making in programs.

The BASIC statement IF is used for selection in BASIC programs. IF is accompanied by the BASIC reserved words THEN and ELSE.

WHILE has some similarities to FOR—it causes your program to iterate, or repeatedly execute, a block of lines. Like FOR, which is accompanied by the BASIC statement NEXT to identify the end of the loop, WHILE is accompanied by the BASIC statement WEND to define the end of a loop.

IF Allows Selection of Appropriate Action

IF . . . THEN: Selection of Action or No Action
Here is a simple example of the IF statement.

```
NEW
Ok
10 LET SALES.TAX.RATE = .06
20 INPUT "What is the purchase price"; PRICE
30 INPUT "Is this a taxable item (yes or no)"; TAXABLE$
40 IF TAXABLE$ = "yes" THEN LET PRICE = PRICE * (1 + SALES.TAX.RATE)
50 PRINT USING "Please pay $$##,###.##"; PRICE
60 END
RUN
What is the purchase price? 100
Is this a taxable item (yes or no)? no
Please pay $100.00
Ok
RUN
What is the purchase price? 100
Is this a taxable item (yes or no)? yes
Please pay $106.00
Ok
```

Line 40 of this example is an IF statement. It starts with

1. the statement IF, followed by
2. a logical condition (TAXABLE\$ = "yes"), followed by
3. the reserved word THEN, followed by
4. a BASIC statement [LET PRICE = PRICE * (1 + SALES.TAX.RATE)].

In this case the IF statement must make a decision: should sales tax be applied to the purchase? If the item is taxable, the LET statement following the THEN is executed. If the item is not taxable, the LET statement is bypassed.

The LET statement following the THEN in this example could just as easily have been any other BASIC statement, such as INPUT or PRINT.

IF X <> 0 THEN INPUT "Enter next value"; X
IF X > 3 THEN PRINT "Value exceeds 3"

BASIC uses the symbol > to mean greater than, the symbol < to mean less than, and the double symbol <> or >< to mean not equal.

When BASIC reaches an IF statement, it stops to evaluate whether the logical condition is currently true or false. If the condition is true, the statement following THEN is executed. If the condition is false, the statement following THEN is bypassed and ignored. Logical conditions are more properly called logical expressions, so we will use that terminology from now on.

IF . . . THEN . . . ELSE: Selection of One Action or Another

The form of IF used in the preceding section chooses either to execute a statement or to bypass it. It is far more common to want your program to choose between two alternative actions. To do this, use an ELSE in your IF statement.

Suppose we want the program to do one thing if the item is taxable and another if it is not. The pseudocode would be as follows:

IF the item is taxable (TAXABLE\$ = "yes")
    THEN LET SALES.TAX = PRICE * SALES.TAX.RATE
    ELSE LET SALES.TAX = 0

• THE IF STATEMENT •

IF expression THEN . . .
IF expression is true, execute statement(s) following THEN.

IF expression THEN . . . ELSE . . .
IF expression is true, execute statement(s) following THEN.
IF expression is false, execute statement(s) following ELSE.

To be written as a line of code in a program this expression must be one continuous statement, as is shown in line 40 of the following program:

```
NEW
Ok
10 LET SALES.TAX.RATE = .06
20 INPUT "What is the purchase price"; PRICE
30 INPUT "Is this taxable (yes or no)"; TAXABLE$
40 IF TAXABLE$ = "yes" THEN LET SALES.TAX = PRICE * SALES.TAX.RATE
     ELSE LET SALES.TAX = 0
50 PRINT USING "Please pay $$##,###.##, including $$###.## sales tax.";
     PRICE + SALES.TAX,SALES.TAX
60 END
RUN
What is the purchase price? 100
Is this taxable (yes or no)? no
Please pay $100.00, including $0.00 sales tax.
Ok
RUN
What is the purchase price? 100
Is this taxable (yes or no)? yes
Please pay $106.00, including $6.00 sales tax.
Ok
```

If the condition is true, the statement following the THEN is executed; if the condition is false, the statement following the ELSE is executed. Only one of the statements (the one following the THEN or the one following the ELSE) will be executed. This is why this structure is called selection. Figure 5.1 illustrates the selection process of IF statements with flowcharts.

Using IF and ELSE with Multiple Statements: Using the ":"

There are times when you want BASIC to choose, based on some condition, whether to execute, not one, but a series of statements. BASIC allows you to put more than one statement, separated by colons (:) after THEN, after ELSE, or both. An example of pseudocode using this construction would be as follows:

```
IF TAXABLE$ = "yes"
     THEN LET SALES.TAX = PRICE * SALES.TAX.RATE
        PRINT "The sales tax is $XXXX.XX"
     ELSE LET SALES.TAX = 0
        PRINT "No sales tax"
```

```
NEW
Ok
10 LET SALES.TAX.RATE = .06
20 INPUT "What is the purchase price";PRICE
30 INPUT "Is this item taxable (yes or no)";TAXABLE$
40 IF TAXABLE$ = "yes" THEN LET SALES.TAX = PRICE * SALES.TAX.RATE:
        PRINT USING "The sales tax is $$###.##." ; SALES.TAX
```

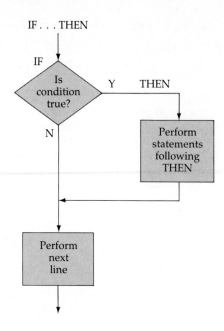

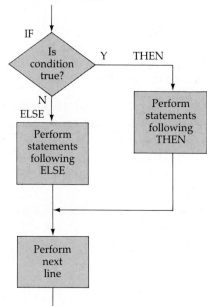

FIGURE 5.1 ·
*Flowcharts of IF
statements*

```
      ELSE LET SALES.TAX = 0: PRINT "No sales tax."
50 PRINT USING "Please pay a total of $$##,###.##."; PRICE + SALES.TAX
60 END
RUN
What is the purchase price? 100
Is this item taxable (yes or no)? no
No sales tax.
Please pay a total of $100.00.
Ok
RUN
What is the purchase price? 100
Is this item taxable (yes or no)? yes
The sales tax is $6.00.
Please pay a total of $106.00.
Ok
```

In this example BASIC must choose between two sets of statements, depending on the value of TAXABLE$. If TAXABLE$ = "yes" is true, BASIC executes the two statements between THEN and ELSE. If the logical expression is false, BASIC executes the two statements following ELSE.

This feature of BASIC is extremely powerful, but there is a very important limit to keep in mind: no line in your program can be more than 254 characters long, including the line number and all spaces in the line. This means that the entire IF-THEN-ELSE statement, including all statements following the ELSE, which are to be executed under the "false" condition, must be 254 or fewer characters in length.

Recall that to type a line longer than 80 characters (the width of the screen), you type the first 80 characters and then continue typing. The display will show the characters after the 80th on the next screen line. Everything that you have typed is still all part of one logical line, which ends when you press the Enter key. You may add spaces in your lines, as we have done, to make them more readable; just remember to count those spaces when figuring the length of the line.

The following line from a program will not work; the ELSE is on a line with a different number than the IF.

```
1000 IF A = B THEN PRINT "Hello"
1010 ELSE PRINT "Goodbye"            ←— | ERROR! |
```

You can also use multiple statements on a single logical line when you use the IF statement with only THEN and not ELSE. Just remember that BASIC will ignore all statements following THEN on the same line if the logical expression is false, whether you intended them to be a part of the IF statement or not! Keep this in mind when putting more than one statement on a line in your program; each IF statement should be given a line of its own.

Nested IFs
We stated earlier that you can use any BASIC statement following a THEN or an ELSE. This includes other IFs! When one IF statement is used inside another IF

statement, the result is called **nested IFs.** An example of this construction in pseudocode would look like the following:

INPUT the Total Sales and the Margin
IF the Margin is less than 1, print the message "Margin is too low."
IF the Margin is greater than 100, print the message "Margin is too high."
IF the Margin is 1 through 100, calculate and print the profit

Another way to write this is:

```
INPUT SALES, MARGIN
IF MARGIN < 1
     THEN PRINT "Margin is too low."
     ELSE
          IF MARGIN > 100
               THEN PRINT "Margin is too high."
               ELSE PRINT USING "Gross profit = ##,###.##";
                  SALES * MARGIN/100
```

The two logical expressions, MARGIN < 1 and MARGIN > 100 test to make sure that MARGIN is between the legal bounds for this percentage.

Figure 5.2 is the flowchart for this program.

```
NEW
Ok
10 INPUT "Enter total sales: ",SALES
20 INPUT "Enter the gross margin as percent of sales: ", MARGIN
30 IF MARGIN < 1 THEN PRINT "Margin is too low." ELSE IF MARGIN > 100
      THEN PRINT "Margin is too high."
      ELSE PRINT USING "Gross profit = ##,###.##"; SALES * MARGIN/100
40 END
RUN
Enter total sales: 1000
Enter the gross margin as percent of sales: .10
Margin is too low.
Ok
RUN
Enter total sales: 1000
Enter the gross margin as percent of sales: 1000
Margin is too high.
Ok
RUN
Enter total sales: 1000
Enter the gross margin as percent of sales: 10
Gross profit = 100.00
Ok
```

In this example there is an "IF within an IF." BASIC interprets line 30 by first looking at the opening IF. It has a logical expression, MARGIN < 1. If this expression is true, BASIC executes the statement following the first THEN, PRINT

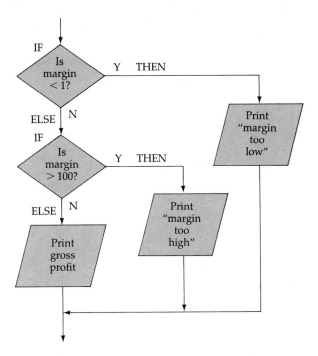

FIGURE 5.2 •
Flowchart of a
nested IF . . .
THEN . . .
ELSE

"Margin is too low." BASIC then skips the rest of the line, since it comes after the ELSE.

If MARGIN < 1 is false, BASIC skips the statement between THEN and the first ELSE and executes the statement following the first ELSE. That this is another IF does not matter to BASIC. BASIC then looks at the next logical expression, MARGIN > 100. If this is true, BASIC executes the statement, PRINT "Margin is too high." If this is false, BASIC executes the statement following the next ELSE, which calculates and prints the answer.

You can use an IF statement between THEN and ELSE. Such a statement would look something like the following:

IF A THEN IF B THEN C ELSE D ELSE E

Visualize this as:

```
IF A
      THEN IF B
                  THEN C
                  ELSE D
      ELSE E
```

where A and B are logical expressions and C, D, and E are any statements. But be aware that nested IF statements are difficult to code correctly and so require caution in their use. In the next chapter we will learn about ON . . . GOSUB as one alternative to nested IFs.

BASIC always groups such a statement such that the first ELSE is matched up with the nearest unmatched IF, the next ELSE with the next unmatched IF to the left, and so forth. In this case BASIC matches the first ELSE to the second IF to form the substatement "IF B THEN C ELSE D." The second ELSE is matched to the first IF.

The following is a nested IF that tests the hours worked to determine the overtime rate. If the person has worked 40 hours or less, the overtime rate will be 0. If he or she has worked more than 40 but not more than 60, the overtime rate is to be 1.5. If the person has worked more than 60 hours, the overtime rate is to be 2. This is shown first in pseudocode as a way to visualize it, then as one program line.

```
IF HOURS > 40
    THEN
    IF HOURS > 60
        THEN LET OT.RATE = 2
        ELSE LET OT.RATE = 1.5
    ELSE LET OT.RATE = 0
```

The flowchart for this program is Figure 5.3.

```
10 IF HOURS > 40 THEN IF HOURS > 60 THEN LET OT.RATE = 2
   ELSE LET OT.RATE = 1.5 ELSE LET OT.RATE = 0
```

The next series of nested IFs tests two items, the gross sales and the bonus rate. If the gross sales is greater than 20,000 and the bonus rate is 2, the commission

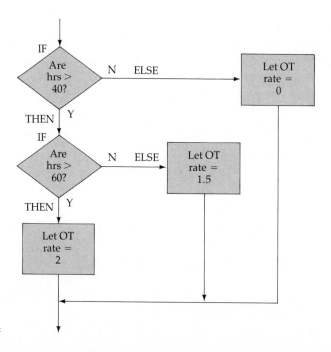

FIGURE 5.3 •
Flowchart of a different nested IF . . . THEN . . . ELSE

factor is to be 4. If the gross sales is greater than 20,000, but the bonus rate is not 2, then the commission factor is to be 3. If the gross sales is less than 20,000 but greater than 10,000, the commission factor is to be 2. Under all other conditions the commission factor is to be 1.

```
IF GROSS.SALES > 20000
      THEN
      IF BONUS.RATE = 2
            THEN LET COMMISSION.FACTOR = 4
            ELSE LET COMMISSION.FACTOR = 3
      ELSE
      IF GROSS.SALES > 10000
            THEN LET COMMISSION.FACTOR = 2
            ELSE LET COMMISSION.FACTOR = 1
```

```
50  IF GROSS.SALES > 20000 THEN IF BONUS.RATE = 2 THEN LET COMMISSION.FACTOR = 4
    ELSE LET COMMISSION.FACTOR = 3 ELSE IF GROSS.SALES > 10000
    THEN LET COMMISSION.FACTOR = 2 ELSE LET COMMISSION.FACTOR = 1
```

Figure 5.4 is a flowchart of this set of nested IF statements.

One of the most common uses of nested IFs is to select separate actions for each of a set of possible values of a variable. The general model is something like this:

IF V = E1 THEN C1 ELSE IF V = E2 THEN C2 ELSE IF V = E3 THEN C3 ELSE C4

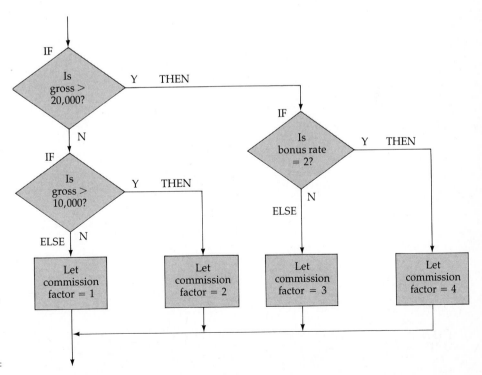

FIGURE 5.4 • *Flowchart of two sets of nested IF . . . THEN . . . ELSE*

or

```
IF V = E1
    THEN C1
    ELSE
    IF V = E2
        THEN C2
        ELSE
        IF V = E3
            THEN C3
            ELSE C4
```

V is any variable name. E1, E2, and E3 are any three possible values for that variable. C1, C2, C3, and C4 are any BASIC statements. C1 is executed if the variable has value E1, C2 if it has the value E2, C3 if it has the value E3, and C4 if it has any value other than those three.

The following program chooses a discount percentage based on the quantity purchased. A series of IFs is used to select the discount range applicable to the entered quantity.

Here is the logic for the selection:

```
IF QTY < 100
    THEN DISCOUNT.RATE = 0
    ELSE
    IF QTY < 200
        THEN DISCOUNT.RATE = .05
        ELSE
        IF QTY < 500
            THEN DISCOUNT.RATE = .10
            ELSE
            IF QTY < 1000
                THEN DISCOUNT.RATE = .15
                ELSE DISCOUNT.RATE = .20
```

See the flowchart in Figure 5.5.

```
10 'Program to Compute Discount from Quantity Ordered and List Price
20 '  and to demonstrate the use of nested IF statements
30 '
40 'Variable Name            Meaning                    Type
50 'QTY               number ordered          single precision
60 'DISCOUNT.RATE                             single precision
70 'LIST.PRICE        price before discount   single precision
80 'UNIT.LIST         price for one           single precision
90 'DISCOUNT.AMT      amount deducted for discount   single precision
100 'NET              cost after discount is taken   single precision
110 '
120 INPUT "What Quantity has been ordered";QTY
130 INPUT "What is the unit list price"; UNIT.LIST
```

```
140 IF QTY < 100 THEN LET DISCOUNT.RATE = 0 ELSE IF QTY < 200 THEN LET
    DISCOUNT.RATE = .05 ELSE IF QTY < 500 THEN LET DISCOUNT.RATE = .1 ELSE IF
    QTY < 1000 THEN LET DISCOUNT.RATE = .15 ELSE LET DISCOUNT.RATE = .2
150 LET LIST.PRICE     = QTY * UNIT.LIST
160 LET DISCOUNT.AMT   = LIST.PRICE * DISCOUNT.RATE
170 LET NET            = LIST.PRICE - DISCOUNT.AMT
180 PRINT USING "List price: $$#,###.##, less $$#,###.## discount; net price:$$
#,###.##"; LIST.PRICE, DISCOUNT.AMT, NET
190 END
```

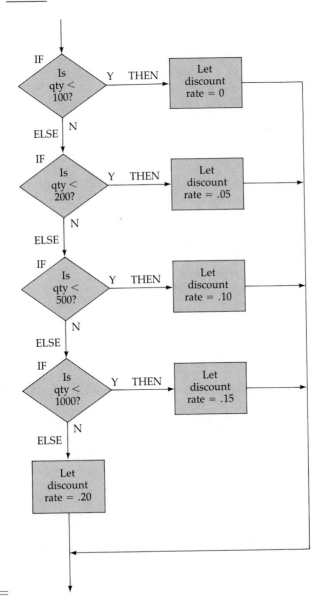

FIGURE 5.5 •
Flowchart of a
series of nested
IF . . .
THEN . . .
ELSE

```
RUN
What Quantity has been ordered? 10
What is the unit list price? 1.00
List price:     $10.00, less      $0.00 discount; net price:     $10.00
Ok
RUN
What Quantity has been ordered? 100
What is the unit list price? 2.50
List price:    $250.00, less     $12.50 discount; net price:    $237.50
Ok
RUN
What Quantity has been ordered? 10000
What is the unit list price? 3.50
List price: $35,000.00, less  $7,000.00 discount; net price: $28,000.00
Ok
```

Comparing Numbers: More Combinations of Equal, Less, and Greater

BASIC provides a number of operators with which to construct logical expressions in IF statements. Most logical expressions are based on a comparison of two values. Here is a complete list of operators you can use to compare two numbers, numeric variables, or arithmetic expressions:

$a > b$ true if a is greater than b

$a >= b$ true if a is greater than or equal to b

$a => b$ same as $a >= b$

$a < b$ true if a is less than b

$a <= b$ true if a is less than or equal to b

$a =< b$ same as $a <= b$

$a = b$ true if a is equal to b

$a <> b$ true if a is not equal to b

$a >< b$ same as $a <> b$

Using this list, you can compare any two numbers in an IF statement. These operators are most commonly called **relational operators.**

A common business problem is to keep just the right kinds of inventory items in stock. Not having a popular item in stock leads to lost sales and lost goodwill, while keeping the wrong items in stock leads to wasted space (which costs money) and wasted capital. One way to evaluate which items deserve to be kept in stock is through evaluating how many of each item are sold in some period, such as a year, compared with how many are kept in inventory. This is called the inventory turn rate.

The following program evaluates turn rates and reports to management if an item is an exception—that is, if an item has a turn rate less than a criterion set by management. The computer does not decide—it provides information to management to aid in *management's* decision.

```
NEW
Ok
1 'Inventory Turn Rate Exception Reporting
10 INPUT "Enter total sales:", SALES#
20 INPUT "Enter total inventory:", INVENTORY#
30 LET INVENTORY.TURN.RATE# = SALES#/INVENTORY#
40 PRINT "Inventory turn rate ="; INVENTORY.TURN.RATE#;
50 IF INVENTORY.TURN.RATE# < 10 THEN PRINT "<- Report "
            ELSE PRINT    ' print message only if less than 10
60 END
RUN
Enter total sales:100
Enter total inventory:10
Inventory turn rate = 10
Ok
RUN
Enter total sales:50
Enter total inventory:10
Inventory turn rate = 5 <-Report
Ok
```

Comparing Strings Following Alphabetical Order, but Uppercase < Lowercase

It is possible to use all of the relational operators with strings, but the meanings are a little different. A$ > B$ means "A$ is greater than B$," but when is one string greater than another?

Think for a moment of a dictionary. It is full of strings — we call them words. They are sorted in alphabetical order. BASIC sorts strings in much the same way. A$ > B$ is true if, in a dictionary, the value of A$ would come after B$ in dictionary order. The expression "banana" > "apple" is true, since the word *banana* comes after *apple* in the dictionary. The same logic applies to the other relational operators >=, <, and <= when used with strings.

The equals (A$ = B$) expression is true only when all characters of the two strings match; in other words, they must be identical. The not equals (A$ <> B$) expression is true whenever any character does not match.

Actually, these definitions using "dictionary" order are not quite complete. BASIC has some conventions that do not apply to dictionaries. One is that all uppercase letters are logically less than all lowercase letters. Thus, Z < a is true, because Z is uppercase and a is lowercase.

Other conventions apply to nonletters, such as the digits 0–9 and special characters such as # and &. BASIC has an assigned order for all possible characters, including letters, digits, and special characters.

The ASCII table in Appendix A lists all BASIC characters in ascending sequence. Notice that numbers appear before uppercase letters, and both appear before lowercase letters. (We will discuss the ASCII value of characters in more detail in Chapter 11.)

Two strings are compared one character at a time, from left to right according to this list. If all the characters in each string are exactly the same, the strings are considered equal. As soon as two different characters are reached, the strings are considered unequal, and the string with the character that has the lower value is considered the lesser. If, before unequal characters occur, one string ends before the other, the shorter one is considered lesser. Blanks, both leading and trailing, are counted as characters for comparison.

The following are examples of string comparisons.

VARIABLE A$	VARIABLE B$	CONDITION
"ZEBRA"	"ELEPHANT"	A$ > B$
"friendship"	"friendly"	A$ > B$
"Thompson"	"Thompson"	A$ = B$
"Thompson, Jane"	"Thompson, Jane C."	A$ < B$
"McDonald"	"Mc Donald"	A$ > B$
"Jan. 3, 1986"	"Jan 3, 1986"	A$ > B$
"JONES, BILL"	"JONES,BILL"	A$ < B$
"Garcia, Marie"	"GARCIA, MARIE"	A$ > B$
"YES"	"yes"	A$ < B$
"NO"	"N"	A$ > B$

These last two are very important to remember. When you write a program that asks the user to enter a yes-no response, be sure that you show the user whether the response is to be uppercase or lowercase and whether the full word *yes* or *no* is to be entered or just the letters *y* or *n*.

Does 1234 = "1234"? No, you cannot compare apples and oranges, nor can you compare numbers and strings. If you try to do so, you will get the error message "Type mismatch."

AND, OR, and NOT: Logical Operators

It is possible to construct more complicated logical expressions by using the logical operators AND, OR, and NOT.

•THE THREE LOGICAL OPERATORS•

AND—True if all expressions are true.
OR—True if any one of the expressions is true.
NOT—Changes true expression to false and false expression to true.

AND

AND joins two or more expressions and is written as:

expression1 AND expression2

In order for the condition to be true, all of the expressions joined by the AND must be true. If any one of them is false, the entire condition will be false.

For example,

17 > 15 AND "YES" > "NO"

is true, because (17 > 15) is true and ("YES" > "NO") is true.

17 > 15 AND "YES" = "NO"

is false, because one of the two expressions (the right one) is false.

OR

OR also joins two or more expressions and is written:

expression1 OR expression2

The condition is evaluated as true if any one or both of the expressions joined by the OR is true.

For example,

17 > 15 OR "YES" = "NO"

is true because at least one of the expressions (the left one) is true. An OR expression is only false when both the left and right expressions are false, as in the following:

17 = 15 OR "YES" = "NO"

NOT

NOT reverses the normal meaning of an expression.

If A is true, then NOT A is false.

NOT (A > B) is the exact opposite of (A > B).

If a condition is true, NOT makes the condition false. If a condition is false, NOT makes the condition true. Here is a handy way to understand the relationship between NOT and the operators.

A > B	is the same as	NOT (A <= B)
A >= B	is the same as	NOT (A < B)
A < B	is the same as	NOT (A >= B)
A <= B	is the same as	NOT (A > B)
A = B	is the same as	NOT (A <> B)
A <> B	is the same as	NOT (A = B)

As you can see, there is some overlap in the logical operators, and it is frequently possible to express the same condition in more than one way.

Examples Using AND, OR, and NOT
The following is a short program demonstrating use of the logical operators.

```
10 LET A = 10: LET B = 50: LET C = 100: LET X = 1: LET Y = 5:
   LET AN$ = "yes"
20 '
30 IF A > Y AND B < C THEN PRINT "TRUE" ELSE PRINT "FALSE"
40 '
50 IF A > Y AND B > C THEN PRINT "TRUE" ELSE PRINT "FALSE"
60 '
70 IF NOT C > 100 THEN PRINT "TRUE" ELSE PRINT "FALSE"
80 '
90 IF AN$ = "yes" OR B > A THEN PRINT "TRUE" ELSE PRINT "FALSE"
100 '
110 IF (C - B) > A OR (C/Y) > A THEN PRINT "TRUE" ELSE PRINT "FALSE"
120 '
130 IF B + C = A OR NOT AN$ = "yes" THEN PRINT "TRUE" ELSE PRINT "FALSE"
140 '
150 IF (C/Y + B) < 80 AND NOT A > B THEN PRINT "TRUE" ELSE PRINT "FALSE"
160 '
170 IF A < B AND C = 100 AND B/X = B THEN PRINT "TRUE"
      ELSE PRINT "FALSE"
180 '
190 END
```

Before you look at the results of running this program, try to figure out what they will be. Until you become comfortable with using these logical operators, you may want to use a test program such as the preceding to check out the results. This is what you will get when you run that program.

```
RUN
TRUE
FALSE
TRUE
TRUE
TRUE
FALSE
TRUE
TRUE
Ok
```

Logical Operators in Combination: Order of Precedence
Using combinations of AND, OR, and NOT, you can build logical expressions of great complexity. As with arithmetic operators, there is an order of precedence for processing the logical operators when used in combination:

NOT is processed first, followed by
AND, followed by
OR

Since one line may contain arithmetic operators, relational operators, and logical operators, the order of precedence followed by BASIC is:

1. arithmetic operators (in the order discussed in Chapter 1)
2. relational operators
3. logical operators (in the order described earlier in this chapter)

If there are two or more operators of the same level, they are processed from left to right. An example of two logical operators in one expression is:

IF A = 2 * 5 OR B = 5 AND C = 100 THEN . . .

The arithmetic operators (+,−,^, *,/,\) are evaluated first. So 2 * 5 is evaluated first and becomes 10. Next the relational operators are evaluated. Since AND takes precedence over OR, B = 5 AND C = 100 is evaluated first and is true only if B has the value 5 and if C has the value of 100. Next the OR is evaluated. For the following values of A, B, and C the entire expression will be evaluated as follows:

A = 10, B = 15, C = 100   true (because A = 10)
A = 5, B = 5, C = 100   true (both B = 5 and C = 100)
A = 5, B = 5, C = 20   false (neither side of the OR is true)
A = 5, B = 15, C = 100   false (neither side of the OR is true)
A = 10, B = 5, C = 20   true (A = 10)

As with arithmetic operators, the order of execution can be changed by the use of parentheses; operators within parentheses are evaluated before those without the parentheses.

If we change the expression we just looked at by using parentheses, the results will change:

IF (A = 10 OR B = 5) AND C = 100 THEN . . .

Now, the OR will be evaluated first. It will be true if either A = 10 OR if B = 5. The entire expression will be true only if the OR expression is true and if C = 100.

A = 10, B = 15, C = 100   true
A = 5, B = 5, C = 100   true
A = 5, B = 5, C = 20   false
A = 5, B = 15, C = 100   true
A = 10, B = 5, C = 20   false

Evaluation of Logical Operators: An Example
Here is a program demonstrating the order of evaluation.

```
10 INPUT "AGE "; AGE: INPUT "YEARS OF EDUCATION "; EDUCATION
20 '
30 ' THIS WILL PRINT "TRUE" FOR A PERSON OVER 40 WITH AT LEAST 8 YEARS
40 '     OF EDUCATION OR A PERSON OVER 20 WITH AT LEAST 12 YEARS OF
        EDUCATION
50 '
60 IF AGE > 40 AND NOT EDUCATION < 8 OR AGE > 20 AND EDUCATION > = 12
        THEN PRINT "TRUE" ELSE PRINT "FALSE"
70 END
```

```
RUN
AGE ? 45
YEARS OF EDUCATION ? 15
TRUE
Ok
RUN
AGE ? 45
YEARS OF EDUCATION ? 8
TRUE
Ok
RUN
AGE ? 50
YEARS OF EDUCATION ? 6
FALSE
Ok
RUN
AGE? 35
YEARS OF EDUCATION ? 10
FALSE
Ok
RUN
AGE ? 35
YEARS OF EDUCATION ? 12
TRUE
Ok
RUN
AGE ? 15
YEARS OF EDUCATION ? 14
FALSE
Ok
```

This next program demonstrates the change in how an expression will be evaluated when parentheses are used:

```
10 ' TEST OF LOGICAL COMPARISONS IN SERIES
20 '
30 INPUT "A, B, C, D "; A, B, C, D
40 '
50 PRINT " WITHOUT PARENTHESES"
60 '
70 IF A > B AND C = D OR C > 100 THEN PRINT "TRUE" ELSE PRINT "FALSE"
80 '
90 PRINT " WITH PARENTHESES"
100 '
110 IF A > B AND ( C = D OR C > 100 ) THEN PRINT "TRUE" ELSE PRINT "FALSE"
RUN
A, B, C, D ? 10,5,20,20
    WITHOUT PARENTHESES
TRUE
    WITH PARENTHESES
```

```
TRUE
Ok
RUN
A, B, C, D ? 5,10,200,300
     WITHOUT PARENTHESES
TRUE
     WITH PARENTHESES
FALSE
Ok
RUN
A, B, C, D ? 5,10,20,20
     WITHOUT PARENTHESES
FALSE
     WITH PARENTHESES
FALSE
Ok
```

Remember, the order of evaluation is first NOT, then AND, then OR unless changed by the use of parentheses. Whenever an expression gets complicated, it is best to use parentheses to make the meaning clear and to ensure your program operates as you believe it will.

Table 5.1 summarizes the operators AND, OR, and NOT, along with three less frequently used operators: XOR, EQV, and IMP. We mention these last three for completeness only. They are not very useful for business programming.

Danger of the Double Negative

When you studied grammer, you were cautioned not to use a double negative. (An example of a double negative is the sentence "I did not go to no party.") A similar warning exists in BASIC. Consider the following line of code.

```
IF NOT A = 1 OR NOT A = 2 THEN PRINT "done"
    ELSE PRINT "not done"
```

One side of this expression will always be true, since if A equals 1, it cannot also equal 2 and vice versa. Therefore the entire expression will always be evaluated as true, and the statement following ELSE will never be executed.

What happens when AND is used?

TABLE 5.1 · *Table of Truth Values for Logical Operators*

| | | | TRUTH VALUE OF CONDITION WHEN X AND Y ARE AS SHOWN ON THE LEFT | | | | |
X	Y	NOT X	X AND Y	X OR Y	X XOR Y	X EQV Y	X IMP Y
TRUE	*TRUE*	FALSE	TRUE	TRUE	FALSE	TRUE	TRUE
TRUE	*FALSE*	FALSE	FALSE	TRUE	TRUE	FALSE	FALSE
FALSE	*TRUE*	TRUE	FALSE	TRUE	TRUE	FALSE	TRUE
FALSE	*FALSE*	TRUE	FALSE	FALSE	FALSE	TRUE	TRUE

·THE XOR, EQV, AND IMP OPERATORS·

XOR — eXclusive OR
Is true if *one* and *only one* of the expressions X and Y is true.

EQV — EQuiValent
Is true if *both* X and Y are true or if *both* are false.

IMP — IMPlies
Is true if *both* expressions X and Y are true or if the *first* is false.

```
IF NOT A = 1 AND NOT A = 2 THEN PRINT "done"
   ELSE PRINT "not done"
```

In this case both sides can never be true at the same time. Therefore the expression will always be evaluated as false, and the statement following THEN will never be executed.

Be very careful when using NOT so that you get the results you intended.

Some More Notes on Comparing

There are times when you wish to test if a numeric variable is equal to zero. If you are testing an integer, there will be no problem since you are dealing with only a whole number. If you are using single- or double-precision variables, because of rounding and fractional parts, a number may not exactly equal zero. One way to adjust for this is to test that your number is less than a particular value. For example, if you are dealing with dollars and cents, you would consider a number equal to zero if it is less than .005 (half a cent). You would write your test as:

```
IF A < .005 THEN . . .
```

where A is the variable you are testing.

If A could be positive or negative, you would write the test as:

```
IF A < .005 AND A > -.005 THEN . . .
```

There is a similar problem if you are testing if two variables are equal. If you wish to test that A and B are equal, you could write:

```
IF (A - B) < .005 AND (A - B) > -.005 THEN . . .
```

Value of TRUE and FALSE

When BASIC evaluates whether a condition is true or false, it assigns a value to the condition. If it is true, the condition is assigned the value −1, and if it is false, it is assigned the value 0.

```
PRINT 1 = 1 ' This is a TRUE condition
-1
Ok
```

```
PRINT 1 = 2 ' This is a FALSE condition
 0
Ok
```

Even though the condition true is assigned the value of −1, BASIC interprets any nonzero value as true. In the following example, if any nonzero value is entered, A is evaluated as true. If zero is entered, A is evaluated as false.

```
NEW
Ok
10 INPUT A
20 IF A THEN PRINT "A is true" ELSE PRINT "A is false"
RUN
? 5
A is true
RUN
? 0
A is false
```

WHILE and WEND — Repetition

The BASIC instruction pair WHILE . . . WEND, like the pair FOR . . . NEXT, is used to make a program repeat, or loop. Here is an example that computes the yield of any number of investments one at a time.

```
NEW
Ok
10 INPUT "Do you want to compute investment yields (yes or no)";
      YES.NO$
20 WHILE YES.NO$ = "yes"
30     INPUT "What is the principal";PRINCIPAL
40     INPUT "What is the interest rate per period (enter as a decimal)";
           INTEREST.RATE
50     INPUT "How many compounding periods";PERIODS
60     LET YIELD = PRINCIPAL * (1+INTEREST.RATE) ^ PERIODS
70     PRINT USING "The yield is $$##,###.##.";YIELD
80     INPUT "Another investment (yes or no)",YES.NO$
90 WEND
100 END
RUN
Do you want to compute investment yields (yes or no)? yes
What is the principal? 1000
What is the interest rate per period (enter as a decimal)? .10
How many compounding periods? 1
The yield is $1,100.00.
Another investment (yes or no)? yes
What is the principal? 1000
What is the interest rate per period (enter as a decimal)? .10
How many compounding periods? 2
The yield is $1,210.00.
Another investment (yes or no)? no
Ok
```

· THE WHILE . . . WEND STATEMENTS ·

WHILE expression

.

.

.

WEND

IF the expression is true, execute the statements between WHILE and
WEND and return to the WHILE.

IF the expression is false, execute the statement following WEND.

The WHILE statement consists of the word WHILE followed by the logical
expression—in this case, YES.NO$ = "yes". You remember that a FOR loop
starts with the FOR statement and continues through all lines to the matching
NEXT statement. The WHILE statement is similar; all lines up to the next WEND
statement are part of the loop. In this example the WHILE loop starts at line 20 and
includes all lines up to line 90, the WEND statement.

The WHILE statement checks to see if the expression following it is true. If it is,
all the statements between it and the WEND will be executed. If it is not true,
processing will skip down to the line immediately after the WEND. This is illustrated by the flowchart in Figure 5.6. In this example as long as YES.NO$ has the
value "yes", the loop repeats.

Comparison Between WHILE . . . WEND and FOR . . . NEXT

The WHILE statement is actually more powerful than the FOR statement. In fact,
it is always possible to write any FOR loop as a WHILE loop. To see this, compare
the following two equivalent programs.

LOOPING WITH WHILE . . . WEND

```
10 LET I = 1
20 WHILE I <= 10
30    PRINT I
40    LET I = I + 1
50 WEND
60 END
```

LOOPING WITH FOR . . . NEXT

```
10 FOR I = 1 TO 10
20    PRINT I
30 NEXT I
40 END
```

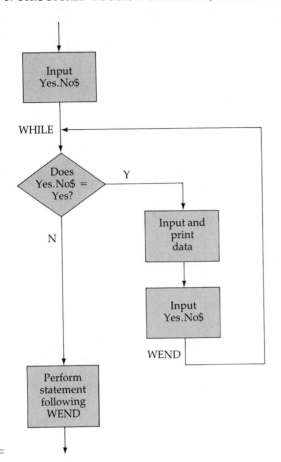

FIGURE 5.6
•
Flowchart of a
simple
WHILE . . .
WEND

It is not possible to write every WHILE loop as a FOR loop. FOR executes the loop a specific number of times, but WHILE can execute a loop an arbitrary number of times based on some logical condition.

When your program must iterate, you must choose between FOR . . . NEXT and WHILE . . . WEND. In general, if the program is to iterate a specific number of times, a FOR loop is called for. In all other cases, use a WHILE loop.

Nested WHILE . . . WEND Loops

As with FOR . . . NEXT, WHILE . . . WEND may also be nested. Each WHILE is matched to the most recent unmatched WEND. The following is an example of a program that calculates the number of months it will take to pay off a loan. The outer loop asks the user if he or she wants to perform another calculation; the inner loop counts the number of months it takes for the outstanding balance to become zero. Figure 5.7 is the flowchart for this program.

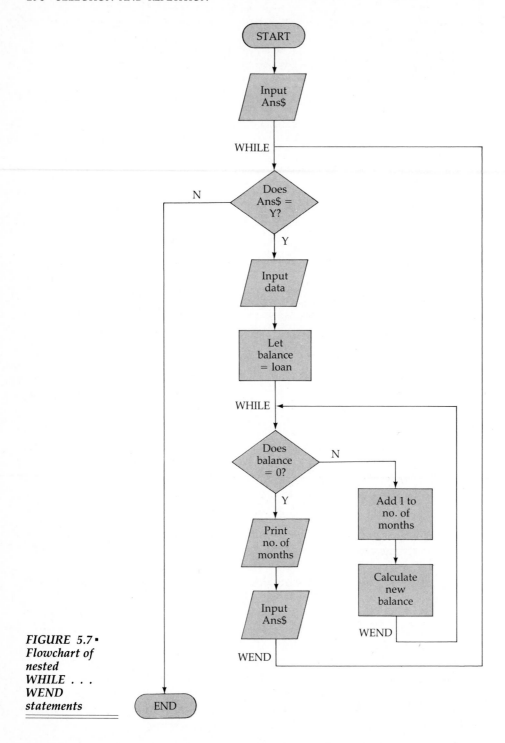

FIGURE 5.7 ·
Flowchart of
nested
WHILE . . .
WEND
statements

```
10 INPUT "Do you want to analyze a loan (Y or N) "; ANS$
20 WHILE ANS$ = "Y"
30    INPUT "Amount of Loan"; LOAN
40    INPUT "Annual Interest Rate (as a decimal)"; INT.RATE
50    INPUT "Monthly Payment"; MO.PMT
60    LET BALANCE = LOAN: LET NO.OF.MONTHS = 0
70    WHILE BALANCE > 0
80      LET NO.OF.MONTHS = NO.OF.MONTHS + 1
90      LET BALANCE = BALANCE - (MO.PMT - BALANCE * (INT.RATE/12))
100   WEND
110   PRINT "Number of Months "; NO.OF.MONTHS
120   INPUT "Do you want to analyze another loan (Y or N) "; ANS$
130 WEND
140 END
```

USING WHILE . . . WEND with INPUT for Data Validation

One of the most common uses of WHILE loops is to ask the user for one or more parameters using INPUT, execute the bulk of a program, then ask for the next set of parameters. This avoids the need to have the user type in RUN for every set of parameters. For this reason, many programs are structured as one big WHILE . . . WEND loop. The preceding example is such a program.

WHILE . . . WEND is also useful when you wish to make sure that the data a user has entered are valid (called **data validation** or **input validation**).

The following simple program asks the user for a yes or no answer. It will not accept any incorrect entry, only yes or no. You might use the equivalent of this sample whenever your program asks a yes or no question.

```
NEW
Ok
10 INPUT "yes or no"; YES.NO$
20 WHILE YES.NO$ <> "yes" and YES.NO$ <> "no"
30    INPUT "Please enter either yes or no"; YES.NO$
40 WEND
50 PRINT YES.NO$
60 END
RUN
yes or no? maybe
Please enter either yes or no? why not
Please enter either yes or no? YES
Please enter either yes or no? n
Please enter either yes or no? yes
yes
Ok
RUN
yes or no? no
no
Ok
```

Notice that only yes or no was allowed as a valid entry; YES is not the same as yes.

It is almost always a good idea to validate any data entered by the user. If your program relies on an answer being yes or no, your program should make sure the user entered one of those values. The same holds if a number entered is supposed to be within a specific range or be one of a specific set of values.

The following is an example of a series of statements that ensure that the value input for the variable AMOUNT will be within the range 0 to 9999.

```
10 INPUT "Enter Amount"; AMOUNT
20 WHILE AMOUNT < 0 OR AMOUNT > 9999
30   INPUT "Amount must be between 0 and 9999. Please reenter "; AMOUNT
40 WEND
```

Simple WHILE . . . WEND loops like these can provide input validation that can be critical to the success of your program.

Avoid Infinite WHILE . . . WEND Loops

One caution when using WHILE . . . WEND: it is possible to create infinite WHILE . . . WEND loops. Consider the following:

```
10 INPUT "Enter Amount"; AMOUNT
20 WHILE AMOUNT < 0 OR AMOUNT > 9999
30   INPUT "Amount must be between 0 and 9999. Please reenter "; AMT
40 WEND
```

In this case, once the loop is entered AMOUNT is never changed, since the variable used in the INPUT statement is AMT rather than AMOUNT. Check your loops carefully to make sure you have allowed a way for it to end. The only way to get out of an infinite loop such as the one shown here is to use Ctrl-Break (hold down the Ctrl key and press Break).

THE STORY'S END

Filled with ideas for how to use IF and WHILE for an investment analysis program, Terry quickly drafted specifications for the program.

Investment Program Specifications

General Purpose

This program computes the future value of a series of investments, each of which is described by parameters entered by the user. Two different types of investments are allowed: "load" and "no-load." In a "no-load" investment, such as a bank account, no commissions are charged. In a "load" investment a commission is charged on the initial investment. In addition, a commission may be charged on reinvestments of interest back into the fund.

• PARABLES FOR PROGRAMMERS •

Murphy Was a Computer User

Once upon a time a brilliant young programmer worked for a major corporation writing accounting programs. This programmer's programs were known far and wide as being superbly designed and written, thoroughly tested, well-documented, and very efficient.

Then one day, shortly after the close of the corporation's fiscal year, an accountant used one of this programmer's programs. As it was supposed to do, the program asked the accountant, "Do you wish to purge all journal entries?" The accountant, knowing that the journal entries were needed until all accounting for the year was completed, answered, "nno," misspelling the intended answer, "no."

This turned out to be a costly mistake, for the program was written to assume that no one would ever enter an answer other than "yes" or "no." Since the answer was not "no," the program, logically enough, concluded that the answer must have been "yes"! It purged the files.

"It's not my fault," the programmer said to the head of the data processing department. "It was user error."

"No," the manager replied, "data entry errors are inevitable, and you should have taken that into account. From now on, write your programs so that they can handle *any* input from users, even incorrect data, without causing havoc."

MORAL: A program that does not validate input is a disaster waiting to happen.

All investments are assumed to pay interest at a fixed annual percentage rate (APR); investments where the rate varies may be analyzed by using the average APR. The investment period must be some number of years.

Output
The output of the program, for each investment, includes the following information:

Investment name: aaaaaaaaaaaaaaaaaaaaaaaaaa
Future value: #,###,###.##

The future value is calculated as described in a separate section of this document.

Input

When the program begins, it asks the user to enter the principal to be invested and the number of years of the investment. Then, for each investment, the program asks the user to enter the following:

1. The name of the investment (string)
2. The number of compounding periods per year
3. The annual percentage rate, as a decimal (APR)
4. Whether the investment charges commissions and, if so, the commission percentage on the initial investment and on reinvestments

All dollar amounts will be less than $10,000,000.00

Calculations of Future Values

The basic calculation for the future value is

```
FV = PV * (1 + I) ^ PERIODS
```

where FV is the future value, PV is the present value of the investment (i.e., the initial principal), I is the interest rate per compounding period, and PERIODS is the number of compounding periods in the life of the investment. If PERIODS.PER.YEAR is the number of compounding periods in a year, APR is the annual percentage rate paid, PRINCIPAL is the initial principal invested, and YEARS is the number of years of the investment, then for a no-load fund,

```
I = APR/PERIODS.PER.YEAR,
PV = PRINCIPAL, and
PERIODS = YEARS * PERIODS.PER.YEAR.
```

For a load fund,

```
PV = PRINCIPAL * (1 - INITIAL.COMMISSION) and
I = APR/PERIODS.PER.YEAR * (1 - REINVEST.COMMISSION),
```

where INITIAL.COMMISSION and REINVEST.COMMISSION are the commission percentages (expressed as decimals) charged on the initial investment and reinvestments of interest, respectively.

Structure Charts and Flowcharts

In addition to these specifications, Terry was determined to write the program in such a way that all data entered by the user are validated by the program. Armed with the specifications and this goal, Terry developed a structure chart (Figure 5.8) and flowchart (Figure 5.9).

Data Dictionary

ANOTHER$	Holds response to "another investment?"
APR	Annual percentage rate (interest)

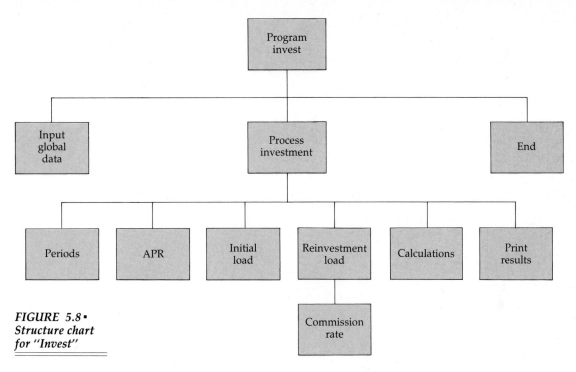

*FIGURE 5.8 ▪
Structure chart
for "Invest"*

COMMISSION.RATE	Cost of purchase and/or reinvestment
FV#	Future value of investment
I	Loop counter
INITIAL.LOAD$	YES or NO (YES if purchase commission is charged)
INVESTMENT.NAME$	Identifier of the investment
PERIODS%	Number of times investment is compounded
PERIODS.PER.YEAR%	Number of times per year interest is compounded
PRINCIPAL#	Amount of investment
PV#	Principal minus commission
REINVEST.LOAD$	YES or NO (YES if reinvestment commission is charged)
YEARS%	Number of years of investments

Pseudocode

<u>MAIN</u>
    DO Input-Global-Data
    WHILE there are more investments
        DO PROCESS-INVESTMENTS

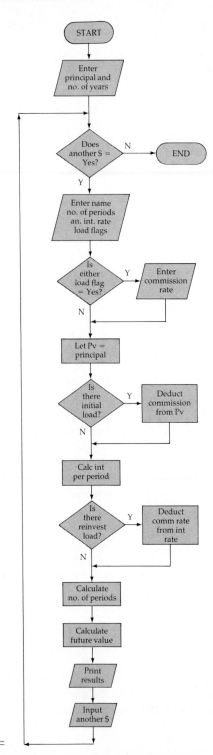

FIGURE 5.9 ▪
Flowchart of
investment
program

           WEND
<u>INPUT-GLOBAL-DATA</u>
           get amount to invest and years to invest

<u>PROCESS-INVESTMENTS</u>
           get investment name
           get number of periods
           get apr
           get initial investment load
           get reinvestment load and commission rate
           calculate yield
           print results

Program Listing

```
100 ' 6-21-88 BY TERRY
110 ' PROGRAM HISTORY
120 '*********************************************************
130 '
140 '
150 '
160 ' ASK THE USER FOR GLOBAL PARAMETERS
170 ' ENTER PRINCIPAL; MUST BE POSITIVE
180 '
190   INPUT "ENTER THE AMOUNT TO INVEST: ", PRINCIPAL#
200   WHILE PRINCIPAL# <= 0
210      PRINT "PRINCIPAL must be positive"
220      INPUT "PLEASE ENTER PRINCIPAL AGAIN: ", PRINCIPAL#
230   WEND
240 '
250 ' ENTER THE NUMBER OF YEARS TO INVEST; FROM 1 TO 99, INCLUSIVE
260 '
270   INPUT "ENTER THE NUMBER OF YEARS TO INVEST: ", YEARS%
280   WHILE YEARS% <= 0 OR YEARS% >= 100
290      PRINT "THE NUMBER OF YEARS MUST BE BETWEEN 1 AND 100"
300      INPUT "REENTER THE NUMBER OF YEARS TO INVEST: ", YEARS%
310   WEND
320 '*********************************************************
330 ' NOW LOOP THROUGH EACH INVESTMENT UNTIL THE USER SAYS TO STOP
340 '
350 INPUT "DO YOU WISH TO PROCESS AN INVESTMENT (YES or NO)", ANOTHER$
360 WHILE ANOTHER$ = "YES"
370   INPUT "ENTER THE NAME OF THE INVESTMENT: ", INVESTMENT.NAME$
380   INPUT "ENTER THE INTEREST PERIODS PER YEAR", PERIODS.PER.YEAR%
390   WHILE PERIODS.PER.YEAR% < 1 OR PERIODS.PER.YEAR% > 366
400      PRINT "THE PERIODS PER YEAR MUST BE BETWEEN 1 AND 366"
410      INPUT "PLEASE REENTER THE INTEREST PERIODS PER YEAR: ",
               PERIODS.PER.YEAR%
420   WEND
```

```
430  '
440      INPUT "ENTER THE ANNUAL INTEREST PERCENTAGE RATE: ", APR
450      WHILE APR <= 0 OR APR >= 1
460         PRINT "INTEREST RATE MUST BE BETWEEN .01 AND .99"
470         INPUT "PLEASE REENTER THE ANNUAL INTEREST PERCENTAGE RATE: ",
                   APR
480      WEND
490      INPUT "IS THERE A COMMISSION ON THE INITIAL INVESTMENT";
                INITIAL.LOAD$
500      WHILE INITIAL.LOAD$ <> "YES" AND INITIAL.LOAD$ <> "NO"
510         PRINT "answer must be YES or NO"
520         INPUT "PLEASE REENTER RESPONSE ", INITIAL.LOAD$
530      WEND
540      INPUT "IS THERE A COMMISSION ON THE REINVESTMENT OF INTEREST";
                REINVEST.LOAD$
550      WHILE REINVEST.LOAD$ <> "YES" AND REINVEST.LOAD$ <> "NO"
560         PRINT "answer must be YES or NO"
570         INPUT "PLEASE REENTER RESPONSE ", REINVEST.LOAD$
580      WEND
590      LET COMMISSION.RATE = 0
600      WHILE COMMISSION.RATE <= 0 AND (INITIAL.LOAD$ = "YES" OR
                REINVEST.LOAD$ = "YES")
610         INPUT "ENTER THE COMMISSION RATE: ", COMMISSION.RATE
620         IF COMMISSION.RATE <= 0 OR COMMISSION.RATE >= 1
                THEN PRINT "ENTER A RATE BETWEEN .01 AND .99"
630      WEND
640  '
650  ' ********************************************************
660  '
670  '   CALCULATE INTERMEDIATE VALUES
680  '
690      LET PV# = PRINCIPAL#
700      IF INITIAL.LOAD$ = "YES" THEN LET PV# = PV# * (1 - COMMISSION.RATE)
710      LET I = APR/PERIODS.PER.YEAR%
720      IF REINVEST.LOAD$ = "YES" THEN LET I = I * (1 - COMMISSION.RATE) >
730      LET PERIODS% = YEARS% * PERIODS.PER.YEAR%
740  '
750  ' ********************************************************
760  '
770  '   ** CALCULATE THE FUTURE VALUE
780  '
790      LET FV# = PV# * (1 + I) ^PERIODS%
800  '
810  ' ********************************************************
820  '
830  '   ** PRINT OUT THE FINAL RESULTS
840      PRINT ' a blank line
850      PRINT "INVESTMENT NAME: ";INVESTMENT.NAME$
860      PRINT USING "FUTURE VALUE: $$,########.##";FV#
870      PRINT ' a blank line
```

```
880 '
890 ' *********************************************************
900 '
910 '   ** PROMPT THE USER TO RUN THE PROGRAM AGAIN
920 '
930    PRINT "PRESS <RETURN> TO TERMINATE; OR ENTER";
940    INPUT " 'YES' <RETURN> TO CONTINUE", ANOTHER$
950    *********************************************************
960 WEND     ' end of processing loop
970 '
980 '*********************************************************
990 '
1000   END
```

Program Output

```
DO YOU WISH TO PROCESS AN INVESTMENT (YES or NO)? YES
ENTER THE AMOUNT TO INVEST: 10000
ENTER THE NUMBER OF YEARS TO INVEST: 15
ENTER THE NAME OF THE INVESTMENT: First National Bank
ENTER THE INTEREST PERIODS PER YEAR: 1
ENTER THE ANNUAL INTEREST PERCENTAGE RATE: .12
IS THERE A COMMISSION ON THE INITIAL INVESTMENT? YES
IS THERE A COMMISSION ON THE REINVESTMENT OF INTEREST? YES
ENTER THE COMMISSION RATE: .005


INVESTMENT NAME:   First National Bank
FUTURE VALUE:      $54,025.99


PRESS <RETURN> TO TERMINATE; OR ENTER 'YES' <RETURN> TO CONTINUE YES
ENTER THE NAME OF THE INVESTMENT: Second National Bank
ENTER THE INTEREST PERIODS PER YEAR: 365
ENTER THE ANNUAL INTEREST PERCENTAGE RATE: .115
IS THERE A COMMISSION ON THE INITIAL INVESTMENT? NO
IS THERE A COMMISSION ON THE REINVESTMENT OF INTEREST? NO


INVESTMENT NAME:   Second National Bank
FUTURE VALUE:      $56,107.68


PRESS <RETURN> TO TERMINATE; OR ENTER 'YES' <RETURN> TO CONTINUE
Ok
```

▪QUICK REFERENCE FOR LESSON 5▪

IF Selects Between Two Alternative Courses of Action

IF evaluates an expression and executes specified statements based on whether the expression is true or false. The expression is any valid logical expression; most commonly, it is a comparison of two numbers or strings.

IF Expression THEN Statement: Statement: . . .

Any number of statements separated by colons may follow THEN. If the expression is true, all the statements following THEN will be executed. If the expression is false, the statements will not be executed.

IF Expression THEN Statement(s) ELSE Statement(s)

If the expression is true, all the statements following THEN will be executed. If the expression is false, all the statements following the ELSE will be executed. The entire IF-THEN-ELSE statement must be on one program line. If there are multiple statements following THEN or ELSE, they must be separated by colons.

Relational Operators

Logical expressions may use relational operators to compare two values.

These operators are:

=	Equal to
<	Less than
>	Greater than
<= or =<	Less than or equal to
>= or =>	Greater than or equal to
<> or ><	Not equal to

If the values being compared are strings, BASIC uses an extension to the "dictionary order concept," using the sort order of the ASCII table.

Logical Operators

More complex logical expressions may be formed using the logical operators AND, OR, and NOT.

A AND B	True when both A and B are true.
A OR B	True when either A or B is true, or both.
NOT A	True when A is false; false when A is true.

Parentheses may be used in complex logical expressions to make the meaning more clear or to alter the normal order of evaluation.

WHILE . . . WEND

Execute a series of statements as long as a given expression is true.

```
WHILE expression
statement
statement
  .
  .
  .
WEND
```

When BASIC reaches the WHILE statement and the logical expression is true, the loop body (statements between the WHILE and WEND) is executed, and BASIC returns to the WHILE statement. This process will be repeated as long as the expression remains true. If the expression is false when it is tested by the WHILE statement, processing will go to the statement following the WEND.

Comparison of WHILE . . . WEND and FOR . . . NEXT

FOR . . . NEXT (with a Positive Step)

FOR A = X TO Y STEP Z
> (Initialize A with the value of X. Is A greater than Y? If it is, then go to the statement immediately after the NEXT. If it is not, process the statements that follow.)

statement
statement
.
.
.

NEXT A
> (Increment A by Z [or by 1 if the STEP is not indicated] and go back to the FOR statement.)

1. BASIC initializes the counter and automatically increments it.
2. The loop is performed a set number of times. For a loop that is incremented by 1, such as in FOR A = X TO Y, the loop will be performed Y − X + 1 times.

WHILE . . . WEND

WHILE expression
> (Is the expression true? If it is, then perform the following statements. If it is not, then go to the statement immediately following the WEND.)

statement
statement
.
.
.

WEND (Go back to the WHILE.)

1. The programmer must set the expression to its initial value and must write any statements to change its value.
2. The loop may be performed any number of times.

• EXERCISES •

Short Answer

1. FOR . . . NEXT is an example of selection. (T/F)

2. WHILE . . . WEND is used for decision making. (T/F)

3. The IF . . . THEN . . . ELSE statement is generally written on three separate lines. (T/F)

4. In order for the condition *expression1 AND expression2* to be true, at least one of the expressions must be true. (T/F)

5. NOT reverses the normal meaning of an expresssion. (T/F)

6. It is possible to write any FOR loop as a WHILE loop, but it is not possible to write any WHILE loop as a FOR loop. (T/F)

7. The three major programming structures are _____, _____, and _____.

8. When one IF . . . THEN statement is included within another IF . . . THEN statement, it is called _____.

9. AND, OR, and NOT are called _____.

10. WHILE . . . WEND is similar to _____ in that they are both used to make a program loop.

11. Define the following relational operators:

> _____   >= _____
= _____   < _____
<= _____   <> _____

12. Which of the following string comparisons are true and which are false?
    a. "TOM" < "tom"
    b. "YES" > "Y"
    c. "Ann M. Murray" > "Ann Murray"
    d. "hello" = "HELLO"
    e. "1985" > "June 1, 1985"

13. Assuming the following values, which of the statements below are true?
    $A = 20$ $B = 5$ $C = 25$ $D = 10$
    a. NOT (A > B)
    b. (C < 20) OR (D < 20)
    c. (A - B) > (C - D)
    d. (A = 20) AND ((B = 5) OR (C = 101))

14. Describe the three major programming structures.

15. What is the difference between using the IF . . . THEN statement and using the IF . . . THEN . . . ELSE statement? When would you need to use one over the other?

16. What is the difference between logical expressions and logical operators?

17. Explain the difference between the WHILE . . . WEND statement and the FOR . . . NEXT statement.

18. What is data validation? Give an example of code that is used for such a purpose.

Analyzing Code

19. Something is wrong with many of the following IF statements. Identify the errors and suggest appropriate corrections.
    a. IF A > B THEN "A is greater than B"
    b. IF A > B THEN PRINT "A is greater than B" ELSE "A
          is not greater than B"
    c. IF A > B THEN PRINT "Hello" PRINT "there" ELSE
          PRINT "Good" PRINT "bye"
    d. IF A = "banana" THEN PRINT "It's a banana"
    e. IF A = 1 OR 2 THEN PRINT "A equals 1 or 2" ELSE
          PRINT "A equals something else"

f. IF A = NOT 1 THEN LET X = 17 ELSE LET X = 34
g. IF NOT (A = 1) THEN PRINT "A equals 1" ELSE PRINT
      "A does not equal 1"
h. IF X$ = "Niagara Falls District" : THEN PRINT
      NIAGARA.FALLS.TOTAL

20. DEBUGGING: Study the following program to see if you can find a problem with it. Enter it into your computer and test it.

```
LET ANS$ = "YES": LET TOTAL% = 0: LET COUNT% = 0
20 WHILE ANS$ <> "NO"
30     INPUT "Do you have any more (YES or NO) "; ANS$
40     INPUT "Amount "; AMOUNT%
50     LET TOTAL% = TOTAL% + AMOUNT%
60     LET COUNT% = COUNT% + 1
70     PRINT COUNT%, AMOUNT%
80 WEND
90 PRINT "The total is: "; TOTAL%
100 END
```

What happens when you answer NO to the question "Do you have any more?" Why? Correct the problem and try running it again.

What happens if you answer yes or Y? What happens if you answer WHAT? Change the program so that YES or NO are the only acceptable responses.

Programming

For the following programs:
    a. Write a structure chart.
    b. Write a flowchart.
    c. Write pseudocode.
    d. Code the program.

21. Practice with IF
    a. Write a program that asks the user to enter either a 1 or a 2. If the user enters a 1, print the word *one*. If the user enters a 2, print the word *two*.
    b. Write a program that asks the user to enter two numbers. If the first number is greater or equal to the second, ask for a third number and print the sum of all three numbers. If the first number is less than the second, print their product.
    c. Write a program that asks the user to enter an integer, then asks the user to enter that number of double-precision values one at a time, then prints out the minimum, maximum, and average of the entered double-precision values. (Hint: use a FOR loop.)
    d. Write a program that asks the user to enter a single letter. If the letter is *a*, print "a is for apple." If the letter is *b*, print "b is for banana." If the letter is *c*, print "c is for cucumber." If the value entered is anything other than these three values, print the message, "illegal value entered." Use a single IF statement. Can you think of a valid way to break this one IF statement into several smaller IFs on separate lines, each of which handles one specific case?

22. Practice with WHILE . . . WEND
    a. Write a program that asks the user to enter a double-precision value, then asks whether he or she desires to enter another value, and continues looping as long as

the answer is yes. When the user is through entering values, print the sum, minimum, maximum, and average of the values entered.

b. Write a program that asks the user to enter one of the letters *a, b,* or *c*. If the user enters any other value, your program should print an error message, then allow the user to try again.

23. LOAN AMORTIZATION
    a. Write a program that which prints a loan amortization schedule. The user should input the annual percentage rate (APR), the loan amount, and the monthly payment. For each month, compute the interest payment as the monthly interest rate (APR/12) times the outstanding balance. Subtract this from the payment to get the amount to apply toward the principal. Continue applying monthly payments until the principal is paid off. Keep a total of the interest paid over the life of the loan and the number of months it takes to repay the loan. The output of the report should look like this:

```
Loan amount: ###,###.##
Annual Interest Percentage Rate: ##.##%
Monthly Payment: ###,###.##
Month      Interest      Principal      Balance
-----------------------------------------------
  1        ###,###.##    ###,###.##    ###,###.##
  2        ###,###.##    ###,###.##    ###,###.##
  .            .             .             .
  .            .             .             .
  .            .             .             .
-----------------------------------------------
Total interest paid: ###,###.##
```

Make sure your program takes the last month into account properly. If the balance plus interest in the last month is less than the usual payment, the amount paid in the last month must be adjusted accordingly.

Also, include directions to the user whether the interest rate is to be entered as a percent or as a decimal. Is a 12.5 percent interest rate to be entered as 12.5 or as .125? If it is to be entered as a percent, be sure to convert it to a decimal before you do your calculations.

b. Add to the preceding program data validation. Both the loan amount and the monthly payment must be positive and not greater than 999,999.99. The interest rate must also be positive and not greater than 99 percent.

24. SALES COMMISSION: XYZ Corporation pays its salespeople commissions based on total sales for each week in addition to their salaries. Salespeople receive no commission on the first $500 in sales. They receive as a commission 15 percent of sales over $500 up to and including $1000, 17 percent on sales over $1000 up to and including $2000, and 20 percent of sales over $2000. For example, if a salesperson's sales for the week are $1200, the commission is 15 percent × $500 plus 17 percent × $200.

Write a program that computes sales commissions. The program asks the user to enter each salesperson's name and the amount of sales, then prints the commission due that salesperson. Do not allow the user to enter an amount less than $0 or an amount of $10,000 or over.

Have your program loop to allow the user to perform the computations for an arbitrary number of salespeople. When the user is through entering values, print the total sales of all salespeople, the total of all commissions earned, the percentage of total sales represented by commissions, and the average commission paid. Also, for the salespeople with the highest and lowest total sales of the group, print their names, total sales, and commissions earned.

25. MULTIPLYING FLIES: Assume that there are two flies in a room. By the end of the day they will produce two more flies, and by the end of the second day these four will have produced eight more. In other words, the fly population doubles each day.
   a. Write a program that will print the fly population for the first ten days. Write it two ways: one using a FOR-NEXT loop and one using WHILE-WEND.
   b. Now you want to know how many days it will take before the fly population reaches 10,000. Write the program so that it prints each day's population and stops when the number is equal to or greater than 10,000. (Can you do this with a FOR-NEXT?)

26. CHECKBOOK: Write a program that will keep track of your checkbook balance. It should first ask you to input your beginning balance. While this balance is greater than zero, the program should ask you to input your check number, the date, and the amount of the check (entered as a negative number). You will also need to be able to enter deposits, using a check number of 0000. For each entry, have the program print the check number, the date, the amount, and the current balance. When the balance is zero or less, the program should print the message, "WARNING—you are overdrawn!" and end.
   All amounts will be in the range −99,999.99 to +99,999.99.
   Additions to the program:
   a. Verify that the check numbers are within the range 0–9999 and that the amount is within the range specified above.
   b. The program as specified earlier allows no way out unless the balance reaches zero. Modify it so that the user is asked if there are anymore entries. Use a nested WHILE-WEND.

27. MEASURING PACKAGES: Depending on its weight, height, and width a package will be sent by different mail services. If the package weighs less than 1 pound, it will be sent first class no matter what the size. If it weighs less than 25 pounds, and the height times the width (in inches) is not greater than 526, then it will be sent third class. Otherwise it will be sent parcel post.
   Write a program that asks the user to enter the weight, height, and width and that prints a message indicating which way the package is to be sent.

28. PRODUCTION MEASUREMENT: Three measurements are taken of a product during a particular point in its production: the temperature measured to the tenth of a degree, the weight measured to the nearest pound, and the acidity measured as a fraction. If the temperature is less than 100.00 degrees, the weight is 50 pounds or less, and the acidity is greater than .75, the product is accepted. If the temperature is less than 100.00 and the weight is over 75, or if the temperature is over 125.00 and the acidity is less than .25, the product is rejected. Otherwise the product is sent back for modification.
   Write a program that asks the user to input these measurements and prints a message indicating into which of the three groups the product falls. Be careful that your line does not exceed the maximum length.

MODULAR PROGRAMMING WITH GOSUB

SOFTWARE ENGINEERING AND STRUCTURED PROGRAMMING

Pat and Chris are sitting in the cafeteria talking over coffee. After the usual idle chatter, the conversation turns to computer programming.

PAT: I understand you're involved in a big project up there in Data Processing.

CHRIS: Yes, we're implementing a corporate-wide management information system. I'm one of the senior software engineers on the project.

PAT: Software engineer, huh? It seems like everyone is an engineer these days. Housewives are "domestic engineers." The drivers of our waste disposal trucks want to be called "sanitary engineers." When I think of engineers, I think of people who build bridges and dam rivers.

CHRIS (a little testily): I'll try not to get mad over that remark because I've heard it before. "Computer programming is an art form, practiced by long-haired, precocious kids in blue jeans." That's a lot of bunk. Developing computer software is every bit as much an engineering task as building a skyscraper.

PAT: Sorry, I was just trying to make a joke. No offense was meant.

CHRIS: Pat, I know that you've been studying programming in BASIC a lot since we worked together on that depreciation program. You've also recently made your first step up the management rung at Con. Glomerate, so you're going to have to deal with computers and computer people the rest of your career. I think it's important for you to learn the difference between developing big programs and developing small programs.

Big Programs Are Fundamentally Different from Small Programs

PAT: I think I know the difference already. Some of the BASIC programs I've written are a couple of hundred lines long. Boy, are they tough to write! So many things to take into account at once!

CHRIS: Do you find yourself bogging down when your program, excluding comments, starts reaching about one hundred lines?

PAT (contemplates for a moment): Well, I never stopped to count lines, but that sounds about right. At somewhere around a hundred lines, a program suddenly seems to get extremely difficult. Some programs fifty lines long are extremely difficult to write, while others that are two hundred lines seem to be easy, but the one-hundred-line average seems pretty close.

CHRIS: Most people experience the same pattern. Some programming geniuses, called "super programmers" by some, can write programs several times that length using seat-of-the-pants methods, but they are rare.

PAT: So you have to be a genius to be a software engineer?

CHRIS: No, because even being able to write five-hundred-line programs would not be enough. Most practical business programs are between one thousand and ten thousand lines long. Some libraries of programs used by a major corporation such as Con. Glomerate may total millions of lines. It is beyond the capacity of the species *Homo sapiens* to deal with that much complication at one time. Genius is not what's needed, just a new approach to computer software.

PAT: I'm confused. You just said that Con. Glomerate has millions of lines of programs, yet no one can deal with that much complication. Isn't that a contradiction?

CHRIS: No, because Con. Glomerate's Data Processing shop, like all good data processing departments, uses special techniques to deal with programs and libraries of programs that are too big for one mind to handle. The use of these techniques is called **software engineering.** The basic idea is to chop huge software projects into manageable chunks. If you write any sizable programs, or if, as a manager, you work with computer professionals to specify and test large programs, you will have to become familiar with these techniques.

PAT: Does the term *software engineering* apply only to programs written in BASIC?

CHRIS: No. In fact, almost all of the principles of software engineering are independent of the programming language used. Con. Glomerate uses programs developed in at least four different programming languages, yet our software engineering approach is pretty much the same across the board. Each language has its own special considerations, but they concern methods of implementing the techniques, not the concepts behind them.

PAT: Isn't this a lot of puffery on the part of computer people? I mean, it's obvious that it should take ten times longer to write a one-thousand-line program than it takes to write a one-hundred-line program. What's so fundamentally different, other than time?

CHRIS: You claim that it is "obvious" that the time taken on a program is proportional to its length, but I can tell you from experience that that's not so. In practice the person who attempts to write a large, say, over one-thousand-line, program without using software engineering techniques usually either never finishes or takes more than ten times as long as someone writing a one-hundred-line program.

PAT: I'd like to believe that, but it doesn't make sense to me.

CHRIS: The fact is that the complexity of a program increases exponentially with its length. A one-thousand-line program may be a thousand times more complex than a one-hundred-line program. Without using good engineering principles, you may never successfully complete a one-thousand-line program in such a way that it is thoroughly tested and easily changed as needs change.

PAT: I'm still not convinced. Can you give me an analogy I can relate to?

CHRIS: Sure. You're probably handy enough with a hammer and saw to build a kid's clubhouse in, say, a weekend, aren't you?

PAT: I guess so.

CHRIS: A skyscraper is maybe one hundred times as tall as a clubhouse. Do you think you could build a skyscraper in one hundred weekends?

PAT: No, of course not.

CHRIS: Well, computer programming is the same way. When you go from the clubhouses of programming to the skyscrapers, suddenly the whole picture changes. More people, more complex definitions of the problem, and more complex calculations are involved. The programs have more variables, more lines, and more IF statements that result in more possible combinations of the outcome. All of this complexity expands at an exponential not a proportional, rate. It takes engineering techniques to build a large building, and it takes engineering techniques to write a large program.

PAT: What are these techniques?

Specifications as a Software Engineering Technique Ensure Solving the Right Problem

CHRIS: You've already learned one of them: specifications. One of the biggest problems with any programming project is maintaining clear communications between technical and nontechnical people in the project. This becomes more essential the more people get involved. Specifications have the effect of providing a common ground for everybody. A programmer need not learn everything about a user's job—just understand the specifications. Similarly, a user need not understand computers, just the specifications. This reduces the complexity of agreeing on just what problem the program is to solve.

PAT: Do specifications become more important as the size of the project increases?

CHRIS: Very much so. Think again about our analogy to building buildings. You could probably build a clubhouse without using a blueprint, because you could plan the whole thing in your head. But you wouldn't even attempt to build a real house, let alone a skyscraper without blueprints. The project is just too complex to carry around in your mind. The same is true of computer programs. The larger the project, the more important the specifications become.

PAT: I can see that now. What else?

Modules Are Understandable Chunks

CHRIS: There is a process called **structured design.** This is a method used to design a program before you start writing code. At the core of structured design is the idea of breaking up the problem into modules, each of which has a very small number, preferably one, of purposes. Each module is then broken down into smaller modules and so forth until the modules are so detailed that they can be directly translated into the programming language.

PAT: I learned something about modules when I learned the REM statement in BASIC. REM allows me not only to put comments into a program but to break it up into visually distinct modules, each of which accomplishes one purpose.

CHRIS: Then you've already gained some experience with modularity. BASIC provides several other statements that aid modularity, foremost among them the GOSUB and ON . . . GOSUB statements.

PAT: GOSUB? I think that's the next lesson in my BASIC book.

CHRIS: Excellent! When you read about GOSUB, keep this conversation in mind.

PAT: Is there an analogy between structured design and building buildings?

CHRIS: Yes. Think of the way one would design a skyscraper. You wouldn't plunge in right away designing executive washrooms. First, you would decide how many floors, how many square feet, and other general considerations. Then, you might break the problem down into the design of the structural components, the electrical system, the plumbing, and so forth. Once the problem was broken down in this way, you would then deal with one area at a time, say, the electrical system. This, in turn, would break down into successively smaller problems, until finally you reached the level of wires and outlets.

PAT: And if I were the architect or engineer and I developed the specifications for the electrical system properly at the highest level, I might even turn over the detailed design to someone else, subject to my approval.

CHRIS: You've got pretty good insight, Pat. That's exactly how programming projects involving more than one person work. Modularity has many advantages.

Top-Down Design Defers Details to Later

PAT: I think what you're saying is that to design a program, one starts with an overview, consisting of a few steps, then breaks each of those steps into more steps, and so forth until each step can be directly translated into one or a few lines of BASIC.

CHRIS: Exactly. This is also called **hierarchical design,** or **top-down design,** because you start at the "top," or most general, level, then work your way down to the detailed solution. The advantage of this method is that you have to deal only with a small module and a small number of concepts at any one time, yet all the modules fit into an easily understood overall design.

PAT: So, for example, I might write a program in which each module of the actual BASIC code was a few lines of code. Each module would be one step in a higher-level module, each higher-level module would be a step in a still higher-level module, and so forth up to the highest level. To design such a program you would start with a definition of the highest level, then successively break it down into more detail.

CHRIS: Now you've got it! A person can easily deal with five or so lines of BASIC, or five steps in the definition of any one module. It's when a person has to deal with all of the complexity at once that confusion develops. By breaking the problem down hierarchically, you guarantee that you can deal with the problem one small, manageable module at a time. Again, the key word is complexity. By arranging things so that you can deal with a module at a time, you've drastically reduced the complexity of writing a large program.

PAT: Is five lines or steps a magic number?

CHRIS: No, the number of lines or step in a module will vary. In general, however, it is best to keep it down to less than ten lines, but the idea is to break the program down in the easiest-to-understand way, not to meet some arbitrary, standard number of lines per module.

PAT: Are there any other techniques I should know?

Top-Down Programming and Testing Uncover Errors in a Manageable Manner

CHRIS: Once you have designed your program using top-down or modular methods, you should write and test it the same way — in modules. Start from the top-level module and write a BASIC program that simulates the steps in that module. Don't worry at the moment that each step must later be broken down into more detail. Just put in dummy PRINT statements for each step, to be replaced later by more detailed code. Then, after you get that dummy version of the top-level module working, choose a step and replace the dummy PRINT statement with the next level of detail for that step. Test the program that way, then fill in more detail. Proceed one module at a time in this way until the program is complete.

PAT: I think I'll have to see an example of that.

CHRIS: OK. When you've finished with the GOSUB lesson, we'll work through a real example.

PAT: This is all so complicated. Isn't it enough to learn the BASIC statements?

CHRIS: Don't worry. All it takes is practice. And yes, it is vitally important to understand the fundamental principles of software engineering. The ability to use these techniques is what separates the "hacker" from the "pro." Even if you don't ever write a large program, as a manager you will have to understand these issues in order to deal with computer professionals in the future.

PAT: Hmmmm. This puts programming into an altogether different light. If I understand you correctly, programming is more of a general problem-solving discipline than just the ability to use a language like BASIC.

CHRIS: You learn fast, Pat. I think you'll go far at Con. Glomerate.

PAT: What do I have to do to learn to use structured programming techniques? Go to graduate school?

CHRIS: As I said, the most important thing is practice — and an awareness of the philosophy that underlies structured programming.

PAT: Thanks, Chris. Every time we talk about programming I learn something new.

CHRIS: I enjoy bringing others along into the world of structured programming. Give me a call when you're ready to meet again.

·*THE ABCS OF BASIC ON THE IBM PERSONAL COMPUTER*·

LESSON 6: GOSUB AND GOTO SEND PROCESSING TO ANOTHER PROGRAM LINE

Your earliest programs involved only LET and PRINT. They started execution at the line with the lowest line number and proceeded through successively higher line numbers until they reached the end of the program. The order of execution never varied from a strict line-number order.

IF was a slight change from that routine; it allowed some statements to be executed while others were skipped. FOR . . . NEXT and WHILE . . . WEND

·**TECHNIQUES OF STRUCTURED PROGRAMMING**·

Specifications define what the program is to do.

Modularity means breaking a program into small blocks of commands.

Structured design means using an orderly, modular method of designing programs.

Top-down design means starting with an overview of the way the program will work, then breaking that overview into successive levels of detail. Top-down design is one method of structured design.

Top-down programming and testing mean writing a program as a general outline, then writing and testing more detailed modules one at a time.

changed the strict line-number order of execution even more by allowing your program to repeat a block of line numbers.

This lesson is concerned with four more statements that allow a program to execute in other-than-line-number order: GOSUB (with its companion statement RETURN), ON . . . GOSUB, GOTO, and ON . . . GOTO.

GOSUB and ON . . . GOSUB are particularly important tools in organizing a program into modules, called **subroutines.** The proper use of GOSUB and ON . . . GOSUB allows a large program to be divided into manageable, smaller problems.

You will also learn that, while GOTO has some important uses, it is also the most abused statement in all of BASIC. This lesson will show when to and when not to use GOTO.

GOSUB and RETURN Allow for Modular Programming

GOSUB and RETURN allow you to formally define a block of lines in a BASIC program as a subroutine. GOSUB tells BASIC to temporarily branch to a subroutine, while RETURN tells BASIC to go back to wherever it came from before the subroutine was called by GOSUB. This is almost like having a program execute another smaller program. Study this example carefully.

```
NEW
Ok
10 PRINT "I am at line 10"
20 GOSUB 1000 ' Tells BASIC to temporarily jump to line 1000
30 PRINT "I am at line 30"
40 END
1000 REM This and lines 1010 and 1020 constitute a subroutine
1010 PRINT "   I am at line 1010"
1020 RETURN ' Tells BASIC to go back to just after the GOSUB
RUN
I am at line 10
   I am at line 1010
I am at line 30
Ok
```

Line 20 contains the statement "GOSUB 1000." This statement tells BASIC to immediately begin processing the program at line 1000.

BASIC will comply by executing line 1000 next, then 1010, and so on until it reaches a RETURN statement. RETURN tells BASIC that the subroutine is done; BASIC remembers where the GOSUB was that sent it to the subroutine and resumes execution at the next statement after the GOSUB.

The order in which the lines will be executed is thus 10, 20, 1000, 1010, 1020, 30, 40 (see Figure 6.1). Lines 1000–1020 together constitute a subroutine. (Some people refer to subroutines as *subprograms;* we will use the term *subroutine.*)

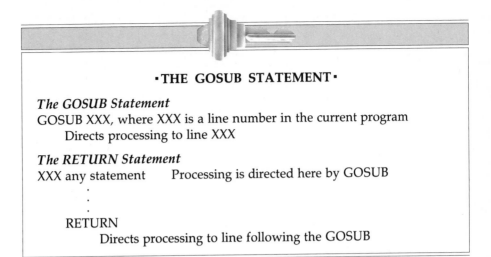

·THE GOSUB STATEMENT·

The GOSUB Statement
GOSUB XXX, where XXX is a line number in the current program
    Directs processing to line XXX

The RETURN Statement
XXX any statement   Processing is directed here by GOSUB
       .
       .
       .
    RETURN
      Directs processing to line following the GOSUB

To illustrate subroutines, suppose you are interested in reading about the platypus. You pick up an encyclopedia and flip to the section on the platypus and begin reading. Pretty soon you come to the term *marsupial*. Wishing to know more about marsupials before reading on, you put a bookmark at the page you are currently reading, then switch to the section on marsupials. When you are through reading about marsupials, you return to the page you marked and continue where you left off.

GOSUB and RETURN work much the same way. GOSUB tells BASIC to mark its current location so that it can later resume processing at this point, then to branch to some other part of the program. RETURN tells BASIC to go back to the "bookmark."

FIGURE 6.1·
Sequence of
processing for
GOSUB . . .
RETURN

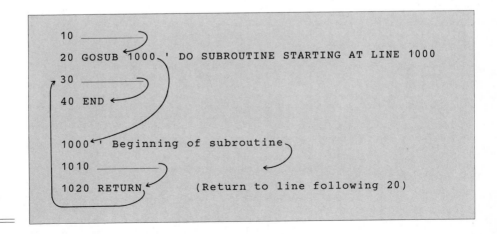

The general format of a GOSUB statement is the word *GOSUB* followed by a line number—for example, GOSUB 3050. The RETURN statement contains only the word *RETURN*. Your program can have as many subroutines as you like.

One subroutine can call another subroutine and so forth; this is called **nesting** subroutines and is very common. Let's modify the preceding example to use a nested subroutine.

First we will change line 1020 to a GOSUB statement.

```
1020 GOSUB 2000 ' A nested subroutine call
```

Next we will add the following lines:

```
1030 PRINT " I am at line 1030"
1040 RETURN ' Return to the line after the GOSUB on line 20
2000 REM This is another subroutine
2010 PRINT "        I am at line 2010"
2020 RETURN ' Return to the line after the GOSUB on line 1020
```

This program now looks as follows:

```
LIST
10 PRINT "I am at line 10"
20 GOSUB 1000 ' Tells BASIC to temporarily jump to line 1000
30 PRINT "I am at line 30"
40 END
1000 REM This and lines 1010 and 1020 constitute a subroutine
1010 PRINT "    I am at line 1010"
1020 GOSUB 2000 '  A nested subroutine call
1030 PRINT "    I am at line 1030"
1040 RETURN ' Return to the line after the GOSUB on line 20
2000 REM This is another subroutine
2010 PRINT "        I am at line 2010"
2020 RETURN ' Return to the line after the GOSUB on line 1020
RUN
I am at line 10
   I am at line 1010
      I am at line 2010
   I am at line 1030
I am at line 30
Ok
```

Figure 6.2 shows the order in which the lines were executed.

TRON and TROFF Provide for Tracing Program Flow

BASIC includes a feature called a **trace** which prints each line number as it is executed. This feature is activated by using the BASIC command TRON, which —aside from being the name of a motion picture about computer programs— means TRace ON.

TRON is useful for following the flow of execution of BASIC lines.

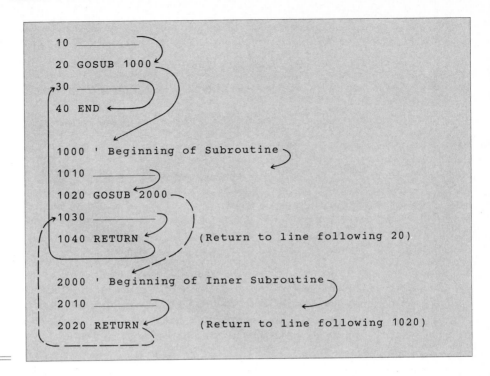

FIGURE 6.2 ·
Nested
subroutine

TRON is canceled with the command TROFF, which stands for TRace OFF. We can use this feature to list the sequence in which the lines in the preceding program are executed.

```
TRON
Ok
RUN
[10]I am at line 10
[20][1000][1010]   I am at line 1010
[1020][2000][2010]      I am at line 2010
[2020][1030]   I am at line 1030
[1040][30]I am at line 30
[40]
Ok
TROFF
Ok
```

This means that line 10 was executed (and it printed "I am at line 10"), then lines 20, 1000, 1010, and so on were executed. The numbers within the brackets indicate lines that were executed.

By examining the trace listing, we note that if subroutines are nested and BASIC encounters a RETURN statement, the program returns to the statement after the most recently executed GOSUB statement. In other words, BASIC

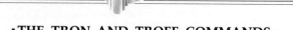

·THE TRON AND TROFF COMMANDS·

TRON—Turn on trace.
TROFF—Turn off trace.

Two commands to turn on and off tracing of program execution.

always keeps track of how it got to the current subroutine and can find its way back via RETURNs.

In the preceding example the first GOSUB sends BASIC to the subroutine on line 1000. The second GOSUB sends BASIC to the subroutine on line 2000. When BASIC finds a RETURN on line 2020, it remembers the most recent GOSUB and returns there. In this program BASIC returns from subroutine 2000 to line 1030, the statement after the calling GOSUB. When BASIC finds the second RETURN on line 1040, it remembers which GOSUB sent it to the current subroutine and returns to the statement after that GOSUB, on line 30.

Why Use GOSUB?

Even though GOSUB is such a simple statement, it is extremely powerful; here are some of the reasons:

1. GOSUB allows you to design and write your program in a "top-down" fashion.
2. If you use GOSUB, your program will be easier to read and maintain.
3. Setting up a subroutine can help avoid having to duplicate lines in different parts of your program; instead, the same subroutine can be called from as many places in your program as you please.
4. GOSUB can help overcome the 254 character per line limitation, especially in complicated IF statements.

Because each of these is so important, let's explore each in detail.

Top-Down Programming Defers Details Until Later

Suppose you want to write a program that calculates salaries and payroll deductions. A general outline of such a program might be as follows:
While there is another payroll to compute, do the following:

1. Ask for the data (hours worked, etc.)
2. Calculate gross salary.
3. Calculate all deductions.
4. Print the results.

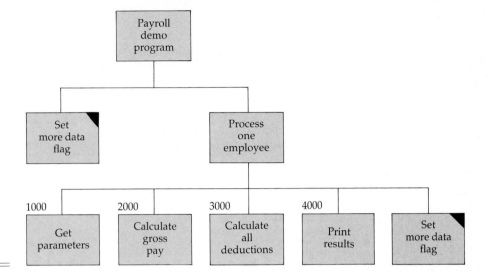

FIGURE 6.3 •
Upper level of
structure chart
for payroll
demonstration
program

We can translate this outline into the top levels of a structure chart without any need to go into greater detail (see Figure 6.3). From there, we can develop pseudocode and BASIC code for each module.

```
NEW
Ok
10 ' Payroll Demonstration
20 '
100 INPUT "Do you wish to process another employee (yes or no)"; YES.NO$
110 WHILE YES.NO$ = "yes"
120   GOSUB 1000 ' Ask user for parameters
130   GOSUB 2000 ' Calculate gross salary
140   GOSUB 3000 ' Calculate all deductions
150   GOSUB 4000 ' Print results
160   INPUT "Another employee (yes or no)"; YES.NO$
170 WEND
180 END
```

Program Stubs Allow Top-Down Testing

Will this program work? No, because there are no subroutines yet at lines 1000, 2000, 3000, and 4000. For the moment, let's put in "dummy" or "stub" subroutines at those lines that do nothing.

```
1000 ' Ask the user for parameters
1010 PRINT "Subroutine 1000, ask for parameters"
1020 RETURN
2000 ' Calculate gross salary
2010 PRINT "Subroutine 2000, calculate gross salary"
2020 RETURN
3000 ' Calculate deductions
```

```
3010 PRINT "Subroutine 3000, calculate deductions"
3020 RETURN
4000 ' Print results
4010 PRINT "Subroutine 4000, print results"
4020 RETURN
RUN
Subroutine 1000, ask for parameters
Subroutine 2000, calculate gross salary
Subroutine 3000, calculate deductions
Subroutine 4000, print results
Another employee (yes or no)? yes
Subroutine 1000, ask for parameters
Subroutine 2000, calculate gross salary
Subroutine 3000, calculate deductions
Subroutine 4000, print results
Another employee (yes or no)? no
Ok
```

We now have a working outline of the program. We can now fill in more detail at our leisure. Let's start with subroutine 1000.

```
1000 ' Ask the user for parameters
1010 INPUT "What is the employee's name";EE.NAME$
1020 INPUT "What is the employee's hourly rate"; HOURLY.RATE
1030 INPUT "How many hours did the employee work"; HOURS
1040 RETURN
```

Without altering any other modules, we have filled in the first subroutine. Let's fill in subroutine 2000, calculate gross salary.

```
2000 ' Calculate gross salary
2010 IF HOURS <= 40
        THEN LET REGULAR.HOURS = HOURS: LET OVERTIME.HOURS = 0
        ELSE LET REGULAR.HOURS = 40: LET OVERTIME.HOURS = HOURS - 40
2020 LET REGULAR.PAY = REGULAR.HOURS * HOURLY.RATE
2030 LET OVERTIME.PAY = OVERTIME.HOURS * HOURLY.RATE * 1.5
2040 LET GROSS.SALARY = REGULAR.PAY + OVERTIME.PAY
2050 RETURN
```

We don't have to fill in the details in subroutine order. In this case we might want to test the subroutines we have developed so far by filling in subroutine 4000.

```
4000 ' Print results
4010 PRINT "Employee name: ";EE.NAME$
4020 PRINT USING "Regular hours: ###.##, Overtime hours: ###.##";
            REGULAR.HOURS, OVERTIME.HOURS
4030 PRINT USING "Regular pay: $$##,###.##, Overtime pay: $$##,###.##";
            REGULAR.PAY, OVERTIME.PAY
4040 PRINT USING "Gross salary: $$##,###.##"; GROSS.SALARY
4050 RETURN
```

```
RUN
What is the employee's name? Jane Doe
What is the employee's hourly rate? 17.50
How many hours did the employee work? 50
Subroutine 3000, calculate deductions
Employee name: Jane Doe
Regular hours: 40.00, Overtime hours: 10.00
Regular pay:     $700.00, Overtime pay:    $262.50
Gross salary:    $962.50
Another employee (yes or no)? no
Ok
```

So far the program works without a hitch. It remains only to fill in the deduction calculations. Because the actual calculations involved in computing payroll taxes are complex, filling in this subroutine is left as an exercise (see Exercise 17).

Notice that we only had to deal with one part of the problem at a time. We started with a high-level definition of the program, then proceeded to fill in detail. Suppose that more detail is needed. For example, in subroutine 1000, we have not applied any input validation to the hours worked or the pay rate. Without disturbing anything else in the program, we can now fill in such detail.

```
LIST 1000-1999
1000 ' Ask the user for parameters
1010 INPUT "What is the employee's name";EE.NAME$
1020 INPUT "What is the employee's hourly rate"; HOURLY.RATE
1030 INPUT "How many hours did the employee work";HOURS
1040 RETURN
Ok
```

Change line 1020 as follows:

```
1020 GOSUB 1200 ' Get the hourly rate
```

Add the following lines:

```
1200 ' Ask the user for the hourly pay rate, which must be
1210 '     between $3.50 and $30.00
1220 INPUT "What is the Hourly Rate", HOURLY.RATE
1230 WHILE HOURLY.RATE < 3.50 OR HOURLY.RATE > 30.00
1240    INPUT "Enter a rate between 3.50 and 30.00 "; HOURLY.RATE
1250 WEND
1260 RETURN
```

Structured Program Design Lets Programs Add New Features Easily

In this way we can add new features to the program without renumbering the entire program to make room. More importantly the changes are isolated to only specific modules, so we don't have to worry so much about the impact the change might have on far-flung parts of the program.

While we are mentioning renumbering, remember that if you use the RENUM command to renumber lines of your program that contain GOSUBs, BASIC will change the numbers in your GOSUB statement so that it refers to the proper line even if its number is now different. Remember also that any reference to line numbers in a REMark will not be changed.

```
NEW
Ok
10    GOSUB 2010 ' Go to subroutine at line 2010
20    PRINT "WE ARE BACK"
30    END
2010 PRINT "We are at the subroutine"
2020 RETURN ' Return to line 20
RENUM 100
Ok
LIST
100 GOSUB 130 ' Go to the subroutine at line 2010
110 PRINT "WE ARE BACK"
120 END
130 PRINT "We are at the subroutine"
140 RETURN ' Return to line 20
```

As you can see, the line number in the GOSUB was changed correctly, but the comments are now wrong. For this reason it is good programming practice not to put line numbers in comments.

Another advantage to top-down programming is that you can test each module as you write it. By putting PRINT statements at strategic parts of the program, you can make sure that each new module works before adding the complication of another module. This greatly speeds up the testing process.

To see this, suppose that we had implemented the entire program at one shot and the results were incorrect. It would be difficult to know where to look for the problem. Suppose instead that the high-level module is thoroughly tested, and each module is thoroughly tested as it is implemented. Then whenever an error occurs, you will know where to look: the problem must be either in or directly related to the new module.

In practice, therefore, if you were writing a payroll program, you would put temporary PRINT subroutines into your program before and after a new module to make sure it worked. These temporary PRINT subroutines should print out the values of all variables used by the calling subroutine. Once the module is thoroughly tested, the GOSUB to this temporary PRINT subroutine can be removed or made into a REMark.

Here is an example of a PRINT subroutine used for debugging modules:

```
64000 'Debug Subroutine
64010 PRINT "Hourly Rate:";HOURLY.RATE
64020 PRINT ""EE.Name:";EE.NAME$
 . . .
64100 RETURN
```

GOSUB Makes Programs Easier to Read and Maintain

You have seen that using GOSUB allows you to write and test programs in a top-down fashion. The second advantage to using GOSUB that was pointed out earlier is that programs written with GOSUBs are generally easier to read and maintain than those written without GOSUB.

Look again at the payroll program. If this had been written without subroutines, it would have looked like one big program of dozens of lines. With subroutines you can read the program in stages, starting with:

```
100 INPUT "Do you wish to process another employee (yes or no)"; YES.NO$
110 WHILE YES.NO$ = "yes"
120     GOSUB 1000 ' Ask user for parameters
130     GOSUB 2000 ' Calculate gross salary
140     GOSUB 3000 ' Calculate all deductions
150     GOSUB 4000 ' Print results
160     INPUT "Another employee";YES.NO$
170 WEND
180 END
```

This gives a quick overview of the program that would be impossible without subroutines. If you want to see more detail on any one subroutine, you can jump right to that section of the program and, again, deal with only a few lines at a time. This is much easier than reading a program that does not use subroutines to organize into modules.

We also stated that modular programs with GOSUBs are easier to maintain. Maintenance involves two activities: fixing bugs and making changes.

You have already seen that by using GOSUBs you can test one subroutine at a time, thereby reducing the number of sources of error to a manageable number. This makes it less likely that your program will have any bugs when it is released. Should one or more bugs later crop up, you can hunt for them one module at a time by retesting each module separately with dummy PRINT statements. This is considerably easier than hunting for a bug that could be anywhere in a large program — hunting for a needle in a haystack is frequently easier.

You have also seen that GOSUBs make it easier to implement changes to a program. The fact that a program is organized into modules makes it likely that any given change will affect only one or a small number of modules. When changes are made, they are easier to test, since their effect is limited to certain modules.

GOSUB Reduces Duplicate Lines

Let's look at a good general-purpose subroutine. Suppose you want to have a subroutine to handle responses to a yes-no question. You could put your question into a string variable and use a subroutine as follows:

```
160 LET QUESTION$ = "Another employee": GOSUB 5000
5000 ' Ask a yes or no question. Accept "y", "yes", "Y",
5010 '      and "YES" as positive responses; "n", "no",
5020 '      "N", and "NO" as negative answers. When this
5030 '      subroutine returns, the variable YES.NO$ contains
5040 '      "yes" for any positive response, "no" for any
5050 '      negative response. Before calling this
5060 '      subroutine, put the question to be asked into
5070 '      the variable QUESTION$.
5080 LET YES.NO$ = ""
5090 WHILE YES.NO$ = ""
5100    PRINT QUESTION$; ' semicolon means cursor stays at question
5110    INPUT YES.NO$
5120    IF YES.NO$ = "y" OR YES.NO$ = "yes" OR YES.NO$ = "Y" OR
        YES.NO$ = "YES" THEN LET YES.NO$ = "yes"
5130    IF YES.NO$ = "n" OR YES.NO$ = "no" OR YES.NO$ = "N" OR
        YES.NO$ = "NO" THEN LET YES.NO$ = "no"
5140 ' If the reply is invalid, set YES.NO$ to "" to continue loop
5150    IF YES.NO$ <> "yes" AND YES.NO$ <> "no" THEN LET YES.NO$ = ""
5160 WEND
5170 RETURN
```

Most programs ask many yes-no questions. If you want to verify the answer to each one, then without using subroutines, you would have to put code similar to lines 5000–5170 in every spot in the program where a yes-no question is asked. This is annoying, because it means lot of typing. If your program asks twenty yes-no questions, and it takes five lines each time, this means a hundred lines of code just to accomplish this simple task!

Even more serious, suppose you wanted to implement a universal change for all yes-no questions? Suppose, for example, that your yes-no questions had previously only accepted "yes" and "no" as answers, and you decided that they should accept "y" and "n" as well. This means making changes in many different parts of the program.

By creating a general-purpose subroutine like the preceding, you isolate all yes-no questions (or any other functions to one subroutine that is easily maintained or changed). We can now call this subroutine from our program as we did with the line:

```
160 LET QUESTION$ = "Another employee": GOSUB 5000
```

When showing on a structure chart a subroutine that is reused a number of places, draw the box for the subroutine for each place it is called. Then darken the upper-right corner of each of these boxes to indicate that it is a reused subroutine.

Passing Parameters to Subroutines
Lets Subroutines Be General Purpose

This example illustrates the passing of variables to and from subroutines. The contents of the variable QUESTION$ is set by the program before subroutine

5000 is called. In different parts of the program, different messages will be placed in QUESTION$ to be displayed by the subroutine. QUESTION$ is an example of a **parameter** or input to the subroutine. When processing returns from subroutine 5000 the value of YES.NO$ has been set to either **yes** or **no.** This is an example of a **return value** or output of the subroutine. Theoretically, if you specify for a subroutine what its parameters (inputs) and return values (outputs) are, and what computations and actions are to take place inside the subroutine (processes), the subroutine is completely defined, independent of what occurs in the rest of the program.

As part of the comments at the beginning of every subroutine, you should clearly state what inputs and outputs apply and what processes take place, as in the comments in subroutine 5000.

GOSUBs Make IFs Readable

This last consideration is fairly minor but refreshing. Instead of an incomprehensible line like

```
100 IF A < B THEN LET C = D: LET E = F: PRINT "hello" ELSE IF A = B THEN LET G =
H * 17 + (52/I): LET C = G * 23: PRINT "goodbye" ELSE LET G = H * 17 + (13/J):
LET C = G * 23 + 12: PRINT "hello again"
```

you can write a simple line like

```
100 IF A < B THEN GOSUB 1000 ELSE IF A = B THEN GOSUB 2000 ELSE GOSUB 3000
```

The latter approach is easier to type and understand than the former. It also allows adequate room for REMs to explain what is going on — one on the IF line and as many as are needed in the subroutines themselves.

In complex IF statements it may be more than a convenience to use GOSUBs; it may be the only way to fit everything on one line. Remember: your entire IF statement, including the ELSE clause and any nested IF- ELSEs, must all fit on one line of not more than 254 characters!

The basic use of GOSUB and RETURN is pretty simple. The implications of subroutines and modules created using GOSUB are profound. GOSUB is the single most valuable tool available in BASIC for organizing a large, complicated program into manageable modules.

The following outline summarizes the specific techniques for structured design and testing that are made possible by using GOSUB.

Structured Program Design and Testing Using GOSUB

    I. Specifications
        A. Write an outline of the program in English.
        B. Define output desired and input necessary to obtain it.
        C. List processes that program must perform.
            1. Defer details of how it will do process until later.
            2. Begin to create list of variables and their names (a data dictionary).

II. Design and Testing
   A. Separate processes into three major groups of modules.
      1. Process performed once at beginning of program—initialize
      2. Repeated processes—main body of program
      3. Processes performed at end of program—termination
   B. Write each module in pseudocode.
      1. Begin at highest level (manager modules).
      2. Defer details of lower level (grunt modules) until later.
   C. Translate pseudocode into BASIC statements.
      1. Begin at highest level.
         a. For every subroutine called at this level, put in a "stub" or "dummy" subroutine.
         b. Test program at this level before proceeding further.
         c. Use temporary PRINT statements inserted in strategic locations as needed.
      2. Take a subroutine, replace the stub, and write a code for it.
         a. If new subroutines are called, write stubs for them.
         b. Retest program.
         c. Remove any temporary PRINT statements that are no longer needed.
      3. Repeat the process until each subroutine has been coded and tested.

ON . . . GOSUB Directs Processing to Selected Subroutine

The ON . . . GOSUB statement is very similar to the GOSUB statement, but it provides the ability to select which subroutine to call based on an **index,** where index is a number, numeric variable, or numeric expression.

```
NEW
Ok
10 LET KEEP.GOING% = 1 ' while loop will continue as long as this is 1
20 WHILE KEEP.GOING% = 1
30     CLS
40     PRINT "Customer record maintenance menu"
50     PRINT TAB(10);"1. Stop the program"
60     PRINT TAB(10);"2. Enter a customer record"
70     PRINT TAB(10);"3. Delete a customer record"
80     PRINT TAB(10);"4. Change a customer record"
90     INPUT "Select an option:",CHOICE%
100    ON CHOICE% GOSUB 1000,2000,3000,4000
110 WEND
120 END
1000 ' Stop the program
1010 LET KEEP.GOING% = 0
1020 RETURN
```

In addition to the portion of the program just shown, subroutines would be placed at lines 2000, 3000, and 4000 for customer record creation, deletion, and

•THE ON . . . GOSUB STATEMENT•

ON N GOSUB XXX, YYY, ZZZ . . . where XXX, YYY, ZZZ, and so on are line numbers in the current program.

IF N is 1, processing will be directed to the subroutine beginning at the first line number after GOSUB.

IF N is 2, processing will be directed to the subroutine beginning at the second line number after GOSUB.

And so on.

The RETURN at the end of each subroutine will return processing to the line following the ON . . . GOSUB.

modification, respectively. This program is an example of a **menu-driven program** in which the user chooses from a set of options displayed on the screen. Menus are programmers tools for making programs easy to use.

Menu-Driven Programs Using ON . . . GOSUB

The ON . . . GOSUB statement on line 100 selects which subroutine to execute based on the value of CHOICE%. If CHOICE% is 1, the program calls the first subroutine on the list, subroutine 1000. If CHOICE% is 2, the program calls subroutine 2000, and so forth. The whole program is one big WHILE loop that

1. Displays the menu.
2. Asks the user to choose an option.
3. Executes the subroutine corresponding to the option chosen.
4. Goes back to step 1 until the user says to stop.

You may wonder what happens if the user does not enter a number from 1 to 4, inclusive. There are two possibilities. If the value is less than 0 or greater than 255, BASIC will stop processing and give the error message "Illegal Function Call." If the value given is within this limit, but greater than the number of items in the list (here, 4), or is 0, BASIC ignores the ON . . . GOSUB and continues processing with the next line (here, line 110).

For this reason, it is good practice to validate your index before using ON . . . GOSUB. One possible set of code that will validate the index is the following:

```
90 INPUT "Select an option:", CHOICE%
92 WHILE CHOICE% < 1 OR CHOICE% > 4
94    INPUT "Please enter a 1, 2, 3, or 4"; CHOICE%
96 WEND
```

As you can see from subroutine 1000, each subroutine takes the same form regardless of whether it is intended to be called using GOSUB or ON . . . GOSUB; that is, it must have a RETURN statement at the end that returns the program to the statement after the GOSUB or ON . . . GOSUB. In fact, your program can call any subroutine using GOSUBs, ON . . . GOSUBs, or both, depending on the need of each part of the program.

Notice that ON . . . GOSUB is a convenient alternative to a complicated IF-ELSE chain. Line 100 of the preceding program could have been written like this:

```
100 IF CHOICE% = 1 THEN GOSUB 1000 ELSE IF CHOICE% = 2 THEN GOSUB 2000 ELSE
        IF CHOICE% = 3 THEN GOSUB 3000 ELSE IF CHOICE% = 4 THEN GOSUB 4000
```

FIGURE 6.4 ·
Comparison of
nested IF and
ON . . .
GOSUB. The
half-circle is a
flowchart symbol
used for
ON . . .
GOSUB.

This is obviously not as easy to read as an ON . . . GOSUB. Figure 6.4 shows a flowchart of this statement and its corresponding flowchart of a similar ON . . . GOSUB.

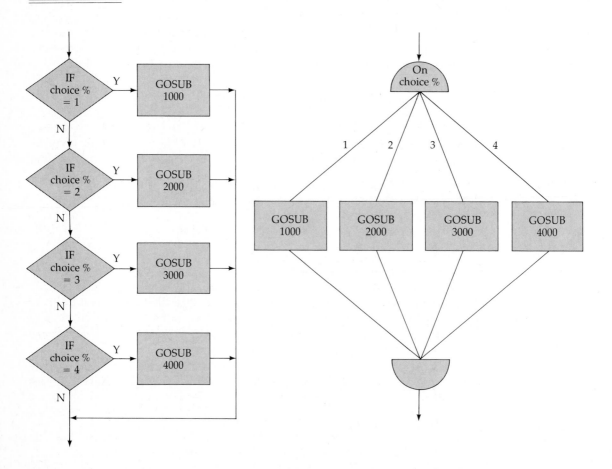

A final note on ON . . . GOSUB: the "index" (CHOICE% in the example) may be a number, a variable, or a mathematical expression. Although in most cases the index used with ON . . . GOSUB will be an integer it is not required to be one. If it is not an integer, BASIC will round it to the closest integer while processing the statement. The only restriction is that the number must have a value between 0 and 255 or BASIC will give you an error message.

As an exercise try putting stubs in for subroutines 2000, 3000, and 4000, which do nothing but print a message saying that the program reached the subroutine, then execute the program.

All of the arguments in favor of using the GOSUB statement apply equally well to the ON . . . GOSUB statement.

Common Errors with GOSUB

One of the most common errors in writing programs using GOSUB is forgetting to place RETURN at the end of the subroutine. If there is no RETURN, BASIC will continue processing with the next statement until a RETURN is encountered or the end of the program is reached. While this causes no syntax error, the results are probably not what you wanted.

Another less obvious error can occur when your program calls one subroutine from another. In the following example the subroutine beginning at line 50 calls the subroutine at line 90. The subroutine at line 90 in turn calls the subroutine at line 50. This creates an endless loop. The "Out of memory" error message occurred because BASIC sets aside a certain amount of memory that it uses to keep track of the line to which it must return for each GOSUB. The endless looping in the example exhausted this space.

```
10 ' Program to demonstrate endless repetition of subroutines
20   GOSUB 50 ' go to first subroutine
30   END
40 ' This subroutine calls another which in turn calls it
50 PRINT "First ";
60 GOSUB 90    ' go to second subroutine
70 RETURN
80 '    This is the second subroutine
90 PRINT "Second ";
100 GOSUB 50   ' go back to first subroutine
110 RETURN


run
First Second First Second First Second First Second First Second First Second
First Second First Second First Second First Second First Second First Second
First Second First Second First Second First Second First Second First
Out of memory in 90
Ok
```

Avoid Using GOTO

For such a simple statement, GOTO has generated more controversy in the computer industry than any other statement. What is GOTO? Here is an example to illustrate how GOTO works.

```
NEW
Ok
10 PRINT "I am at line 10"
20 GOTO 100
30 PRINT "I am at line 30"
100 PRINT "I am at line 100"
110 END
RUN
I am at line 10
I am at line 100
Ok
```

Line 20, GOTO 100, told BASIC to go to line 100 immediately, skipping any lines in between the current line and that line. The order of execution of the lines is, therefore, 10, 20, 100, 110 — with 30 left unexecuted.

GOTO is similar to GOSUB in that it causes BASIC to branch to another, possibly distant, part of the program. Unlike GOSUB, there is no analogy to the RETURN statement for use with GOTO. Once you use GOTO to jump to a new line, BASIC does not keep track of how it got to that line and cannot return unless you use another GOTO explicitly to get back.

Although there was considerable controversy about GOTOs in the late 1960s, today virtually every computer expert agrees that GOTOs should be used sparingly in BASIC programs and only under specific circumstances. Most of the time when a GOTO could be used, an IF, WHILE, FOR, or GOSUB can and should be used instead. If you feel you must use a GOTO, follow these rules to guide you in using it properly:

1. See if there is a way to avoid using GOTO by using IF, FOR, WHILE, or GOSUB.
2. Use GOTO only to branch downward in your program; for example, if your GOTO is on line 100, do not jump to a line before line 100, only after.

·THE GOTO STATEMENT·

GOTO XXX, where XXX is a line number in the current program

Directs processing to line number XXX.
Does not provide a way to get back.

3. Do not use GOTO to jump to a spot in the program far removed from the line on which the GOTO occurs. A reasonable guide is to avoid jumping more than roughly ten lines ahead. Use subroutines if necessary to enforce this rule.
4. Never use a GOTO to jump out of the middle of a FOR loop, a WHILE loop, or a subroutine. Always exit through the corresponding NEXT, WEND, or RETURN.
5. Never use a GOTO to jump into the middle of a FOR loop, a WHILE loop, or a subroutine.
6. You may use GOTOs within a loop to jump directly to the NEXT or WEND at the end of the loop.
7. You may use GOTOs within a subroutine to jump directly to the RETURN command for that subroutine.

Almost all of the valid uses of GOTO in BASIC fall into category 6 or 7 — that is, branching immediately to the end of a loop or subroutine. This is called a **forward transfer of control.** To understand how to avoid GOTO, consider the following problem: Within a subroutine, how can you branch around a series of statements? You should use only one RETURN in a subroutine. Although IBM BASIC will allow more than one RETURN, doing so makes the logic more difficult to follow and the program more difficult to test. Here are two ways to handle this.

1. A valid use of GOTO

   ```
   1000 ' This is a subroutine
   1010 IF SOME.CONDITION$ <> "yes" THEN GOTO 1500
   1020 ' a long series of statements
      .
      .
      .
   1500 RETURN ' Return to main program
   ```

   The GOTO was used to direct the flow of processing to the line containing the RETURN statement.
2. A better way that doesn't use GOTO

   ```
   1000 ' This is a subroutine
   1010 IF SOME.CONDITION$ = "yes" THEN GOSUB 2000
   1500 RETURN ' Return to main program
   2000 ' Subroutine with a long series of statements
      .
      .
      .
   2500 RETURN ' Return to Line 1500
   ```

   In this case the test was reversed, and the process was written as a subroutine.

Even these uses should be limited; GOSUBs wisely used make for better programs. As for other uses, the best rule of all is number 1: if you don't use GOTO, you can't abuse it!

Example of Bad Code Misusing GOTOs

```
10 'This is an example of unstructured, "spaghetti" code
20 'See if you can figure out what this program does
30 GOTO 130
40 GOTO 100
50 LET B = A * (A + 1)/2
60 IF B > 100 THEN GOTO 200
70 PRINT A,B
80 LET AT = AT + A
90 LET BT = BT + B
100 IF A > 10 THEN GOTO 200
110 LET A = A + 1
120 GOTO 50
130 LET A = 0
140 LET AT = 0
150 LET BT = 0
160 GOTO 40
170 PRINT "------------------------"
180 PRINT AT,BT
190 GOTO 210
200 GOTO 170
210 END
```

Now imagine that, instead of being only 21 lines long, this program and others like it were 21,000 lines long, and you had the job of fixing it. It would take you a long time just to figure out what the program is supposed to do, and then it would take you an even longer time to discover why it does not do what it is supposed to. And you could never be sure that you had tested all the program.

How much easier it is to understand the following version of the program, written in a structured fashion. (And for those of you readers who test out the first version, you will note that the first version has a subtle error. The test in line 100 for ending the loop is incorrect. The program prints the information for 1 through 11 instead of 1 through 10.)

```
10    'This is an example of using structured programming techniques
20    ' to make a program understandable and maintainable
30    ' This program prints each of the integers 1 through 10, along with
40    ' the sum of all integers up to and including that number.
50    ' It then prints the accumulated totals of each column.
60    GOSUB 1000           'initialize the totals
70    FOR A = 1 TO 10      'column a
80       GOSUB 2000        'compute and print sum of digits, accumulate totals
90    NEXT A
100   GOSUB 3000           'print totals
110   END
120   '
1000  '                Initialize
1010  LET TOTAL.A = 0           'accumulator for A's
1020  LET TOTAL.B = 0           'accumulator for B's
```

```
1030  RETURN
1040  '
2000  'compute and print sum of digits, accumulate totals
2010  LET B = A * (A + 1)/ 2      'sum of digits 1, . . . ,a
2020  LET TOTAL.A = TOTAL.A + A
2030  LET TOTAL.B = TOTAL.B + B
2040  PRINT A,B
2050  RETURN
2060  '
3000  '              print totals
3010  PRINT "-------------------"
3020  PRINT TOTAL.A, TOTAL.B
3030  RETURN
3040  '              END OF LISTING
```

ON . . . GOTO Is Also Undesirable

Only slightly less harmful than GOTO is ON . . . GOTO. ON . . . GOTO is identical to ON . . . GOSUB except that it executes a GOTO to the line number listed, not a GOSUB. As with GOTO, there is no way back from an ON . . . GOTO jump analogous to the RETURN used with ON . . . GOSUB. Whenever you are tempted to use an ON . . . GOTO, stop to first consider whether an ON . . . GOSUB will work instead; 99 times out of 100 it will do just as well.

Careful Planning and Testing Pay Off

At this point while you are writing simple programs, this emphasis on documentation, structured design, and structured programming may feel like it's more trouble than it's worth. But as many programmers have discovered, developing these habits as you are learning will save you and others hours of frustrating toil as you create and maintain complex programs.

·THE ON . . . GOTO STATEMENT·

ON N GOTO XXX, YYY, ZZZ, . . . , where XXX, YYY, ZZZ are line numbers in the current program.

IF N equals 1, processing is directed to line XXX
IF N equals 2, processing is directed to line YYY.
And so on.

Does not provide any way to get back.

•PARABLES FOR PROGRAMMERS•

The Tortoise and the Hare

The Hare challenged the Tortoise to a race one day, but it was not to be an ordinary footrace. The Hare claimed that he could write programs faster than anyone on earth and wanted to prove it by putting the plodding Tortoise to shame.

They selected a very difficult problem, then both set out to write the programs. The Tortoise started by completing the specifications; the Hare plunged right in and started writing BASIC statements. The Tortoise then wrote a top-down design; the Hare snorted as he raced further into the program. The Tortoise methodically wrote the program in a top-down fashion, thoroughly testing the program as he went. The Hare, yelling, "Damn the torpedos, full speed ahead," just began by plunging into details.

It seemed to all the spectators that the Tortoise had no chance to win the race, or even to make a respectable showing, for the Hare was almost through by the time the Tortoise began his top-down writing and testing. But then a curious thing happened. The Tortoise kept plodding along, filling in one subroutine at a time, making slow but steady progress. The Hare, meanwhile, wrote slower and slower as his program grew. He started sweating as complicated bugs cropped up. In his panic he started writing more and more statements at a shot before testing, which only made the situation worse.

Three times the Hare proudly proclaimed that his program was finished, only to have the judge each time find a bug that had to be fixed. Finally, as night fell, the Tortoise turned his program over to the judge. It worked the first time. The Tortoise wandered off to eat a sumptuous dinner and go to bed, while the Hare continued frantically working on his program far into the night. By morning, the Hare had given up, "Bah," he said to the Tortoise, "I was just unlucky. If I hadn't run into those bugs, I would have won by a mile." The Tortoise just smiled.

MORAL: It pays to be methodical.

How to Design a Program

Here is an eight-step procedure to design and write programs. The eight steps are as follows:

1. Define the specifications and develop preliminary test data.
   UNTIL the structure chart is complete

    2. Decompose the functions.

    3. Develop the structure chart.

    4. Develop the data dictionary.

END-UNTIL

5. Write pseudocode for each module of the structure chart.

UNTIL the full program is debugged

    6. Code BASIC for each module from the pseudocode.

    7. Test using top-down testing.

END-UNTIL

8. Document the complete program by

- Adding REMarks in the code describing the program and its operation.
- Adding flowcharts where necessary.

Define the Specifications and Develop Test Data

The most common programming error is also the most fatal: *solving the wrong problem.* Usually the person requesting the program has only a fuzzy idea of what he or she wants, and so, after the results of the program are used, the program needs to be changed to meet the requestor's real needs.

In the field you may be given absolute specifications (such is the case if your program segment must interface with other program segments). But most likely, you will be working from a set of specifications that are not set in concrete. So you should program for great flexibility. Quite likely, the program will be changed many times over its life.

As part of your review of the specifications, develop some preliminary test data. These test data should exercise all the conditions the data might conceivably take. For example, if you are writing a payroll program, your test data for hours worked might include the values of $-40, 0, 40, 39, 41,$ and 200 hours. (Note that there are only 168 hours in a week, and so 200 represents an abnormal high condition.)

These next two steps are repeated until you have developed a satisfactory structure chart.

Decompose the Functions

A function is some task that must be done as part of completing the program specifications. Most business problems need functions to do these three major tasks:

1. Tasks that are done once only, at the start of processing

2. Tasks that are done repetitively, once per data record

3. Tasks that are done once only, at the end of processing

Arrange the Functions into a Structure Chart

Arrange the functions you have decomposed under the proper module (things done once at start, repetitively, or once at end).

Develop the Data Dictionary

Create a list of all of the variables you will be using. This is called the **data dictionary.** Separate the list by kinds of variables, such as input variable names, constants, and working variables such as accumulators, and so on. Refer to this list as you write the pseudocode and program code so that you are sure to spell the variable name the same way each time it is used. This document will become part of your documentation for the program.

For Each Module of the Structure Chart, Write Pseudocode

This is self-explanatory. Typically, each module will require only a few lines of pseudocode.

For Each Module, Starting from the Top, Translate the Pseudocode in BASIC

Top-Down Test

Debug your code as you enter each module, module by module, using top-down testing. Use the test data that you created in the first step to verify the operation of your program.

Add Documentation

The documentation for your program should include:

1. Structure chart
2. Data dictionary
3. Pseudocode
4. Program listing

Some programmers prefer placing the data dictionary as remarks in the program. This is particularly helpful if the variable names are not self-explanatory.

Review the program listing, inserting remarks where they will help the understanding of the program or aid in separating sections of the program.

If any module of your program is confusing to others, add a flowchart to your external documentation.

THE STORY'S END

Pat and Chris are back in the cafeteria, discussing modularity and structured programming.

PAT: You were sure right, Chris. GOSUB really makes it easy to organize programs. The ABCs book talked about a lot of the same things we talked about: modularity, top-down design, top-down testing. I understand a little better what you said the other day about treating programming as an engineering discipline, not just writing instructions in BASIC.

CHRIS: Most people who hear these ideas resist them at first, but later on, when they see them in action, they quickly come around.

PAT: The book really stressed the evils of the GOTO statement. Is GOTO really all that bad?

CHRIS: Some of the biggest disaster stories I've been involved with in programming have been the result of indiscriminate use of GOTOs. Yes, they really are all that bad. In fact, there are some modern programming languages that don't even provide the equivalent of a GOTO.

PAT: You said we could work through a real example once I mastered the lesson on GOSUB.

CHRIS: And so we shall. Have you a pet project we can use for illustration?

PAT: Well, now that you mention it, there is a program I've had on the back burner for a while. What I want is a program that allows me to solve a variety of financial calculations.

CHRIS: What calculations?

PAT: There are four calculations I'm interested in. First, given an interest rate, a term, and an investment amount, I want to calculate the future value of the investment. This is the old formula

$$FV = PV * (1 + I) \wedge N.$$

Second, I want to turn that formula around. Given the desired future value, the interest rate, and the term, I want to calculate the amount I have to invest today. This version of the formula is

$$PV = FV/(1 + I) \wedge N$$

Third, given an interest rate, a term, and a periodic payment amount, I want to calculate the future value of those payments at the end of the term. The formula for this is

$$FV = PMT * ((1 + I) \wedge N - 1)/I$$

Fourth, given the future value, interest rate, and term, I want to know what periodic payment to make to achieve that future value. This formula is

$$PMT = FV * (I/((1 + I) \wedge N - 1))$$

CHRIS: That's all pretty straightforward. It also looks like it would be a useful program for an accountant like yourself.

PAT: I can't count the number of times I go through similar calculations. What I need is a single program that allows me to do any of these. Unfortunately, until now I haven't been able to figure out how to organize a program that does more than one of these calculations.

CHRIS: Enter GOSUB and ON . . . GOSUB!

PAT: Right.

CHRIS: What we can do is set up subroutines for each calculation, then provide a menu followed by an ON . . . GOSUB that branches to the appropriate subroutine.

PAT: Like the "customer record maintenance" menu in the ABCs book?

CHRIS: Yes.

Program Specifications

Pat and Chris wrote specifications based on the formulas above, then proceeded to design the program.

Functions

From the specifications, they made the following list of functions.
While the user wants to continue, do the following;

A. Display menu of options; ask which is desired
B. Perform the desired computation
  1. Compute future value given present value
  2. Compute present value given future value
  3. Compute future value given payment amount
  4. Compute payment amount given future value

Structure Chart

The next step was the structure chart. Their final version is shown in Figure 6.5.

Data Dictionary

They selected the following names for the variables they would need to perform the calculations:

FV	Future value (double precision)
PV	Present value (double precision)
PMT	Amount of payment
APR	Entered annual percentage rate of interest, as a decimal number
ANNUAL.PERIODS	Entered number of compounding periods per year
YEARS	Entered number of years for the investment
I	Periodic interest rate, APR/ANNUAL.PERIODS
N	Number of periods of the investment, YEARS * ANNUAL.PERIODS
CHOICE	The value of the menu option selected by the user (integer)

Pseudocode

For each module of the structure chart, they wrote pseudocode before starting to code the program. As they did this, they realized that the interest rate and number

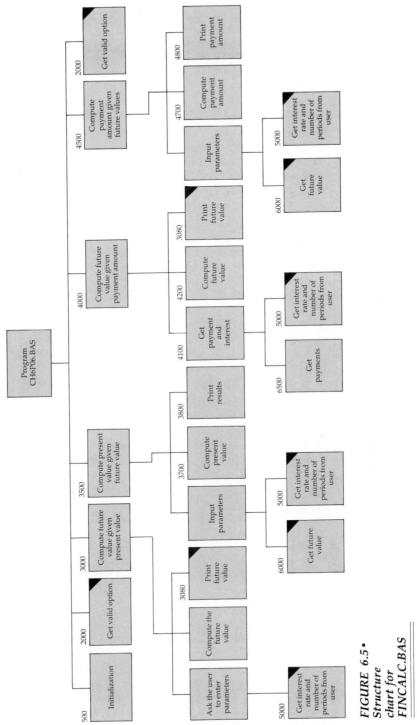

FIGURE 6.5 ▪
Structure chart for FINCALC.BAS

of periods would have to be entered for all four types of computations. Chris and Pat decided to set up one subroutine that would handle this function for all four computations. They noted this subroutine in the pseudocode and added it to the structure chart.

MAIN-LINE
    Do INITIALIZATION
    WHILE CHOICE is not equal to 5 (5 indicates ready to end program)
        ON CHOICE GOSUB
            CHOICE = 1: Do COMPUTE-FV-GIVEN-PV
            CHOICE = 2: Do COMPUTE-PV-GIVEN-FV
            CHOICE = 3: Do COMPUTE-FV-GIVEN-PMT
            CHOICE = 4: Do COMPUTE-PMT-GIVEN-FV
      Do GET-VALID-OPTION
    WEND
    END
INITIALIZATION
    DEFINT C (CHOICE is integer)
    DEFDBL F, P (FV, PV and PMT are double precision)
    KEY OFF
    Do GET-VALID-OPTION
GET-VALID-OPTION
    Clear Screen
    PRINT Options 1 through 5
    INPUT CHOICE
    WHILE CHOICE is less than 1 or greater than 5
        PRINT message to reenter
        INPUT CHOICE
    WEND
COMPUTE-FV-GIVEN-PV
    INPUT Present Value
    Do GET-INTEREST-RATE-AND-NUMBER-OF-PERIODS
    Compute Future Value given Present Value
    Do PRINT-FUTURE-VALUE
COMPUTE-PV-GIVEN-FV
    Do GET-FUTURE-VALUE
    Do GET-INTEREST-RATE-AND-NUMBER-OF-PERIODS
    Compute Present Value given Future Value
    Do PRINT-PRESENT-VALUE
COMPUTE-FV-GIVEN-PMT
    Do GET-PAYMENT-AMOUNT
    Do GET-INTEREST-RATE-AND-NUMBER-OF-PERIODS
    Compute Future Value given Payment Amount
    Do PRINT-FUTURE-VALUE
COMPUTE-PMT-GIVEN-FV
    Do GET-FUTURE-VALUE
    Do GET-INTEREST-RATE-AND-NUMBER-OF-PERIODS

      Compute Payment Amount given Future Value
      Do PRINT-PAYMENT-AMOUNT
<u>GET-INTEREST-RATE-AND-NUMBER-OF-PERIODS</u>
      INPUT Annual Percentage Rate (APR)
      WHILE APR less than or equal to 0 or greater than or equal to 1
         Display message to enter as decimal
         INPUT APR
      WEND
      INPUT Number of Compounding Periods per year (ANNUAL.PERIODS)
      WHILE ANNUAL.PERIODS is less than or equal to 0 or greater than 366
         Display message to enter number between 1 and 366
         INPUT ANNUAL.PERIODS
      WEND
      Compute Periodic Interest Rate (I)
      INPUT Number of Years for Investment (YEARS)
      WHILE Years is less than 0 or greater than 99
         Display message to enter number between 1 and 99
         INPUT YEARS
      WEND
      Compute Total Number of Compounding Periods (N)
<u>PRINT-FUTURE-VALUE</u>
      PRINT Future Value
      Wait for User to press ENTER
<u>GET-FUTURE-VALUE</u>
      INPUT Future Value (FV)
      WHILE FV is less than or equal to 0
         Display message that FV must be positive
         INPUT FV
      WEND
<u>PRINT-PRESENT-VALUE</u>
      PRINT Present Value (PV)
      Wait for User to press ENTER
<u>GET-PAYMENT-AMOUNT</u>
      INPUT Payment Amount (PMT)
      WHILE PMT is less than or equal to zero
         Display message that PMT must be positive
         INPUT PMT
      WEND
<u>PRINT-PAYMENT-AMOUNT</u>
      PRINT Payment Amount
      Wait for User to press ENTER

Program Listing

They then wrote this outline as the beginning of a BASIC program. Line numbers less than 1000 were used for comments; the instructions began on line number 1000.

```
1000 ' ------------ Main Line of Program ---------------------------
1010 GOSUB 1500                    'Initialization
1030 WHILE CHOICE <> 5
1040     CLS
1050     ON CHOICE GOSUB 3000,3500,4000,4500
1060     GOSUB 2000               'get valid option
1070 '
1080 WEND
1090 END
1100 ' -------------- END OF PROCESSING -----------------------
1110 '
1120 ' =============================================================
1500 ' -------------- Initialization ------------------------
1510 DEFINT C
1520 DEFDBL F,P
1530 KEY OFF                      'turn off key display on 25th line
1540 GOSUB 2000                   'get valid option
1550 RETURN
1560 '
1570 ' =============================================================
2000 ' ------- Display menu and ask user which option is desired.----
2010 CLS
2020 PRINT "Financial Calculator Options"
2030 PRINT TAB(10) "1. Compute future value given present value"
2040 PRINT TAB(10) "2. Compute present value given future value"
2050 PRINT TAB(10) "3. Compute future value given payment amount"
2060 PRINT TAB(10) "4. Compute payment amount given future value"
2070 PRINT TAB(10) "5. End the program"
2080 '
2090 INPUT "Please select your option (1,2,3,4, or 5) ",CHOICE
2100 WHILE CHOICE < 1 OR CHOICE > 5
2110     PRINT
2120     INPUT "Please enter a 1 or a 2 or a 3 or a 4 or a 5 . . . ",CHOICE
2130 WEND
2140 RETURN
2150 '
2160 ' =============================================================
3000 ' ------- Compute future value given present value -------
3010 PRINT "Subroutine 3000, compute future value given present value"
3020 RETURN ' -------------------------------------------------
3500 ' --------- Compute present value given future value -----
3510 PRINT "Subroutine 3500, compute present value given future value"
3520 RETURN ' -------------------------------------------------
4000 ' ----- Compute future value given payment amount -------
4010 PRINT "Subroutine 4000, compute future value given payment amount"
4020 RETURN ' -------------------------------------------------
4500 ' ------- Compute payment amount given future values ----
4510 PRINT "Subroutine 4500, compute payment amount given future value"
4520 RETURN ' -------------------------------------------------
```

From this much of an outline they ran the program to make sure that the menu worked and that the right subroutines were being reached at the right time.

Next Pat and Chris designed the first computation module, "compute future value given present value," or COMPUTE-FV-GIVEN-PV, as they called it in their pseudocode. Armed with this, they went to the next level of detail in their program.

```
3000 ' ------- Compute future value given present value -------
3010 '
3020 INPUT "What is the present value";PV
3030 INPUT "What is the annual percentage rate"; APR
3040 INPUT "Number of compounding periods per year";ANNUAL.PERIODS
3050 LET I = APR/ANNUAL.PERIODS
3060 INPUT "Number of periods of investment";N
3070 ' ----------- Compute the future value -----------------
3080 LET FV = PV * (1 + I) ^ N
3090 PRINT "Future Value is "; FV ' Print out the results
3100 RETURN
```

Chris and Pat chose to be careful, testing the program thoroughly before proceeding further. They then wrote the subroutine to input and validate the interest rate and number of periods.

```
5000 ' -- Get interest rate and number of periods per year from user -----
5010 INPUT "What is the annual percentage rate (as a decimal)"; APR
5020 WHILE APR <= 0 OR APR >= 1
5030    INPUT "Enter as a decimal number; (Enter .10 for 10%) ", APR
5040 WEND
5050 '
5060 ' -- Get the number of compounding periods per year --------
5070 '
5080 INPUT "How many compounding periods are in a year"; ANNUAL.PERIODS
5090 WHILE ANNUAL.PERIODS <= 0 OR ANNUAL.PERIODS > 366
5100    INPUT "Please enter a number between 1 and 366, inclusive",
              ANNUAL.PERIODS
5110 WEND
5120 LET I = APR/ANNUAL.PERIODS      ' Compute the periodic interest rate
5130 '
5140 ' Enter the number of periods in the investment
5150 '
5160 INPUT "How many years does the investment run"; YEARS
5170 WHILE YEARS < 0 OR YEARS > 99
5180    INPUT "Please enter a number between 1 and 99, inclusive ", YEARS
5190 WEND
5200 LET N = YEARS * ANNUAL.PERIODS
5210 RETURN
```

They modified subroutine 3000 to call this subroutine.

```
3000 ' ------- Compute future value given present value -------
3010 '
3020 INPUT "What is the present value";PV
3030 GOSUB 5000              ' get interest rate and number of periods
3070 ' ----------- Compute the future value ----------------
3080 LET FV = PV * (1 + I) ^ N
3090 PRINT "Future Value is "; FV ' Print out the results
3100 RETURN
```

Once again, they thoroughly tested the program with the new subroutine in place, fixing bugs as they were found.

The process seemed to Pat to be a little cumbersome, but then they began work on the next module that computed present value. It was then that Pat appreciated the value of modularity. They had already written and tested subroutines that asked for the interest rate, the number of periods, and the number of years. They had only to add another subroutine that asked for the future value, then call the subroutines from wherever they were needed.

Pat also was amazed at how few bugs there were using this top-down method and how easy it was to fix bugs when they did occur. Because they tested each module as it was added, the bugs were almost always isolated to the new module, which was never more than a few lines long.

Best of all, the pace was steady. From the time they started to the time they finished, Pat and Chris ran into no stumbling blocks that brought them to a halt. Chris seemed to take this in stride, but it was a radical change from Pat's experience in developing programs this size. Pat was used to forging ahead quickly, then bogging down when some complicated problem arose. With modules simply defined and small in size, it seemed that complicated problems almost melted by being successively reduced into simpler problems.

Following is the final version of the program. Once they finished testing it, Pat never found another bug. In fact, it proved so easy to maintain that Pat was later able to add several more types of computations to the same program in practically no time. Pat was convinced that modularity and top-down programming and testing were the only right way to program.

```
10   ' Program Name : FINCALC.BAS
20   ' Date Written : 06/17/88
30   ' Written by:    Chris and Pat
40   ' Program Description:
50   '          User may select one of the following calculations
60   '              1. Compute Future Value given the Present Value
70   '              2. Compute Present Value given the Future Value
80   '              3. Compute Future Value given the Payment Amount
90   '              4. Compute Payment Amount given the Future Value
100  ' Program History:
110  '              none to date
500  ' Variables Used:
```

```
510  '    Entered for all calculations
520  '         APR Annual Percentage Rate (as a decimal)
530  '         ANNUAL.PERIODS Number of compounding periods per year
540  '         YEARS Number of years investment runs
550  '    Other variables calculated or entered
560  '         FV      Future Value
570  '         PV      Present Value
580  '         PMT     Payment Amount
590  '         I       Interest Rate per Period
600  '         N       Number of Compounding Periods
610  '         CHOICE Menu Option selected by user
620  '
1000 ' ------------ Main Line of Program ----------------------------
1010 GOSUB 1500                    'Initialization
1030 WHILE CHOICE <> 5
1040    CLS
1050    ON CHOICE GOSUB 3000,3500,4000,4500
1060    GOSUB 2000                 'get valid option
1070 '
1080 WEND
1090 END
1100 ' ------------- END OF PROCESSING -----------------------
1110 '
1120 ' ===========================================================
1500 ' ------------- Initialization -------------------------
1510 DEFINT C
1520 DEFDBL F,P
1530 KEY OFF                       'turn off key display on 25th line
1540 GOSUB 2000                    'get valid option
1550 RETURN
1560 '
1570 ' ===========================================================
2000 ' ------- Display menu and ask user which option is desired.----
2010 CLS
2020 PRINT "Financial Calculator Options"
2030 PRINT TAB(10) "1. Compute future value given present value"
2040 PRINT TAB(10) "2. Compute present value given future value"
2050 PRINT TAB(10) "3. Compute future value given payment amount"
2060 PRINT TAB(10) "4. Compute payment amount given future value"
2070 PRINT TAB(10) "5. End the program"
2080 '
2090 INPUT "Please select your option (1,2,3,4, or 5) ",CHOICE
2100 WHILE CHOICE < 1 OR CHOICE > 5
2110    PRINT
2120    INPUT "Please enter a 1 or a 2 or a 3 or a 4 or a 5 . . . ",CHOICE
2130 WEND
2140 RETURN
2150 '
2160 ' ===========================================================
```

```
3000 ' ------- Compute future value given present value -------
3010 '
3020 INPUT "What is the present value"; PV
3030 GOSUB 5000                ' get interest rate and number of periods
3040 LET FV = PV * (1 + I) ^ N  ' compute Future Value
3050 GOSUB 3080                ' print Future Value
3060 RETURN
3070 '
3080 ' ------------- Print Future Value-------------------
3090 '
3100 PRINT USING "The future value is ##,###,###.##"; FV
3110 INPUT ''Press ENTER key to continue . . . ", DUMMY$
3120 RETURN
3130 '
3140 ' ==============================================================
3500 ' --------- Compute present value given future value -----
3510 CLS
3520 GOSUB 6000                ' get Future Value
3530 GOSUB 5000                ' get Interest Rate and Number of Periods
3540 LET PV = FV/(I + 1) ^ N ' compute Present Value
3550 GOSUB 3580                ' print Present Value
3560 RETURN
3570 '
3580 ' --------- print Present Value -------------------
3590 PRINT USING "Present value: #####,##.##";PV
3600 INPUT "Press ENTER to continue . . . ",DUMMY$
3610 RETURN
3620 '
3630 ' ==============================================================
4000 ' ----- Compute future value given payment amount -------
4010 GOSUB 6500                ' get Payment Amount
4020 GOSUB 5000                ' get Interest Rate and Number of Periods
4030 LET FV = PMT * (((I + 1) ^ N) - 1)/I' compute Future Value from PMT
4040 GOSUB 3080                ' print Future Value
4050 RETURN
4060 '
4070 ' ==============================================================
4500 ' ------- Compute payment amount given future value ----
4510 GOSUB 6000                'get Future Value
4520 GOSUB 5000                ' get Interest Rate and Number of Periods
4530 LET PMT = FV/(((( I + 1) ^ N) - 1)/I)
4540 GOSUB 4570                ' print the Payment Amount
4550 RETURN
4560 '
4570 ' ---------- print Payment Amount ----------
4580 PRINT USING "Payment amount: ########,#.##"; PMT
4590 INPUT "Press ENTER to continue . . . ",DUMMY$
4600 RETURN
4610 '
```

```
4620 ' ==============================================================
5000 ' -- Get interest rate and number of periods from user -----
5010 INPUT "What is the annual percentage rate (as a decimal)"; APR
5020 WHILE APR <= 0 OR APR >= 1
5030    INPUT "Enter as a decimal number; (Enter .10 for 10%) ", APR
5040 WEND
5050 '
5060 ' -- Get the number of compounding periods per year --------
5070 '
5080 INPUT "How many compounding periods are in a year"; ANNUAL.PERIODS
5090 WHILE ANNUAL.PERIODS <= 0 OR ANNUAL.PERIODS > 366
5100    INPUT "Please enter a number between 1 and 366, inclusive",
              ANNUAL.PERIODS
5110 WEND
5120 LET I = APR/ANNUAL.PERIODS      ' Compute the periodic interest rate
5130 '
5140 ' Enter the number of years in the investment runs
5150 '
5160 INPUT "How many years does the investment run"; YEARS
5170 WHILE YEARS < 0 OR YEARS > 99
5180    INPUT "Please enter a number between 1 and 99, inclusive ", YEARS
5190 WEND
5200 LET N = YEARS * ANNUAL.PERIODS
5210 RETURN
5220 '
5230 ' ==============================================================
6000 ' ---------- get future value ----------------------
6010 INPUT "What is the future value";FV
6020 WHILE FV <= 0
6030       PRINT "Future Value must be positive"
6040       INPUT "What is the future value";FV
6050 WEND
6060 RETURN
6070 '
6080 ' ==============================================================
6500 ' --------- get payment amount --------------------
6510 INPUT "What is the periodic payment"; PMT
6520 WHILE PMT <= 0
6530       PRINT "Payment must be a positive amount!"
6540       INPUT "What is the periodic payment";PMT
6550 WEND
6560 RETURN
6570 ' ==============================================================
6580 ' ------------------ end of listing ------------------
6590 ' ==============================================================

RUN

        (screen clears)
```

```
Financial Calculator Options
        1. Compute future value given present value
        2. Compute present value given future value
        3. Compute future value given payment amount
        4. Compute payment amount given future value
        5. End the program
Please select your option (1,2,3,4, or 5) 4
```

(screen clears)

```
What is the future value? 100000
What is the annual percentage rate (as a decimal)? .12
How many compounding periods are in a year? 12
How many years does the investment run? 10
Payment amount:        434.71
Press ENTER to continue . . .
```

(screen clears)

```
Financial Calculator Options
        1. Compute future value given present value
        2. Compute present value given future value
        3. Compute future value given payment amount
        4. Compute payment amount given future value
        5. End the program
Please select your option (1,2,3,4, or 5) 2
```

(screen clears)

```
What is the future value? 10000
What is the annual percentage rate (as a decimal)? .12
How many compounding periods are in a year? 12
How many years does the investment run? 10
Present value:    3,029.95
Press ENTER to continue . . .
```

(screen clears)

```
Financial Calculator Options
        1. Compute future value given present value
        2. Compute present value given future value
        3. Compute future value given payment amount
        4. Compute payment amount given future value
        5. End the program
Please select your option (1,2,3,4, or 5) 5
Ok
```

·QUICK REFERENCE FOR LESSON 6·

GOSUB . . . RETURN

GOSUB and its companion statement, RETURN, allow you to break your program into small, manageable modules. The format of a GOSUB statement is

GOSUB line number, where "line number" is the number of any line in the
program. This causes BASIC to temporarily jump to that line number.

RETURN. When BASIC encounters a RETURN statement, it goes back to the
statement after the most recent GOSUB.

GOSUBs may be nested; in fact, it is very common to do so.

ON . . . GOSUB . . . RETURN

The format of ON . . . GOSUB is ON index GOSUB line, line, line, . . . where "index"
is a number, a variable, or a mathematical expression and "line" is a line number in your
program.

BASIC evaluates the index to decide which line number to use; if the value is 1, BASIC
GOSUBs to the first line number in the list; if the value is 5, BASIC GOSUBs to the fifth line
number in the list, and so on.

The index must evaluate to a number in the range 0 to 255, inclusive, or BASIC gives an
error message.

If the index is 0 or greater than the length of the list of line numbers, BASIC ignores the
ON . . . GOSUB statement and proceeds to the next statement in the program.

RETURN. When RETURN is encountered, BASIC executes the statement following the
ON . . . GOSUB.

GOTO

The format of a GOTO statement is GOTO line number, where "line number" is any line
in your program.

The GOTO statement causes BASIC to immediately jump to that line number and begin
processing at that point.

(There is no return statement associated with GOTO; GOTO provides no way to get
back to the place from where you came.)

ON . . . GOTO

The format of an ON . . . GOTO statement is ON index GOTO line, line, line, . . . ,
where "index" is a number, variable, or mathematical expression and "line" is any line
number in the program.

BASIC evaluates "index" to determine which line number in the list to choose; if the
value is 1, it executes a GOTO to the first line in the list; if the value is 3, it executes a GOTO
to the third line number in the list, and so on.

"Index" must evaluate to a number from 0 and 255, inclusive, or BASIC will give an
error message. If it is 0 or greater than the length of the line number list, BASIC ignores the
ON . . . GOTO statement and proceeds with the next statement in the program.

Use of GOTO and ON . . . GOTO

Both GOTO and ON . . . GOTO should be used with great discretion, if at all. Instead,
try to use IF, FOR, WHILE, GOSUB, and ON . . . GOSUB wherever possible.

· EXERCISES ·

Short Answers

1. Why isn't it a good idea to put line numbers in comments?

2. How can GOSUBs be more advantageous than IF . . . THEN statements?

3. What happens if the number entered in response to an ON . . . GOSUB is greater than the number of choices?

4. Why is it a good idea to validate an idex before using it?

5. How is GOTO similar and different from GOSUB?

6. Why is it preferable to use GOSUB over GOTO?

7. Explain what a forward transfer of control is and why it is a valid use of GOTO.

8. What is the difference between GOSUB and ON . . . GOSUB? Give an example of the use of each.

9. What is a "dummy subroutine?" What is is used for?

10. What is the index in an ON . . . GOSUB routine?

11. Describe what is involved in structured programming.

12. What benefits does top-down design have?

Analyzing Code

13. The following program should calculate the factorial of 5 and print the number 5 and its factorial. (The factorial of 5 is 5 * 4 * 3 * 2 * 1.) It does not do this. Find the error and correct it.

```
110 'Program to show that BASIC can use recursion
110 LET FACTORIAL = 1
120 LET N% = 5
130 GOSUB 1000
140 PRINT "The factorial of ";N%;" is ";FACTORIAL
150 END
1000 '    A recursive subroutine
1010 LET FACTORIAL = FACTORIAL * N%
1020 LET N% = N% - 1
1030 IF N% > 1 THEN GOSUB 1000
1040 RETURN
1050 '=============== END OF LISTING ====================
```

14. What will happen when this subroutine is executed and I is greater than zero? Why is this poor programming practice?

```
1000 ' A typical subroutine
1010 IF I > 0 THEN GOTO 100
1020 LET X = X + I
1020 RETURN
```

Programming

For the following programs:
  a. Write a structure chart.
  b. Write a flowchart.
  c. Write pseudocode.
  d. Code the program.

15. Practice with GOSUB
  a. Write a program that asks the user to enter one of the values: "single," "married filing separately," "married filing jointly." Use a subroutine to ask for and validate the answer, then print out the answer in your main program after the subroutine returns.
  b. After your program calls that subroutine, have it call another subroutine that asks you the number of payroll withholding allowances. Make sure the entered number is not negative. If the number is greater than 15, have the program print the message, "Number of allowances is greater than 15, notify IRS."

16. Practice with ON . . . GOSUB
  a. Modify the subroutine you wrote in 15a so that it displays a menu of the options, asks the user to choose one of them, then sets the variable TABLE$ to "single," "married filing separately," or "married filing jointly,'" as appropriate.
  b. The XYZ Corporation carries four products, numbered 1 through 4, respectively. Each has a different discount schedule for high-volume customers:

Product #1: qty 0–100 = 0%,   101–300 = 10%, 301–1000 = 15%, over 1000 = 20%
Product #2: qty 0–10 = 0%,   11–20 = 5%, 21–50 = 10%, over 50 = 15%
Product #3: qty 0–1000 = 5%, 1001–5000 = 10%, over 5001 = 12%
Product #4: no discounts

The list prices on the products are $100, $495, $5.95, and $10,000, respectively, for products 1 through 4.
  Write a program that asks the user for the product number and quantity ordered, then computes the total list price, the discount percentage, and the discounted price. Use one subroutine for each product type to compute discounts and prices. Allow the user to enter a series of product orders, then print out a total for all products ordered.
  (Hint: use an ON . . . GOSUB to branch to the appropriate subroutine.)

17. Payroll: Write a subroutine that asks the user to input the gross income and computes the federal payroll withholding tax for a semimonthly payroll.
  Use the subroutines from Exercise 15 that input and validate whether the employee is married or single and the number of allowances.
  For all employees: Multiply the number of allowances times $41.66 (the amount deducted for each allowance) to give the total allowance deduction.
  Subtract the total allowance deduction from the gross salary. The result is the amount subject to withholding.
  If the employee is single:
  Calculate the amount of income tax to be withheld using the table on page 250.

Single — Biweekly Payroll

AMT. SUBJECT TO WITHHOLDING

OVER	BUT NOT OVER	AMOUNT TO WITHHOLD IS:	
$ 0	$ 58	$ 0.00	
$ 58	$ 171	$ 0.00	plus 12% of amount over $ 58
$171	$ 396	$13.56	plus 15% of amount over $117
$396	$ 600	$47.31	plus 19% of amount over $396
$600	$ 917	$86.07	plus 25% of amount over $600
$917	$1158	$165.32	plus 30% of amount over $917
$1158	$1379	$237.62	plus 34% of amount over $1158
$1379		$312.76	plus 37% of amount over $1379

For example, if the amount subject to withholding is $495, the withholding tax = 47.31 + (495 − 396) * .19

18. Rewrite the following programs from Chapter 5's exercises using subroutines.
a. Exercise 23
b. Exercise 24
c. Exercise 26

More About BASIC

Introduction to Part II

THUS FAR, IN Part I, you've learned how to use some of the fundamental tools of BASIC. In Part II we'll take a step further and explore the language's capabilities for working with data in the real business world.

A number of the techniques in Part II are aimed at helping you to write programs that solve a greater variety of problems. In business you will often need to solve problems larger in scale than the sample problems you've seen in the early chapters. For instance, most business applications involve large volumes of data. You must be able to access data quickly and efficiently and present it to others in a meaningful way.

An important part of handling large quantities of data is storage. In Chapter 7 we'll discuss sequential files, which provide a means to put data in files and access it when necessary.

Chapters 8 and 9 describe arrays. These allow you to use one variable name for a whole list of data items. Multidimensional arrays, covered in Chapter 9, hold tables of data.

In Chapters 10 and 11 you'll see how numeric and string functions enable the user to perform a sequence of operations with one instruction. Numeric functions operate on numeric data, and string functions manipulate string data.

Chapter 12 looks at several features of BASIC that can be used to make a program "friendlier"—that is, simpler to use and more accessible.

To allow you immediate access to data stored in files, Chapter 13 explains Random Access files.

Finally, Chapter 14 portrays some of the graphics capabilities of BASIC.

As you read the chapters of Part II, you may wish also to read the cases presented in Part III. The first case supplements Chapter 7. The later cases require information found in later chapters. (The introduction to Part III tells which chapters need to be read before attempting each case.) Part II and Part III go hand in hand in developing your skills to write application programs in BASIC.

SEQUENTIAL FILES

AUTOMATING RECEIVABLES WITH A SEQUENTIAL FILE

Capital Portable X-Ray is a small firm consisting of six x-ray technicians and an office staff of four. It provides the community with the service of taking x-rays at the client's place of residence. Most of the clients are elderly, living in convalescent hospitals. The alternative to bringing the x-ray machine to the patient is to bring the elderly patient, via ambulance, to a hospital for x-rays. The latter alternative is expensive and uncomfortable.

The office staff use programs written in BASIC to maintain the customer records. Using BASIC allows them to develop new reports as required by law and/or business necessity.

Capital Portable X-Ray discovered that many of its accounts were "slipping through the cracks." A yearly audit found over $10,000 in unpaid bills more than six months old. Particularly in dealing with ailing, elderly customers, the older the bill, the less likely the bill will be paid. They realized that they needed a way to keep on top of unpaid bills so that they could send reminders on a regular basis.

Jesse had the job of writing the programs to produce the required reports. Although he knew how the customer data were stored, he figured that a short refresher on sequential files was in order. Turning to Lesson 7 in *The ABCs of BASIC*, Jesse read about using sequential files.

LESSON 7: SEQUENTIAL FILES

By now you have written some useful BASIC programs. However, most of your programs did a lot of computations on a few key variables. In the business world most problems do not fit this mold. Most practical business programs process large amounts of data, such as a list of hundreds or thousands of names and addresses.

In a manual system large amounts of data are kept in files, such as in filing cabinets, index card boxes, or Rolodex files. Likewise, a computer system can store data in **files.** You have already learned how to store a program as a file on your disk; in this lesson you will learn how to store data as well.

You will learn about sequential files and the statements that allow you to use them: OPEN, CLOSE, PRINT #, WRITE #, and INPUT #. This lesson will also cover the techniques for sequential file updating, appending to the end of a file, and end-of-file handling.

Data Files: General Information

Files Have Names

There are a few terms and concepts with which you should be familiar when using data files. In a manual system you give a name to a particular file, such as "Payroll" or "Customer Record," so that you will know which drawer of the file cabinet to open to get the data contained in the file. In the same way a computer system also gives names to files. As you will learn shortly, the rules for naming program files also apply to naming data files. If in the manual system the data about customers were kept in an index card file called the "Customer Record" file, we might transfer that data into a computer file and name that file "CUSTOMER.DAT."

Files Contain Records

Each card in the manual file holds all of the data about one customer: the account number, customer name, address, account balance, and so on. It is our record on that customer. Likewise, all of the data about one entity, such as customer, that are put into a data file are referred to as a **record** (see Figure 7.1). This is also called a **logical record** since it is a collection of all of the data items that logically belong together. (A physical record refers to aspects of the hardware and how data are physically stored on the disk. We will not be concerned with physical records at this point.)

Records Contain Fields

Each record for a customer will contain all of the data items we kept on the index card, such as customer name, address, account number, and so on. These items

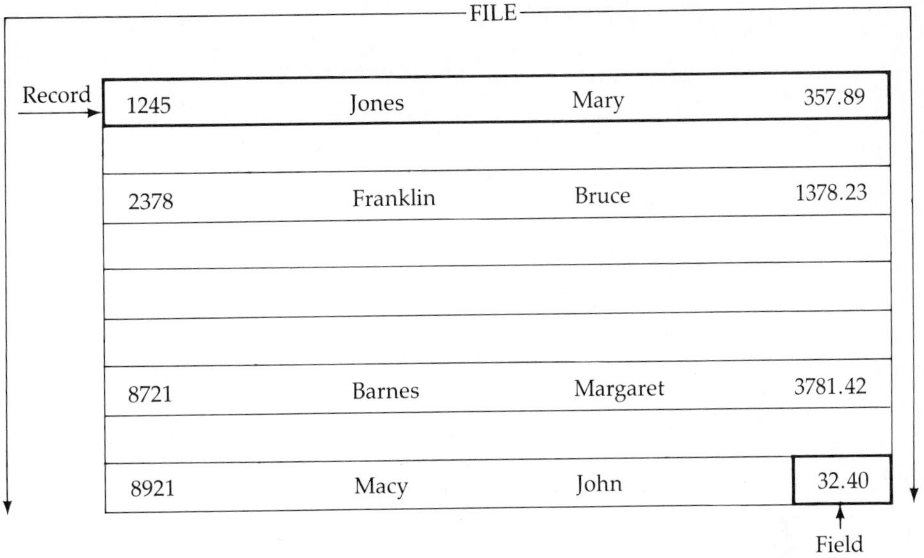

FIGURE 7.1 •
A file is a series
of records.
Records are
composed of
fields.

are called **fields.** We might store the customer's account number in the account number field.

Record Layout

When designing any information system, manual or automated, you should try to make it easy to use and understand. For this reason in our manual system we design the index cards so that all the data on all cards will always be in the same place. For example, we put the account number in the upper left corner, the name on the second line, the current balance in the box on the fifth line, and so on. Anyone using the file thus always knows where to find any particular item of data. The same rules apply for designing a computer data record.

Before you begin to write BASIC instructions, lay out all of the fields that will appear in your record in the order in which they will appear. This **record layout** should be a permanent part of your documentation. Special forms are available just for this purpose. Table 7.1 is the record layout for the Customer Record.

Variable Length Versus Fixed Length

In the record layout we indicated a size range for each field, but the actual data for each record could be of any length within that range. The name could be short

TABLE 7.1 • Record Layout for File: BALANCES.DAT

FIELD #	NAME	DATA TYPE	DESCRIPTION
1	CUSTOMER.NUMBER	Integer	0 to 9999
2	CUSTOMER.NAME	Strong	Up to 35 characters
3	BALANCE	Double precision	From −9999.99 to +9999.99

(JOE LEE) or long (KATHERINE ELIZABETH JOHANSEN). Although each Customer Record will always consist of the same three fields, each will not always be of the same physical length. These are referred to as **variable length records.** When each field in each record is of the same length the records are known as **fixed length records.** We will discuss fixed length records in more detail when we cover random access files (see Chapter 13).

Types of File Access

Once you have decided what data you are going to keep in your file, you need to decide what *type* of file you wish to use. BASIC supports two different types of files: sequential and random access. In a **sequential file** data are written and are read in the same order. You start at the beginning of the file and process the records, one by one, in the order they were written. If you want to look at the 35th record, you must pass over the previous 34 records before you can get that record. In contrast, **random access files** allow you to go directly to the record you wish without having to pass over all of the previous ones. Depending on the needs of the application you will select whether your file is to be sequential or random access. We will discuss sequential files in this chapter and will cover random access files in Chapter 13. (See Figure 7.2.)

Sequential Files

Imagine that you need to prepare a list of customer numbers, names, and account balances and store that list for later use. This list is an example of a data file. You already keep data files manually. BASIC also lets you create and use automated data files.

A stack of plates is like a sequential file. You must take each plate in turn— from top to bottom without skipping any.

Sequential Access

A file drawer is like a random access file. You can take out or add a folder at any place.

FIGURE 7.2•
Sequential versus
random access

Random Access

BASIC's automated files are very easy to use. You already know most of what you need in order to use these files. To print data on the screen, you use the PRINT statement. To store that same data in a file, you use a simple variation on the same PRINT statement or a new statement, WRITE. To ask the user to enter data from the keyboard, you use the INPUT statement. A simple variation on that same INPUT statement reads the data from an existing data file. Let's see how easy BASIC files are to use.

Here is a program that asks the user for a customer number, name, and account balance and then displays the number, name, and balance on the screen.

```
100 DEFINT C
110 DEFDBL B
120 INPUT "Customer Number (enter 0 to end)"; CUSTOMER.NUMBER
130 WHILE CUSTOMER.NUMBER <> 0          '0 means no more customers
140     INPUT "Customer Name"; CUSTOMER.NAME$
150     INPUT "Account Balance"; BALANCE
160     PRINT CUSTOMER.NUMBER, CUSTOMER.NAME$, BALANCE
170     INPUT "Customer Number (0 to end)"; CUSTOMER.NUMBER
180 WEND
190 END
```

This program is admittedly not very useful; it merely echoes back the data that you supply, as you supply it. However, let's try a slightly different version. Instead of displaying the data on the screen, let's put it into a data file on the magnetic disk, so that it can be recalled later. This involves only a simple change to the preceding program.

OPEN Associates a Filename with a File Number

The first step is to tell the computer where the data is to go. Just as your programs, when stored on disk, have filenames, so data files have filenames. The statement to tell the computer where to put the data is OPEN. To create a file called "BALANCES.DAT" and set it up to receive data from a program, use the statement

```
115 OPEN "BALANCES.DAT" FOR OUTPUT AS #1
```

In this statement "BALANCES.DAT" is the name of the file, chosen by you. A file of data is stored much the same way as a program file, so the same rules apply to naming data files. The name consists of two parts: a file name of up to eight characters and an optional extension of a period and up to three characters. "BALANCES.DAT" is a legitimate filename, with "BALANCES" as the name and ".DAT" as the extension. It is a common convention in BASIC on the IBM PC to use the extension ".DAT" for all data filenames. However, BASIC does not enforce this practice.

FOR OUTPUT Creates a New File
The FOR OUTPUT part of the OPEN statement indicates that data will be put into the file. As you will see later in the section entitled "INPUT #" later in this

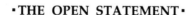

· THE OPEN STATEMENT ·

$$OPEN \textit{ "Filename" for } \begin{Bmatrix} INPUT \\ OUTPUT \\ APPEND \end{Bmatrix} \textit{ as } \#n$$

Readies the named file for input or output.

Assigns the number n to the file.

is optional.

n is an integer whose value is from 1 to the maximum number of files allowed (normally three, but can be changed with the /F: switch when BASIC is invoked).

chapter, data can also be retrieved from an existing file by changing this to FOR INPUT.

AS #1 means that, from now on, the program will refer to the file that we have named "BALANCES.DAT" as file #1. BASIC refers to files by numbers instead of the names that you and I use. The OPEN statement gives BASIC the number it wants (#1) and gives us the name that we want (BALANCES.DAT). We could assign "BALANCES.DAT" the file #2 or #3 if we wish; just remember that whatever number we assign it in the OPEN statement is the number that BASIC will use to refer to that file until the file is closed. The # is optional with the OPEN statement (as is also true with the CLOSE statement about which you will learn shortly).

Number of Open Files

Normally, IBM PC BASIC can have at most three files OPEN at once. However, it is possible to have as many as 15 files OPEN at the same time. To do this you must tell BASIC that you want to change the default rules when you first invoke BASIC by typing

BASIC /F:15 if you are using standard BASIC
BASICA /F:15 if you are using advanced BASIC

OPEN Can Erase Files

When you give the statement to OPEN a file FOR OUTPUT, if a file with the same name already exists in the current directory, *it will be erased* from your disk. For this reason it is essential that you keep track of your file names. (Later in this chapter when we discuss APPEND, you will learn a way to open a file to put data into it without destroying the former file.)

CLOSE: Disassociates File and File Number

The CLOSE statement is the opposite of the OPEN statement. After a file is closed, it is no longer available to the program unless it is reopened, and the file number may be used to OPEN a different file.

CLOSE also makes sure that the last record is written correctly and places a special character called the end-of-file character (EOF) at the end of the file. We'll discuss EOF in detail later in this chapter.

It is a good idea to CLOSE a file as soon as you are through with it. First, a limited number of files can be open at one time. But, most importantly, while a file is open, it is vulnerable to losing data if the system power supply fails.

As with the OPEN statement, the # is optional in the CLOSE statement.

CLOSE #1 or CLOSE 1   . . . makes BASIC forget what file is #1
CLOSE #1,#2 or CLOSE 1,2 . . . same, for both files #1 and #2
CLOSE   . . . CLOSEs all OPEN files

Neglecting to close a file may lead to disks or files that are no longer usable. (It will not hurt the hardware, just the data on your diskette.)

Fortunately, when BASIC encounters an END statement, or the commands NEW or SYSTEM (the command that takes you back to DOS), or if you edit a line, BASIC will CLOSE any OPEN files for you. The STOP statement does not have this effect.

PRINT # Sends Data to a Disk File

Once a file has been OPENed for OUTPUT, we can put data into it by using one of two statements: PRINT # or WRITE #.

PRINT # sends the same data to disk that PRINT sends to the screen. The format of the PRINT # statement is:

```
PRINT #n, variable, . . . ,variable
```

• THE CLOSE STATEMENT •

CLOSE #n, #m
Makes files *n* and *m* unaccessible.
Disassociates file numbers *n* and *m* from filename assigned in OPEN
    statement.
is optional.

CLOSE
Closes all files.

•THE PRINT #*n* STATEMENT•

PRINT #n, variable, variable, . . .
Writes data to disk file #*n* in same format PRINT writes to the screen.
File must have been opened FOR OUTPUT (or FOR APPEND).

where *n* is the number you have assigned to the file. In this statement the # is required, and the file number must be followed by a comma. The space between PRINT and # is optional. Here are some examples:

```
100 OPEN "MYFILE" FOR OUTPUT AS #2
200 PRINT #2, 1
300 CLOSE #2
```

The number 1 will be placed in file #2, which we know as "MYFILE." Change line 200 as follows:

```
200 PRINT #2, A,B,C
```

The contents of the variables A, B, and C will be placed in "MYFILE" with the same number of spaces between them as if we were using the regular PRINT statement.

```
200 PRINT #2, A;B;C
```

The contents of the variables A, B, and C will now be placed in the file with the same spacing that numeric variables have when the PRINT statement is used.

There is a problem with using PRINT #. In most cases you will want to be able to retrieve the data that you have stored in a file for further processing. The statement you will use to access this data is INPUT #. Like the INPUT statement with which you are familiar, if a series of items are to be entered using a single INPUT # statement, they must be separated by commas. For example, consider the following statement:

```
INPUT A,B,C,D,E
```

If we key 1 2 3 4 5 and press Enter, the following message will be displayed:

```
??redo from start
```

The correct way to key these numbers is: 1,2,3,4,5, putting commas between each number. The INPUT statement will then assign the value 1 to the variable A, the value 2 to the variable B, and so on. Therefore, we need a way to put commas between each field as the data are stored in the file.

The PRINT # statement, just like the PRINT statement, does not put commas between items. We could put them there ourselves by creating a string variable with a single comma in it and placing it in the file. Our sample program would then look like this:

```
050 LET COMMA$ = ","
100 OPEN "MYFILE" FOR OUTPUT AS #2
200 PRINT #2, A;COMMA$;B;COMMA$;C
300 CLOSE #2
```

The commas would now be placed on the file between the values of A, B and C.

This is a cumbersome method and, as you can imagine, one that is prone to programming errors. What we need is a statement to put all the commas onto the disk for us. This is exactly what the WRITE # statement is designed to do.

WRITE # Adds Commas and Quotes Automatically

While the WRITE # statement is designed for putting data into files, you can see how it differs from the PRINT statement by using it without the # to WRITE to the screen. The WRITE statement automatically puts commas between items and quotes around string variables. Try this:

```
PRINT 1,2,3
 1              2              3
Ok
WRITE 1,2,3
1,2,3
Ok
```

(Note that the commas appear on the screen.)

```
PRINT 1;2;3
 1 2 3
Ok
WRITE 1;2;3
1,2,3
```

(Note that semicolons are replaced by commas.)

```
Ok
PRINT "THANKS FOR THE NEW STATEMENT"
THANKS FOR THE NEW STATEMENT
Ok
WRITE "THANKS FOR THE NEW STATEMENT"
"THANKS FOR THE NEW STATEMENT"
Ok
LET A$ = "Hi, There"
PRINT A$
Hi, There
WRITE A$
"Hi, There"
```

(Note that with WRITE the quotes appear on the screen, while with PRINT they do not.)

Just as PRINT has its counterpart PRINT # to print data to a file, so WRITE has its file counterpart WRITE #. The format is the same as that for PRINT #:

•THE WRITE #*n* STATEMENT•

WRITE #n, variable, variable, . . .
Writes data to disk file with commas between values and quotes around
string values for later input by INPUT #*n* statement.
File must have been opened FOR OUTPUT (or FOR APPEND).

```
WRITE #n, variable, . . . ,variable
```

where *n* is the number of the file and "variable, . . . ,variable" are one or more
variables separated by commas or semicolons.

Now the problem of having to insert all those commas and quotes between
items when putting data into a file has been solved. Our preceding program can
now be written as:

```
100 OPEN "MYFILE" FOR OUTPUT AS #2
200 WRITE #2, A,B,C
300 CLOSE #2
```

The contents of the variables A, B, and C will now be written on the file with the
commas between them so that they can be read back in correctly at a later time.

At the end of the list of variables written to the file by each PRINT # or WRITE
statement, two special characters are placed on the disk: a carriage return
character followed by a line feed character. These can be ignored for the present,
but they will become important during our discussion of random access files in
Chapter 13.

Adding Data File to Program Example

Our previous example of entering customer balances can now become a useful
process if each entry is written out to a file after it is entered:

```
100 DEFINT C
110 DEFDBL B
115 OPEN "BALANCES.DAT" FOR OUTPUT AS #1
120 INPUT "Customer Number (enter 0 to end)"; CUSTOMER.NUMBER
130 WHILE CUSTOMER.NUMBER <> 0    '0 means no more customers
140     INPUT "Customer Name"; CUSTOMER.NAME$
150     INPUT "Account Balance"; BALANCE
160     WRITE #1, CUSTOMER.NUMBER, CUSTOMER.NAME$, BALANCE
170     INPUT "Customer Number (0 to end)"; CUSTOMER.NUMBER
180 WEND
185 CLOSE #1
190 END
```

In this example the data that are written out to the file each time the WRITE # is executed will be the customer number (an integer), a comma, the customer name (a string), another comma, the balance (a double-precision number), a carriage return, and a line feed. The following is a sample of data that could be entered:

Customer Number	Customer Name	Balance
111	Mary Jones	124.73
23721	Jackson Sanders	5689.30
42	Fred Simpson	−15.65

This data would be written on the file as follows:

111,"Mary Jones",124.73{CR LF}23721,"Jackson Sanders",5689.30{CR LF}42,"Fred Simpson",−15.65{CR LF}

(We have used {CR LF} to indicate the carriage-return line-feed sequence.)

INPUT # Inputs Values from a Disk File

Now that we have put all this data out on a file, we need a way to get it back. We can do this with the INPUT # statement.

However, before we can use the INPUT # statement we must OPEN the file FOR INPUT. To OPEN the file called "BALANCES.DAT" we write

```
OPEN "BALANCES.DAT" FOR INPUT AS #1
```

As has been mentioned before, when a file is OPENed FOR OUTPUT, any previously existing file with the same name is erased. However, when a file is OPENed FOR INPUT, the file must already exist in the system. If a file by the name specified in the OPEN FOR INPUT statement does not exist, you will get the error message:

```
File not found
```

INPUT # operates in a manner similar to the INPUT statement we have used for entering data on the screen. The format is:

```
INPUT #n, variable, . . . ,variable
```

where *n* is the number assigned to the file. This number must be followed by a comma. The # is required.

·THE INPUT #*n* STATEMENT·

INPUT #n, variable, variable, . . .
Inputs next field from disk file into variable(s) named.
File must have first been opened FOR INPUT.

After the comma one or more variable names may appear. The first INPUT # statement encountered after the OPEN will assign the first item in the file to the first variable named in the INPUT # statement. It will proceed item by item through the file, assigning each sequentially to the variables that appear in the INPUT # statement(s).

For example, suppose we wrote the following data onto a file using the following program:

```
100 LET LABEL$ = "TEST FILE"
120 LET MSG$ = "HI"
130 LET ONE = 1
200 OPEN "TESTFILE" FOR OUTPUT AS #1
300 WRITE #1, LABEL$,5,20,MSG$,ONE,"BYE"
400 CLOSE #1
500 END
```

The file looks essentially like this:

```
"TEST FILE",5,20,"HI",1,"BYE" (CR LF)
```

Now let's retrieve this data with the INPUT # statement in the following program:

```
100 OPEN "TESTFILE" FOR INPUT AS #1
200 INPUT #1, TITLE$,A,B,MSG$,C,LAST$
300 CLOSE #1
400 PRINT TITLE$
500 PRINT A
600 PRINT B
700 PRINT MSG$
800 PRINT C
900 PRINT LAST$
1000 END
RUN
TEST FILE
 5
 20
HI
 1
BYE
Ok
```

Notice that we gave the variables different names when we input them from disk and when we wrote them to disk. The name given a variable is only for the use of the program in which it appears. When it is written to the file, only the data are stored. When we input data, the variables to which we assign them can have any variable name we wish. The only rule is that the name used must be consistent with the data type (string, integer, etc.)

We would get the same results by changing the INPUT # statement to any of the following:

```
200 INPUT #1, TITLE$
210 INPUT #1, A,B
220 INPUT #1, MSG$,C,LAST$
```

or

```
200 INPUT #1, TITLE$, A, B
210 INPUT #1, MSG$, C, LAST$
```

or even

```
200 INPUT #1, TITLE$
210 INPUT #1, A
220 INPUT #1, B
230 INPUT #1, MSG$
240 INPUT #1, C
250 INPUT #1, LAST$
```

The important thing to remember is that the appropriate types of variable names are used for the items that are to be INPUT from files. Mismatching data type with variable type will lead to erroneous results.

EOF(*n*) Indicates Whether File #*n* Is at End of File

If you were taking pages from a file folder and had just taken the last page, you would know it and would not try to take any more. If BASIC is retrieving data from a file, it needs to know if it has just input the last item, so that it will not try to input any more. If you attempt to input past the end of a file, you will get the error message:

```
.Input past end
```

The **end-of-file (EOF) character** that is written at the end of an output file by the CLOSE statement is a solution to this situation. When the last data item is input, this character signals to BASIC that the end of the file has been reached by setting the EOF function for that file to true. In your program you can test whether the

·THE EOF FUNCTION·

EOF(n)
Returns the value of −1 (logical TRUE) when the last data item of a file has been input.
Otherwise, returns the value of 0 (logical FALSE).

end-of-file has been reached by checking the value of EOF for the file being processed.

BASIC calls the end-of-file condition for file #1, EOF(1). EOF(1) is true (has the value of −1) when BASIC is at the end of the file for file #1 and there is no more data to input. As long as there is more data to input from file #1, EOF(1) will be false (it will have the value of zero).

Note that with OPEN and CLOSE, the pound sign (#) in front of the number is optional. You can use OPEN #1 or OPEN 1. But with EOF, you may not use the #. Typing EOF(#1) will cause a syntax error.

We can use EOF(*n*) (where *n* is the file number) with the WHILE statement and IF statement to select what action to take if there is or is not more data to read.

Example Using EOF(*n*), OPEN, CLOSE, and INPUT

With this last bit of knowledge we can now take that data we earlier entered into the file "BALANCES.DAT" and INPUT it to print a report.

```
10   '   Program Example to print contents of file as a report
100 DEFINT C
110 DEFDBL B
120 OPEN "BALANCES.DAT" FOR INPUT AS #3
130 WHILE NOT EOF(3)
140    INPUT #3, CUSTOMER.NUMBER, CUSTOMER.NAME$, BALANCE
150    PRINT USING "###### \                \ ######.##";
          CUSTOMER.NUMBER, CUSTOMER.NAME$, BALANCE
160 WEND
170 CLOSE #3
180 END
RUN
     111 Mary Jones           124.73
   23721 Jackson Sanders      5689.30
      42 Fred Simpson          -15.65
Ok
```

There are several important concepts to remember with INPUT #

Values Must Be Input in the Same Order as They Were Written
INPUT # reads data from a file one variable at a time, starting with the beginning of the file and proceeding sequentially through the file. This is why it is so important that your file record layout be clearly documented. In the preceding program we may have thought that customer name should come before customer number and have written lines 140 and 150 as follows:

```
140 INPUT # 3, CUSTOMER.NAME$, CUSTOMER.NUMBER, BALANCE
150 PRINT USING "\                \ ######## ######.##";
          CUSTOMER.NAME$, CUSTOMER.NUMBER, BALANCE
```

The results would be as follows:

```
111                    0        0.00
124.73             23721        0.00
Sanders"            5689       42.00
Input past end in 140
```

We will not go into the details of what happens when you read data into a variable of the incorrect data type. However, this example clearly demonstrates that the result of mismatching input data and variable type is garbage.

All Fields Must Be Input Even If Not All Will Be Used

What if in our preceding example we wanted to print only the number and the balance? All we need from the file is the customer number and the balance. But if we were to use the statement:

```
INPUT #3, CUSTOMER.NUMBER, BALANCE
```

we would have similar garbage to the earlier example since the first customer name would be read into BALANCE and from then on nothing would be correct. One way to accomplish the desired results is to leave the INPUT # line just as is and print only the number and the balance. Just because we read in the name, we are not forced to use it for anything. Another way to write the line would be:

```
INPUT #3, CUSTOMER.NUMBER, DUMMY$, BALANCE
```

This indicates that we are reading in a string data item, but we have given it the name DUMMY$ to show to anyone reading the program that we do not plan to use it for anything.

Data Names on Input and Output Programs Need Not Be the Same — Only of the Same Type

This reinforces an important point made earlier. When we created the file, we used the variable name CUSTOMER.NAME$. Just now we used DUMMY$ for the same data. Is it okay to do this? The answer is yes. When you create a file, the variable names you use are only a part of that program. When the data are written to the file, only the data are put on the file; there is no name associated with the data on the file. When you read the data back in, you can give it any name you wish as long as it is consistent with the data type (string, integer, etc.) For consistency we usually give the data the same name both when writing it and when reading it, but it is not mandatory that we do so.

Remember that variable names are transient; they are in existence only while the program that uses them is running. The file name, however, is permanently assigned to a file. If you give the file the name "BALANCES.DAT" when you create it, you must use that name in any other program that accesses it.

Remember also that the file number assigned by the OPEN statement is a temporary number used by BASIC to refer to that file only until it is CLOSEd. In the earlier examples we OPENed the file "BALANCES.DAT" as file #1 when we created it, and we OPENed it as #3 when we read from it, but in both cases we called it by the name "BALANCES.DAT".

PRINT #*n*, USING Writes Formatted Output to a File

You may want to write formatted output temporarily to a file. This file can later be displayed on the screen using the DOS command TYPE filename or printed on the printer using the DOS command PRINT filename. The BASIC statement that writes formatted output to a file is:

```
PRINT #n, USING MASK$; VARIABLE, . . . , VARIABLE
```

Note that the punctuation is a comma after the file number and a semicolon after the mask.

```
2100 PRINT #1, USING "#####        #####"; FIRST, SECOND
2110 PRINT #3, USING "The answer is $***#####,.##"; DOLLAR.AMT
```

There is no WRITE # USING statement since WRITE # is not designed for formatting output.

APPEND Adds Data to the End of an Existing Data File

Suppose we want to add (append) data to the end of a file that already exists. If we OPEN it FOR OUTPUT, the existing file will be erased, and if we OPEN it FOR INPUT, we will not be able to WRITE to it. The way around this dilemma is to OPEN it FOR APPEND as follows:

```
OPEN "MYFILE" FOR APPEND AS #2
```

When a file is OPENed for APPEND, BASIC looks to see if a file with that name already exists in the current directory. If one does, data written to that file are added to the end of the file. If one does not already exist, BASIC acts as if the file were opened for OUTPUT; it creates the new file.

Files OPENed FOR APPEND are output files. You can only write to them. You cannot read from them (without closing the file and reOPENing it FOR INPUT). To summarize, the three modes used to open a sequential file are as follows:

1. FOR OUTPUT—Erases any former file with same name and readies new file to receive data.

·THE PRINT #*n* USING STATEMENT·

PRINT #n, using MASK$; variable, . . .
Writes data to disk file #*n* in same format PRINT USING writes to the screen.
File must have been opened FOR OUTPUT (or FOR APPEND).

2. FOR APPEND—Readies file for adding records to end of file. If file does not already exist, a new one will be created.
3. FOR INPUT—Readies a file for input. File must already exist.

Using the customer file "BALANCES.DAT" from our earlier examples, we can now write a program to add records to the end of it. In most applications you do not want to reenter all the data every time you want to add more records. The only change we need to make to our earlier program is to change line 115 to read FOR APPEND instead of FOR OUTPUT.

```
100 DEFINT C
110 DEFDBL B
115 OPEN "BALANCES.DAT" FOR APPEND AS #1
120 INPUT "Customer Number (enter 0 to end)"; CUSTOMER.NUMBER
130 WHILE CUSTOMER.NUMBER <> 0     '0 means no more customers
140    INPUT "Customer Name."; CUSTOMER.NAME$
150    INPUT "Account Balance"; BALANCE
160    WRITE #1, CUSTOMER.NUMBER, CUSTOMER.NAME$, BALANCE
170    INPUT "Customer Number (0 to end)"; CUSTOMER.NUMBER
180 WEND
185 CLOSE #1
190 END
```

Summary of Sequential Files Statements

Let's summarize what we have learned about sequential files so far.

1. To use a file, first you must OPEN it.
2. Files from which you wish to input data must already exist and must be OPENed FOR INPUT. (FOR INPUT means input *from* the file *to* the program.)
3. Files to which you wish to PRINT or WRITE data may be OPENed FOR OUTPUT or OPENed for APPEND. FOR OUTPUT will erase any previous file with the same name. (OUTPUT means output *from* the program *to* the file.)
4. BASIC reads from a file using the INPUT #n, statement.
5. BASIC writes to a file using the PRINT #n, PRINT #n, USING mask$, and WRITE #n statements.
6. After the last data in a file #1 is INPUT, EOF(1) becomes true. This is useful in setting up a WHILE NOT EOF(1) loop.
7. Files should be CLOSEd as soon as they are no longer needed by the program.

Sequential Files: One More View

Before leaving the subject of sequential files, we want to make sure you fully understand their characteristics. Suppose you have a roll of microfilm and a

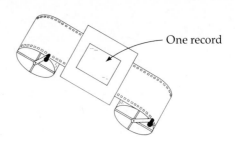

One record

FIGURE 7.3 •
*Microfilm's
similarity to a
sequential file*

The reel moves forward one frame
at a time. Only one record
at a time may be read from
or written onto.

microfilm reader that moves in a forward direction only, and that each frame on
the microfilm has a picture of one customer record (or any other kind of record)
(see Figure 7.3).

To access any one record on the microfilm, you first thread the film onto the
take-up spool. Then you start looking through the records (frames) one by one,
starting at the beginning, until you find the one you want. When you finish, you
rewind the film and put it away.

This is quite similar to the way sequential files work. The OPEN statement is
analogous to threading the film onto the take-up spool. It tells BASIC to find the
right "film" (file), then prepare to start processing records starting at the beginning of the file. The INPUT# statement is equivalent to what you would do with
your eyes on a microfilm reader—namely, "read" one record at a time. CLOSE is
equivalent to rewinding the spool and putting it away.

With sequential files there is no way to get directly to the middle of the file. You
must always start with the first record, then "wind" through the file, looking at
each record in turn to see whether it is the one you want. Random access files,
which overcome this limitation, will be discussed in Chapter 13.

Altering Data in Sequential Files: Sequential File Update

Using sequential files, you cannot select a record, update it, and place it back in
the same file. If you want to alter records in a file, you must create a new file for
output. You must successively read records from the original file, make any
alterations, and write the revised record to the output file. If you do not wish to
make any changes to a particular record, you will still need to write the record to
the new file if you wish to keep it as a part of your file. When this process is
finished, there will be two files: the original, unchanged file and the new, updated
file. Since you cannot have two files with the same name, the new file must be
given a different name from the original.

For example, suppose that we have a file named CUSTMAST.DAT in which
we keep the following data about each customer:

CUST.NBR	Customer number	Positive whole number less than 99999
CUST.NAME$	Customer name	String, up to 35 characters

CUST.ADDR$	Customer address	String, up to 50 characters
BAL.CURRENT	Current balance	Single precision
BAL.OVER.30	Balance 31 to 60 days	Single precision
BAL.OVER.60	Balance 61 to 90 days	Single precision
BAL.OVER.90	Balance over 90 days	Single precision

At the end of each month the balances need to be shifted. The current balance must be moved to the over 30 day, the balance over 30 must be moved to over 60, and over 60 must be must be added to over 90.

Naming Updated Files

This is a fairly simple process (see the program in "The Story's End"), but what shall we do about naming the files? Since the input and output files cannot have the same name, we can give the output file a temporary name, such as CUST-TEMP.DAT, while we write to it. We now have a problem. The new, updated file is the one we now wish to use in all other programs that will be using this data. Those programs use the filename "CUSTMAST.DAT" which is the name of the old file, not the updated one. We obviously do not want to change the filename in all those programs; what we need to do is to change the names of the files. There are several ways to do this.

One way would be to kill the original file and then to rename the new file with the name "CUSTMAST.DAT". The disadvantage of this way is that the original data are now gone, and if an error occurs, we may have no data at all. In any case we may wish to keep this data for historical purposes and to be able to rerun the program if we accidentally destroy the new file.

A better way would be to first rename the original file, then rename the new file to the original filename. We can rename the original file any name at all (other than a filename of an existing file on the disk). To avoid problems of duplicate names the next time the program is run, the program can ask the user to enter some identifying information, such as year and month, which can be used to give each file a unique name.

The initialization section of the program would include the following lines:

```
2040 OPEN "CUSTMAST.DAT" FOR INPUT AS #1
2050 OPEN "CUSTTEMP.DAT" FOR OUTPUT AS #2
2054 INPUT "Last two digits of this year: ", ACCT.YR$
2056 INPUT "Two digits for current month: ", ACCT.MO$
```

After updating is completed, execution will pass to the ending routine, which will include the following lines:

```
5050 LET NEW.NAME$ = "AR" + ACCT.YR$ + ACCT.MO$ + ".DAT"
5060 NAME "CUSTMAST.DAT" AS NEW.NAME$
5070 NAME "CUSTTEMP.DAT" AS "CUSTMAST.DAT"
5080 PRINT "Old file is named "; NEW.NAME$
```

Notice the use of concatenation in line 5050 to create the filename.

Balanced Line Algorithm for Sequential File Updating

One of the most commonly used algorithms for solving the general file updating problem is called the **balanced line algorithm.** There are several forms of this algorithm; the form shown here is closest to that of Barry Dwyer's.

Imagine that you are a clerk who has the job of keeping the customer account file current. You have a file drawer with the current customer data, which are kept in sequence by customer number, and an update file of changes, which is also put in numerical order. Your job then is to go through the two files. If the change has the same number as the master record, you apply the change; if it does not, you leave the master record as is and flip to the next master record to see if it needs changing. If the customer number on the change does not match a number in the master file, this is an "error" condition, which should be noted and investigated at a later time. Also, your auditor has asked that as an audit trail you keep some record of the changes that are applied.

In a general update problem you would not only make changes to existing records, but also add new customers or delete old ones. For the current discussion we will focus on the more limited problem of only changing some of the master records, but the value of the balanced line algorithm is that it can be used with all three kinds of updates.

The Algorithm

This algorithm assumes that both master records and update records are in order by a *key field,* where the key may be anything that identifies each master record. In our example the customer number is the key field.

The algorithm has three parts: a start, a repetitive process, and a finish. You may find it helpful to follow the path of each of the conditions through the flowchart in Figures 7.4, 7.5, and 7.6 as we discuss the algorithm.

THE START.   We will be dealing with at least three files: the old master file, the update or transaction file, and the new master file which we create to hold the updated master records. We may also create other files to hold an audit trail, errors, and so on.

We read the first record of the old master file and of the transaction file. We then determine which of these records holds the lower value for the key field and set the variable LOW-KEY to the lower value. LOW-KEY will be used to keep track of the customer number that is currently being processed. As new master and transaction records are read, the values of their key fields will be compared to LOW-KEY to determine whether it is time to process a transaction, to write a new master, or to write an error message.

REPETITION.   This loop is repeated once for each value of LOW-KEY. During each pass through the loop one of the following will occur:

1. If a master record has matching transaction records, all the transactions that match will be applied to the master and an updated master will be written.

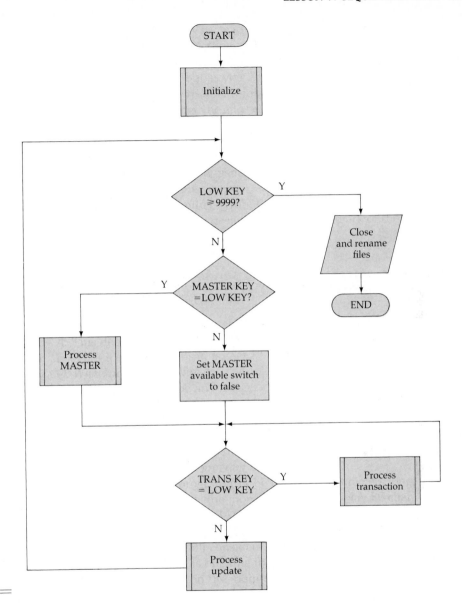

FIGURE 7.4 ▪
Flowchart for
balanced line
algorithm

2. If a master has no matching transactions, the unchanged master record will be written.
3. If any transactions are encountered that do not match a master record, they will be written to an error file.

Since LOW-KEY holds the value of the customer number being examined, each value of LOW-KEY will yield either a record in the updated master file or a record in the error file.

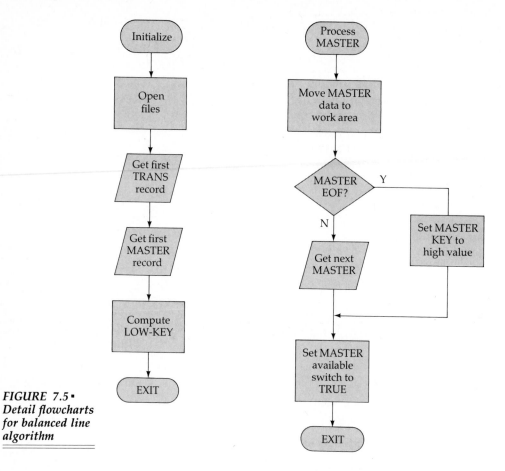

FIGURE 7.5 •
Detail flowcharts
for balanced line
algorithm

Now let's look at how each of the conditions just described is processed.

1. *Master with Matching Transaction*

   MASTER.KEY = LOW.KEY = TRANS.KEY

   We first test to see if the old master record key equals the LOW-KEY. If this is true, we know that the master record is ready to be processed. We move it to a work area for processing, set a switch to indicate that a master record is available for processing, and read the next old master record.

   Then we test to see if the transaction record key also equals the LOW-KEY. This is true, and the switch indicating a master is available has been set; therefore we apply the transaction and read the next transaction record. Deviating from our procedure with the master record, we *repeat* this process until the key of the transaction record that is input no longer equals the LOW-KEY.

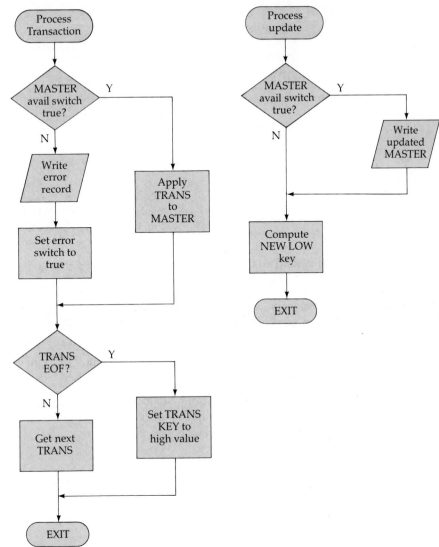

FIGURE 7.6 •
*Detail flowcharts
for balanced line
algorithm*

At this point we verify that the master available switch has been set, write the updated master record to the new master record file, compute a new value for LOW-KEY, and return to the start of the loop. Since the next master record was read immediately after the current record was moved to the work area and the next transaction was read during the transaction processing loop, LOW-KEY will contain the lower of the two.

2. *Master with No Matching Transactions*

MASTER.KEY = LOW.KEY <> TRANS.KEY

▪ *PARABLES FOR PROGRAMMERS* ▪

Murphy Was a Programmer

"It's not my fault," cried an exasperated Yorick. "I only write programs, and this was a hardware problem!"

Yorick, a programmer, and Ophelia, an irate user of Yorick's programs, leaned over the supervisor's desk heatedly pleading their respective cases. "One at a time!" bellowed the supervisor. "Yorick, Ophelia claims your program destroyed a month's worth of data. What's your side of the story?"

"It's really very simple," explained Yorick. "My program handles end-of-month reporting for an accounting application. It prints a report from the file containing the current month's transactions, then empties the file in preparation for the following month's entries. The program works, but this month Ophelia's printer, didn't; it jammed in the middle of printing the report. The program kept on printing, then emptied the file as it was supposed to. The program had no way to know the printer was jammed and the report scrambled. Like I said, a hardware problem."

"Hardware, shmardware," huffed Ophelia. "All I know is that because your program emptied the file, we can't rerun the report. All that data is lost."

The supervisor seemed lost in thought for a moment, then turned to Ophelia. "Ophelia, didn't you make a backup copy of the data before you ran such a critical program?" Turning bright crimson, Ophelia admitted she hadn't. "Did you keep an eye on the printer to watch for problems?" Again, the answer was no.

Turning to Yorick's smug smile, the supervisor said, "Alas, poor Yorick, you are also not without fault. You, more than Ophelia, knew the potential for harm when this program is interrupted in midstream, yet your instructions on its use did not clearly state that a backup should be done before using the program. It is also bad practice to try to have one program do too many things at once. Had you split the program into two separate programs, one of which printed the report and the other of which emptied the file, Ophelia would have had the opportunity to rerun the report program before running the purge program.

"The real lesson each of you should learn from this is that anything that can go wrong with a program or computer eventually will, but that good planning can overcome all but the worst problems. Instead of pointing fingers, why don't you two discuss how both of you can minimize our risk in the future."

MORAL: An ounce of prevention, in computers as in life, is worth a pound of cure.

Since the master key equals LOW-KEY, it will be readied for processing and the next master read in. There are no transactions with the same key; therefore, the transaction processing routine will not be executed. Execution will proceed to the next step, in which the unchanged master record will be written and LOW-KEY recomputed with the next master.

3. *Transactions with No Matching Master*

MASTER.KEY <> LOW.KEY = TRANS.KEY

When this occurs, the key of the transaction will be less than the key of the master. When LOW-KEY is calculated, it will equal the transaction key but not equal the master key. The master will not be moved to the work area, nor will the master available switch be set.

Since the transaction key equals LOW-KEY, the transaction processing routine will be executed. However, the master available switch was not set; therefore, the transaction will be written to an error file and the next transaction input.

When all unmatched transactions with this key are processed, we will exit from the loop, compute LOW-KEY, and begin the loop again.

FINISH. At the time either of the files is input we test first to see if the end-of-file has been reached. If is has, we set key field for that file to a value higher than the last valid value for that file. In our case, we will set it to 99999. (For an alphabetic field we might use "ZZZZZZZZZZZ".) This will force any remaining records in the other file to be processed. When both files have reached the end, LOW-KEY will have the value of 99999, and we will exit the loop.

At this point we close the files, rename them, and perhaps write a message to the operator.

Coding the Algorithm
We are now ready to write the program to update the customer balances. The structure chart is shown in Figure 7.7.

Notice that since this program uses more than three files (it uses five), we must invoke BASIC using the command BASICA /F:5

Pseudocode

```
PROGRAM:  BALANCE
      DO INITIALIZATION
      WHILE LOW.KEY < 99999
          DO UPDATE-RECORD-WITH-LOW.KEY
      WEND
      DO FINISH
      END
```

```
INITIALIZATION
      OPEN files
      INPUT TODAY$ (today's date)
```

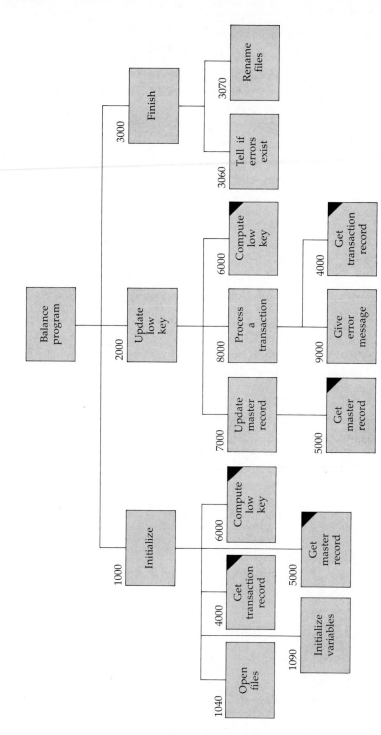

FIGURE 7.7 ▪
Structure chart
for balanced line
program

```
    PRINT header to to audit trail file
    Initialize variables
    DO GET-TRANS
    DO GET-MASTER
    DO COMPUTE-LOW-KEY
GET-TRANS
    IF end of trans file [eof (2)]
        THEN LET trans.key = 99999
        ELSE INPUT from customer trans file, transrecord
GET.MASTER
    IF end of master file [eof (1)]
        THEN LET master.key = 99999
        ELSE INPUT from customer master file, master record
COMPUTE-LOW.KEY
    IF master.key <= trans.key
        THEN low.key = master.key
        ELSE low.key = trans.key
```

```
UPDATE-RECORD-WITH-LOW.KEY
    IF master.key = low.key
        THEN DO UPDATE-MASTER
        ELSE LET record.available = false
    WHILE trans.key = low.key
        DO PROCESS-A-TRANSACTION
    WEND
    IF record.available = true
        THEN WRITE to updated master file, temprecord
            PRINT to audit trail,"Done",temp.master.key,temp.bal.current
    DO COMPUTE-LOW.KEY
UPDATE-MASTER
    PRINT to audit trail, "Start", master.key, bal.current
    Move master record fields to work area
    DO GET-MASTER
    LET record.available = true
PROCESS-A-TRANSACTION
    IF record.available = true
        THEN LET temp.bal.current = temp.bal.current + trans.amt
            PRINT to audit trail,"Apply",trans.key,trans.amt
        ELSE DO ERROR
    DO GET-TRANS
```

```
FINISH
    CLOSE files
    PRINT "Processing has finished"
    IF error.flag = true
        THEN PRINT "Error occurred . . ."
```

       Rename files
<u>ERROR</u>
       WRITE to error file, trans.key, trans.date, trans.desc$, trans.amt
       LET error.flag = true

Program Listing

```
10    '===============================================================
20    '             PROGRAM NAME:   BALANCE.BAS
30    '===============================================================
40    '   Author    : Jesse Mears
50    '   Date of Installation:  Aug. 7, 1988
60    '   Program Description:
70    '        Updates Current Balance in Customer Master Record
80    '   Files Used:
90    '        CUSTMAST.DAT-Customer Master Records
100   '        CUSTTRAN.DAT-Customer Transaction Records
110   '        UPDATED.REC-Temporary Name for Updated Master Records
120   '        AUDIT_F.ILE-Audit Trail of Processing
130   '        ERRORS_L.IST-Unmatched Transactions
140   '
150   '   ** must use BASICA/F:5  when BASIC is invoked ***
500   '===============================================================
510   '                    MAIN LINE
520   '===============================================================
530 GOSUB 1000                                    'initialization
540 WHILE LOW.KEY < 99999!
550     GOSUB 2000                                'update low key
560 WEND
570 GOSUB 3000                                    'finish
580 END
590   '===============================================================
600   '                 END OF PROCESSING
1000  '===============================================================
1010  '                  INITIALIZATION                             '
1020  '===============================================================
1030 CLS
1040 OPEN "CUSTMAST.DAT" FOR INPUT AS #1            ' open files
1050 OPEN "CUSTTRAN.DAT" FOR INPUT AS #2
1060 OPEN "UPDATED.REC" FOR OUTPUT AS #3
1070 OPEN "AUDIT_F.ILE" FOR OUTPUT AS #4
1080 OPEN "ERRORS_L.IST" FOR OUTPUT AS #5
1090 INPUT "Please enter today's date as mm/dd/yy ", TODAY$
1100 PRINT #4, TODAY$,"Audit Trail"
1110 PRINT #4, " "
1120 LET TRUE = -1
1130 LET FALSE = 0
1140 LET ERROR.FLAG = FALSE
1150 '                                           get values
```

```
1160 GOSUB 4000                               'get transaction record
1170 GOSUB 5000                               'get master record
1180 GOSUB 6000                               'compute low key
1190 RETURN
2000 '=========================================================================
2010 '              UPDATE ONE RECORD FOR THIS GIVEN LOW KEY VALUE         '
2020 '=========================================================================
2030                                          'either update master or
2040                                          'turn available flag false
2050 IF MASTER.KEY = LOW.KEY THEN GOSUB 7000 ELSE LET RECORD.AVAILABLE = FALSE
2060                                          'now work on transactions
2070                                          'with this same low key
2080 WHILE TRANS.KEY = LOW.KEY
2090     GOSUB 8000                           'process a transaction
2100 WEND
2110 IF RECORD.AVAILABLE = TRUE THEN WRITE #3,TEMP.MASTER.KEY,TEMP.CUST.NAME$,
     TEMP.CUST.ADDR$, TEMP.BAL.CURRENT, TEMP.BAL.OVER.30, TEMP.BAL.OVER.60,
     TEMP.BAL.OVER.90: PRINT #4,"Done",TEMP.MASTER.KEY,TEMP.BAL.CURRENT:
     PRINT #4, " "
2120 GOSUB 6000                               'compute low key
2130 RETURN
3000 '=========================================================================
3010 '                        FINISH
3020 '=========================================================================
3030 CLOSE
3040 CLS
3050 PRINT "Processing has finished"
3060 IF ERROR.FLAG = TRUE THEN PRINT
       "Error occurred-not all transactions matched master records":
       PRINT "Check file ERRORS_L.IST for details"
3070 OPEN "OLDMAST.DAT" FOR APPEND AS #1      ' if old back up exists
3080 CLOSE                                    '     erase it
3090 KILL "OLDMAST.DAT"
3100 NAME "CUSTMAST.DAT" AS "OLDMAST.DAT"
3110 NAME "UPDATED.REC"  AS "CUSTMAST.DAT"
3120 RETURN
4000 '=========================================================================
4010 '            GET A TRANSACTION RECORD                                   '
4020 '=========================================================================
4030 IF EOF(2) THEN LET TRANS.KEY = 99999!
       ELSE INPUT #2, TRANS.KEY,TRANS.DATE,TRANS.DESC$,TRANS.AMT
4040 RETURN
5000 '=========================================================================
5010 '         GET A MASTER RECORD'
5020 '=========================================================================
5030 IF EOF(1) THEN LET MASTER.KEY = 99999!
       ELSE INPUT #1, MASTER.KEY, CUST.NAME$,CUST.ADDR$, BAL.CURRENT,
       BAL.OVER.30, BAL.OVER.60, BAL.OVER.90
5040 PRINT "Processing Master Record for Customer: "; MASTER.KEY
5050 RETURN
```

```
6000 '=================================================================
6010 '              COMPUTE LOW KEY'
6020 '=================================================================
6030 IF MASTER.KEY <= TRANS.KEY THEN LET LOW.KEY = MASTER.KEY
        ELSE LET LOW.KEY = TRANS.KEY
6040 RETURN
7000 '=================================================================
7010 '              UPDATE A MASTER RECORD'
7020 '=================================================================
7030 PRINT #4, "Start", MASTER.KEY, BAL.CURRENT       'audit file entry
7040 '                                                move master to temp
7050 LET   TEMP.MASTER.KEY = MASTER.KEY
7060 LET   TEMP.CUST.NAME$ = CUST.NAME$
7070 LET   TEMP.CUST.ADDR$ = CUST.ADDR$
7080 LET   TEMP.BAL.CURRENT = BAL.CURRENT
7090 LET   TEMP.BAL.OVER.30 = BAL.OVER.30
7100 LET   TEMP.BAL.OVER.60 = BAL.OVER.60
7110 LET   TEMP.BAL.OVER.90 = BAL.OVER.90
7120 '
7130 GOSUB 5000                                       'get master record
7140 LET RECORD.AVAILABLE = TRUE
7150 RETURN
8000 '=================================================================
8010 '     APPLY ONE TRANSACTION RECORD TO MASTER, OR GIVE ERROR       '
8020 '=================================================================
8030 IF RECORD.AVAILABLE = TRUE THEN LET TEMP.BAL.CURRENT = TEMP.BAL.CURRENT
        + TRANS.AMT: PRINT #4,"Apply",TRANS.KEY,TRANS.AMT ELSE GOSUB 9000
                '9000 is error routine
8040 GOSUB 4000                                       'get transaction
8050 RETURN
9000 '=================================================================
9005 '              ERROR IN TRANSACTION NOT MATCHING A MASTER RECORD   '
9010 '=================================================================
9020 WRITE #5, TRANS.KEY, TRANS.DATE, TRANS.DESC$, TRANS.AMT
9030 LET ERROR.FLAG = TRUE
9040 RETURN
9999 '===================== END OF LISTING =============================
```

Systems of Programs: Different Programs Use the Same Data Files

Sequential files introduce a new element in computer programming: sharing data between two or more programs. With data stored on a disk, dozens of different programs may use the same files.

Consider the two files we have been discussing: CUSTMAST.DAT and CUST-TRAN.DAT. We have mentioned one program that shifts the balances in CUST-MAST.DAT and have shown another program in which the records stored in CUSTTRAN.DAT are processed to update current the balances stored in CUST-

MAST.DAT. How were these files created? Some other programs must have asked the user for the data and created the files. It is likely that other programs will generate reports from the data in these files.

This implies that for this simple example no fewer than four programs use the same data files. A collection of programs that work together to allow a user to process an application is called a **system of programs.** A system of programs introduces the need for documentation beyond that you have used so far. Comments embedded in one program describing a data file are not adequate to document all the programs that use that same file. Instead, an external document should be prepared that describes the data file and, in general terms, the programs that operate on it. Only in this way can a programmer working on one program be assured that changes will not have a "side effect" on some other program or programs. This set of documents is called **systems documentation.**

Figure 7.8 shows a system flowchart that illustrates the programs and the files that process customer accounts. The following are documents that would appear in the systems documentation:

CUSTOMER ACCOUNT SYSTEM

FILES USED
    CUSTTRAN.DAT
        Fields

Account Number	####, integer greater than 0
Date	yymmdd
Description	string, max of 30 characters
Amount	####.##, positive or negative

        Used in Programs

ENTRTRAN.BAS	Enter Transactions
BALANCE.BAS	Update Current Balance

    CUSTMAST.DAT
        Fields

Account Number	####, integer greater than 0
Name	string, max of 35 characters
Address	string, max of 50 characters
Current Balance	#####.##, positive or negative
Balance over 30 days	#####.##, positive or negative
Balance over 60 days	#####.##, positive or negative
Balance over 90 days	#####.##, positive or negative

        Used in Programs

BALANCE.BAS	Update Current Balance
AGEDAR.BAS	Age Account Balances

SEQUENCE OF PROCESSING
    DAILY
        RUN ENTRTRAN.BAS   Enter Transactions
            Uses file CUSTTRAN.DAT
            Transactions entered from the keyboard are appended to
                the file CUSTTRAN.DAT

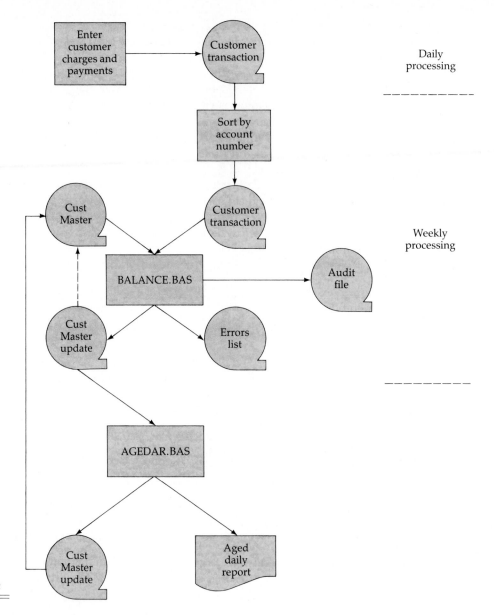

FIGURE 7.8 ▪
Customer
accounts system

WEEKLY
    Sort CUSTTRAN.DAT into account number sequence using one of
        the sort programs
    RUN BALANCE.BAS   Update Current Balance
        Uses files CUSTTRAN.DAT and CUSTMAST.DAT
        Transactions in CUSTTRAN.DAT are applied to balance in
            CUSTMAST.DAT

Unmatched transactions stored in ERRORS__L.IST
Audit trail stored in AUDIT__F.ILE
Original master file renamed as OLDMAST.DAT
Back Up
Format a disk, label with this week's date and copy
OLDMAST.DAT and CUSTTRAN.DAT
Kill CUSTTRAN.DAT on daily disk before ENTRTRAN.BAS is run
again
MONTHLY
RUN AGEDAR.BAS   Age Account Balances
Uses file CUSTMAST.DAT
Prints balances and shifts balances to next age field
Original master file renamed to "ARyymm.DAT"
where yy is year and mm is month
Back Up
Copy "ARyymm.DAT" to historical disk

THE STORY'S END

Jesse could now write the programs to update the aged balances and to print a report.

The company figured that this report enabled them to follow up quickly on the delinquent accounts and collect at least 60 percent of the accounts that they had formerly had to write off.

Specifications

Aged balances for each customer are stored in the file "CUSTMAST.DAT". (See file layout in "Systems of Programs—Different Programs Use the Same Data Files.")

This program will be run at the end of each month.

A report will be printed listing each customer name, number, and the amount in each of the balance fields. At the end of the report the total of each of the fields for all customers will be printed.

The customer account will then be "aged" by adding the balance over 60 days old to the balance over 90 and then moving each remaining balance to the next older field.

At the end of the processing the old file will be renamed using the year and month entered by the user, and the new, updated file will be renamed "CUST-MAST.DAT".

Functions

A. Verify user's intent to age accounts
B. Initialization

  C. Process each record
   1. INPUT customer record from file
   2. PRINT data
   3. Age balances and add to final totals
   4. WRITE updated record
  D. Closing routines
   1. PRINT totals
   2. Rename files

Structure Chart

Jesse drew the structure chart shown in Figure 7.9.

Data Dictionary

Files   *Fields*
CUSTMAST.DAT   input
    CUST.NBR
    CUST.NAME$
    CUST.ADDR$ (not used)
    CURRENT.BAL
    BAL.OVER.30
    BAL.OVER.60
    BAL.OVER.90
CUSTTEMP.DAT   output
   same fields as CUSTMAST.DAT

Working Variables
ACCT.YR$ Current year as yy
ACCT.MO$ Current month as mm
ACCT.DAY$ Current day as dd
TODAY$ Today's date as mm/dd/yy
NEW.NAME$ File name for CUSTMAST.DAT
           after update
PAGE.NUMBER   Current page number
REC.COUNT   Number of records printed so far on
           this page
LINES.PER.PAGE   Max number of lines on one page
MASK$ Mask for detail lines
TOTAL.MASK$ Mask for total line

Switches
ANSWER$ C or c indicates ok to process any
           other value indicates abort process

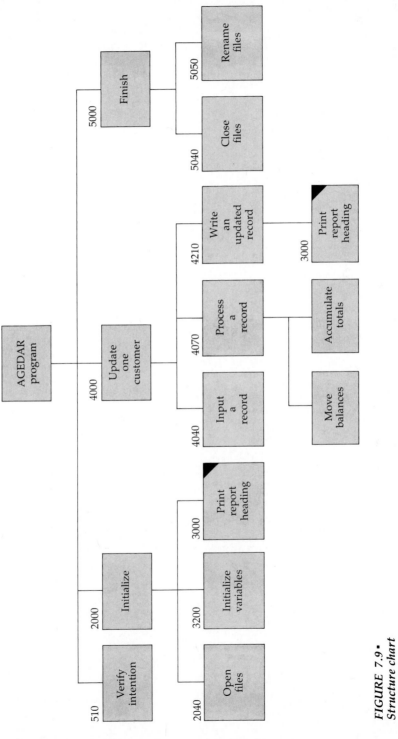

FIGURE 7.9 ·
Structure chart
for AGEDAR
program

Accumulators

TOTAL.CURRENT	Total of BAL.CURRENT
TOTAL.OVER.30	Total of BAL.OVER.30
TOTAL.OVER.60	Total of BAL.OVER.60
TOTAL.OVER.90	Total of BAL.OVER.90

Pseudocode

<u>MAIN LINE</u>
    DO VERIFY-INTENTION
    IF ANSWER$ <> Continue THEN END
    DO INITIALIZATION
    WHILE NOT END OF FILE
        DO UPDATE-ONE-CUSTOMER-RECORD
    WEND
    DO FINISH
    END

<u>VERIFY-INTENTION</u>
    INPUT ANSWER$
        C or c to continue with process
        Any other character to abort

<u>INITIALIZATION</u>
    OPEN FILES
        CUSTMAST.DAT for INPUT
        CUSTTEMP.DAT for OUTPUT
    DO INITIALIZE-VARIABLES
    DO PRINT-REPORT-HEADING
<u>INITIALIZE VARIABLES</u>
    INPUT year, month and day
    Set counters and accumulators to zero
<u>PRINT-REPORT-HEADING</u>
    Increment PAGE.NBR
    Set REC.COUNT to zero
    PRINT heading

<u>UPDATE-ONE-CUSTOMER-RECORD</u>
    INPUT Customer Record from file
    Increment REC.COUNT
    IF REC.COUNT > LINES.PER.PAGE
        THEN DO PRINT-REPORT-HEADING
    PRINT customer data
    Add balances to totals

> Move balances to next fields
> WRITE customer data to temp file

FINISH
> CLOSE files
> Rename files
> PRINT totals
> PRINT name of old file

Program Listing

```
100  '======================================================================
110  '                        Program: AGEDAR.BAS
120  '======================================================================
130  'Author: Jesse Mears
140  'Date of Installation: Sept. 19, 1988
150  ' Program Description
160  '        Prints Aged Accounts Receivable Report
170  '        Moves Balances to Next Period
180  ' File Used:
190  '        CUSTMAST.DAT-renamed to ARyymm at end of processing
200  '        CUSTTEMP.DAT-temporary name until processing is complete
210  '                    renamed to CUSTMAST.DAT at end of processing
220  '
230  '
500  '======================================================================
510  GOSUB 1500       'Verify Intention
520  IF ANSWER$ <> "C" AND ANSWER$ <> "c"
         THEN GOTO 1080 'User does not want to continue
1000 '======================================================================
1010 '                    MAIN LINE OF PROGRAM
1020 '======================================================================
1030 GOSUB 2000         'Initialize
1040 WHILE NOT EOF(1)
1050      GOSUB 4000          'Update One Customer Record
1060 WEND
1070 GOSUB 5000       'Finish
1080 END
1090 '======================================================================
1100 '                    END OF PROCESSING
1500 '======================================================================
1510 '                    Verify Intention
1520 '======================================================================
1530 CLS
1540 PRINT "THIS PROGRAM WILL AGE THE ACCOUNT RECEIVABLE BALANCES"
1550 INPUT "Enter C to CONTINUE-Enter any other key to ABORT ", ANSWER$
1560 RETURN
1570 '======================================================================
```

```
2000 '=======================================================================
2010 '                            INITIALIZE
2020 '=======================================================================
2030 '           Open Files
2040 OPEN "CUSTMAST.DAT" FOR INPUT AS #1
2050 OPEN "CUSTTEMP.DAT" FOR OUTPUT AS #2
2060 GOSUB 3200       'Initialize Variables
2070 GOSUB 3000       'Print Report Heading
2080 RETURN
3000 '=======================================================================
3010 '                        Print Report Heading
3020 '=======================================================================
3030 LET PAGE.NBR = PAGE.NBR + 1
3040 PRINT:PRINT:PRINT:PRINT 'skip down 4 lines
3050 PRINT "              AGED ACCOUNT RECEIVABLE REPORT"
3060 PRINT "                   FOR "; TODAY$
3070 PRINT "                       PAGE: "; PAGE.NBR
3080 PRINT
3090 PRINT
"      NAME          NUMBER        0-30         31-60         61-90        over 90"
3100 PRINT
3110 LET MASK$ =
"\             \    ######  ###,###.##    ###,###.##    ###,###.##    ###,###.##"
3120 LET TOTAL.MASK$ =
"\            \            #,###,###.## #,###,###.## #,###,###.## #,###,###.##"
3130 LET REC.COUNT = 0
3140 RETURN
3200 '=======================================================================
3210 '              Initialize Variables
3220 '=======================================================================
3230 INPUT "Please enter the last two digits of the year:  ", ACCT.YR$
3240 INPUT "Please enter two digits for the current month: ", ACCT.MO$
3250 INPUT "Please enter two digits for the day:           ", ACCT.DAY$
3260 LET TODAY$ = ACCT.MO$ + "/" + ACCT.DAY$ + "/" + ACCT.YR$
3270 DEFINT C
3280 DEFDBL B,T
3290 LET REC.COUNT = 0
3300 LET LINES.PER.PAGE = 10
3310 LET TOTAL.CURRENT = 0: LET TOTAL.OVER.30 = 0
3320 LET TOTAL.OVER.60 = 0: LET TOTAL.OVER.90 = 0
3330 RETURN
4000 '=======================================================================
4010 '                         Update One Customer
4020 '=======================================================================
4030 '                                            input a record
4040 INPUT #1, CUST.NBR, CUST.NAME$, DUMMY$, BAL.CURRENT, BAL.OVER.30,
              BAL.OVER.60, BAL.OVER.90
4050 IF REC.COUNT => LINES.PER.PAGE THEN GOSUB 3000
4060 LET REC.COUNT = REC.COUNT + 1
4070 PRINT USING MASK$; CUST.NAME$, CUST.NBR, BAL.CURRENT, BAL.OVER.30,
              BAL.OVER.60, BAL.OVER.90
```

```
4080 '
4090 '                              Accumulate Totals
4100 LET TOTAL.CURRENT = TOTAL.CURRENT + BAL.CURRENT
4110 LET TOTAL.OVER.30 = TOTAL.OVER.30 + BAL.OVER.30
4120 LET TOTAL.OVER.60 = TOTAL.OVER.60 + BAL.OVER.60
4130 LET TOTAL.OVER.90 = TOTAL.OVER.90 + BAL.OVER.90
4140 '                              Move Balances
4150 LET BAL.OVER.90 = BAL.OVER.90 + BAL.OVER.60
4160 LET BAL.OVER.60 = BAL.OVER.30
4170 LET BAL.OVER.30 = BAL.CURRENT
4180 LET BAL.CURRENT = 0
4190 '
4200 '                                        Write Updated File
4210 WRITE #2, CUST.NBR, CUST.NAME$, DUMMY$, BAL.CURRENT, BAL.OVER.30,
              BAL.OVER.60, BAL.OVER.90
4220 RETURN
5000 '====================================================================
5010 '                              Finish
5020 '====================================================================
5030 '                                        Close Files
5040 CLOSE #1,#2
5050 LET NEW.NAME$ = "AR" + ACCT.YR$ + ACCT.MO$ + ".DAT"
5060 NAME "CUSTMAST.DAT" AS NEW.NAME$
5070 NAME "CUSTTEMP.DAT" AS "CUSTMAST.DAT"
5080 '                                        Print Totals
5090 PRINT
5100 PRINT USING TOTAL.MASK$; "TOTALS", TOTAL.CURRENT, TOTAL.OVER.30,
              TOTAL.OVER.60, TOTAL.OVER.90
5110 PRINT
5120 PRINT "Old file is named "; NEW.NAME$
5130 RETURN
5140 '============================= END OF LISTING =======================
```

•QUICK REFERENCE FOR LESSON 7•

DATA FILES: Data May be Stored on Disks in Data Files

Files usually consist of a series of logical records, which contain all of the data about one transaction.

Logical record are divided into fields, which hold various items of data.

There are two types of data files: sequential and random access.

Sequential files are input and output in sequential order, from beginning to end. Data is input in the same order in which it was written. New records may be added to the end of an existing sequential file, but may not be inserted into the middle of an existing file.

Random access files allow data to be retrieved from or written to any place in the file. (They will be discussed in Chapter 13.)

OPEN Makes Ready a File for Input or Output

OPEN Filename FOR Mode AS #*n*
Modes for sequential files are:

> OUTPUT will ready the file for being written onto disk. If a file with the same name already exists in the current directory, it will be erased.
>
> INPUT will ready the file for being read from disk. A file with the name specified must exist in the current directory or the error message "File not found" will occur.
>
> APPEND will ready the file for additional records to be added to the end. If a file with the name specified does not exist on the disk, one will be created; if one does exist, all current records will be preserved.
>
> #*n* is an integer that is assigned to the file specified and may not exceed the maximum allowed number of open files.
>
> Disk BASIC allows a maximum of 3 files open at one time unless the /F: option is used when BASIC is invoked from DOS. The maximum may be increased up to 15 by loading
>
> BASIC with the command: BASICA /F:m (or BASIC /F:m), where m is the maximum number that may be open at one time.
>
> The # may be omitted.

PRINT #n, Writes Data to a Sequential Disk File

PRINT # writes data to disk in the same format PRINT writes to the screen. Punctuation is *not* automatically placed between items.

#*n* refers to the file number that was assigned by the OPEN statement. The file must have been opened FOR OUTPUT or FOR APPEND.

The # is required.

> ### PRINT #*n*, variable (or expression)
> Writes a single variable to the file assigned the number *n*.
> ### PRINT #*n*, variable, variable, . . .
> Writes the indicated variables to the file. The variables are written with the same print zone spacing between them as they would be if PRINTed to the screen.
> ### PRINT #*n*, variable; variable; . . .
> Writes the indicated variables to the file. As with PRINT, the semicolon suppresses the print zones. The variables will have the same spacing as they would with PRINT.

PRINT #n, USING MASK$; Variable, Variable, . . .

Writes data to a sequential file in the same manner PRINT USING writes to the screen.

WRITE #n,

Writes data to a sequential file with correct punctuation for later INPUT from the file.

#*n* refers to the file number that was assigned by the OPEN statement. The file must have been opened FOR OUTPUT or FOR APPEND.

The # is required.

WRITE #n, Variable (or Expression), Variable, . . .
Quotation marks are placed around string variables.
Numeric variables are written without leading or trailing spaces.
Commas are placed between each variable in the file.

INPUT #n, Inputs Data from a Sequential Disk File

#n refers to the file number that was assigned by the OPEN statement. The file must have been opened FOR INPUT.

INPUT #n, Variable, Variable, . . .
Inputs the next data items into the variable(s) specified. To avoid errors, the variable type names in the INPUT statement must match the variable types of the data in the file. The data items are read sequentially.

If an attempt is made to input data past the last item in the file, the message "Input past end" will occur.

CLOSE Removes a File from Ready Status

CLOSE #n, #m, . . . will close only the files assigned the numbers specified. The # may be omitted.

CLOSE will close all files.

CLOSE disassociates the file name from the file number that was assigned by the OPEN statement.

CLOSE also ensures that the last data are written to the file and places an EOF marker at the end of the file.

All open files are also closed by executing any one of the following: END, NEW, SYSTEM, RUN (STOP does *not* close any files).

EOF(n): Function Indicates the End of the File

n refers to the file number that was assigned by the OPEN statement. The file must have been opened FOR INPUT.

The # may *not* be used with EOF.

When the last item of data has been INPUT from a sequential file, the EOF function for that file is set to the value of TRUE. This function can be tested to prevent attempting to input past the end of the file.

·EXERCISES·

Short Answer

1. Define the different parts of a computer file (file, record, field). Using a Rolodex as an example, give the corresponding parts.

2. What is the difference between sequential and random access files?

3. What statement creates a new file?

4. What is the difference between the PRINT # and WRITE # statements? When would you use one over the other?

5. What is the difference between the PRINT and PRINT # statements? the WRITE and WRITE # statements?

6. What might happen if you don't CLOSE a file?

7. What is the statement to open an already existing file?

8. What does EOF stand for? What does it do?

9. What happens when string data is input into a numeric variable?

10. What statement would you use to write formatted output?

11. Explain the differences among the following statements: OPEN FOR INPUT, OPEN FOR OUTPUT, OPEN FOR APPEND.

12. Explain the process for updating a sequential file. Give the results of each step.

13. Is it necessary for the variable names used to input and output data in a file to be the same name and type? Why or why not?

14. If you want to have more than three files open at once, what must you do?

15. How many files can you have open if:
    a. you type BASIC or BASICA?
    b. you type BASIC/F:13 or BASICA/F:13?

16. What is a sequential file? If you want to process the twenty-first record in the file, how do you get to it?

17. How are the terms *files, records,* and *fields* related?

18. Which of the following data file names are invalid?
    a. TEMP
    b. TEMP.COM
    c. FILE1.DATA
    d. MASTER-FILE.DAT
    e. MASTER-1.DAT

Analyzing Code

19. What will happen if you run the following program?

```
10 LET CONTINUE.SWITCH$ ="YES"
20 WHILE CONTINUE.SWITCH$ = "YES"
30    INPUT #1, THE.NAME$, THE.ADDRESS$
40    INPUT  "IF YOU WISH TO GET ANOTHER NAME AND ADDRESS
             ENTER 'YES'"; CONTINUE.SWITCH$
50 WEND
60 END
```

20. What, if anything, is wrong with the following?

```
10 OPEN "ACCTREC.DAT" FOR INPUT AS #1
20 WHILE NOT EOF
30   INPUT #1, THE.NAME$, THE.ADDRESS$
```

```
40    PRINT THE.NAME$, THE.ADDRESS$
50 WEND
60 STOP
```

21. Using the INPUT # statement, write a line of code that reads data from the following fields for the file that we will call "EMPLOYEE.DAT".
    a. Employee's Social Security number (format: 999999999)
    b. Employee's first name
    c. Employee's last name
    d. Previous title
    e. Current title
    f. Previous salary (format: 9999.99)
    g. Current salary (format: 9999.99)

22. What will happen in the following lines of code?

```
10 OPEN "INV.DAT" FOR INPUT AS #1
20 OPEN "INV.DAT" FOR OUTPUT AS #2
30 END
```

23. If you wanted to add data to the end of the INV.DAT how would you open the file?

Programming

24. CREATE A FILE
    a. Write a program to create a data file called "PAYROLL.DAT". The fields for each record are as follows:

    Social Security number
    Employee name
    Cumulative gross pay
    Cumulative taxes withheld
    Cumulative net pay.

    There may be up to 99 employees.
    The program should prompt the user to enter the Social Security number and employee name. The other fields will be set to zero.
    b. Now write a program to print an employee listing from this file—just print the Social Security number and name for each employee.

25. UPDATING A FILE: Using the data file "PAYROLL.DAT" described in Exercise 24, write a program that reads each employee name and prompts the user to enter the gross wages and taxes withheld. (Net pay equals gross minus the amount withheld.)
    Add the amounts entered to the balances in the file and write the updated record.
    When processing is completed, the updated file should be named "PAYROLL.DAT". The original file should be kept and given a name that will identify the period to which this processing applies. For example, you might prompt the user to enter the current month (a number between 1 and 12) and then prompt the user for the last two digits of the year. These numbers will be concatenated to a string such as "PAY" + PAY.MONTH$ + PAY.YEAR$ + ".DAT".

26. PRINT REPORT: Modify the preceding program so that it prints the following report as the data are entered.

```
                    EMPLOYEE PAYROLL REPORT
                 FOR MONTH OF _____ , 19___

              TOTALS THIS PERIOD              CUMULATIVE TOTALS
              ==================              =================

EMPLOYEE:     xxxxxxxxxxxxxxxxxx     SOCIAL SECURITY NO. 999-99-9999
GROSS PAY:             $99,999.99      GROSS PAY:     $999,999.99
WITHHOLDING:           $9,999.99       WITHHOLDING:   $ 99,999.99
NET PAY:              $99,999.99       NET PAY:       $999,999.99


EMPLOYEE:     xxxxxxxxxxxxxxxx       SOCIAL SECURITY NO. 999-99-9999
GROSS PAY: . . . . . .                 GROSS PAY: . . . . . . .
        .                                      .
        .                                      .
        .                                      .
        .                                      .
```

27. INVENTORY

   a. Write a program that creates a master file named "PARTMAST.DAT" for the parts in inventory. For each part the following data are stored:

   Part number   positive integer, maximum value 9999
   Part description   string, maximum of 30 characters

   b. Customers send in orders for these parts. Write a second program that creates a file of parts ordered in the following manner.

   Input a record from "PARTMAST.DAT" and display the part number and description.

   Ask the user to enter all the orders for this part by entering the customer number and quantity ordered. Create a file named "ORDER.DAT" that contains for each order:

   Part number   positive integer, maximum value 9999
   Customer number   positive integer, maximum value 9999
   Quantity ordered   positive whole number, maximum value 99999

   There may be any number of orders for a particular part. If there are no orders for a part, do not write an order record.

   c. Write a program that inputs both "PARTMAST.DAT" and "ORDER.DAT" (both files are in part number sequence) and prints the following report.

```
            PARTS ORDERED
    PART NUMBER: ####     DESCRIPTION: XXXXXXXXXXXXXXXXXXXXXXXXXXXXXX
         CUST NUMBER: #### QUANTITY:    ##,###
         CUST NUMBER: #### QUANTITY:    ##,###
              .         .
              .         .
              .         .
            TOTAL ORDERED                 #,###,###
    PART NUMBER: ####     DESCRIPTION: XXXXXXXXXXXXXXXXXXXXXXXXXXXXXX
         .              .
         .              .
         .              .
```

As the report is printed, create a filed named "TOTORDER.DAT" that contains the part number and total ordered. If no orders have been placed for that part, do not write a record to this file.

If the part number in "ORDER.DAT" does not equal the part number in "PARTMAST.DAT", write the record to an error file.

28. UTILITY BILLING

Natural gas is measured in therms. Assume that the utility company charges the following rates for gas usage:

First 100 therms $0.25 per therm
Next 100 therms $0.43 per therm
All additional $1.01 per therm

a. Write a program that prompts the user to input the customer account number and the total gas usage (in therms) and writes the account number and total therms to a file named "CUSTUSE.DAT". Calculate and display the total charge. Verify that the account number is greater than 0 and less than 10,000. The total number of therms may range from 0 to 2000.

b. Write another the program to read the file "CUSTUSE.DAT" and print the following report. There are an unknown number of customers.

ACCOUNT #	TOTAL THERM	0-100 CHARGE	101-200 CHARGE	OVER 200 CHARGE	TOTAL CHARGE
11111	10	2.50	0.00	0.00	$2.50
22222	120	25.00	8.60	0.00	$33.60
33333	210	25.00	43.00	10.10	$78.10
TOTAL	340	52.50	51.60	10.10	$134.20

29. CUSTOMER TRANSACTIONS

a. Write the program ENTRTRAN.BAS described in the last text section, "Systems of Programs." The program should ask the user to enter the account number, the date of the transaction, a description of the transaction, and the amount. Each entry should be appended to the file CUSTTRAN.DAT. Validate all numeric entry.

b. Before each record is written, allow the user to change any of the fields.

30. EXCEPTION REPORT: Using the file CUSTMAST.DAT described in the chapter, write a program to print a list of all accounts with a value greater than $1.00 in the over-90-days field. The report should show name, address, and balance over 90 days. If the balance is over $150, print three asterisks in front of the name.

STORING LISTS IN ARRAYS

PICKING THE TOP PERFORMERS IN SALES

"Hello, MIS. This is Agatha speaking. May I help you?"

"I sure hope you can help. This is Christi in marketing. I'm one of the people who uses the weekly sales report."

"Yes," responded Agatha. "I'm familiar with that report. It lists each salesperson with his or her sales amount for the previous week, month, and year. It is used by the sales manager to keep track of changes in performance of each salesperson. A year ago I modified the program to create an exception report showing which salespersons have sales this week sharply differing from the previous week. This allows the sales manager to focus on those whose performance is exceptional, good or bad."

Christi blurted out, "Well, I have a problem. My boss, the sales manager, wants me to develop a list of the top ten sales performers each week."

"What's the problem?" Agatha asked.

"It took me two hours this first week, and (don't tell my boss) I'm not sure that my list is correct. Since I'm using the computer list you prepare, isn't this the type of thing you can have the computer do at the push of a button?"

Agatha flinched at the phrase "at the push of a button" and responded coldly, "Yes, creating a sorted list can be done by computer, but nothing is easy. I have invested hundreds of hours of my time in the weekly sales report program.

Programs are not created at the push of a button." Having vented a little anger, Agatha continued in a more friendly voice, "I'll be over to check out the specifications of the program with you. How about Tuesday at 2:00?"

"Is it really necessary for us to meet?" Christi asked. "I've already told you what I want."

"Yes. It is necessary."

"All right. Tuesday at 2:00."

In preparation for the meeting Agatha reviewed the material on arrays and sort routines in her BASIC text.

·*THE ABCS OF BASIC ON THE IBM PERSONAL COMPUTER*·

LESSON 8: ARRAYS

In this lesson we will look at arrays, which represent a way to use one variable name for an entire list of values or data items. We will also discuss the statements that pertain to arrays: DIM, ERASE, and OPTION BASE. As it explores the role of arrays in BASIC, this lesson will describe the techniques of using parallel arrays, loading an array from a file, searching an array using a linear search, searching an array using a binary search, sorting using a bubble sort, and sorting using a Shell sort.

Using Arrays Reduces the Number of Variable Names Required

TABLE 8.1 ▪
Sales by Month of Product QPX

MONTH	SALES ($M)
1	123.00
2	234.00
3	124.57
4	23.00
5	45.00
6	231.00
7	1234.70
8	12.00
9	456.00
10	2341.00
11	34.00
12	65.00
⋮	⋮
24	700.00

Up to now, every time we needed a new variable we had to define a new variable name. However, some data naturally arrange themselves into lists or tables. Consider the list of sales by month of a new product of the XYZ Corporation shown in Table 8.1. The total dollar sales are "indexed" by month—that is, for each month there is a dollar amount corresponding to it. If we wished to use this list for 24 months in a program, we could name 24 separate variables and input the data as follows:

```
2100 INPUT "Sales for Month 1 "; SALES.MO1
2110 INPUT "Sales for Month 2 ": SALES.MO2
2130 INPUT "Sales for Month 3 "; SALES.MO3
       .
       .
       .
2340 INPUT "Sales for Month 24"; SALES.MO24
```

An Array Is a Named List

The series of INPUT statements is cumbersome and time consuming to write, especially if we have a large number of items to enter. BASIC provides a simple way of storing data in a special type of list called an **array.** Each of the data items in the list is called an **element** of the array. The array is assigned a name, and each element is identified by the array name followed by a number within parentheses indicating the position of the element in the array. This position indicator is called a **subscript.** For the list of monthly sales, we will select SALES as the name of the array. If we wish to refer to a particular element in the array, we do so by putting the number that represents its position in the array into the subscript. The first element in the array is identified by the name SALES(1), the second by SALES(2), and so on. These elements are called **subscripted variables** (see Figure 8.1). The same rules that apply to naming variables also apply to naming arrays.

An array such as this, which represents a list, has only one subscript for each element and is called a one-dimensional array. In the next chapter we will discuss multidimensional arrays that represent tables.

Dimension Sets the Size of an Array

Before we use an array we must tell BASIC the maximum number of elements the array may have so that BASIC can allocate space for these elements. The statement that tells BASIC to reserve space for the elements of an array is the DIMension statement.

The dimension statement (written as DIM) consists of two parts: the name of the array and the maximum value that the subscript for that array may have. For the array SALES we will use the following DIMension statement to allow the 24 months of data to be stored in it:

```
2100 DIM SALES(24)
```

If we have more than one array to dimension, we can use more than one DIM statement, or we can name more than one array in a single DIM statement.

```
1111 DIM FIRST(3), SECOND(24), THIRD(22)
```

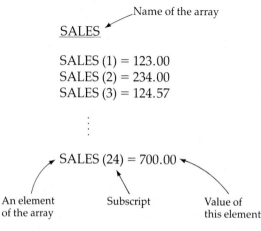

Name of the array

SALES

SALES (1) = 123.00
SALES (2) = 234.00
SALES (3) = 124.57

⋮

SALES (24) = 700.00

FIGURE 8.1 ▪
Components of
an array

An element   Subscript   Value of
of the array   this element

Since the effect of the DIM statement is to tell BASIC how much space to set aside for the array, when the program is run, the DIM statement must be encountered before the array is used in the program. Usually DIM statements are placed in the initialization section of a program. In this way they can be easily located when changes need to be made.

Using Arrays Reduces Program Size

One advantage of using subscripted variables such as SALES(1) in place of the simple variable SALES.MO1 is that the subscript may also be a variable. This allows us to greatly simplify the process of entering all of the data into our program, as shown by the following statements, which ask the user to input values for the elements SALES(1) through SALES(24).

```
2120 FOR MONTH = 1 TO 24
2130    INPUT "Sales for next month "; SALES(MONTH)
2140 NEXT MONTH
```

We have reduced 24 lines of code to 3. If we had a larger number of items to enter, instead of adding more lines, all we need to do is increase the ending value for MONTH in the FOR . . . NEXT loop.

Implicit Dimension of Single-Dimension Arrays

If BASIC encounters a single-dimension array variable before it encounters a DIM statement for the array, it will automatically dimension the array so that the maximum subscript is 10. This is called an implicit definition.

For example, if BASIC encounters the subscripted variable WHO(3) in a LET statement and it has not processed a DIM statement for the array WHO, it will act as if it had encountered DIM WHO(10) prior to this.

Good programming practice dictates that you should always explicitly define arrays with DIM statements for the following reasons:

1. If you know there are fewer than ten elements, space will not be wasted.
2. More importantly, another person looking through your program will be able to see quickly the sizes of your arrays.

Error Message for Using Subscripts Greater Than Dimensioned

It is important that we correctly dimension each array. Once the size of the array has been dimensioned, BASIC will not accept a subscript greater than that maximum set implicitly or explicitly. That is, if we dimension the array SALES to have as its greatest element SALES(24) by using the statement, DIM SALES(24), and if at some point in the program we use SALES(25), we will get the error message:

```
Subscript out of range
```

ERASE Deletes an Array

Arrays may be quite large, thereby taking a considerable amount of memory, yet used in only a portion of a program. The ERASE statement deletes the specified array(s) with all of the elements, releasing that space for other uses. Since it also erases all the values of the variables, you would not want to do this if you wish to preserve the values.

The following statement would erase the values that were stored in the array SALES and free that space:

```
ERASE SALES
```

The next statement would erase both the array named SECOND and the array named THIRD:

```
ERASE SECOND, THIRD
```

OPTION BASE Changes the Starting Reference to an Array

There is one more feature of arrays you need to know. When the statement

```
2100   DIM SALES(24)
```

is given, BASIC actually sets aside space for 25, not 24, elements with the subscripts SALES(0) through SALES(24). Unless we tell BASIC otherwise, it will start counting array elements from element 0, not 1.

Much of the time we want to start counting with 1, not 0, and may just not use the element with the subscript of 0. In the array we have been discussing, the fact that the space reserved for SALES(0) is wasted may not bother us since it is just one element in one array. In more complicated programs with several multidimensional arrays (as we will see in the next chapter) this wasted space can be substantial. If we wish to begin all our arrays with the subscript 1 instead of 0, we can eliminate the wasted space by using the statement

```
2000   OPTION BASE 1
```

·THE DIM AND ERASE STATEMENTS·

DIM ARRAY.NAME (n)
Allocates storage space for an array of up to *n* elements and assigns the array the name specified.

ERASE ARRAY.NAME
Removes the array specified and frees the space for other arrays.

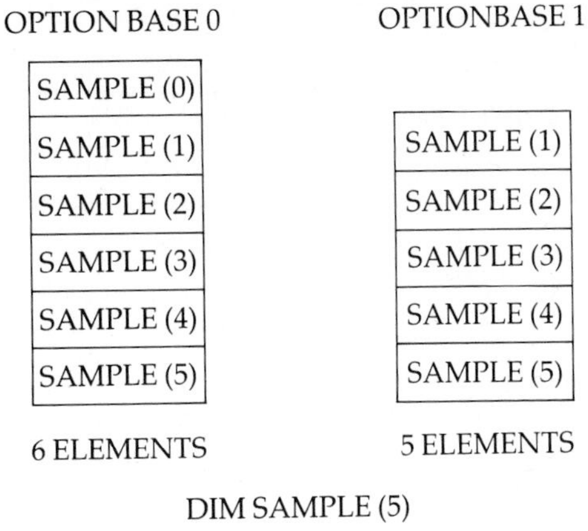

OPTION BASE 0   OPTIONBASE 1

| SAMPLE (0) |
| SAMPLE (1) |
| SAMPLE (2) |
| SAMPLE (3) |
| SAMPLE (4) |
| SAMPLE (5) |

| SAMPLE (1) |
| SAMPLE (2) |
| SAMPLE (3) |
| SAMPLE (4) |
| SAMPLE (5) |

6 ELEMENTS   5 ELEMENTS

FIGURE 8.2 •
OPTIONBASE 1
starts all arrays
with subscript 1

DIM SAMPLE (5)

This tells BASIC to begin *all* arrays in this program with the subscript 1. It is used only once in the program and must be executed before any arrays are dimensioned or used (see Figure 8.2).

Array Elements Are Each Separate Variables, But All Are of the Same Type

Even though an array is a collection of variables with the same name, differing only in subscript, each array element is independent. It contains its own value. For example, if you want to add 100 to the eighth element of the array, you can do so by writing:

```
3500 LET SALES(8) = SALES(8) + 100
```

We can use a subscripted variable (array element) in any of the ways we can use a nonscripted variable.

Arrays may be of the data type integer, single precision, double precision, or string. The same conventions that we used for naming simple (unsubscripted) variables apply to arrays.

For example, SALES in the sample program holds single-precision values. DIM SALES%(6) would set up an array of integer values; DIM SALES#(6) double-precision values; and DIM SALES$(6) string values. SALES$(1) holds a string, while SALES#(1) is a different variable that holds a double-precision numeric value. We could use all four of these arrays in the same program since each has been defined as a different data type; however, it is good programming practice not to use names that could be easily confused.

An Example of a Program Using an Array

Now let's write a program to do the following:

1. Ask the user to input sales for 12 months and put these values into an array.
2. After the array has been entered, print the data.

3. Find and print the lowest month, the highest month, and the average monthly sales.

Figure 8.3 shows the structure chart for this program. We will write the program in modules and discuss each separately.

The main body of the program will list the four main subroutines.

```
10  ' Program Name:   YRSALES.BAS
20  ' Written by:     A. Brewster
30  ' Date written:   11/14/86
40  '
50  ' This program does the following:
60  '     input sales for 12 months
70  '     print sales figures followed by
80  '         month and amount of lowest sales
90  '         month and amount of highest sales
100 '         average monthly sales
110 '
500 GOSUB 1000      ' Initialize
510 GOSUB 2000      ' Enter sales data
520 GOSUB 3000      ' Print data and find lowest, highest, and average
530 GOSUB 4000      ' Print lowest, highest and average
540 END             ' END OF PROCESSING
550 '
```

Since we are interested in the elements 1 through 12, we will use OPTION BASE 1. We will also define MONTH as an integer.

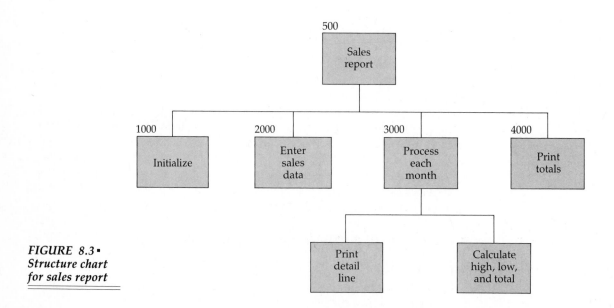

FIGURE 8.3 ▪
Structure chart
for sales report

```
1000 '
1010 ' *** INITIALIZATION ***
1020 '
1030 OPTION BASE 1
1040 DIM SALES(12) ' SALES is array of sales data
1050 DEFINT M
1060 RETURN
1070 '
```

As the user enters the sales data, we will verify that it is in the range 0 to 99,999, the valid range for this particular example.

```
2000 ' * * * INPUT SALES FIGURES * * *
2010 '
2015 CLS
2020 FOR MONTH = 1 TO 12
2030     PRINT "MONTH "; MONTH;
2040     INPUT " AMOUNT OF SALES IS ", SALES(MONTH)
2050     WHILE SALES(MONTH) > 99999 OR SALES(MONTH) < 0
2060         PRINT "Sales figures are too high or too low"
2070         INPUT "Please reenter amount of sales: ",SALES(MONTH)
2080     WEND
2090 NEXT MONTH
2100 RETURN
2110 '
```

Notice the use of a FOR . . . NEXT loop to build the array. This is the most common way of looping through all or a range of subscripts of an array. WHILE loops are used for sequential files because the number of records in the file is not known in advance. Since you will usually know in advance how many elements are in the array, a FOR . . . NEXT loop is appropriate.

Finding the Highest Value of an Array

Here is one way to find the highest value in the array. First, we will initialize two variables. The one that we have named HIGHEST.SALES will hold the highest value for sales that we have found so far. We will initially set this to a value lower or equal to the lowest value possible in the array, in this case zero. The second variable, MONTH.OF.HIGHEST, will hold the month in which the highest sales occurred. We will also initialize this to zero.

For each element in the array, we will compare the value of the element to the variable HIGHEST.SALES. If the value of this element is greater than HIGH-EST.SALES, we will replace the value in HIGHEST.SALES with the value of this element and store the subscript of this element in MONTH.OF.HIGHEST. If it is not greater, we will not replace the values. In this way HIGHEST.SALES will contain the highest sales so far, and MONTH.OF.HIGHEST will contain the month in which it occurred.

Finding the Lowest Value

To find the element with the lowest value, the same technique is used, except the variable LOWEST.SALES, which is used for the comparison, must be initialized to the highest value possible for the array, in this case 99,999. Figure 8.4 shows the flowchart for this process.

```
3000 '
3010 ' * * * PRINT ARRAY AND FIND LOWEST, HIGHEST, AND AVERAGE * * *
3020 '
3030 LET LOWEST.SALES = 99999: LET MONTH.OF.LOWEST = 0
3040 LET HIGHEST.SALES = 0 :   LET MONTH.OF.HIGHEST = 0
3050 LET TOTAL.SALES = 0
3060 CLS
3061 PRINT "     SALES REPORT"
3062 PRINT
3063 PRINT "Month        Sales"
3064 PRINT
3070 FOR MONTH = 1 TO 12
3080    PRINT USING "  ##     $$##,###.##"; MONTH, SALES(MONTH)
3090    IF SALES(MONTH) < LOWEST.SALES THEN
          LET LOWEST.SALES = SALES(MONTH): LET MONTH.OF.LOWEST = MONTH
3100    IF SALES(MONTH) > HIGHEST.SALES THEN
          LET HIGHEST.SALES = SALES(MONTH): LET MONTH.OF.HIGHEST = MONTH
3110    LET TOTAL.SALES = TOTAL.SALES + SALES(MONTH)
3120 NEXT MONTH
3130 RETURN
3140 '
```

There is another way the variables LOWEST.SALES and HIGHEST.SALES could be initialized. We could place the value of the first element into both of these variables before we begin the loop and set both MONTH.OF.HIGHEST and MONTH.OF.LOWEST to 1. The remainder of the program would remain the same. If an element that was greater or lower than the first was found, its values would be placed in the appropriate variables. Lines 3030 and 3040 would be written as:

```
3030 LET LOWEST.SALES = SALES(1): LET MONTH.OF.LOWEST = 1
3040 LET HIGHEST.SALES = SALES(1): LET MONTH.OF.HIGHEST = 1
```

Now that the highest and lowest have been found, they can be printed. Since the subscripts of these elements have been saved in MONTH.OF.HIGHEST and MONTH.OF.LOWEST, we can pick those elements out of the array to print them.

```
4000 '
4010 ' * * * PRINT LOWEST, HIGHEST, AND AVERAGE * * *
4020 '
4030 PRINT
4040 PRINT USING " LOWEST SALES WERE $$##,###.## IN MONTH ##";
          SALES(MONTH.OF.LOWEST), MONTH.OF.LOWEST
```

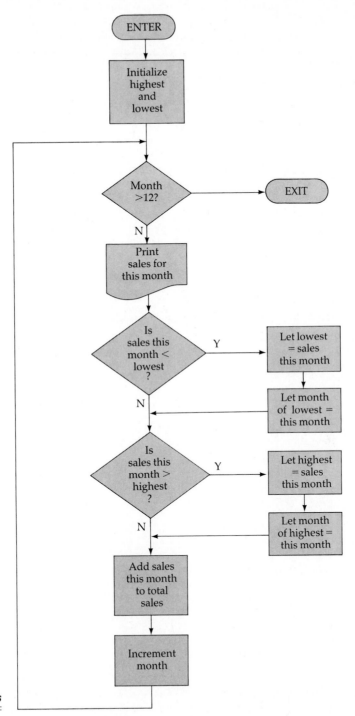

FIGURE 8.4 ▪
Flowchart for
finding highest
and lowest values

```
4050 PRINT USING "HIGHEST SALES WERE $$##,###.## IN MONTH ##";
          SALES(MONTH.OF.HIGHEST), MONTH.OF.HIGHEST
4060 LET AVERAGE.SALES = TOTAL.SALES/12
4070 PRINT
4080 PRINT USING "AVERAGE SALES WERE $$##,###.##"; AVERAGE.SALES
4090 RETURN
4100 '
```

The following is a sample run of the program:

```
RUN
MONTH 1    AMOUNT OF SALES IS 123
MONTH 2    AMOUNT OF SALES IS 234
MONTH 3    AMOUNT OF SALES IS 124.57
MONTH 4    AMOUNT OF SALES IS 23
MONTH 5    AMOUNT OF SALES IS 45
MONTH 6    AMOUNT OF SALES IS 231
MONTH 7    AMOUNT OF SALES IS 1234.70
MONTH 8    AMOUNT OF SALES IS 12
MONTH 9    AMOUNT OF SALES IS 456
MONTH 10   AMOUNT OF SALES IS 2341
MONTH 11   AMOUNT OF SALES IS 34
MONTH 12   AMOUNT OF SALES IS 65
(Clear screen.)
     SALES REPORT


Month          Sales

  1          $123.00
  2          $234.00
  3          $124.57
  4           $23.00
  5           $45.00
  6          $231.00
  7        $1,234.70
  8           $12.00
  9          $456.00
 10        $2,341.00
 11           $34.00
 12           $65.00


LOWEST SALES WERE       $12.00 IN MONTH  8
HIGHEST SALES WERE   $2,341.00 IN MONTH 10


AVERAGE SALES WERE      $410.27
Ok
```

Loading an Array From a File

In the preceding example we entered the data for the array from the keyboard. Because an array is in memory, once the system is turned off, all of the data in the array are gone. For our example this did not matter, but in most applications it is more likely that the data will be stored in a file so that it does not have to be rekeyed every time. We can store the sales figures on a file by changing lines 540 and 550 and adding this subroutine to the program.

```
540 GOSUB 5000        ' Save sales data to file "SALES.DAT"
550 END               ' END OF PROCESSING
 . . .
5000 ' Write array to file named SALES.DAT
5010 '
5020 OPEN "SALES.DAT" FOR OUTPUT AS #1
5030 FOR MONTH = 1 TO 12
5040     WRITE #1, SALES(MONTH)
5050 NEXT MONTH
5060 CLOSE #1
5070 RETURN
```

On the other hand, if the data have already been stored in the file SALES.DAT by some other program, we can retrieve it by rewriting lines 2020 to 2090 as:

```
2020 OPEN "SALES.DAT" FOR INPUT AS #1
2030 FOR MONTH = 1 TO 12
2040     INPUT #1, SALES(MONTH)
2050 NEXT MONTH
2060 CLOSE #1
```

Parallel Arrays and File Header Record

One powerful feature of arrays is the ability they give us to link together several pieces of data about a specific topic. Suppose we wish to record and store the following items about all of our employees:

Employee number
Employee name
Employment date
Supervisor's name
Address
Phone number
Job classification

The data are stored in a file named "EMPLOYEE.DAT". We want to read these data into memory and store it in arrays. In order to use arrays we need to know how large to dimension them. In our earlier example of sales for each month of the year, we knew that there would always be 12 elements. But in this case if the number of employees varies, how are we going to get this information?

The solution is to store the current number of employees as the first item of data in the file. This can be read into the program and that number used to dimension the arrays. Information stored at the beginning of the file that tells about the remaining data is called a **file header record** (see Figure 8.5)

Following the header record is the information for each of the employees in the order listed earlier: first the employee number, then the employee name, and so on. To put these data into arrays, we set up an array for each of the items, then read the file into these arrays. In the previous example we knew exactly how many elements were in the array as we wrote the program. In this case we will not know until we read the number from the file. We can write the DIM statements using a variable to indicate the size as long as that variable has been given a value before the DIM statements are encountered. We must make sure the file is opened and the total number of employees read before the DIM statements are encountered. The following subroutines can be used to accomplish this.

```
1000 '  **** Initialization ****
1080 OPTION BASE 1
1090 DEFINT E         ' Numeric variables starting with E will be integers
1100 OPEN "EMPLOYEE.DAT" FOR INPUT AS #1
1110 INPUT #1, NUM.OF.EMPL ' read total number of employees from file
1120 ' dimension the arrays
1130 DIM EMPL.NO(NUM.OF.EMPL),       EMPL.NAME$(NUM.OF.EMPL)
1140 DIM EMPL.DATE$(NUM.OF.EMPL),    EMPL.SUPV$(NUM.OF.EMPL)
1150 DIM EMPL.ADDRESS$(NUM.OF.EMPL), EMPL.PHONE$(NUM.OF.EMPL)
1160 DIM EMPL.JOB.CLASS(NUM.OF.EMPL)
1170 LET TRUE = -1: LET FALSE = 0
1080 RETURN
```

As shown, one DIMension statement can be used to dimension several arrays. Both string and numeric arrays can be defined with one statement. In our case we want all of the arrays to be the same size, but different size arrays also can be defined by one DIM statement.

```
2200 ' read the file and put into arrays
2220 FOR INDEX = 1 TO NUM.OF.EMPL
2230   INPUT #1, EMPL.NO (INDEX), EMPL.NAME$ (INDEX), EMPL.DATE$ (INDEX),
              EMPL.SUPV$(INDEX), EMPL.ADDRESS$ (INDEX),
              EMPL.PHONE$ (INDEX), EMPL.JOB.CLASS (INDEX)
2240 NEXT INDEX
2250 CLOSE #1
2260 RETURN
```

There are now seven arrays in memory, each containing one category of data about each employee. These are called **parallel arrays** because, if you were to put them in the form of tables, all the data for each employee would appear on parallel lines through the tables.

File: EMPLOYEE.DAT

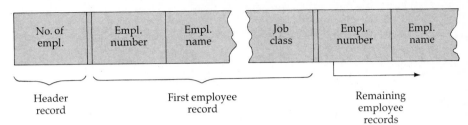

FIGURE 8.5 •
File with header
record

No. of empl.	Empl. number	Empl. name	Job class	Empl. number	Empl. name

Header record   First employee record   Remaining employee records

SUBSCRIPT	EMPL.NO	EMPL.NAME$	EMPL.DATE$
1	2456	JONES, EDITH	78/02/01
2	1865	HOWARD, SAMUEL	83/05/15
3	0076	COLE, JANET	82/10/20
4	2397	BARNES, RICHARD	79/04/25
⋮	⋮	⋮	⋮

In this table, with just three of the arrays shown, the third element in each array gives the information for the same employee. If we wished to print the information for this employee, we could do so as follows:

```
PRINT EMPL.NO(3) TAB(8) EMPL.NAME$(3) TAB(50) EMPL.DATE$(3)
 76    COLE, JANET                                   82/10/20
Ok
```

If we wished to write a set of instructions that allows the user to enter the subscript of the employee to be retrieved, we could write it as follows:

```
3300 ' print number, name and date of hire for one employee
3310 INPUT "Which employee do you wish to see", THIS
3320 PRINT EMPL.NO(THIS) TAB(8) EMPL.NAME$(THIS) TAB(50) EMPL.DATE$(THIS)
3330 RETURN
```

Searching an Array

Sequential Search

In the preceding example we had to know the position in the array of the data we wanted. In most cases we do not know the position of the data, but we do know the value of some identifying item of data, such as a particular employee's number. What we would like to be able to do is to input the employee number and have the program search the arrays for all the other data that correspond to this person. To do this we will input the employee number and, beginning with the first element in the array EMPL.NO, compare the number that was entered until we find a match in the array. We will have to allow for the fact that there may not be a matching number in the array.

```
4300 ' ** input employee number for search **
4310 INPUT "What is the employee number "; TARGET
4320 ' ** search employee number array for matching number **
4330 '    ** search ends when either a match is found **
4340 '    ** or INDEX becomes greater than the number of employees **
4350 LET INDEX = 1
4360 WHILE INDEX <= NUM.OF.EMPL AND FOUND = FALSE
4370   IF EMPL.NO(INDEX) <> TARGET THEN LET INDEX = INDEX + 1 ELSE LET FOUND = TRUE
4380 WEND
4390 ' ** if match is found, EMPL.NO(INDEX) will equal TARGET **
4400 IF INDEX > NUM.OF.EMPL THEN PRINT "NO MATCH FOUND"
          ELSE PRINT EMPL.NO(INDEX) TAB(8) EMPL.NAME$(INDEX)
               TAB(50) EMPL.JOB.CLASS(INDEX)
4410 RETURN
```

Since we used OPTION BASE 1, all the arrays will begin with the subscript 1. Therefore, we set the variable INDEX to 1 to begin the search with the first element in the array. The value of the employee number we want to find is stored in the variable TARGET. As the WHILE . . . WEND loop is executed, the value of each element in the array EMPL.NO is compared to the value in TARGET. If they are equal, the looping ends and the value of INDEX will indicate the position in the arrays of the matching employee. If no match is found, when the looping ends, the value of INDEX will be one greater than NUM.OF.EMPL.

Binary Search

The sequential search through an array will always work. If the list contains 100 items, on the average a sequential search will find the match after searching through 50 items. In the worst case, it will have to look through all 100 items.

Often lists of items, such as employee numbers, are kept in numeric (or alphabetic) order. In this case there is a more efficient search procedure. This search procedure involves first looking in the *middle* of the list. The value of the middle element is compared against the search or target element. If the middle element is greater than the target, the target must be in the lower half of the list. If the middle is less than the target, the target must be in the upper half. Having determined which half of the remaining list is to be searched, the *middle of that half* is compared against the target. This continues until a match is found (or until no more elements remain). Because the list is always divided in half, this search procedure is called a **binary search.**

To understand this procedure, consider the guessing game "Guess My Number." In this game, you have to guess which integer between 0 and 100 I have selected.

Using a sequential search, you would guess "Is it 1?" "Is it 2?" and so on until you guessed my number. This is a slow and laborious method.

Since I am willing to tell you if your guess is too high or too low, you could use a binary search. Here you always guess the middle number in the range of possible numbers. For example, if my number is 64, we might have the following encounter (since all guesses must be integers, we have indicated integer division):

Your Guess		*My Answer*
50	middle of 1 to 100 or (1 + 100)\2	too low
75	middle of 50 to 100 or (50 + 100)\2	too high
62	middle of 50 to 75 or (50 + 75)\2	too low
68	middle of 62 to 75 or (62 + 75)\2	too high
65	middle of 62 to 68 or (62 + 68)\2	too high
63	middle of 62 to 65 or (62 + 65)\2	too low
64	middle of 63 to 64 or (63 + 65)\2	That's It!

You can see how quickly you guessed the number. In this, the worst case of finding the correct number in a list of 100 items (1 through 100), it took seven guesses. This, the worst case of this binary search, is better than the average case of a sequential search (see Figure 8.6)

This procedure could be written in pseudocode as follows:

Establish BOTTOM = Bottom of Range
            TOP = Top of Range
            TARGET = Search Value
WHILE there are more elements in the array and no match has been found
      LET INDEX = middle of remaining range (TOP + BOTTOM)\2

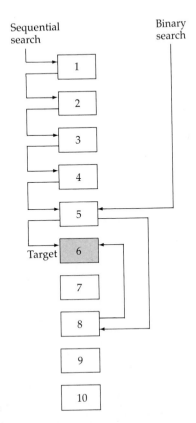

FIGURE 8.6 •
Sequential and
binary search for
the number 6

> IF element(INDEX) > TARGET
>> THEN set TOP of Remaining Range to INDEX
>> ELSE set BOTTOM of Remaining Range to INDEX
> Repeat WHILE loop

Since we are continually dividing the range in half, we will never actually reach the bottom or top of the range. Therefore, we must set the search range to at least one beyond the actual top and bottom values in which we are searching. Again we use integer division so that the subscript will always have an integer value.

The following program demonstrates a binary search. First it creates an array with values equal to the multiples of 5 from 5 through 50. It then asks the user to input a number and uses a binary search to locate that value in the array.

```
10 ' SAMPLE PROGRAM TO DEMONSTRATE BINARY SEARCH ------------------------
20 '===================== INITIALIZE ===================================
30 '      Store Multiples of Five as Array Elements 1 through 10
40 LET N = 10                     ' N is number of elements in the array
50  OPTION BASE 1
60  DIM A(N)
70 FOR I = 1 TO N
80     LET A(I) = I * 5           ' A(1) = 5 . . . A(10) = 55
90 NEXT
100                               ' set boundaries for range of search
110 LET TOP = N + 1               ' TOP = top of search range
120 LET BOTTOM = 0                ' BOTTOM = bottom of search range
130 LET INDEX = (TOP + BOTTOM)\2  ' initialize INDEX to middle of range
140 '==================== ASK FOR SEARCH VALUE ========================
150 INPUT "For What Value Do You Want To Search"; TARGET
160 ' ===================== SEARCH ====================================
170 WHILE (TOP-BOTTOM) > 1 AND A(INDEX) <> TARGET
180    LET INDEX = (TOP + BOTTOM)\2
190    IF A(INDEX) > TARGET THEN LET TOP = INDEX ELSE LET BOTTOM = INDEX
200 WEND
210 ' ======================= PRINT SEARCH RESULTS ====================
220 IF A(INDEX) <> TARGET THEN PRINT "NO MATCH" ELSE PRINT "No. is"; A(INDEX)
230 END
```

Try entering this program and experimenting with different target values.

Now, let's modify the employee program to use a binary search. In order to use a binary search, the array elements must be in ascending (or descending) order by employee number.

```
4300 ' input employee number for search
4310 INPUT "What is the employee number "; TARGET
4320 ' search employee number array for matching number
4330 LET BOTTOM = 0: LET TOP = NUM.OF.EMPL + 1     ' set range limits
4335 LET INDEX = (TOP + BOTTOM)\2
4340 WHILE (TOP - BOTTOM) > 1 AND EMPL.NO(INDEX) <> TARGET
4350    LET INDEX = (TOP + BOTTOM)\2
```

```
4355     IF EMPL.NO(INDEX) > TARGET THEN LET TOP = INDEX
             ELSE LET BOTTOM = INDEX
4360 WEND
4370 '  if match is found, EMPL.NO(INDEX) will equal TARGET
4380 IF EMPL.NO(INDEX) <> TARGET THEN PRINT "NO MATCH FOUND"
         ELSE PRINT EMPL.NO(INDEX) TAB(8) EMPL.NAME$(INDEX)
             TAB(50) EMPL.JOB.CLASS(INDEX)
4390 RETURN
```

Sorting Single Subscript Arrays

We were able to use the binary search because we had kept the EMPL.NO array in order. Sort routines will take an array whose values are unordered and put them in order so the lowest value is first, the next lowest value next, and so on. To do this, we swap array elements to put them in the correct order.

SWAP Exchanges the Values of Two Variables

IBM PC BASIC offers us a simple statement called SWAP, to swap the value stored in one variable with that stored in another variable. The syntax is quite simple: SWAP A,B will swap the values stored in variables A and B.

```
LET A = 5
LET B = 10
PRINT A,B
 5               10
SWAP A,B
PRINT A,B
 10              5
```

This SWAP statement accomplished with one statement the equivalent of the following three statements.

```
LET TEMP = A
LET A = B
LET B = TEMP
```

Not all BASICs have a SWAP statement. Its presence in IBM PC BASIC makes the coding of sort routines much simpler.

•THE SWAP STATEMENT•

SWAP VARIABLE.A, VARIABLE.B
Exchanges the values of two variables. Both variables must be of the same data type.

The Bubble Sort

The simplest sort to code is also the least efficient. Like the sequential search compared to the binary search, the bubble sort uses brute force to "push" an element in an array to its proper place.

The **bubble sort,** like a bubble floating to the top, compares each element with every other element in an array. If the two are in proper order, nothing happens. But if they are not in order, the sort swaps their values.

The bubble sort to put the values of an array in ascending sequence begins by comparing the value of the first element with the value of all other elements in the array. If the other element's value is less than the first element's value, the values are swapped. When the last element of the array is reached, the first position will contain the lowest value.

The bubble sort then takes the second element and compares its value with all remaining elements, swapping values when a lesser one is encountered. This continues, position by position, until the final comparison of the next-to-last element with the last element. At this point the values will be in ascending numeric sequence.

The pseudocode for this sort is:

For CURRENT.POSITION = FIRST.ELEMENT to (LAST.ELEMENT − 1)
   For COMPARE.TO.POSITION = (CURRENT.POSITION + 1) to
      LAST.ELEMENT
      Compare ARRAY(CURRENT.POSITION) to
         ARRAY(COMPARE.TO.POSITION)
      If ARRAY(COMPARE.TO.POSITION) is less than
         ARRAY(CURRENT.POSITION) then SWAP values
   Next COMPARE.TO.POSITION (increment compare to position so that
      the next comparison will compare the CURRENT.POSITION to the
      next element in the array)
Next CURRENT.POSITION (increment CURRENT.POSITION and repeat
   comparison with all remaining elements)

The following program demonstrates a bubble sort. It asks the user to input five numbers, then arranges them into ascending sequence. In this example we have not used OPTION BASE 1, so the first element in the array is assigned the subscript 0 and the last element the subscript 4. In the outer loop, I is the subscript of the current position. As the inner J loop is executed, ARRAY(I) is compared with each of the remaining elements in the array. The values of I and J, as well as the values of the elements in the array, are printed at each step so you can follow the sort.

```
10 ' demonstration of BUBBLE SORT
20 ' input values to be sorted
30 DIM ARRAY(5)
40 LET LAST = 4
50 FOR I = 0 TO LAST
60    INPUT "next value "; ARRAY(I)
```

```
70 NEXT
80 PRINT "Values to be sorted are:"
90 PRINT TAB(15) ARRAY(0); ARRAY(1); ARRAY(2); ARRAY(3); ARRAY(4)
100 ' sort values
110 FOR I = 0 TO LAST - 1
115     PRINT
120     PRINT "I IS "; I
130     FOR J = I + 1 TO LAST
140         PRINT " J IS "; J;
150         IF ARRAY(J) < ARRAY(I) THEN SWAP ARRAY(J), ARRAY(I)
160         PRINT TAB(15)  ARRAY(0); ARRAY(1); ARRAY(2); ARRAY(3); ARRAY(4)
170     NEXT J
180 NEXT I
RUN
next value ? 101
next value ? 34
next value ? 56
next value ? 3
next value ? 98
Values to be sorted are:
              101   34   56    3    98
```

```
I IS 0          (compare first position to all other positions)
    J IS 1     34   101   56    3   98     ARRAY(1) [34]    <    ARRAY(0) [101]  SWAP
    J IS 2     34   101   56    3   98     ARRAY(2) [56] not < ARRAY(0) [34] no SWAP
    J IS 3      3   101   56   34   98     ARRAY(3) [3]     <    ARRAY(0) [34]   SWAP
    J IS 4      3   101   56   34   98     ARRAY(4) [98] not < ARRAY(0) [3]   no SWAP
    (The lowest value [3] is now in the first position of the array.)
I IS 1          (compare second position to remaining positions)
    J IS 2      3    56   101   34   98    ARRAY(2) [56]    <    ARRAY(1) [101]  SWAP
    J IS 3      3    34   101   56   98    ARRAY(3) [34]    <    ARRAY(1) [56]   SWAP
    J IS 4      3    34   101   56   98    ARRAY(4) [98] not < ARRAY(1) [34] no SWAP
    (Second lowest value [34] is now in second position.)
I IS 2          (compare third position to remaining positions)
    J IS 3      3    34   56   101   98    ARRAY(3) [56]    <    ARRAY(2) [101]  SWAP
    J IS 4      3    34   56   101   98    ARRAY(4) [98] not < ARRAY(2) [56] no SWAP
    (Third lowest value [56] is now in third position.)
I IS 3          (compare fourth position to last position)
    J IS 4      3    34   56    98  101    ARRAY(4) [98]    <    ARRAY(3) [101]  SWAP
    (All values are now in order.)
```

A subroutine that sorts an array in which the number of elements is equal to LAST (and OPTION BASE is 0) could be written as follows:

```
2000 '============bubble sort for array===============
2010 FOR I = 0 TO LAST -1
2020     FOR J = I + 1 TO LAST
2030         IF ARRAY(J) < ARRAY(I) THEN SWAP ARRAY(J), ARRAY(I)
2040     NEXT J
2050 NEXT I
2060 RETURN
```

The sort is easy to code but can be very time consuming to run. It is adequate for arrays with fewer than 100 or so elements. When you are sorting a large number of elements, you should use a smarter sort routine, such as the Shell sort.

Shell Sort Is More Efficient Than Bubble for Large Number of Items

The **Shell sort** routine was developed in 1959 by Donald Shell. It is to the bubble sort what the binary search is to the sequential search. Following is the sample program changed to use the Shell sort. Notice that the innermost FOR . . . NEXT loop has a STEP clause. Instead of always comparing an element with its neighbor, we compare it with a value GAP elements away. First the GAP is half the size of the array, then a quarter, and so forth until the GAP is finally less than one. At that point all the elements in the array are in sorted order. We have added comments to the output as well as underlined the elements that are compared to illustrate how the Shell sort operates on the sample values we have used.

With only five elements, the Shell sort is not faster than the bubble sort; however, its power becomes evident when there are a large number of elements.

```
10 ' demonstration of SHELL SORT
20 ' input values to be sorted
30 DIM ARRAY(5)
40 LET LAST = 4
50 FOR I = 0 TO 4
60    INPUT "next value "; ARRAY (I)
70 NEXT
80 PRINT "Values to be sorted are:"
90 PRINT TAB(15) ARRAY(0); ARRAY(1); ARRAY(2); ARRAY(3); ARRAY(4)
100 ' sort values
105 LET GAP = LAST\2
106 WHILE GAP >= 1
110    FOR I = 0 TO GAP
120    PRINT "I IS "; I
130      FOR J = I TO LAST - GAP STEP GAP
140        PRINT "   J IS "; J;
150        IF ARRAY (J) > ARRAY(J + GAP) THEN SWAP ARRAY(J), ARRAY(J + GAP)
160        PRINT TAB(15)   ARRAY(0); ARRAY(1); ARRAY(2); ARRAY(3); ARRAY(4)
170      NEXT J
180    NEXT I
190 LET GAP = GAP\2
200 WEND
RUN
next value ? 101
next value ? 34
next value ? 56
next value ? 3
next value ? 98
```

```
Values to be sorted are:
              101 34 56 3 98
(Line 105 sets the initial value of GAP to 2)
(WHILE GAP >= 1)
(GAP = 2)
I IS 0
   J IS 0     56 34 101 3 98     ARRAY(0) [101]  >     ARRAY(2) [56]     SWAP
   J IS 2     56 34 98 3 101     ARRAY(2) [101]  >     ARRAY(4) [98]     SWAP
I IS 1
   J IS 1     56 3 98 34 101     ARRAY(1) [34]   >     ARRAY(3) [3]      SWAP
I IS 2
   J IS 2     56 3 98 34 101     ARRAY(2) [98] not >   ARRAY(4) [101] no SWAP
(GAP = 1)
I IS 0
   J IS 0     3 56 98 34 101     ARRAY(0) [56]   >     ARRAY(1) [3]      SWAP
   J IS 1     3 56 98 34 101     ARRAY(1) [56] not >   ARRAY(2) [98]  no SWAP
   J IS 2     3 56 34 98 101     ARRAY(2) [98]   >     ARRAY(3) [34]     SWAP
   J IS 3     3 56 34 98 101     ARRAY(3) [98] not >   ARRAY(4) [101] no SWAP
I IS 1
   J IS 1     3 34 56 98 101     ARRAY(1) [56]   >     ARRAY(2) [34]     SWAP
   J IS 2     3 34 56 98 101     ARRAY(2) [56] not >   ARRAY(3) [98]  no SWAP
   J IS 3     3 34 56 98 101     ARRAY(3) [98] not >   ARRAY(4) [101] no SWAP
```

Sorting Parallel Arrays

At this point we know how to sort an array. But if we have parallel arrays, such as employee number, name, employment date, and so on, how do we put them all in order?

The secret is that when we sort one array, such as EMPL.NO, we swap not only the EMPL.NO elements but also the corresponding elements of EMPL.NAME$ and EMPL.DATE$.

For example, we wish to sort all our employee records to put them in order by EMPL.NO, using a Shell sort. We might code the following subroutine:

```
2000 '==============sort array=========================
2010 LET GAP = LAST\2
2020 WHILE GAP >= 1
2030 FOR I = 0 TO GAP
2040   FOR J = I TO LAST - GAP STEP GAP
2050       IF EMPL.NO(J) > EMPL.NO(J + GAP) THEN
              SWAP EMPL.NO(J),EMPL.NO(J + GAP):SWAP EMPL.NAME$(J),
              EMPL.NAME$(J + GAP):SWAP EMPL.DATE$(J),EMPL.DATE$(J + GAP)
2060   NEXT J
2070 NEXT I
2080 LET GAP = GAP\2
2090 WEND
2100 RETURN
```

We only compare on employee number. But when we swap elements in one array, we also swap elements in each of the other parallel arrays. That is, we swap all of the data about an individual or item as we sort on one of its attributes.

THE STORY'S END

The following Tuesday Agatha and Christi met to discuss their program.

"We are meeting," Agatha began, "to develop a set of specifications for the program I will write for you. This meeting is necessary because as a programmer I can't know what you want unless you tell me. We both want you to have a program that meets your needs. Would you please tell me one more time exactly what you want?"

An incredulous look appeared on Christi's face. Then, with resignation, she exhaled and said, "I need a list of our top ten sales representatives, based on their sales the previous week."

"Okay. Here is a mock-up report that I drew last week after your call. Does this meet your needs?"

TOP TEN SALESPEOPLE

JONES
ABLE
BAKER
CAT
DOG
ELEPHANT
FOX
GRIFFIN
HEATH
ISLE

Christi looked at the report for a moment, then snapped "No! Where are the sales figures?"

Agatha calmly wrote down "name and sales."

"And," added Christi, "would it be very hard to number each name?"

"No problem at this stage. Would you like today's date on the top of the report?"

"Oh yes, please." Christi was mellowing as she realized that what was obvious to her was not obvious to someone else; she would have to explicitly state what she wanted in the report. "Let's change the report title to TOP SALES REPORT."

"Fine." Agatha sketched away and asked without looking up, "Do you ever need greater than or fewer than ten top sales reps on the report?"

"Yes, once a month I need a list of the top 25. Is that a problem?"

"No problem at this stage. Here, take a look at this mock-up report. Does this meet your needs?"

Order in the Court

"Uh-oh," thought Perkins, "here comes the Judge. What is it this time?"

"Perkins," thundered the Judge, "what is the meaning of this?"

"The meaning of what, your honor?"

"I mean this list of cases to be heard before this court." The Judge stooped under the weight of a thick sheaf of paper. "I ask for a list of today's cases and you hand me *this*, a report five hundred pages long! It looks to me like every case we've ever heard or ever will hear is in this report!"

Perkins grinned with satisfaction. "Precisely, your honor. Here, in one master report is all the information you will ever need to know about the court docket; all past, present, and scheduled future cases are all here in this one, handy place. Our computer programmer designed it that way to save programming costs."

The Judge turned scarlet. "I don't want a five-hundred page report; I want a simple, one- or two-page summary of today's cases! Now! How am I supposed to use something like this from the bench?"

"Well, your honor," Perkins stammered, "the information's all there. Just flip through the report looking for today's date. It, uh, might take awhile, though . . . the report is sorted by offense and defendant name, not by date."

"Perkins, this report is worse than useless to me. Using it is like trying to take a sip of water from a fire hose. I'd sooner keep track of the information by hand than have to wade through this pile of paper. Tell that programmer to give us some way to select only the information we want, and to specify the order in which it is to appear, or we'll find another programmer."

MORAL: A short report in the proper order is frequently better than a long one.

TOP SALES REPORT AS OF MM/DD/YY

	NAME	SALES
1	JONES	$10,000.00
2	ABLE	$ 9,000.00
3	BAKER	$ 8,000.00
·	·	·
·	·	·

Christi examined the second mock-up carefully. "Yes, this is what I want."

Agatha stood up. "Then thank you, Christi. I can get this program written and on the system for you by Monday. Is that okay?"

Christi also rose and said her thanks as Agatha left.

"Now that I know what she wants," thought Agatha, "I'll begin programming."

Here are the notes Agatha wrote.

Program Specifications

This program will typically be run weekly on the same day as the weekly sales report program. It is being created as a separate program since it may be requested at other times.

It will list the name and prior week's sales of the *n* sales representatives with the greatest sales figures. The value of *n* will be entered by the user with a default value of ten.

The maximum sales per week is $999,999.99 and the maximum number of sales representatives is 200.

The sales figures are stored in the file WEEKLY.SLS.

Functions

    A. Initialization
        1. Input today's date
        2. Input number to be reported
        3. Input data from file
    B. Sort for requested number of top sales reps
    C. Print report

Structure Chart

Figure 8.7 is the structure chart Agatha developed.

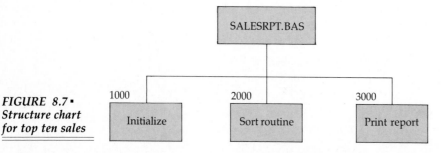

FIGURE 8.7 ·
Structure chart
for top ten sales

Data Dictionary

Files
WEEKLY.SLS

SALESPERSON.ID	Integer	Not used in this program
SALESPERSON.NAME$	String	Last name
	(maximum of 25 characters)	
SALES.REGION	String	Not used in this program
SALESPERSON.SALES	Single Precision	Prior week's sales
SALESPERSON.MONTH	Single Precision	Not used in this program
SALESPERSON.YEAR	Single Precision	Not used in this program

Working Variables

TODAY$	Today's date in form mm/dd/yy
NBR.OF.TOP.EMPS	Number of sales reps to be printed
MAX.NBR.EMPS	Maximum number of sales reps, currently 200
NBR.EMPS	Actual number of sales reps on file

Pseudocode

MAIN LINE
    DO INITIALIZATION
    DO SORT.ROUTINE
    DO PRINT.REPORT
INITIALIZATION
    Enter TODAY$
    Enter number of sales reps to be printed (NBR.OF.TOP.EMPS)
    Set variables to initial values
    Dimension arrays SALESPERSON.NAME$ and SALESPERSON.SALES
    OPEN "WEEKLY.SLS" for input
    PRINT message that files are being read
    WHILE not end of file
        Increment number of employees (NBR.EMPS)
        INPUT SALESPERSON.NAME$(NBR.EMPS) and
        SALESPERSON.SALES(NBR.EMPS)
        (use DUMMY$ for unused fields)
    WEND
    CLOSE file
SORT.ROUTINE
    FOR I = 1 TO NBR.OF.TOP.EMPS (stop sort after requested number are
      found)
        FOR J = I + 1 TO NBR.EMPS
            IF SALESPERSON.SALES(I) < SALESPERSON.SALES(J) THEN
                SWAP SALESPERSON.SALES and SALESPERSON.NAME$
        NEXT J
    NEXT I

<u>PRINT.REPORT</u>
>   PRINT heading
>   FOR I = 1 TO NBR.OF.TOP.EMPS
>   PRINT I, SALESPERSON.NAME$(I) and SALESPERSON.SALES(I)
>   NEXT I

Program Listing

Agatha was now ready to begin coding and testing the program.

```
10    'Program: SALESRPT.BAS
20    'Author: Agatha Simms
30    'Installation: Con. Glomerate
40    ' Date Written: 10/24/88
50    ' Program Description:
60    '          Ask user to specify # of top employees to be found
70    '          Inputs sales data from WEEKLY.SLS file
80    '          Finds employees with top sales and prints report
90    ' File used:
100   '          WEEKLY.SLS as input
110   '
120   '
480   '======================================================================
490   '======================================================================
500    GOSUB 1000          'Initialization
510    GOSUB 2000          'Sort Routine
520    GOSUB 3000          'Print Report
530    END
1000  '======================================================================
1010  '                              Initialization
1020  '======================================================================
1030  '        Set Values
1040  CLS
1050  PRINT "Top Sales Report "
1060  INPUT "Please enter today's date as MM/DD/YY ", TODAY$
1070  INPUT "How many top sales reps do you wish printed (press ENTER for 10)";
            NBR.OF.TOP.EMPS
1080  IF NBR.OF.TOP.EMPS = 0 THEN LET NBR.OF.TOP.EMPS = 10
1090  LET NBR.EMPS = 0
1100  LET MAX.NBR.EMPS = 200
1110  OPTION BASE 1
1120  DIM SALESPERSON.NAME$(MAX.NBR.EMPS)
1130  DIM SALESPERSON.SALES(MAX.NBR.EMPS)
1140  '                                                  Fill Arrays
1150  OPEN "WEEKLY.SLS" FOR INPUT AS #1
1160  PRINT " ** READING SALES DATA *** PLEASE WAIT **
1170  WHILE NOT EOF(1)
1180     LET NBR.EMPS = NBR.EMPS + 1
```

```
1190     INPUT #1, DUMMY$, SALESPERSON.NAME$(NBR.EMPS), DUMMY$,
                  SALESPERSON.SALES(NBR.EMPS), DUMMY$, DUMMY$
1200 WEND
1210 CLOSE #1
1220 RETURN
2000 '=================================================================
2010 '                           Sort Routine
2020 '=================================================================
2030 '       This is a bubble sort which sorts into descending sequence
2040 '       The sort ends when the number of positions sorted
2050 '        equals NBR.OF.TOP.EMPS
2060 '  ------------------------------------------------------------------
2070 FOR I = 1 TO NBR.OF.TOP.EMPS
2080    FOR J = I + 1 TO NBR.EMPS
2090       IF SALESPERSON.SALES(I) < SALESPERSON.SALES(J) THEN
                  SWAP SALESPERSON.SALES(I), SALESPERSON.SALES(J):
                  SWAP SALESPERSON.NAME$(I), SALESPERSON.NAME$(J)
2100    NEXT J
2110 NEXT I
2120 RETURN
3000 '=================================================================
3010 '                           Print Report
3020 '=================================================================
3030 '                                              Print Headings
3040 CLS
3050 PRINT "            TOP SALES REPORT"
3060 PRINT "               AS OF "; TODAY$
3070 PRINT
3080 PRINT TAB(5) "NAME" TAB(30) "SALES"
3090 PRINT
3100 '                                              Print Detail Line
3110 FOR I = 1 TO NBR.OF.TOP.EMPS
3120    PRINT USING "## \                \        $###,###.##";
                  I, SALESPERSON.NAME$(I), SALESPERSON.SALES(I)
3130 NEXT I
3140 RETURN
3150 '====================End of Listing===================================
```

Program Output

Christi and Agatha tested the program by listing the top five salespersons with the following results.

```
Top Sales Report
PLEASE ENTER TODAY'S DATE AS MM/YY/DD 11/24/88
HOW MANY TOP EMPLOYEES TO YOU WISH PRINTED (PRESS ENTER FOR 10)? 5
```

The screen cleared and the following list was displayed.

```
                 TOP SALES REPORT
                  AS OF 09/01/88

         NAME                    SALES

       1 ZEEK                 $132,173.34
       2 RESNICK              $106,392.75
       3 FISH                 $102,682.29
       4 ERMAN                $ 97,336.85
       5 WILSON               & 93,873.38
```

▪QUICK REFERENCE FOR LESSON 8▪

Arrays

Arrays are named lists of variables.
The variables of an array are its elements.
An element is identified by the array name followed by a subscript.

DIMension Allocates Storage for Arrays

DIM ARRAY.NAME(*n*), . . .

ARRAY.NAME is the name assigned to the array.
n is the maximum element number that will be in the array.
   (Maximum allowed by BASIC is 255.)
Statement reserves enough space for *n* number of elements.
It must be executed before any element of the array is used.
It may be omitted for single-dimension arrays only.
   If it is omitted, a single-dimension array will be dimensioned to 10.

ERASE Deletes the Array

ERASE ARRAY.NAME, . . .

All of the elements of the named array will be eliminated.
The space reserved for the array is released for other uses.

OPTION BASE 1 Causes Minimum Value of Subscript for All Arrays to Be One

The statement must be executed before any array is dimensioned or used.
If it is not executed, the OPTION BASE is 0.
   Minimum value of subscript for all arrays will be 0.

SWAP Exchanges Values of Two Variables

SWAP VARIABLE.A, VARIABLE.B

The value of VARIABLE.A is exchanged with the value of VARIABLE.B.
Both variables must be of the same data type.

· EXERCISES ·

Short Answer

1. What is meant by a subscripted variable?

2. What are the two parts of the DIM statement?

3. Why should you explicitly dimension arrays? What happens when you don't?

4. What happens when you ERASE an array?

5. What does the statement OPTION BASE do?

6. Which data types can be used in arrays?

7. What would you use to build an array that stores account balances for 100 accounts: FOR-NEXT or WHILE-WEND? Why?

8. What is a file header record? What is it used for?

9. What are parallel arrays?

10. Describe the steps involved in a sequential search of an array.

11. Describe the differences between a sequential search and a binary search.

12. What is necessary in order to do a binary search?

13. What does the SWAP statement do?

14. Explain the difference between the bubble sort and Shell sort. When would you use one over the other?

15. Should you rely on implicit dimension of arrays? Why or why not?

16. An array with a DIMension of 100 has the capacity to hold how many elements?

17. What purpose do parallel arrays serve and how are they used?

18. Which of the sort routines will work best when:
    a. you have 10 or less items?
    b. you have 100 or more items?

Analyzing Code

19. Assume that you have arrays with the names PRICE, COST, and PROFIT. How would the following statements affect the data in each of these arrays?
    a. 100   ERASE
    b. 100   ERASE COST, PRICE

20. Will the following execute properly? If not, why?
    a. 10   DIM TABLE$(100)
       20   LET A.DOUBLE.PRECISION# = 79.87
       30   LET TABLE$(50) = A.DOUBLE.PRECISION#
    b. 10   DIM TABLE(100)
       20   LET A.STRING$ = "STRUCTURED CODE"
       30   LET TABLE(50) = A.STRING$

21. What will happen when this program is executed?

```
10   LET MY.FIRST.NAME$ = "FIRST NAME"
20   LET MY.LAST.NAME$ = " LAST NAME"
30   SWAP MY.FIRST.NAME$, MY.LAST.NAME$
40   PRINT MY.LAST.NAME$; MY.FIRST.NAME$
```

Programming

22. a. Write a program that prompts the user to enter the description and cost for nine products. Place this data into two single-dimension arrays. After the entry is complete, write the description and cost for each item to a file named "PRODUCT.DAT".

   b. Write a second program that reads the file "PRODUCT.DAT" into two arrays. For each product, display the name and price and ask the user to enter the quantity desired (0 through 999 items may be ordered). Store the response in a third array. When entry is completed, print out a report listing the name, price, quantity ordered, and total cost for the items ordered. If 0 is ordered for a particular item, do not print it.

   At the end of the list, print the total cost for all items.

23. a. Write a program that will load the following sales data into an array (use the input statement to load the array interactively):

100,000	200,100	100	98,776.88	747.35
747,707.99	16,000	54.98	121,456.78	123,456,789.99
345.99	66,000.87			

   Initially DIMension your array to 30. Load the data into the elements beginning with subscript 1. Keep a count of the total entries in your array and place this count in the element with the subscript of 0.

   b. Print the contents of the array described in (a), starting at the beginning of the array using a FOR . . . NEXT loop. Then print the array in reverse order.

   c. Modify the program in (a) so that after the data have been entered, the program creates a second array, which is DIMensioned to the value stored in position zero of the already existing array. Sort the values of the first array into ascending sequence and store them in the second array. Then purge the original array.

   Print the contents of this second array and check that the elements are in the correct order.

24. There are five manufacturing areas in the company. Management wants a comparative analysis of the output of each of the areas over a six-month period. Write a program to do the following:

   Ask the user to enter for each of the five departments: the department name and for each of the six months, the total output as a whole, single-precision number. Place this data in parallel arrays.

   Total the output for each department and compute the average total output.

   Find the department with the highest and lowest total output.

   Print a report listing the departments in sequence by total output, with the department that has the highest output first on the list.

   For each department list the department name, the output for each of the six months, the total output, and the amount by which this is over or under the average.

25. a. A company keeps data on its distributors in a disk file named "PRODDIST.DAT." The file has a header record that stores the number of distributors in the file. For each distributor it also stores the city, state, name of the company, and product. Write a program to create this file and enter the following data.

Header Record:

	DATA RECORDS		
CITY	STATE	COMPANY	PRODUCT
Boise	Idaho	Tech-City Suppliers	80 meg hard disks
Citrus Heights	California	Micropute Int'l	Graphics boards
Colorado Springs	Colorado	The Diskettes	Floppy disks
Salem	Oregon	Keys-R-Us	Keyboards
Tucson	Arizona	Inside Looking Out	Monitors
Salt Lake City	Utah	Speed of Light	Ink jet printers
Elko	Nevada	White & Bright	Fanfold paper

Once your program has created this file, read the header record to determine how many suppliers are present. Then dimension four parallel arrays to this number. Load the arrays with their respective data (name the arrays: CITY$, STATE$, COMPANY.NAME$, and PRODUCT$). Lastly, create a listing of all suppliers, locations, and products with the appropriate headings.

b. Add additional modules to the program described in part a of this exercise to allow the user to input a product, location, or company and to receive, printed on the screen, all pertinent information stored in the respective arrays. This is an on-line inquiry.

c. Add to the program the necessary code to sort the data, after it has been entered, into alphabetic sequence by distributor name using a binary sort.

d. Change the program to use a Shell sort instead of a binary sort.

MULTIDIMENSIONAL ARRAYS

KEEPING TRACK OF A FULL HOUSE

As manager of the local movie theater, Charlie had to be innovative to keep his business successful. He faced competition from the growing field of entertainments from which his patrons could choose. Even within the area of films, many customers were finding it more comfortable and less expensive to view films on their VCRs at home.

Charlie's theater showed the best of first-run films, and these movies were often popular enough to fill his house, especially on weekends. But sometimes this very popularity caused problems. The long lines and confusion at the box office over the number of available seats frustrated some patrons. Each performance some customers were not seated until the movie had started, disrupting the show for all. If the patrons were discouraged in this way too many times, they would not return.

Knowing he had to make it more convenient for people to come to his theater, Charlie decided to offer reserved seating. That way customers could buy seats in advance and be assured of a good seat. This arrangement would also relieve the long lines on weekends and help to spread out the theater's business.

When he first suggested his plan to his assistants, they were happy. It would certainly make their jobs easier. But then one of the ushers asked how they were going to keep track of the reservations. The theater had 800 seats. Monitoring reservations by hand would be a nightmare. Charlie, who had been reading *The ABCs of BASIC on the IBM Personal Computer,* tried to calm his employees' apprehensions. He felt sure, he told them, that his computer "could take care of that."

Privately, though, Charlie was worried, too. Thus far he had found no answer to this particular problem. With the approach of a big weekend's premiere, he had to find a solution fast. As he read Lesson 9, Charlie grew excited. This looked like just what he was looking for.

•*THE ABCS OF BASIC ON THE IBM PERSONAL COMPUTER*•

LESSON 9: ARRAYS KEEP TRACK OF ROWS AND COLUMNS

Recall that single-dimensional arrays in BASIC hold lists of items. Two-dimensional arrays hold tables.

We are all familiar with tables. For example, in third grade we learned about the multiplication table. Here is a small extract from the multiplication table:

×	1	2	3	4	5	6	7	8
1	1	2	3	4	5	6	7	8
2	2	4	6	8	10	12	14	16
3	3	6	9	12	15	18	21	24
4	4	8	12	16	20	24	28	32
5	5	10	15	20	25	30	35	40

In third grade we learned to write $2 \times 3 = 6$. Let's learn a new way to write this: X(2,3) is 6. What is X(3,7)? It is 21. Here we have a table called X. The value of X(3,7) is the number at the intersection of the third row and the seventh column.

The row is our first subscript. The column is our second subscript.

Much of what we learned in the previous chapter about single-dimension arrays applies directly to multidimensional arrays (see Figure 9.1)

DIMensioning a Multidimensional Array

Here is an example of dimensioning two-, three-, and four-dimension arrays.

```
DIM TWO(9,17), THREE$(20,3,6), FOUR#(4,5,3,4)
```

To dimension an array, just issue a DIM statement showing the maximum subscript in each dimension.

As mentioned in Lesson 8, using a single subscripted array before it has been DIMensioned implicitly DIMensions it to size 10. There is no corresponding

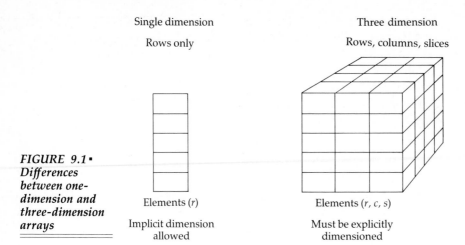

Single dimension

Rows only

Three dimension

Rows, columns, slices

Elements (r)

Elements (r, c, s)

Implicit dimension allowed

Must be explicitly dimensioned

FIGURE 9.1 •
Differences
between one-
dimension and
three-dimension
arrays

implicit DIMensioning of multisubscripted arrays. Multisubscripted arrays must be explicitly DIMensioned before use.

OPTION BASE

The rules for OPTION BASE 0 or 1 are exactly the same. OPTION BASE, if used, must be issued before any array is DIMensioned or even referenced.

Limits on the Size of Arrays

The maximum number of dimensions for an array is 255, and the maximum number of elements per dimension is 32767. In reality the number of dimensions will be limited by two other factors:

1. A statement line can be no more than 255 characters; therefore, any line referencing an element of the array with all of its subscripts must fit on one line.
2. The amount of memory available is limited. If you dimension an array that uses more memory than is available, you will get the error message, "Subscript out of range". (A better message for this error would have been "Not enough memory.") In most cases this will be the factor that limits the size of the array you can use in your program.

In business applications arrays are most commonly of one or two dimensions.

Loading Arrays

Suppose we have the following table, which represents data on sales by product for each of three years. We need to load these data into an array to be used in a program we are writing.

Sales

	YEAR		
PRODUCT	1	2	3
1	100	160	80
2	80	190	80
3	110	180	90
4	130	140	145
5	140	110	90
6	160	120	140

How are we going to get these data into an array? There are several different ways in which we can do this.

Loading an Array From an External Source Using INPUT

One way to place the data into the array is to have the user enter the figures from the keyboard with a subroutine such as the following:

```
500 ' Enter data for SALES array
510   OPTION BASE 1
520   DIM SALES(6,3)
530   FOR PRODUCT = 1 TO 6
540       FOR YEAR = 1 TO 3
550           PRINT USING "Product ## Year ## "; PRODUCT, YEAR;
560           INPUT " Sales "; SALES(PRODUCT, YEAR)
570       NEXT YEAR
580   NEXT PRODUCT
590   RETURN
```

Since this approach requires that the entire table be keyed by the user each time the program is run, it is a time-consuming process for a large table. Also, since we humans are prone to making entry errors, this method of loading the data into the array is likely to produce invalid data.

Loading an Array From an External File Using INPUT

A more efficient way to load a table is to first store the data in a file with another program. In this way the data are entered only once, reducing the chance for entry errors and improving the time taken to load the array. This method also allows data that are calculated by one program to be stored in a file to be used by another program. Let's assume that the product sales data for each year were calculated by another program and stored in the file "PRODSALE.DAT". We can load these data into an array using the following subroutine:

```
500 ' Enter SALES data
510   OPTION BASE 1
520   DIM SALES(6,3)
530   OPEN "PRODSALE.DAT" FOR INPUT AS #1
540   FOR PRODUCT = 1 TO 6
```

```
550          FOR YEAR = 1 TO 3
560              INPUT #1, SALES(PRODUCT,YEAR)
570          NEXT YEAR
580      NEXT PRODUCT
590      CLOSE #1
600      RETURN
```

Loading an Array Internally Using LET Statements

In both the previous methods the data were entered from a source external to the program. In the first case the entry was done manually, and in the second case it was done from a file created by another program. These methods are good for data that change frequently, but what about data that remains constant, such as the names of the months, or data that change infrequently, such as census data? In these cases we would like to have the data internal to the program, or "hard coded," so that no external source is required.

One way to do this is to use a series of LET statements, using one LET statement for each element of the array.

```
500    ' Enter SALES data
510    OPTION BASE 1
510    DIM SALES (6,3)
520    LET SALES (1,1) = 100
530    LET SALES (2,1) = 80
540    LET SALES (3,1) = 110
550    LET SALES (4,1) = 130
560    LET SALES (5,1) = 140
570    LET SALES (6,1) = 150
580    LET SALES (1,2) = 160
590    LET SALES (2,2) = 190
           .   .   .   .
690    LET SALES (6,3) = 140
700    RETURN
```

Loading an Array Internally Using READ . . . DATA

Another, less cumbersome method for placing data within a program makes use of two new statements: DATA and READ. The DATA statements hold the data, and the READ statements assign the values of the data to variables. You can think of DATA statements as statements that set up a sequential file within your program. The READ statement is then similar to INPUT#, retrieving the data, one item after another from the internal sequential file.

We will first look at the DATA statement to see how the data are placed in the program, and then we will examine the READ statement.

DATA Statements Store Data in a Program

To use the DATA statement you write DATA followed by the data you wish to be used, separating each item of data with a comma. The DATA statement to enter the numbers 50, 100, and 150 is:

·THE DATA AND READ STATEMENTS·

DATA Stores Constants Within a Program

DATA CONSTANT, CONSTANT, . . .
Constants are stored sequentially in the order they appear in the program listing.

READ Assigns Constants Stored by DATA to Variables

READ VARIABLE.A, VARIABLE.B, . . .
Takes the next, unread constant in the DATA list and assigns it to the variable indicated.

```
1120 DATA 50, 100, 150
```

DATA statements may also be used for string constants. String data do not need to be surrounded by quotes unless they contain commas or colons:

```
1130 DATA Sacramento, CA 95831, "July 25, 1987"
```

The quotes were required around *July 25, 1987* because that string contained a comma. Leading and trailing spaces are eliminated unless they are within quotes:

```
1140 DATA   " ONE ",  TWO
```

ONE will have a space before and after it, but TWO will not.
Both numeric and string constants can be placed in the same DATA statement:

```
1150 DATA 3.27, San Francisco, 35.067, NEW YORK
```

All of the technical details of how these constants are stored with DATA statements are not important to know. The easiest way to conceive of it is to visualize that as the program is loaded line by line into memory, the constants are stored sequentially in memory in a single list or stack. (Figure 9.2 shows the data list created by the earlier lines 1110 through 1150.) Since this occurs before the program is executed, technically it does not matter where the DATA statements are placed. However, there are several schools of thought on the most logical place to put them. Wherever they are placed, they should be easy to locate in case changes need to be made. Before structured programming, most programmers placed them at the end of the program, and this is still preferred by many. With structured programming, others now feel that the correct location is in the initialization module. As we discuss READ and RESTORE, you will also see that, done carefully, DATA statements may also be placed near the READ statements that use the constants.

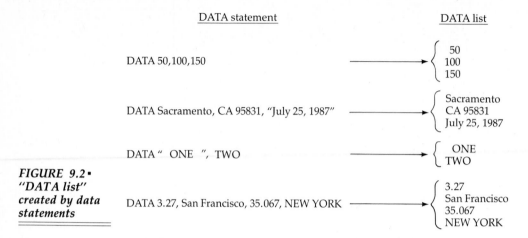

FIGURE 9.2 •
"DATA list"
created by data
statements

READ Statements Read Constants Stored by DATA Statements and Assign Them to Variables

The READ statement takes the next unread constant in the DATA list and assigns it to the variable named. One or more variables may be named in a READ statement. If the lines 1120 through 1150 used earlier are the DATA statements in a program, and if the first READ statement executed is:

```
3040 READ A, B
```

the statement will read the first two constants in the DATA list (50 and 100) into the variables A and B (see Figure 9.3).

```
3050 READ C, D$, E$
```

will read the next three constants (50, Sacramento, and CA 95831). Notice that D$ and E$ are string variable names. Both numeric and string constants can be read

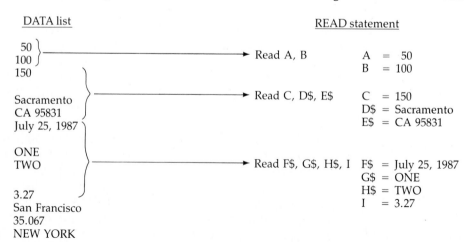

FIGURE 9.3 •
READ retrieves
values from the
"DATA list"

by a single READ statement. What is important is that the data type of the variable name matches the data type of the constant.

```
3060 READ F$, G$, H$, I
```

reads the next four constants.

If we were to print the variables at this point, we would get the following:

```
PRINT A; B; C; D$; E$
 50 100 150 SacramentoCA 95831
```

The positive numeric constants have the customary space before and after them. The string variables D$ and E$ do not have any leading or trailing spaces.

```
PRINT F$; G$; H$; I
July 25, 1987 ONE TWO 3.27
```

In this case the quotes caused the trailing spaces to be stored as part of the constant.

In the discussion so far we have assumed that all the DATA statements are in one location in the program. They do not have to be, but it is important to remember that the DATA list is created from the DATA statements in line number sequence. Consider the following excerpts from a program:

```
100 GOSUB 1000
200 GOSUB 2000
 .  .  .
 .  .  .
1000 READ A,B,C,D,E
1010 DATA 1,2,3,4,5
1020 RETURN
 .  .  .
 .  .  .
2000 READ X,Y,Z
2010 DATA 98,99,100
2020 RETURN
```

Now reverse the content of lines 100 and 200.

```
100    GOSUB 2000
200    GOSUB 1000
```

The DATA constants will be placed in the DATA list in the same sequence in both instances because when the program is loaded, line 1010 is encountered before line 2010. However, in the second instance, when the program is run, line 2000 is the first READ executed. Therefore, X will be assigned the value of 1, Y the value of 2, and so on (see Table 9.1)

RESTORE Statement With READ . . . DATA

As you just saw, READ reads DATA constants from the top of the program to the bottom. Sometimes it would be useful to reread the list or to begin reading at a

TABLE 9.1 • DATA Statements Place Values in Sequence as Program Is Loaded

DATA LIST	FIRST ORDER OF EXECUTION	SECOND ORDER OF EXECUTION
1	READ A,B,C,D,E	READ X,Y,Z
2	A = 1	X = 1
3	B = 2	Y = 2
4	C = 3	Z = 3
5	D = 4	READ A,B,C,D,E
98	E = 5	A = 4
99	READ X,Y,Z	B = 5
100	X = 98	C = 98
	Y = 99	D = 99
	Z = 100	E = 100

selected point in the list. Fortunately, there is a feature that allows you to do this: the RESTORE statement.

RESTORE by itself tells BASIC to start READing at the first DATA statement all over again. RESTORE line number tells BASIC to start READing with the first DATA statement at or after the line number. We can use RESTORE to avoid the errors in the preceding example.

```
1000 RESTORE 1020
1010 READ A,B,C,D,E
1020 DATA 1,2,3,4,5
1030 RETURN
 . . .

 . . .
2000 RESTORE 2020
2010 READ X,Y,Z
2020 DATA 98,99,100
2030 RETURN
```

By using RESTORE with the appropriate line number, you can place DATA statements in the subroutine in which they are to be READ.

Error Message With READ

If you attempt to READ past the last item in the DATA list, you will receive the error message "Out of Data". Each variable used in a READ statement must match up with a constant in a DATA statement. To reuse a DATA statement, the RESTORE statement must be used.

Using READ and DATA to Load Data into an Array

Now we can illustrate how to load the sales figures into an array using READ and DATA.

•THE RESTORE STATEMENT•

RESTORE
Next READ will start with first DATA constant in the program.

RESTORE **nnn**
Next READ will start with DATA constant specified on or after line number *nnn*.

```
500  ' Enter SALES data
510  OPTION BASE 1
520  DIM SALES(6,3)
530  FOR PRODUCT = 1 TO 6
540      FOR YEAR = 1 TO 3
550          READ SALES(PRODUCT,YEAR)
560      NEXT YEAR
570  NEXT PRODUCT
580  DATA     100,  160,  80
590  DATA      80,  190,  80
600  DATA     110,  180,  90
610  DATA     130,  140,  145
700  DATA     140,  110,  90
710  DATA     160,  120,  140
720  RETURN
```

How many data items are placed in each DATA statement is left to the discretion of the programmer. Good programming practice is to put data in a DATA statement so that each READ matches up to one DATA statement, but BASIC does not require this. In the preceding example the DATA statements replicated the table with six lines of three constants each.

Abuses of READ . . . DATA

Some authors allow READ . . . DATA to be used for a wide variety of purposes. We feel, however, that READ . . . DATA is most appropriate for storing **parameter** data. Parameter data, as we are using the term here, are values that will not change within one run of the program. They may, however, change over the shelf life of the program.

An example of parameter data is the tax rate. Tax rates may change often in business, sometimes more than once a year. However, they usually remain constant for a period of months. They are not changed in a program while the program is running.

Placing the tax rates in DATA statements eliminates the need to reinput them each time the program is run. They need to be entered only once.

An example of nonparameter data, in contrast, is employee name. For each employee we process, the value of the variable EMPLOYEE.NAME$ changes.

Generally nonparameter data are handled using INPUT or INPUT#. We certainly would not put all the employees' names and other data in DATA statements. Doing so would be tedious and would render this data unavailable to other programs. Here inputting values from a file is preferable.

To change data stored in a DATA statement requires rewriting part of the program (the DATA statements themselves.) Any change to a program introduces the possibility of introducing a bug and so should be composed thoughtfully. Users should never need to modify a program.

For this reason we believe that READ . . . DATA should not be used as an alternative to INPUT and INPUT#. READ . . . DATA has a unique purpose — to store parameter values.

Searching a Two-Dimensional Array

We have already seen how to search a one-dimensional table sequentially. Here is a program that demonstrates how to search a two-dimensional table for some target value:

```
10 'Program to demonstrate searching a two-dimensional table
20 '
30 OPTION BASE 1
40 DIM TABLE(10,10)
50 LET FALSE = 0
60 LET TRUE = -1
70 LET TARGET = 100
80 '
90 'BASIC initializes numeric elements and variables to zero.
100 'Let us put the target value in one element as the object of the search.
110 LET TABLE(6,4) = TARGET
120 '
130 'Here is the search
140 LET I = 1
150 LET FOUND.IT = FALSE
160 WHILE I <= 10 AND FOUND.IT = FALSE
170     LET J = 1
180     WHILE J <= 10 AND FOUND.IT = FALSE
190             IF TABLE(I,J) = TARGET THEN LET FOUND.IT = TRUE
                                ELSE PRINT I;J, :LET J = J + 1
200     WEND
210     IF FOUND.IT = FALSE THEN LET I = I + 1
220 WEND
230 '
240 IF FOUND.IT = TRUE THEN PRINT "Found target value at cell ";I;J
ELSE PRINT "Target value is not in the table"
250 END
```

·*PARABLES FOR*
PROGRAMMERS·

Let Users Be Users

Once upon a time a programmer named Nancy wrote a program that calculated the return on investment of a stock. Given the appropriate information about the stock's price, past performance, and the like, the program advised its user whether to invest in the stock and to what degree.

The program worked spectacularly well when tested by Nancy and her colleagues, but somehow things always went wrong when the program was put in front of computer users. It seemed that the users had trouble following Nancy's instructions.

"After starting up BASIC, enter your stock parameters by modifying lines 100 through 130 of the program," read one part of the instructions, and therein lay the problem. Those lines defined the parameters for the problem, and in order to analyze a particular stock, the user had to actually modify the program text. Unfortunately, the users tended to make mistakes that resulted in not only wrong answers but often error messages the users just couldn't understand.

For some time Nancy berated the users for their clumsiness and concentrated on making the instructions ever simpler and more detailed. Alas, it was in vain, for users continued to change the wrong lines or to make editing errors they did not understand. Still Nancy persisted in believing that "user error" was the root cause of the problem.

One day Nancy herself noticed what looked like particularly attractive stocks and decided to analyze them. Although she knew the program thoroughly and understood BASIC's error messages, Nancy still made several mistakes of the type the users complained about. A glimmer of understanding shone through, and by nightfall, Nancy had rewritten the program to ask the users for the parameters one at a time, catching most common errors. Never again did she rely on a user to change a program.

MORAL: Users are users and programmers are programmers and never the twain shall meet.

RUN

1	1	1	2	1	3	1	4	1	5
1	6	1	7	1	8	1	9	1	10
2	1	2	2	2	3	2	4	2	5
2	6	2	7	2	8	2	9	2	10
3	1	3	2	3	3	3	4	3	5
3	6	3	7	3	8	3	9	3	10
4	1	4	2	4	3	4	4	4	5

```
4   6          4   7          4   8          4   9          4  10
5   1          5   2          5   3          5   4          5   5
5   6          5   7          5   8          5   9          5  10
6   1          6   2          6   3          Found target value at cell  6   4
Ok
```

You see that to search a two-dimensional table we search one row (or one column) at a time. The crux of the search is searching one dimension at a time in lines 180 to 200. Lines 160, 170 and 210, 220 advance the search to the next row.

In this demonstration we have printed the subscripts as each element is searched. Normally these subscripts would not be displayed.

THE STORY'S END

Charlie was able to solve his reservation problem quite simply now that he knew how to use arrays with more than one dimension.

The seats in a theater can easily be expressed in a two-dimensional array in which the two dimensions represent row and seat number. By adding a third dimension for day, Charlie created an array to represent the theater reservations for different dates (see Figure 9.4). The following code would create an array to store one week's reservations in a theater with 40 rows of 20 seats each:

```
1100    OPTION BASE 1
1110    DIM THEATER (7,40,20)
```

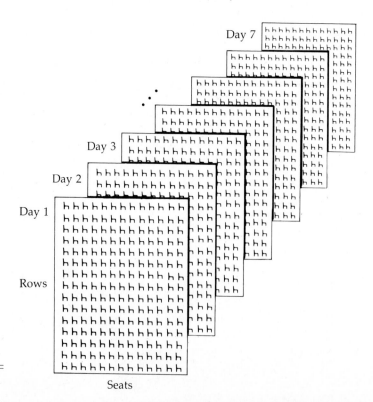

FIGURE 9.4 •
The array:
theater (date,
row, seat)

Program Specifications

Create an array that will hold the reservations. Each element will represent a particular seat in a particular row on a particular day. All of the elements will initially be set to zero to represent unreserved seats. This array will then be stored on a disk file.

When reservations are to be made, the reservation file will be input into an array. The program will prompt the user to input the day, row, and seat that is desired. If the seat is available (has the value zero), the program will reserve the seat by changing the value of the element to one and display a message to the user that the seat has been reserved.

If the seat is already reserved (is not zero), the program will inform the user and ask the user to enter another choice.

When the user has no more reservations to make, the array will be written back to the disk.

To allow flexibility, the file will contain a header record in which the number of days, the number of rows, and the number of seats are stored. This header record will also store the date of the last update.

Functions

A. Initialize
  1. Read the reservation file into a table
B. Process Reservations
  1. Input user's request for a date, row, and seat
  2. Verify that the requests are valid
  3. Execute a table lookup based on the user's request
  4. If the seat is taken, display a message; if not, reserve the seat
C. Finish
  1. Write the updated file from the table

Structure Chart

Charlie drew the structure chart shown in Figure 9.5.

Data Dictionary

File RESERVE.DAT
  (header)
  OLD.DATE$ Date file was last updated
  NBR.DAYS Number of days for reservations
  NBR.ROWS Number of rows in theater
  NBR.SEATS Number of seats in each row
  (records)
  0 or 1 for each seat in each row on each day

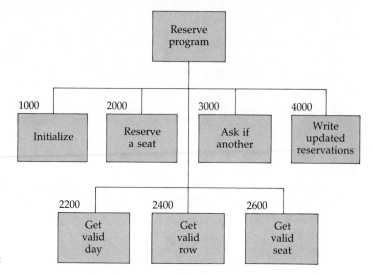

FIGURE 9.5 •
Structure chart
for reserving
theater seats

Array THEATER
Three-dimensional array with the following subscripts:
    DAY   Number of days
    ROW   Number of rows
    SEAT   Number of seats

Variables
    ANSWER$ Switch controling the main processing loop
    TODAY$ Current date

Pseudocode

MAIN
    DO INITIALIZE
    DO MORE?
    WHILE ANSWER$ = "Y" or "y"
        DO RESERVE-A-SEAT
        DO MORE?
    WEND
    DO WRITE-UPDATED-FILE
INITIALIZE
    OPEN FILE "RESERVE.DAT"
    INPUT header data from file
    PRINT message that file is being read

Both the inputting and writing of the file take time, so a message is displayed letting the user know that the program is working. It is good programming to show the user that the program has not "bombed" whenever operations take more than a few seconds.

INPUT file data into array THEATER
CLOSE FILE

After the data are input into the array, the file is not used again until the end of the program. Therefore, it is closed immediately after the input is completed.

MORE?
    Ask user if more to do
    Place response of Y or N in ANSWER$
RESERVE A SEAT
    DO GET-VALID-DAY
    DO GET-VALID-ROW
    DO GET-VALID-SEAT
    IF seat is not reserved [THEATER(DAY,ROW,SEAT) = 0]
        THEN set element to 1, print message confirming reservation
        ELSE print message that seat is already reserved
GET-VALID-DAY
    Enter DAY
    WHILE DAY is less than 1 or greater than NBR.DAYS
        PRINT error message
        Enter DAY
    WEND
GET-VALID-ROW
    Enter ROW
    WHILE ROW is less than 1 or greater than NBR.ROWS
        PRINT error message
        Enter ROW
    WEND
GET-VALID-SEAT
    Enter SEAT
    WHILE SEAT is less than 1 or greater than NBR.SEATS
        PRINT error message
        Enter SEAT
    WEND
WRITE-UPDATED-FILE
    PRINT message that file is being written
    OPEN FILE for OUTPUT
    WRITE updated header
    WRITE each seat
    CLOSE FILE

Program Listing

Before this program can be run, the file "RESERVE.DAT" must be created with the header information and all of the seat reservations set to zero. The following program creates the file for seven days and for a theater with 40 rows and 20 seats per row.

```
          10 'sample program to create RESERVE.DAT
          20 '
          30 OPEN "RESERVE.DAT" FOR OUTPUT AS #1
          40 WRITE #1, "11/11/88",7,40,20
          50 FOR D = 1 TO 7
          60     FOR R = 1 TO 40
          70         FOR S = 1 TO 20
          80             WRITE #1, 0
          90         NEXT S
          100    NEXT R
          110 NEXT D
          120 CLOSE
          130 END
```

Now that the file is created, the program can be coded and run.

```
10      'Program: RESERVE.BAS
20      'Author: Charlie Logan
30      'Date written: 11-15-88
40      'Program Description:
50      '     Inputs current reservations from file RESERVE.DAT
60      '     Asks user for day, row and seat
70      '     If seat is not taken, reserves that seat
80      '     If seat is taken, displays message to user
90      '     Writes updated reservations to RESERVE.DAT
100         '
110         '
120         '
500  ' ===============================================================
510  '                    MAIN LINE OF PROCESSING
520  ' ===============================================================
530     GOSUB 1000        'Initialize
540     GOSUB 3000        'Ask if wish to make reservation
550     WHILE ANSWER$ = "Y" OR ANSWER$ = "y"
560             GOSUB 2000        'Reserve 1 Seat
570             GOSUB 3000        'Ask if Wish to Reserve Another
580     WEND
590     GOSUB 4000        'Write Updated Reservations to File
600     END
610  ' ===============================================================
620  '                    END OF PROCESSING
630  ' ===============================================================
1000 ' ===============================================================
1010     '                    INITIALIZE
1020 ' ===============================================================
1030    CLS
```

```
1040      OPEN "RESERVE.DAT" FOR INPUT AS #1
1050      INPUT #1, OLD.DATE$, NBR.DAYS, NBR.ROWS, NBR.SEATS  ' Input Header
1060      PRINT "THIS FILE WAS LAST UPDATED ON "; OLD.DATE$
1070      INPUT "WHAT IS TODAY'S DATE"; TODAY$
1080  ' ----------  Input File   ----------------
1090      PRINT " ** Reading Current Reservations   ** Please Wait ** "
1100      OPTION BASE 1
1110      DIM THEATER (NBR.DAYS, NBR.ROWS, NBR.SEATS)
1120      FOR DAY = 1 TO NBR.DAYS
1130          PRINT "READING DAY NUMBER "; DAY
1140          FOR ROW = 1 TO NBR.ROWS
1150              FOR SEAT = 1 TO NBR.SEATS
1160                  INPUT #1, THEATER (DAY, ROW, SEAT)
1170              NEXT SEAT
1180          NEXT ROW
1190      NEXT DAY
1200      CLOSE #1
1210      CLS
1220      RETURN
2000  ' ===============================================================
2010      '                  RESERVE 1 SEAT
2020  ' ===============================================================
2030      GOSUB 2200      'Get Valid Day
2040      GOSUB 2400      'Get Valid Row
2050      GOSUB 2600      'Get Valid Seat
2060      IF THEATER(DAY,ROW,SEAT) = 0
              THEN LET THEATER(DAY,ROW,SEAT) = 1: PRINT "THE SEAT IS NOW RESERVED"
              ELSE PRINT "SORRY, THIS SEAT IS ALREADY TAKEN"
2070      PRINT
2080      RETURN
2200  ' ===============================================================
2210      '                  GET VALID DAY
2220  ' ===============================================================
2230      INPUT "Please enter the DAY:   ", DAY
2240      WHILE DAY < 1 OR DAY > NBR.DAYS
2250          PRINT "VALID RESPONSES ARE WHOLE NUMBERS FROM 1 TO "; NBR.DAYS
2260          INPUT "ENTER THE DAY"; DAY
2270      WEND
2280      RETURN
2400  ' ===============================================================
2410      '                  GET VALID ROW
2420  ' ===============================================================
2430      INPUT "Please enter the ROW:   ", ROW
2440      WHILE ROW < 1 OR ROW > NBR.ROWS
2450          PRINT "VALID RESPONSES ARE WHOLE NUMBERS FROM 1 TO "; NBR.ROWS
2460          INPUT "ENTER THE ROW"; ROW
2470      WEND
2480      RETURN
```

```
2600 ' ================================================================
2610    '                   GET VALID SEAT
2620 ' ================================================================
2630    INPUT "Please enter the SEAT: ", SEAT
2640    WHILE SEAT < 1 OR SEAT > NBR.SEATS
2650        PRINT "VALID RESPONSES ARE WHOLE NUMBERS FROM 1 TO "; NBR.SEATS
2660        INPUT "ENTER THE SEAT"; SEAT
2670    WEND
2680    RETURN
3000 ' ================================================================
3010    '         ASK IF WISH TO RESERVE ANOTHER SEAT
3020 ' ================================================================
3030    INPUT "DO YOU WISH TO MAKE ANOTHER RESERVATION (Y or N)"; ANSWER$
3040    WHILE ANSWER$ <> "Y" AND ANSWER$ <> "y" AND ANSWER$ <> "N" AND
            ANSWER$ <> "n"
3050        INPUT "PLEASE ANSWER Y OR N ", ANSWER$
3060    WEND
3070    RETURN
4000 ' ================================================================
4010    '               FINISH - WRITE FILE
4020 ' ================================================================
4030    CLS
4040    PRINT "** Writing Updated File ** Please Wait **"
4050    OPEN "RESERVE.DAT" FOR OUTPUT AS #1
4060    WRITE #1, TODAY$, NBR.DAYS, NBR.ROWS, NBR.SEATS
4070    FOR DAY = 1 TO NBR.DAYS
4080        PRINT "WRITING DAY NUMBER "; DAY
4090        FOR ROW = 1 TO NBR.ROWS
4100            FOR SEAT = 1 TO NBR.SEATS
4110                WRITE #1, THEATER(DAY, ROW, SEAT)
4120            NEXT SEAT
4130        NEXT ROW
4140    NEXT DAY
4150    CLOSE #1
4160    RETURN
4170 ' ================================================================
4180 '                   END OF LISTING
4190 ' ================================================================
```

Program Output

```
THIS FILE WAS LAST UPDATED ON 12/01/88
WHAT IS TODAY'S DATE? 12/02/88
 ** Reading Current Reservations ** Please Wait **
READING DAY NUMBER  1
READING DAY NUMBER  2
READING DAY NUMBER  3
READING DAY NUMBER  4
READING DAY NUMBER  5
```

```
READING DAY NUMBER  6
READING DAY NUMBER  7
DO YOU WISH TO MAKE ANOTHER RESERVATION (Y or N)? y
Please enter the DAY:   4
Please enter the ROW:   3
Please enter the SEAT:  10
THE SEAT IS NOW RESERVED

DO YOU WISH TO MAKE ANOTHER RESERVATION (Y or N)? y
Please enter the DAY:   4
Please enter the ROW:   3
Please enter the SEAT:  10
SORRY, THIS SEAT IS ALREADY TAKEN

DO YOU WISH TO MAKE ANOTHER RESERVATION (Y or N)? y
Please enter the DAY:   8
VALID RESPONSES ARE WHOLE NUMBERS FROM 1 TO 7
ENTER THE DAY? 7
Please enter the ROW:   85
VALID RESPONSES ARE WHOLE NUMBERS FROM 1 TO 40
ENTER THE ROW? 40
Please enter the SEAT:  112
VALID RESPONSES ARE WHOLE NUMBERS FROM 1 TO 20
ENTER THE SEAT? 20
THE SEAT IS NOW RESERVED

DO YOU WISH TO MAKE ANOTHER RESERVATION (Y or N)? n
** Writing Updated File ** Please Wait **
WRITING DAY NUMBER  1
WRITING DAY NUMBER  2
WRITING DAY NUMBER  3
WRITING DAY NUMBER  4
WRITING DAY NUMBER  5
WRITING DAY NUMBER  6
WRITING DAY NUMBER  7
Ok
```

Charlie's seat reservation system worked like a charm. After a few months Charlie modified the program to insert the price of each ticket sold, instead of a 1, to show that the seat was sold. This allowed Charlie to use the RESERVE.DAT file with another program that totaled the income for each performance.

▪QUICK REFERENCE FOR LESSON 9▪

ARRAY May Have More Than One Dimension

Arrays with more than one dimension must be explicitly dimensioned.

DIM ARRAY.NAME (a, b, . . .)

where *a*, *b*, and so on are numeric values that indicate the maximum number of elements in the corresponding dimension.

DATA Stores Constants in a Program

DATA Constant, Constant, . . .

Constants may be numeric or string.
String constants do not require quotes unless the strings contain commas, colons, or leading or trailing spaces.
Constants in DATA statements are placed in a sequential list at the time the program is loaded.
Constants stored by DATA statements may be retrieved by the READ statement.

READ Retrieves Constants Stored by the DATA Statement

READ Variable, Variable, . . .

Constants are read sequentially.
The variable type in the READ statement must agree with the data type of the constant.
If the READ statement(s) specifies more variables than are in the DATA list, the error message "Out of Data" will result.

RESTORE Allows Next READ to Begin at DATA in a Specified Line Number

RESTORE

Next READ will begin with the first DATA statement in the program.

RESTORE Line Number

Next READ will begin with DATA starting in the line number specified.

•EXERCISES•

Short Answer

1. Does the OPTION BASE statement operate the same for both single-dimension and multidimension arrays? The DIM statement?

2. Describe the procedure for using the DATA and READ statements.

3. Where in the program should you place the DATA statements?

4. What does the RESTORE statement do?

5. When would you load data into an array directly from the program? from an external file?

6. If you have one program that requires access to the same data each run, and these data are seldom changed, what statement would you issue to accomplish this?

Analyzing Code

7. Consider the following tables and identify which are the rows and which are the columns.
   a. PRODUCT.TABLE (PRODUCT.NUMBER, PRICE)
   b. PROFIT.TABLE (PRODUCT.NUMBER, VOLUME, PRICE)

8. How would you set up a three-dimensional table that represented the 12 months of a year, and for each month, represents the salespeople (five total) and the volume of four different products that each sells?

9. What will happen if the following program is run?

```
10   DIM LOCATION.TABLE (21,8)
20   FOR PROCESS.COUNTER = 1 TO 21
30     FOR INNER.LOOP = 1 TO 8
40       PRINT "FOR SALES LOCATION " ;PROCESS.COUNTER;
50       PRINT " WHAT IS THE VOLUME FOR PRODUCT #:"; INNER.LOOP;
60       INPUT LOCATION.TABLE(INNER.LOOP,PROCESS.COUNTER)
70     NEXT INNER.LOOP
80 NEXT PROCESS.COUNTER
90 END
```

10. Which of the following are valid two-dimensional arrays?
    a. DIM TABLE#(X#,Y#)
    b. DIM TABLE$(X,Y)
    c. DIM TABLE#(X,Y)
    d. DIM TABLE$(X$,Y$)
    e. DIM TABLE%(X%,Y%)
    f. DIM TABLE%(X,Y)
    g. DIM TABLE(X,Y)
    h. DIM TABLE(X$,Y$)
    i. DIM TABLE(X,Y), SALES%(X,Y), ONE.D(SUBSCRIPT)

11. What will happen if the following is executed?

```
10 WHILE COUNT = 0
20       GOSUB 80
30 WEND
40 END
50 '
80 READ MY.DATA
90 PRINT MY.DATA
100 RETURN
110 DATA 9,12,90,848,63333,,32767,0,999
```

12. Correct the program shown in Exercise 11, using the value 999 as a trailer value (a value that will indicate the end of the program or loop).

13. What will be placed in ARRAY by the following program?

```
10   WHILE NUMBER <> 99
20       READ NUMBER
30       LET SUBSCRIPT = SUBSCRIPT + 1
```

```
40          LET ARRAY(SUBSCRIPT) = NUMBER
50    WEND
60    DATA 1,100,6.7,400,100000,9,99
```

14. a. If the DATA statement in line 60 of Exercise 13 were changed to

```
60    DATA 1,100,6.7,400,100000,9,2,3,4,5,6,7,99
```

would the program still work? If not, how would you change it?

b. If you did not want the ending value of 99 to be placed in the array, how would you change the program?

Programming

15. Write a short program to build and enter the data for the table described in Exercise 8.

16. EXPENSE ACCOUNTS: Expenses that have been turned in during the week are entered at the end of the week. Twelve employees submit expenses. Write a program that prompts the user to enter the employees ID (five letters), the day (1 through 7) of the expense, and the amount. Store the total for each employee for each day in a two-dimensional array. At the end of entry, print out a report showing total expenses for each employee each day, as shown here. An employee may turn in any number of expenses for a single day, and the data are not sorted into any sequence before entry.

```
        SUMMARY OF EXPENSES FOR THE WEEK ENDING:  xx/xx/xx
EMPL ID   DAY 1    DAY 2    DAY 3    DAY 4    DAY 5    DAY 6    DAY 7
XXXXX   ####.## ####.## ####.## ####.## ####.## ####.## ####.##
XXXXX   ####.## ####.## ####.## ####.## ####.## ####.## ####.##
  .               .                 .                 .
  .               .                 .                 .
  .               .                 .                 .
TOTAL   ####.## ####.## ####.## ####.## ####.## ####.## ####.##
```

17. TRAVEL TOURS: You have just been hired by the Travel Tours to Tahoe Bus Company, which has two buses to take people from the valley to Lake Tahoe. You are to write a program that will keep track of the available seats on each bus.

You will accomplish this objective by designing two two-dimensional tables representing both of the buses. The buses hold twenty people, sitting four across and five rows deep; therefore, each table should have four rows and five columns—the first two rows represent the left side of the bus, and the second two rows represent the right side of the bus.

The program should ask the user which bus (bus 1 or 2) he or she would like to make a reservation on.

The passenger is assigned the next available seat, starting with the front row. In each row the seats are filled from left to right.

Put the initials of the passenger in the element of the array that represents the seat assigned to that passenger.

If the bus requested is full, ask the user if he or she would like to try the other bus.

When both buses are filled, display a message that both are filled, and write the contents of each table to a data file. Also allow the user to indicate that there are no more reservations, and write the file with all the reservations that have been entered.

Now close the file, reopen it for input, and print a list of passengers for each bus using the following format:

```
            TRAVEL TOURS TO TAHOE BUS COMPANY'S
                       PASSENGER LIST
   BUS 1:
        PASSENGERS:    1. DPT    2. EBC    3. JMM    4. HDT
                       5. KR     6. GRC    7. WKE    8. CMO
                         .         .         .         .
                         .         .         .         .
                         .         .         .         .
                      17. FKD   18. JLT   19. FDR   20. HST
   BUS 2:
        PASSENGERS:    1. SMF    2. PDX    3. LAX . . . . .
```

18. Change the program in Exercise 17 to use one three-dimensional array instead of two two-dimensional arrays.

19. (This is challenging.) Input the file that was written in Exercise 17 and print a listing of the passengers, in alphabetical sequence, that shows the bus, row, and seat assigned to each passenger.

20. a. Modify the program "RESERVE.BAS" to keep track of the price of each ticket as mentioned at the end of the story. At the point the program currently displays the message "THE SEAT IS NOW RESERVED," change it to print the message "THIS SEAT AVAILABLE. PLEASE ENTER PRICE (or 0 if seat is not desired)." Store the price that is entered in the array. If 0 is entered, do not reserve the seat. Validate that the price is greater than 0 and less than $99.99.

   b. Write a program that retrieves the data from the file "RESERVE.DAT" and prints a report listing the total price of tickets sold for each day. Today's date should appear at the top of the report.

   To get the total price for each day, total the price of all the seats in all rows for each of the days.

Numeric Functions

The Value of a Function

Phil's Roofing must provide fast, accurate estimates. When customers call Phil's Roofing for a bid, they are ready to buy a new roof. If his estimators can't give them a price within a day or two, the customer will hire a competitor, even if Phil can do the job for less. Not only are his estimators sluggish, they are not known for their accuracy.

Phil's office manager, who is taking classes at the city's college, suggested getting advice from some business students. Phil arranged for a student to intern with him. After studying Phil's office, the student made these suggestions:

"First, a standard formula should be used for each type of roof. For example, the formula for the cost of a tar and gravel roof should be: $103 for fixed cost of office staff plus $425 for each 10 squares, or part there of, for equipment setup plus $141 per square for materials and labor." (A square is 100 square feet.)

The student explained that this formula separates the costs of (1) office staff, (2) equipment and labor to set up equipment, and (3) materials and installation labor, thereby giving a better estimation.

"We charge $103 for each job to cover the costs of office space and staff to answer phones, do billing, and so on. Since the roofers can cover no more than 10 squares of roof in a day, and since we must move the truck and equipment to the job site each day, we charge $425 in setup costs for each on-the-job day. Lastly, we charge for the actual installation (labor and materials).

"Also, since the staff doing the estimates are better at sales than they are at determining areas, we ask them to measure the roof, and we let the computer figure the area and the cost. We will ask them to measure the roof as a number of rectangles, triangles, and semicircles. We will enter these measurements into the computer, which will provide the estimated cost."

Phil was so pleased with these suggestions that he hired the intern to write the required program.

Thinking "I'd better bone up on BASIC if I am to deliver what I promised," the intern opened *The ABCs of BASIC for the IBM PC* to Lesson 10.

•THE ABCS OF BASIC ON THE IBM PERSONAL COMPUTER•

LESSON 10: NUMERIC FUNCTIONS

For programming many business applications the statements and commands you have learned in BASIC are adequate. However, other applications take advantage of additional features of BASIC such as **built-in functions** and **user-defined functions.**

A BASIC statement or command tells BASIC to do something: print something on the monitor, write a record to a file, and so on. Functions are different. They can be thought of as instructions, all within one BASIC statement, that perform some sequence of operations on the data specified and return the result of those operations to the program. In addition to using the functions built-in (preprogrammed) to BASIC, you may define your own functions.

The main purpose of functions is to reduce both the time and space needed to write the code for operations that are frequently performed. Operations provided by BASIC are those that are commonly used, such as taking the square root of a number. Users may find they have other operations that are used repeatedly throughout a program. These can be defined once and called as needed in the program.

In this lesson we will discuss **numeric functions.** These are functions that operate on numeric data and that return numeric values. Except for a few that are

•FUNCTIONS•

Functions consist of instructions to perform a sequence of operations to return a value. BASIC provides some "built-in" functions. Others may be defined by the programmer. Functions may have one or more arguments or no arguments at all.

so described, numeric functions return as values only integer or single-precision numbers. Lessons 11 and 12 cover the string functions and input/output functions.

SQR(): A Numeric Function for Taking Square Roots

Let's plunge into numeric functions by showing a sample program that asks the user for a number, then displays its square root.

```
10 INPUT "Enter a positive number"; N
20 LET S = SQR(N) ' Take the square root of N
30 PRINT "The square root of ";N; " is "; S
40 END
run
Enter a positive number? 45
The square root of  45  is  6.708204
Ok
run
Enter a positive number? 201
The square root of  201  is  14.17745
Ok
```

The function SQR() returns as its value the square root of the number in parentheses, in this case the value of N. SQR is the **name** of the function. N is the **argument** to the function. Notice that the value of N (the argument of the function) is not changed by the function. The function performed the operation of computing the square root of N and returned that value. The program assigned that value to the variable named S. When both N and S are printed, N still has its original value.

All functions have the same form: name(argument, argument, . . .). Some functions have only one argument, while others have two or more. Certain special-purpose functions have no arguments at all. When speaking of functions, programmers commonly refer to them by their name followed by empty parentheses—for example, SQR(). However, in order to use a function you must supply it with appropriate argument(s).

SQR() takes as its argument a numeric expression. That expression may be a numeric constant, such as 17; a variable, such as N; or a more complicated expression, such as $2 * (3 + N)$. Like all numeric-valued functions, SQR() can be used in the same way as a numeric constant or a variable. Thus, the above program could have been simplified by using SQR() directly in the PRINT statement.

```
10 INPUT "Enter a positive number";N
20 PRINT "The square root is "; SQR(N)
30 END
```

Functions may even be used as all or part of the arguments to the same or other functions. SQR(SQR(N)) takes the square root of the square root of N.

SQR(3 * (4/SQR(N))) is also legal. Here is a program that computes the length of the diagonal of a rectangle.

```
10 INPUT "Enter the length and width";L,W
20 PRINT "The diagonal is ";SQR(L * L + W * W)
30 END
```

The diagonal is the square root of the sum of the squares of the sides. The rest of this lesson looks at other numeric functions:

ABS() Returns the Absolute Value of a Number

ABS() expects one argument. ABS(X) returns the positive equivalent of the argument. In other words, if the argument is zero or positive, the value returned by ABS() is the same as the argument. If the argument is negative, the value returned is that number without the minus sign.

```
PRINT ABS (345.27), ABS (0), ABS (-345.27)
 345.27          0             345.27
```

One use of ABS() is to test whether two numbers are approximately equal. Because of rounding errors that are too small to concern us, X may not exactly equal Y, and the condition X = Y would test false. In Chapter 5 we took this into consideration and tested whether the difference between X and Y was between −.005 and +.005 using the following condition:

```
IF (X - Y) < .005 OR (X - Y) > -.005 THEN . . .
```

With ABS() we can shorten this test to:

```
IF ABS(X - Y) < .005 THEN . . .
```

If the two values differ by less than .005, we will call them the same.

Here is another example. Let's assume that a company that manufactures auto glass needs to make sure that the measurements of its windshields fall within certain specifications. The desired length is stored in the variable COR-RECT.SIZE, and the actual measurement is entered into the variable AC-TUAL.SIZE. Assuming that a deviation of .04 is acceptable, the following use of ABS() can be used to test for measurements that are out of spec and to direct processing to a subroutine:

```
7230 IF ABS(CORRECT.SIZE - ACTUAL.SIZE) > .04 THEN GOSUB 8500 ' test
                                         for acceptable measurements
```

SGN() Determines the Sign of a Numeric Value

SGN() is used as a way of easily determining if a number is negative, zero, or positive. SGN() expects one argument and returns −1 if that value is less than 0, 0 if the value of the argument is 0, and 1 if the value of the argument is greater than 0. The following equivalent statements show the power of well-used functions:

▪THREE FUNCTIONS: SQR(), ABS(), SGN()▪

SQR(X) returns the square root of X, where X is not negative.

ABS(X) returns the absolute value of X. Absolute value is always positive or zero.

SGN(X) returns the value of:

> 1 if X is positive
> 0 if X is zero
> −1 if X is negative

```
LET I = SGN(CUSTOMER.BALANCE)
```

is equivalent to

```
IF CUSTOMER.BALANCE < 0 THEN LET I = -1 ELSE IF CUSTOMER.BALANCE = 0
   THEN LET I = 0 ELSE LET I = 1
```

SGN() could be used in a program to print a special message that the balance became negative. The test for this could be written as:

```
IF SGN(CUSTOMER.BALANCE) = -1 THEN GOSUB 2000 ' negative balance
```

For example, the local public radio station wants to print a report comparing donations received to pledges made. The report needs to show the subscriber's name and the pledge in the first two columns and the actual donation in one of three columns depending on whether the donation is less than the pledge, equal to the pledge, or greater than the pledge. The subscriber's name is in the array S.NAME$(), the pledge in the array PLEDGE(), and the donation in the array DONATION(). The subscript identifying the person is the variable SUBS.

```
5999 PRINT S.NAME$(SUBS) TAB(15) PLEDGE(SUBS)
        TAB(50 + 15 * SGN(PLEDGE(SUBS) - DONATION(SUBS))) DONATION(SUBS)
```

If the pledge is less than the donation, SGN will return the value −1 and the TAB will be to column 35. If the pledge equals the donation, the TAB will be to column 50, and if the pledge is greater than the donation, the TAB will be to position 65.

CINT() Converts to the Nearest Integer

There are many occasions when you wish to round a noninteger number to the nearest integer. You have already seen two ways in which nonintegers can be converted or rounded to whole numbers. PRINT USING rounds values to fit the print mask.

```
PRINT USING "The integer is ####"; 345.789
The integer is 346
Ok
```

The LET statement can also be used to assign to one variable the integer value of another noninteger variable. This process also rounds to the closest integer.

```
10 LET DBL.PRES# = 12345.678999#
20 LET INTGR% = DBL.PRES#
30 PRINT DBL.PRES#; INTGR%
 12345.67899  12346
```

Since we do not have to do anything explicit to cause this conversion to take place, the conversion process is said to be *implicit.*

For some applications this is fine. However, BASIC contains functions that allow us to request explicitly that a variable of one precision be used to generate a number of another precision. CINT() is one such function. CINT() returns an integer value equal to its argument, rounded to the nearest whole number.

That is, for a single- or double-precision argument, CINT() returns that value rounded to the nearest integer. Since integers must be from −32768 to +32767, the argument of CINT() must round to within those limits. If it rounds to a value outside those limits, you will get the error message "Overflow."

```
PRINT CINT(345.789)
 346
Ok
PRINT CINT(-345.789)
-346
Ok
PRINT CINT(32767.499999)
 32767
Ok
PRINT CINT(32767.500)
Overflow
Ok
```

Converting to an integer value can speed processing. It will also conserve memory space. A *byte* is the amount of memory required to store one character. Integers require only two bytes of memory while single precision requires four and double precision take eight.

Two Functions That Return Whole Numbers

Two other numeric functions, INT() and FIX(), return whole numbers. They are similar in that both INT() and FIX() return a number that is the same precision as that of the argument and both return whole numbers. (In contrast, CINT() returns only values of type integer.) However, they differ from one another in how they handle the decimal portion of the number.

·THREE FUNCTIONS: CINT(X), INT(X), FIX(X)·

CINT(X) returns the integer nearest to X (the rounded integer value of X).
INT(X) returns the greatest whole number equal to or less than X (does not round).
FIX(X) returns the value of X truncated to a whole number.
For positive numbers, INT(X) and FIX(X) will return the same results.
For negative numbers, INT(X) will return a whole number less than FIX(X).

INT() Returns the Greatest Whole Number That Is Equal to or Less Than

INT() does not round; instead INT() returns the greatest whole number that is less than or equal to the argument. The simplest way to visualize this is to think of the number line (see Figure 10.1). For whole numbers, INT() will return that whole number; for numbers with a decimal portion, INT() will return the whole number to the left of the argument on the number line.

For positive numbers this is equivalent to truncating the decimal portion of the number. For example:

```
PRINT INT(1.6); INT(15.99); INT(0.6278); INT(4)
 1  15  0  4
```

For negative numbers, since the rule is to return a whole number equal to or less than the argument, the result is to return the whole number to the left of it on the number line. For example:

```
PRINT INT(-1.6); INT(-15.99); INT(-0.6278); INT(-4)
 -2 -16 -1 -4
```

Remember that −2 is less than −1.6.

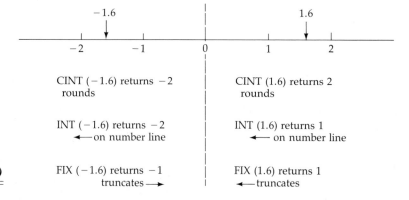

FIGURE 10.1 •
Differences
between CINT(),
INT(), and FIX()

ROUNDING Using INT()

Here is an example of using INT() to round to the nearest thousandth. To do this we can use INT() as follows:

```
LET A = 35.7658
LET A = INT(A * 1000 + .5)/1000
PRINT A
 35.766
```

To round to the nearest hundreds, we can write the following:

```
LET A = 13789
LET A = INT(A/100 + .5) * 100
PRINT A
 13800
```

FIX() Truncates to a Whole Number

FIX() is similar to INT(), except that the decimal portion of the argument is always truncated ("lopped off ").

FIX retains the precision of the argument. For positive numbers, INT and FIX give identical results. For negative numbers, FIX gives a value one more than INT, because FIX lops off the decimal portion, which yields a number closer to zero than the original. INT, in contrast, yields a value less than (or equal to) the original in all cases.

Comparing INT(), FIX(), and CINT()

Let's compare the results of INT(), FIX(), and CINT(). Although both INT() and FIX() return whole numbers, they retain the precision of the original argument; CINT(), on the other hand, returns an integer.

```
5 PRINT "I","INT","FIX","CINT"
10 FOR I = -1.6 TO 1.6 STEP .45      ' I is single precision
20      PRINT I,INT(I),FIX(I),CINT(I)
30 NEXT I
40 END
run
```

I	INT	FIX	CINT
-.6	-2	-1	-2
-1.15	-2	-1	-1
-.7000001	-1	0	-1
-.2500001	-1	0	0
.1999999	0	0	0
.6499999	0	0	1
1.1	1	1	1
1.55	1	1	2

Notice that the functions behave as expected. Also notice the way in which I is printed. Where we expected −.7, I took the value of −.7000001. This is due to the way in which numbers are stored internally. BASIC stores numbers in binary format. In binary format, .1 cannot be represented exactly, which results in numbers not appearing exactly as we would expect. This is the reason for rounding to the desired number of places before a number is printed.

Two Other Functions That Convert Precision: CSNG() and CDBL()

We have already discussed CINT(), which is used to convert a numeric value to an integer. A comparable function to converting to single precision is CSNG(); a function for converting to double precision is CDBL().

CSNG(): Convert to a Single-Precision Value

CSNG() returns the single-precision value of the argument. Since single-precision values take only four bytes, while double-precision take eight bytes, if double-precision accuracy is no longer needed, CSNG() can be used to reduce memory requirements.

```
LET DBL.PRES# = 1.2345679999
PRINT CSNG(DBL.PRES#)
  1.234568
```

Because it is desirable that all of the values have the same precision when performing arithmetic calculations, CSNG() can be used explicitly to return the single-precision value before the calculation is executed. BASIC will convert variable type as needed in any case.

```
LET RESULT = (SUB.TOTAL - .5 * CSNG(COUNT%))/.55
```

CDBL() Converts a Value to Double Precision

There are probably few times when CDBL() will be used. Converting an integer or single-precision value to double precision does not increase precision. As you learned in Chapter 4, converting single precision to double precision does not increase accuracy; it may, however, lead to erroneous results.

In general, whole numbers of seven or fewer digits of length can be converted to double precision without causing problems, but this is often not the case with other values. Consider the following example in which CDBL() returns values with erroneous data:

```
PRINT CDBL(1.234567)
  1.234567046165466
PRINT CDBL(1.234568)
  1.234567999839783
PRINT CDBL(1234567)
  1234567
```

To make matters worse, even if you do not *explicitly* convert a single-precision value to double, BASIC will implicitly do so and possibly introduce errors in precision should you use any double-precision variable in the same expression as the single-precision variable.

RND() Returns a Random Number

RND() is a function. It can be used with or without an argument to return a randomly generated single-precision number from 0 to .9999999. There are several ways in which RND() can be used. In the following program RND is used with no argument to produce and print five random values. (The values you get might be different; the sequence generated depends upon your machine and the version of BASIC that you are using.)

```
NEW
Ok
10 FOR I = 1 TO 5
20      PRINT RND
30 NEXT I
40 END
RUN
 .7151002
 .683111
 .4821425
 .9992938
 .6465093
Ok
```

Now let's try running the program a second time.

```
RUN
 .7151002
 .683111
 .4821425
 .9992938
 .6465093
```

•THE RND FUNCTION•

RND returns a random number between 0 and 1.

RND with no argument and RND(X), where X is positive, return the next random number.

RND(0) repeats the last random number that was generated.

RND(X), where X is negative, initiates the particular random sequence associated with X.

The exact same "random" sequence was repeated. On your machine the numbers may be different than those shown here but each time you run this program or any other program using this format for RND, you will get the same sequence. This is both a blessing and a curse. It is helpful because any given run can be replicated (i.e., rerun with the same results), which is particularly useful when testing a program. It is harmful in that since the same sequence is always generated, it does not constitute a true random sampling.

Fortunately, BASIC allows us to change the starting point at which the random generator begins. This starting point is called the **seed.**

Reseeding the Random Number Generator: RND() With Negative Argument

We can reseed the RND() function in two ways. The first way is by using the RND() function with a negative argument. For each given negative value, a particular sequence is generated. As an example, we can cause a different sequence to be generated in the sample program we've been using by adding this line:

```
5 PRINT RND (-4)
```

Now when we run it, we will get this result:

```
RUN
 .8188288
 .2677991
 8.733116E-02
 7.081251E-02
 .8175731
 .5208339
```

Line 05 "reseeded" the random generator so that it generated the sequence associated with the seed of −4. In the example we printed RND (−4). This is not necessary; we could reseed using a "dummy" LET statement such as:

```
5 LET DO.NOTHING = RND(-4)
```

If we run the program now, only the five values generated by the FOR . . . NEXT loop will print.

```
RUN
 .2677991
 8.733116E-02
 7.081251E-02
 .8175731
 .5208339
```

Although this did change the sequence, we still have a problem because each time we run this using RND(−4) we will get the same sequence. We could ask the user to enter the seed by changing the program with these lines:

```
 5 INPUT "Enter any number ", SEED
06 LET POS.SEED = ABS(SEED)         ' Get positive value
07 LET DO.NOTHING = RND(-POS.SEED)  ' Argument must be negative
```

With these lines we take whatever value the user enters, positive or negative, transform the value to a positive number using ABS(), then precede it with a minus sign for the RND() function.

RND() With Positive or Zero Argument

Before going on to the second way to reseed the random number generator, we should mention what happens when RND() is used with a positive number or the value of zero as the argument.

RND() with a positive argument is the same as with no argument. The generator is not reseeded and the next random number in the sequence is generated.

RND(0) will repeat the last number generated.

To demonstrate this we will enter the following:

```
NEW
Ok
```

Issuing the NEW command reinitializes the random generator at its original starting point.

```
PRINT RND
 .7151002
Ok
```

This is the first random number our machine generates when it is not reseeded. We saw this number a few paragraphs back.

```
PRINT RND (345)
 .683111
Ok
```

This is the second number in the sequence we saw earlier. Since the argument was positive, it did not change the sequence.

```
PRINT RND (0)
 .683111
Ok
```

The argument of zero caused the last number that was generated to be repeated.

```
PRINT RND (456.38)
 .4821425
Ok
```

Again, a positive argument generates the next number in the sequence.

RANDOMIZE Reseeds the RND Function

You can also reseed the RND function by using the RANDOMIZE statement. When BASIC encounters the RANDOMIZE statement, it stops processing and issues the following message:

```
Random number seed (-32768 to 32767)?
```

The user then types in a number within the range specified. Entering a number outside of these limits will give the error message "Overflow." We can change our sample program to use this statement.

```
 5 RANDOMIZE
10 FOR I = 1 TO 5
20     PRINT RND
30 NEXT I
40 END
RUN
Random number seed (-32768 to 32767)? 34
 .1565455
 3.840159E - 02
 .3539538
 .5708105
 .3711072
```

RANDOMIZE With Variable or Constant
RANDOMIZE may also be used with a numeric variable or constant. For example, we could write line 05 as follows:

```
05 RANDOMIZE 2435
```

When BASIC encounters the statement RANDOMIZE 2435, it reseeds the random number generator with the number specified and does not ask the user for a seed. While RANDOMIZE used alone allows only the values between the limits of −32768 and 32767 to be entered, in BASIC 2.0 and later RANDOMIZE *n* allows *n* to be any number.

Since the message "Random number seed (−32768 to 32767)" may be unclear to some user, you may wish to use this version of RANDOMIZE to create your own message as follows:

```
3 INPUT "Enter any number ", SEED
5 RANDOMIZE SEED
```

RANDOMIZE TIMER: Another Way to Reseed
The RANDOMIZE TIMER statement allows for a technique that will give different random numbers each time the program is run. This technique uses the function TIMER, which returns the number of seconds on the system clock. (TIMER is not available in versions prior to BASIC 2.0.)

```
PRINT TIMER
 56407.67
Ok
```

This tells us that 56407.67 seconds have elapsed since the system clock was set to 00:00:00. Since this is a constantly changing number, the statement RANDOMIZE TIMER will give different random numbers each time the program is run—a different set for each second of the day.

·**THE RANDOMIZE STATEMENT**·

RANDOMIZE reseeds the random number generator.

RANDOMIZE used by itself will cause program to pause and prompt user for a value between −32768 and 32767.

RANDOMIZE (*n*), where *n* is an integer or integer expression, will reseed the generator based on the value of *n*.

RANDOMIZE TIMER (not available in BASIC prior to version 2.0) uses the number of seconds since midnight to reseed the generator.

```
 5 RANDOMIZE TIMER
10 FOR I = 1 TO 5
20     PRINT RND
30 NEXT I
40 END
```

Techniques in Using Random Numbers

All of the numbers we have generated have been from 0 to .9999999. Typically we want random numbers not just between 0 and 1 but also between other values, such as between 1 and 6. How do you generate numbers greater than 1?

While there is not a function to do this directly in BASIC, using some of the functions we have just learned, we can easily write our own set of statements to give us what we want.

If we want to simulate the roll of dice, we need to generate whole numbers from 1 through 6. Since RND varies between 0 and 1, 6 * RND generates numbers from 0 to 5.999999. To get whole numbers we could use the function INT(). INT (6 * RND) will give the whole numbers 0 through 5. (We could also use FIX() in place of INT() since they give the same results for positive numbers.) To get the range 1 through 6, all we need to do is to add 1 to the number we have just generated.

```
PRINT INT (6 * RND) + 1 ' a random digit 1 through 6
```

In general, to generate whole numbers in the range 1 to N, use the expression INT (N * RND) + 1. To generate a random, single-precision number between 1 and N, use the expression (N − 1) * RND + 1.

For example, since there are 13 face values for playing cards, to simulate the drawing of a card we can use the following statement:

```
PRINT INT (13 * RND) + 1
```

Uses of Random Numbers

There are many times when we want a program to return a random sequence of values. This is important in many areas of computer programming, such as in generating data to test a program. Nowhere, however, is returning random values more important than in simulations.

A program that simulates some aspect of the real world must recognize that certain events are inherently unpredictable. For example, it is not certain on any given day whether the stock market will go up or down, or by how much. A program that tests a theory on stock market behavior needs to generate a random series of numbers to represent buying and selling of stock. The idea of simulations will be explored in detail in the Case Studies (see Case VI).

Remaining Numeric Functions

There are six more numeric functions intrinsic to BASIC. You should be aware of them in case the need arises; they are less commonly used in business.

EXP() Returns e to the Xth Power

Some computations involve raising the constant e (2.71828) to a power. EXP(X) returns as its value e raised to the Xth power. The following are some examples:

```
LET E.TO.THE.FOURTH = EXP(4)
PRINT E.TO.THE.FOURTH
 54.59815
PRINT EXP(4 * 2)
 2980.958
Ok
```

LOG() Returns the Natural Logarithm of a Number

The flip side of EXP() is LOG(), which returns as its value the power to which e must be raised in order to equal the argument of LOG(). These two functions are useful in financial calculations.

```
PRINT LOG (54.59815)
 4
```

Trigonometric Functions: ATN(), COS(), SIN(), TAN()

The functions ATN(), COS(), SIN(), and TAN() are the trigonometric functions of BASIC. All expect a single numeric argument and return numeric values. In each case angles are measured in radians. ATN() returns the arctangent of the argument; COS() the cosine; SIN() the sine; and TAN() the tangent.

A circle is 360 degrees, which is also equal to 2 * PI radians, where PI = 3.14159. . . . Therefore, you can convert from X degrees to radians by using the statement

LET RADS = X * (2 * 3.14159)/360

Another way to express this relationship would be as follows:

degrees = (radians * 180)/PI
radians = (degrees * PI)/180,

where

PI = 3.141593

DEF FN Creates Your Own Functions

There are times when BASIC's set of functions is not enough and you will wish to define your own function. This is particularly true when you have a complicated set of calculations or operations that will be repeated in different parts of the program. Creating a function allows you to write the code and test it once, ensuring that each time that function is called the calculations will be performed accurately and in a uniform manner. It also allows for ease in maintenance. Should you need to make a change in the series of operations or calculations (and, inevitably, you will), you will only need to make the change in one place.

As a simple example we will create a function to calculate profit margin. For a given price and cost, the profit margin is the difference between the price and cost divided by the price.

The first step is to give the function a name. The first two letters must be FN. (Now you see why variable names may not begin with the letters FN.) Other than that, the rules for naming functions are the same as for naming variables. They may contain the letters of the alphabet, digits 0 through 9, and the decimal point, and they may not be longer than 40 characters.

The name of a user-defined function determines its type in the same way that the name of a variable determines its type. A name ending in # returns a double-precision value; a name ending in % returns an integer value; a name ending in $

·THE DEF FN STATEMENT·

DEF FN name(argument,argument, . . .) = expression
Name is the name given to the function. It must be a valid variable name.
Argument(s) are the names of variables that are used in the expression.
Expression is a valid BASIC expression that tells how this function will
 operate upon the arguments.

Example: Function that calculates the area of a circle. The radius is the argument of the function.

DEF FNCIRCLE.AREA (RADIUS) = RADIUS ^ 2 * 3.14159

returns a string value (more about string functions in the next lesson). Unless overridden by a DEFINT, DEFDBL, or DEFSTR statement, a name that does not end in any of the three characters #, %, or $ returns a single-precision value.

The name we will give to the function that returns the value of the profit margin is FNMARGIN. Since we have not indicated otherwise, the value will be single precision.

To define this function we first write: DEF FNMARGIN. In parentheses we place the names of the arguments — in our case, PRICE and COST. We then write the equal sign followed by the formula. The full statement defining this function is:

```
1150 DEF FNMARGIN(COST,PRICE) = ( PRICE - COST )/PRICE
```

Now when you want to perform this calculation somewhere in the program, you can call the function by giving its name followed by the arguments with parentheses. Here are two examples that could be used:

```
2200 PRINT FNMARGIN(8,10)          ' margin for cost of 8 and price of 10
```

or

```
5550 LET SELL.PRICE = 100
5560 LET COST.TO.US = 60.58
5570 PRINT "The Margin is "; FNMARGIN(COST.TO.US, SELL.PRICE)
```

Once defined, the function FNMARGIN() may be used any number of times any place in your program. However, the DEF FN statement must be executed before the function is called and would normally be placed in the initialization module. For purposes of structuring programs, you may think of defined functions in the same light as subroutines. Remember that subroutines are also used both to avoid duplicating the same statements in several places and to structure a program in a natural, readable manner.

DEF FN is easy to use, but there are a few subtleties of which you should be aware. When you define the function with the DEF FN statement, the names that you give to the arguments are merely placeholders or dummy variable names. They can be used in the program without affecting the function.

```
10 DEF FNDIAGONAL(X,Y) = SQR (X * X + Y * Y)
20 LET X = 6: LET Y = 8
30 LET BOTTOM = 700: LET SIDE = 900
40 PRINT "The diagonal length is "; FNDIAGONAL(BOTTOM,SIDE)
50 PRINT X, Y
60 END
RUN
The diagonal length is  1140.175
6               8
Ok
```

The placeholder names X and Y are used in the definition of the function FNDIAGONAL. These same names are used for the numeric variables in line 20, which sets their values to 6 and 8, respectively. Later in the program, FNDIAGONAL is called with arguments BOTTOM and SIDE. Even though FNDIAGONAL uses the arguments named X and Y in the DEF FN statement, when the function is called with the arguments BOTTOM and SIDE, the variables named X and Y retain their values of 6 and 8. It is poor programming practice to use the same variable name for two different purposes; we did so here just to illustrate the point.

Example: A Random Number Function

Suppose we need a convenient way to generate a random number on demand. Let's make a function FNRAN(N), which will yield a number between 1 and N.

```
1170 DEF FNRAN(N) = (N - 1) * RND + 1
```

Then whenever we want a random number between 1 and N, we will invoke the function. For example, to obtain a random number between 1 and 5, we could use the following:

```
3350  LET A.RANDOM.NUMBER = FNRAN (5)
```

What if we want only integers between 1 and N? We could use INT (N * RND) + 1, but then we must define our function as integer (DEF FNRAN%(N)) if we want the result to be an integer.

```
1170 DEF FNRAN%(N) = INT(N * RND) + 1
```

To generate a random whole number between max and min, the function is as follows:

```
1170 DEF FNRAN%(MAX,MIN) = INT( RND * (MAX - MIN) + MIN)
```

Example of a Rounding Function

We discussed earlier a way to round numbers using INT(). Now let's make this into a user-defined function that will have as its arguments the number we wish rounded and the power of ten to which we wish it rounded. If we wish to round to the nearest thousand, that is ten to the third power; the nearest thousandth is ten to the minus third power.

```
1090 DEF FNROUND(VALUE,POWER) = INT(VALUE/10 ^ POWER + .5) * 10 ^ POWER
```

To use this function to round the variable ANY.NUMBER to the nearest hundredth, we can write:

```
4090 LET ANY.NUMBER = FNROUND(ANY.NUMBER, -2)
```

Example of a Function to Convert Fahrenheit to Centigrade

Suppose you have a program in which you frequently need to convert Fahrenheit to Centigrade. You can create a function to perform this calculation so you won't have to write the formula each time you want to make the conversion. In the following sample program we have defined the function FNCONV.TO.CENT, which returns the Centigrade equivalent of the argument. When the report is printed, we want the Centigrade degrees rounded to the nearest integer. We have used CINT() to get the integer value to illustrate that a function can be the argument of another function; we could have defined the function to be of type integer.

```
10 ' Program Name: TEMPDEMO.BAS"
20 ' Date Written: 03/04/88
30 ' Description
40 '     Program asks user to input maximum, minimum, and average temp
50 '     Centigrade temps are calculated and printed with Fahrenheit
60 ' ================================================================
70 '
80 ' =======    Define Function to Convert Fahrenheit to Centigrade ===
90 '
100 DEF FNCONV.TO.CENT(FAHREN.TEMP) = (FAHREN.TEMP - 32) * 5/9
110 '
120 '=======     Input Temperatures =======
130 '
140 CLS
150 INPUT "Please enter maximum temperature (in Fahrenheit) ", MAX.TEMP
160 INPUT "Please enter minimum temperature (in Fahrenheit) ", MIN.TEMP
170 INPUT "Please enter average temperature (in Fahrenheit) ", AVG.TEMP
180 '
190 '=======     Print Report =======
200 '
210 CLS
220 PRINT ,"*****", "TEMPERATURE REPORT", "*****"
230 PRINT
240 PRINT ,,"Fahren", "Cent"
250 PRINT "Maximum Degrees", MAX.TEMP, CINT(FNCONV.TO.CENT(MAX.TEMP))
260 PRINT "Minimum Degrees", MIN.TEMP, CINT(FNCONV.TO.CENT(MIN.TEMP))
270 PRINT "Average Degrees", AVG.TEMP, CINT(FNCONV.TO.CENT(AVG.TEMP))
280 END
RUN
(screen clears)
Please enter maximum temperature (in Fahrenheit) 115
Please enter minimum temperature (in Fahrenheit) 48
Please enter average temperature (in Fahrenheit) 84
(screen clears)
                *****        TEMPERATURE REPORT        *****

                             Fahren                    Cent
Maximum Degrees              115                        46
Minimum Degrees              48                         9
Average Degrees              84                         29
Ok
```

A More Advanced Example of User-Defined Functions

```
10 ' A FUNCTION TO YIELD THE GREATER OF TWO NUMBERS
20    DEF FNMAX(A,B) = - ( A > B ) * A + - ( B >= A ) * B
30    LET X = 5: LET Y = 6
40    PRINT FNMAX(X,Y)
RUN
 6
```

Here we defined a maximum function; it returns the value of the higher of two numbers. It does this by using the logical expressions (A > B) and (B >= A). The expression A > B is true when A is greater than B. A true expression has the value of -1; an expression that is false has the value of 0. So, if A is greater than B, then FNMAX(A,B) $= -(-1) * A + 0 * B$, or A.

If B is greater than A, then FNMAX(A,B) $= -(0) * A + -(-1) * B = B$

THE STORY'S END

After reading Lesson 10, Phil set out to transform lengthy engineering calculations into BASIC programs.

"I used to have to perform every calculation twice to check its accuracy. Now that I've debugged and thoroughly tested my program, I don't need to recheck my figures. I just have BASIC echo back to the printer the figures I give it along with the results. Then I recheck to make sure that I entered the correct figures. If the results are in the right 'ball park,' I go with them.

"Building a BASIC program was a big chore, but now I would never go back to my manual system. In fact, some of the subroutines we wrote for this program we will use again in some new programs I have in mind."

Program Specifications

This program will assist the user by calculating the cost to roof a house. The user will enter the measurements of the roof as a combination of three geometric shapes: triangle, rectangle, and semicircle.

The program will calculate the number of square feet in the roof and determine the number of "squares" in the roof. A "square" is 100 square feet of roof. If the result is not a whole number, it will be rounded to the next highest whole number.

The estimated cost of the roof will be based on the formula:

```
COST = FIXED OFFICE COST of $103 plus
           SETUP FIXED COST of $425 for each 10 squares plus
           MATERIALS COST of $1.41 per square foot.
```

The output will present the square footage, the number of squares, and the estimated cost.

·*PARABLES FOR*
PROGRAMMERS·

Think Ahead

The Beaver had noticed recently that the Otter always seemed to have a lot of free time to cavort on the river bank. It had not always been so: when they had both started programming, the Otter spent as much time as the Beaver on its programs. Wondering how the Otter managed to become so much more productive, the Beaver one day took the Otter aside.

"Otter," began the Beaver, "why is it that you seem to have so much leisure time these days while I work my tail off writing programs? Have you quit programming?"

"No," replied the Otter, with a sly grin. "In fact, I produce more programs now than ever before, and in less time."

"Well, then, the answer is obvious; you must be writing only simple programs, which would naturally take less time."

The Otter slid into the water and swam several circles around the bewildered Beaver. "As a matter of fact, I am now tackling more difficult programs than ever before."

"Aha!" exclaimed the Beaver. "You must have hired a programmer or two to help!"

The Otter ran merrily up and down the bank, laughing, "Who, me? Hired help? Why, I have so much free time now, I don't think I could find a use for more!"

"What is it, then? Have you learned a new style of programming? Do you use a different programming language? A new computer? How do you accomplish so much in so little time when I barely have time to eat?"

The Otter ran up to the Beaver, leaned close, and said, "The secret is my library. We both started programming at the same time, but while you have tackled each program as a unique project, I have taken to time to isolate those parts of my programs that might have use in future programs. I save these subroutines and, where appropriate, use them or modify them slightly for each new program. Over time, I've accumulated such a fine library that most of my programs these days can be pieced together from subroutines already written and tested.

"This also means that I spend less time fixing bugs. Since the library subroutines are pretty well tested by repeated use, bugs come up less often."

MORAL: A good library will pay for itself many times over.

Functions

A. Initialize
 1. Display instructions
 2. Initialize variables
 3. Define functions
B. Figure area
 1. Enter measurements of rectangles
 2. Calculate and total the area of every rectangle
 3. Enter measurements of triangles
 4. Calculate and total the area of every triangle
 5. Enter measurements of circular portions
 6. Calculate and total the area of every semicircle
 7. Calculate total based on the sum of the three areas
C. Print estimate
 1. Calculate and print the number of squares
 2. Compute and print the estimate

Structure Chart

The structure chart for this program is seen in Figure 10.2.

Data Dictionary

Files: none

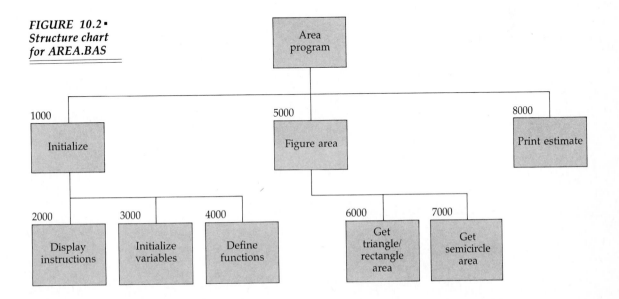

FIGURE 10.2 •
Structure chart
for AREA.BAS

Constants

OFFICE.FIXED.COST	Cost to handle order, set to $103
SET.UP.FIXED.COST	Cost per 10 squares, set to $425
MATERIALS.COST	Cost of material per square ft, set to $1.41

Measurements Input by User

LENGTH	Length of a rectangle or triangle
HEIGHT	Height of a rectangle or triangle
RADIUS	Radius of the circular portion
PROPORTION	Proportion of a circle that the circular figure represents

Working Variables

DUMMY$	Used only for determining if key is pressed
LABEL$	Used to store identification (triangle or rectangle) of calculation in progress
MULTIPLIER	Allows the function FNAREA to operate on either a rectangle (multiplier set to 1) or a triangle (multiplier set to .5)
TEMP.TOTAL	Temporary accumulator used in GET TRIAG/RECT AREA module
RECT.TOTAL	Total area of all rectangles
TRIAG.TOTAL	Total area of all triangles
SEMI.TOTAL	Total area of all circular areas
TOTAL.AREA	Sum of REC.TOTAL, TRIAG.TOTAL, and SEMI.TOTAL

User-Defined Functions

FNAREA	Calculates the area of a triangle or rectangle
FNSEMI	Calculates the area of a circular figure
FNSQUARES	Rounds the total area to the nearest 100
FNESTIMATED	Calculates an estimated cost for roofing

Pseudocode

MAIN
    DO INITIALIZE
    DO FIGURE-AREA
    DO PRINT-ESTIMATE

INITIALIZE
    display instructions
    initialize each variable
    define each function
FIGURE-AREA
    Set LABEL$ to "RECTANGLE" and MULTIPLIER to 1
    DO GET-TRIANG/RECT AREA
    LET RECT.TOTAL = TEMP.TOTAL
    Set LABEL$ to "TRIANGLE" and MULTIPLIER TO .5
    DO GET-TRIANG/RECT AREA
    LET TRIAG.TOTAL = TEMP.TOTAL
    DO GET-SEMICIRCLE-AREA
    sum all areas giving TOTAL.AREA
GET-TRIANG/RECT-AREA
    set TEMP.TOTAL to zero
    get first LENGTH
    WHILE LENGTH > 0
        get height
        figure area and add to TEMP.TOTAL
        get next LENGTH
    WEND
GET-SEMICIRCLE-AREA
    get first RADIUS
    WHILE RADIUS > 0
        get PROPORTION
            WHILE PROPORTION > 1 OR < 0
                give error message
                get PROPORTION
            WEND
        figure area of this semicircle and add to SEMI.TOTAL
        get next RADIUS
    WEND
PRINT-ESTIMATE
    PRINT TOTAL.AREA
    Compute and PRINT number of squares
    Compute estimate cost using TOTAL.AREA
    PRINT estimated cost

Program Listing

```
10    'Program: AREA.BAS
20    'Author: Hal Lockwood, intern for Phil's Roofing
30    'Date Written: 4-15-88
40    'Program Description:
50    '   Asks user to input area of roof as series of
```

```
60   '       rectangles, triangle and semicircles
70   '    Calculates areas of figures
80   '    Computes cost based on sum of:
90   '       (1) OFFICE.FIXED.COST        Processing cost. Same for each job.
100  '       (2) Cost to Send Truck and Crew Each Day Required to Complete Job
110  '              Crew can complete 10 squares (1000 sq ft) each day
120  '              Cost per day is SET.UP.FIXED.COST
130  '       (3) Cost of Materials
140  '              Cost per square foot is MATERIALS.COST
150  '
160  '
500  '================================================================
510  '                    Main Line
520  '================================================================
530  GOSUB 1000                                      'Initialize
540  GOSUB 5000                                      'Figure Area
550  GOSUB 8000                                      'Print Estimate
560  END
1000 '================================================================
1010 '                    Initialize
1020 '================================================================
1030 GOSUB 2000                                      'Display Instructions
1040 GOSUB 3000                                      'Zero Out Variables
1050 GOSUB 4000                                      'Define Functions
1060 '     Wait for user to read instructions
1070 INPUT "Press ENTER to continue", DUMMY$
1080 RETURN
2000 '================================================================
2010 '                    Display Instructions
2020 '================================================================
2030 KEY OFF
2040 CLS
2050 PRINT "You will be prompted to enter the dimensions of all the "
2060 PRINT "rectangles, triangles, and semicircles that compose the roof"
2070 PRINT "of the house you are estimating."
2080 PRINT
2090 PRINT "If there are multiple figures, the program will total their"
2100 PRINT "areas for you.  After you have entered all of the rectangles,"
2110 PRINT "enter the dimensions for the triangles and then the semicircles."
2120 PRINT
2130 PRINT
2140 PRINT
2150 RETURN
3000 '================================================================
3010 '                    Zero Out Variables
3020 '================================================================
3030 LET TEMP.TOTAL = 0                    'used by subroutine
3040 LET RECT.TOTAL = 0                    'holds total area of rectangles
3050 LET TRIAG.TOTAL = 0                   'holds total area of triangles
3060 LET SEMI.TOTAL = 0                    'holds total area of semicircles
```

```
3070 LET TOTAL.AREA = 0                  'sum of above three
3080 LET LENGTH = 0                      'length entered by user
3090 LET HEIGHT = 0                      'height entered by user
3100 LET RADIUS = 0                      'radius entered by user
3110 LET OFFICE.FIXED.COST = 103           'cost to handle order
3120 LET SET.UP.FIXED.COST = 425          'cost to send truck (per day)
3130 LET MATERIALS.COST   =   1.41        'cost for 1 sq ft
3140 RETURN
4000 '=====================================================================
4010 '                     Define Functions
4020 '=====================================================================
4030 DEF FNAREA(LENGTH,HEIGHT,MULTIPLIER) = LENGTH * HEIGHT * MULTIPLIER
4040 DEF FNSEMI(RADIUS,PROPORTION) = 3.1415 * RADIUS^2 * PROPORTION
4050 DEF FNSQUARES(AREA) = INT((AREA - 1)/100 ) + 1
4060 DEF FNESTIMATED(AREA) = OFFICE.FIXED.COST+
     SET.UP.FIXED.COST * ((FNSQUARES(AREA) - 1)\10 + 1) + MATERIALS.COST
     * AREA          'Estimated cost
4070 RETURN
5000 '=====================================================================
5010 '                     Figure Area
5020 '=====================================================================
5030 LET LABEL$ = "RECTANGLE"
5040 LET MULTIPLIER = 1
5050 GOSUB 6000        'Get Triag/Rect Area
5060 LET RECT.TOTAL = TEMP.TOTAL
5070 '
5080 LET LABEL$ = "TRIANGLE"
5090 LET MULTIPLIER = .5
5100 GOSUB 6000        'Get Triag/Rect Area
5110 LET TRIAG.TOTAL = TEMP.TOTAL
5120 '
5130 GOSUB 7000        'Get Semicircle Area
5140 LET TOTAL.AREA = TRIAG.TOTAL + RECT.TOTAL + SEMI.TOTAL
5150 RETURN
6000 '=====================================================================
6010 '                     Get Triag/Rect Area
6020 '=====================================================================
6030 CLS
6040 LET TEMP.TOTAL = 0
6050 PRINT "In this module, you will enter the length and height of each ";
          LABEL$
6060 PRINT
6070 INPUT "Enter the first LENGTH (or press RETURN to exit) ",LENGTH
6080 WHILE LENGTH > 0
6090    INPUT "Now please enter the HEIGHT ", HEIGHT
6100    LET TEMP.TOTAL = TEMP.TOTAL + FNAREA(LENGTH, HEIGHT, MULTIPLIER)
6110    PRINT "Accepted"
6120    INPUT "Enter the next LENGTH (or press ENTER to exit) ",LENGTH
6130 WEND
6140 RETURN
```

```
7000 '================================================================
7010 '                     Get Semicircle Area
7020 '================================================================
7025 CLS
7030 PRINT "In this module, you will enter the radius of each semicircle"
7040 PRINT "and the proportion it is of a full circle.  You will enter "
7050 PRINT "that proportion as a decimal number, such as .50"
7060 PRINT
7070 INPUT "Enter the radius of the first semicircle (or press ENTER to exit) ",
RADIUS
7080 WHILE RADIUS > 0
7090         INPUT "Now enter the proportion in the form .xx (or press ENTER to
            cancel) ",PROPORTION
7100        WHILE PROPORTION > 1 OR PROPORTION < 0
7110           PRINT
7120           INPUT "Please enter a decimal point and two digits ",PROPORTION
7130        WEND
7140        LET SEMI.TOTAL = SEMI.TOTAL + FNSEMI(RADIUS,PROPORTION)
7150        INPUT "Please ENTER the radius of the next semicircle (or press
            ENTER to exit) ", RADIUS
7160 WEND
7170 RETURN
8000 '================================================================
8010 '                     Print Estimate
8020 '================================================================
8030 CLS
8040 PRINT USING "The total roof area is #####,## sq ft";TOTAL.AREA
8050 PRINT USING "(#,###) squares ";FNSQUARES(TOTAL.AREA)
8060 LET ESTIMATED = FNESTIMATED(TOTAL.AREA)
8070 PRINT USING "I recommend estimating the cost at $$#####,###";ESTIMATED
8080 RETURN
9999 '===================== END OF LISTING ===========================
```

Program Output

```
You will be prompted to enter the dimensions of all the
rectangles, triangles, and semicircles that compose the roof
of the house you are estimating.

If there are multiple rectangles, the program will total their
areas for you. After you have entered all of the rectangles,
enter the figures for the triangles and semicircles.




Press ENTER to continue
```

(screen clears)

```
In this module, you will enter the length and width. of each RECTANGLE

Enter the first LENGTH (or press RETURN to exit) 25
Now please enter the width ? 23
Accepted
Enter the next length (or press ENTER to exit) 21
Now please enter the width ? 26
Accepted
Enter the next length (or press ENTER to exit) (ENTER is pressed)
```

(screen clears)

```
In this module, you will enter the length and width. of each TRIANGLE

Enter the first LENGTH (or press RETURN to exit) 10
Now please enter the width ? 12
Accepted
Enter the next length (or press ENTER to exit) 11
Now please enter the width ? 12
Accepted
Enter the next length (or press ENTER to exit) (ENTER is pressed)
```

(screen clears)

```
In this module, you will enter the radius of each semicircle
and the proportion it is of a full circle. You will enter
that proportion as a decimal number, such as .50

Enter the radius of the first semi-circle (or press ENTER to exit) 16
Now enter the proportion in the form .xx (or press ENTER to cancel) .5
Please enter the radius of the next semicircle (or press ENTER to exit) (ENTER)
```

(screen clears)

```
The total roof area is     1,649 sq ft
(   17) squares
I recommend estimating the cost at        $2,853
Ok
```

• QUICK REFERENCE FOR LESSON 10 •

FUNCTIONS

A function returns a value. The value returned is usually used in a LET or PRINT statement, but it may be used anywhere a variable is permitted in an expression.

To call a function, use the function name followed by its arguments in parentheses: name (arg1, arg2, . . .). Functions may have zero or more arguments.

Some functions return numeric values; others return string values, while still others return a logical value (true or false). Arguments may be numeric expressions or string expressions, depending on the particular function being used. This lesson has covered those functions that accept numeric arguments and return numeric values.

Numeric Functions

The following is a table of functions discussed in this lesson.

NAME	ARGUMENT TYPE	VALUE
ABS(X)	Numeric	$-X$ is negative, X otherwise
CDBL(X)	Numeric	X as a double-precision value
CINT(X)	Numeric	X as an integer value
CSNG(X)	Numeric	X as a single-precision value
INT(X)	Numeric	greatest whole number less than or equal to X
FIX(X)	Numeric	number obtained by truncating decimal portion of x
SGN(X)	Numeric	-1 if $X < 0$, 0 if $X = 0$, 1 if $X > 0$
SQR(X)	Numeric	square root of X
EXP(X)	Numeric	$e \wedge X$
LOG(X)	Numeric	n such that $e \wedge n = X$
ATN(X)	Numeric	arctangent of X (where X is radians)
COS(X)	Numeric (radians)	cosine of X
SIN(X)	Numeric (radians)	sine of X
TAN(X)	Numeric (radians)	tangent of X
RND	None	next random number ($0 <= RND < 1$)
RND(X)	Numeric < 0	"seeds" random sequence
RND(X)	Numeric > 0	same as RND
RND(0)		repeat previous random number

Statements Used With Random Numbers

RANDOMIZE nnn	Seeds RND with the number nnn
RANDOMIZE	Asks the user for a number to seed RND
RANDOMIZE TIMER	Reseeds RND using the time since midnight

User-Defined Functions

Functions may also be defined by you, the programmer, using the DEF FN statement. The format of this statement is DEF FNname (arg1,arg2, . . .) = expression.

Name is the name of the function you have defined.

The names *arg1, arg2,* and so on are names of the arguments to your function. These names may be used in the expression to represent the values passed as arguments at the time the function is called. Argument names have no relationship whatever to variable names.

Expression is a numeric or string expression, which may be built of constants, variable names, argument names, and the various BASIC operators (e.g., +, −). The type of the expression (integer, single-precision, double-precision, or string) must match that of the name of the function.

The DEF FN statement(s) may appear anywhere in your program, but a function must have been defined by executing the DEF FN statement before it can be called from elsewhere in the program.

Short Answer

1. Describe the difference between BASIC statements, expressions, and functions.

2. What are the different parts of a function?

3. What is the ABS() function used for?

4. What does the SGN() function do?

5. Give examples of three different ways to round a number to the nearest integer.

6. Describe the differences between the INT(), FIX(), and CINT() functions.

7. Give examples of two ways to convert a value to a double-precision form.

8. Discuss the necessity and process of reseeding a RND() function.

9. Why is it necessary to use the formula INT (N * RND) + 1 rather than a simple function to generate random integers?

10. What is the DEF FN function? Give its format and define each part of the statement.

Analyzing Code

11. Consider the following:

```
10   LET A = 36
20   PRINT SQR(A)
```

What is the value of A at this point in the program?

12. Evaluate the results of the following functions and give the precision of the results.
    a. ABS(-12 * (64 - 52))
    b. SQR(ABS(-12 * (64 - 52))
    c. CINT(A) if A = 12.445
    d. CINT(A) if A = 45008
    e. INT(A) if A = -24.99
    f. INT(A) if A = 24.49
    g. INT(A#) if A# = -12345.6789
    h. FIX(0)
    i. FIX(-23.68)
    j. FIX(23.999)

Programming

13. Using the RANDOMIZE n statement, write a program that will generate numbers from -25 to 25. Your program should loop at least 25 times; each pass determines the square root, absolute value, INT, FIX, and SGN of each value. Note, if the value is negative, print "N/A" for the square root. The output should be designed as follows:

NUMBER	SQUARE ROOT	ABSOLUTE VALUE	INT	FIX	SIGN
25	5	25	25	25	+
-25	N/A	25	-25	-25	-
.	.	.	.	.	.
.	.	.	.	.	.

14. The formula for the future value of an amount P is P(1 + I) ^ N, where I is the interest rate per period and N is the number of compounding periods.

The formula for continuous compounding is similar: P * e ^ IN, where e is the natural log of 1, or 2.718 (see the EXP() function). For interest rates between 5 percent and 15 percent write a program that uses a user-defined function to calculate the future value based on the first formula and based on the continuous compounding method. Display the results in the form of a comparison table.

15. Assume that you have to make payments of AMT for T periods and the opportunity cost of money is I (I = interest rate). The formula to determine what the present value of this series of payments is as follows: PV = AMT(1/(1 + I) ^ 0) + AMT(1/(1 + I) ^ 1) . . . + AMT(1/(1 + I) ^ (T − 1). That is, if T = 4 years the formula would be PV = AMT(1/(1 + I) ^ 0) + AMT(1/(1 + I) ^ 1) + AMT(1/(1 + I) ^ 2) + AMT(1/(1 + I) ^ 3).

Given this information (referred to as the present value of an annuity), develop a program that will allow the user to determine the present value of ten annuities based on interest rates of 8, 10, and 15 percent. Use a user-defined function for the formula. Print the results in a narrative form as follows:

```
The present value of ## payments of $#,### at an interest rate of ##% is
    $##,###.
```

16. The program "AREA.BAS" currently gives estimates only for tar and gravel roofs. Phil would like to be able to use the program to estimate other types of roofs, such as shake or tile. The computation for these roofs is essentially the same; the only thing that changes is the setup cost and materials cost (the office processing cost is the same for all types of roofs).

For a shake roof, the daily setup cost is $550 for each ten squares, and the materials cost is $389 per square.

For a tile roof, the daily setup cost is $600 for each ten squares, and the materials cost is $527 per square.

Modify the function to ask the user for the type of roof and give the estimate for that type. Do this in such a way that the user may get an estimate of all three types of materials for the same house without having to reenter the measurements three times.

Change the function FNESTIMATED so that instead of the one argument AREA, it uses three arguments: AREA, SET.UP.FIXED.COST and MATERIALS.COST. This function can then be used for all three types of roofs by just changing the values of the arguments.

PROCESSING CHARACTERS USING STRING FUNCTIONS

LIVING WITH LETTERS

"How's it going?" Pat asked, seeing Willie in front of the company mailroom.

"Boy, am I glad that I ran into you!", Willie said. "You know how I've been doing my part to computerize our business? Well, I've run into a blank wall."

Willie, who had started out in the mailroom just six months ago, had already turned that old-fashioned department into one of the most modern in the company. At the time the Top Brass wanted all the departments to use desktop computers, most were reticent. Willie, however, not only requested one for the mailroom but actually submitted a proposal showing what the PC could do for the department. Management could not refuse.

Although Pat normally tried to avoid getting involved in someone else's dilemma, Pat liked Willie's enthusiasm. "What can I do for you, Willie?"

"I can't get BASIC to decode my addresses. I've entered all of these city, state, and zip codes into a string, and now I want to break apart the string into separate strings for city, state, and zip code."

Pat looked relieved. "Oh, I can help you with that. The answer is in Lesson 11 of *The ABCs of BASIC for the IBM PC*."

As Willie started reading the text, Pat walked away, silently wishing all problems were so easily solved.

LESSON 11: STRING FUNCTIONS AND STATEMENTS

In the last lesson we discovered what numeric functions BASIC offers us. In this chapter we will explore string functions. We will look at functions that work with strings, either accepting string variables, expressions, or constants as parameters, or returning string constants.

First, let's examine a function useful for making borders on reports.

STRING$() Generates a Row of Any Character

The function STRING$() creates a string of any single character that you want. For example, to print a row of asterisks across a page write:

```
PRINT STRING$(70,"*")
**********************************************************************
```

The number of times you want the character is written first, followed by a comma, and then, in quotes, the character that you wish. You will find this function useful when designing reports and screen displays. If you want a line of equal signs to print across the screen, it is much easier to write PRINT STRING$(80,"=") than to write a string with 80 equal signs. If you should place a string with more than one character within the quotes, only the first character of that string will be used by STRING$(). For example, STRING$(3,"ELI") is "EEE".

Suppose you want to print on the screen a report or message that uses some of the more unusual characters, such as a solid box or an arrow. You can't put quotes around the characters because these characters are not on the keyboard. But there are ways you can generate them.

Recall that a byte is a collection of eight bits, each bit being in an on (1) or off (0) state. Within a string of eight on-off bits, there are 256 (2 to the eighth power) possible combinations of ons and offs. These 256 possible combinations form a code that BASIC uses to display or print characters. Most computer manufacturers have agreed to use the same code, called **ASCII** (American Standard Code for Information Interchange). An ASCII table (see Appendix A) lists these combinations and their translations. Rather than list the binary representation, the table gives its decimal value. For example, A is represented by the *binary* 01000001, which is equivalent to *decimal* 65; therefore, A is given the *ASCII* value of 65.

STRING$() allows you to use the ASCII values to generate the characters that are not on the keyboard. As you look down the table, note that the solid box has the ASCII value of 219. Try the following statement:

```
PRINT STRING$(50, 219)
```

This will print a bar of 50 solid boxes on the screen. Look through the ASCII table and try some of the other values. If you have a printer available, try using LPRINT

• THE STRING$() AND SPACE$() FUNCTIONS •

STRING$() returns a string of characters.

Form 1: STRING$(*n*,"*") returns a string of *n* asterisks.
Form 2: STRING$(*n*,A$) returns a string repeating the first character of A$ *n* times.
Form 3: STRING$(*n*,*x*) returns a string with the character that has the ASCII value of *x*, *n* times.

SPACE$(*n*) returns a string of *n* spaces. For example:
LET A$ = SPACE$(19).

with some of these values. You may or may not get the results you expect depending on your printer. While the IBM PC printer will print all the characters correctly, some other printers may not.

We can also use STRING$ to print spaces.

```
PRINT "TOM"; STRING$ (10," "); "BROWN"
TOM          BROWN
```

Ten spaces were printed between TOM and BROWN.

SPACE$() Generates a Row of Spaces

Since a string of spaces is frequently desired, there is a special function called SPACE$ just for generating spaces. SPACE$(10) is the same as STRING$(10," ").

```
PRINT "TOM"; SPACE$ (10); "BROWN"
TOM          BROWN
```

CHR$() Generates Any Character Using Its ASCII Value

We discussed earlier how you can get some of the special characters not on the keyboard by giving their ASCII value as one of the arguments for STRING$. Often you will want to generate only a single character. For example, suppose you want to have the symbol for pi printed on the screen. The ASCII value of the pi symbol is 227. Rather than write PRINT STRING$(1,227), you can use the function CHR$() and write PRINT CHR$(227).

CHR$() accepts as its argument a whole number from 0 through 255 and returns the character with that ASCII value.

On the ASCII list you will also notice there are some things that are not characters but signals to the computer.

Beside the value of 7 is listed "beep." Printing CHR$ (7) will cause the computer to beep. Another control character is CHR$ (13), the carriage return. It is the same character the keyboard sends when the Enter key is pressed.

ASC() Returns the ASCII Code for a Character

ASC is the inverse of CHR$. While CHR$() accepts a numeric value for its argument and returns as a string value the character that has the ASCII value of the argument, ASC() accepts a string argument and returns as a numeric value the ASCII code for the character. For example:

```
PRINT ASC("A")
 65
```

If the argument is longer than one character, ASC returns the value for the first character only.

```
LET TRY$ = "BANANA"
PRINT ASC(TRY$)
 66
```

(The ASCII code for *B* is 66.)

The ASC function is very useful. For example, we can use it to make sure that all the alphabetic characters are in uppercase. Using both ASC() and CHR$(), you can write a simple routine to convert lowercase to uppercase (or vice versa).

On the ASCII table notice that uppercase letters have the ASCII values 65 through 90 and lowercase 97 through 122. In other words, the uppercase letter has an ASCII value 32 less than the corresponding lowercase letter. A subroutine to convert a lowercase letter to uppercase would do the following:

1. Find the ASCII value of the character.
2. Test that this value is from 97 to 122.
3. Subtract 32 from the ASCII value.
4. Replace the lowercase letter with CHR$() of the new value.

Here is the code for a subroutine that does this:

```
2250 ' **** Subroutine to Convert Lowercase to Uppercase
2260 '      Character to be converted has been placed in variable
2270 '           HOLD.CHAR$
2280 LET HOLD.ASCII = ASC(HOLD.CHAR$)          ' find ASCII value
2290 IF HOLD.ASCII > 96 AND HOLD.ASCII < 123
        THEN LET HOLD.ASCII = HOLD.ASCII - 32 ' if lower, change to upper
2300 LET HOLD.CHAR$ = CHAR$(HOLD.ASCII)       ' replace lowercase
2310 RETURN
```

LEN() Determines the Number of Characters in a String

We often want to know the length of a string — that is, how many characters there are in a string. A function in BASIC called LEN() will tell us this. To find the length of the string named ANY.STRING$, we would write the following:

```
LEN(ANY.STRING$)
```

·THE CHR$() AND ASC() FUNCTIONS·

CHR$(*n*) returns the character that has the ASCII value of *n*. For example:

PRINT CHR$(65)
A

ASC(A$) returns the ASCII value of the first character of A$. For example:

PRINT ASC("IBM")
 73

·PARABLES FOR PROGRAMMERS·

A Cure for the Common Code

"Jones! How do I delete this record?"

"Use code 48, Boss," replied Jones.

"Jones! How do I print a list of our customers?" continued the Boss.

"Code 17," replied Jones.

"Jones! What is it doing? I used code 17, and it's telling me to enter an accounting transaction!" Jones could sense the Boss's patience wearing thin.

"Oops! That should have been code 27, not 17. Use codes 92, 13, and 15 to get back to where you were, then try code 27."

"Jones! On this report, the customer's status just lists numbers like 11 and 3. And this one, 5559672. What does that mean? How do I tell who is over their credit limit, or who is behind in paying our bills? Wait . . . don't tell me. Those are just . . ." Jones chimed in with the Boss, "more codes."

"11 means a customer has exceeded a credit limit, 3 means there are no invoices outstanding, and 5559672 is just that customer's telephone number."

"Jones, I don't like codes," fumed the Boss. "If I want to delete something, why can't I just type in 'delete'? If I want to print something, why can't I just type in 'print'? Bank account numbers, Social Security numbers, license plate numbers, numbers, numbers, numbers . . . there are too many numbers in this world. Find me a program that speaks my language!"

MORAL: Avoid using artificial codes in a computer program: if a string is available that naturally describes an action or condition, use it.

LEN() will count the characters in the string ANY.STRING$ and return that numeric value. LEN() counts all characters including spaces and commas. If the string is null, LEN() returns the value of zero.

```
PRINT LEN("This")
 4
Ok
PRINT LEN("THIS IS A STRING")
 16
Ok
LET CITY.STATE$ = "Sacramento, CA 95831"
Ok
PRINT LEN(CITY.STATE$)
 20
Ok
LET NULL$ = ""
Ok
PRINT LEN(NULL$)
 0
Ok
```

To store the value that is returned by LEN in the numeric variable SIZE, write:

```
LET SIZE = LEN(ANY.STRING$)
```

SIZE now holds the number of characters in the string ANY.STRING$.

An Example of Using LEN()

Here is a routine that will center a message, given a set left margin and right margin. Note that in line 1040 we have used concatenation to join the strings.

```
100 LET LEFT.MARGIN = 1
110 LET RIGHT.MARGIN = 80
120 INPUT "Please Enter your Message: ", MESSAGE$
130 GOSUB 1000                  ' centering routine
140 PRINT CMESSAGE$             ' centered message
150 END
160 ' --------------------------------------------------
1000 'Routine to center a heading message MESSAGE$
1010 LET PRLEN = RIGHT.MARGIN - LEFT.MARGIN ' Number of available spaces
1020 LET ML = LEN(MESSAGE$)                 ' length of message
1030 LET PADDING$ = SPACE$((PRLEN-ML)/2)
1040 LET CMESSAGE$ = SPACE$(LEFT.MARGIN) + PADDING$ + MESSAGE$
1050 RETURN
run
Please Enter your Message: This is a Message!
                        This is a Message!
Ok
run
Please Enter your Message: a short msg
                            a short msg
```

```
Ok
run
Please Enter your Message: A very, very, very long message to be centered.
?Redo from start
Please Enter your Message: "A very, very, very long message to be centered."
            A very, very, very long message to be centered.
```

"?Redo from start" appeared because there are commas in the message entered. Without quotes around the message, BASIC interprets the entry as three separate values. Placing quotes around the message indicates that the commas are part of the data, not separators.

Another Example Using LEN()

The following program prints a box of asterisks around a name. The value returned by LEN() has been used as the argument for other functions (STRING$() and space$()) and to calculate the ending value for a FOR . . . NEXT loop. We have used different methods to print the top and bottom lines of asterisks to illustrate that there is usually more than one way to accomplish the same thing.

```
10 ' sample program illustrating the use of LEN to print box of
20 '    asterisks around the name that is input
30 INPUT "Please enter name ", C.NAME$
40 PRINT STRING$( (LEN(C.NAME$) + 4), "*")    ' print top of box
50 PRINT "*";SPACE$(LEN(C.NAME$) + 2); "*"    ' print second line
60 PRINT "* "; C.NAME$; " *"                  ' print name
70 PRINT "*"; SPACE$(LEN(C.NAME$) + 2); "*"   ' print next line
80 FOR I = 1 TO (LEN(C.NAME$) + 4)            ' print bottom line
90      PRINT "*";
100 NEXT I
110 END
RUN
Please enter name Christopher Robbins
**********************
*                    *
* Christopher Robbins *
*                    *
**********************
```

INSTR(): Where in a String Are Specific Characters?

There are times when you wish to see if a particular character or sequence of characters occurs in a string. For example, suppose the city, state, and zip code have been entered into a string named CITY.STATE$ in the following format:

```
CITY, ST 12345
```

Thus, we have city followed by a comma and one space, then two letters for state, one more space, and finally a five-digit zip code. You wish to find if CA has been entered as the state.

You can use the INSTR() function to search one string (in this case, CITY.STATE$), for a substring (CA). INSTR will return a value that tells you at which position IN the STRing the substring begins. Positions in a string are counted from left to right, with the left-most position counted as position number one.

If the substring does not occur in the major string, the value of zero will be returned. (Remember, the value of a logical false is zero.)

The general format for INSTR() is:

```
INSTR(MAJOR.STRING$, SUB.STRING$)
```

where MAJOR.STRING$ and SUB.STRING$ may be string variables, string expressions, or string constants. The function will search the first named string and return the number of the position in the first named string where the second named string begins. For example,

the value of	is
INSTR ("ABCDE","D")	4
INSTR ("ABCDE","F")	0
INSTR ("Oh, what a beautiful morning", "Oh, what")	1
INSTR ("Oh, what a beautiful morning", "beau")	12

Notice that the positions taken by commas and spaces are counted.

If we want to select all addresses in the state of California, we must find if and where the letters *CA* occur in CITY.STATE$. We can do this with the following:

```
3320 LET WHERE = INSTR (CITY.STATE$, "CA")
```

If CITY.STATE$ contains the letters *CA*, WHERE will indicate the position (1) at which they are found. For example, if CITY.STATE$ contains "Sacramento, CA 95831", the value of WHERE will be 13. If *CA* did not appear in the string, WHERE would have the value of zero.

INSTR() looks for an exact match. If the characters for state in CITY.STATE$ are *ca* or *Ca* instead of *CA*, INSTR() will return the value of zero. Therefore, if CITY.STATE$ contains "San Francisco, Ca 94901", WHERE will have the value of zero.

Specifying the Starting Point

In the preceding examples, because we did not specify otherwise, INSTR() began its search with the first position. There is another format of INSTR() that allows us to specify the position at which we wish INSTR() to begin its search:

```
INSTR(N, MAJOR.STRING$, SUB.STRING$)
```

where N is a numeric expression from 1 to 255.

In our example, if we know that all cities have at least five characters, we could have INSTR begin the search starting with the sixth position by writing:

```
3320 LET WHERE = INSTR(6, CITY.STATE$, "CA")
```

Testing Your Understanding

Using the first version of line 3320, what will happen if CITY.STATE$ contains "Calexico, CA 90111"? What about "CALISTOGA, CA 96789"? What will be the results using the second version?

Using INSTR() for Data Validation

Another use of INSTR() is to test that a valid character has been entered into a particular variable. Suppose that our program contains a screen display such as the following, which asks the user to enter one digit from 1 through 6 to select which process to execute next. The character the user enters is stored in the variable CHOICE$. (Even though a number is being entered, we have input it into a string variable because INSTR() operates only on string variables.)

```
*** Mailing Program ***
1. Enter Customer Address
2. Change Customer Address
3. Delete Customer Address
4. Sort Addresses by Zip Code
5. Print Mailing Labels
6. Exit From Program
Please enter your selection -
```

To test if CHOICE$ contains a valid entry we will create a string that contains all the valid characters:

```
1500 LET VALID.CHAR$ = "123456"
```

To find out if CHOICE$ is one of the characters in VALID.CHAR$ we can use the following:

```
2550 INPUT "Please enter your selection ", CHOICE$
2560 LET VALID.POSITION = INSTR(VALID.CHAR$, CHOICE$)
```

If VALID.POSITION has the value of zero, we know that CHOICE$ was not one of the digits 1 through 6. If VALID.POSITION is not zero, we know CHOICE$ was a valid entry.

Another Example Using INSTR()

Suppose we are conducting a survey of our product and want to focus on responses from only a selection of states. INSTR() has a starring role in the routine we will write to select responses from "valid" states.

Initially, in line 1010, we store the abbreviations of valid states in the variable VALID.STATE$. STATE$ contains the state abbreviation for the current survey response. Line 1020 will return a value from 0 (for not a valid state) to 22 (for AK). Line 1040 branches execution to the proper subroutine, depending on this number.

```
1000 '  **  Select processing based on STATE$
1010 LET VALID.STATE$ = "AZ,CA,WA,NV,OR,TX,HI,AK"   ' States wanted
1020 LET WHICH = INSTR(VALID.STATE$,STATE$)
1030 LET CHOICE = FIX(( WHICH + 2)/3 + 1)
```

```
1040 ON CHOICE GOSUB 2000,3000,4000,5000,6000,7000,8000,9000,10000
1050 RETURN
1060 '
2000 PRINT "Not one of the specified states"
2010 RETURN
3000 '     Arizona
3010 PRINT "Arizona"
3020 RETURN
4000 '     California
4010 PRINT "California"
4020 RETURN
5000 '     Washington
5010 PRINT "Washington"
5020 RETURN
6000 '     Nevada
6010 PRINT "Nevada     "
6020 RETURN
7000 '     Oregon
7010 PRINT "Oregon     "
7020 RETURN
8000 '     Texas
8010 PRINT "Texas      "
8020 RETURN
9000 '     Hawaii
9010 PRINT "Hawaii "
9020 RETURN
10000 '    Alaska
10010 PRINT "Alaska "
10020 RETURN
```

We used the comma after each state abbreviation for two reasons. First, it makes the program easier to read. Second, and most importantly, it avoids wrongly accepting two letters that just happen to be beside one another. Without the comma between AZ and CA, ZC would be accepted as valid. (In the previous example, 12 and 123 *could* be accepted.)

Let's look at line 1030 in more detail. Once the position where the state begins is stored in WHICH, it needs to be converted into a value that can be used as the index for an ON . . . GOSUB. First we take the value in WHICH, add 2 and divide by 3. The value of WHICH for CA is 4, (4 + 2)/3 is 2, and CA is the second valid state. We FIX this number, since we only want the integer portion. We want processing to go to the initial subroutine if the state is not one of the ones selected for the survey. We do this by adding 1 to the index. All the state subroutines then move down one (CA becomes the third subroutine in the ON . . . GOSUB).

MID$() Extracts Data From the Middle of a String

Now that we have located where a particular set of characters or substring occurs within a string, how can we extract those characters? In our earlier example we discovered that CA began in the 13th position of the string CITY.STATE$ when

·THE LEN() AND INSTR() FUNCTIONS·

LEN(A$) returns the number of characters in the string A$.
  Usage: FOR I = 1 to LEN(A$) will repeat a loop the number of times
    equal to the number of characters in A$.
INSTR() returns the position at which one string begins within another
string. If the string is not found, a value of zero is returned.
  Form 1: INSTR(MAJOR.STRING$,SUB.STRING$) returns the position
    within MAJOR.STRING$ where SUB.STRING$ begins.
  Usage: INPUT "Enter a Y or N", AN$
      LET REPLY = INSTR("YN",AN$)
  Form 2: INSTR(n,MAJOR.STRING$,SUB.STRING$) same as above
    except the search begins at the nth character in MAJOR.STRING$.
  Usage: LET DATE$ = "85/06/06"
      LET MATCH = INSTR(7,DATE$,"06")

that string contained *Sacramento, CA 95831*. Suppose we now want to place those two characters into the variable STATE$. The MID$() function will enable us to do this.

MID$() function returns a copy of a portion of a string argument. It requires three arguments: the name of the string from which you wish to extract the copy, the position within that string where you wish to begin, and the number of characters you wish to extract.

MID$() returns a copy of the selected characters. It does not alter the original string. For example:

```
LET CITY$ = "SACRAMENTO"
LET X$ = MID$ (CITY$, 5, 2)
PRINT X$; CITY$
AM SACRAMENTO
```

The MID$() function began at the fifth character of CITY$, which was an *A* and took two characters, the *A* and the *M* (SACRAMENTO). The LET statement placed these two characters into X$.

If the last parameter of MID$() is omitted, MID$() will return all of the characters to the end of the string. For example, MID$(CITY$,5) is "AMENTO".

Going back to our variable CITY.STATE$, once we have found that CA begins in the 13th position of CITY.STATE$, we can retrieve a copy of these characters with the following statement.

```
4910 LET STATE$ = MID$(CITY.STATE$, 13,2)
```

When CITY.STATE$ contains "Sacramento, CA 95831" this line places the characters CA into the variable STATE$. But what if CITY.STATE$ contains a city with a different number of characters? The state is not going to always be in the 13th position.

Combining INSTR() and MID$()

We can use both INSTR() and MID$() to locate and extract the state from the string CITY.STATE$ no matter what the length of the city. First we will find the position in which the comma following the city appears:

```
4910 LET COMMA.LOC = INSTR(CITY.STATE$, ",")
```

The state begins two places past the comma:

```
4920 LET STATE.LOC = COMMA.LOC + 2
```

Now, instead of using a constant to specify the exact location at which MID$() is to begin, we can use the variable STATE.LOC.

```
4930 LET STATE$ = MID$(CITY.STATE$, STATE.LOC, 2)
```

User Function With MID$

Here is a user function we can define if we want only one character from the string ANY.STRING$. This function is useful when making vertical report headings.

```
1100 DEF FNDECODE$(ANY.STRING$,NTH) = MID$(ANY.STRING$,NTH,1)
```

This will always bring the Nth character in the string named ANY.STRING$.

This short program will print the contents of ANY.STRING$ vertically down the screen.

```
10 ' Program to illustrate user defined function with MID$()
20 '    User enters the name of a city
30 '    The program prints the name vertically on the screen
100 ' ======= Define the Function =========
110 DEF FNDECODE$(ANY.STRING$, NTH) = MID$(ANY.STRING$,NTH,1)
200 ' ======= Ask User for Input =========
210 INPUT "City Name"; ANY.STRING$
300 ' ======= Print Name of City =========
310 FOR NTH = 1 TO LEN(ANY.STRING$)
320     PRINT FNDECODE$(ANY.STRING$, NTH)
330 NEXT
400 END
RUN
City Name? SACRAMENTO
S
A
C
R
A
M
E
N
T
O
```

LEFT$() and RIGHT$() Return the Left or Right Part of a String

There are occasions when we want only the beginning (left-most) or ending (right-most) characters of a string. The next two functions are similar to MID$ since they extract characters from a string, but they take either from the left side or from the right side.

LEFT$ extracts the number of characters we specify beginning with the left-most character. Consider, again, the string ANY.STRING$. The following statement

```
LET LEFT.5.CHAR$ = LEFT$(ANY.STRING$, 5)
```

will examine the first five positions of ANY.STRING$ and copy their contents into the string LEFT.5.CHAR$. If ANY.STRING$ has less than five characters, then LEFT$ will take only as many characters as are in ANY.STRING$. If there are only three characters in ANY.STRING$, there will be only three in LEFT.5.CHAR$.

Using the preceding statement, we would get the following results:

ANY.STRING$	LEFT.5.CHAR$
Constantinople	Const
An Example	An Ex
ONE	ONE

The number of characters specified may be 0 to 255; if 0 is specified, the result will be a null.

An Example Using LEFT$()

Using the variable CITY.STATE$ that we have been discussing, we can use a combination of INSTR() and LEFT$() to extract the city. We do not know how many characters there are in the city, but we can find out where it ends using INSTR() again to find the comma:

```
5910 LET COMMA.LOC = INSTR(CITY.STATE$, ",")
```

The number of characters in the city will be one less than the location of the comma.

```
5920 LET CITY.SIZE = COMMA.LOC - 1
```

To extract the city, we can use the following LEFT$() statement:

```
5930 LET CITY$ = LEFT$(CITY.STATE$, CITY.SIZE)
```

An Example Using RIGHT$()

RIGHT$() is similar to LEFT$() except that it extracts the right-most characters. In our example of CITY.STATE$ we know that the last five characters are the zip code. To take out the zip code, we can use:

```
5840 LET ZIP$ = RIGHT$(CITY.STATE$, 5)
```

Obviously for routines such as these, the entry of the string we called CITY.STATE$ must be consistent. We will not get what we expect if someone

▪THE MID$(), LEFT$(), AND RIGHT$() FUNCTIONS▪

MID$(A$,*b*,*n*) returns a string containing *n* characters of A$ beginning at position *b*.

LEFT$(A$,*n*) returns a string containing the *n* left-most characters of A$.

RIGHT$(A$,*n*) returns a string containing the *n* right-most characters of A$.

Examples:

```
LET A$ = "123456789"
PRINT MID$(A$,4,3)
456
PRINT LEFT$(A$,3)
123
PRINT RIGHT$(A$,3)
789
```

forgets to put the comma after the city, puts more than one space after the comma, or uses a nine-digit zip code or none at all.

STR$() Changes Numbers to Strings

STR$() will return the string representation of the value of a numeric variable or expression. For example:

```
LET NEW.STRING$ = STR$(OLD.NUMBER)
```

will place the string representation of OLD.NUMBER in the string NEW.STRING$. If the numeric variable is positive, the first character of the string will be a space; if it is negative, the first character will be a minus sign.

```
10 'DEMONSTRATE STR$
15 PRINT "Numeric" TAB(20) "String"
20 READ I
30 WHILE I <> 99
40      PRINT I TAB(20) STR$(I)
50      READ I
60 WEND
70 END
80 '
90 DATA 123,-123,12E10,123456789987654321,123D12,99
Ok
RUN
Numeric             String
```

```
  123                      123
- 123                    - 123
    1.2E+11                  1.2E+11
    1.234568E+17             1.234568E+17
    1.23E+14                 1.23E+14
```

As you see, STR$() creates a string variable that contains an image of the number in exactly the form that BASIC would use to print the number. Remember, the two output columns in the preceding example do not contain the same things: one contains a number and the other a string. They just look the same. But you cannot multiply or perform other arithmetic operations on the result of STR$().

Here is an example of using STR$(). Suppose the zip code has been entered as a numeric variable, ZIP.CODE. You want to join it with the variables CITY$ and STATE$ to create the variable CITY.STATE$ (using the same format we used earlier). CITY$ and STATE$ have been entered as string variables, so we could join them using string concatenation, but ZIP.CODE is a numeric variable and would give the Type mismatch error if we were to try to concatenate it. We can get the string representation of ZIP.CODE as follows:

```
5850 LET ZIP.CODE$ = STR$(ZIP.CODE)
```

Now we can join the three variables together:

```
5860 LET CITY.STATE$ = CITY$ + ", " + STATE$ + ZIP.CODE$
```

We did not have to put the space between state and zip code, because STR$ places a space in front of all positive numbers.

VAL() Changes Strings Into Numeric Values

VAL converts a string variable into a number with the same value, removing the leading zeros in the process. For example, VAL("123") is the number 123. VAL("000123") also is 123.

If the first character of the string is not a number, VAL returns a zero. If the first character is a number but the string contains other characters that BASIC cannot convert into numbers, VAL will convert all the characters up to the first that cannot be converted.

Here is an example. It is the program we used earlier, modified to demonstrate VAL(). It also contains a second DATA line (line 100) that shows how VAL converts only the numeric portion of a street address into a number.

```
10 'DEMONSTRATE VAL
15 DEFSTR I
18 PRINT "String" TAB(20) "Numeric"
20 READ I
30 WHILE I <> "99"
40      PRINT I TAB(20) VAL(I)
50      READ I
```

```
60 WEND
70 END
80 '
90 DATA 123,-123,12E10,123456789987654321,123D12
100 DATA 12garbage, 6401 Street-Address, 99
RUN
String                  Numeric
 123                      123
-123                     -123
 12E10                    120000000000
 123456789987654321       1.234567899876543D+17
 123D12                   123000000000000
 12garbage                12
 6401 Street-Address     6401
Ok
```

VAL() can be used to strip leading zeros or blanks from a number. For example, LET AMOUNT = VAL (AMOUNT$) will put the value of AMOUNT$ into the numeric variable AMOUNT without any leading zeros. For example:

```
100 LET A$ = "000123"
200 LET A = VAL(A$ )      ' A is now 123
300 LET A$ = STR$( A)     ' A$ is now " 123"
```

If *A* is negative, the first character of STR$(A) is a minus sign. If it is positive, the first character is a space.

In the section earlier in this chapter, "Using INSTR() for Data Validation," the user's entry of a 1 through 6 was stored in the variable CHOICE$. We can use VAL() to return a numeric value as branch to the appropriate subroutine as follows:

```
2580 ON VAL(CHOICE$) GOSUB . . .
```

LSET and RSET Assign Characters Into an Existing String

Two other tools helpful in making professional-looking reports are LSET and its counterpart RSET. They are used to left-justify or to right-justify. These statements typically are used for random access file processing (see Chapter 13), but

▪THE STR$() AND VAL() FUNCTIONS▪

STR$(X), where X is a numeric expression, returns the string equivalent of X.

VAL(A$) returns the numeric value of A$. If the first character of A$ is not numeric, VAL(A$) returns a zero.

they are also very useful for generating report headings. They copy the contents of one variable into another, either left- or right-justifying and filling the remaining places with spaces. The following lines define two variables with 20 periods. A string is left-justified into the first with LSET and right-justified into the second using RSET. The results are then printed.

```
10 LET TWENTY.DOTS$ = STRING$(20,".")
20 LET TWENTY.DOTS2$ = STRING$(20,".")
30 PRINT TWENTY.DOTS$
40 PRINT TWENTY.DOTS2$
50 LSET TWENTY.DOTS$ = "Jo Do"
60 RSET TWENTY.DOTS2$ = "Jo Do"
70 PRINT TWENTY.DOTS$
80 PRINT TWENTY.DOTS2$
RUN

....................
....................
Jo Do
                Jo Do
```

As an example, let's say that we have two variables we want to print on a line. The variables are placed in the arrays CUSTOMER.NAME$ and CUSTOMER.NUMBER. We want the customer name to be left-justified in a column of 20 spaces followed by the customer number, right-justified in its own column of 20 spaces.

We will first set up two variables containing 20 spaces. We will then use LSET and RSET to left- and right-justify the variables into these fields. Since LSET and RSET operate only on string variables, we use the STR$() function to get the string equivalent of CUSTOMER.NUMBER.

```
1100 '    ** Justify and Print elements **
1110 FOR EMPL.NUM = 1 TO NUM.OF.EMPL
1120     LET TWENTY.SPACES1$ = SPACE$(20)     ' define variables of 20 spaces
1130     LET TWENTY.SPACES2$ = SPACE$(20)
1140     LSET TWENTY.SPACES1$ = CUSTOMER.NAME$(EMPL.NUM)
1150     RSET TWENTY.SPACES2$ = STR$(CUSTOMER.NUMBER(EMPL.NUM))
1160     PRINT TWENTY.SPACES1$, TWENTY.SPACES2$
1170 NEXT EMPL.NUM
1180 RETURN
```

MID$ as a Statement Replaces Characters in an Existing String

Recall that BASIC offers a general purpose function, MID$(), and two variations on it, LEFT$() and RIGHT$(), which are more special purpose.

BASIC also offers a general purpose version of LSET and RSET. It is the *statement* MID$(). MID$() is one feature that can be either a function or a statement.

As with LSET and RSET, MID$() will insert new values into an existing string. The string keeps the same length, as it does with RSET and LSET; however, there are some differences. The major difference is that when LSET and RSET place characters into the string, the unused positions are replaced with spaces; with the statement MID$, the unused positions are left unchanged.

The syntax of the *statement* MID$() is very similar to that of the *function* MID$(). The difference is that the statement MID$ appears on the left side of the equal sign, while the function MID$ appears on the right side.

```
MID$(A$, BEGIN, LENGTH) = NEWVALUE$
```

where A$ and NEWVALUE$ are string variables and BEGIN and LENGTH are integers. (Note that a space may *not* be placed between the $ symbol and the parenthesis when using MID$. Doing so will give a syntax error.) When executing this statement, BASIC starts with the position in A$ indicated by the number BEGIN and replaces the number of characters indicated by the number LENGTH with the same number of characters from NEWVALUE$. For example:

```
10 LET A$ = "abcdefghijk"
20 MID$(A$, 3, 2) = "++++++"
30 PRINT A$
run
ab++efghijk
```

The length of A$ stays the same. BASIC began at the third position in A$ and replaced two characters with the first two characters from the string "++++++". The remaining characters of A$ were unchanged.

The length parameter may be omitted, in which case characters will be replaced until the end of either string is reached. Here is an example.

```
10 LET A$ = "abcdefghijk"
20 MID$(A$,3) = "++++++"
30 PRINT A$
run
ab++++++ijk
```

The string of plus signs is shorter than A$; therefore, the letters *ijk* are not replaced.

```
10 LET A$ =    "abcdefghijk"
20 MID$(A$,3) = "+++++++++++++"
30 PRINT A$
run
ab+++++++++
```

This time the string of plus signs is longer than A$; therefore, all of the characters from *c* to the end of A$ are replaced.

Comparison of LSET, RSET, and MID$

The following program demonstrates the differences among these three statements.

```
2000  '  Define Three Fields of 20 Asterisks
2010  LET AST.ONE$ = STRING$ (20, "*")
2020  LET AST.TWO$ = STRING$ (20, "*")
```

```
2030   LET AST.THREE$ = STRING$ (20, "*")
2040   PRINT AST.ONE$
2042   PRINT AST.TWO$
2044   PRINT AST.THREE$
2050   PRINT
2060   '  Place String "test" into each field
2070   LET TEST$ = "test"
2080   LSET AST.ONE$ = TEST$
2090   RSET AST.TWO$ = TEST$
2100   MID$(AST.THREE$, 6, 4) = TEST$
2110   '  Print fields again
2120   PRINT AST.ONE$
2122   PRINT AST.TWO$
2124   PRINT AST.THREE$
2130   END
RUN
*******************
*******************
*******************

test
                    test
*****test**********
```

As you can see, LSET and RSET replaced the asterisks in the unused positions with spaces while MID$ did not change them.

Uses of MID$() Statement

MID$() can be used for centering titles in a way more elegant than using LEN() alone.

```
100    LET LEFT.MARGIN = 1
110    LET RIGHT.MARGIN = 80
120    INPUT "Enter message: ",MESSAGE$
130    GOSUB 1000          'place centered message in CMESSAGE$
140    PRINT CMESSAGE$
150    END
1000   '  ## Centering routine using MID$ statement ##
1010   LET CMESSAGE$ = SPACE$(RIGHT.MARGIN)
1020   LET START = LEFT.MARGIN + ((RIGHT.MARGIN - LEFT.MARGIN) - LEN(MESSAGE$))/2
1030   MID$(CMESSAGE$,START) = MESSAGE$
1040   RETURN
RUN
Enter message: a short message
                        a short message

RUN
Enter message: a long message which has many many words
                a long message which has many many words
```

To right-justify the text in the above program, change line 1020 to:

```
1020 LET START = LEFT.MARGIN + ((RIGHT.MARGIN - LEFT.MARGIN) - LEN(MESSAGE$))
```

which is the same as

```
1020 LET START = RIGHT.MARGIN - LEN(MESSAGE$)
```

To left-justify it, change the line to:

```
1020 LET START = LEFT.MARGIN
```

·THE MID$ STATEMENT AND FUNCTION·

MID$ may be used as either a statement or as a function.

When used as a function, MID$ appears to the right of the equal sign:

PART$ = MID$(WHOLE$,3,5)

When used as a statement, MID$ appears to the left of the equal sign:

MID$(BIG.STRING$,4,2) = SMALL.STRING$

·THE LSET, RSET, AND MID$ STATEMENTS·

LSET copies the contents of one string variable into another and left-justifies it. Any unused positions are filled with spaces.

A$ | * | * | * | * | * | B$ | H | I |
LSET A$ = B$
A$ | H | I | | | | B$ | H | I |

RSET is similar to LSET except the characters are right-justified.

A$ | * | * | * | * | * | B$ | H | I |
RSET A$ = B$
A$ | | | | H | I | B$ | H | I |

MID$ used as a statement copies a specified number of characters from one string into another. Unused spaces are left unchanged.

In MID$(A$,n,m) = B$, the first m characters of B$ are placed into A$, beginning at position n in A$. If m is omitted, all of B$ will be used.

A$ | * | * | * | * | * | B$ | H | I |
MID$(A$,3,2)
A$ | * | * | H | I | * | B$ | H | I |

DATE$ and TIME$ Are Both Variables and Statements

When you turned on your computer, you were asked for the current date and time. Your responses reset the time stored in the system's clock. BASIC can access the system's clock to determine the date and time.

DATE$, the Variable, Contains the Current Date

The system's date is accessible in BASIC in the variable DATE$. DATE$ is of the form "12-31-1988", where the first two digits represent the month, followed by a hyphen. The next two digits show the day of the month, followed by a hyphen. The last four digits show the year.

You can use the date when printing reports.

DATE$, the Statement

BASIC lets you change the date stored in the system's clock by using the statement DATE$.

For example, to change the date to May 21, 1988, you would use the statement

```
DATE$ = "05-21-1988" or
DATE$ = "05-21-88"   or
DATE$ = "05/21/88"   or
DATE$ = "05/21/1988"
```

Note that we did not use the LET statement with the DATE$. You cannot change the date using LET DATE$ = "05-21-88" since this is an error in syntax.

TIME$, the Variable, Contains the Current Time

The time is stored in the variable TIME$ in the form 23:59:59. The first two digits represent the hour (using the 24-hour clock). The next two digits represent the minutes. The last two digits represent the seconds.

One use of TIME$ is in documenting reports. Another use is in timing an event, such as how long it takes a program or a portion of a program to run. For example, printing the start and stop times in a log file or audit file would enable us later to determine how long a program has taken.

For calculating durations, however, TIMER (which we used with RANDOMIZE) is far better. Here is an example of measuring durations.

```
10 LET TIMSTART = TIMER
20 'put timed process here
30 LET DURATION = TIMER - TIMSTART
```

TIME$, the Statement

You can set the system time from within BASIC using the TIME$ statement. Here are three forms of the statement:

```
TIME$ ="23:59:58"   set hour to 11pm, min to 59, seconds to 58
TIME$ ="15:25"      set hour to 3pm, min to 25, seconds to zero
TIME$ ="05"         set hour to 5am, min and seconds to zero
```

THE STORY'S END

Willie felt excitement and fear as the Top Brass paid a visit to the mailroom. They were there to see Willie's creation.

"Let me show you some of the features of my program," Willie said. "I enter the weight of the parcel and the address, and using the rate charts that I've stored in it, my program tells me which shipping carrier is the least expensive, and prints the mailing labels and other forms. It also stores the costs for latter use.

"I computed the savings of always shipping with the least expensive carrier."

"And," asked the Top Brass with dollar signs reflecting in their smiles.

"$54,291 a year, assuming we do not grow. However, if we assume a continued growth of 12 percent annually, as we have experienced in the past, over a four-year system life this project will save the company about a third of a million dollars.

The president of the company put an arm around Willie and proclaimed, "We should get together over golf, let's say this Sunday. I have plans for you, Willie."

"But I don't play golf," protested the clerk.

"Don't worry, you'll learn. In fact, I'd say that in two or three years, Arnold Palmer will be the one to worry."

Program Specifications

The program will ask the user to enter the weight of a package, the state to which it is being shipped, and the complete mailing address. Based on the weight and the state of destination, the program will determine which of two carriers is the least expensive for that package and display that information to the user.

It will also print the mailing label for the package.

After all labels have been printed, the program will print a report showing, for each carrier, the number of packages shipped and the cost of shipping. It will also print the total number of packages and the total cost.

Functions

A. Initialize
   1. Initialize variables
   2. Load in rate tables
B. Get package information
   1. Enter data
   2. Determine best carrier and postage
   3. Print shipping label
C. Print end-of-day report

Structure Chart

The structure chart for this program appears in Figure 11.1.

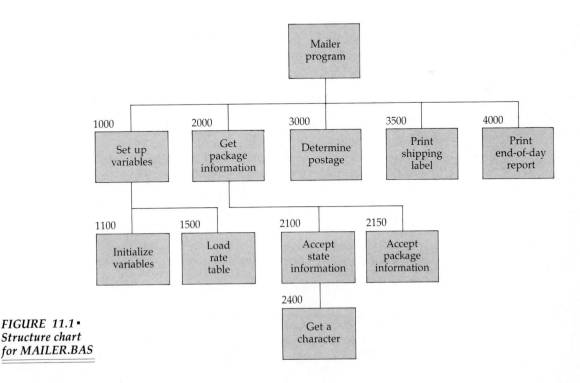

FIGURE 11.1 •
Structure chart
for MAILER.BAS

Data Dictionary

Arrays

FIRST.POUND	For each state, the cost of the first pound for both carriers one and two
ADDITIONAL.POUNDS	For each state, the cost of any additional pounds for both carriers
USE	Stores the number of times each carrier is used
COST	Stores the total cost for using each carrier

Constants

FALSE	Set to 0, value of logical false
TRUE	Set to -1, value of logical true
FORM.FEED	Form feed control character [chr$(12)]
NBR.OF.CARRIERS	Number of carriers this program deals with
NBR.OF.STATES	Initialized to 51 (incl. District of Columbia)

Variables Entered by User

STATE.CODE$	Two-letter abbreviation plus a space
ADDRESS1$	Shipping address line one
ADDRESS2$	Shipping address line two
ADDRESS3$	Shipping address line three
ADDRESS4$	Shipping address line four
PACKAGE.WEIGHT	Weight of package to be shipped

Variables Used as Subscripts

STATE.NBR	Subscript that indicates state in arrays FIRST.POUND and ADDITIONAL.POUNDS
CARRIER.NBR	Subscript that indicates carrier in arrays FIRST.POUND and ADDITIONAL.POUNDS
BEST.WAY	Subscript of carrier that offers lowest cost in arrays USE and COST

Working Variables

REPORT.DETAIL.LINE$	Format for detail line on report
TOTAL.LINE$	Format for the total line on report
STATE$	All state's abbreviations concatenated into one string
A.STATE$	Used in READ statement to retrieve state abbreviation from DATA statements
DUMMY	Used in READ statement to bypass weight data
DUMMY$	Used as input for statement that pauses
TOTAL.USE	Sum of usages for both carriers
TOTAL.COST	Sum of costs for both carriers
CHAR$	One character of a state's abbreviation
HOLD.ASCII	ASCII value of letter used to convert to uppercase
CARRIER.COST	Cost of postage for carrier being processed
LOWEST.COST	Holder of cost for lowest carrier

| EACH.STATE | Loop counter |
| CARRIER.COUNT | Loop counter |

Switches

ANSWER\$	Ends label entry loop when user enters *Q* or *q*
MORE.TO.DO	True/false switch controlling main loop
VALID.STATE	True/false indicating if state entered is valid

Pseudocode

<u>MAIN</u>
>   DO SET-UP
>   DO GET-PACKAGE-INFORMATION
>   WHILE MORE.TO.DO
>   DO DETERMINE-POSTAGE
>   DO PRINT-SHIPPING-LABEL
>   DO GET-PACKAGE-INFORMATION
>   WEND
>   DO PRINT-END-OF-DAY-REPORT

<u>SETUP</u>
>   Initialize all variables
>   READ state abbrev into STATE\$
>   Dimension arrays
>   READ the rates from DATA statements into arrays
>   Display message about forms to user

<u>GET-PACKAGE-INFORMATION</u>
>   Ask whether to Quit or Continue
>   IF ANSWER\$ is not Quit
>   THEN DO ACCEPT-STATE-INFO
>   DO ACCEPT-PACKAGE-INFO
>   ELSE set MORE.TO.DO to FALSE

<u>ACCEPT-STATE-INFO</u>
>   LET VALID.STATE = FALSE
>   WHILE VALID.STATE = FALSE
>   Enter two letters and convert to uppercase
>   LET STATE.CODE\$ equal letters entered plus a space
>   Use INSTR to find STATE.CODE\$ in STATE\$
>   IF STATE.CODE\$ is not in STATE\$
>   THEN PRINT error message
>   ELSE LET VALID.STATE = TRUE

<u>ACCEPT-PACKAGE-INFO</u>
>   Enter PACKAGE.WEIGHT
>   Enter four address lines

<u>DETERMINE-POSTAGE</u>
>   Initialize BEST.WAY and LOWEST.COST
>   FOR each carrier

Compute this carrier's cost
IF this carrier's cost < LOWEST.COST
    THEN set BEST-WAY to this carrier
        set LOWEST-COST to this carrier's cost
NEXT carrier
Add 1 to this carrier's USE
Add carrier's cost to this carrier's COST
PRINT-SHIPPING-LABEL
Tell the user how to ship and cost
PRINT the label
PRINT-END-OF-DAY-REPORT
Ask user to set up printer for report
PRINT report heading
FOR each carrier
    PRINT number of time carrier was used and cost
NEXT
PRINT grand totals of use and cost

Program Listing

```
10       'Program Name: MAILER.BAS
20       'Author:       William Burnside
30       'Date Written: 2-21-88
40       'Program Description:
50       '   Asks the user to input the state and weight for packages
60       '   Determines and displays best carrier and cost
70       '   Prints mailing label
80       '   After all labels are printed, prints summary report
90       '
100      '
500      ' -------------------------------------------------------------
510      '              MAIN LINE
520      ' -------------------------------------------------------------
530      GOSUB 1000      'Set Up
540      GOSUB 2000       'Get First Package Information
550      WHILE MORE.TO.DO
560            GOSUB 3000        'Determine Postage
570            GOSUB 3500        'Print Shipping Label
580            GOSUB 2000        'Get Next Package Information
590      WEND
600      GOSUB 4000            'Print End of Day Report
610      END
620      ' -------------------------------------------------------------
630      '              END OF PROCESSING
640      ' -------------------------------------------------------------
1000     ' -------------------------------------------------------------
1010     '              SET UP
1020     ' -------------------------------------------------------------
```

```
1030     KEY OFF
1040     CLS
1050     PRINT TAB(15) "MAILING LABEL PROGRAM"
1060     LET FORM.FEED$ = CHR$(12)                ' Set form feed
1070     GOSUB 1200        'Initialize Variables
1080     GOSUB 1500        'Load Rate Table
1090     RETURN
1100     '
1200     ' ------------------------------------------------------------
1210     '              Initialize Variables
1220     ' ------------------------------------------------------------
1230     LET REPORT.DETAIL.LINE$ =
              "    #                     ####           $##,###.##"
1240     LET TOTAL.LINE$ =
              "TOTALS                    ####           $##,###.##"
1250     LET TRUE = -1
1260     LET FALSE = 0
1270     LET MORE.TO.DO = TRUE    'used to stop processing
1280     LET NBR.OF.CARRIERS = 2 'number of carriers in system
1290     LET CARRIER.NBR = 0        'which carrier
1300     LET NBR.OF.STATES = 51
1310     LET STATE.NBR = 0          'which state
1320     LET STATE.CODE$ = ""       'two-letter state code plus space
1330     LET ADDRESS1$ = ""         'following four hold package address
1340     LET ADDRESS2$ = ""
1350     LET ADDRESS3$ = ""
1360     LET ADDRESS4$ = ""
1370     LET PACKAGE.WEIGHT = 0
1380     LET VALID.STATE = FALSE
1390     LET STATE$ =""
1400     FOR EACH.STATE = 1 TO NBR.OF.STATES          ' create STATE$
1410         READ A.STATE$,DUMMY,DUMMY                '  to hold all valid
1420         LET STATE$ = STATE$ + A.STATE$ + " "     '  state abbreviation
1430     NEXT EACH.STATE
1440     RESTORE                                 'return to beginning of DATA list
1450     RETURN
1500     ' ------------------------------------------------------------
1510     '              Load Rate Tables
1520     ' ------------------------------------------------------------
1530     OPTION BASE 1
1540     DIM FIRST.POUND(NBR.OF.STATES,NBR.OF.CARRIERS)
1550     DIM ADDITIONAL.POUNDS(NBR.OF.STATES,NBR.OF.CARRIERS)
1560     FOR CARRIER.NBR = 1 TO NBR.OF.CARRIERS
1570         FOR STATE.NBR = 1 TO NBR.OF.STATES
1580             READ DUMMY$,FIRST.POUND(STATE.NBR,CARRIER.NBR),
                      ADDITIONAL.POUNDS(STATE.NBR,CARRIER.NBR)
1590         NEXT STATE.NBR
1600     NEXT CARRIER.NBR
1610     DIM USE(NBR.OF.CARRIERS)              ' Will hold # of uses for each carrier
1620     DIM COST(NBR.OF.CARRIERS)             ' Will hold total cost for each carrier
```

```
1700    ' ------------------------------------------------------------
1710    '                     Display Message to User
1720    ' ------------------------------------------------------------
1730    PRINT "This program determines the cost and best carrier for your
packages."
1740    PRINT "  It will print mailing labels for each package as you enter
the information"
1750    PRINT "  A printed report follows the labels"
1760    PRINT "  Be sure you have the proper forms ready before proceeding."
1770    PRINT
1780    PRINT "Press any key to continue": LET DUMMY$ = INPUT$(1)
1790    RETURN
2000    ' ------------------------------------------------------------
2010    '                     GET PACKAGE INFORMATION
2020    ' ------------------------------------------------------------
2030    PRINT "PRESS Q TO QUIT FOR DAY"
2040    PRINT "PRESS ANY OTHER KEY TO CONTINUE"
2050    LET ANSWER$ = INPUT$(1)
2060    IF ANSWER$ <> "Q" AND ANSWER$ <> "q"
            THEN GOSUB 2100: GOSUB 2300
            ELSE LET MORE.TO.DO = FALSE
2070    RETURN
2100    ' ------------------------------------------------------------
2110    '                     Accept State Info
2120    ' ------------------------------------------------------------
2130    CLS
2140    LET VALID.STATE = FALSE
2150    WHILE VALID.STATE = FALSE
2160       INPUT "ENTER THE TWO LETTER STATE ABBREVIATION --> ", STATE.CODE$
2170       FOR I = 1 TO 2
2180          LET CHAR$ = MID$(STATE.CODE$,I,1)
2190          GOSUB 2400      'Convert To Upper Case
2200          MID$(STATE.CODE$,I,1) = CHAR$
2210       NEXT I
2220       LET STATE.CODE$ = LEFT$(STATE.CODE$,2) + " "
2230    '------ Find if state entered is in STATE$ ---------------
2240       LET STATE.NBR = (INSTR(STATE$, STATE.CODE$) + 2)/3
2250       IF STATE.NBR < 1 THEN PRINT "THAT STATE IS NOT VALID"
               ELSE LET VALID.STATE = TRUE
2260    WEND
2270    RETURN
2300    ' ------------------------------------------------------------
2310    '                     Accept Package Info
2320    ' ------------------------------------------------------------
2330    INPUT "WHAT IS THE PACKAGE WEIGHT IN POUNDS "; PACKAGE.WEIGHT
2340    PRINT "NOW ENTER THE FOUR LINES FOR THE ADDRESS"
2350    LINE INPUT "ENTER ADDRESS LINE 1: ";ADDRESS1$
2360    LINE INPUT "ENTER ADDRESS LINE 2: ";ADDRESS2$
```

```
2370     LINE INPUT "ENTER ADDRESS LINE 3: ";ADDRESS3$
2380     LINE INPUT "ENTER ADDRESS LINE 4: ";ADDRESS4$
2390     RETURN
2400     '------ Get A Character And Convert To Uppercase ----------
2410     LET HOLD.ASCII = ASC(CHAR$)
2420     IF HOLD.ASCII > 96 AND HOLD.ASCII < 123
             THEN LET HOLD.ASCII = HOLD.ASCII - 32
2430     LET CHAR$ = CHR$(HOLD.ASCII)
2440     RETURN
3000     ' -------------------------------------------------------
3010     '              DETERMINE POSTAGE
3020     ' -------------------------------------------------------
3030     '--------- Initialize lowest cost and best way ------------
3040     LET LOWEST.COST = 99999!
3050     LET BEST.WAY = 0
3060     FOR CARRIER.NBR = 1 TO NBR.OF.CARRIERS
3070       LET CARRIER.COST = FIRST.POUND(STATE.NBR,CARRIER.NBR) +
               (PACKAGE.WEIGHT - 1) * ADDITIONAL.POUNDS(STATE.NBR,CARRIER.NBR)
3080       IF CARRIER.COST < LOWEST.COST THEN
               LET LOWEST.COST = CARRIER.COST:
               LET BEST.WAY = CARRIER.NBR
3090     NEXT CARRIER.NBR
3100     '------- Accumulate Totals for Carrier Selected ----------
3110     LET USE(BEST.WAY) = USE(BEST.WAY) + 1            'increment count
3120     LET COST(BEST.WAY) = COST(BEST.WAY) + LOWEST.COST 'add to cost
3130     RETURN
3500     ' -------------------------------------------------------
3510     '              PRINT SHIPPING LABEL
3520     ' -------------------------------------------------------
3530     CLS
3540     PRINT "SHIP THROUGH CARRIER NUMBER ";BEST.WAY
3550     PRINT "THE SHIPPING COST IS ";LOWEST.COST
3560     PRINT
3570     PRINT "PRESS ANY KEY WHEN THE PRINTER IS READY FOR LABELS"
3580     LET DUMMY$ = INPUT$(1)
3590     LPRINT "FROM:           CONSOLIDATED GLOMERATE"
3600     LPRINT "               CON GLOM DRIVE"
3610     LPRINT "               WHATLUCK, CA 99999"
3620     LPRINT
3630     LPRINT
3640     LPRINT
3650     LPRINT
3660     LPRINT "TO:             ";ADDRESS1$
3670     LPRINT "               ";ADDRESS2$
3680     LPRINT "               ";ADDRESS3$
3690     LPRINT "               ";ADDRESS4$
3700     LPRINT: LPRINT: LPRINT
3710     RETURN
```

```
4000    ' ---------------------------------------------------------
4010    '                   PRINT END OF DAY REPORT
4020    ' ---------------------------------------------------------
4030    PRINT "PRESS ANY KEY WHEN THE PRINTER IS READY TO PRINT THE "
4040    PRINT "              END-OF-DAY REPORT"
4050    LET DUMMY$ = INPUT$(1)
4060    LPRINT FORM.FEED$
4070    LPRINT "            END-OF-DAY SHIPPING REPORT"
4080    LPRINT "                  FOR " DATE$"
4090    LPRINT
4100    LPRINT
4110    LPRINT
4120    LPRINT
4130    LPRINT "                      SUMMARY"
4140    LPRINT
4150    LPRINT " CARRIER              USES              COST"
4160    LPRINT "--------             ----              ----
4170    FOR CARRIER.COUNT = 1 TO NBR.OF.CARRIERS
4180       LPRINT USING REPORT.DETAIL.LINE$; CARRIER.COUNT,
                   USE(CARRIER.COUNT),COST(CARRIER.COUNT)
4190      LET TOTAL.USE = TOTAL.USE + USE(CARRIER.COUNT)
4200      LET TOTAL.COST = TOTAL.COST + COST(CARRIER.COUNT)
4210    NEXT CARRIER.COUNT
4220    LPRINT
4230    LPRINT USING TOTAL.LINE$;TOTAL.USE, TOTAL.COST
4240    LPRINT FORM.FEED$
4250    RETURN
9000    ' ---------------------------------------------------------
9010    ' ---------------------------------------------------------
9020    '-------- Data statements for read at line 1560 ----------
9030    '-------- state, first pound, additional pounds ----------
9040    '
9050    '    *************        data for carrier 1
9060    DATA AL,11,9
9070    DATA AK,12,8
9080    DATA AZ,12,7
9090    DATA AR,13,6
9100    DATA CA,13,5
9110    DATA CO,13,4
9120    DATA CT,14,5
9130    DATA DE,14,6
9140    DATA DC,14,7
9150    DATA FL,14,8
9160    DATA GA,15,9
9170    DATA HI,15,7
9180    DATA ID,15,8
9190    DATA IL,15,5
9200    DATA IN,15,6
9210    DATA IA,16,7
```

```
9220      DATA KS,16,6
9230      DATA KY,16,8
9240      DATA LA,16,8
9250      DATA ME,16,8
9260      DATA MD,16,9
9270      DATA MA,17,5
9280      DATA MI,17,6
9290      DATA MN,17,7
9300      DATA MS,17,8
9310      DATA MO,17,8
9320      DATA MT,17,5
9330      DATA NE,17,5
9340      DATA NV,16,8
9350      DATA NH,16,9
9360      DATA NJ,16,4
9370      DATA NM,16,2
9380      DATA NY,16,3
9390      DATA NC,16,8
9400      DATA ND,15,5
9410      DATA OH,15,5
9420      DATA OK,15,5
9430      DATA OR,15,9
9440      DATA PA,15,7
9450      DATA RI,14,6
9460      DATA SC,14,8
9470      DATA SD,14,5
9480      DATA TN,14,4
9490      DATA TX,13,3
9500      DATA UT,13,2
9510      DATA VT,13,7
9520      DATA VA,13,9
9530      DATA WA,13,8
9540      DATA WV,12,7
9550      DATA WI,12,7
9560      DATA WY,10,7
9570      '     *************          data for carrier 2
9580      DATA AL,17,2
9590      DATA AK,17,3
9600      DATA AZ,17,4
9610      DATA AR,17,4
9620      DATA CA,17,2
9630      DATA CO,17,4
9640      DATA CT,17,6
9650      DATA DE,18,8
9660      DATA DC,10,9
9670      DATA FL,18,6
9680      DATA GA,19,9
9690      DATA HI,20,4
9700      DATA ID,18,3
```

```
9710       DATA IL,18,7
9720       DATA IN,16,6
9730       DATA IA,17,8
9740       DATA KS,15,4
9750       DATA KY,15,5
9760       DATA LA,15,4
9770       DATA ME,15,8
9780       DATA MD,10,9
9790       DATA MA,15,4
9800       DATA MI,15,5
9810       DATA MN,15,7
9820       DATA MS,10,6
9830       DATA MO,14,4
9840       DATA MT,18,3
9850       DATA NE,13,2
9860       DATA NV,13,6
9870       DATA NH,13,8
9880       DATA NJ,13,8
9890       DATA NM,10,8
9900       DATA NY,18,4
9910       DATA NC,18,4
9920       DATA ND,18,3
9930       DATA OH,18,6
9940       DATA OK,18,5
9950       DATA OR,15,6
9960       DATA PA,14,5
9970       DATA RI,13,6
9980       DATA SC,12,8
9990       DATA SD,11,5
10000      DATA TN,11,3
10010      DATA TX,11,6
10020      DATA UT,11,2
10030      DATA VT,19,8
10040      DATA VA,10,2
10050      DATA WA,10,4
10060      DATA WV,14,2
10070      DATA WI,14,3
10080      DATA WY,10,3
10090      ' ----------------------------------------------------------------
10100      ' -----        END OF LISTING         ---------------------------
10110      ' ----------------------------------------------------------------
```

Program Output

Willie demonstrated his programs by printing the labels as shown in Figure 11.2.
These were followed by the following report.

```
                     END-OF-DAY SHIPPING REPORT
                          FOR 09-14-1988


                              SUMMARY

        CARRIER                 USES                    COST
           1                      1            $       22.00
           2                      3            $      143.00

        TOTALS                    4            $      165.00
```

FIGURE 11.2 ▪
Sample mailing
labels

```
    FROM:     CONSOLIDATED GLOMERATE        FROM:     CONSOLIDATED GLOMERATE
              CON GLOM DRIVE                          CON GLOM DRIVE
              WHATLUCK, CA 99999                      WHATLUCK, CA 99999


    TO:       Mr. J. R. Richardson          TO:       E. Leslie Johnston
              California Headquarters                 Company of New York
              1415 Any Street                         New York, NY 10096
              Some City, CA 98345


    FROM:     CONSOLIDATED GLOMERATE        FROM:     CONSOLIDATED GLOMERATE
              CON GLOM DRIVE                          CON GLOM DRIVE
              WHATLUCK, CA 99999                      WHATLUCK, CA 99999


    TO:       Ms. Janice Eaglesmith         TO:       David R. Mears
              Nevada Test Company                     123 Any Street
              5729 High Street                        City Station, CA 94026
              Reno, NV 80024
```

▪QUICK REFERENCE FOR LESSON 11▪

String Functions

String functions accept strings as arguments and/or return string values.

ASC(A$)

This returns the ASCII value of the first character of A$. (Function.)

CHR$(n)

CHR$($n$) returns the character that has the ASCII value of n. (Function.) The value of n must be from 0 to 255.

DATE$

DATE$ may be a variable or a statement.

As a variable, the current date as read from the system is stored in DATE$ in the form mm-dd-yyyy, where mm is the month, dd is the day, and yyyy is the year.

As a statement, DATE$ will change the value stored in the variable DATE$. Any of the following formats are acceptable to BASIC.

DATE$ = "mm-dd-yy"
DATE$ = "mm/dd/yy"
DATE$ = "mm-dd-yyyy"
DATE$ = "mm/dd/yyyy"

The year must be from 1980 to 2099; if the first two digits of the year are omitted, 19 will be inserted.

INSTR

This statement returns the position at which one string begins within another. (Function.)

INSTR(BIG.STRING$, SMALL.STRING$) returns the position IN STRing BIG.STRING$ where the first character of SMALL.STRING$ begins.

INSTR(n, BIG.STRING$, SMALL.STRING$) is the same as the first version, except the search begins at position n in BIG.STRING$.

LEFT$(A$, n)

LEFT$(A$, n) returns a string containing the n left-most characters of A$. (Function.)

LEN(A$)

This statement returns the number of characters in the string named. (Function.) Spaces and punctuation characters are included in the count.

LSET and RSET

These copy the contents of one string into another. (Statement.)

LSET A$ = B$

The contents of B$ are copied into A$ and left-justified. Any unused positions in A$ are filled with spaces.

RSET A$ = B$

The contents of B$ are copied into A$ and right-justified. Any unused positions in A$ are filled with spaces. With both statements, if B$ is longer than A$, only as many characters of B$ as will fit into A$ are copied, beginning with the left-most character of B$.

MID$

MID$ may be a function or a statement.

As a function, MID$ will appear on the right of the equal sign. LET B$ = MID$(A$, b, n) returns a string containing n characters of A$ beginning at position b. If n is omitted, all of the characters to the right of position *b* are returned. If *n* is zero or if *b* is greater than the length of A$, a null string is returned.

As a statement, MID$ will appear on the left of the equal sign. MID$(C$, *b*, *n*) = B$ causes the first *n* characters of B$ to be copied into C$ beginning at position *b* in C$. There must not be a space between MID$ and the opening parenthesis. If *n* is omitted, all of B$ will be copied. If *n* is greater than the number of positions following *b* in C$, only the number of characters equal to the remaining positions in C$ will be copied.

RIGHT$(A$, n)

RIGHT$(A$, *n*) returns a string containing the *n* right-most characters of A$. (Function.)

SPACE$(n)

This returns a string of *n* spaces. (Function.) The value *n* must be from 0 to 255.

STR$(x)

This command returns the string equivalent of the numeric expression *x*. (Function.) If *x* is positive, STR$(*x*) will have a leading space. If *x* is negative, STR$(*x*) will have a minus sign in the first space.

STRING$

This returns a string of characters. (Function.)

STRING$(*n*, "char") repeats the characters within the quotes *n* times.
STRING$(*n*, A$) repeats the first character of A$ *n* times.
STRING$(*n*, *x*), where *x* represents the ASCII value of a character, repeats the character with the ASCII value of *x*, *n* times.

n and *x* must be 0 to 255.

TIME$

TIME$ may be a variable or a statement.

As a variable, TIME$ stores the time on the system clock in the form hh:mm:ss, where hh is the hours (00 to 24), mm is the minutes, and ss is the seconds.

As a statement, TIME$ will change the value stored in the variable TIME$. Any of the following may be used:

TIME$ = "hh:mm:ss"
TIME$ = "hh:mm"   ss will be set to zero
TIME$ = "hh"   mm and ss will be set to zero

VAL(A$)

VAL(A$) returns the numeric value of A$. (Function.) If the first character of A$ is not numeric, VAL(A$) returns a zero. If the first character is numeric, but other non-numeric characters appear in A$, VAL(A$) will return the numeric value of up to the first non-numeric character.

```
▪EXERCISES▪
```

Short Answer

1. Write a statement to print a row (65 characters across) of # signs.

2. Give three examples of ways to print the following line:

   ```
   Page 1                                           July 1985
   ```

3. Describe some of the uses of the INSTR() function.

4. What are the three variables needed in the MID$() functions?

5. What are the differences and similarities among the LEFT$(), RIGHT$(), and MID$() functions?

6. How do you convert a numeric variable into a string variable? a string variable into a numeric variable?

7. What is the difference between the CHR$() and ASC() functions?

8. Describe the differences between MID$() when it appears on the left side of the equal sign versus on the right side.

9. Give two examples of ways to format the following lines:

   ```
                    Financial Report
                      For XYZ Co.
   July                                                 1985
   ```

Analyzing Code

10. Evaluate the following series of statements. If they are valid, explain what they will do; if they are invalid, explain why.

    ```
    a. 10 DATA.STRING$ = "THE CAR"
       20 READTHE.STRING$
       30 PRINT INSTR(3,MID$(DATA.STRING$,3,1),"E")
       40 DATA "THE CAR",THE CAR,THE,CAR
    b. 10 LET A = 100
       20 PRINT LEN(A)
    c. 10 PRINT STRING$(70,CHR$(61)
    d. 10 PRINT STRING$(ASC(B),CHR$(61))
    e. 10 FOR HEARING = 1 TO 100
       20     PRINT CHR$(7)
       30     LPRINT CHR$(13) + CHR$(10) +CHR$(12)
       40 NEXT HEARING
    f. 10 DATA.STRING$ = "THE DATA"
       20 FIRST$ = RIGHT$(DATA.STRING$,8)
       30 LAST$ = LEFT$(DATA.STRING$,3)
       40 PRINT LEN(INSTR(FIRST$,LAST$))
    ```

    g. Substitute the following for line 40 in Exercise 10f.

    ```
    40 PRINT STR$(INSTR(FIRST$,LAST$))
    50 PRINT LEN(STR$(INSTR(FIRST$,LAST$)))
    ```

```
h. 10 PRINT STRING$(10,CHR$(42))
   20 FOR I = 1 TO 10
   30    PRINT "*" + SPACE$(9) + "*"
   40 NEXT I
   50 PRINT STRING$(10,"*")
i. 10 DATA.STRING$ = "999D5"
   20 PRINT VAL(DATA.STRING$)
```

11. Are the following true or false?
   a. `CHR$(66) = ASC("B")`
   b. `CHR$(70) = "f"`
   c. `ASC(65) = A`
   d. `ASC(E$) = 116 given that E$ = CHR$(ASC("T") + 32)`
   e. `E$ = "t" given that E$ = CHR$(ASC("T") + 32)`

Programming

12. Write a short program that prompts the user to enter his or her first name, then last name. Using only SPACE$, INPUT, LEN, MID$, and PRINT, print the first name right-justified in the first 40 columns, and print the last name, left-justified in the second 40 columns. Leave a space between the first and last name. For example:

```
columns 1-40          > <  columns    41-80
               YENRAB RELLIM
          FRANKLIN ROOSEVELT
```

13. Write a program that accomplishes the same output as described in Exercise 12; however, use the LSET and RSET statements in lieu of the MID$ statement.

14. Write a program that generates random whole numbers from 65 to 90. Convert the numbers to characters. Also, produce the lowercase counterpart of each character. Print the results as follows:

```
                     UPPERCASE          LOWERCASE
ASCII VALUE          CHARACTER          CHARACTER
   77                    M                  m
```

Your program should process 20 random numbers.

15. Write a program that will create a data file with the following data:

```
88              #2 PENCILS        47.85
California      Z4321             473
-107.2          43%
```

Once the file has been created, reopen the file and read in each data item. Determine if the data are numeric; if they are, store them in an numeric array.

Sort the array in descending order, and in position zero of the array store the sum of the elements in the array. Print out each element in the array in the center of the screen using right-justification at column 40.

16. Write a program that will simulate a roll of a pair of dice. Use the random-number-generating function of BASIC to generate randomly numbers between 1 and 6 for each die.

In a table dimensioned to 12, keep a count of the total tosses in the element with subscript 0 and a count of the combinations of dice rolled in the remaining elements. For instance, if a roll generated a 2 and a 1 for a total of 3, add 1 to the element with subscript 3 and also add 1 to position 0. Simulate at least 100 rolls of the dice.

Upon completion, print out the percentage of 2s, 3s, 4s, . . . , 12s.

17. Make the following changes to the program "MAILER.BAS":
  a. Currently the user may enter a string of any length into the ADDRESS variables. Change the program to allow a maximum of 30 characters in each line. If more than 30 are entered, display a message and allow the user to reenter the line.
  b. Alter the instructions given to the user during initialization (lines 1700–1790) to allow the option of printing a dummy label to check the forms alignment. The company return address appears on the dummy label and a string of 30 *x*s is printed in each of the address fields.

     Allow the user to reprint the dummy label as many times as desired.
  c. Instead of printing the labels as they are entered, have the program write the address and weight data to file. Create a separate file for each carrier.

     When entry is completed, instruct the user to set up the labels for carrier 1. After printing this message, read the records for carrier 1 into arrays (maximum size 25). Sort the addresses into zip code order. You may assume that the zip code is the last five characters of ADDRESS4$. (This means that the city, state, and zip *must* be placed in address line 4. You may wish to add instructions to that effect to the user.) After the sort is completed, inquire if the dummy labels described in (b) are desired. Print the labels for carrier 1, then repeat the process for carrier 2. Since the labels may differ, again provide the option of printing dummy labels.

DESIGNING FRIENDLIER PROGRAMS

GOOD SOFTWARE NEEDS PIZZAZZ

"We have the best project management software in the business and yet we are going broke. Why?" Anderson asked. "We have all the features, more than any of our competitors' products. But the public continues to buy their tinsel programs over ours. Tell me why, Harris."

"Maybe we should add a few things to our programs", answered Harris.

Anderson looked annoyed. "I've been in this business for 20 years. Maybe I don't understand the microcomputer market as well as I do the mainframe software market, but I refuse to have my programs waste CPU time having a little mouse run across the screen chasing a cat as one of our competitor's products does."

"Excuse me, Boss," interrupted Harris," but I didn't mean that we should add 'tinsel.' What I am saying is that we should add user-friendly features to make our product easier to use. My market study showed that our programs take a longer training time than our competitors' products. Our users see our programs as difficult to operate."

"What do you have in mind, Harris?"

Harris pulled out some notes from a folder and continued. "Here are some specific changes I recommend:

1. Add an option that will show a menu of available commands at each stage. Structure it so experienced users can turn off this option.

2. Have our displays use the screen like a drawing board so that the cursor may be moved to different parts of the screen as needed. Our current output might as well be printed on a 1950 teletype machine, line by line.
3. Let users provide password security for their project files.
4. Fashion error messages to blink or to be accompanied by a beep to catch the users' attention.
5. Wherever feasible, reduce the number of keystrokes needed to execute a feature.
6. Validate all user entries.
7. Make messages to the user easy to understand."

"Yes, user friendly! That term has been around for awhile, but you, Harris, have given it significance. Why, we could even make our manuals easier to understand, separating the tutorial material from the reference material. Yes! Harris, get on it right away."

▪THE ABCS OF BASIC ON THE IBM PERSONAL COMPUTER▪

LESSON 12: INPUT AND OUTPUT STATEMENTS, FUNCTIONS, AND VARIABLES

In this lesson we will discover ways to make programs easier for the user to operate. We will cover the input and output functions, variables, and statements that will enable us to create "user-friendly" programs. These new BASIC features are INPUT$(), INKEY$, LINEINPUT, COLOR, BEEP, LOCATE, POS(), and CSRLIN.

We will also discuss menu-driven programs and logical devices.

Menu-Driven Programs

A **menu-driven program** is one in which a list of options is displayed on the screen. The user selects the option he or she wishes from this menu by entering the character or characters specified on the menu. In some cases one option may lead to another submenu from which the user can again select the desired operation. The following is an example of a menu for a project management program. It clearly states the functions to be performed and what the user must do to select one of the options.

```
            PROJECT MANAGEMENT-MAIN MENU
    1)     ADD OR CHANGE DATA
    2)     PRINT CHARTS
```

```
3)    PRINT STATISTICAL REPORTS
X)    EXIT FROM PROGRAM
Please enter the character corresponding to your selection
```

Another important aspect of menu-driven programs is the "exit principle." *Always* leave the user an exit. The main menu should allow the user to exit, for instance, back to BASIC or to DOS. Submenus must also have an exit, thus giving the user the opportunity to continue processing at that level or return to the main menu.

Well-written menu-driven programs are easy to use, or **user friendly.** However, there are several more aspects to being user friendly.

User-Friendly Features

One aspect of user friendly is good data validation, which prevents the program from "bombing" on the user. The program should be written to consider every possible action taken by an uninformed user — a gorilla should be able to run the program and not have it blow up because of incorrectly entered data. User friendly implies that you devote a significant amount of your logic to input validation.

What if the menu offers the user options numbered 1 through 5 and the user enters a 7? Will the program execute one of the selections even though an incorrect number was entered? Will it automatically end the program? Or will it give a brief, clear message that an incorrect response has been entered and ask that it be reentered?

Clear, unintimidating messages in the event of an error are another aspect of being user friendly. For instance, if you are asking the user to enter a number to select an option from a menu with the statement

```
1010 INPUT "Enter Choice: ", OPTION.NUMBER
```

and the user enters a character other than a number, BASIC will return the message "?Redo from start." This is anything but user friendly. What the program should do is give a clear message to the user that an incorrect response has been entered and ask that the selection be reentered. The program should have manners; it should use the words *please* and *thank you* in instructions. A good error message should alert the user in a way that does not frustrate, scare, or insult.

One method is to have all error messages displayed on the bottom line of the screen, line 25. The message can be accompanied by a beep and flashing asterisks at either end of the message. It is best not to have the message itself flash, because a flashing message is difficult to read.

Now that we have introduced you to some of the necessary features we will discuss the BASIC functions and statements that will allow you to move the cursor around the screen, cause the computer to sound a beep, or flash messages.

·PARABLES FOR
PROGRAMMERS·

A Most Unusual Restaurant

"I've discovered a most unusual restaurant," said Jo. "They put new customers through a one-day training course, during which time you are expected to memorize everything that the restaurant sells."

"That is strange," replied Dennis. "Why is that necessary? You can always look at the menu."

"Ah, but that is where it gets even stranger," said Jo. "They don't use menus! The waiter expects you to know just how to order every course. You have to remember that the steak comes with your choice of salad or soup, while the hamburgers come with french fries, baked potatoes, or rice. If you order a salad, you must remember what kinds of dressings are available."

"How odd! But what happens if you forget? Suppose I order soup with my hamburger?"

"The waiter will tell you, 'Input Error' and wait for you to try again. Of course, in some cases, you can order wrong and the waiter won't say anything at all; he'll just bring something crazy from the kitchen. Last week I forgot to tell him how to cook my steak; when I got it, it hadn't been cooked *at all.* You see, the default choice is 'uncooked.'"

"I can't understand how they could stay in business," observed Dennis. "A lot of customers must make mistakes and end up unhappy."

"Aha, but that is the beauty of the setup. Once customers have completed the training course, they are reluctant to admit that they don't remember how to order, so a lot of problems go unreported. And, of course, the restaurant management can always blame mistakes on 'customer error.' Few customers can overcome the guilt associated with this explanation, so they accept responsibility. Besides, the food is so good that the customers put up with it."

"Incredible! Who would have thought that such a setup would work?!"

"Well, it won't work for long," replied Jo. "There's a new restaurant down the street. Their food is just as good, and they do have menus. The old restaurant is losing business fast."

MORAL: Menus make happy customers—in restaurants and computer programs.

Two Alternatives to INPUT Statement for Entering Data From the Keyboard

INPUT$() Returns a String of Specified Length

The INPUT statement with which you are familiar takes data from the keyboard and places it in to one or more variables. It also echoes (displays back) the keystrokes on the screen. Processing pauses until the user presses the Enter key. INPUT$(*n*) is different.

INPUT$(*n*) returns a string of *n* characters from the keyboard. Unlike INPUT, INPUT$(*n*) does not require the user to press Enter for processing to continue. INPUT$(1) proceeds after one keystroke, INPUT$(2) after two, and so on. Also, it does not produce a question mark on the screen, nor does it echo the characters pressed back to the screen.

When the program encounters INPUT$(1), it waits until the user presses any one key, assigns the value of the key pressed to INPUT$(1), and proceeds with the processing. If an *A* was pressed, INPUT$(1) returns the value *A*.

INPUT$() also differs from INPUT by what values it will accept. Only INPUT$() will accept Backspace, Escape, Return, and other control characters as input. For example,

```
1080 PRINT "Please press any key to continue"
1090 LET CONTINUE$ = INPUT$(1)
```

As soon as any key is pressed the program will continue. The key pressed will not appear on the screen.

```
2080 PRINT "Enter your password"
2090 LET PASSWORD$ = INPUT$(5)
```

A five-character string will be placed in the variable PASSWORD$. As is proper for passwords, the characters entered will not appear on the screen.

Another form of INPUT$ reads from files. For example,

```
INPUT$(N, #1)
```

will read *n* characters from file #1. (The # may be omitted.)

The following is a program that reads a file named INFILE one character at a time, converts all uppercase letters to lowercase, then writes the results to a file named OUTFILE. It uses the ASCII values of the characters to determine which are uppercase letters. This is one case in which PRINT # is used instead of WRITE # because we do not want each letter to be written as a separate field.

```
10 'program to convert uppercase text into lowercase
20 '   ascii codes 65 . . . 90 represent upper case A . . . Z
30 '   ascii codes 97 . . . 122 represent lower case a . . . z
40 OPEN "INFILE" FOR INPUT AS #1
50 OPEN "OUTFILE" FOR OUTPUT AS #2
60 DEFINT I
65 '  Following statement inputs a single character from the file
```

```
66 '       and places its ASCII code in the variable I
70 LET I = ASC(INPUT$(1, #1) )
80 WHILE NOT EOF(1)
90      IF I > 64 AND I < 91 THEN LET I = I + 32 ' convert to lowercase
100     PRINT #2, CHR$(I);         ' convert back to character and write
110     LET I = ASC(INPUT$(1, #1) )
120 WEND
130 CLOSE
140 END
```

▪ THE INPUT$() FUNCTION ▪

INPUT$(*n*) returns a string of *n* characters entered on the keyboard. The characters entered do not appear on the screen.

INPUT$(*n*, #*m*) or INPUT$(*n*, *m*) returns a string of *n* characters from file number *m*.

INKEY$ Reads a Character from the Keyboard

INKEY$ is a variable that contains a single character showing which key is currently being pressed. For example,

```
LET CHOICE$ = INKEY$
```

will place a character from the keyboard into the variable CHOICE$. Unlike INPUT or INPUT$, INKEY$ acts so that BASIC does not pause and wait for the user's entry. Instead INKEY$ will take whatever key is being pressed at the moment the statement containing INKEY$ is executed. If no character is entered, INKEY$ will place a null character in the variable.

We might try using INKEY$ to accept the selection entered by the user after a menu has been displayed. What happens if we write the following?

```
1050 PRINT "Please enter your choice: "
1060 LET CHOICE$ = INKEY$
1070 ON VAL (CHOICE$) GOSUB 2000, 3000, 4000, 5000
```

Because INKEY$ does not wait, the user would not have time to press any key before the statement with INKEY$ was executed. One solution to this problem is to create a small loop that is repeated until some value other than a null is read by INKEY$. The preceding lines would be rewritten as:

```
1050 PRINT "Please enter your choice: "
1060 LET CHOICE$ = "" ' initialize CHOICE$ to null
1063 WHILE CHOICE$ = ""
1065     LET CHOICE$ = INKEY$
1067 WEND
1070 ON VAL (CHOICE$) GOSUB 2000, 3000, 4000, 5000
```

INKEY\$, like INPUT\$(), does not echo the character to the screen.

We can rewrite the examples that were used earlier with INPUT\$ to use INKEY\$.

```
1080 PRINT "Please press any key to continue"
1090 LET I$ = INKEY$
2000 WHILE I$ = ""
2010     LET I$ = INKEY$
2020 WEND
```

and

```
2080 PRINT "Enter your password"
2090 LET PASSWORD$ = ""
2100 FOR K = 1 to 5
2110       'get a character and pack into password$
2120     LET I$ = ""
2130     WHILE I$ = ""
2140         LET I$ = INKEY$
2150     WEND
2160     LET PASSWORD$ = PASSWORD$ + I$
2170 NEXT K
```

INKEY\$ cannot be used to read from a file.

The power of using INKEY\$ can be seen by changing line 2030 to include a counter that limits the amount of time a user can take in entering the password. This feature is not available using just INPUT\$().

```
2080 PRINT "Enter your password"
2090 LET PASSWORD$ = ""
2095 LET J = 0
2100 FOR K = 1 to 5
2110       'get a character and pack into password$
2120     LET I$ = ""
2130     WHILE I$ = ""
2140         LET I$ = INKEY$
2145         LET J = J + 1
2150     WEND
2160     LET PASSWORD$ = PASSWORD$ + I$
2170 NEXT K
2180 IF J < 1000 THEN GOSUB 3000
        ELSE PRINT "Too much time taken-please see the supervisor"
2190 END
```

LINE INPUT Reads an Entire Line

Sometimes a simple INPUT statement will not do. For example, if your program requests a person's name with the statement:

•THE INKEY$ VARIABLE•

INKEY$ is a special variable that contains the value of the key being pressed on the keyboard. For example:

LET RESPONSE$ = INKEY$

```
5530 INPUT "Enter customer name ", CUST.NAME$
```

and you enter the person's name as *Wendell Wentworth, III,* BASIC will give the message "?Redo from start." This happens because a comma was used when the name was entered. BASIC interprets this as two separate variables, and since the INPUT statement specifies only one item, BASIC gives the error message.

To solve this problem, you could ask the user to put quotes around all names with commas, but this would be cumbersome. Fortunately, BASIC provides the LINE INPUT statement, which accepts all the characters (up to a maximum of 254) that are entered, including commas, semicolons, and quotes.

The problem with the preceding line can now be solved by changing INPUT to LINE INPUT.

```
5530 LINE INPUT "Enter customer name ", CUST.NAME$
```

Prompts can be used with LINE INPUT just as with INPUT. However, LINE INPUT does not generate a question mark when the prompt is followed by a semicolon as does INPUT. Therefore, it does not matter whether you follow the prompt with a comma or with a semicolon. If you want a question mark, you must include it within the prompt.

Also, as with INPUT, you can suppress the movement of the cursor to next line when Enter is pressed by placing a semicolon directly after the word *INPUT.*

```
100 LINE INPUT; "Name ", CUST.NAME$
110 LINE INPUT " Address "; CITY.STATE$
120 PRINT CUST.NAME$; SPACE$(2); CITY.STATE$
RUN
Name Wendell Wentworth, III Address Sacramento, CA
Wendell Wentworth, III Sacramento, CA
```

As similar as LINE INPUT is to INPUT, there is a very important difference. LINE INPUT may be used only with string variables. With INPUT you can enter numeric data into a numeric variable with the statement:

```
INPUT "Please enter the zip code: ", ZIP.CODE
```

If you changed this statement to LINE INPUT, you would get a "Type mismatch" error message because ZIP.CODE is a numeric variable. The statement would have to be written as:

•THE LINE INPUT STATEMENT•

LINE INPUT accepts up to 254 characters of input including commas and other punctuation.

LINE INPUT ANY.STRING$ does not cause a question mark to appear on the screen.

LINE INPUT "prompt"; ANY.STRING$ causes a prompt to display on the screen.

LINE INPUT *n*, ANY.STRING$ accepts one line from file *n*.

```
LINE INPUT "Please enter the zip code: "; ZIP.CODE$
```

Another version of LINE INPUT will read from file #*n*:

```
LINE INPUT #n, A$
```

As with the version that accepts data from the keyboard, this version will input commas, quotes, and so on until it reads a carriage return/line feed pair (as mentioned in Chapter 7), or 254 characters, whichever occurs first, and assign these characters to the variable A$. LINE INPUT # is most commonly used to read data that were written to a file with the PRINT # statement.

COLOR Changes How Things Appear

The COLOR statement has various options, depending upon whether you are using a color or monochrome video board and monitor. The most important aspect of the COLOR statement for business processing, regardless of what kind of monitor you have, is the ability to cause messages to blink and thus attract attention.

For all monitors you can change the color of the **foreground** (the color in which the characters print) and the color of the **background** (the color of the box in which they print) and change the intensity of the foreground characters or cause them to blink.

Each of the colors is assigned a numeric value as follows:

0	black	8	gray
1	blue	9	light blue
2	green	10	light green
3	cyan	11	light cyan
4	red	12	light red
5	magenta	13	light magenta
6	brown	14	yellow
7	white	15	high-intensity white

The normal setting is a white (7) foreground on a black (0) background. (Some monochrome monitors have a green or amber screen. In that case "white" will appear as green or amber.) You can change the default setting with the COLOR statement. The format for the COLOR statement is:

```
COLOR foreground, background
```

Any of the colors may be used for the foreground, but only 0 through 7 may be used for background. Thus the statement:

```
COLOR 0, 7
```

will reverse the colors on the screen, displaying black characters on a white background.

With a monochrome monitor you will not be able to get all of the colors. For the foreground, COLOR setting 0 will display as black and 2 through 7 will display as white. On the monochrome monitor only, a setting of 1 will display as a white foreground with underline. For the background on a monochrome monitor, 0 through 6 will display as black and 7 will display as white.

On all of the monitors you can cause the characters to blink by setting the foreground to the color you want plus 16. Thus the statement:

```
COLOR 23, 0
```

will produce blinking white characters on a black background. The statement:

·THE COLOR AND BEEP STATEMENTS·

COLOR Foreground Color, Background Color, Border Color

Regular		Intense	
Number	*Color*	*Number*	*Color*
0	black	8	gray
1	blue	9	light blue
2	green	10	light green
3	cyan	11	light cyan
4	red	12	light red
5	magenta	13	light magenta
6	brown	14	yellow
7	white	15	high-intensity white

For blinking add 16 to the above number.

Reverse video: COLOR 0, 7
Reset to normal: COLOR 7, 0

BEEP has the same effect as printing CHR$(7);.

```
COLOR 31, 0
```

will produce blinking high-intensity white on a black background. Only the foreground can be made to blink or to display in high intensity.

The following is a short program that demonstrates how the display can be changed to attract the user's attention. The line asking for input is displayed in reverse color to make it stand out. The phrase "Your name is:" is printed in high-intensity white on a black background, and the name that was entered is displayed as blinking. If there is no change to be made to the background, the setting does not have to be specified. Therefore, in lines 80 and 100 we did not have to give a background setting. Line 100 returns the COLOR setting to the default setting. It is important to remember to do this. The color will remain at whatever the last setting was until changed or until you exit from BASIC.

```
10 CLS
20 COLOR 7,0              ' default setting (white on black)
30 PRINT "This is the normal setting"
40 COLOR 0,7              ' reverse (black on white)
50 INPUT "Please enter your name ", NA$
60 COLOR 15,0             ' high-intensity white on black
70 PRINT "Your name is: ";
80 COLOR 23               ' blinking white foreground
90 PRINT NA$
100 COLOR 7               ' return to default
```

On a PC equipped for color you may also change the color of the border. The border is the area around the perimeter of the screen in which no characters are printed. You do this by specifying the color of the border as the third parameter.

```
COLOR 9, 4, 2
```

will cause the characters to be printed in light blue on a red background with a green border.

Be careful not to make the foreground color the same as the background color. Doing so will make the characters invisible! Changing either the foreground or background to a different color will restore visibility.

BEEP Also Attracts Attention

Execution of the statement BEEP causes the PC to sound a beep. It is particularly useful to include a BEEP statement when announcing to the user an unexpected occurrence, such as an entry error.

```
4210 IF ANSWER$ <> "y" or ANSWER$ <> "n" THEN BEEP:
         PRINT "Please Reenter"
```

Moving Around the Screen

There are times when we want to move the cursor to a specific location on the screen. For example, we might want to have all error messages print on the bottom line of the screen and then have the cursor return to the spot where it was before. We can do this by using LOCATE, CSRLIN, and POS(0).

LOCATE Positions the Cursor at the Desired Location

It would be helpful if we were able to paint the screen, putting data where we want. BASIC gives us this capability by allowing us to position the cursor where we want it with the LOCATE statement.

As you remember, the screen has 25 rows (or lines) and 80 columns. With the LOCATE statement, you specify the row and the column at which you wish to cursor be positioned:

```
LOCATE row, column
```

For example:

```
LOCATE 10, 75
```

will move the cursor to row 10, column 75. See Figure 12.1.

We can give a third specification with LOCATE, which will turn the cursor on or off (now you see it, now you don't). LOCATE r, c, 0 will move it to row r, column c, and turn it off, while LOCATE r, c, 1 will turn it on. (LOCATE ,,0 and LOCATE ,,1 will turn the cursor off and on without moving it.)

We may want to use the bottom (25th) row of the screen to display an error message. In order to move to line 25, we must first turn off the Function key display using the statement KEY OFF.

```
KEY OFF
LOCATE 25, 1, 1
```

turns off the Function key display on line 25, moves the cursor to the first column of line 25, and makes the cursor visible.

CSRLIN AND POS(0) Report the Position of the Cursor

With CSRLIN and POS(0) we can find the row and the column at which the cursor is currently positioned. CSRLIN (cursor line) is a variable containing the number of the line on which the cursor lies. POS(0) is a function that returns the column number of the cursor position on that line. The argument of the POS() function is actually a dummy argument; any number can be used and the result will always be the current column of the cursor.

These two statements, along with the statement LOCATE, allow us to change the cursor position in interesting ways. For example, the following statement will move the cursor position up one line.

```
LOCATE CSRLIN - 1, POS(0)
```

One use of CSRLIN and POS(0) is to keep track of where the cursor is so that we can move it to a new location using LOCATE and then return it to its former position. We make use of this in the following subroutine.

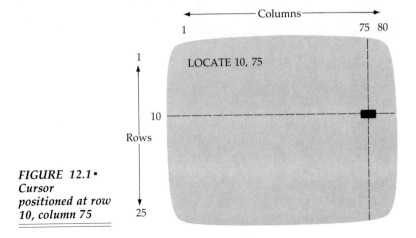

FIGURE 12.1 ·
Cursor
positioned at row
10, column 75

This routine will move the cursor to the bottom of the screen, sound a beep, print the error message in reverse image with flashing arrows before and after it, then return the cursor to its former position

```
8500 '   ******* Error Message Subroutine   *******
8510 '       Message must be placed in ERROR.MSG$
8520 '       before this subroutine is entered
8530 '   ******************************************
8540 KEY OFF                    ' Turn off function key display
8550 LET ROW = CSRLIN          ' Keep current cursor position
8560 LET COL = POS(0)
8570 LOCATE 25, 1              ' Move cursor to bottom line
8575 BEEP
8580 COLOR 31                  ' Blinking, high-intensity
8590 PRINT ">>>   ";
8600 COLOR 0, 7                ' Reverse image, non-blinking
8610 PRINT ERROR.MSG$;
8620 COLOR 31                  ' Blinking, high-intensity
8630 PRINT "  <<<"
8640 COLOR 7,0                 ' Return to normal color
8650 LOCATE ROW, COL           ' Return cursor to former position
8660 RETURN
```

Input/Output Devices as Files

Up to now we have used PRINT when we wanted to display on the screen and LPRINT to print on the printer. However, BASIC allows the input/output devices to be treated as files and assigns them the following names:

·THE LOCATE, CSRLIN, AND POS() FEATURES·

LOCATE row, column, on.off, where *row* is the row number (1–25) (use
   KEY OFF first to clear row 25). *Column* is the column number (1–80).
   on.off is 1 to turn cursor on, 0 to turn cursor off.
CRSLIN is a variable containing the line number where the cursor is located.
POS(*n*) is a function that returns the number of the column position of
   the cursor. *n* is a dummy argument. Any number may be used.
   Usually zero is used.

Output Devices

SCRN:	Screen
LPT1:	Line Printer #1
LPT2: and LPT3:	Line printers #2 and #3, if available

Input Device

KYBD:	Keyboard

To use the device as a file we open it just as we would a disk file, and we use
PRINT# or WRITE# to write to it or INPUT# to input from it. As you can imagine,
SCRN: and LPT1: can be opened only for output and KYBD: only for input.

You may be wondering, "Why go to all the trouble of setting up the screen or
printer as a file when it is simpler just to use PRINT or LPRINT?" In most cases
you would be right; however, there are times when we want to allow the user a
choice of where output is to be printed: to the screen, to the printer or to a file. In
other words, we want the user to be able to select which output device is to be
used.

In this following excerpt of a program that generates a report, the user is asked
to indicate whether the report should be displayed on the screen, printed on the
printer, or sent to a data file for later use.

```
1000 CLS
1010 PRINT "Where do you wish for me to send the output?"
1020 PRINT "              P -> to the printer"
1030 PRINT "              S -> to the screen"
1040 PRINT "              F -> to a file"
1050 LET WHICH = 0
1060 '
1070 WHILE WHICH = 0
1080    LOCATE 6,1,1: BEEP
1090    PRINT "Enter one letter P, S, or F for your choice: "
1100    LET WHICH = (INSTR ("PpSsFf", INPUT$(1)) + 1)\2
```

```
1110 WEND
1120 '
1130 IF WHICH = 1 THEN LET FSPEC$ = "LPT1:"
1140 IF WHICH = 2 THEN LET FSPEC$ = "SCRN:"
1150 IF WHICH = 3 THEN INPUT "Enter the name of the file on which the
report is to be printed: ", FSPEC$
1160 '
1170 OPEN FSPEC$ FOR OUTPUT AS #1
1180 PRINT #1, "the report goes here"
1190 CLOSE #1
1200 END
```

The Story's End

Harris was proud of the program.

"We started with a good project management program and made it better. Now our customers love us.

"Our program has all the bells and whistles, or beeps, so to speak. Users can password their projects to keep roving eyes out of their project. And input and output are much more sophisticated than simple INPUT and PRINT.

"We have already gained an extra 2 percent of the market share. That may not sound like much, but that means we have a 30 percent increase in sales. And that is good business!" (While Harris could not let us print the project management aspects of the program, which sells for $495, we are allowed to see how the selection of options is menu-driven.)

Program Specifications

All of the menus will be displayed inside a box that is drawn in the center of the screen. The menu will show the options available from that menu and direct the user to enter one of the options. If the user enters an invalid option, the computer will sound a beep and display a message with blinking asterisks at the bottom of the screen informing the user of the error.

The main menu will lead the user to one of three submenus, which will also be displayed in a box on the screen.

All of the menus will use the same character (an *x*) for the user to indicate exit from the current menu.

The three processing options from the main menu are:

1. Add or change data.
2. Print charts.
3. Print statistical reports.

All users will be allowed access to options two and three, but a password must be entered before access to option one is allowed. The user will be asked to enter a five-character password, which must not be shown as the screen as it is being entered. If an invalid password is entered, a message will display in reverse video, informing the user that the correct password was not entered.

Functions

A. Initialize
1. Initialize variables
2. Read password table
B. Display menus
1. Display main menu
2. Input response and do one of the following
a. Display add/change menu
b. Display print charts menu
c. Display print statistical reports menu
d. Exit from program
3. End processing

Structure Chart
Harris drew the detailed structure chart shown in Figure 12.2 before beginning to
write the program.

Data Dictionary

ANS$	Y/N switch used to confirm exit from program
DUMMY$	Pause for output displays
EXIT.SUB	Set true when user wishes to exit the subroutine
EXIT.SWITCH	Set true when the user wishes to exit the program
FALSE	Logical value of false (0)
FNRESPONSE(SUB)	Decoder for the user's response into a value
I	Counter in FOR . . . NEXT loops
J	Counter in FOR . . . NEXT loops
LEFT.MARGIN	Parameter holding position of left margin
MAIN.MENU$	Holder for all legal responses to menu menu query
MENU.1$	Holder for all legal responses to menu 1 query
MENU.2$	Holder for all legal responses to menu 2 query
MENU.3$	Holder for all legal responses to menu 3 query
MENU.HEIGHT	Loop variable used in displaying menus
NUM.PASSWORDS	Loop variable used in reading passwords
OK.PASSWORD	Logical variable set to true if legal password is given
PASSWORD$(SUB)	List of legal passwords
RIGHT.MARGIN	Parameter holding value of right margin
TEMP.PASS$	Variable holding password given by user
TRUE	Logical true (−1)
VALID$	Placeholder variable used in defining the function

Pseudocode

MAIN
    DO INITIALIZE
    WHILE EXIT.SWITCH = FALSE

```
        DO BUILD-SCREEN-BORDER
        DO DISPLAY-MAIN-MENU
        DO GET-RESPONSE
Depending on response,
        DO GIVE-ERROR-MESSAGE or
        DO ADD-OR-CHANGE, or
        DO PRINT-CHARTS, or
        DO PRINT-REPORTS, or
        DO EXIT
WEND
```

FIGURE 12.2 ▪
Structure chart
for MENU.BAS

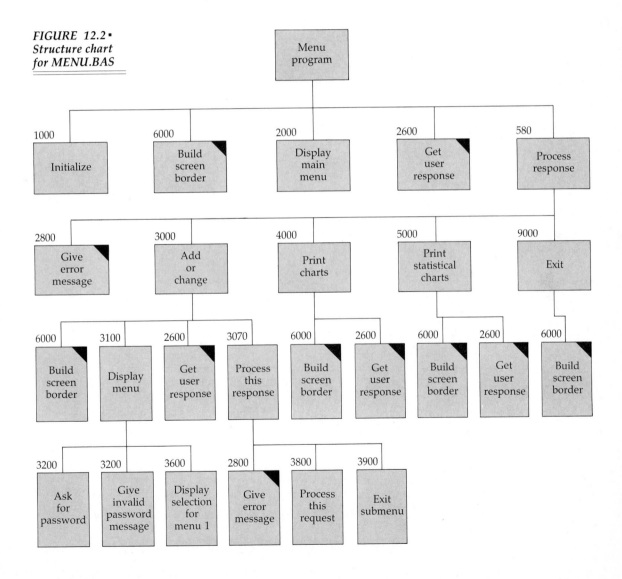

<u>INITIALIZE</u>
    Initialize variables
    Read in passwords from DATA statements into array PASSWORD$
        (In this program the passwords are stored as DATA statements within
        the program. This means that anyone can discover the passwords by
        looking at a listing of the program. In this application, as in many
        business applications, the purpose of the password is to prevent
        someone not familiar with the correct procedures for updating a file
        from inadvertently doing so, rather than for security. Therefore, it is
        not critical that the passwords be kept completely secret.)
<u>BUILD-SCREEN-BORDER</u>
    Draw a box for the menu
<u>DISPLAY-MAIN-MENU</u>
    Print the options
<u>GET-RESPONSE</u>
    Print message to enter response
<u>GIVE-ERROR-MESSAGE</u>
    Blink, say selection is invalid
    Wait for user to read
<u>ADD-OR-CHANGE</u>
    LET EXIT.SUB = FALSE
    WHILE EXIT.SUB = FALSE
        DO BUILD-SCREEN-BORDER
        DO DISPLAY-MENU-1-AND-GET-PASSWORD
        IF password is valid
            THEN DO GET-RESPONSE
                Depending on response
                    DO GIVE-ERROR-MESSAGE, or
                    DO DUMMY-PROCESS, or
                    DO EXIT-FROM-SUBMENU
    WEND
<u>DISPLAY-MENU1-AND-GET-PASSWORD</u>
    DO ASK-FOR-PASSWORD
    IF password not valid
        THEN display bad password message
            LET EXIT.SUB = TRUE
        ELSE display submenu 1
<u>ASK-FOR-PASSWORD</u>
    Display message and underline field for password
    FOR I = 1 TO 5
        Accept 1 character using INPUT$(1)
        Append character to TEMP.PASS$
        PRINT X in password field
    NEXT I

```
        FOR J = 1 TO number of passwords
            IF TEMP.PASS$ = PASSWORD$()
                THEN LET OK.PASSWORD = TRUE
        NEXT J
DUMMY-PROCESS
        Temporary stub that will later be replaced
EXIT-FROM-SUBMENU
        Set EXIT.SUB to TRUE
PRINT-CHARTS
        DO BUILD-SCREEN-BORDER
        Print message that this is a dummy module
        DO GET-RESPONSE
PRINT-REPORTS
        DO BUILD-SCREEN-BORDER
        Print message that this is a dummy module
        DO GET-RESPONSE
EXIT
        DO BUILD-SCREEN-BORDER
        Verify that user indeed intends to exit
        IF ANS$ is "Y" or "y"
                THEN set EXIT.SWITCH to TRUE
```

Program Listing

```
10      ' Program Name: MENU.BAS
20      ' This is a sample of a user-friendly, menu-driven
30      ' program-the Submenu # comments refer to modules
40      ' that will most likely be menu-driven as well
50      '
500     ' -----------------------------------------------
510     ' ----------  MAIN LINE  ---------------------
520     ' -----------------------------------------------
530     GOSUB 1000                ' Initialization
540     WHILE EXIT.SWITCH = FALSE
550         GOSUB 6000 ' Build the screen border
560         GOSUB 2000 ' Display Main Menu
570         GOSUB 2600 ' Enter response
580         ON FNRESPONSE(MAIN.MENU$) + 1
                GOSUB 2800, 3000, 4000, 5000, 9000, 9000
590     '   2800-Error Message for incorrect response
600     '   3000-Submenu #1: Adds or Changes
610     '   4000-Submenu #2: Print Charts
620     '   5000-Submenu #3: Print Statistical Reports
630     '   9000-Exit
640     WEND
650     END
```

```
1000   ' ------------------------------------------------
1010   '                  INITIALIZATION
1020   ' ------------------------------------------------
1030   KEY OFF
1040   LET LEFT.MARGIN = 10: LET RIGHT.MARGIN = 70   'set margins for display
1050   LET TRUE = -1: LET FALSE = 0
1060   LET EXIT.SWITCH = FALSE
1070   '
1080   DEF FNRESPONSE(VALID$) = INSTR(VALID$, INPUT$(1))
1090   '  FNRESPONSE will input a single character and return a numeric value.
1100   '      If the character entered appears in its argument,
1110   '          FNRESPONSE will return the position of that character.
1120   '      If the character entered does not appear in its argument,
1130   '          FNRESPONSE will return a zero.
1140   '
1150   '      VALID RESPONSES-X or x indicates exit from menu
1160   LET MAIN.MENU$ = "123Xx"          ' Valid responses for main menu
1170   LET MENU.1$    = "12Xx"           ' Valid responses for menu 1
1180   LET MENU.2$    = "123Xx"          ' Valid responses for menu 2
1190   LET MENU.3$    = "123Xx"          ' Valid responses for menu 3
1200   '
1210   '    Read Password Table
1220   OPTION BASE 1
1230   READ NUM.PASSWORDS
1240   DIM PASSWORD$(NUM.PASSWORDS)
1250   FOR I = 1 TO NUM.PASSWORDS
1260      READ PASSWORD$(I)
1270   NEXT I
1280   RETURN
2000   ' ------------------------------------------------
2010   '                  Display Main Menu
2020   ' ------------------------------------------------
2030      LOCATE 7,25
2040         PRINT "PROJECT MANAGEMENT - MAIN MENU"
2050      LOCATE 10, LEFT.MARGIN + 5
2060         PRINT "1)    ADD OR CHANGE DATA"
2070      LOCATE 12,LEFT.MARGIN + 5
2080         PRINT "2)    PRINT CHARTS"
2090      LOCATE 14,LEFT.MARGIN + 5
2100         PRINT "3)    PRINT STATISTICAL REPORTS"
2110      LOCATE 16, LEFT.MARGIN + 5
2120          PRINT "X)    EXIT FROM PROGRAM"
2130      RETURN
2600      ' ----------------------------------------------------
2610      '                  Accept Response
2620      ' ----------------------------------------------------
2630      LOCATE 19,LEFT.MARGIN + 5
2640         PRINT "Please enter the character corresponding to "
```

```
2650        LOCATE 20, LEFT.MARGIN + 10
2660           PRINT "your selection"
2670        RETURN
2800        ' ----------------------------------------------------
2810        '              ERROR MESSAGE
2820        ' ----------------------------------------------------
2830        BEEP
2840        LOCATE 25, 2: COLOR 31: PRINT "**";      ' Blinking asterisks
2850        COLOR 7:LOCATE 25, 5
2860        PRINT "INVALID SELECTION-PLEASE PRESS ANY KEY TO RETURN TO MENU";
2870        DUMMY$ = INPUT$(1)
2880        RETURN
3000        '----------------------------------------------------
3005        '            Submenu #1-Add or Change Data
3010        '----------------------------------------------------
3020        LET EXIT.SUB = FALSE
3030        WHILE EXIT.SUB = FALSE
3040           GOSUB 6000      'Build the screen border
3050           GOSUB 3100      'Display Menu and get password
3060        IF OK.PASSWORD = TRUE THEN GOSUB 2600      ' input response
3070        IF OK.PASSWORD = TRUE THEN ON FNRESPONSE(MENU.1$) + 1
                 GOSUB 2800, 3800, 3800, 3900, 3900 'write process routines later
3080        WEND
3090        RETURN
3100        '----------------------------------------------------
3110        '           Display Submenu #1 and Get Password
3120        '----------------------------------------------------
3130        LOCATE 8, 32: PRINT "ADD OR CHANGE DATA"
3140        GOSUB 3200                       ' Ask for password
3150        IF OK.PASSWORD = FALSE THEN GOSUB 3400
                 ELSE GOSUB 3600     ' display error message or rest of menu
3160        RETURN
3200        '----------------------------------------------------
3210        '              Ask for Password
3220        '----------------------------------------------------
3230        LOCATE 10, LEFT.MARGIN + 5
3240        PRINT "Enter your 5 character password: ";
3250        PRINT "_____";                 ' Print underlines
3260        LOCATE ,POS(0) - 5               ' Return cursor to first underline
3270        LET TEMP.PASS$ = ""
3280        FOR  I = 1 TO 5                   ' Enter 5 characters
3290           LET TEMP.PASS$ = TEMP.PASS$ + INPUT$(1)
3300           PRINT "X";                     ' Print X as character is entered
3310        NEXT I
3320        LET OK.PASSWORD = FALSE
3330        FOR J = 1 TO NUM.PASSWORDS       ' Test for valid password
3340          IF TEMP.PASS$ = PASSWORD$(J) THEN LET OK.PASSWORD = TRUE
3350        NEXT J
3360        RETURN
```

```
3400     '----------------------------------------------------------
3410     '                     Invalid Password Message
3420     '----------------------------------------------------------
3430     COLOR 0,7                'Reverse colors
3440     LOCATE 12, LEFT.MARGIN + 10: PRINT "  Your password does not permit   "
3450     LOCATE 13, LEFT.MARGIN + 10: PRINT "      adding or changing data      "
3460     LOCATE 15, LEFT.MARGIN + 10: PRINT "   With your password you may      "
3470     LOCATE 16, LEFT.MARGIN + 10: PRINT " print reports but not alter data "
3480     LOCATE 18, LEFT.MARGIN + 10: PRINT " HIT ANY KEY TO RETURN TO MENU "
3490     LET DUMMY$ = INPUT$(1)
3500     COLOR 7,0            ' Return to normal colors
3510     LET EXIT.SUB = TRUE            ' exit submenu if invalid password
3520     RETURN
3600     '----------------------------------------------------------
3610     '             Display Selections for Submenu #1
3620     '----------------------------------------------------------
3630     '         Clear line with password message
3640     LOCATE 10, LEFT.MARGIN + 1: PRINT SPACE$(RIGHT.MARGIN - LEFT.MARGIN - 1)
3650     '          Print Selections
3660     LOCATE 12, LEFT.MARGIN + 10
3670        PRINT "This menu should give the user the ability to"
3680     LOCATE 13, LEFT.MARGIN + 10
3690        PRINT "enter 1 to add new data"
3700     LOCATE 14, LEFT.MARGIN + 10
3710        PRINT "enter 2 to change existing data"
3720     LOCATE 15, LEFT.MARGIN + 10
3730        PRINT "or enter X to return to the MAIN menu"
3740     RETURN
3800     '----------------------------------------------------------
3810     '        ** TO BE REPLACED BY PROCESSING ROUTINES **
3820     '----------------------------------------------------------
3830     RETURN
3900     '----------------------------------------------------------
3910     '             Exit from Submenu
3920     '----------------------------------------------------------
3930      LET EXIT.SUB = TRUE
3940      RETURN
4000     ' ---------------------------------------------------------
4010     '               Submenu #2
4020     ' ---------------------------------------------------------
4030     GOSUB 6000              ' Build screen border
4040     LOCATE 12, 18
4050        PRINT "Develop a menu for selection of charts"
4060     GOSUB 2600                ' Enter response
4070     LET DUMMY$ = INPUT$(1)
4080     RETURN
5000     ' ---------------------------------------------------------
5010     '               Submenu #3
5020     ' ---------------------------------------------------------
5030     GOSUB 6000              ' Build screen border
5040     LOCATE 12, 15
```

```
5050          PRINT "Develop a menu for selection of statistical reports"
5060     GOSUB 2600                    ' Enter response
5070     LET DUMMY$ = INPUT$(1)
5080     RETURN
6000     ' ----------------------------------------------------
6010     '                 Build the screen border
6020     ' ----------------------------------------------------
6030     CLS
6040     LOCATE 5, LEFT.MARGIN: PRINT STRING$(61,CHR$(220))   ' Print top line
6050     FOR MENU.HEIGHT = 6 TO 20                            ' Print sides
6060          LOCATE MENU.HEIGHT,LEFT.MARGIN
6070          PRINT CHR$(221)
6080          LOCATE MENU.HEIGHT,RIGHT.MARGIN
6090          PRINT CHR$(222)
6100     NEXT MENU.HEIGHT
6110     LOCATE MENU.HEIGHT, LEFT.MARGIN
6120     PRINT STRING$(61,CHR$(223))                          ' Print bottom line
6130     RETURN
9000     ' ----------------------------------------------------
9010     '                 Exit from Program
9020     ' ----------------------------------------------------
9030     GOSUB 6000                         'Build screen border
9040     LOCATE 12, LEFT.MARGIN + 5
9050        PRINT "Please confirm that you wish to end processing"
9060     LOCATE 14, LEFT.MARGIN + 10
9070        PRINT "Y = Yes, I wish to EXIT"
9080     LOCATE 15, LEFT.MARGIN + 10
9090        PRINT "N = No, I wish to return to the MAIN MENU"
9100     LET ANS$ = INKEY$
9110     WHILE ANS$ <> "Y" AND ANS$"y" AND ANS$ <> "N" AND ANS$ <> "n"
9120        LOCATE 17, LEFT.MARGIN + 10: PRINT "Please enter a Y or N: ";
9130        LET ANS$ = INKEY$
9140     WEND
9150     IF ANS$ = "Y" OR ANS$ = "y" THEN LET EXIT.SWITCH = TRUE: CLS:
             PRINT "End of Project Management Program"
9160     RETURN
9170     ' ----------------------------------------------------
9180     DATA 4, JESSI, ELIZB, TONKA, LESLI
9190     ' ----------------------------------------------------
9200     '                 End of Listing
9210     ' ----------------------------------------------------
```

·QUICK REFERENCE FOR LESSON 12·

BEEP

BEEP is a statement that causes the PC to sound a beep. The statement BEEP is equivalent to the statement PRINT CHR$(7);.

COLOR

This is a statement that sets the colors on the screen. The format is COLOR foreground, background, border. The colors are assigned numeric values 0 through 15. The foreground can be made to blink by adding 16 to the value of the color.

CSRLIN

CRSLIN is a variable that contains the number of the line in which the cursor is currently located.

INKEY$

This variable contains the value of the key being pressed on the keyboard.

INPUT$()

This function returns a string of characters.

INPUT$(n) returns a string of n characters entered from the keyboard.
INPUT$(n, #m) returns a string of n characters entered from file number m.

The characters entered do not appear on the screen.

LINE INPUT

LINE INPUT is a statement that accepts a line of input, including commas and other punctuation. LINE INPUT does not cause a question mark to appear on the screen.

LINE INPUT A$ — All the data entered from the keyboard until Enter is pressed are placed into the variable A$.
LINE INPUT "prompt"; A$ displays the prompt within the quotes.
LINE INPUT; "prompt"; A$ is the same as the preceding but suppresses movement of the cursor to the next line after input.
LINE INPUT #n, A$ inputs data from file #n up to a carriage return/line feed pair into the variable A$.

LOCATE

LOCATE controls the placement of the cursor. The format is LOCATE row, column, on.off

row indicates the row (1 to 25) to where the cursor is to move.
column indicates the column (1 to 80).
on.off — the value of 1 will turn the cursor display on; the value of 0 will turn the cursor display off.

Logical Devices

The input/output devices of the screen, printer, and keyboard may be opened just like files and data sent to them. They are assigned the following names:

NAME	DEVICE	FUNCTION
"KYBD:"	Keyboard	Input
"SCRN:"	Screen	Output
"LPT1:"	Line Printer #1	Output
"LPT2:"	Line Printer #2	Output

POS(0)

This function returns the number of the column in which the cursor is currently located. Any number may used as the argument; it is a dummy argument that is not used. Most commonly, zero is used as the argument.

· EXERCISES ·

Short Answer

1. Explain the differences between INPUT and INPUT$() and between INPUT and LINE INPUT.

2. When would you use INPUT$() over INPUT? INPUT over INPUT$()?

3. Describe the differences and similarities between INPUT$() and INKEY$. When would you use one over the other?

4. What statement would you use to create a screen with a black background, cyan foreground, and magenta border?

5. What are the advantages of creating menu-driven programs?

6. Write a statement to place the cursor in the center of the screen.

7. CSRLIN and POS() are commonly used for what purpose?

Analyzing Code

8. What will appear on the screen if the following statement is encountered?

```
10 LET DATA.ENTRY$ = INPUT$(3)
```

9. If a user enters "123456" in response to the statement described in Exercise 8, what will be the value of DATA.ENTRY$?

10. How many times will the message "ENTER NOGO TO EXIT" be printed if the following lines of code are executed?

```
10 LET A$ = "NOGO"
20 WHILE A$ = "NOGO"
30     PRINT "ENTER NOGO TO EXIT"
40     LET A$ = INKEY$
50 WEND
```

11. What are the necessary modifications to the preceding lines of code to give the user control over the exit of the loop by hitting any key? (Hint: will the user have complete control over the exit if INKEY$ is used?)

12. Consider the following two series of statements. How would you write these routines using INPUT$() and using INPUT? How does each of these affect what is displayed on the screen, and what the user must do? How would you decide when to use one of these instead of the others?

a.
```
10  PRINT "ENTER YOUR CHOICE"
20  LET CHOICE$ = ""
30  WHILE CHOICE$ = ""
40       LET CHOICE$ = INKEY$
50  WEND
60  ON VAL(CHOICE$) GOSUB 1000,2000,3000
```
b.
```
10  PRINT "HIT ANY KEY TO CONTINUE"
20  LET A$ = ""
30  WHILE A$ = ""
40       LET A$ = INKEY$
50  WEND
```

13. If you wanted to allow a user to enter his or her address as follows: 7007 Microway, Elko, Nevada, would you use LINE INPUT or INPUT, and why?

14. What will happen to the cursor if the following statement is executed?

```
10  LOCATE 26, 49
```

15. Where will you see the cursor after the following line is executed?

```
10  LOCATE 12, 12, 0
```

16. How is a cursor turned on and off with the LOCATE statement? Will the cursor move if these lines are executed?

```
10  LOCATE,,0
20  LOCATE,,1
```

17. What will happen if the following lines are executed?

```
10  KEY OFF
20  LOCATE 25, 10: COLOR 7
30  PRINT "*****";:COLOR 31
40  PRINT " ERROR";:COLOR 7
```

18. Is this legal?

```
10  LET CSRLIN = 10
```

Programming

19. Write a program that requires the knowledge of a password to run the program.

The password is stored on a file called "PASS.DAT", which you will have to create separately. The original password should be "CSUS, Sacramento".

Allow the user three attempts at the password. Each failure should be brought to the user's attention by displaying an error message on line 25 in inverse video. Upon successful password entry, clear the error message from the bottom of the screen.

If the user is successful at entering the correct password, he or she is given the opportunity to change the password to any combination of letters, commas, and spaces. The new password is written to "PASS.DAT". When the user is finished changing the password, clear the screen, print "End of Password Program" in the center of the screen, and surround the exit message with a box of flashing asterisks.

20. Write a program that directs the user to enter a string of up to eight uppercase letters (*A–Z*) and to press Enter when the last one is keyed. The directions print in the top eight rows of the screen.

    The first character entered should appear in the center of the screen. Each character should be displayed on the screen and validated as soon as it is entered.

    If the character is not valid, display an error message in inverse video on line 25. Pause for the user to read the message and press any key to continue. At that point erase the error message and erase the invalid character from the end of the string.

    Once a carriage return has been pressed, the length of the string is to be evaluated. If it is larger than eight, print an error message in inverse video on line 25. Pause for the user to read the message and press any key to continue. Erase the error message and all of the characters that have been entered, but do not erase the directions at the top of the screen.

    When the user has entered up to eight correct characters, the program will cause the computer to sound a beep and print a message congratulating the user for successful completion of the task. This message will display in rows 16 through 20 with a row of 20 blinking, high-intensity "#" above and below the message.

21. Develop a menu-driven program which will initially display an identification screen as follows:

```
**************************************************
*   INVENTORY AND PERSONNEL MASTER FILE UPDATE   *
**************************************************


        This program allows entry of
        new inventory items or
        new employees


        Press any key to continue
```

The next screen that should appear is as follows:

```
==================================================================
                        MASTER FILE UPDATE
==================================================================
INVENTORY DATA:
        Item number ---->?
        Description:
        Quantity:
        Price:
        Quantity on order:


PERSONNEL DATA:
        Employee ID:
        Employee name:
        Salary:
        Position:
        Comments:
```

```
- - - - - - - - - - - - - - - - - - - - - - - - - - - - - - - - - - - - - - - - - - -
        To enter Inventory data, please enter "I".
        To enter Personnel data, please enter "P".
        To END processing, please enter an "X".
- - - - - - - - - - - - - - - - - - - - - - - - - - - - - - - - - - - - - - - - - - -
```

If the user presses either *I* or *P* (accept either uppercase or lowercase), erase the instructions. Display the prompt "---->?" after the first field in the category the user has selected. Once the user presses return, the prompt should automatically drop to the next field within the record. This prompt should blink.

After the last field in the record has been entered, clear all the fields that have been entered (without clearing the descriptions) and display the instructions again.

Validate all numeric fields, ensuring that only numbers are entered. Use LINE INPUT for the description and comment fields, and allow only 30 characters. If more than 30 characters are entered, this is an error and an error message should be displayed in inverse video at the bottom of the screen. Also, blank fields are considered as errors.

Write the incoming data to the respective files—INV.DAT and EMP.DAT.

If you have a color system, print the screen heading one color, the INVENTORY fields a second color, the PERSONNEL a third, and the instructions a fourth. Experiment with different foreground and background colors to find combinations that are easy to read on your monitor. Try printing the instructions in inverse video.

RANDOM ACCESS
FILES

AL'S EFFICIENCY EXPERT

Jay, a data processing troubleshooter for Con Glomerate, Inc., was sent to a subsidiary, Al's Auto Parts (AAP). When Jay arrived at the store, he found the inventory system to be inadequate. On the positive side the store had a computer and employees could get inventory reports out on time. The computer even recommended which items to reorder. Rosie, the inventory manager, had done a good job in getting that done.

But the inventory system did not keep the current information on line and easily accessible. If an employee needed to know the current inventory status of blue widgets, the program would search through the inventory file, item by item, until it found blue widgets.

AAP needed a program that would directly access blue widgets. They needed new programming. Jay didn't want to replace the existing system with a new one. To do so would cause unnecessary turmoil, retraining, and employee dissatisfaction. Rather, Jay wanted to supplement the existing system with a new application. The new application would meet the requirements for direct access to any inventory record. The new application would have to be designed so as to work with the existing, sequential access files.

"My job is to reduce trouble, not create it," Jay said. "I'm going to work with a systems analyst and later a programmer to get AAP what it needs to be a profitable business. The systems analyst, Vicki, will define what the new portion of the system will do, and how it will interact with the existing system. The programmer, Dave, will write new BASIC programs, using Random Access, to meet these needs."

•*THE ABCS OF BASIC ON THE IBM PERSONAL COMPUTER*•

LESSON 13: RANDOM ACCESS FILES

In Chapter 7 you learned about sequential files. To use a sequential file you need to take these three steps:

1. OPEN the file, giving BASIC the name of the file, the number to be associated with this file, and the use of the file (FOR INPUT if you want to read the file, FOR OUTPUT if you want to write a new file, or FOR APPEND if you want to add data to the end of an existing file).
2. Process the file using INPUT #, PRINT #, or WRITE #.
3. CLOSE the file when you are finished with it.

Assume that we have placed information about our employees (employee name, employee address, and so on) into a sequential file and that we now need to access data about a specific employee. We could read this file into an array (in memory); however, in a large company it is likely that the entire file will be larger than can be held in memory at one time. Therefore, we need another solution.

One approach would be to search the file for the employee we need. Suppose the data we need right now are stored in the 140th record in our file. Since our file is too large to read into an array, the only way we can get this data is to read through all of the 139 employee records in the file before reaching the one that we want. This will waste a lot of time.

After processing the information for the employee in the 140th record, we need information about the person in the 138th record. The only way to get it (using what we know so far) is to go back to the beginning and go through the first 137 again.

You can see that this is no way to run a business.

The limitation of sequential files is that we cannot directly access any one specific record at a time. We can only read the next record on the file. BASIC does offer a way to write and read specific records: Random Access files.

As we stated in an earlier lesson, sequential files are like DATA statements; constants in DATA statements can be accessed only sequentially. In contrast, random files are like arrays; if you know the index of the array element, you can directly access it. Random Access files allow you to directly access any record in the file by its record number. Figure 13.1 illustrates some of the important points about random access.

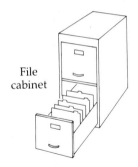

File cabinet

- Any record can be accessed directly.

- All records are the same size.

- A record can be added at any time.

FIGURE 13.1 •
Random Access
files

Record Length: Fixed Length Versus Variable Length

To use Random Access files we must tell BASIC the exact size that each record will be in terms of number of characters. Random Access requires that all records be exactly the same length.

For example, if we need 25 characters for employee name and 40 for employee address, and these are the only two fields in the record, then our record needs to be 65 characters long. Even if we only need 14 characters for Elizabeth Boyd's name, to use random access, we must allocate 25 characters for her name.

When we created sequential files, we did not worry about how many characters were in each field or record. With WRITE # and INPUT # all we needed to do was indicate the name and sequence of the variables. WRITE # and INPUT # kept track of where each field began and ended.

As you might guess, random file processing does not use WRITE # and INPUT #. Instead it uses GET # and PUT #. But both sequential and random file processing use the statement OPEN.

Opening a Random Access File

We tell BASIC that we want to access a file as a Random Access file by using different forms of the OPEN statement than what we have used in the past. One of these new forms is as follows:

```
OPEN "FILENAME.DAT" AS #1
```

Notice that the words FOR INPUT, FOR APPEND, or FOR OUTPUT are omitted. This is because when a file is opened for Random Access, we can both read from it and write to it, as well as append to it.

In the preceding example because we did not specify the record length, it was automatically set to 128, the default record length. If we do not wish our records to be 128 characters long, we can change the record length by stating the length we wish in the OPEN statement. To create records that are 44 characters in length we would use the following form of the OPEN statement:

```
OPEN "FILENAME.DAT" AS #1 LEN = 44
```

If we want our record to contain more than 128 characters, there is one additional thing we must do. We need to tell BASIC, at the time it is loaded, to allocate more space for its buffers. We do this by invoking BASIC with the /S switch following its name:

```
BASIC /S:n
```

or

```
BASICA /S:n
```

where n is the maximum number of characters contained in one record in any file written or read by the program. The maximum record size allowed by BASIC is 32767 characters.

GET # Replaces INPUT

For sequential files, to access the next items of data on the file opened as #1 we use INPUT #1, A, B, and so on. For Random Access we use GET #1. GET #1 will access the next record. GET #1, 5 will access the fifth record; GET #1, 1 will access the first record.

In other words, GET #1, n will get the nth record, and GET #1 (with nothing after the #1) will access the next record. If we have just opened the file, GET #1 will access the first record. If we have just accessed the fifth record, GET #1 will get the sixth record.

Notice that we said GET accesses *a record*, not *a data item* as we did for sequential files. GET # brings in the entire record, not just one field of data. We will show you how to separate the record into fields in just a few moments.

PUT # Replaces WRITE

Similarly PUT #1 writes the information in the next record. We can specify which record if we want a specific record written. For example, PUT #1, 5 will write information to the fifth record of the file. Figure 13.2 summarizes the GET # and PUT # statements.

·THE OPEN STATEMENT FOR RANDOM ACCESS FILES·

OPEN file spec AS #n LEN = m, where file spec is the filename, n is the filenumber, and m is the length of the record.

If $m > 128$, BASIC must be invoked as BASIC /S:m or BASICA /S:m.

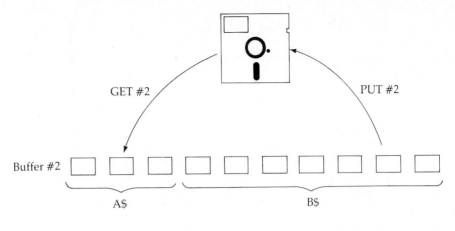

GET #2, 15   Put the 15th record into buffer for file #2.

PUT #2, 15   Place the contents of buffer #2 into the 15th record of the OPENed file.

FIGURE 13.2 •
GET # and PUT #
transfer
information
between BASIC
and a disk file

What Information Is Read or Written?

You recall that we specified the size of the record in the OPEN statement with the LEN= clause. (If we omitted LEN=, a record length of 128 was assumed.) Suppose for the moment that each record in the file takes up 44 characters and that the record length for the file is set to 44. When we execute the GET statement, BASIC puts all 44 characters that make up the contents of the file record into an area of memory called a **buffer.** The buffer has been set to the same size as the record length. From this buffer we can extract the data we need for our program. Likewise, once our program stores information in this buffer, we can use the PUT # statement to write the record to disk.

Note that this random access buffer is not the same as the DOS buffer.

Getting Information Into and Out of the Buffer: The FIELD Statement

Now we must introduce a new statement that has no parallel in sequential processing: the FIELD statement. FIELD lets us "pack" and "unpack" the buffer using BASIC variables. For example, if our 44-character record is composed of two items—Employee Name, which is 20 characters in length, and Employee Address, which is 24 in length—the following statement will associate the first 20 characters of the buffer with EMP.NAME$ and the remaining 24 characters with EMP.ADDRESS$:

```
FIELD #1, 20 AS EMP.NAME$, 24 AS EMP.ADDRESS$
```

The Mythical Microsecond

The Hawk and the Eagle were renowned for the speed with which their programs ran. Give them a program that took an hour to run and they would make it run in 15 minutes — or less. In fact, they frequently undertook to speed up programs just for the sheer challenge. Yet, in spite of their legendary talents, they went largely unappreciated.

The Owl, for example, had recently been promoted to Project Leader. "A duffer," said the Eagle, pointing to one of the Owl's programs while the Hawk shook its head. "Look at this program! If I shortened these variable names, packed more statements on each line, and shortened the comments, this program would run several times faster." "Not only that," chimed in the Hawk, "the Owl used an inefficient algorithm. Let's see how much faster we can make this program run." And off they went.

Five weeks later, the Hawk and the Eagle had, indeed, sped up the program by a factor of four! They confronted the Owl the next day.

"Oh, that program," replied the Owl after listening to their barbed presentation. "I don't want to throw cold water on your heroic efforts, but I think you've missed the point. I knew when I wrote that program that it wasn't as fast as it could have been, but I also knew it would take a long time to make it faster. You say it took you five weeks between you? For the cost of that personnel time, I could have simply purchased a faster computer, which would have sped up all our programs."

"But . . ." squawked the Hawk.

"In addition," continued the Owl, ignoring the Hawk, "the program was written with two goals in mind: that it work and that it be maintainable. The original program meets those goals. Your program may run faster, but in the long run it will cost more than it saves. It takes longer to understand a program written purely for speed, with abbreviated variable names and comments and obscure algorithms. This means it costs more in personnel time to maintain. Not only that, but I see from this printout that it contains a bug. Not surprising, since the program is obscure enough to be difficult to test."

"But . . ." chirped the Eagle, squirming.

The Owl continued, undaunted. "All of which is quite beside the point. When the specifications for the program were drafted, acceptable performance was clearly spelled out. The program meets those criteria and no one has yet complained about how long it takes. Put bluntly, 'if it ain't broke, don't fix it.' The time you spent was better devoted elsewhere."

The Hawk and the Eagle flew off in a rage, but on later reflection realized, for the first time, that there was more to computer programming than speed.

MORAL: In computer programming, speed for its own sake is rarely worth the effort.

EMP.NAME$ is now defined as a **fielded variable** and is different from other string variables. Its purpose is to point to the proper place in the buffer and to assign that portion of the buffer a name. When you use the statement PRINT EMP.NAME$, in effect you are telling BASIC to print the portion of the buffer that has been assigned the name EMP.NAME$. You may use a fielded variable name to retrieve data as in a PRINT statement or as the right side of a LET statement. But be careful not to use any fielded variable name in an INPUT or on the receiving (left) end of a LET statement. BASIC will not give you any error message, but the FIELD statement will no longer be active. The variable name will now refer to an ordinary string variable, not a portion of the buffer. One other rule: the file must be opened before the FIELD statement is executed. Figure 13.3 illustrates the FIELD statements and the buffer.

Retrieving a Specific Record

Now that you know how to set up a Random Access file, it is a simple matter to retrieve a specific record. The following is a set of instructions that will GET and PRINT the 140th and then the 1st record of the file we have been discussing. Assume this file was created by an earlier program and given the name "EMPINFO.DAT".

```
100 OPEN "EMPINFO.DAT" AS #1 LEN = 44
110 FIELD #1, 20 AS EMP.NAME$, 24 AS EMP.ADDRESS$
120 GET #1, 140
130 PRINT EMP.NAME$, EMP.ADDRESS$
140 GET #1, 1
150 PRINT EMP.NAME$, EMP.ADDRESS$
160 CLOSE #1
170 END
```

As you can see, it is just as easy to access the 140th record in the file as it is to access the 1st record.

How to Put Characters Into the Buffer Without Using LET

BASIC will not let us use the LET statement to copy characters into a fielded variable. So how do we copy characters into the buffer? Recall that in Chapter 11 we used LSET and RSET to make fancy headings. LSET moves and left-justifies

FIGURE 13.3 ▪
The buffer and
the FIELD
statement

The OPEN statement creates a buffer; the FIELD statement associates names with positions in the buffer

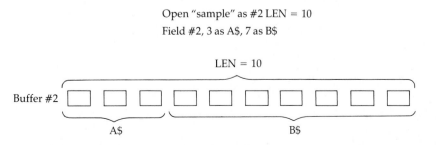

data from one string variable into another. Similarly, RSET moves and right-jus-
tifies string data. LSET and RSET are precisely the statements we need to copy and
justify string data into fielded variables. Here is an example of using LSET.

```
100 OPEN "EMPINFO.DAT" AS #1 LEN = 44
110 FIELD #1, 20 AS EMP.NAME$, 24 AS EMP.ADDRESS$
120 INPUT "WHAT IS THE EMPLOYEE'S NAME AND ADDRESS";
        EMPLOYEE.NAME$, EMPLOYEE.ADDRESS$
130 LSET EMP.NAME$ = EMPLOYEE.NAME$
                              .
                              .
                              .
```

Here line 130 causes as much of EMPLOYEE.NAME$ as will fit to be copied
into the fielded variable EMP.NAME$. EMP.NAME$ is exactly 20 characters
long. Therefore, LSET can copy no more than 20 characters into EMP.NAME$. If
EMPLOYEE.NAME$ is shorter than 20 characters, LSET will copy all of it into the
first (left-most) positions. All remaining positions will be filled with spaces.

If line 130 had contained RSET instead of LSET, the result would be similar,
with the following exception. If EMPLOYEE.NAME$ is shorter than 20 charac-
ters, RSET would right-justify it within EMP.NAME$. RSET would fill the first,
unused positions of EMP.NAME$ with spaces.

Similarly, the line

```
140 LSET EMP.ADDRESS$ = EMPLOYEE.ADDRESS$
```

will copy the first 24 characters of the string variable EMPLOYEE.ADDRESS$
into positions 21 through 44 of the buffer. These are the positions assigned to
EMP.ADDRESS$ in the field statement. If EMPLOYEE.ADDRESS$ is fewer than
24 characters long, the address will start filling in at position 21 and continue
filling for the length of EMPLOYEE.ADDRESS$. The remaining positions up to
position 44 will be filled with spaces. Figure 13.4 illustrates the usage of the LSET
and RSET statements.

How to Put Numeric Data Into the Buffer

FIELDed variables are of type string, not of type numeric. How then can we write
numeric data to a Random Access file? We need some way to convert numeric
data to string data.

We could use the function STR$() and its counterpart, the function VAL(). As
you recall from Chapter 11, STR$ converts a numeric value into a string value.
VAL() returns the numeric value of a string. However, there is a drawback. After

```
LSET A$ = "XX"
RSET B$ = "YY"
```

FIGURE 13.4 •
The effect of
LSET and RSET
on a buffer

STR$() converts a value into a string, the length of the string is not constant. STR$(3) is shorter than STR$(3000), even though both 3 and 3000 might be integer values.

BASIC offers a better way to convert string values to and from numeric values. This method takes advantage of how BASIC stores numbers internal to itself.

To store an integer value, BASIC takes 2 bytes of memory. Similarly, BASIC uses 4 bytes to store single-precision numbers. To store double-precision values, BASIC uses 8 bytes.

So what we need are functions that will convert an integer into a 2-byte string, a single-precision number into a 4-byte string, and a double-precision number into a 8-byte string.

We also need corresponding functions to convert each of these strings into an integer, single-precision or double-precision value.

In short, we need three functions to MaKe a string; one for Integer, one for Single precision, and one for Double precision. These functions are called MKI$(), MKS$(), and MKD$().

MKI$() takes an integer argument and returns a 2-byte string value. MKS$() takes a single-precision argument and returns a 4-byte string. MKD$() takes a double-precision argument and returns an 8-byte string.

Such strings typically are LSET into a buffer. How do we ConVert buffer variables back into numeric variables? BASIC provides corresponding functions CVI(), CVS(), and CVD().

CVI() takes a 2-byte string argument and returns an integer value. CVS() takes a 4-byte string argument and returns a single-precision value. CVD() takes an 8-byte string argument and returns a double-precision value.

Here is an example that uses these functions:

```
10 OPEN "TEMP" AS #1 LEN = 14
20 FIELD #1, 2 AS A$, 4 AS B$, 8 AS C$
30 LSET A$ = MKI$(321)
40 LSET B$ = MKS$(12.3)
50 LSET C$ = MKD$(1.23D+21)
60 PUT #1,1
70 GET #1,1
80 PRINT CVI(A$), CVS(B$), CVD(C$)
90 END
RUN
  321             12.3            1.23D+21
```

Table 13.1 summarizes these functions.

Points to Remember

In order to access a file correctly we must know its structure—that is, how it was created. For both Sequential and Random Access Files we need to know the sequence in which the data are stored and what variables are used. For Random Access we also must know the length of the records and the length of each field within the record.

TABLE 13.1 ▪ *Functions for Data Storage Using Random Access Files*

NUMBER	STRING	NUMBER
Integer $\Rightarrow$	MKI\$() $\Rightarrow$ CVI()	$\Rightarrow$ Integer
Single precision $\Rightarrow$	MKS\$() $\Rightarrow$ CVS()	$\Rightarrow$ Single precision
Double precision $\Rightarrow$	MKD\$() $\Rightarrow$ CVD()	$\Rightarrow$ Double precision

Creating a File Accessible via Both Sequential and Random Access

When BASIC stores sequential files, it does two things automatically that we will have to do manually in order to make our Random Access files accessible sequentially. These two things are:

1. At the end of each record in a sequential file, BASIC stores two characters, the carriage return character (ASCII value 13) followed by the line feed character (ASCII value 10).
2. At the end of the file it stores an end-of-file character (ASCII value 26).

We can take these steps into account when creating a random access file as shown in the following examples. The first program creates a file "TESTRAN.DAT," which is accessible both by Random Access and by Sequential Access techniques. The carriage return and line feed are written at the end of each record, and the end-of-file marker is written at the end of the file.

```
10 OPEN "TESTRAN.DAT" AS #1 LEN = 7
20 FIELD #1,5 AS A$,1 AS CR$,1 AS LF$
30 LSET CR$ = CHR$(13)        'Carriage Return
40 LSET LF$ = CHR$(10)        'Line Feed
50 INPUT I$                   'Data to be stored
60 WHILE I$ <> "end"
70     LSET A$ = I$
80     PUT #1
90     INPUT I$
100 WEND
110 LSET A$ = CHR$(26)        'Store End-of-File mark
120 PUT #1
130 CLOSE #1
140 END
```

This next program shows the file being read using the Random Access GET# statement. Notice that to detect the end of the file, we test for the presence of the end-of-file character CHR\$(26) in position 1 of the buffer.

```
10 OPEN "TESTRAN.DAT" AS #1 LEN = 7
20 FIELD #1, 5 AS A$, 2 AS DUMMY$
30 GET #1
35 WHILE LEFT$(A$,1) >< CHR$(26)
40      PRINT A$
50      GET #1
60 WEND
70 END
```

Next we see the file being accessed using the sequential file INPUT# statement.

```
10 OPEN "TESTRAN.DAT" FOR INPUT AS #1
20 INPUT #1,A$
30 WHILE NOT EOF(1)
40      PRINT A$
50      INPUT #1,A$
60 WEND
70 END
```

THE STORY'S END

"It really was not hard getting Al's Auto Parts inventory system into shape," reported Jay at the end of the project.

"I created an inventory file that could be accessed both sequentially and randomly. This allowed them to use their old programs and just add a new one to access each record as needed when inventory came in or went out. It's all in a day's work for a troubleshooter."

Program Specifications

Inventory data are stored in a file named "INVENTRY.DAT". The file contains the following fields:

ITEM NUMBER	integer
DESCRIPTION	string, 30 characters
QUANTITY	integer

The first record is a header record and contains the next available part number in the ITEM NUMBER field. Part numbers begin with #2 and are assigned sequentially by the program. Therefore, the part number is the same as the record number.

This program will allow the user to add to, delete from, and inquire about existing inventory items. As new items are added, they are assigned the next available part number and added to the end of the file.

All user input is validated, and appropriate error messages are displayed.

Lastly, there is a provision to print a report listing each inventory item, its description, and its quantity.

Functions

A. Initialization
   1. Open file and read header
   2. Initialize variables
B. Process inventory transactions
   1. Display main menu
   2. Based on menu selection do one of the following
      a. Process part received
         (1) Add to existing inventory or
         (2) Add new item
      b. Process part requisition
      c. Process inquiry
      d. Print report
C. Close
   1. Write updated header
   2. Close file

Structure Chart

Figures 13.5 through 13.9 show the structure charts for this program. Figure 13.10 shows sample screens.

FIGURE 13.5 ▪
Structure chart
for
INVENTRY.BAS

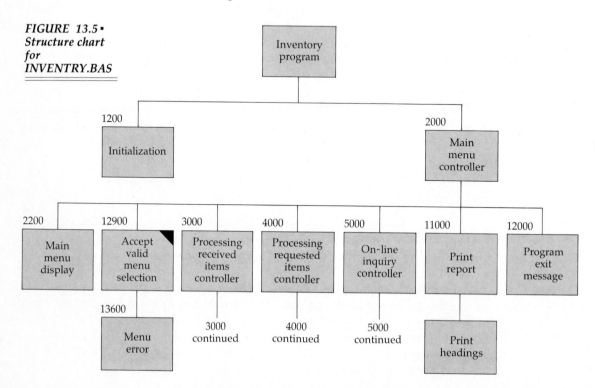

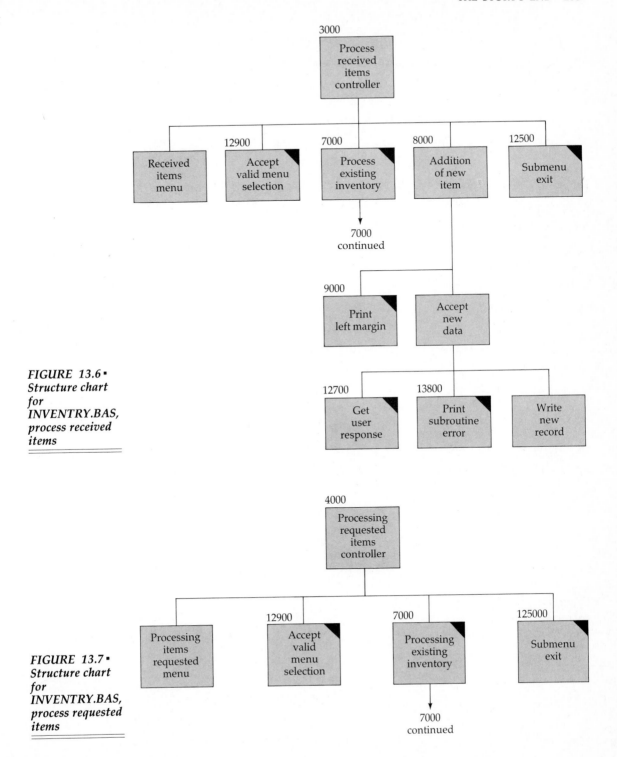

FIGURE 13.6 •
Structure chart
for
INVENTRY.BAS,
process received
items

FIGURE 13.7 •
Structure chart
for
INVENTRY.BAS,
process requested
items

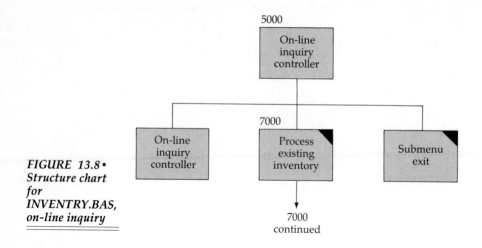

FIGURE 13.8 ·
Structure chart
for
INVENTRY.BAS,
on-line inquiry

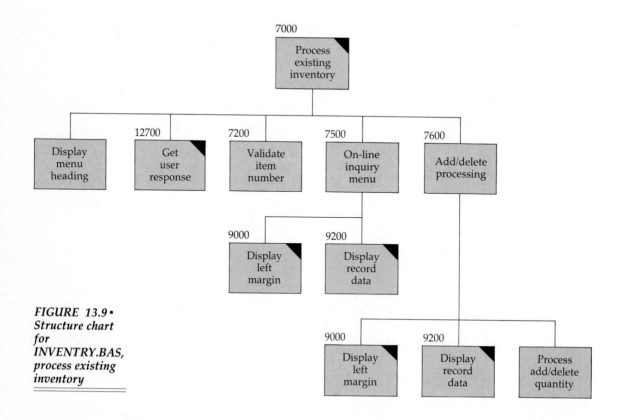

FIGURE 13.9 ·
Structure chart
for
INVENTRY.BAS,
process existing
inventory

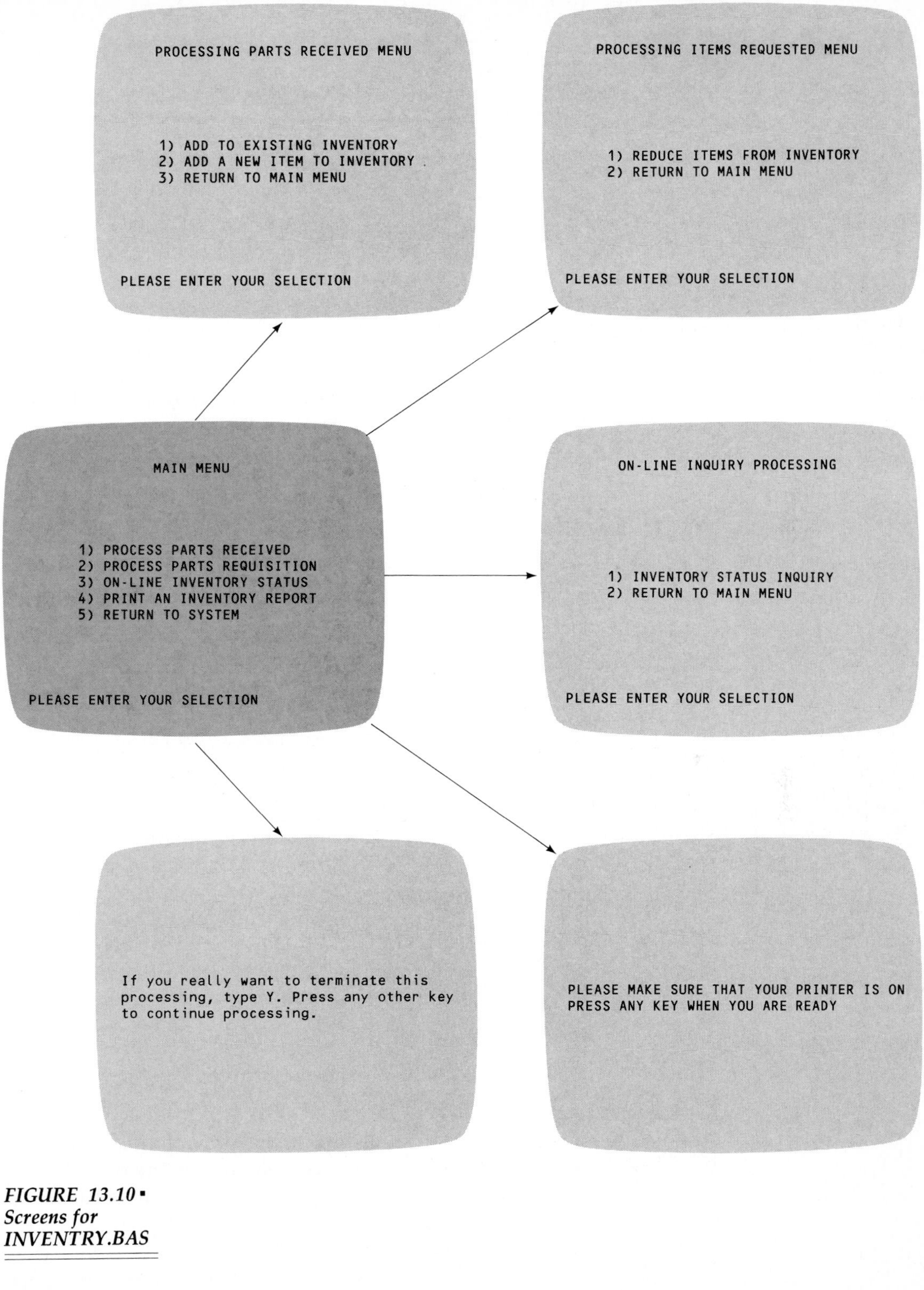

PROCESSING PARTS RECEIVED MENU

1) ADD TO EXISTING INVENTORY
2) ADD A NEW ITEM TO INVENTORY
3) RETURN TO MAIN MENU

PLEASE ENTER YOUR SELECTION

PROCESSING ITEMS REQUESTED MENU

1) REDUCE ITEMS FROM INVENTORY
2) RETURN TO MAIN MENU

PLEASE ENTER YOUR SELECTION

MAIN MENU

1) PROCESS PARTS RECEIVED
2) PROCESS PARTS REQUISITION
3) ON-LINE INVENTORY STATUS
4) PRINT AN INVENTORY REPORT
5) RETURN TO SYSTEM

PLEASE ENTER YOUR SELECTION

ON-LINE INQUIRY PROCESSING

1) INVENTORY STATUS INQUIRY
2) RETURN TO MAIN MENU

PLEASE ENTER YOUR SELECTION

If you really want to terminate this
processing, type Y. Press any other key
to continue processing.

PLEASE MAKE SURE THAT YOUR PRINTER IS ON
PRESS ANY KEY WHEN YOU ARE READY

FIGURE 13.10 ▪
Screens for
INVENTRY.BAS

Data Dictionary

File Used : INVENTRY.DAT

PART.NBR$	Integer, sequentially assigned to parts as new items are added to inventory, minimum value is 2
PART.DESCRIPTION	Description of part, 30 characters
PART.QUANTITY$	Integer, current number of items on hand

First record is a header record. The next available part number is stored in the part number field of this record.

Constants

CLEAR.LINE$	Blank line used to erase a screen line
DUMMY$	Dummy input field to suspend processing until user presses any key
LOWEST.PART.NUMBER	Set to 2, lowest part number in system
HIGHEST.PART.NUMBER	Next available part number
MAX	Set to maximum number of options for menu
MENU.SELECTION	Menu option input by user, used to pass processing via ON GOSUB
MENU.HEADING$	Holds heading of current process for display
VALID.CHARACTER$	String of digits 0–9 plus Enter and Backspace, used to validate numeric input

Working Variables

COLUMN	Holds cursor column position
COMPLETE.NUMBER$	String of valid digits input by user
EACH.CHARACTER$	Single character input by user
NEW.QUANTITY%	Quantity on hand plus quantity input
PART.NUMBER	Part number input by user
QUANTITY%	Quantity to be added or deleted, input by the user
SHORT.STRING$	Holds COMPLETE.NUMBER$ less last digit
THE.LINE	Holds cursor line position

Variables Used for Printing of Report

DETAIL$	Detail line format for report
HEADING1$ thru HEADING4$	Page headings for report
LINES.PER.PAGE	Number of lines per page (currently 15)

PAGE.ADVANCE	Value is CHR$(12), which is a form feed
LINE.COUNT	Line counter checked against lines per page
PAGE.COUNT	Page counter used to print a page number

Switches and Flags

ADD.DELETE.SWITCH$	Determines whether to add to or delete from inventory
ANY.ERROR	Set to zero if EACH.CHARACTER$ is not valid
CONTINUE.SWITCH	Controls main menu loop, set to FALSE when user selects ending option
ERROR.FLAG	Set to TRUE when invalid character is entered
INQUIRY.SWITCH	Set in on-line inquiry process, used in processing of existing inventory to differentiate online inquiries from add/deletes
INVALID.ENTRY.SWITCH	Error switch set in SUBROUTINE-ERRORS to indicate invalid entry
RETURN.TO.MAIN$	Enables a return to the main menu after processing either parts requisition or prior to printing
SUB.MENU.SWITCH	Controls submenu loop, set to FALSE in SUB-MENU-EXIT
THE.ERROR	Determines which error message to display

Pseudocode

INVENTORY UPDATE PROGRAM
    DO INITIALIZATION
    WHILE user indicates wish to continue (CONTINUE.SWITCH = TRUE)
        Do MAIN-MENU-CONTROLLER
    WEND
    END
INITIALIZATION
    Set print headings and page length
    OPEN "INVENTRY.DAT" (LEN = 36)
    FIELD record
        PART.NBR$, PART.DESCRIPTION$, PART.QUANTITY$
    Initialize working variables

    CLEAR.LINE$, TRUE, FALSE, VALID.CHARACTER$
GET header record
IF part number = 0
    THEN LET HIGHEST.PART.NUMBER = 2
    ELSE HIGHEST.PART.NUMBER = part number

Part numbers will begin at 2, since record number 1 is reserved for the header.

    LET LOWEST.PART.NUMBER = 2
    LET CONTINUE.SWITCH = TRUE

MAIN-MENU-CONTROLLER
    Do MAIN-MENU-DISPLAY
    LET MAX = 5 (there are five possible valid selections from main menu)
    LET SUBMENU.SWITCH = TRUE
    Do ACCEPT-VALID-MENU-SELECTION

ACCEPT-VALID-MENU-SELECTION is a subroutine used throughout the program to accept and validate a menu selection.

    ON MENU.SELECTION GOSUB
        Do PROCESS-RECEIVED-ITEMS-CONTROLLER
        Do PROCESS-REQUESTED-ITEMS-CONTROLLER
        Do ONLINE-INQUIRY-CONTROLLER
        Do PRINT-REPORT
        Do PROGRAM-EXIT
MAIN-MENU-DISPLAY
    Clear Screen
    Display Five Options
ACCEPT-VALID-MENU-SELECTION
    LET MENU.SELECTION = 0
    WHILE MENU.SELECTION = 0
        PRINT message at bottom of display to enter selection
        PRINT flashing arrows
        Input single character from keyboard
        IF character entered is > 0 and < (Max + 1)
            THEN LET MENU.SELECTION = character entered
            ELSE Do MENU-ERROR
    WEND
    PRINT SPACE$ in message display area to clear it
MENU-ERROR
    PRINT message showing valid range at bottom of screen
    PRINT spaces over invalid entry

PROCESS-RECEIVED-ITEMS-CONTROLLER
    LET MENU.HEADING$ = "PROCESSING ITEMS RECEIVED"
    WHILE SUBMENU.SWITCH = TRUE

```
            Do DISPLAY-ITEMS-RECEIVED-MENU
            LET MAX = 3 (there are three valid menu selections for items received)
            Do ACCEPT-VALID-MENU-SELECTION
            LET ADD.DELETE.SWITCH$ = " ADD TO "
            ON MENU.SELECTION GOSUB
                Do PROCESS-EXITING-INVENTORY
                Do ADD-NEW-ITEM
                Do SUBMENU-EXIT
        WEND
    DISPLAY-ITEMS-RECEIVED-MENU
        Clear Screen
        Display Three Options
```
- -
```
    PROCESS-REQUESTED-ITEMS-CONTROLLER
            LET MENU.HEADING$ = "PROCESSING REQUESTED ITEMS"
            WHILE SUBMENU.SWITCH = TRUE
                Do DISPLAY-ITEMS-REQUESTED-MENU
```

There is only one option; therefore, no selection is requested.

```
            LET ADD.DELETE.SWITCH$ = " DELETE FROM "
            Do PROCESS-EXISTING-INVENTORY
            PRINT message asking if user wishes to return to main menu
            INPUT RETURN.TO.MAIN$
            IF RETURN.TO.MAIN$ is "Y" or "y"
                THEN Do SUBMENU-EXIT
            PRINT CLEAR.LINE$ to clear message line
        WEND
```
- -
```
    ON-LINE-INQUIRY-CONTROLLER
        LET MENU.HEADING$ = "ON LINE INQUIRY"
        WHILE SUBMENU.SWITCH = TRUE
            LET INQUIRY.SWITCH = TRUE
            Do ON-LINE-INQUIRY-MENU
```

There is only one option; therefore, no selection is requested.

```
            Do PROCESS-EXISTING-INVENTORY
            PRINT message asking if user wishes to return to main menu
            INPUT RETURN.TO.MAIN$
            IF RETURN.TO.MAIN$ is "Y" or "y"
                THEN Do SUBMENU-EXIT
            PRINT CLEAR.LINE$ to clear message line
        WEND
        LET INQUIRE.SWITCH = FALSE
```
- -

PRINT-REPORT
    Clear Screen
    PRINT message to confirm report is to be printed
    INPUT response
    IF response is not "N" or "n"
        THEN Do REPORT
REPORT
    Clear Screen
    PRINT message to turn on printer and press any key when ready
    LET DUMMY$ = INPUT$(1)—halt processing until any key is pressed
    LET LINE.COUNT = 99 (will force heading)
    LET PAGE COUNT = 0
    FOR I = LOWEST.PART.NUMBER TO HIGHEST.PART.NUMBER − 1
        GET #1, I (get record for each part number)
        Increment LINE.COUNT
        IF LINE.COUNT > LINES.PER.PAGE
            THEN Do PRINT-HEADING-ON-NEW-PAGE
        LPRINT part number, part description, part quantity
    NEXT I
    Clear Screen
    Advance Page
PRINT-HEADING-ON-NEW-PAGE
    Advance Page
    Increment PAGE.COUNT
    PRINT Heading Lines
    LET LINE.COUNT = 0

PROGRAM-EXIT
    Clear Screen
    PRINT message confirming user wishes to exit
    IF response is "Y" or "y"
        THEN LET CONTINUE.SWITCH = FALSE
            PUT HIGHEST.PART.NUMBER in Header Record (record 1)
            CLOSE File

PROCESS-EXISTING-INVENTORY
    Clear Screen
    PRINT MENU.HEADING$
    PRINT message to enter item number and press Enter
    Do GET-USER-RESPONSE
    PRINT CLEAR.LINE$ to clear message line
    Do VALIDATE-ITEM-NUMBER
    IF item number is valid (INVALID.ENTRY.SWITCH = FALSE)
        THEN IF INQUIRY.SWITCH = TRUE
            THEN Do ONLINE-INQUIRY-PROCESSING
            ELSE Do ADD/DELETE-PROCESSING

GET-USER-RESPONSE
    LET ERROR-FLAG = FALSE
    LET EACH.CHARACTER$ and COMPLETE.NUMBER$ = null
    WHILE EACH.CHARACTER$ does not equal ENTER (CHR$(13))
        Do CHARACTER-INPUT-VALIDATION

Note: here we will accept user entry keystroke by keystroke and validate each character entered.

    IF EACH.CHARACTER$ is not ENTER and is not BACKSPACE
        THEN PRINT EACH.CHARACTER$
            Append EACH.CHARACTER$ to COMPLETE.NUMBER$
        IF EACH.CHARACTER$ is a BACKSPACE
            THEN Do ERASE-CHARACTER
    WEND
CHARACTER-INPUT-VALIDATION
    Input single character into EACH.CHARACTER$
    Test if EACH.CHARACTER$ is one of the valid characters in
        VALID.CHARACTER$
    If it is not a valid character
        THEN LET ERROR.FLAG = TRUE
ERASE-CHARACTER
    PRINT space over character just entered
    Set SHORT.STRING$ equal to COMPLETE.NUMBER$ without last
        character
    SWAP SHORT.STRING$, COMPLETE.NUMBER$
VALIDATE-ITEM-NUMBER
    LET INVALID.ENTRY.SWITCH = FALSE
    IF ERROR.FLAG = TRUE

(Set to TRUE in CHARACTER-INPUT-VALIDATION if invalid character is entered.)

        THEN LET THE.ERROR = 1 and Do PRINT-ERROR-MESSAGE
        ELSE IF PART.NUMBER < LOWEST.PART.NUMBER
      OR > HIGHEST.PART.NUMBER − 1
        THEN LET THE.ERROR = 2 and Do PRINT-ERROR-MESSAGE
PRINT-ERROR-MESSAGE
    Clear Screen
    PRINT MENU.HEADING$
    IF THE.ERROR = 1
        THEN PRINT "YOU ENTERED A NONNUMERIC CHARACTER"
        ELSE IF THE.ERROR = 2
            THEN PRINT "THE ITEM NUMBER DOES NOT EXIST"
            ELSE PRINT "THERE IS INSUFFICIENT INVENTORY"
    PRINT message to press any character to continue
    LET INVALID.ENTRY.SWITCH = TRUE

ON-LINE-INQUIRY-PROCESSING
    Do PRINT-LEFT-MARGIN-HEADINGS
    GET #1, PART.NUMBER (record for part number entered)
    Do PRINT-RECORD-INFORMATION
    LET INQUIRY.SWITCH = FALSE
ADD/DELETE-PROCESSING
    Do PRINT-LEFT-MARGIN-HEADINGS
    GET #1, PART.NUMBER (record for part number entered)
    Do PRINT-RECORD-INFORMATION
    Do QUERY-FOR-ADD/DELETE-QUANTITY
    IF QUANTITY entered is not zero
        THEN add quantity entered to existing quantity
            LET THE.ERROR = 3
            IF new quantity is not negative
                THEN Store new quantity in record
                PUT updated record
                ELSE Do PRINT-ERROR-MESSAGE
PRINT-LEFT-MARGIN-HEADINGS
    PRINT screen labels on left side of screen
PRINT-RECORD-INFORMATION
    PRINT PART.NBR$, PART.DESCRIPTION$, PART.QUANTITY$ on right
    side of screen
QUERY-FOR-ADD/DELETE-QUANTITY
    PRINT message for quantity using ADD.DELETE.SWITCH$ as part of
    message
    Do GET-USER-RESPONSE
    IF ERROR.FLAG = TRUE
        THEN LET THE.ERROR = 1
            LET quantity entered = 0
            Do PRINT-ERROR-MESSAGE
        ELSE IF ADD.DELETE.SWITCH$ = " DELETE FROM "
            THEN change quantity entered to negative value

ADD-NEW-ITEM
    Clear Screen
    Do PRINT-LEFT-MARGIN-HEADINGS
    DO ACCEPT-NEW-DATA
ACCEPT-NEW-DATA
    PRINT HIGHEST.PART.NUMBER (next available part number)
    LINE INPUT DESCRIPTION$
    Do GET-USERS-RESPONSE (input quantity)
    LET QUANTITY$ = COMPLETE.NUMBER$
    IF ERROR.FLAG = TRUE (invalid character was input)
        THEN LET THE.ERROR = 1
            Do SUBROUTINE.ERRORS
        ELSE Do WRITE-NEW-RECORD

WRITE-NEW-RECORD
    Place data entered in fields
    PUT #1, HIGHEST.PART.NUMBER (write new record)
    GET #1, 1 (header record)
    Increment HIGHEST.PART.NUMBER
    PUT #1, 1 (write updated header record)

SUB-MENU-EXIT
    LET SUB.MENU.SWITCH = FALSE

Program Listing

```
10  '-------------------------------------------------------------
20  ' Program Name:   INVENTRY.BAS
30  ' Date Written:   09/15/88
40  ' Written by:     Jay Blue
50  '
60  '
70  '  File used:  INVENTRY.DAT
75  '
80  ' General Overview: This program adds records to the end of an
90  ' inventory file, updates records (adding to or deleting from
100 ' stock), allows for an on-line inventory status, and allows for
110 ' printing an updated inventory list.   The program uses random
120 ' file access-this is accomplished by assigning the part number
130 ' to the relative record number.  The part numbers for new items
140 ' are computed by the program, and the header record keeps track
150 ' of the highest part number for successive runs. The program
160 ' is essentially bomb-proof, only valid responses will be processed
170 '
500 '-------------------------------------------------------------
510 '                INVENTORY UPDATE PROGRAM
520 '-------------------------------------------------------------
530 GOSUB 1000             'Initialization
540 WHILE CONTINUE.SWITCH = TRUE
550      GOSUB 2000        'Main Menu Controller
560 WEND
570 END
1000 '-------------------------------------------------------------
1010 '                INITIALIZATION
1020 '-------------------------------------------------------------
1030 KEY OFF: CLS
1040 LET CLEAR.LINE$ = SPACE$(80)
1050 '                define detail and heading lines
1060 LET DETAIL$   = " #####           \                          \          ####"
1070 LET HEADING1$ = "                  INVENTORY REPORT        Page"
1080 LET HEADING2$ = "                  AS OF "
1090 LET HEADING3$ = "PART NUMBER            DESCRIPTION                 QUANTITY"
1100 LET HEADING4$ = "===========   ==============================   =========="
```

```
1110 LET FALSE = 0: LET TRUE = -1
1120 LET LINES.PER.PAGE = 15
1130 LET PAGE.ADVANCE$ = CHR$(12)
1140 '                file controls
1150 OPEN "INVENTRY.DAT" AS 1 LEN = 36
1160 FIELD #1, 2 AS PART.NBR$, 30 AS PART.DESCRIPTION$, 2 AS PART.QUANTITY$,
              2 AS CRLF$
1170 '                define valid characters
1180 LET VALID.CHARACTER$ = "0123456789" + CHR$(13) + CHR$(8)
1190 '                get highest record number from header
1200 GET #1,1
1210 IF CVI(PART.NBR$) = 0
        THEN LET HIGHEST.PART.NUMBER = 2
        ELSE LET HIGHEST.PART.NUMBER = CVI(PART.NBR$)
1220 '                set lowest part number to 2, since record 1
1230 '                is reserved as a header record
1240 LET LOWEST.PART.NUMBER = 2
1250 '                set continue switch to the on position
1260 LET CONTINUE.SWITCH = TRUE
1270 RETURN
2000 '------------------------------------------------------------
2010 '                MAIN MENU CONTROLLER
2020 '------------------------------------------------------------
2030 GOSUB 2200           'MAIN MENU DISPLAY
2040 '                get selection and validate it
2050 LET MAX = 5              'highest selection is 5
2060 LET SUB.MENU.SWITCH = TRUE
2070 GOSUB 12900           'ACCEPT VALID MENU SELECTION
2080 ON MENU.SELECTION GOSUB 3000,4000,5000,11000,12000
2090 RETURN
2200 '------------------------------------------------------------
2210 '                MAIN MENU DISPLAY
2220 '------------------------------------------------------------
2230 CLS
2240 LOCATE 5,36: PRINT "MAIN MENU"
2250 LOCATE 9,29: PRINT "1)   PROCESS PARTS RECEIVED"
2260 LOCATE 11,29:PRINT "2)   PROCESS PARTS REQUISITION"
2270 LOCATE 13,29:PRINT "3)   ON-LINE INVENTORY STATUS"
2280 LOCATE 15,29:PRINT "4)   PRINT AN INVENTORY REPORT"
2290 LOCATE 17,29:PRINT "5)   RETURN TO SYSTEM"
2300 RETURN
3000 '------------------------------------------------------------
3010 '                PROCESSING RECEIVED ITEMS CONTROLLER
3020 '------------------------------------------------------------
3030 LET MENU.HEADING$ = "PROCESSING ITEMS RECEIVED"
3040 WHILE SUB.MENU.SWITCH = TRUE
3050    GOSUB 3200       'display processing received items menu
3060    LET MAX = 3
3070    GOSUB 12900      'accept valid menu selection
3080    LET ADD.DELETE.SWITCH$ = " ADD TO "
```

```
3090     ON MENU.SELECTION GOSUB 7000, 8000, 12500
3100 WEND
3110 RETURN
3200 '------------------------------------------------------------
3210 '                DISPLAY PROCESSING RECEIVED ITEMS MENU
3220 '------------------------------------------------------------
3230 CLS
3240 LOCATE 5,29: PRINT "PROCESSING PARTS RECEIVED MENU"
3250 LOCATE 11,29:PRINT "1)   ADD TO EXISTING INVENTORY"
3260 LOCATE 13,29:PRINT "2)   ADD A NEW ITEM TO INVENTORY"
3270 LOCATE 15,29:PRINT "3)   RETURN TO MAIN MENU"
3280 RETURN
4000 '------------------------------------------------------------
4010 '                PROCESSING REQUESTED ITEMS CONTROLLER
4020 '------------------------------------------------------------
4030 LET MENU.HEADING$ = "PROCESSING REQUESTED ITEMS"
4040 WHILE SUB.MENU.SWITCH = TRUE
4050     GOSUB 4200        'display processing items requested
4060     LET ADD.DELETE.SWITCH$ = " DELETE FROM "
4070     GOSUB 7000        'processing existing inventory
4080     LOCATE 22,5
4090     PRINT "Press Y to return to MAIN MENU or any other key to continue
  processing"
4100     LET RETURN.TO.MAIN$ = INPUT$(1)
4110     IF RETURN.TO.MAIN$ = "Y" OR RETURN.TO.MAIN$ = "y" THEN GOSUB 12500
4120     LOCATE 22,1: PRINT CLEAR.LINE$
4130 WEND
4140 RETURN
4200 '------------------------------------------------------------
4210 '                DISPLAY PROCESSING ITEMS REQUESTED MENU
4220 '------------------------------------------------------------
4230 CLS
4240 LOCATE 5,29: PRINT "PROCESSING ITEMS REQUESTED "
4250 RETURN
5000 '------------------------------------------------------------
5010 '                ON-LINE INQUIRY CONTROLLER
5020 '------------------------------------------------------------
5030 LET MENU.HEADING$ = "ON-LINE INQUIRY"
5040 WHILE SUB.MENU.SWITCH = TRUE
5050     LET INQUIRY.SWITCH = TRUE
5060     GOSUB 5200        'display on-line inquiry
5070     GOSUB 7000        'on-line inquire processing
5080     LOCATE 22,5
5090     PRINT "Press Y to return to MAIN MENU; any other key to continue"
5100     LET RETURN.TO.MAIN$ = INPUT$(1)
5110     IF RETURN.TO.MAIN$ = "Y" OR RETURN.TO.MAIN$ = "y" THEN GOSUB 12500
5120     LOCATE 22,1 : PRINT CLEAR.LINE$
5130 WEND
5140 LET INQUIRY.SWITCH = FALSE
5150 RETURN
```

```
5200 '-----------------------------------------------------------
5210 '                 DISPLAY ON-LINE INQUIRY
5220 '-----------------------------------------------------------
5230 CLS
5240 LOCATE 5, 29 : PRINT "ON-LINE INQUIRY PROCESSING"
5250 RETURN
7000 '-----------------------------------------------------------
7010 '                 PROCESSING EXISTING INVENTORY
7020 '-----------------------------------------------------------
7030 CLS: LOCATE 5,29: PRINT MENU.HEADING$
7040 LOCATE 12,15
7050 PRINT "PLEASE ENTER THE ITEM NUMBER THEN <CR> ";
          CHR$(16);CHR$(16);" ";        ' CHR$(16) is an arrow
7060 GOSUB 12700                'get user response
7070 LOCATE 12,1: PRINT CLEAR.LINE$
7080 GOSUB 7200 ' VALIDATE ITEM NUMBER
7090 '              route to add/delete or inquiry processing
7100 IF INVALID.ENTRY.SWITCH = FALSE
        THEN IF INQUIRY.SWITCH = TRUE
             THEN GOSUB 7500 ELSE GOSUB 7600
7110 ' 7500 is On-Line Inquiry, 7600 is Add or Delete Items
7120 RETURN
7200 '-----------------------------------------------------------
7210 '                 VALIDATE ITEM NUMBER
7220 '-----------------------------------------------------------
7230 LET INVALID.ENTRY.SWITCH = FALSE
7240 IF ERROR.FLAG = TRUE
        THEN LET THE.ERROR = 1: GOSUB 13800
        ELSE GOSUB 7270
7250 RETURN
7260 '
7270 '   ---------- check if number is within range -----------
7280    LET PART.NUMBER = VAL(COMPLETE.NUMBER$)
7290    IF PART.NUMBER < LOWEST.PART.NUMBER OR
            PART.NUMBER > HIGHEST.PART.NUMBER -1
          THEN LET THE.ERROR = 2: GOSUB 13800
7300    RETURN
7500 '-----------------------------------------------------------
7510 '                 ON-LINE INQUIRY PROCESSING
7520 '-----------------------------------------------------------
7530 GOSUB 9000               'print left margin headings
7540 GET #1, PART.NUMBER
7550 GOSUB 9200               'print record information
7560 LET INQUIRY.SWITCH = FALSE
7570 RETURN
7600 '-----------------------------------------------------------
7610 '                 ADD/DELETE PROCESSING
7620 '-----------------------------------------------------------
7630 GOSUB 9000              'print left margin headings
7640 GET #1, PART.NUMBER
```

```
7650 GOSUB 9200              'print record information
7660 GOSUB 7800                'query user for add/delete quantity
7670 IF QUANTITY% <> 0 THEN GOSUB 7700
7680 RETURN
7690 '
7700   LET NEW.QUANTITY% = QUANTITY% + CVI(PART.QUANTITY$)
7710   LET THE.ERROR = 3 'prime for insufficient stock
7720   IF NEW.QUANTITY% > -1 THEN RSET PART.QUANTITY$ = MKI$(NEW.QUANTITY%):
                   LSET CRLF$ = CHR$(13) + CHR$(10): PUT #1,PART.NUMBER
            ELSE GOSUB 13800          'low inventory level
7730 RETURN
7800 '-----------------------------------------------------------
7810 '              QUERY USER FOR ADD/DELETE QUANTITY
7820 '-----------------------------------------------------------
7830 LOCATE 20,5
7840 PRINT "PLEASE ENTER THE QUANTITY THAT YOU WISH TO";
          ADD.DELETE.SWITCH$; "INVENTORY";
7850 COLOR 31: PRINT CHR$(26);CHR$(26);: COLOR 7  ' display blinking arrows
7860 GOSUB 12700                            ' get user response
7870 IF ERROR.FLAG = TRUE
          THEN LET THE.ERROR = 1: LET QUANTITY% = 0: GOSUB 13800
          ELSE GOSUB 7890
7880 RETURN
7890 ' -------------- change to numeric ------------------------
7900   LET QUANTITY% = VAL(COMPLETE.NUMBER$)
7910   IF ADD.DELETE.SWITCH$ = " DELETE FROM "
          THEN LET QUANTITY% = -1 * QUANTITY%       'if delete, make negative
7920   RETURN
8000 '-----------------------------------------------------------
8010 '              ADDITION OF NEW ITEM
8020 '-----------------------------------------------------------
8030 CLS: LOCATE 5,29: PRINT MENU.HEADING$
8040 GOSUB 9000             'print left margin
8050 GOSUB 9500             'accept new data
8060 RETURN
9000 '-----------------------------------------------------------
9010 '              PRINT LEFT MARGIN HEADING
9020 '-----------------------------------------------------------
9030 LOCATE 10,10 : PRINT "PART NUMBER:"
9040 LOCATE 12,10 : PRINT "DESCRIPTION:"
9050 LOCATE 14,10 : PRINT "QUANTITY:"
9060 RETURN
9200 '-----------------------------------------------------------
9210 '              PRINT RECORD INFORMATION
9220 '-----------------------------------------------------------
9230 LOCATE 10,22 : PRINT CVI(PART.NBR$)
9240 LOCATE 12,22 : PRINT PART.DESCRIPTION$
9250 LOCATE 14,19 : PRINT CVI(PART.QUANTITY$)
9260 RETURN
```

```
9500 '---------------------------------------------------------------
9510 '                   ACCEPT NEW DATA
9520 '---------------------------------------------------------------
9530 LOCATE 10,22: PRINT HIGHEST.PART.NUMBER
9540 LOCATE 12,22: LINE INPUT;"? ";DESCRIPTION$
9550 LOCATE 14,19: PRINT "? ";
9560 GOSUB 12700                  'get user's response
9570 LET QUANTITY$ = COMPLETE.NUMBER$
9580 IF ERROR.FLAG = TRUE
        THEN LET THE.ERROR = 1: GOSUB 13800
        ELSE GOSUB 10000
9590 RETURN
10000 '---------------------------------------------------------------
10010 '                   WRITE NEW RECORD
10020 '---------------------------------------------------------------
10030 '                   prepare fields to be written
10040 RSET PART.NBR$ = MKI$(INT(HIGHEST.PART.NUMBER))
10050 LSET PART.DESCRIPTION$ = DESCRIPTION$
10060 RSET PART.QUANTITY$ = MKI$(INT(VAL(QUANTITY$)))
10070 LSET CRLF$ = CHR$(13) + CHR$(10)        ' carriage return and line feed
10080 '             write record and update next available record pointer
10090 PUT #1, HIGHEST.PART.NUMBER
10100 GET #1, 1          'access the header record
10110 LET HIGHEST.PART.NUMBER = HIGHEST.PART.NUMBER + 1
10120 LSET PART.NBR$ = MKI$(INT(HIGHEST.PART.NUMBER))
10130 LSET CRLF$ = CHR$(13) + CHR$(10)
10140 PUT #1 ,1
10150 RETURN
11000 '---------------------------------------------------------------
11010 '                   PRINT REPORT
11020 '---------------------------------------------------------------
11030 CLS
11040 LOCATE 12
11050 PRINT "If you do NOT wish to print a report, please press N"
11060 PRINT "  To continue press any other key"
11070 LET RETURN.TO.MAIN$ = INPUT$(1)
11080 IF RETURN.TO.MAIN$ <> "N" AND RETURN.TO.MAIN$ <> "n" THEN GOSUB 11110
11090 RETURN
11100 '
11110     CLS
11120     LOCATE 12,29: PRINT "PLEASE MAKE SURE THAT YOUR PRINTER IS ON"
11130     LOCATE 13,29: PRINT "PRESS ANY KEY WHEN YOU ARE READY"
11140     LET DUMMY$ = INPUT$(1)
11150     CLS
11160     LOCATE 12,32: PRINT "PRINTING IN PROGRESS"
11170     LET LINE.COUNT = 99: LET PAGE.COUNT = 0 'Force a heading
11180     FOR I = LOWEST.PART.NUMBER TO HIGHEST.PART.NUMBER - 1
11190         GET #1,I
11200         LET LINE.COUNT = LINE.COUNT + 1
```

```
11210        IF LINE.COUNT => LINES.PER.PAGE THEN GOSUB 11500
11220        LPRINT USING DETAIL$; CVI(PART.NBR$), PART.DESCRIPTION$,
                              CVI(PART.QUANTITY$)
11230   NEXT I
11240   CLS
11250   LPRINT PAGE.ADVANCE$
11260   RETURN
11500 '-------------------------------------------------------------
11510 '                  PRINT HEADINGS
11520 '-------------------------------------------------------------
11530 LPRINT PAGE.ADVANCE$
11540 LET PAGE.COUNT = PAGE.COUNT + 1
11550 LPRINT
11560 LPRINT
11570 LPRINT
11580 LPRINT HEADING1$; PAGE.COUNT
11590 LPRINT HEADING2$; DATE$
11600 LET LINE.COUNT = 0   'reinitialize line count
11610 FOR J = 1 TO 5
11620     LPRINT
11630 NEXT J
11640 LPRINT HEADING3$
11650 LPRINT HEADING4$
11660 RETURN
12000 '-------------------------------------------------------------
12010 '                  PROGRAM EXIT MESSAGE
12020 '-------------------------------------------------------------
12030 CLS
12040 LOCATE 12,25: PRINT "If you really want to terminate this"
12050 LOCATE 13,30: PRINT "processing, type  Y ."
12060 LOCATE 15,25: PRINT "Press any other key to continue processing."
12070 IF INSTR("Yy",INPUT$(1))
         THEN LET CONTINUE.SWITCH = FALSE: LSET PART.NBR$ = CHR$(26):
              PUT #1, HIGHEST.PART.NUMBER: CLOSE #1
12080 CLS
12090 RETURN
12500 '-------------------------------------------------------------
12510 '                  SUBMENU EXIT
12520 '-------------------------------------------------------------
12530 LET SUB.MENU.SWITCH = FALSE
12540 RETURN
12700 '-------------------------------------------------------------
12710 '                  GET USER'S RESPONSE
12720 '-------------------------------------------------------------
12730 LET ERROR.FLAG = FALSE
12740 LET EACH.CHARACTER$ = ""         ' set to null
12750 LET COMPLETE.NUMBER$ = ""
12760 WHILE EACH.CHARACTER$ <> CHR$(13)        ' CHR$(13) is ENTER
12770     GOSUB 13400        'character input validation
```

```
12780     IF EACH.CHARACTER$ <> CHR$(13) AND EACH.CHARACTER$ <> CHR$(8)
              THEN PRINT EACH.CHARACTER$;:
                 LET COMPLETE.NUMBER$ = COMPLETE.NUMBER$ + EACH.CHARACTER$
12790 ' ------------ CHR$(8) is backspace -----------
12800     IF EACH.CHARACTER$ = CHR$(8) THEN GOSUB 13100 ' erase character
12810 WEND
12820 RETURN
12900 '----------------------------------------------------------------
12910 '                 ACCEPT VALID MENU SELECTION
12920 '----------------------------------------------------------------
12930 LET MENU.SELECTION = 0
12940 WHILE MENU.SELECTION = 0
12950    LOCATE 20,29:PRINT "PLEASE ENTER YOUR SELECTION";
12960    COLOR 31:PRINT CHR$(26);CHR$(26);:COLOR 7
12970    LET MENU.SELECTION$ = INPUT$(1) ' input user's response
12980    PRINT MENU.SELECTION$;
12990    IF VAL(MENU.SELECTION$) > 0 AND VAL(MENU.SELECTION$) < MAX + 1
             THEN MENU.SELECTION = VAL(MENU.SELECTION$)
             ELSE GOSUB 13600      'menu error
13000 WEND
13010 LOCATE 24,1: PRINT SPACE$(79);
13020 RETURN
13100 '----------------------------------------------------------------
13110 '                     ERASE CHARACTER
13120 '----------------------------------------------------------------
13130 LET COLUMN = POS(0)
13140 LET THE.LINE = CSRLIN
13150 LOCATE THE.LINE,COLUMN - 1
13160 PRINT " ";                  'print blank over character
13170 LOCATE THE.LINE,COLUMN - 1
13180 LET SHORT.STRING$ = SPACE$(LEN(COMPLETE.NUMBER$) - 1)
13190 LSET SHORT.STRING$ = COMPLETE.NUMBER$
13200 SWAP SHORT.STRING$, COMPLETE.NUMBER$
13210 RETURN
13400 '----------------------------------------------------------------
13410 '                 CHARACTER INPUT VALIDATION
13420 '----------------------------------------------------------------
13430 LET EACH.CHARACTER$ = INPUT$(1)
13440 LET ANY.ERROR = INSTR(VALID.CHARACTER$,EACH.CHARACTER$)
13450 IF ANY.ERROR = 0 THEN LET ERROR.FLAG = TRUE
13460 RETURN
13600 '----------------------------------------------------------------
13610 '                     MENU ERROR
13620 '----------------------------------------------------------------
13630 LOCATE 24,1:  PRINT SPACE$(79);
13640 LOCATE 24,29: PRINT "PLEASE ENTER A VALID SELECTION ( 1 - ";
                     MAX; ")"; CHR$(7);
13650 LOCATE 20,57: PRINT SPACE$(2)
```

```
13660 RETURN
13800 '-------------------------------------------------------------
13810 '                    SUBROUTINE ERRORS
13820 '-------------------------------------------------------------
13830 CLS
13840 LOCATE 5,29: PRINT MENU.HEADING$
13850 LOCATE 12,29
13860 IF THE.ERROR = 1 THEN PRINT "YOU ENTERED A NONNUMERIC CHARACTER"
        ELSE IF THE.ERROR = 2 THEN PRINT "THE ITEM NUMBER DOES NOT EXIST";
            ELSE PRINT "THERE IS INSUFFICIENT INVENTORY";
13870 LOCATE 15,29: PRINT "PRESS ANY KEY TO CONTINUE"; CHR$(7);
13880 LET DUMMY$ = INPUT$(1)
13890 LET INVALID.ENTRY.SWITCH = TRUE
13900 RETURN
13910 '======================= END OF LISTING =========================
```

Sample Output

After completing the preliminary testing, as he wrote the program, Dave ran it again trying all of the options. Figures 13.11 through 13.13 show some of the results.

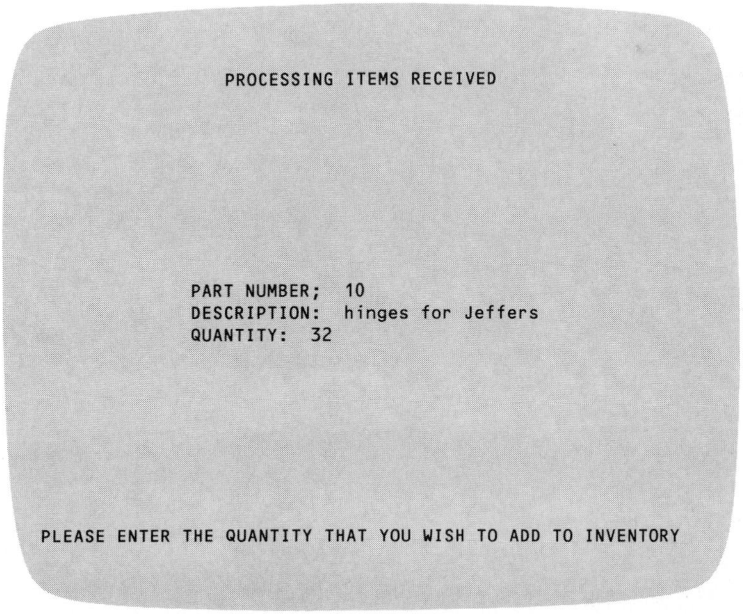

```
              PROCESSING ITEMS RECEIVED




          PART NUMBER;  10
          DESCRIPTION:  hinges for Jeffers
          QUANTITY:  32



   PLEASE ENTER THE QUANTITY THAT YOU WISH TO ADD TO INVENTORY
```

FIGURE 13.11 ·
Add to existing
inventory

```
                        ON-LINE INQUIRY




          PART NUMBER:  10
          DESCRIPTION:  hinges for Jeffers
          QUANTITY:  32




Press Y to return to MAIN key to continue. MENU; any other
```

FIGURE 13.12 ▪
On-line inquiry

```
                    INVENTORY REPORT                    Page 1
                    AS OF 05-11-1988



   PART NUMBER                    DESCRIPTION                    QUANTITY
   ===========        =================================        ========
        2             wing nuts                                     2032
        3             widget fasteners                              9483
        4             bracket, 3"                                   4543
        5             bolts, 3"                                      456
        6             bolts, 2"                                      546
        7             paint brushes                                  54
        8             Jeffers, #3                                   4567
        9             hinges, #4                                    715
       10             hinges for Jeffers                             32
       11             handles                                        43
       12             hangers                                       432
       13             wire links                                    867
       14             plastic coatings                               64
       15             floppy wirettes                               653
       16             wirettes, regular                             843
```

FIGURE 13.13 ▪
*The PRINT
REPORT option
gives this report*

```
                        INVENTORY REPORT                          Page 2
                        AS OF 05-11-1988


PART NUMBER                       DESCRIPTION                    QUANTITY
===========          =================================          ========
     17              wirettes, fancy                                 827
     18              switches, 110                                   823
     19              switches, 220                                   837
     20              nuts, wingless                                 4023
     21              holders #3                                      643
     22              holders, other                                  463
```

FIGURE 13.13
continued

▪QUICK REFERENCE FOR LESSON 13▪

Random Access Files

Random Access files allow direct access to a particular record in a file. Random Access files must consist of fixed-length records—that is, all records must be the same length.

OPEN

OPEN "FILENAME.DAT" AS #1 opens the file for both input and output. Unless specified, the record length is set to 128.

OPEN "FILENAME.DAT" AS #1 LEN = x, where x is 1 to 128. It sets the record length to x characters. If the length is to be greater than 128, BASIC must be invoked using the /S switch as follows:

> BASIC /S:x for standard BASIC
> BASICA /S:x for Advanced BASIC

where x is the greatest length of any record to be used.

GET

GET transfers a record from a file to the file's buffer in memory.

> GET #n, m is a statement that transfers the mth record of file number n into the buffer for file number n.
> GET #n is a statement that transfers the next record of file number n into its buffer.

PUT

This is a statement that transfers a record from the buffer to the file.

> PUT #n, m is a statement that places the contents of the buffer for file number n into the mth record of that file.
> PUT #n is a statement that places the contents of the buffer for file number n into the next record of that file.

FIELD Describes the Layout of the File's Buffer

FIELD #*n*, *w* AS A$, . . .

> *n* is the number assigned to the file.
> *w* is the width of the field.
> A$ is the name assigned to the variable.
> > A$ is called a fielded variable.

Every character in the buffer must be assigned to a fielded variable.

LSET and RSET Are Used to Move String Data Into Fields

MKI$, MKS$, and MKD$

These functions encode numeric data into strings in binary format.
> MKI$ returns an integer as a two-byte string.

> LET A$ = MKI$(some integer)

MKS$ returns a single-precision number as a four-byte string.

> LET B$ = MKS$(some single-precision number)

MKD$ returns a double-precision number as an eight-byte string.

> LET C$ = MKD$(some double-precision number)

CVI, CVS, and CVD

These are functions that decode binary formatted strings into numbers. These functions are used to convert back to numeric format numeric variables that were saved on files in binary format after using the MK functions.

> LET X% = CVI(A$) returns the integer that was encoded with MKI$.
> LET Y = CVS(B$) returns the single-precision number that was encoded with MKS$.
> LET Z# = CVD(C$) returns the double-precision number that was encoded with MKD$.

• EXERCISES •

Short Answer

1. A sequential file is to a DATA statement as a Random Access file is to an array. Explain why this is true.

2. Can a Random Access file have variable-length records? Also, can a Random Access file have variable-length fields?

3. Rewrite the following statement so it is correct: "A Random Access file is unique, for one can read from the file as well as write to the file; however, it must be closed and reopened (FOR APPEND) to append information."

4. Assume that you have a record that has three fields. The first has integer data, the second character data (up to 30 characters), and the third possesses double-precision data. Write the FIELD statement to accommodate these fields.

5. If you want to read the first record in a Random Access file, what statement can you use? If you have just accessed the 21st record and you want to write this information as the third record, what syntax is necessary?

6. If you wished to store a numeric value as a character string in a Random Access file, what function would you use to convert the number to a string, and what function would you use to convert the string to a numeric value?

7. Generally, when Random Access files are used, numeric values are stored in the most efficient manner possible—they are encoded into binary format. What functions encode, what functions decode, and why is this particularly important with respect to building Random Access files?

Analyzing Code

8. What, if anything, is wrong with this code?

```
10    OPEN "PAYROLL.DAT" AS #1 LEN = 22
20    FIELD #1, 22 AS EMP.ADDRESS$
30    INPUT #1, EMP.ADDRESS$
40    PRINT EMP.ADDRESS$
50    INPUT NEW.ADDRESS$
60    LSET EMP.ADDRESS$ = NEW.ADDRESS$
70    WRITE #1 EMP.ADDRESS$
80    CLOSE #1 : END
```

9. After this line is executed

```
10    OPEN "INV.DAT" AS #1 LEN = 254
```

the following error message is displayed.

```
Illegal function call in 10
```

What do you think caused it?

10. Will the following work, or will it cause an error to occur? Correct it if necessary.

```
10    FIELD #1, 9 AS SSN$, 5 AS GROSS.PAY
20    OPEN "EMP.DAT" AS #1 LEN = 14
```

11. What will happen if the following is executed?

```
10 OPEN "EXAMPLE.DAT" AS #1 LEN = 20
20 FIELD #1, 20 AS SAMPLE.DATA$
30 GET #1, 20
40 PRINT SAMPLE.DATA$
50 FOR I = 1 TO 19
60    GET #1 : PRINT SAMPLE.DATA$
65    PRINT SAMPLE.DATA$
70    GET #1,I:PRINT SAMPLE.DATA$
80    PUT #1,I + 19
90 NEXT I
100 END
```

Programming

12. Write a program that will create a data file for an inventory system.

The fields of each record are part number, quantity on hand, description, and quantity on order.

Create at least 10 items with the item numbers ranging from 1 to 10.

Once you have created the inventory file, allow the user an opportunity to modify any field of any record. Prompt the user to enter the part number, which is the Random Access address of that item. Therefore, don't allow the user to modify the part number field. Anytime the user hits a carriage return in response to field modification, leave that field unchanged. When the user has had an opportunity to modify all of the fields, display the modified record to the user. If the user wishes to continue modifying that record, allow him or her to do so. If no more modifications are to be made, write the modifications to the file and prompt the user to either modify another record or exit the program.

The error message and screen display are up to you; however, you must make this a user-friendly program that will validate the incoming changes and display error messages when necessary.

13. Modify the program in Exercise 12 so that the Random Access file will have the necessary components to be read as a sequential file. At the end of the program, print out an updated inventory report by processing the file sequentially. (Hint: close the file, then reopen it for INPUT.)

14. Using the inventory file created in Exercise 12, write a program that allows users to remove items from inventory or to process receipt of shipments. Access to these options will be restricted by passwords. The password XPT45 must be entered in order to take items, and the password AJK87 must be entered to process shipments.
The following must be done while taking items from inventory:

If the quantity on hand is equal to or greater than the quantity requested, reduce the quantity on hand by the quantity requested.

If the quantity on hand is less than the quantity requested, display the number on hand and ask if the user will accept that number.

If the quantity on hand is zero, display a message that this part is currently out of stock.

If the remaining quantity is less than 7, place an order for that item. Do this by displaying to the user the quantities that are currently on order (stored in quantity on order field) and asking if more are to be ordered. If the response is positive, ask for the quantity to be ordered and add this to the quantity already on order. Also, place the part number and the current quantity ordered in an array. At the end of processing, sort this array into part number sequence and print (or display) a listing of the part number, the quantity ordered, and the description. You may assume that there will be a maximum of 25 orders.

The processing of shipments includes the following:

Add the quantity received to the quantity on hand and reduce the quantity on order by the same amount.

Inventory levels that exceed 65 should be brought to management's attention. Create an array containing the part number of any item with quantity on hand over 65. At the end of processing shipments, sort this array by part number and print (or display) a list of the part number, description, and quantity on hand. You may assume a maximum of 25 parts with this condition.

BUSINESS GRAPHICS

A PICTURE IS BETTER THAN A THOUSAND WORDS

The computer department where Micky worked as a programmer needed a new computer to keep up with company growth. Recently, many managers had learned how to use the PCs management had provided. The more they learned, the more analyses they demanded from the mainframe. Soon the demands on the mainframe were outstripping its capacity. Micky's supervisor asked him to develop a cost justification for the proposed new computer and show the proposal to management.

After several weeks of research Micky took his data to a management meeting. To his surprise management reacted coolly. Although the need seemed obvious to Micky, and though he felt his case was strong, they brushed him aside with "we'll get back to you."

"I thought that I did a good job," Micky explained to his friend Judy. "I had all the figures well laid out, showing increased demand, growth by regions, and anticipated future demands."

Judy asked, "Do you have a copy of your sales presentation?"

"Sales? I didn't make a sales presentation. I used reason," Micky said, taking out a thick tome of figures.

Judy flipped through the pages. "These are just numbers. Where are the graphics?"

Micky looked bewildered. "What do you mean? You have all the justification anyone could need for a new computer. How much thicker do you want it to be?"

"Not thicker, understandable", Judy advised. "Do you actually expect anyone to read this and understand the gist of it? Business people are busy, and they want to know the big picture first: the trends and roughly what is going on. If it interests them, they'll look at the numbers. But if it doesn't interest them, they want to quickly move on to something else."

"So what should I do?"

"Some reading." Judy suggested. "Take a look at the graphics chapter in *The ABCs of BASIC on the IBM PC* to see how BASIC can help you put your figures into graphic form."

·*THE ABCS OF BASIC ON THE IBM PERSONAL COMPUTER*·

LESSON 14: GRAPHICS AS A TOOL FOR BUSINESS

Overview

This chapter deals with when and how to use business graphics. Business graphics covered in this chapter include pie charts, line graphs, bar charts, and scatter plots. New BASIC features introduced here include SCREEN, WIDTH, WINDOW, CIRCLE, PAINT, VIEW, LINE, and DRAW. We will cover just the aspects that are needed to create these tools. There is much more that can be done with BASIC graphics, but that is a whole text in itself.

These graphics statements are available for use only on PCs that have the color graphics card installed; they are not available in monochrome PCs. Some PCs with color graphics cards installed have monochrome (composite) displays. They *are* able to use these statements.

These graphic statements also require using BASICA, (the advanced BASIC) version 2.0 or later.

What Are Business Graphics?

Figure 14.1a shows some examples of business graphics; Figure 14.1b shows other "graphics" used in business that are not what we will call business graphics. This difference is worth noting at the start.

Business graphics show *amounts* and/or *trends*. The power of business graphics is that they provide an overview of the data represented so as to show trends and comparisons by deferring details to later.

Earlier, when looking at how to design a program, we saw the necessity of looking at the "big picture" first and deferring details. This important concept is repeated here. Humans have a limited capacity to absorb information; business

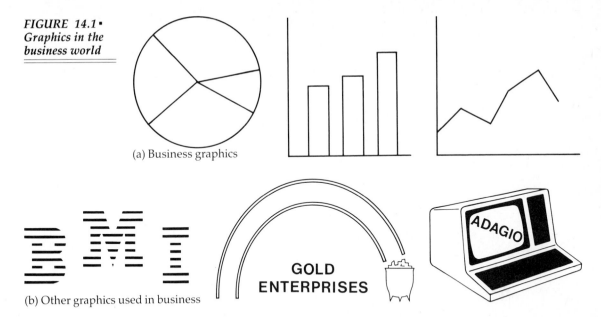

FIGURE 14.1 •
Graphics in the
business world

(a) Business graphics

(b) Other graphics used in business

GOLD
ENTERPRISES

graphics make sure that the most important aspects of the data are presented unobstructed by details.

A second reason why business graphics are important is that they, as pictures, appeal to the intuitive side of the brain. Some researchers believe that one side of the brain understands numbers while the other understands graphics. Using both helps business people to use all of their mental resources.

Why Use Business Graphics?

There are three reasons to use business graphics. The first one we just mentioned: business graphics open up thinking, rather than burying the reader in a sea of details.

A second reason is that business graphics are concise—a picture is worth a thousand words.

The third reason for using business graphics is that they are effective at making one's point. The Wharton School studies have shown that a presentation with graphics is much more effective at convincing than the same presentation without graphics.

How to Use

Good business graphics have two or three components:

1. the graph itself,
2. a caption telling in a few words what the graph shows, and possibly,
3. a table showing the data on which the graph was constructed.

Figure 14.2 shows an example of a business graphic.

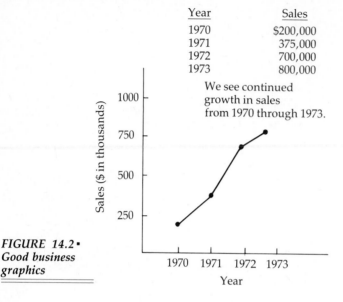

Year	Sales
1970	$200,000
1971	375,000
1972	700,000
1973	800,000

We see continued growth in sales from 1970 through 1973.

FIGURE 14.2 ▪
Good business graphics

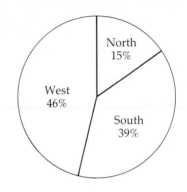

Most sales are from the western region and, secondarily, the southern region.

Volume of sales by region

FIGURE 14.3 ▪
Pie chart

Commonly Used Graphics Tools

A variety of graphs and charts are commonly used in business. These include the pie chart, the bar chart, the line graph, and the scatter plot. Each graph is used for a different purpose. In this section we will describe each of these graphs and give guidelines for when each is appropriate.

Pie Chart (Circle Graph)
A **pie chart** is best used to describe proportion data (which total to 100 percent). For example, regional sales data can be represented in a pie chart, as seen in Figure 14.3.

To avoid having very thin "slices" of the pie, it is common to lump together categories containing less than 5 percent or so into an "other" or miscellaneous category. See Figure 14.4 for an example.

Attention can be drawn to an important category or "slice" of the pie chart by moving it out from the center. This is called an **exploded pie chart.** An example is shown in Figure 14.5.

Bar Chart
One of the requirements for using the pie chart is that the data represent proportions or parts of a whole. Most business data do not sum to 100 percent. For instance, in the preceding example, we may wish to graphically compare sales in the western region to sales in the southern region. A pie chart would not be appropriate since the sales from the two regions do not total to total sales. For this situation a **bar chart** graphically shows the data quite nicely (see Figure 14.6).

In this bar chart the *y* axis (the line going up and down) represents the amount, in dollars. The categories "sit" on the *x* axis (the horizontal line). The height of the bar or box of each category represents the amount of sales.

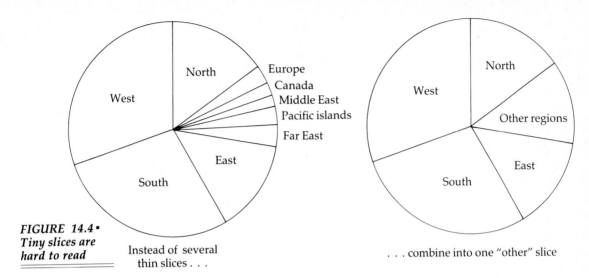

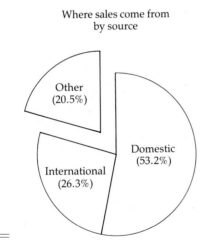

FIGURE 14.4 •
Tiny slices are
hard to read

Instead of several
thin slices . . .

. . . combine into one "other" slice

FIGURE 14.5 •
Exploded pie
chart

Line Graph

In the preceding example western sales and southern sales are two different categories. We can place either one first with equal logic. Where they are placed on the *x* axis does not matter.

Other times we have to graph business data that have a natural ordering. For example, we may wish to plot proceeds from different years. It makes sense to show 1980, then 1981, then 1982 in that order. A bar chart with ordered categories could be used, but a **line graph** is really recommended for this situation.

Figure 14.7 shows an example of a line graph for southern sales for the years 1980 to 1984. As you see, the line graph is like the bar chart in that both have an *x*

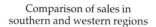

Comparison of sales in
southern and western regions

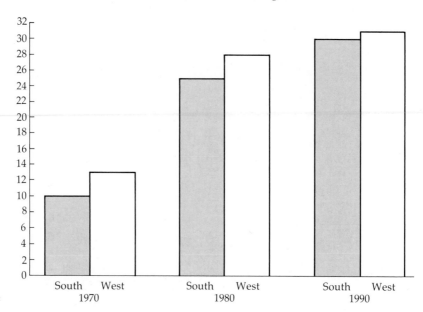

FIGURE 14.6 ·
Bar graph

and *y* axis and both have gradations or tick marks on the *y* axis. However, they differ in two ways.

The line graph also has tick marks on the *x* axis; where the category is placed on the *x* axis is important. The category or bar size in a line graph has been reduced to a point.

The second difference is that in a line graph you do not draw a box to show the category amount; you draw just a point and then connect the dots between neighboring categories with lines.

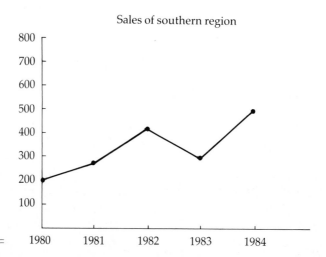

Sales of southern region

FIGURE 14.7 ·
Line graph

Data Year	Southern Sales	Western Sales
1980	200	300
1981	250	500
1982	400	600
1983	300	500
1984	500	700

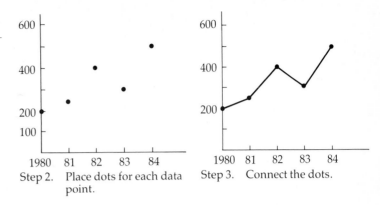

Step 1. Draw x and y axis and define coordinates. Example: x axis will represent year, and y axis will represent sales dollars.

Step 2. Place dots for each data point.

Step 3. Connect the dots.

FIGURE 14.8 •
Steps for creating a line graph

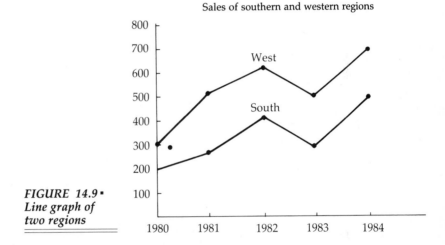

FIGURE 14.9 •
Line graph of two regions

Figure 14.8 shows how to create a line graph.

It is possible to show two or more line graphs in the same figure. Figure 14.9 shows an example of this.

Scatter Plot

To use line graphs, we assumed that all the points we were plotting were for the same business. The line connecting the 1981 and 1982 points showed growth or decline in southern region sales for that one business whose data we plotted.

Some business data are of a different sort. For example, we may wish to use the data on two variables, such as total sales and DP budget, from a large number of businesses in order to discern a possible relationship within the data (see Figure 14.10).

This figure contains a large number of data points; each point represents the total sales (as measured on the y axis) and DP budget (as measured on the x axis). Visual inspection of the data points (called "eye balling") can give the viewer impressions of the relationship between the two variables. For example, this graph indicates that businesses with high sales also have high DP budgets.

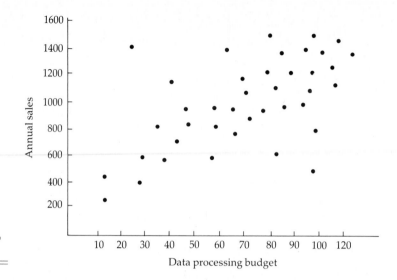

FIGURE 14.10 •
Scatter plot

Although a relationship may exist between the two variables, you cannot automatically assume that one caused the other. The DP manager may wish to use these data to assert that increasing the DP budget will increase sales. It may also be that having a large number of sales caused a need for more computers. Or it could be that a third variable, such as size of business, caused both amount of sales and size of DP budget.

Table 14.1 summarizes the types of business graphics and their uses.

Creating Graphs in BASIC

BASIC provides features that let us create graphs on the screen. The special statements that enable us to create business graphics include SCREEN, WINDOW, VIEW, LINE, CIRCLE, PAINT, and DRAW.

SCREEN Modes and the SCREEN Statement

In all of the previous chapters we have been working in the **text mode,** which is the default or "normal" mode for the screen. This mode allows us to enter and run all of the programs that have been discussed so far and on a color system allows the full use of all the colors; however, it does not allow the use of graphics. The text mode can be set with the statement:

```
1010 SCREEN 0
```

Since this is the default setting, we do not need to use this statement unless one of the graphics modes has been set and we wish to return to text mode.

We have also been working with 80 columns across the screen. In text mode on a color system this can be changed to 40 columns by the statement:

TABLE 14.1 ▪ Each Type of Chart Has a Different Use

TYPE OF CHART	USE
Pie	Shows how 100 percent is divided.
Bar	Compares two or more amounts.
Line	Shows trends.
Scatter	Shows relationship between two variables.

```
1020 WIDTH 40
```

With WIDTH 40 the characters are "fatter," taking twice as much horizontal space on the screen. WIDTH 80 will restore the display to 80 columns.

Execution of either the SCREEN statement or the WIDTH statement that changes the current setting also clears the screen.

Before using the graphics statements described in this section, the user must enter one of the following SCREEN statements to set a graphics mode:

SCREEN 1   Medium-resolution graphics
SCREEN 2   High-resolution graphics

When one of the graphics modes is set, text may also be displayed. When in medium resolution, text will print in the 40 character per row ("fat") format;

▪THE SCREEN STATEMENT▪

SCREEN 0: Text Mode
WIDTH 40 sets 40 columns
WIDTH 80 sets 80 columns
SCREEN 0,0 — color disabled
SCREEN 0,1 — color enabled
No graphics

SCREEN 1: Medium-Resolution Graphics
Text printed 40 characters per row
Limited use of colors
SCREEN 1,0 — color enabled
SCREEN 1,1 — color disabled

SCREEN 2: High-Resolution Graphics
Text printed 80 characters per row
Black and white only

when in high resolution, text will display in the normal 80 characters per row. Executing the statement WIDTH 80 when in medium resolution forces the screen into high resolution. Likewise, executing WIDTH 40 when in high resolution forces the screen into medium resolution.

A second parameter, called **color burst,** may be used with the SCREEN statement. Depending upon the type of monitor you are using, this parameter enables or disables full use of color. On an RGB monitor color burst is always on; however, on a composite monitor, color burst may be turned on or off. In text mode a value of 0 as the second parameter in the SCREEN statement (SCREEN 0,0) disables color and a value of 1 enables it. In graphics mode this is reversed: a value of 0 (SCREEN 1,0) enables color, while a value of 1 disables color.

Color With Medium-Resolution Graphics

Color graphics are allowed in medium-resolution (SCREEN 1) graphics mode only. High-resolution graphics mode (SCREEN 2) displays in black and white only, and execution of the COLOR statement in high-resolution graphics will produce an error message.

The use of color in graphics mode differs from text mode. In text mode you may select from 16 foreground colors and 8 background colors; in graphics you may select a background from one of the 16 colors, but you are limited in your selection of foreground or "drawing" colors. There are two sets of foreground colors called **palettes.** Each of the palettes has three colors, and each of these colors is assigned a number or **color attribute.**

COLOR ATTRIBUTE	PALETTE 0	PALETTE 1
1	Green	Cyan
2	Red	Magenta
3	Brown	White

In text mode the syntax for the COLOR statement is COLOR foreground, background, border. To use the COLOR statement in graphics mode you first give the background color (0 through 15) and the palette (0 or 1), which is to be used for foreground colors:

```
COLOR background, palette
```

This defines the set of colors that may be used by the graphics statements that follow.

Several of the graphics statements, such as CIRCLE, allow you to indicate a color attribute (0 through 3) for the color in which the figure will be drawn. Attribute 0 always refers to the background. Depending on the palette selected, color attributes 1, 2, and 3 will refer to green, red, and brown (palette 0) or cyan, magenta, and white (palette 1). If you do not specify a color attribute, the figure will display in attribute 3 (brown or white), which is considered the default foreground color. Any text on the screen will also appear in attribute 3.

For example:

```
20 SCREEN 1,0
30 COLOR  9,0
```

will display a light blue background and select palette 0 (green, red, and brown). If you create a circle with color attribute 2, you will have a red circle on a light blue background. On the other hand, if you use:

```
30 COLOR  9,1
```

(selecting palette #1), the circle drawn with attribute 2 will now be magenta on the light blue background.

Since you may use attributes 0 through 3, you may have at most four colors on the screen at one time.

Screen Coordinates and the Window Statement

In graphics mode the screen is divided into small graphic rectangles, called **pixels.** A pixel can either be lit or unlit. When BASIC displays anything, it does so by illuminating the appropriate pixels.

In medium-resolution graphics mode (SCREEN 1), there are 200 vertical locations (labeled 0–199) by 320 horizontal ones (labeled 0–319). In high-resolution graphics mode (SCREEN 2), there are 200 by 640 pixels. The (0,0) location is at the upper left corner. Any pixel can be identified by giving its horizontal (x axis) position and its vertical (y axis) position. These are called the **physical coordinates.** As you can see in Figure 14.11a, this coordinate system is backward from the usual system in which the y axis increases in value as you move up.

The WINDOW statement allows us to do two things:

1. change the y axis to increase in value as you move up the screen, making it like the usual coordinate system,
2. define the range of values for the coordinates

For example, suppose we have a graph on which we wish to display the values of x, which vary from −10 to 150, and the values of y, which vary from −10 to 50 (see Figure 14.11b). On this graph the lower left-hand point has the value (−10,−10) and the upper right-hand point has the value (150,50). To set the coordinates of the screen for this graph we issue the statement:

```
1150 WINDOW (-10,-10) - (150,50)
```

This WINDOW statement has reset the coordinates so that now the lower left-hand corner of the screen has the coordinates (−10,−10) and the upper right-hand corner has the coordinates (150,50). We now have 160 (−10 to 150) horizontal points and 60 (−10 to 50) vertical points. Any pair of (x,y) coordinates within this range will identify a specific point on the graph. The coordinates set by a WINDOW statement are referred to as the **world coordinates.** Once the WINDOW statement has been executed, the graphic statements CIRCLE and LINE (which we will discuss in a moment) that follow in the program will use these coordinates.

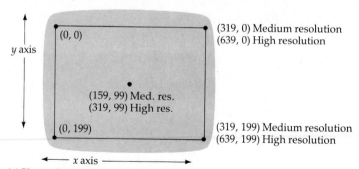

(a) Physical coordinates of point in center are
(159, 99) in medium resolution
(319, 99) in high resolution

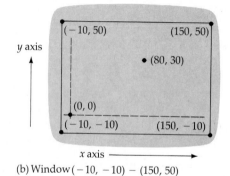

FIGURE 14.11 ·
WINDOW sets
the world
coordinates

(b) Window (− 10, − 10) − (150, 50)

More than one WINDOW statement can appear in a program. Each time WINDOW is executed, the world coordinates are redefined. This allows graphics with differing coordinates to appear on the same screen.

WINDOW by itself, with no coordinates specified, returns the system to the standard physical coordinate setting.

The CIRCLE Statement

A pie chart is a circle divided into slices. BASIC's statement CIRCLE will draw a circle, an arc (a curved line), or a sector (arc with two straight lines to the center like a "pie slice"). To use CIRCLE we state the coordinates of the center of the circle and its radius. For this example we will first issue a WINDOW statement to define the world coordinates, then define a circle with its center at position (0,0) and a radius of 30 (see Figure 14.12).

```
 70  WINDOW (-50,-50) - (50,50)
110 CIRCLE (0,0), 30
```

Since we did not specify a color attribute, the circle will be displayed in either brown or white, depending on whether we have selected palette 0 or 1. If we wish to indicate a different color, we place the attribute after the radius. To display the circle with color attribute 2, we write the statement as:

```
110 CIRCLE (0,0), 30, 2
```

For pie charts we want to be able to draw sectors, not just whole circles. Before we can do this, we must review the use of radians.

As you remember from the earlier discussion of trigonometric functions (see Chapter 10), IBM PC BASIC measures angles in radians instead of degrees. A full circle is composed of 360 degrees, which equals 2 pi radians, or about 6.28 radians. To convert from degrees to radians use the formula: Radians = Degrees * 3.1416/180. A 45-degree angle is approximately .79 radians (see Figure 14.13).

To specify an arc or sector, you must give the beginning point and ending point as measured in radians in a counter-clockwise direction from the x axis. These are the fourth and fifth parameters in the CIRCLE statement. If we do not wish to indicate the color we may omit it, but we must place a comma in the statement to indicate its omission. The statement that defines an arc from 45 degrees to 90 degrees is:

```
5000 CIRCLE (0,0), 30, , .79, 1.57
```

More frequently, you will want to display a sector (pie slice) rather than an arc. To tell BASIC to draw a sector, you use the same syntax as for an arc except that the beginning and ending radians are preceded by a minus sign. The minus signs are signals to draw a straight line to the circle's center (see Figure 14.14). The preceding statement can be changed to display a sector by writing it as follows:

```
5000 CIRCLE (0,0), 30, , -.79, -1.57
```

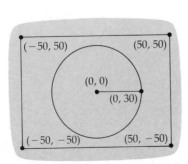

FIGURE 14.12 •
The CIRCLE statements create a circle

Window (−50, −50) − (50, 50)
Circle (0, 0), 30

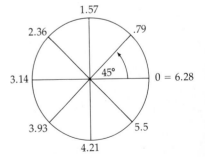

FIGURE 14.13 •
A circle is composed of 360° or 6.28 radians

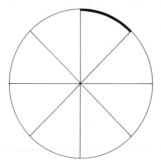

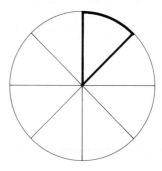

*FIGURE 14.14 ▪
CIRCLE can also
create arcs and
sectors*

Circle (0, 0), 30 , , .79, 1.57
displays an arc

Circle (0,0), 30 , , − .79, − 1.57
displays a sector

PAINT

Often we wish to fill in a sector or other area with some color, pattern, or texture.
The PAINT statement allows us to do this. To use it we must first specify the (x,y)
coordinate of some point *within* the area we wish PAINTed. This point must not
be a pixel touching the border of the area.

▪SYNTAX OF THE CIRCLE STATEMENT▪

CIRCLE (X,Y), R, C, R_1, R_2
(X,Y) are the coordinates of the center.
   R is the radius.
    C specifies color attribute (optional).
       0 through 3 in medium resolution.
       0 or 1 in high resolution.
    R_1 is the starting radian.   ⎫
    R_2 is the ending radian.   ⎬   optional
      If positive, specify start and end of arc.
      If negative, specify start and end of sector.

EXAMPLES:
CIRCLE (0,0), 10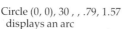
CIRCLE (0,0), 10, , 0, 1
CIRCLE (0,0), 10, , 1, 0
CIRCLE (0,0), 10, , −1, −0

•SYNTAX OF THE PAINT STATEMENT•

PAINT (X,Y), N or A$
(X,Y) must be some point wholly *within* the area to be painted.
N is the numeric expression that specifies the color attribute.
 0 through 3 in medium resolution.
 0 or 1 in high resolution.
 The area will be filled with color specified by the attribute.
A$ is a string expression. The area will be filled with a textured pattern.

The second parameter may be a number 0 through 3 to indicate the color attribute or a string value or variable that specifies the pattern or **tiling.** Rather than go into all of the technical aspects of tiling, for our purposes we can experiment with different strings and observe the results that are produced.

PAINT will fill the entire bounded area with color or texture. If the area PAINTed is not completely bounded by a solid line, the color or pattern will spill over, filling the whole screen.

Pie Chart

Now we are ready to write a program that will draw a pie chart and paint the sectors. This program will do the following:

1. Ask the user to enter a series of values.
2. Total these values. This total equals the value of the whole circle.
3. Display and texture sectors to represent the values entered.

To calculate the portion of the circle that a particular sector should take, we divide the value entered for this sector by the total of all the values. We multiply this by 6.28 to get the size (number of radians) of this sector. To display the sectors, we must find the starting and ending radians for each. We will let the variable START hold the value for the starting radian and DONE hold the value for the ending radian. For each sector, DONE will equal START plus the value we just calculated as the sector size. For the next sector, the value of DONE from the previous sector is moved to START, and a new value for DONE is calculated.

We must next find some point within each sector to be used in the PAINT statement. We first calculate MIDL, which is the value (in radians) halfway between START and DONE. COS(MIDL) will give us the *x* coordinate of a point on a line inside the sector, and SIN(MIDL) will give us the *y* coordinate. Because we want to make sure the coordinates are far enough from the center that it does not touch any of the border of the sector, we multiply the coordinates by 5. This will give us another point on the midline inside the sector, away from the border pixels.

Because we want to be able to calculate various values for the tiling variable, we have used the function CHR$. Any calculation resulting in values from 0 to 255 will work. We found that the calculation used here produced a fairly good variety of patterns. (Experiment with some of your own.)

```
10 'Program to draw pie charts  PIECHART.BAS
20 '
30 GOSUB 500               'initialize values
40 GOSUB 1000              'get data values
50 SCREEN 1, 0             'change to medium resolution
60 CLS
70 WINDOW (-50,-50) - (50,50)
80 '
90 FOR I = 1 TO NUMBER.OF.VALUES
100     LET DONE = VALUE(I)/TOTAL * 6.28 + START
110     CIRCLE  (0,0),30,,-START,-DONE             ' draw each sector
120     LET MIDL = (START + DONE)/2
130     PAINT (5 * COS(MIDL),5 * SIN(MIDL)),CHR$(I * 3 + 90)' and paint it
140     LET START = DONE
150 NEXT I
155 LOCATE 23, 20
156 PRINT "This is a sample of a pie chart"
160 END
500 '---------------------------------------------------------
505                        'initialize values
507 '---------------------------------------------------------
510 KEY OFF
520 CLS
530 OPTION BASE 1
540 DIM VALUE(50)
550 LET NUMBER.OF.VALUES = 1
560 LET TOTAL = 0              ' TOTAL holds sum of all values
570 LET START = 0             ' START is beginning radian
580 RETURN
1000 '---------------------------------------------------------
1005 '             enter up to 50 data values
1007 '---------------------------------------------------------
1010 INPUT "Enter data value or press ENTER to end ",
          VALUE(NUMBER.OF.VALUES)
1020 WHILE VALUE(NUMBER.OF.VALUES) > 0
1030     LET TOTAL = TOTAL + VALUE(NUMBER.OF.VALUES)
1040     LET NUMBER.OF.VALUES = NUMBER.OF.VALUES + 1
1050     INPUT "Enter next value or press ENTER to end ",
             VALUE(NUMBER.OF.VALUES)
1060 WEND
1070 LET NUMBER.OF.VALUES = NUMBER.OF.VALUES - 1
1080 RETURN
```

When you run this program, you will see that it creates a pie chart, plotting each value as its proportion of the total of all values entered. The circle takes up most of the screen, leaving little room for headings and titles (see Figure 14.15).

There is a way to keep the graphics image in only a portion of the screen, called a **view port,** by using the VIEW statement.

VIEW

We can specify to BASIC to take whatever graphic image we create and place it (in reduced, scaled-down size) into a view port. We tell BASIC the size and location of the view port using this syntax:

$$\text{VIEW } (X_1, Y_1) - (X_2, Y_2)$$

where $(X_1, Y_1) - (X_2, Y_2)$ are the physical coordinates of the view window. In both resolutions, the top left-hand corner is (0,0). In medium resolution, the lower right-hand corner is (199,319), while in high resolution it is (199,639).

In order to move the window correctly, VIEW must be executed after WINDOW has been executed. WINDOW establishes the world coordinates that are used to plot points within that window, then VIEW states where on the screen that window is to be displayed and what size the window is to be.

You may fill the view port with a color by adding a color attribute to the statement:

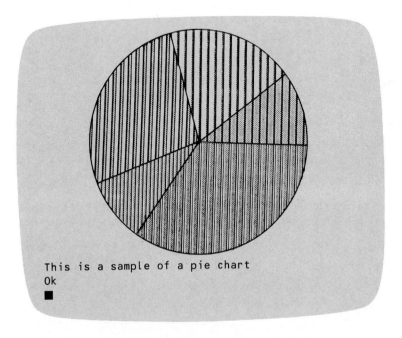

This is a sample of a pie chart
Ok

FIGURE 14.15 •
Pie chart with
textured sectors

```
VIEW (X , Y ) - (X , Y ), c
      1   1      2   2
```

You may also indicate that you wish the border around the view port drawn in a different color by placing a second color attribute following the statement:

```
VIEW (X , Y ) - (X , Y ), c, b
      1   1      2   2
```

If either of these attributes is omitted, the background color will be used. To have a view port filled with the background color and with a border in color attribute 1, you would write:

```
VIEW (X , Y ) - (X , Y ), ,1
      1   1      2   2
```

To have the border appear properly, you must make sure that the view port does not include the edges of the screen.

For example, in the preceding pie chart program, changing line 80 to:

```
80 VIEW (165,25) - (315,130),,1
```

will plot that very same pie chart in just the upper left-hand corner of the screen, in a box with a border around it (see Figure 14.16). Within the view port the x,y "world" coordinates retain the same relative values. The whole graph has been scaled down to fit within the view box.

Once a view port has been defined, the statement CLS will clear only the view port, not the entire screen. To clear the entire screen, you must first issue VIEW with no parameters to disable the view ports.

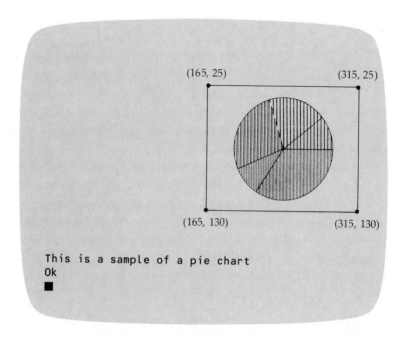

FIGURE 14.16 ·
Textured pie chart in view port

LINE Statement and Bar Charts

To draw a bar chart, we need just one new statement, LINE. The LINE statement can be used to draw a line between two points, or optionally, to draw a box. In the following examples and figures, we assume that the statement:

```
70 WINDOW (-50,-50) - (50,50)
```

has been issued earlier in the program.

To draw a line, we specify the starting and ending points (see Figure 14.17). To draw a line from point (5,10) to point (25,45) the statement is:

```
6900 LINE (5,10) - (25,45)
```

If the first set of coordinates is omitted, the last point drawn is assumed. Therefore, if the preceding line is followed by:

```
6910 LINE - (35,20)
```

a second line will be drawn from (25,45) to (35,20).

If, as in the preceding examples, no color is specified, the line will be drawn in the foreground color. To draw the line in a different color, follow the statement with a comma and the color attribute. To have the line drawn in color attribute 1 instead of 3, change line 6900 to:

```
6900 LINE (5,10) - (25,45), 1
```

To draw an open box, we specify the coordinates of opposite corners and follow the statement with ", c, B". The color attribute is optional. We can change line 6900 to draw a box:

```
6900 LINE (5,10) - (25,45), , B
```

FIGURE 14.17 ·
LINE statements
create lines or
boxes

Window $(-50, -50) - (50, 50)$

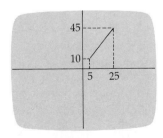

Line (5, 10) − (25, 45)

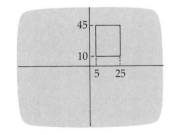

Line (5, 10) − (25, 45) , , B

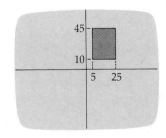

Line (5, 10) − (25, 45) , 1 , BF

To draw a box filled with color, we specify the opposite corners, the color with which to fill the box, and "BF"

```
6900 LINE (5,10) - (25,45), 1, BF
```

This will fill the box with the color associated with the value 1. In medium resolution, we may use color values 0 through 3; in high resolution, we may use only 0 or 1.

Here is a program to draw a bar graph that follows the same general form as the previous program. To scale the graph properly, instead of calculating the total of the values as we did with the pie chart, we find the highest value that is entered. To make the graph fill the window, we use the number of values entered as the ending x coordinate and the highest value as the ending y coordinate in the WINDOW statement. We want only color values 1, 2, and 3; therefore, we used MOD in line 100 to keep the color parameter within this range. Figure 14.18 shows a graph created from this program.

```
10 'Program to demonstrate bar graphs in BASIC   BARVIEW.BAS
20 'In Cohen/Alger/Boyd
30 GOSUB 1000               'initialize values
40 GOSUB 2000               'get data values
50 KEY OFF
60 SCREEN 1,0
70 COLOR 9,0
80 WINDOW (0,0) - (NUMBER.OF.VALUES,HIGH.VALUE)
85 VIEW (165,1) - (315,99),,1
90 FOR I = 1 TO NUMBER.OF.VALUES
100     LINE (I - 1,0) - (I,VALUE(I)),(I MOD 3) + 1,BF
110 NEXT I
120 END
```

·SYNTAX OF THE LINE STATEMENT·

LINE $(X_1,Y_1) - (X_2,Y_2)$, C, B, or BF
   (X_1,Y_1) are the starting coordinates. If omitted, last point referenced will be used.
   (X_2,Y_2) are the ending coordinates.
   C is the color attribute (optional).
   If neither B nor BF is present, a straight line is drawn from (X_1,Y_1) to (X_2,Y_2).
   If B is present, the borders of a rectangle are drawn with (X_1,Y_1) and (X_2,Y_2) as opposite corners.
   If BF is present, a rectangle with (X_1,Y_1) and (X_2,Y_2) as opposite corners is drawn and filled with color.

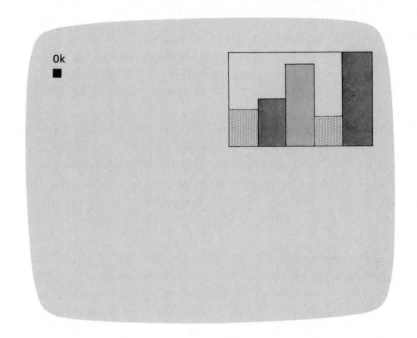

FIGURE 14.18 ·
Bar graph in
view port

```
1000 ' -----------------------------------------------------
1005 '                       initialize values
1010 ' -----------------------------------------------------
1020 CLS
1030 LET HIGH.VALUE = 0
1050 OPTION BASE 1
1060 DIM VALUE(50)
1070 LET NUMBER.OF.VALUES = 1
1080 RETURN
2000 ' -----------------------------------------------------
2005 '                     get data values
2007 ' -----------------------------------------------------
2010 INPUT "Enter data value or press ENTER to end ",
            VALUE(NUMBER.OF.VALUES)
2020 WHILE VALUE(NUMBER.OF.VALUES) > 0
2030    IF VALUE(NUMBER.OF.VALUES) > HIGH.VALUE
           THEN LET HIGH.VALUE = VALUE(NUMBER.OF.VALUES)
2050    LET NUMBER.OF.VALUES = NUMBER.OF.VALUES + 1
2060    INPUT "Enter next value or press ENTER to end ",
            VALUE(NUMBER.OF.VALUES)
2070 WEND
2080 LET NUMBER.OF.VALUES = NUMBER.OF.VALUES - 1
2090 RETURN
2100 --------------- end of listing ---------------------
```

Line Graph

To produce a line graph we connect a series of points using the LINE statement. To simplify running this demonstration program, instead of asking the user to input the data points, we will get the data points from values stored in DATA statements. As these values are read, we determine the highest and lowest values for the *x* coordinate and the *y* coordinate. We want the window to be slightly larger than the range of points, therefore, we multiply these high and low values by 1.1 to set the coordinates in the WINDOW statement (see line 110). The high and low values are also used to draw the *x* and *y* axes (lines 130 and 140).

We will draw small circles to mark each data point.

To demonstrate that the size of the viewport can be modified by the program, we ask the user to specify what percentage (SIZEIN) of the screen should be used for the chart. We do some elementary validation of the entry and convert it into a proportion. We take the square root of SIZEIN in line 620 since both the horizontal and vertical dimensions are changed. Figure 14.19 shows the graph created by this program.

```
10  ' Program to demonstrate Line Graphs  LINEVIEW.BAS
20  '    and to demonstrate making the view port a variable size
30  ' The use of DATA statements for storing variables is not
40  '    recommended in general, and is used here for demonstration only.
50  ' In Cohen/Alger/Boyd
80 GOSUB 500               'initialize values
90 GOSUB 1000              'get data values
100 SCREEN 1, 0: CLS
110 WINDOW (1.1 * LOW.VALUE.X,1.1 * LOW.VALUE.Y) -
           (1.1 * HIGH.VALUE.X,1.1 * HIGH.VALUE.Y)
120 VIEW (1,1) - (SIZE * 315,SIZE * 190),,3
130 LINE (LOW.VALUE.X,0) - (HIGH.VALUE.X,0),2   'draw the axes
140 LINE (0,LOW.VALUE.Y) - (0,HIGH.VALUE.Y),2
150 CIRCLE (LOW.VALUE.X,LOW.VALUE.Y),1            'draw the starting point
160 FOR I = 1 TO NUMBER.OF.VALUES
170     LINE - (VALUEX(I),VALUEY(I))
180     CIRCLE (VALUEX(I),VALUEY(I)),1      'show the intersection as a circle
190 NEXT I
200 END
500 '----------------------------------------------------
510 '                  initialize values
520 '----------------------------------------------------
530 LET HIGH.VALUE.X = 0: LET LOW.VALUE.X = 999999
540 LET HIGH.VALUE.Y = 0: LET LOW.VALUE.Y = 999999
550 DIM VALUESX(50),VALUEY(50)
560 LET NUMBER.OF.VALUES = 1
570 CLS: KEY OFF
580 INPUT "Enter a number between 10 and 100 for what percent of the screen
the graph should take. ",SIZEIN
590 LET SIZEIN = SIZEIN MOD 100                'If too big, cut down to size
```

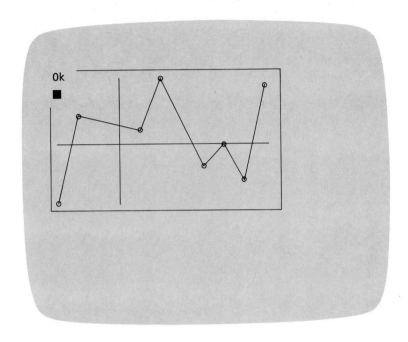

FIGURE 14.19•
Line graph

```
600 IF SIZEIN < 0 THEN LET SIZEIN = -SIZEIN 'If negative, make positive
610 IF SIZEIN < 1 THEN LET SIZEIN = 100      'If too small, make full screen
620 LET SIZE = SQR(SIZEIN/100)               'Change percent into proportion
630 RETURN
1000 ' -------------------------------------------------------------
1005 '                      get data values
1010 ' -------------------------------------------------------------
1015 READ VALUEX(NUMBER.OF.VALUES),VALUEY(NUMBER.OF.VALUES)
1020 WHILE VALUEX(NUMBER.OF.VALUES) >< 99999!
1030    IF VALUEX(NUMBER.OF.VALUES) > HIGH.VALUE.X
           THEN LET HIGH.VALUE.X = VALUEX(NUMBER.OF.VALUES)
1035    IF VALUEX(NUMBER.OF.VALUES) < LOW.VALUE.X
           THEN LET  LOW.VALUE.X = VALUEX(NUMBER.OF.VALUES)
1040    IF VALUEY(NUMBER.OF.VALUES) > HIGH.VALUE.Y
           THEN LET HIGH.VALUE.Y = VALUEY(NUMBER.OF.VALUES)
1045    IF VALUEY(NUMBER.OF.VALUES) < LOW.VALUE.Y
           THEN LET  LOW.VALUE.Y = VALUEY(NUMBER.OF.VALUES)
1050    LET NUMBER.OF.VALUES = NUMBER.OF.VALUES + 1
1055    READ VALUEX(NUMBER.OF.VALUES),VALUEY(NUMBER.OF.VALUES)
1060 WEND
1070 LET NUMBER.OF.VALUES = NUMBER.OF.VALUES - 1
1080 RETURN
```

```
2000 ' ---------------------------------------------------------
2010 '                 points for line graph
2020 ' ---------------------------------------------------------
2030 DATA -30,-80
2040 DATA -20,40
2050 DATA 10,20
2060 DATA 20,90
2070 DATA 30,30
2080 DATA 40,-30
2090 DATA 50,0
2100 DATA 60,-50
2110 DATA 70,80
2120 DATA 99999,99999
3000 ' --------- end of listing ----------------------------
```

Scatter Plot

Now that we have developed the pie chart and line graph, the scatter plot is a piece of cake. It is a line graph in which only the small circles (not the line) are drawn (see Figure 14.20).

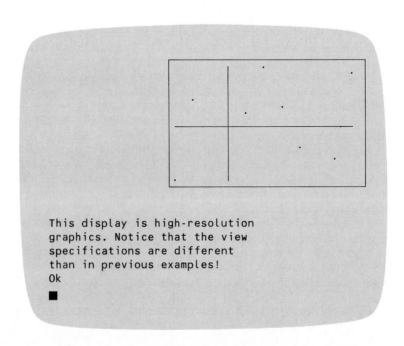

This display is high-resolution graphics. Notice that the view specifications are different than in previous examples!
Ok

FIGURE 14.20 ·
Scatter plot

```
10 'Scatter Plot demonstration Program  SCATTER2.BAS
20 'in Cohen/Alger/Boyd
30 GOSUB 1000                                  'initialize values
40 GOSUB 2000                                  'get data values
50 SCREEN 2                                    'SCREEN 2 = High Resolution
55 CLS
60 WINDOW (1.1 * LOW.VALUE.X,1.1 * LOW.VALUE.Y) -
         (1.1 * HIGH.VALUE.X,1.1 * HIGH.VALUE.Y)
70 VIEW (320,1) - (630,99),,1                  'New view port values
80 LINE (LOW.VALUE.X,0) - (HIGH.VALUE.X,0)     'Draw the axes
90 LINE (0,LOW.VALUE.Y) - (0,HIGH.VALUE.Y)
100 FOR I = 1 TO NUMBER.OF.VALUES              'Draw each data point
110     CIRCLE (VALUEX(I),VALUEY(I)),.25       ' as a small circle
120 NEXT I
130 GOSUB 3000                                 'print message
140 END
1000 ' -----------------------------------------------------------
1005 '                      initialize values
1007 ' -----------------------------------------------------------
1010 LET HIGH.VALUE.X = 0: LET LOW.VALUE.X = 2 ^ 15
1020 LET HIGH.VALUE.Y = 0: LET LOW.VALUE.Y = 2 ^ 15
1030 OPTION BASE 1
1040 DIM VALUEX(50),VALUEY(50)
1050 LET NUMBER.OF.VALUES = 1
1060 KEY OFF
1070 RETURN
2000 ' -----------------------------------------------------------
2005 '                       get data values
2007 ' -----------------------------------------------------------
2010 READ VALUEX(NUMBER.OF.VALUES),VALUEY(NUMBER.OF.VALUES)
2020 WHILE VALUEX(NUMBER.OF.VALUES) >< 99999!
2030     IF VALUEX(NUMBER.OF.VALUES) > HIGH.VALUE.X
            THEN LET HIGH.VALUE.X = VALUEX(NUMBER.OF.VALUES)
2040     IF VALUEX(NUMBER.OF.VALUES) < LOW.VALUE.X
            THEN LET   LOW.VALUE.X = VALUEX(NUMBER.OF.VALUES)
2050     IF VALUEY(NUMBER.OF.VALUES) > HIGH.VALUE.Y
            THEN LET HIGH.VALUE.Y = VALUEY(NUMBER.OF.VALUES)
2060     IF VALUEY(NUMBER.OF.VALUES) < LOW.VALUE.Y
            THEN LET   LOW.VALUE.Y = VALUEY(NUMBER.OF.VALUES)
2070     LET NUMBER.OF.VALUES = NUMBER.OF.VALUES + 1
2080     READ VALUEX(NUMBER.OF.VALUES),VALUEY(NUMBER.OF.VALUES)
2090 WEND
2100 LET NUMBER.OF.VALUES = NUMBER.OF.VALUES - 1
2110 RETURN
3000 ' -----------------------------------------------------------
3005 '                    message for display
3007 ' -----------------------------------------------------------
3010 PRINT
3020 PRINT "This display is in high resolution"
```

```
3030 PRINT "graphics.  Notice that the view"
3040 PRINT "specifications are different"
3050 PRINT "than in previous examples!"
3060 RETURN
4000 ' -----------------------------------------------------------
4010 '                       points for scatter plot
4020 ' -----------------------------------------------------------
4030 DATA -30,-80
4040 DATA -20,40
4050 DATA 10,20
4060 DATA 20,90
4070 DATA 30,30
4080 DATA 40,-30
4090 DATA 50,0
4100 DATA 60,-50
4110 DATA 70,80
4120 DATA 99999,99999
4130 ' ------------   end of listing   -----------------------
```

Notice that here we used high-resolution graphics (SCREEN 2). We were not interested in color here — for scatter plots, it adds nothing. And high-resolution graphics allow us to use text that fits 80 characters to a line, so captions look much better than in medium resolution.

DRAW

We have all but concluded our discussion of business graphics. But BASIC provides one more feature of graphics that may be useful in business — the DRAW statement.

DRAW has many variations; we will discuss one. This variation of DRAW lets you move the cursor leaving a trail behind. It uses a form of "turtle" graphics. Imagine that you have a turtle with ink on its tail. You can direct the turtle to move up the screen, down, left, right, or any of the four sideways directions.

You use DRAW to tell the turtle what directions you want it to move and how far in that direction. Each DRAW statement will begin at the point last referenced. For example, this series of statements will draw a line up 2, to the right 15, and downward 20 on a left diagonal, creating a figure shaped like a seven. The figure begins in the middle of the screen, since both RUN and CLS set the center of the screen as the last point referenced.

```
10 CLS
20 SCREEN 2          ' high-resolution graphics
30 DRAW "U 2"        ' draw line up 2
40 DRAW "R 15"       ' draw 15 to the right
50 DRAW "G 20"       ' draw 20 down and to the left
```

Lines 30 through 50 can be written in one statement as follows:

```
30 DRAW "U 2 R 15 G 20"
```

•SYNTAX OF THE DRAW STATEMENT•

DRAW String
The string contains one or more letters that indicate the direction. Each letter is followed by a number, which indicates how far to move in that direction.

BASIC interprets the letters as indicating direction and the numbers as distance.

The following program allows the user to "draw" on the screen by using the keys on the numeric keypad to indicate the direction. Notice the combination of INPUT$, INSTR, and MID$ in line 120. INPUT$(1) returns the digit that is pressed on the numeric keypad. INSTR returns the position of where that digit appears in the string "824693175". The variable DIRECTION$ holds the letters that are used to indicate direction for the DRAW statement. MID$ returns the letter that is in the position corresponding to the value returned by INSTR. If a 4 is pressed on the keypad, INSTR will return the value 3. (The digit 4 is the third one in the string "824693175".) MID$ will return the third character in DIRECTION$, which is an L. The DRAW statement will now draw one position to the left. Figure 14.21 shows two patterns that were created with this program.

```
10 'Program to demonstrate the use of DRAW     DRAW2.BAS
20 'In Cohen/Alger/Boyd
30 '
100 GOSUB 1000                  'initialize
110 WHILE A$ <> "B"
120      LET A$ = MID$(DIRECTION$,INSTR("824693175",INPUT$(1)),1)
130      DRAW A$
140 WEND
150 END
```

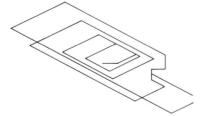
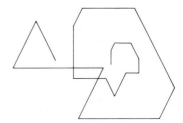

FIGURE 14.21•
Two designs
created with the
DRAW statement

```
1000 ' ------------------------------------------------
1005 '                  Initialize
1007 ' ------------------------------------------------
1010 LET DIRECTION$ = "UDLREFGHB"
1020 KEY OFF
1030 CLS
1040 PRINT "Press the NUM LOCK key to turn the numeric keypad to numbers"
1050 PRINT "Use the NUMERIC KEYPAD as your direction panel for drawing"
1060 PRINT "When you wish to exit, press 5"
1070 PRINT "Now press any key to continue . . . "
1080 LET DUMMY$ = INPUT$(1)
1090 SCREEN 1
1100 LET A$ = ""            'A$ holds the direction to draw
1110 RETURN
1120 ' ----------- end of listing -------------------
```

A Word of Caution

Programming with graphs can be challenging and also a great deal of fun. There is often a temptation to keep working on a program until it is picture perfect. Always keep in mind that the goal of a business program is to solve a business problem within the required time period. No matter how spectacular the output of your program may be, it will be of no use if it is not completed on schedule.

THE STORY'S END

Micky was beaming with joy as he knocked on the door of Judy's office. "Mind if I come in?" he asked.

"I haven't seen you in ages. Where have you been keeping yourself?"

"Let's see, where should I start? Well, I read that BASIC book you told me about. It had programs already written to produce graphs. I used some as is and modified others to produce the graphs as you told me to. I was also able to use the company's color printer to produce color overheads from the graphics screens BASIC produced.

"Then I asked for another chance to represent my proposal to management."

"How did it go, Micky?" Judy asked, sensing his excitement.

"Well, they complimented me on how much my presentation had improved. They also said that this improvement meant that I was a valuable employee to the company. Later, they agreed that we need a new computer. The head of DP met with me privately, and guess what? She asked me to be project leader on the system acquisition project."

"Great, but that's a lot of work."

"Sure, but I get to go to training seminars on it, all expenses paid. And since they don't want to pay me overtime, I got promoted to management."

At this point, although she said nothing, Judy was dismayed. She had been vying for a management position herself, and now someone junior to her got it because of her advice. She felt let down, almost betrayed.

·PARABLES FOR PROGRAMMERS·

The Perfect Program

Albert was a perfectionist. His house was immaculate, his car shiny and well-tuned, his hair just so. As with the rest of his life, Albert considered his computer programming to be more than a living. A computer program was not a means to an end but organization and completeness in their purest, most elegant form.

It happened that one day Albert was told to write a program to analyze sales for the company. Albert tackled the program with his usual relish, starting with the specifications.

"It seems to me," Albert said to his boss, "that we could do a lot better than this. The specifications call for a program that analyzes sales for only one year at a time. Why not make it three years, instead?" Delighted, Albert's boss agreed. "While we're at it, let's take into account future growth. Right now, we only have one office, but suppose we expand nationwide? The program should be able to handle a couple dozen offices, with separate totals for each." Enchanted with the prospect of such spectacular success, Albert's boss quickly agreed to this and Albert's many other "slight improvements."

Albert threw himself into the program but quickly discovered more features that just had to be added. "After all," reasoned Albert, "a good program should be able to handle all foreseeable situations." Almost hourly, Albert marched into his boss's office to propose some new feature. Each change, taken by itself, made so much sense that Albert was always granted permission to enhance the specifications.

This continued for several weeks. Albert's boss, who had originally thought the program would be ready for the sales force in a week or two at the most, nervously started to look in on Albert, who always took the opportunity to propose yet more improvements to the unfinished program. When Albert was asked to estimate how much longer the program would take, he invariably pointed out the many valuable improvements agreed to since the original schedule was drafted and the extra time needed to "get the job done right."

Not being one to argue with perfection, Albert's boss tried hard to remain patient. However, after three months Albert's boss could no longer wait; the original "imperfect" specifications were given to another programmer. The program was completed in two weeks and put to immediate and effective use.

MORAL: A working program is better than dreams of perfection.

But Micky was going on. "Judy, I am going to need good people on my team," he said. "I've asked to have you transferred to the project. Is that okay?"

Judy thought and after a long pause said, "Sure, I'd be pleased to work with someone who improves so quickly." It would be interesting working with a new computer anyway.

"Great, because I told the boss that I owed all this to your advice and told her that you too should be made project team leader and be promoted to management. After all, acquisition is a lot of work."

·QUICK REFERENCE FOR LESSON 14·

Graphics Requirements

In order to use the graphics statements you must be using a PC that has a color graphics card installed. These statements also require that you use BASICA version 2.0 or later.

SCREEN Sets the Mode for the Screen

SCREEN 0: Text Mode (Default Mode)

SCREEN 0,0 — color disabled.
SCREEN 0,1 — color enabled.
Graphics statements cannot be used in this mode.
16 colors may be used for foreground, 8 for background, 8 for border.

SCREEN 1: Medium-Resolution Graphics Mode

SCREEN 1,0 — color enabled.
SCREEN 1,1 — color disabled.
Graphics statements may be used.
Text prints 40 characters per row.
Upper-left coordinate is (0,0); lower-right coordinate is (199,319).
One of 16 colors may be used for background; foreground colors may be selected from one of two palettes.

SCREEN 2: High-Resolution Graphics

Graphics statements may be used.
Text prints 80 characters per row.
Upper-left coordinate is (0,0); lower-right coordinate is (199,639).
Black and white only.

WIDTH Sets Number of Characters per Row

In text mode (SCREEN 0):

WIDTH 40 sets 40 characters per row (on color systems only).
WIDTH 80 sets 80 characters per row (default setting).

In medium-resolution mode (SCREEN 1):

Default setting is WIDTH 40.
WIDTH 80 forces change to high resolution.

In high-resolution mode (SCREEN 2):

Default setting is WIDTH 80.
WIDTH 40 forces change to medium resolution.

COLOR Defines Selection of Colors for the Screen

In text mode the format is: COLOR foreground, background, border. In medium-resolution mode the format is: COLOR background, palette.

COLOR ATTRIBUTE	PALETTE 0	PALETTE 1
1	Green	Cyan
2	Red	Magenta
3	Brown	White

In high-resolution mode the COLOR statement may not be used.

WINDOW

WINDOW defines the coordinates ("world" coordinates) to be used by graphics statements that follow.

WINDOW $(X_1, Y_1) - (X_2, Y_2)$

(X_1, Y_1) is *lower*-left coordinate for figures that follow.
(X_2, Y_2) is *upper*-right coordinate for figures that follow.

VIEW

VIEW defines physical coordinates of the rectangle (view port) into which contents of WINDOW are mapped

VIEW $(X_1, Y_1) - (X_2, Y_2)$

(X_1, Y_1) is *upper* left *physical* coordinate.
(X_2, Y_2) is *lower* right *physical* coordinate.

VIEW is placed *after* the WINDOW statement.

CIRCLE

CIRCLE draws a circle, arc, or sector.

CIRCLE (X, Y), R, C, R_1, R_2

(X, Y) is coordinate of center of circle.
R is radius of circle (in points).
C is the color attribute (optional).
R_1 and R_2 are starting and ending points (in radians). If omitted, a full circle will be

drawn. If positive, just the arc will be drawn. If negative, a line will be drawn to the center, creating a sector.

PAINT

This command fills an area with color or pattern.

PAINT (X,Y), N

Fills the area containing (X,Y) with the color specified by attribute N.
In medium-resolution mode, N may be 0 through 3.
In high-resolution mode, N may be 0 or 1.

PAINT (X,Y), TILE$

Fills the area containing (X,Y) with a pattern specified by the string TILE$.
TILE$ may be any string value.
Different strings produce different patterns.

The point (X,Y) must be entirely within the area, not touching any border. If the area is not completely closed, the entire screen will be painted.

LINE

LINE draws a straight line or rectangle.

LINE $(X_1,Y_1) - (X_2,Y_2)$, C, B, or BF

(X_1,Y_1) is starting point. If not specified, last point referenced will be used.
(X_2,Y_2) is ending point.
C is color attribute (optional).
B or BF creates a rectangle (box).
   If neither is present, a straight line is drawn.
   B draws a box with (X_1,Y_1) and (X_2,Y_2) as opposite corners.
   BF draws a box with (X_1,Y_1) and (X_2,Y_2) as opposite corners and fills it with the color specified. If no color is specified, in medium resolution the box is filled with the color having attribute 3, and in high resolution the box is filled with black.

DRAW

This command draws a line in the direction and distance indicated.

DRAW STRING$

STRING$ contains one or more sets of a letter indicating direction followed by a number indicating distance. Letters indicating direction are:

U   up
R   right
D   down
L   left
E   diagonal up and to the right
F   diagonal down and to the right
G   diagonal down and to the left
H   diagonal up and to the left

· EXERCISES ·

Short Answer

1. Describe three types of business graphics.

2. What is one major factor in choosing a bar chart instead of a pie chart?

3. For full use of color and graphics, what two pieces of hardware must you be using?

4. Describe the three screen modes.

5. Can you print 80 characters of text per row in medium-resolution mode? What happens if WIDTH 80 is executed in medium-resolution mode?

Analyzing Code

6. Describe or draw the figures that would result from the following CIRCLE statements. Assume that lines 100 through 120 have been previously executed:

```
100 SCREEN 1, 0
110 WINDOW (-100, -100) - (100, 100)
120 COLOR 0, 1
```

   a. `210 CIRCLE (0,0), 75, 1`
   b. `230 CIRCLE (0,0), 50, 2, .5, 1.5`
   c. `250 CIRCLE (0,0), 50, , -1.5, -5`
   d. What would you expect to see if lines 210 through 250 were executed in succession?

7. Describe or draw the figures that would result from the following LINE statements. Assume that lines 100 and 110 have been previously executed.

```
100 SCREEN 1,0
110 COLOR 9,0
```

   a. `210 LINE (10,100) - (150,20)`
   b. `310 LINE (10,100) - (150,20), ,B`
   c. `410 LINE (10,100) - (150,20), , BF`
   d. How would these figures change if line 100 were changed to:

   ```
   100 SCREEN 2,0
   ```

   e. How will the figures appear if this line is added to (1)

   ```
   120 WINDOW (0,0) - (200,200)
   ```

8. What would result if the following lines were executed?

```
100  SCREEN 1,0
110  COLOR 1,0
120  WINDOW (-100, -100) - (100,100)
200  LINE (-70,50) - (25, 0)
210  LINE - (50, 75)
230  LINE - (75, -50)
```

Programming

9. Modify the pie chart program in this chapter (PIECHART.BAS) to ask the user to input a title for each segment. Print the titles and values on the screen.

10. Modify the bar graph program in this chapter (BARVIEW.BAS) to produce titles and captions.

11. Change the bar graph program in this chapter to make the bars less wide, so that they do not touch one another.

12. a. Write a program to create a pie chart to represent the following budget:

Personnel   63%
Building   15%
Equipment   10%
Supplies   5%
Other   7%

b. Change the chart to an exploded pie chart with the segment representing Building the one that is pulled out. (To do this, you need to redefine the center of the circle for that segment.)

13. Change the DRAW program so that drawings are stored (up to 255 keystrokes) in a variable B$ so the user can
a. Later DRAW B$ in immediate mode.
b. Store B$ on a file for later retrieval and drawing.
c. Store and later modify B$ and its drawing.

14. a. Write a program asking the user to enter the net profit for the past six months and display the data on a line graph.
b. Now ask the user to enter profit for the same six months the previous year. Display these figures on the same line graph but in a different color.

·P·A·R·T·

III

Solving Business Problems with BASIC

INTRODUCTION TO PART III

NOW THAT YOU have completed Part I (Chapters 1 through 6) and at least some of Part II (Chapters 7 through 14) of this text, you know the ABCs of BASIC. When learning to write essays, first you must learn the alphabet, then words built from the letters. Only then can you place the words into sentences, paragraphs, and essays.

Learning to program is similar. You learned first the individual statements and then organized them into modules and the modules into programs.

One of the best ways to learn style both for essays and for programs is to practice, imitating the works of others. Even following the strict confines of structured programming, there is still room for individual style.

Part III, therefore, consists of case studies. Each case study solves a different business problem. By studying these problems and solutions, which are available *on disk* for you to modify and examine, you will learn not only real business examples but also programming styles.

The cases are so designed that you do not need to have covered all of the chapters. The cases require the following chapters in Part II to have been covered. Some of the exercises for the cases may require knowledge of topics in later chapters. Those that do are so indicated.

Case I	Chapter 7 (Sequential Files)
Case II	Chapters 7 and 8 (Arrays)
Case III	Chapters 7 and 8
Case IV	Chapters 7 through 11 (String Functions)
Case V	Chapters 8 through 12 (Input/Output Functions)
Case VI	Chapters 8 through 12

GENERAL LEDGER— PRINT CHART OF ACCOUNTS

Chapters Required: Part I and Part II, Chapter 7.

PROBLEM SPECIFICATION

Small businesses use the IBM PC for their accounting needs. What are accounting needs? Businesses need to keep track of expense and revenue. All of the expense and income categories are assigned **account numbers.** Separate accounts are kept for payroll expense, supply expense, income from sales, and so on. As expenditures and receipts are recorded, the amounts of the transactions are added to or subtracted from the balance in the appropriate account. This process is called "posting to the accounts."

For this case the description of each account, the number assigned to it, and the current balance of that account are stored in a file on disk. This is the **Chart of Accounts** file and has been given the filename "CHARTOF.ACT".

Periodically the managers want a report of all the accounts and their current balances. This case studies a program to produce that report.

Cases II and III will discuss the programs that create and update the file "CHARTOF.ACT". This case assumes that the file "CHARTOF.ACT" is already on disk. Note that although the case deals with accounting issues, the problem requires no knowledge of accounting. We are merely creating a report that shows in human format what the computer has stored in its own format.

File Layout

CHARTOF.ACT is a sequential file. For each account the following data are in the file:

Account number   Integer, maximum of 4 digits
Account name   String, maximum of 30 characters
Account balance   Double precision, positive or negative, maximum value
                 99,999,999.99

The records are in ascending sequence by account number. The final record is a "dummy" record with account number 9999 used to flag the end of the file.

Report Layout

The report is to appear as follows:

```
                    CHART OF ACCOUNTS AS OF MM/DD/YY
ACCT #      DESCRIPTION                    DEBIT              CREDIT

####    XXXXXXXXXXXXXXXXXXXXXXXXXXXXXX   ##,###,###.##      ##,###,###.##
####    XXXXXXXXXXXXXXXXXXXXXXXXXXXXXX   ##,###,###.##      ##,###,###.##
.
.
####    XXXXXXXXXXXXXXXXXXXXXXXXXXXXXX   ##,###,###.##      ##,###,###.##

TOTALS                                 ###,###,###.##     ###,###,###.##
```

Positive balances are to print in the debit column. Negative balances are to print in the credit column without the minus sign appearing.

FUNCTIONS TO BE PERFORMED

The functions that this program is to perform are outlined as follows:

A. Initialization
   1. Display message to user
   2. Open file
   3. Initialize variables
   4. Print heading
   5. Read a record
B. Print each record
   1. Add balance to appropriate total
   2. If end of screen, print heading
   3. Print detail line showing account data
   4. Read next record
C. Final processing
   1. Close file
   2. Print totals

STRUCTURE CHARTS

Once the functions are outlined, the structure chart can be drawn (see Figure I.1). Note that the boxes representing "Print the Heading" and "Input Record" have been used in more than one place. Therefore the corner of each of these boxes in the structure chart has been darkened to show this.

DATA DICTIONARY

Data from File CHARTOF.ACT
ACT.NO%   Account number
ACCT.NAME$ Account description
ACCT.BAL#   Account balance

Constants
TODAY$ Today's date
PAGE.LEN   Number of lines per page
T   Tab setting

Counters
LINE.COUNT   Number of lines printed so far

FIGURE I.1 •
Structure chart
for COARPT.BAS

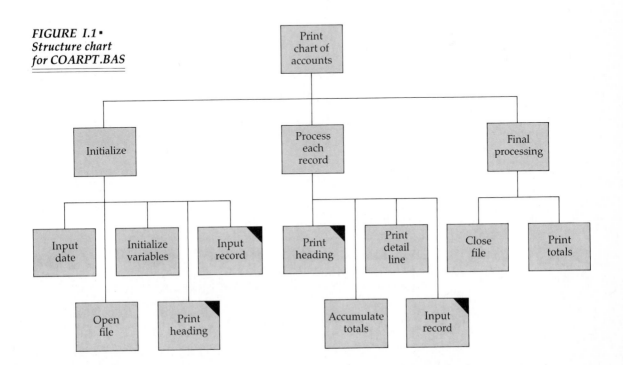

Accumulators

CR.BAL#   Total of credit (negative) balances
DR.BAL#   Total of debit (positive) balances

Format Masks

MASK$ Mask for printing balances

PSEUDOCODE

We are now ready to write the pseudocode for this program. As we write it, we will note any special techniques or any unusual circumstances.

MAIN-LINE
        DO INITIALIZATION
        WHILE not end of file (ACCT.NO% <> 9999)
                DO PRINT-EACH-ACCOUNT-RECORD
        WEND
        DO PRINT-TOTALS

INITIALIZATION
        Clear screen
        OPEN CHARTOF.ACT for INPUT
        Initialize variables
        INPUT today's date (TODAY$)
        DO PRINT-HEADING
        INPUT first record

The first record is input before entering the WHILE . . . WEND loop. All remaining records are input at the end of the loop. This is done so that when the last record containing account number 9999 is read, it will not be processed as a valid record.

PRINT-HEADING
        Reset LINE.COUNT to 0
        Clear screen
        Print heading lines

PROCESS-EACH-ACCOUNT-RECORD
        IF LINE.COUNT is greater than PAGE.LEN
                THEN DO PRINT-HEADING
        IF ACCT.BAL# is negative
                THEN set tab (T) to 60 and add ACCT.BAL# to CR.BAL#
                ELSE set tab (T) to 40 and add ACCT.BAL# to DR.BAL#
        IF ACCT.BAL# is negative, remove sign
        Print ACCT.NO%, ACCT.NAME$ and ACCT.BAL#

Increment LINE.COUNT by 1
INPUT next record

==

PRINT-TOTALS
Close file
Print totals

PROGRAM LISTING

```
10  '   General Ledger System
20  '   Program Name: COARPT.BAS
30  '   Date Written: 4/12/87
40  '   Written by:   F. K. Thompson
50  '   Program Description
60  '           Inputs data from file CHARTOF.ACT
70  '           Prints Account Data and Balances
80  '           Prints total Debit and Credit Balances
90  '   Files Used:
100 '       CHARTOF.ACT - input only
200 ' Program History
210 '           None to date
1000 '============================================================
1010 '                   MAIN LINE
1020 '============================================================
1030 '
1040   GOSUB 2000              ' Initialization
1045   WHILE ACCT.NO% <> 9999
1050     GOSUB 3000            ' Print Each Account
1055   WEND
1060   GOSUB 4000              ' Print Totals
1070   END
1080 '
2000 '============================================================
2010 '                   INITIALIZATION
2020 '============================================================
2025 '                                       message
2030   CLS
2040   PRINT "This Program Prints the Chart of Accounts"
2050   INPUT "Please Enter Today's Date as mm/dd/yy ", TODAY$
2055 '                                       open file
2060   OPEN "CHARTOF.ACT" FOR INPUT AS #1
2065 '                                       initialize variables
2070   LET PAGE.LEN = 15            ' Initialize Page Length
2080   LET LINE.COUNT = 0           '    and Line Count
2090   LET CR.BAL# = 0              ' Initialize Credit Total
2100   LET DR.BAL# = 0              '    and Debit Balance
```

```
2110    LET MASK$ = "###,###,###.##-"    ' Mask for Amounts
2120    GOSUB 5000                       ' Print Heading
2130    INPUT #1, ACCT.NO%, ACCT.NAME$,  ACCT.BAL#      'read first record
2140    RETURN
3000 '=========================================================
3010 '                PROCESS EACH RECORD
3020 '=========================================================
3030 '                                          print heading
3040 IF LINE.COUNT > PAGE.LEN THEN GOSUB 5000   'if needed
3045 LET LINE.COUNT = LINE.COUNT + 1            ' Increment Line Count
3047 '                                          ' add balance to accumulators
3050 IF ACCT.BAL# < 0
        THEN LET T = 60: LET CR.BAL# = CR.BAL# + ACCT.BAL#
        ELSE LET T = 40: LET DR.BAL# = DR.BAL# + ACCT.BAL#
3055 IF ACCT.BAL# < 0 THEN LET ACCT.BAL# = -ACCT.BAL#       'remove sign
3060 PRINT USING "####   \                       \";
        ACCT.NO%, ACCT.NAME$;                    ' Print Line
3070 PRINT TAB(T);
3080 PRINT USING MASK$; ACCT.BAL#
3090 '
3100 INPUT #1, ACCT.NO%, ACCT.NAME$, ACCT.BAL# ' Input Next Record
3120 RETURN
4000 '=========================================================
4010 '                CLOSE FILE AND PRINT TOTALS
4020 '=========================================================
4030    CLOSE #1                         ' Close File
4040    PRINT                            ' Print Totals
4050    PRINT "TOTALS" TAB(40);: PRINT USING MASK$; DR.BAL#;
4060    PRINT TAB(60);: PRINT USING MASK$; -CR.BAL#
4070    RETURN
5000 '=========================================================
5010 '                PRINT HEADING
5020 '=========================================================
5030    LET LINE.COUNT = 0               ' Reset Line Count
5040    CLS                              ' Print Heading
5050    PRINT TAB(20) "CHART OF ACCOUNTS AS OF "; TODAY$
5060    PRINT "ACCT #     DESCRIPTION" TAB(45) "DEBIT" TAB(65) "CREDIT"
5070    PRINT
5080    RETURN
5090 ' =========================================================
5100 '            END OF LISTING
5110 ' =========================================================
```

PROGRAM OUTPUT

This Program Prints the Chart of Accounts
Please Enter Today's Date as mm/dd/yy <u>04/30/87</u>

(screen clears)

CHART OF ACCOUNTS AS OF 04/30/87

ACCT #	DESCRIPTION	DEBIT	CREDIT
1001	Cash in Checking Account	13,875.75	
1010	Petty Cash	50.00	
2010	Assets: Office Furniture	45,700.00	
2020	Assets: Equipment	67,705.86	
2500	Accumulated Depreciation		25,000.00
4100	Withholding Payable		5,600.00
4500	Accounts Payable		23,864.90
4520	Notes Payable		8,525.65
6100	Capital Stock		30,000.00
6200	Retained Earnings	56,188.86	
7100	Income: Sale of Goods		705,976.98
7200	Income: Services		13,000.00
7300	Income: Other		1,059.00
8000	Salaries - Professional	359,700.00	
8100	Salaries - Clerical	125,079.00	
8200	Salaries - Other	50,100.00	

(screen clears)

CHART OF ACCOUNTS AS OF 04/30/87

ACCT #	DESCRIPTION	DEBIT	CREDIT
8300	Employee Benefits	25,100.50	
8500	Expenses: Rent	45,000.00	
8510	Expenses: Utilities	5,836.98	
8700	Expenses: Supplies	3,000.00	
8800	Expenses: Vehicles	15,689.58	
	TOTALS	813,026.53	813,026.53

Ok

• EXERCISES •

1. Run the program "COARPT.BAS" and observe how the accounts are displayed. What suggestions, if any, do you have for improving it?

2. Change the program so that the report is sent to the printer instead of the screen. Print 40 accounts on each page. Add the company name and a page number to the heading.

3. Add to the program an option to display a selected account. Ask the user to enter the account number, then search the file for a matching number.

When a match is found, display the account description and balance. If no match is found, inform the user of this.

4. Currently any characters may be entered into the string TODAY$.
   a. Modify the program so that the date is validated. Month must be from 1 to 12, day from 1 to 31, and year from 85 to 99.
   b. Check that the day entered is valid for that month. For example, August has 31 days, while September has only 30. Remember that February has only 28 days except on leap years.

5. Using what you learned in Chapter 12 about treating I/O devices as files, add a menu to the program to allow the user the choice of either displaying the report on the screen or sending it to the printer.

General Ledger— Build Chart of Accounts

Chapters Required: Part I and Part II, Chapters 7 and 8.

Problem Specification

Case I developed a program that printed a report from the Chart of Accounts file (CHARTOF.ACT). This case examines a program to create that file.

The Chart of Accounts file contains the description of each account, the number assigned to the account, and the balance in that account. In a business environment this program will initially be used to enter the accounts and the beginning balances into the system. Once the accounts have been entered and checked to ensure that all account numbers, descriptions, and initial balances are correct, the user ordinarily will not make changes to existing accounts through this program. While new accounts may be added, any changes to existing accounts should be made through Journal Entries. (See Case III for discussion of the Journal Entries programs.)

For this reason the program that builds the Chart of Accounts (described in this case) is separate from the programs that process Journal Entries (Case III). Prudent business practices dictate separating functions and restricting access to any program that allows directly changing Chart of Account balances. This is good management control.

Some accounts, such as Cash in Checking Account, will have positive balances, while others, such as Accounts Payable, will have negative balances. One of the rules of accounting is that the sum of all account balances must always equal zero. When this is true, the accounts are said to be **in balance.** The program must display the current sum to the user and not allow the file to be written unless the accounts are in balance.

File Layout

CHARTOF.ACT is a sequential file. For each account the following data are in the file:

Account number   Positive integer, not greater than 9999
Account name   String, maximum of 30 characters
Account balance Double precision, positive or negative, maximum value
                 99,999,999.99

The records are in ascending sequence by account number. The final record is a "dummy" record with account number 9999 used to flag the end of the file. The sum of all of the balances must equal zero.

File Handling

We have to solve the problem of how to add new accounts to the file. We cannot use APPEND because that will add a new account to the end of the file rather than insert it in its proper account number position. And what about changes to the file? We might want to make a change to any record, any place in the file. As we know, the only way to make changes to records in a sequential file is to rewrite the file.

These programs are for the "tiny" business; therefore, we have made the restriction that we can have at most 100 different accounts. (Depending on the amount of memory available, this can be increased by modifying the DIMension statement.)

Our method of processing will be to read the entire file into memory as an array, make any changes or additions, resort the array to account number sequence, and write the updated file back to the disk.

FUNCTIONS TO BE PERFORMED

This program contains the following functions.

    A. Initialization
       1. Read existing Chart of Accounts file
    B. Display menu
    C. Based on selection entered by user, do one of following
       1. Add new accounts to the chart
       2. Display the Chart of Accounts on the screen
         a. Allow the user to make changes to any account

3. Print a listing of the Chart
   a. Sort into account number sequence
   b. Debit balances in separate column from credit
   c. Print total debit and total credit balances
4. Write the Chart of Accounts to the file
   a. Sort into account number sequence
   b. Write file only if it is in balance
D. Closing activities

The program will display the menu shown in Figure II.1. The sort has been made a separate option so that it can be called from different places in the processing as well as allowing the user the ability to sort the accounts at any time.

STRUCTURE CHART

Figure II.2 is the structure chart for this program.

DATA DICTIONARY

Data from File, Placed in Arrays
ACCT.NO%()   Account number
ACCT.NAME$()   Account description
ACCT.BAL#()   Account balance

```
           UPDATE CHART OF ACCOUNTS

1 = Add a New Account
2 = Display or Make Changes to Existing Accounts
3 = Sort Chart into Account Number Sequence
4 = Print Listing of Chart of Accounts
5 = Write Chart of Accounts to File
6 = Exit from Program

Please Enter Your Choice (1-6) and press ENTER
```

FIGURE II.1 •
Menu for
program to
create
CHARTOF.ACT

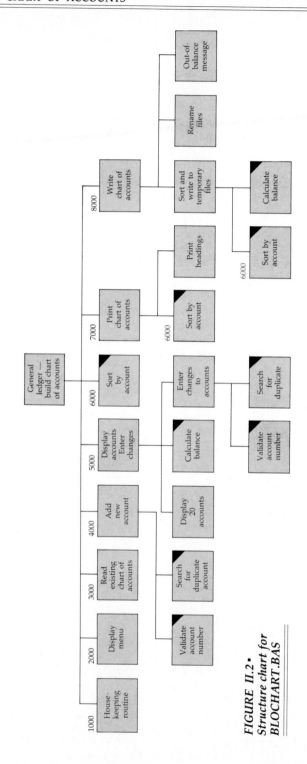

FIGURE II.2 ·
Structure chart for
BLOCHART.BAS

Working Variables	
CHOICE	Option selected by user
TRUE	Initialized to -1
FALSE	Initialized to 0
I	Number of accounts
TEMP.ACCT.NO	Account number as entered
INT.ACCT.NO	Integer equivalent of TEMP.ACCT.NO
NUM.DISPLAY	Number of accounts to be displayed on current screen
SELECTION	Number of line to be changed
ANS$	Field to be changed
PAUSE$	Dummy variable
Accumulators	
BALANCE#	Total of all account balances
DBL.CK.BAL#	Total of all account balances calculated as file is written
Switches	
MORE.TO.DO	TRUE until exit option is selected
VALID	TRUE if account number is integer between 0 and 9999
DUPLICATE	TRUE if account number is a duplicate
YES.NO$	Yes or no switch
FILE.WRITTEN	TRUE after file has been written
Counters	
INDEX.DUP	Counter in FOR . . . NEXT loop that checks for duplicates
INDEX	Used as FOR . . . NEXT loop index
INDEX20	Used as FOR . . . NEXT loop index
J	Used as FOR . . . NEXT loop index
K	Used as FOR . . . NEXT loop index

Pseudocode

<u>MAIN LINE</u>
    DO INITIALIZATION
    WHILE MORE.TO.DO
        DO DISPLAY-MENU
        ON choice
            DO ADD-NEW-ACCOUNT or
            DO DISPLAY-AND-EDIT ACCOUNT or
            DO SORT-ACCOUNTS or

```
          DO PRINT-ACCOUNT-LISTING or
          DO WRITE-ACCOUNTS-TO-FILE or
          DO EXIT-FROM-PROGRAM
     WEND
```

===

INITIALIZATION
     Initialize variables
     Dimension arrays (ACCT.NO%, ACCT.NAME$, ACCT.BAL#)
     DO INPUT-CHARTOF.ACT-FILE-INTO-ARRAY
-|---

INPUT-CHARTOF.ACT-FILE-INTO-ARRAY
     PRINT message telling user file is being read
     OPEN CHARTOF.ACT FOR APPEND
     WRITE dummy ending record with ACCT.NO% = 9999
     CLOSE CHARTOF.ACT

Because this program will be used to create or modify the Chart of Accounts file, it must work for the instance when the file does not yet exist and for when it has already been created. Opening the file for APPEND and writing the "dummy" record guarantees that there will be at least one record in the file.

```
     OPEN "CHARTOF.ACT" FOR INPUT
     WHILE not last record (account number <> 9999)
          Increment subscript (I)
          INPUT ACCT.NO%, ACCT.NAME$, ACCT.BAL# from file into arrays
     WEND
     Subtract 1 from I
```

The dummy record was included in the count. We must subtract 1 from I to give the number of actual accounts.

```
     CLOSE file
```

===

DISPLAY-MENU
     PRINT lines describing options
     INPUT CHOICE

===

ADD-NEW-ACCOUNT
     INPUT first account number (TEMP.ACCT.NO)
     WHILE account number is not 9999
          DO VALIDATE-ACCOUNT-NUMBER
          IF number is valid DO CHECK-FOR-DUPLICATE
          IF number is valid and not a duplicate DO ENTER-NAME-AND-
               BALANCE
          INPUT next account number
     WEND
```
```

Placing the first input before entering the WHILE . . . WEND loop and the remaining ones at the end of the loop allows an exit from the loop immediately after the account number 9999 is entered.

VALIDATE-ACCOUNT-NUMBER
    IF within range 1 through 9999 and integer
        THEN let VALID = TRUE
        ELSE let VALID = FALSE and PRINT error message
CHECK-FOR-DUPLICATE
    FOR INDEX.DUP = 1 to end of array (I)
        If account number entered equals any account number in array
            THEN let DUPLICATE = TRUE and PRINT error message
            ELSE let DUPLICATE = FALSE
    NEXT INDEX.DUP
ENTER-NAME-AND-BALANCE
    Increment number of accounts (I)
    LET ACCT.NO% = Validated account number
    INPUT ACCT.NAME$ and ACCT.BAL#

===

DISPLAY-ACCOUNTS-AND-ENTER-CHANGES
    FOR INDEX = 1 to I STEP 20
        DO DISPLAY-NEXT-20-ACCOUNTS
        DO CALCULATE-BALANCE
        PRINT balance
        INPUT number of line to be changed
        IF line number is 1 through 20 DO ENTER-CHANGES
    NEXT INDEX

We want to display the accounts 20 at a time on the screen. We use one counter (INDEX) that is incremented using a STEP of 20 each time a screen is displayed until it equals or exceeds the total number of records (I). Each time through the loop, INDEX will equal the subscript of the first account to be displayed on that screen. When the first screen is displayed it will equal 1, when the second is displayed it will equal 21, and so on.

DISPLAY-NEXT-20-ACCOUNTS
    Calculate number to display on this screen (NUM.DISPLAY)

The total number of accounts will probably not be an even multiple of 20, so how do we handle the last screen? Each time a new screen is started, 20 is added to the current value of INDEX. As long as this new value is not greater than I, there are at least 20 more accounts to display. If it is greater than I, we need to figure out how many are left. Since INDEX equals the subscript of the first account to be displayed on the current screen, INDEX − 1 equals the number that have been displayed so far. The number left to be displayed is I less the number displayed so far (I − (INDEX − 1) = I − INDEX + 1) The variable NUM.DISPLAY is used to hold the actual number to be displayed for each "page." For example, if there are 28 records, I equals 28, and the first time through the outer loop, INDEX equals 1 and INDEX plus 20 equals 21. Since this is less than I, NUM.DISPLAY is set to 20. The second time through the outer loop, INDEX equals 21 and INDEX plus 20 equals 41. This is greater than I, therefore, NUM.DISPLAY is set to I (28) minus INDEX (21) plus 1 or a value of 8, the number of remaining records.

    FOR INDEX20 = 1 to NUM.DISPLAY

The second counter (INDEX20) equals the line number within each screen.

      Display line number, acct number, name & balance
    NEXT INDEX20

CALCULATE-BALANCE
    Let balance = zero
    FOR K = 1 TO I
      Add account balance to balance
    NEXT K

As accounts are being added and changed, it is important that the user know if the accounts are in balance. Each time a new screen is printed, the total is recalculated and displayed.

ENTER-CHANGES
    Redisplay selected line (J = Subscript of selected account)
    Select field to be changed
      If change is to ACCT.NO%, DO CHANGE-ACCOUNT-NUMBER
      If change is to ACCT.NAME$, input new name
      If change is to ACCT.BAL#, input new balance
      Reset INDEX to redisplay same screen
    NEXT INDEX
CHANGE-ACCOUNT-NUMBER
    Enter account number
    DO VALIDATE-ACCOUNT-NUMBER
    IF valid DO CHECK-FOR-DUPLICATE
    If valid and not duplicate
      THEN change account number
      ELSE print error message
===
SORT-ACCOUNTS
    Use bubble sort to sort on account number
    Display message to user that file is being sorted
===
PRINT-CHART-OF-ACCOUNTS

This is the same as the report in Case I, except that the data are taken from the array rather than from the file. Rather than repeat the discussion here, the writing of this report is left as an exercise (see Exercise 3).

```
===========================================================
WRITE-ACCOUNTS-TO-FILE
        DO CALCULATE-BALANCE
        If BALANCE# equals zero
                THEN DO WRITE-FILE
                ELSE PRINT error message
-------------------------------------------------------
WRITE-FILE
        DO SORT-ARRAY
        Print message to user that file is being written
        OPEN "TEMP.COA" for output
```

The array is first written to a temporary file. In this way, if there is an interruption, such as a power outage in the middle of writing the file, the original file will still be intact. As the new file is written, the balance is again calculated and checked. If the balance is zero, the old file is killed and the temporary file is renamed to be the new CHARTOF.ACT file.

```
        FOR INDEX = 1 to End of Array
                WRITE ACCT.NO%, ACCT.NAME$, ACCT.BAL#
        NEXT
        WRITE "dummy" ending record
        CLOSE file
        IF new balance equals zero
                THEN DO RENAME-FILES
                ELSE DO FILE-NOT-RENAMED
-------------------------------------------------------
RENAME-FILES
        Kill CHARTOF.ACT
        Rename TEMP.COA to be CHARTOF.ACT
        Let FILE.WRITTEN equal TRUE
-------------------------------------------------------
FILE-NOT-RENAMED
        Kill TEMP.COA
        Print error message
===========================================================
EXIT-FROM-PROGRAM
        If file has not been written (FILE.WRITTEN = FALSE)
                Confirm user wishes to exit
        let MORE.TO.DO equal FALSE
===========================================================
```

PROGRAM LISTING

```
10    ' GENERAL LEDGER SYSTEM
20    ' Program Name : BLDCOA.BAS
30    ' Date Written:  3/25/87
40    ' Written by:    F. K. Thompson
50  ' Program Description
60  '     This program updates the Chart of Accounts File-CHARTOF.ACT
70  '     User may add new accounts or change existing ones
80  '     The file is not rewritten unless the total of the balances
90  '          of all accounts equals zero
100 '  Program History
110 '      None to Date
120 ' ================================================================
500 ' ================================================================
510 '                     MAIN LINE
520 ' ================================================================
530 GOSUB 1000                         ' Initialization
540 WHILE MORE.TO.DO
550    GOSUB 2000                      ' Display Menu
560    ON CHOICE GOSUB 4000, 5000, 6000, 7000, 8000, 9000
570 '              4000 - Add New Account
580 '              5000 - Display and Change Existing Accounts
590 '              6000 - Sort Accounts
600 '              7000 - Print Listing of Accounts
610 '              8000 - Write Chart of Accounts to File
620 '              9000 - Exit from Program
630    WEND
640    END
1000 ' ================================================================
1010 '                     INITIALIZATION
1020 ' ================================================================
1030 KEY OFF
1040 OPTION BASE 1
1050 DEFINT I, J, K
1060 LET TRUE = -1: LET FALSE = 0
1070 LET MORE.TO.DO = TRUE: LET FILE.WRITTEN = FALSE
1080 DIM ACCT.NO%(100), ACCT.NAME$(100), ACCT.BAL#(100)
1200 ' ****************************************************************
1210 '              Read in Existing File
1220 ' ****************************************************************
1230 CLS: PRINT
1240 PRINT " ***    Reading in Chart of Accounts File ***"
1250 '  ----------------------------------------------------
1260 '  ****  Make Certain CHARTOF.ACT File Exists    ****
1270 '  ----------------------------------------------------
1280 OPEN "CHARTOF.ACT" FOR APPEND AS #3
1290    WRITE #3, 9999, "END OF FILE", 0
```

```
1300 CLOSE #3
1310 ' -------------------------------------------------
1320 ' ****Read in Existing Chart of Accounts     *****
1330 ' -------------------------------------------------
1340 OPEN "CHARTOF.ACT" FOR INPUT AS #3
1350 LET I = 0              '  I = Number of Accounts
1360 LET ACCT.NOX% = 0   '  ACCT.NOX% used to Test for Ending Record
1370 WHILE ACCT.NOX% <> 9999
1380    LET I = I + 1
1390    INPUT #3, ACCT.NO%(I), ACCT.NAME$(I), ACCT.BAL#(I)
1400    LET ACCT.NOX% = ACCT.NO%(I)
1410 WEND
1420 LET I = I - 1         ' Do not Count Ending Record
1430 CLOSE #3
1440 RETURN
2000 ' ============================================================
2010 '                    DISPLAY MENU
2020 ' ============================================================
2030 CLS                            ' Clear Screen
2040 PRINT TAB(25)  "UPDATE CHART OF ACCOUNTS
2050 PRINT
2060 PRINT " 1 = Add a New Account"
2070 PRINT " 2 = Display or Make Changes to Existing Accounts"
2080 PRINT " 3 = Sort Chart into Account Number Sequence"
2090 PRINT " 4 = Print Listing of Chart of Accounts"
2100 PRINT " 5 = Write Chart of Accounts to File"
2110 PRINT " 6 = Exit from Program"
2120 PRINT
2130 INPUT "Please Enter Your Choice (1-6) and press ENTER ", CHOICE
2140 WHILE CHOICE < 1 OR CHOICE > 6
2150    INPUT "Please Enter a 1, 2, 3, 4, 5, or 6 ", CHOICE
2160 WEND
2170 RETURN
4000 ' ============================================================
4010 '               ADD NEW ACCOUNT
4020 ' ============================================================
4030  CLS
4040  PRINT "ADD NEW ACCOUNTS TO CHART OF ACCOUNTS"
4050  INPUT "Please Enter the Account Number (9999 to exit) ", TEMP.ACCT.NO
4060  WHILE TEMP.ACCT.NO <> 9999
4070    GOSUB 4200                              ' Validate Account Number
4080    IF VALID = TRUE THEN GOSUB 4400        ' Check for Duplicate
4090    IF VALID AND NOT DUPLICATE THEN GOSUB 4600   ' Enter Name and Balance
4100    PRINT
4110    INPUT "Please Enter the Next Account Number (9999 to exit) ",
              TEMP.ACCT.NO
4120  WEND
```

```
4130   RETURN
4200 ' ***********************************************************
4210 '           Check for Valid Account Number
4220 ' ***********************************************************
4230   LET VALID = TRUE
4240   IF TEMP.ACCT.NO < 1 OR TEMP.ACCT.NO > 9999 THEN LET VALID = FALSE
4250   IF VALID = TRUE THEN LET INT.ACCT.NO = TEMP.ACCT.NO 'Test for Integer
4260   IF VALID = TRUE AND INT.ACCT.NO <> TEMP.ACCT.NO
           THEN LET VALID = FALSE
4270   IF VALID = FALSE THEN PRINT
           "* INVALID * Account Number must be an Integer 1 through 9999"
4280     RETURN
4400 ' ***********************************************************
4410 '           Check For Duplicate Account Number
4420 ' ***********************************************************
4430   LET DUPLICATE = FALSE
4440   FOR INDEX.DUP = 1 TO I            ' Check all existing accounts
4450       IF INT.ACCT.NO = ACCT.NO%(INDEX.DUP) THEN LET DUPLICATE = TRUE
4460   NEXT INDEX.DUP
4470   IF DUPLICATE = TRUE THEN PRINT "Duplicate Account Number"
4480   RETURN
4600 ' ***********************************************************
4610 '           Enter Account Name and Balance
4620 ' ***********************************************************
4630   LET I = I + 1
4640   LET ACCT.NO%(I) = INT.ACCT.NO
4650   INPUT "Enter Account Name:    ", ACCT.NAME$(I)
4660   INPUT "Enter Account Balance: ", ACCT.BAL#(I)
4670   RETURN
5000 ' ===========================================================
5010 '               DISPLAY AND ENTER CHANGES
5020 ' ===========================================================
5030 FOR INDEX = 1 TO I STEP 20         ' Display next 20 accounts
5040     GOSUB 5200                     '   Display accounts
5050     GOSUB 5400                     '   Calculate Balance
5060     PRINT USING "  >> Current Balance is ###,###,###.##    "; BALANCE#
5070     INPUT "Enter line number to be changed (1-20) Press RETURN if no
 correction: ", SELECTION
5080     IF SELECTION > 0 AND SELECTION < 21 THEN GOSUB 5600 ' enter changes
5090 NEXT INDEX
5100 RETURN
5200 ' ***********************************************************
5210 '               DISPLAY NEXT 20 ACCOUNTS
5220 ' ***********************************************************
5230 CLS
5240 '     Set NUM.DISPLAY to 20 or to number remaining if there are < 20
5250 IF INDEX + 20 > I THEN LET NUM.DISPLAY = I - INDEX + 1
                     ELSE LET NUM.DISPLAY = 20
```

```
5260 FOR INDEX20 = 1 TO NUM.DISPLAY
5270     LET J = INDEX20 + INDEX - 1        ' J = subscript in array
5280     PRINT USING
         "Line ## Acct #### Name \                   \ Balance ##,###,###.##";
             INDEX20, ACCT.NO%(J), ACCT.NAME$(J), ACCT.BAL#(J)
5290 NEXT INDEX20
5400 ' ************************************************************
5410 '            Calculate Balance
5420 ' ************************************************************
5430  LET BALANCE# = 0                ' BALANCE# = total of all accounts
5440  FOR K = 1 TO I
5450     LET BALANCE# = BALANCE# + ACCT.BAL#(K)
5460  NEXT K
5470  RETURN
5600 ' ************************************************************
5610 '            Enter Changes
5620 ' ************************************************************
5630  LET J = INDEX + SELECTION - 1         ' J = subscript in array
5640  PRINT , ACCT.NO%(J), ACCT.NAME$(J), ACCT.BAL#(J)
5650  INPUT "Enter field to edit: (N)umber, (D)escription, (B)alance or(Q)uit:
",    ANS$
5660  IF ANS$ = "N" OR ANS$ = "n" THEN GOSUB 5810  ' Change Acct No
5670  IF ANS$ = "D" OR ANS$ = "d" THEN
          INPUT "Enter New Account Name: ", ACCT.NAME$(J)
5680  IF ANS$ = "B" OR ANS$ = "b" THEN
          INPUT "Enter New Balance: ", ACCT.BAL#(J)
5690  LET INDEX = INDEX - 20           ' Set index to redisplay last 20
5700  RETURN
5800 ' ----------------------------------------------------------
5810 ' ********  Change Account Number  ******************
5820 ' ----------------------------------------------------------
5830  INPUT "Enter New Account Number: ", TEMP.ACCT.NO
5840  GOSUB 4200                       ' Check for Valid Account Number
5850  IF VALID = TRUE THEN GOSUB 4400  ' Check for Duplicate Number
5860  IF VALID AND NOT DUPLICATE THEN LET ACCT.NO%(J) = INT.ACCT.NO
             ELSE INPUT "press RETURN to reenter change", PAUSE$
5870  RETURN
6000 ' ==========================================================
6010 '            SORT INTO ACCOUNT NUMBER SEQUENCE
6020 ' ==========================================================
6030  CLS
6040  PRINT "  *** SORTING ACCOUNTS - PLEASE WAIT ***"
6050  FOR K = 1 TO I - 1
6060     FOR J = K + 1 TO I
6070        IF ACCT.NO%(J) < ACCT.NO%(K) THEN SWAP ACCT.NO%(J), ACCT.NO%(K):
             SWAP ACCT.NAME$(J),ACCT.NAME$(K): SWAP ACCT.BAL#(J),ACCT.BAL#(K)
6080     NEXT J
6090  NEXT K
6100  RETURN
```

```
7000 ' =============================================================
7010 '               PRINT CHART OF ACCOUNTS
7020 ' =============================================================
7030   PRINT   "Insert print routine from CASE I here"
7040   INPUT   "Press RETURN to return to menu", PAUSE$
7050   RETURN
8000 ' =============================================================
8010 '            WRITE CHART OF ACCOUNTS TO FILE
8020 ' =============================================================
8030   GOSUB 5400                      ' Calculate Balance
8040 '    Write File Only If Balance Equals Zero
8050   IF BALANCE# > -.005 AND BALANCE# < .005 THEN GOSUB 8100
          ELSE PRINT " Balance not Zero - File will not be Written":
                INPUT "Press RETURN and Enter Correction", PAUSE$
8060 RETURN
8100 ' ************************************************************
8110 '             Ok to Write File
8120 ' ************************************************************
8130   GOSUB 6000                      ' Sort Accounts
8140   LET DBL.CK.BAL# = 0          ' DBL.CK.BAL# used to check balance as write
8150   PRINT: PRINT "        *** WRITING FILE ***"
8160 ' ----------------------------------------------------
8170 '        Write to Temporary File
8180 ' ----------------------------------------------------
8190   OPEN "TEMP.COA" FOR OUTPUT AS #1    ' Write to Temporary File
8200   FOR INDEX = 1 TO I
8210      WRITE #1, ACCT.NO%(INDEX), ACCT.NAME$(INDEX), ACCT.BAL#(INDEX)
8220      LET DBL.CK.BAL# = DBL.CK.BAL# + ACCT.BAL#(INDEX)
8230   NEXT INDEX
8240   WRITE #1, 9999, "END OF FILE", 0     ' Write Ending Record
8250   CLOSE #1
8260 ' ----------------------------------------------------
8270 '    Check that Balance Still Equals Zero
8280 ' ----------------------------------------------------
8290   IF DBL.CK.BAL# > -.005 AND DBL.CK.BAL# < .005
          THEN GOSUB 8400    ELSE  GOSUB 8500
8300 RETURN
8400 ' ----------------------------------------------------
8410 '  ****    IN BALANCE-Rename Files              ****
8420 ' ----------------------------------------------------
8430   KILL "CHARTOF.ACT"
8440   NAME "TEMP.COA" AS "CHARTOF.ACT"
8450   LET FILE.WRITTEN = TRUE
8460   RETURN
8500 ' ----------------------------------------------------
8510 '  ****    OUT OF BALANCE-DO NOT Rename Files ****
8520 ' ----------------------------------------------------
8530   KILL "TEMP.COA"
```

```
8540   PRINT "   *** Out of Balance-File Not Changed ***"
8550   INPUT "Press RETURN to return to Menu", PAUSE$
8560   LET FILE.WRITTEN = FALSE
8570   RETURN
9000   ' ===========================================================
9010   '            EXIT FROM PROGRAM
9020   ' ===========================================================
9030 LET MORE.TO.DO = FALSE
9040 LET YES.NO$ = "Y"
9050   '    Verify that File has been Written
9060 PRINT
9070 IF FILE.WRITTEN = FALSE THEN INPUT
        "File not yet written-Do you want to QUIT anyway (Y/N)"; YES.NO$
9080 WHILE YES.NO$<>"Y" AND YES.NO$<>"y" AND YES.NO$<>"N" AND YES.NO$<>"n"
9090     INPUT "Please enter Y or N ", YES.NO$
9100   WEND
9110 IF YES.NO$ = "N" OR YES.NO$ = "n" THEN LET MORE.TO.DO = TRUE
9120 RETURN
9130 '===========================================================
9140 '          END OF LISTING
9150 '===========================================================
```

PROGRAM OUTPUT

Here is what appears on the screen as the account for petty cash is added to the chart.

(screen clears)

```
ADD NEW ACCOUNTS TO CHART OF ACCOUNTS
Please Enter the Account Number (9999 to exit) 1010
Enter Account Name:   Petty Cash
Enter Account Balance: 50
```

After the accounts have been added, option 2 displays them, 20 at a time, and asks if changes are to be made. The first 20 accounts appear as follows.

(screen clears)

```
Line  1 Acct 1001 Name Cash in Checking Acc Balance    13,875.75
Line  2 Acct 1010 Name Petty Cash           Balance        50.00
Line  3 Acct 2010 Name Assets: Office Furni Balance    45,700.00
Line  4 Acct 2020 Name Assets: Equipment    Balance    67,705.86
Line  5 Acct 2500 Name Accumulated Deprecia Balance   -25,000.00
Line  6 Acct 4100 Name Withholding Payable  Balance    -5,600.00
Line  7 Acct 4500 Name Accounts Payable     Balance   -23,864.90
Line  8 Acct 4520 Name Notes Payable        Balance    -8,525.65
Line  9 Acct 6100 Name Capital Stock        Balance   -30,000.00
Line 10 Acct 6200 Name Retained Earnings    Balance    56,188.86
```

```
Line 11 Acct 7100 Name Income: Sale of Good Balance   -705,976.98
Line 12 Acct 7200 Name Income: Services     Balance   -13,000.00
Line 13 Acct 7300 Name Income: Other        Balance    -1,059.00
Line 14 Acct 8000 Name Salaries - Professio Balance   359,700.00
Line 15 Acct 8100 Name Salaries - Clerical  Balance   125,079.00
Line 16 Acct 8200 Name Salaries - Other     Balance    50,100.00
Line 17 Acct 8300 Name Employee Benefits    Balance    25,100.50
Line 18 Acct 8500 Name Expenses: Rent       Balance    45,000.00
Line 19 Acct 8510 Name Expenses: Utilities  Balance     5,836.98
Line 20 Acct 8700 Name Expenses: Supplies   Balance     3,000.00
   >> Current Balance is              0.00
Enter line number to be changed (1-20) Press RETURN if no correction:
```

· EXERCISES ·

1. Run the program "BLDCOA.BAS" and do the following:
   a. Add Acct 8400 with the name Expenses: Outside Services and a balance of $10,250.
   b. Display the accounts. What is the current balance?
   c. Try option 5, Write Chart of Accounts. What happened?
   d. Modify the balance in the following two accounts:

   7200 Income: Services—New Balance   −23,000.00
   7300 Income: Other—New Balance   −1,309.00

   e. Now try option 5.
   f. Experiment with adding some accounts of your own.
   Remember, if you exit the program before writing the file, the changes you enter will not be saved in the file.

2. Add a routine that asks the user to enter a password before the menu is displayed. If the password entered by the user does not match the one you have stored, do not allow the user to proceed.
   You can put the password in a DATA statement (Chapter 9) or develop some techniques of your own.
   If you have covered Chapter 12, use INPUT$ or INKEY$ so that the characters input do not display on the screen.

3. Complete the routine to print the Chart of Accounts report. (See Case I for report specifications.) Sort the array before the report is printed. If you have access to a printer, produce the report on the printer; if not, display it on the screen. If you choose the screen, have the program pause at the end of each screen and wait for the user to press Enter before the next screen is displayed.

4. Option 2 in "BLDCOA.BAS" currently displays all of the accounts. Modify this option to give the user the choice of displaying all the accounts as is currently done, or displaying just a single account. If the user selects the latter option, request that the account number be entered and search the array for that number. You may use either a linear or a binary search. (Remember that if you use a binary search, you must be certain the accounts are in numeric sequence before you begin.)

5. (Requires Chapters 11 and 12.) Modify the screen display for option 1, Add a New Account, to make it more appealing. Using the techniques covered in Chapters 11 and 12, print the error messages at the bottom of the screen. Use your imagination in creating borders and making use of BEEP, blinking characters, or inverse video.

6. Add an option to delete an account. One way to do this is to "mark" an account in the array for deletion and, at the time the file is written, not to write the account to file. You will need to modify the write routine to test for this "mark." The "mark" could be changing the account name to "DELETE" or some other combination of characters.

   Another way to delete would be to move each account after the one to be deleted forward one place in the array.

GENERAL LEDGER—
ENTER AND POST
JOURNAL ENTRIES

Chapters Required: Part I and Part II, Chapters 7 and 8.

PROBLEM SPECIFICATION

As business expenditures occur and income is received, these transactions are recorded in journals. These **Journal Entries** may be made in manual ledgers or in disk files. Periodically, these entries are **posted** to the Chart of Accounts, updating the balances in the appropriate accounts.

This case discusses the two programs needed to accomplish posting to the Chart of Accounts using disk files. The first program allows the user to create Journal Entries and saves them on disk. The second program processes the Journal Entries to update the balances in the Chart of Accounts file.

What Is a Journal Entry?

A Journal Entry records the transfer of money between accounts. This transfer is recorded as a credit to one or more accounts and a debit to another account or accounts. To keep the accounts in balance, the total amount credited must always equal the total amount debited.

An example of a Journal Entry to record the salary paid to an employee is written as follows:

J E Number: 31
Date: 05-15-87
Description: Wages paid to M. Mouser
    Acct 1001: Cash in Checking Account   1000.00
    Acct 4100: Withholding Payable   500.00
    Acct 8000: Salaries — Professional   1500.00

Each Journal Entry consists of two parts. The first part is data that identify the entry (Journal Entry number, date, description), and the second part consists of the accounts and the amounts that are to be debited (added) or credited (subtracted) to the balance. There will always be just one descriptive part for each Journal Entry, but there may be any number of items in the second part.

File Layout

How shall we store these data in the system? One way to solve this would be to decide on the maximum number of transactions that would be allowed for any Journal Entry and make all Journal Entries large enough to hold this information. Two drawbacks to this potential solution are that it limits the number of entries available for any Journal Entry and it wastes an enormous amount of space.

The solution we have selected is to build two files to store the journal data. One file will contain the descriptive information for the Journal Entry (JETITLES) and the second will contain the detail data (JEDETAIL). The Journal Entry Number (JE.NO) will appear in both files and will be the link between the two.

File JETITLE: Descriptive Part of Journal Entry
Sequential file. Records are stored in the sequence in which they are entered.

JE.NO — Up to four digits used to identify this event
JE.DATE — mmddyy
JE.DESC$ — Up to 30 characters of descriptive data

File JEDETAIL: Transaction Part of Journal Entry
Sequential file. Records are stored in the sequence in which they are entered.

JE.NO — Same four-digit number used in the descriptive part
JE.ACCT — Number of the account (in the Chart of Accounts) that is to be updated
JE.AMT — Amount that is to be posted to the account. Debit entries will be entered as positive amounts. Credit entries will be entered as negative amounts.

Remember that within any Journal Entry as well as within the Chart of Accounts as a whole, the total of the amounts must always equal zero for it to be "in balance."

We will also use the Chart of Accounts file for both programs.

File CHARTOF.ACT: Chart of Accounts
Sequential file in order by account number. For each account the following data are in the file:

ACCT.NO   Positive integer, not greater than 9999
ACCT.NAME$ String, maximum of 30 characters
ACCT.BAL#   Double precision, positive or negative, maximum value
              99,999,999.99

The records are in ascending sequence by account number. The final record is a "dummy" record with account number 9999 used to flag the end of the file.

Discussion of Processing to Be Performed

Enter Journal Entries
Making a Journal Entry is straightforward. The program will first ask for a Journal Entry number to identify this entry, the date of the entry, and description.

It will next ask for transactions, one at a time. For each transaction it will ask for the account number and the amount of the transaction. The program will check that the account number already exists in the chart of accounts (CHARTOF.ACT file). If it does, the name of the account will be displayed and the user asked to verify that this is the correct account.

As the transactions amounts are entered, the program will total them and display this total. The Journal Entry will not be written unless the total of the transaction amounts is zero.

When all the transactions for this Journal Entry have been entered and the total of the transaction amounts is zero, the descriptive data will be written to the file JETITLE and the transactions will be written to the file JEDETAIL. We will keep the Journal Entry files in sequence by order of entry. This feature, which has the virtue of simplicity, serves as an audit trail.

Although the program will verify that the account number is valid and that the total of the transactions is zero, how will we handle the case when the user enters an incorrect amount or, after having entered several transactions, realizes that one of the account numbers is incorrect? The program solves this by asking the user, "OK to write entry?" before the entry is written. If the response is no, the Journal Entry will not be written to the file and the user may reenter it. (We have left as an exercise adding the ability to display and edit a Journal Entry before it is written. See Exercise 3.)

However, once an entry is written, the only way to correct the error is by making a reversing entry. A reversing entry is one that backs out the former transaction by crediting the account with the amount that was originally debited (or vice versa) and then debiting (or crediting) the correct account. While this may sound cumbersome, it is good accounting practice. (No one erases the books, only points out errors, and shows how the error was reversed.)

We have dimensioned the arrays to accept up to 25 transactions per Journal Entry. This should be ample for most businesses but could be changed if needed by a particular business by altering the dimension statements. We have also planned for up to 1500 Journal Entries to be made each month. (This number provides for 60 Journal Entries each business day. It is a sufficient number for a small business.)

Post Journal Entries to the Chart of Accounts

Posting will be done on a periodic basis depending on the needs of the organization. For this case we have assumed it is done once each month.

We mentioned an audit trail earlier. For all accounting systems there needs to be a way that all changes to the accounts can be traced. Therefore, a permanent trail should be kept of all transactions. The report that is printed as the accounts are updated is one such trail. It is also good practice to keep copies of the files involved in the updating process. Not only will this provide additional documentation, should anything happen to the file after posting is completed (such as being accidentally erased), it will also allow the process to be repeated. In order to facilitate making the copies, the program asks the user to enter a three-letter identification for the month of processing. At the end of the posting process the original files are renamed using this identifier as the extension.

As the posting is done, for each account the beginning balance will be printed, followed by all the transactions that update it. The new balance will be calculated and written to a file as well as printed on the report.

After all the transactions have been posted to the accounts, the program will verify that the general ledger is "in balance."

If it is, the file containing the Chart of Accounts with the beginning balances for that month and the files with the Journal Entries for that month will be renamed using the month designator. These files can be copied to another disk for permanent storage and erased from the current disk to make space for the next month's entries. Figure III.1 illustrates the relationship between these files and programs.

FUNCTIONS TO BE PERFORMED

Enter Journal Entries

A. Initialization.
    1. Read in the Chart of Accounts file (CHARTOF.ACT)
B. Enter Journal Entries
    1. Verify that Journal Entry number is an integer
    2. Enter descriptive data
    3. Enter transaction data
        a. Verify that account number is valid
        b. Enter amounts

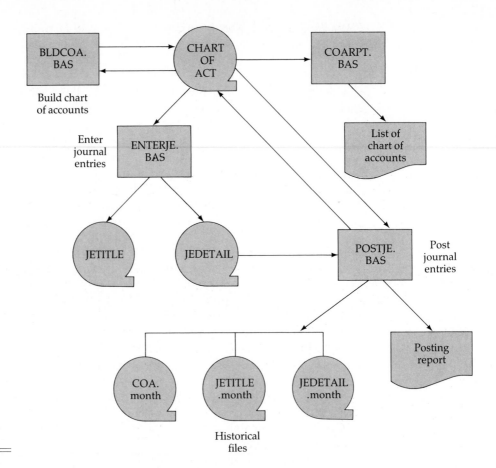

FIGURE III.1 •
General ledger
programs and
files

    4. If total transactions equal zero, write Journal Entry
  C. Close files

Post Journal Entries to Account Balances

  A. Initialization
    1. Read in Chart of Accounts and Journal Entry files
  B. For each account
    1. Print the beginning account balance
    2. Find all Journal Entries for this account
    3. Print the entry and add to account balance
    4. Print the ending account balance
    5. Write account with new balance to file
  C. Closing activities
    1. Close files
    2. If balance of all accounts equals zero rename files

STRUCTURE CHART

Figures III.2 and III.3 show the structure charts for both these programs.

At this point we will go through the remaining steps for the program to enter Journal Entries (ENTERJE.BAS) and then the program to post them (POSTJE.BAS).

DATA DICTIONARY FOR **ENTERJE.BAS**

DATA in File JETITLE
JE.NOX%   Journal Entry number
JE.DATE$ Journal Entry date
JE.DESC$ Journal Entry description

DATA in File JEDETAIL
JE.NOX%   Journal Entry number matches
                                    JE.NOX% in JETITLE
JE.ACCT%()   Number of account to be updated
                                    placed in array, dimensioned at 25
JE.AMT#()   Amount of transaction placed in
                                    array, dimensioned at 25

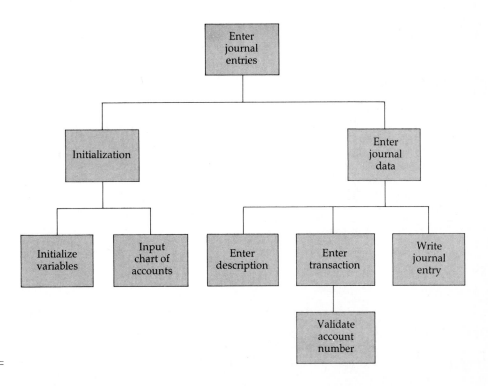

FIGURE III.2 •
Structure chart
for
ENTERJE.BAS

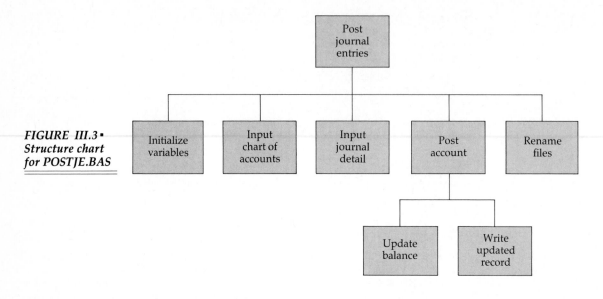

FIGURE III.3 ▪
Structure chart
for POSTJE.BAS

DATA from File CHARTOF.ACT

ACCT.NO%()	Account number placed in array, dimensioned at 100
ACCT.NAME$()	Description of account placed in array, dimensioned at 100
DUMMY#	Unused account balance

Working Variables

TRUE	Initialized to −1
FALSE	Initialized to 0
I	Number of accounts
TEMP.JE.NOX	Journal Entry number as entered
TEMP.ACCTX	Account number as entered

Accumulators

TEMP.BALANCE#	Total of transaction amounts

Counters

INDEX	Number of transactions in journal entry
J	Counter used during search for acct no
K	Counter in FOR . . . NEXT loop

Switches

ANY.MORE.ENTRIES	TRUE until user signals exit
VALID.JE	TRUE if JE.NOX is positive integer
A$	Yes or no switch
IN$	Yes or no switch

PSEUDOCODE FOR **ENTERJE.BAS**

MAIN LINE
    DO INITIALIZATION
    WHILE ANY.MORE.ENTRIES
        DO ENTER-JOURNAL-ENTRIES
    WEND

==

INITIALIZATION
    Initialize variables
    Dimension arrays
    DO READ-IN-CHART-OF-ACCOUNTS

READ-IN-CHART-OF-ACCOUNTS
    OPEN CHARTOF.ACCT
    PRINT message telling user file is being read
    WHILE not last record (ACCT.NO <> 9999)
        Increment subscript (I)
        INPUT ACCT.NO and ACCT.NAME
    WEND
    Subtract 1 from subscript (I)
    CLOSE file

Only the account number and name are needed from the Chart of Accounts file. Therefore, no array is dimensioned for the account balance. But because the balance does exist on the file, it must be identified in the INPUT# statement. The variable is given the name DUMMY# to indicate it is not used in this program.

==

ENTER JOURNAL ENTRIES
    DO INPUT-JE-NO
    IF JE.NO is not zero DO ENTER-JE-DATA

INPUT-JE.NO
    WHILE journal entry number (JE.NO) is not valid
        INPUT journal entry number
        If a positive integer
            THEN let VALID.JE = TRUE
            ELSE let VALID.JE = FALSE
    WEND

DO ENTER-JE-DATA
    INPUT journal entry date (JE.DATE$)
    INPUT journal entry description (JE.DESC$)
    INPUT account number (TEMP.ACCTX)
    WHILE TEMP.ACCTX is not zero
        DO FIND-ACCOUNT-IN-CHART

        PRINT account description
        IF account number is in chart DO CONFIRM-ACCOUNT
        IF account number is in chart and has been confirmed
            DO ENTER-TRANS-AMOUNT
        INPUT next account number (TEMP.ACCTX)
   WEND
   IF total of transactions is zero
        THEN DO WRITE-JOURNAL-ENTRY
        ELSE PRINT error message

FIND-ACCOUNT-IN-CHART
   LET J = 1
   WHILE TEMP.ACCTX does not equal account number in array
    (ACCT.NO(J)) AND J is less than or equal to I
       LET J = J + 1
   WEND
   IF J is less then equal to I (match was found)
       THEN LET VALID.NUM = TRUE and LET acct
        descrip = ACCT.NAME$(J)
       ELSE LET VALID.NUM = FALSE and LET acct descrip = error
       message

CONFIRM ACCOUNT
   Ask user if this is right account
   IF user answers "yes"
       THEN LET VALID = TRUE
       ELSE LET VALID = FALSE

ENTER-TRANS-AMOUNT
   Increment Subscript for Transaction (INDEX)
   LET JE.ACCT%(INDEX) = TEMP.ACCTX
   INPUT Amount (JE.AMT#)
   Add Amount to Journal Entry Balance (TEMP.BALANCE#)
   Print Balance and Warning if not Zero

===

WRITE-JOURNAL-ENTRY
   Ask user if OK to write entry
   IF answer is "yes" THEN DO OK-TO-WRITE

OK-TO-WRITE
   PRINT message that entry is being written
   OPEN JETITLE and JEDETAIL files for APPEND
   WRITE Description Data to JETITLE
   FOR J = 1 TO INDEX (INDEX equals the number of transactions)

```
              WRITE Transaction Data to JEDETAIL
          NEXT J
          CLOSE Files
```

PROGRAM LISTING FOR ENTERJE.BAS

```
10  '   General Ledger System - Enter Journal Entries
20  '   Name of Program:   ENTERJE.BAS
30  '   Date Written:      05-28-87
40  '   Written by:        K. F. Simpson
50  '   Program Description
60  '      Inputs Data for Journal Entries
70  '      Descriptive Data is Saved in file JETITLE
80  '          Fields are:JE.NOX%, JE.DATE$ and JE.DESC$
90  '      Transactions are Saved in file JEDETAIL
100 '          Fields are:JE.NOX%, JE.ACCT%, JE.AMT#
200 ' Program History
210 '      None to Date
220 '
500 ' ================================================================
510 '               MAIN LINE
520 ' ================================================================
530 GOSUB 1000                      'initialize variables
540 WHILE ANY.MORE.ENTRIES     'enter journal entries
550      GOSUB 2000
560 WEND
570 END
580 '   *****    end of processing  ******
1000 ' ================================================================
1010 '               INITIALIZATION
1020 ' ================================================================
1030 KEY OFF
1040 LET TRUE = -1: LET FALSE = 0
1050 LET ANY.MORE.ENTRIES = TRUE
1060 DEFINT I, J, K
1070 OPTION BASE 1
1080 DIM JE.ACCT%(25), JE.AMT#(25)        ' journal entry transactions
1090 DIM ACCT.NO%(100), ACCT.NAME$(100) ' chart of accounts
1100 ' ***********************************************************************
1110 '               Read in Chart of Accounts
1120 ' ***********************************************************************
1130 OPEN "CHARTOF.ACT" FOR INPUT AS #1
1140 CLS
1150 PRINT "Reading in Chart of Accounts"
1160 LET I = 0: LET ACCT.NOX% = 0
1170 WHILE ACCT.NOX% <> 9999
1180      LET I = I + 1
```

```
1190          INPUT #1, ACCT.NO%(I), ACCT.NAME$(I), DUMMY#
1200          LET ACCT.NOX% = ACCT.NO%(I)
1210 WEND
1220 LET I = I - 1
1230 CLOSE #1
1240 RETURN
1250 '
2000 ' ================================================================
2010 '               ENTER JOURNAL ENTRIES
2020 ' ================================================================
2030 CLS
2040 LET VALID.JE = FALSE
2050 WHILE VALID.JE = FALSE
2060    INPUT "Enter Journal Entry Number (ENTER to quit) ", TEMP.JE.NOX
2070    IF TEMP.JE.NOX < 0 OR TEMP.JE.NOX > 32767
           THEN LET VALID.JE = FALSE
           ELSE LET VALID.JE = TRUE
2080    IF VALID.JE = TRUE THEN LET JE.NOX% = TEMP.JE.NOX
2090    IF VALID.JE = TRUE AND JE.NOX% <> TEMP.JE.NOX
           THEN LET VALID.JE = FALSE
2100    IF VALID.JE = FALSE
           THEN PRINT "Number must be an Integer between 0 and 32767"
2110 WEND
2120 IF JE.NOX% <> 0 THEN GOSUB 2300 ELSE LET ANY.MORE.ENTRIES = FALSE
2130 RETURN
2300 ' ************************************************************
2310 '               Enter Journal Entry Description
2320 ' ************************************************************
2330 INPUT "Enter journal entry date as mmddyy ", JE.DATE$
2340 INPUT "Enter journal entry description    ",JE.DESC$
2350 LET INDEX = 0
2360 INPUT "Please Enter General Account Number (ENTER to quit)"; TEMP.ACCTX
2370 WHILE TEMP.ACCTX <> 0
2380    GOSUB 2600                              'find account in chart
2390    PRINT "Account Name: "; ACCT.NAMEX$
2400    IF VALID.NUM THEN GOSUB 2700           ' confirm account
2410    IF VALID AND VALID.NUM THEN GOSUB 2800  ' enter amount
2420    INPUT "Please Enter General Account Number (ENTER to quit)";
              TEMP.ACCTX
2430 WEND
2500 '       -----------------------------------------
2510 '          VERIFY BALANCE IS ZERO BEFORE WRITING
2520 '       -----------------------------------------
2530 IF TEMP.BALANCE# > -.005 AND TEMP.BALANCE# < .005 THEN GOSUB 4000
        ELSE PRINT " * OUT OF BALANCE - Journal Entry Not Saved *":
              INPUT "Press ENTER to re-enter Journal", PAUSE$
2540 RETURN
2600 ' -----------------------------------------------------------
2610 '               Find Account in Chart
```

```
2620 ' ------------------------------------------------------------
2630 LET J = 1
2640 WHILE TEMP.ACCTX <> ACCT.NO%(J) AND J <= I
2650     LET J = J + 1
2660 WEND
2670 IF J <= I THEN LET VALID.NUM = TRUE: LET ACCT.NAMEX$ = ACCT.NAME$(J)
               ELSE LET VALID.NUM = FALSE: LET ACCT.NAMEX$ = "Account not Found"
2680 RETURN
2700 ' ------------------------------------------------------------
2710 '         Confirm Account Name
2720 ' ------------------------------------------------------------
2730 INPUT "Is this the right one (Y or N)"; A$
2740 WHILE A$ <> "Y" AND A$ <> "y" AND A$ <> "N" AND A$ <> "n"
2750     INPUT "Please answer Y or N ", A$
2760 WEND
2770 IF A$ = "Y" OR A$ = "y" THEN LET VALID = TRUE ELSE LET VALID = FALSE
2780 RETURN
2800 ' ----------------------------------------------------------
2810 '              Enter Amount
2820 ' ----------------------------------------------------------
2830 LET INDEX = INDEX + 1
2840 LET JE.ACCT%(INDEX) = TEMP.ACCTX
2850 INPUT "Please Enter Amount ", JE.AMT#(INDEX)
2860 LET TEMP.BALANCE# = TEMP.BALANCE# + JE.AMT#(INDEX)
2870 PRINT "Current Balance Is"; TEMP.BALANCE#;
2880 IF TEMP.BALANCE# < -.005 OR TEMP.BALANCE# > .005
        THEN PRINT "* Journal Entry Cannot be Saved Until In Balance *"
2890 PRINT
2900 RETURN
4000 ' **************************************************************
4010 '              Write Journal Entry
4020 ' **************************************************************
4030 '          Confirm OK to Write
4040 PRINT: INPUT "OK to WRITE ENTRY (Y/N)" ; IN$
4050 WHILE IN$ <> "Y" AND IN$ <> "y" AND IN$ <> "N" AND IN$ <> "n"
4060     INPUT "Please answer Y or N ", IN$
4070 WEND
4080 IF IN$ = "Y" OR IN$ = "y" THEN GOSUB 4100
4090 RETURN
4100 ' ----------------------------------------------------------
4110 '          OK to Write
4120 ' ----------------------------------------------------------
4130 PRINT "Saving Journal Entry"
4140 OPEN "JEDETAIL" FOR APPEND AS #1
4150 OPEN "JETITLE" FOR APPEND AS #2
4160 WRITE #2, JE.NOX%, JE.DATE$, JE.DESC$ ' Write Description
4170 FOR K = 1 TO INDEX                    ' Write Transactions
4180     WRITE #1, JE.NOX%, JE.ACCT%(K), JE.AMT#(K)
4190 NEXT K
```

```
4200 CLOSE
4210 RETURN
5000 ' =============================================================
5010 '                END OF LISTING
5020 ' =============================================================
```

PROGRAM OUTPUT FOR ENTERJE.BAS

The following sequence shows entry of two Journal Entries using this program.

```
Reading in Chart of Accounts

(screen clears)

Enter Journal Entry Number (ENTER to quit) 15
Enter journal entry date as mmddyy 051087
Enter journal entry description   May rent payment
Please Enter General Account Number (ENTER to quit)? 1001
Account Name: Cash in Checking Account
Is this the right one (Y or N)? y
Please Enter Amount -9000
Current Balance Is-9000 * Journal Entry Cannot be Saved Until In Balance *

Please Enter General Account Number (ENTER to quit)? 8500
Account Name: Expenses: Rent
Is this the right one (Y or N)? y
Please Enter Amount 9000
Current Balance Is 0
Please Enter General Account Number (ENTER to quit)? <ENTER>
OK to WRITE ENTRY (Y/N)? y
Saving Journal Entry

(screen clears)

Enter Journal Entry Number (ENTER to quit) 31
Enter journal entry date as mmddyy 051587
Enter journal entry description   wages paid to M. Mouser
Please Enter General Account Number (ENTER to quit)? 1001
Account Name: Cash in Checking Account
Is this the right one (Y or N)? y
Please Enter Amount -1000
Current Balance Is-1000 * Journal Entry Cannot be Saved Until In Balance *

Please Enter General Account Number (ENTER to quit)? 4100
Account Name: Withholding Payable
Is this the right one (Y or N)? y
Please Enter Amount -500
Current Balance Is-1500 * Journal Entry Cannot be Saved Until In Balance *

Please Enter General Account Number (ENTER to quit)? 8000
Account Name: Salaries - Professional
```

```
Is this the right one (Y or N)? y
Please Enter Amount 1500
Current Balance Is 0
Please Enter General Account Number (ENTER to quit)? <ENTER>
OK to WRITE ENTRY (Y/N)? y
Saving Journal Entry
Enter Journal Entry Number (ENTER to quit) <ENTER>
Ok
```

DATA DICTIONARY FOR POSTJE.BAS

Data from File JEDETAIL

JE.NO%()	Journal Entry number placed in array, dimensioned at 1500
JE.ACCT%()	Number of account to be updated placed in array, dimensioned at 1500
JE.AMT#()	Amount of transaction placed in array, dimensioned at 1500

Data from File CHARTOF.ACT

ACCT.NO%()	Account number placed in array, dimensioned at 100
ACCT.NAME$()	Description of account placed in array, dimensioned at 100
ACCT.BAL#()	Account balance

Working Variables

AMT.MASK$	Mask for printing amounts
NO.OF.ACCOUNTS	Number of accounts
NO.OF.JE	Number of Journal Entries

Accumulators

BALANCE#	Total of all updated account balances

Counters

INDEX	Counter in FOR . . . NEXT loop
COUNT	Counter in FOR . . . NEXT loop

Switches

ANS$	Yes or no switch
KEEP.ON.GOING	TRUE or FALSE switch that controls main loop

PSEUDOCODE FOR POSTJE.BAS

MAIN-LINE
    DO INITIALIZATION
    DO VERIFY-READY-TO-PROCESS

```
        WHILE KEEP.ON.GOING = TRUE
            DO INPUT-CHART-OF-ACCOUNTS
            DO INPUT-JOURNAL-ENTRIES
            DO ENTER-MONTH-AND-OPEN-OUTPUT-FILES
            DO POST-ACCOUNTS-AND-PRINT-REPORT
            DO RENAME-FILES
        WEND
```

===

INITIALIZATION
    Initialize variables
    Dimension arrays

===

VERIFY-READY-TO-PROCESS
    PRINT message reminding user to have backup copies of files
    Ask user if ready to continue with process
    IF answer is "yes"
        THEN LET KEEP.ON.GOING = TRUE
        ELSE LET KEEP.ON.GOING = FALSE

===

INPUT-CHART-OF-ACCOUNTS
    PRINT message that file is being read
    OPEN CHARTOF.ACT for INPUT
    WHILE not last record (ACCT.NO <> 9999)
        Increment NO.OF.ACCTS
        INPUT ACCT.NO, ACCT.NAME$. ACCT.BAL
    WEND
    CLOSE file
    Subtract 1 from NO.OF.ACCTS (NO.OF.ACCTS = number of accounts in
       chart)

===

INPUT-JOURNAL-ENTRIES
    PRINT message that file is being read
    OPEN JEDETAIL for INPUT
    WHILE end of file
        Increment NO.OF.JE (NO.OF.JE will equal number of transactions)
        INPUT JE.NO, JE.ACCT, JE.AMT
    WEND
    CLOSE file

===

ENTER-MONTH-AND-OPEN-OUTPUT-FILE
    INPUT posting month (MONTH$)
    OPEN COA.TMP for OUTPUT

===

POST-ACCOUNTS-AND-PRINT-REPORT

```
        FOR INDEX = 1 TO NO.OF.ACCTS
            DO PROCESS-NEXT-ACCOUNT
        NEXT INDEX
-----------------------------------------------------------
PROCESS-NEXT-ACCOUNT
        PRINT account number, name, and beginning balance
        FOR COUNT = 1 TO NO.OF.JE
            IF journal entry account number equals this account
                THEN DO POST-MATCHING-JOURNAL-ENTRIES
        NEXT COUNT
        PRINT ending balance
        WRITE updated account to COA.TMP
        Add ending balance to BALANCE#
-----------------------------------------------------------
POST-MATCHING-JOURNAL-ENTRIES
        PRINT journal entry number and amount
        Add journal entry amount to account balance
===========================================================
RENAME-FILES
        WRITE dummy record to COA.TMP
        PRINT current balance (BALANCE#)
        IF balance equals zero
            THEN DO OK-TO-RENAME
            ELSE PRINT error message
        LET KEEP.ON.GOING = FALSE
-----------------------------------------------------------
OK-TO-RENAME
        PRINT message that files are being renamed
        NAME old chart of accounts file as COA. followed by month indicator
        NAME COA.TMP as CHARTOF.ACT
        NAME old JETITLE as JETITLE. followed by month indicator
        NAME old JEDETAIL as JEDETAIL. followed by month indicator
        PRINT message showing names of old files
===========================================================
```

PROGRAM LISTING FOR POSTJE.BAS

```
10  '   General Ledger - Post Journal Entries to Accounts
20  '   Program Name:  POSTJE.BAS
30  '   Date Written:  06-06-88
40  '   Written by:    F. K. Thompson
50  '   Program Description
60  '      Posts transactions from Journal Entry Files
70  '              to balances in Chart of Accounts Files
80  '      Files used:
```

```
90  '            CHARTOF.ACT        Chart of Accounts
100 '              JEDETAIL         Journal Entry Transactions
110 '      Program History:
120 '              None to date
130 '
140 '
500 '  ============================================================
510 '              MAIN LINE
520 '  ============================================================
530 GOSUB 1000                       ' Initialization
540 GOSUB 2000                       ' Verify Ready to Process
550 WHILE KEEP.ON.GOING = TRUE
560    GOSUB  3000                   ' Input Chart of Accounts from file
570    GOSUB  3500                   ' Input Journal Entries from file
580    GOSUB  4000                   ' Enter Month and Open Output File
590    GOSUB  5000                   ' Post to Account and Print Report
600    GOSUB  6000                   ' Rename Files
610 WEND
620 END
630 '  ============================================================
640 '              END OF PROCESSING
650 '  ============================================================
1000 '  ============================================================
1010 '              INITIALIZATION
1020 '  ============================================================
1030 LET TRUE = -1: LET FALSE = 0
1040 LET BALANCE# = 0
1045 LET AMT.MASK$ = "###,###,###.##"
1050 OPTION BASE 1
1060 DIM ACCT.NO%(100), ACCT.NAME$(100), ACCT.BAL#(100)
1070 DIM JE.NO%(1500), JE.ACCT%(1500), JE.AMT#(1500)
1080 RETURN
2000 '  ============================================================
2010 '              VERIFY READY TO PROCESS
2020 '  ============================================================
2030   CLS
2040   PRINT "**  This Program Will Update The Chart of Account Balances **"
2050   PRINT "    Be sure you have current backup copies of the files before
you continue"
2060   INPUT "    Do you wish to continue with this process (Y or N)"; ANS$
2070   WHILE ANS$ <> "Y" AND ANS$ <> "y" AND ANS$ <> "N" AND ANS$ <> "n"
2080       INPUT "Please enter Y or N ", ANS$
2090   WEND
2100   IF ANS$ = "Y" OR ANS$ = "y" THEN LET KEEP.ON.GOING = TRUE
          ELSE LET KEEP.ON.GOING = FALSE
2110   RETURN
3000 '  ============================================================
3010 '              READ CHART OF ACCOUNTS FILE
```

```
3020  ' ================================================================
3030  PRINT: PRINT " >>>   READING CHART OF ACCOUNTS   <<<"
3040  OPEN "CHARTOF.ACT" FOR INPUT AS #1
3050  LET NO.OF.ACCTS = 0: LET ACCT.NO% = 0
3060  WHILE ACCT.NO% <> 9999
3070     LET NO.OF.ACCTS = NO.OF.ACCTS + 1
3080     INPUT #1, ACCT.NO%(NO.OF.ACCTS), ACCT.NAME$(NO.OF.ACCTS),
                     ACCT.BAL#(NO.OF.ACCTS)
3090     LET ACCT.NO% = ACCT.NO%(NO.OF.ACCTS)
3100  WEND
3200  CLOSE #1
3210  LET NO.OF.ACCTS = NO.OF.ACCTS - 1
3220  RETURN
3500  ' ================================================================
3510  '               READ JOURNAL ENTRY DETAIL FILE
3520  ' ================================================================
3530  PRINT: PRINT ">>>   READING JOURNAL ENTRY FILE   <<<"
3540  OPEN "JEDETAIL" FOR INPUT AS #2
3550  LET NO.OF.JE = 0
3560  WHILE NOT EOF(2)
3570  LET NO.OF.JE = NO.OF.JE + 1
3580  INPUT #2, JE.NO%(NO.OF.JE), JE.ACCT%(NO.OF.JE), JE.AMT#(NO.OF.JE)
3590  WEND
3600  CLOSE #2
3610  RETURN
4000  ' ================================================================
4010  '             ENTER MONTH AND OPEN OUTPUT FILE
4020  ' ================================================================
4030  PRINT
4040  INPUT "Please enter 3 letters to identify the posting month: ",
            MONTH$
4050  OPEN "COA.TMP" FOR OUTPUT AS #3
4060  RETURN
5000  ' ================================================================
5010  '             POST TO ACCOUNTS AND PRINT REPORT
5020  ' ================================================================
5030  FOR INDEX = 1 TO NO.OF.ACCTS
5040     GOSUB  5100              'Process Next Account
5050  NEXT INDEX
5060  RETURN
5100  ' *******************************************************
5110  '             Process Next Account
5120  ' *******************************************************
5130  PRINT USING "Acct: #### Name\                        \ ";
                  ACCT.NO%(INDEX), ACCT.NAME$(INDEX);
5135  PRINT TAB(55) "Beg Bal:" TAB(65);
5137  PRINT USING AMT.MASK$; ACCT.BAL#(INDEX)
```

```
5140 FOR COUNT = 1 TO NO.OF.JE        ' Post Matching Journal Entries
5150     IF JE.ACCT%(COUNT) = ACCT.NO%(INDEX) THEN GOSUB 5300
5160 NEXT COUNT
5170 PRINT TAB(55) "End Bal:" TAB(65);
5180 PRINT USING AMT.MASK$; ACCT.BAL#(INDEX)
5185 PRINT
5190 WRITE #3, ACCT.NO%(INDEX), ACCT.NAME$(INDEX), ACCT.BAL#(INDEX)
5200 LET BALANCE# = BALANCE# + ACCT.BAL#(INDEX)
5210 RETURN
5300 ' -----------------------------------------------------
5310 '          Post Matching Journal Entries
5320 ' -----------------------------------------------------
5330 PRINT USING "                    JE No: #####"; JE.NO%(COUNT);
5340 PRINT TAB(65);: PRINT USING AMT.MASK$; JE.AMT#(COUNT)
5345 LET ACCT.BAL#(INDEX) = ACCT.BAL#(INDEX) + JE.AMT#(COUNT)
5350 RETURN
6000 ' =====================================================
6010 '          RENAME FILES
6020 ' =====================================================
6030 WRITE #3, 9999, "END OF FILE", 0          ' Write Ending Record
6040 CLOSE #3
6050 PRINT
6060 PRINT USING " >>>>>  BALANCE IS >>>>>  ###,###,###.##"; BALANCE#
6070 IF BALANCE# > -.005 AND BALANCE# < .005 THEN GOSUB 6200
        ELSE PRINT " ** WARNING!! OUT OF BALANCE!! FILES NOT RENAMED!!"
6080 LET KEEP.ON.GOING = FALSE
6090 RETURN
6200 ' -----------------------------------------------------------
6210 '          Ok to Rename Files
6220 ' -----------------------------------------------------------
6230 CLS
6240 PRINT "Processing Successful - Files are now being Renamed"
6250 NAME "CHARTOF.ACT" AS "COA." + MONTH$
6260 NAME "COA.TMP"     AS "CHARTOF.ACT"
6270 NAME "JETITLE"     AS "JETITLE." + MONTH$
6280 NAME "JEDETAIL"    AS "JEDETAIL." + MONTH$
6290 PRINT
6300 PRINT   "Old files are named:"
6310 PRINT   "    Previous Chart of Accounts:    "; "COA." + MONTH$
6320 PRINT   "    Previous Journal Entry Title: "; "JETITLE." + MONTH$
6330 PRINT   "    Previous Journal Entry Detail: "; "JEDETAIL." + MONTH$
6340 PRINT
6350 PRINT   "PLEASE MAKE COPIES OF THESE FILES FOR HISTORICAL RECORDS"
6360 PRINT   "    THEN ERASE THEM FROM THE DISK"
9000 ' =====================================================
9010 '          END OF LISTING
9020 ' =====================================================
```

PROGRAM OUTPUT FROM POSTJE.BAS

We will now run this program to post the two Journal Entries shown in "Program Output for ENTERJE.BAS."

```
**  This Program Will Update The Chart of Account Balances **
    Be sure you have current backup copies of the files before you continue
    Do you wish to continue with this process (Y or N)? y
```

[(screen clears)]

```
 >>>   READING CHART OF ACCOUNTS  <<<

 >>>   READING JOURNAL ENTRY FILE  <<<

Please enter 3 letters to identify the posting month: MAY
```

[(screen clears)]

```
Acct: 1001 Name Cash in Checking Account    Beg Bal:      13,875.75
               JE No:    15                               -9,000.00
               JE No:    31                               -1,000.00
                                            End Bal:       3,875.75


Acct: 1010 Name Petty Cash                  Beg Bal:          50.00
                                            End Bal:          50.00


Acct: 2010 Name Assets: Office Furniture    Beg Bal:      45,700.00
                                            End Bal:      45,700.00


Acct: 2020 Name Assets: Equipment           Beg Bal:      67,705.86
                                            End Bal:      67,705.86


Acct: 2500 Name Accumulated Depreciation    Beg Bal:     -25,000.00
                                            End Bal:     -25,000.00


Acct: 4100 Name Withholding Payable         Beg Bal:      -5,600.00
               JE No:    31                                 -500.00
                                            End Bal:      -6,100.00


Acct: 4500 Name Accounts Payable            Beg Bal:     -23,864.90
                                            End Bal:     -23,864.90


Acct: 4520 Name Notes Payable               Beg Bal:      -8,525.65
                                            End Bal:      -8,525.65


Acct: 6100 Name Capital Stock               Beg Bal:     -30,000.00
                                            End Bal:     -30,000.00
```

```
Acct: 6200 Name Retained Earnings          Beg Bal:     56,188.86
                                           End Bal:     56,188.86


Acct: 7100 Name Income: Sale of Goods      Beg Bal:   -705,976.98
                                           End Bal:   -705,976.98


Acct: 7200 Name Income: Services           Beg Bal:    -13,000.00
                                           End Bal:    -13,000.00


Acct: 7300 Name Income: Other              Beg Bal:     -1,059.00
                                           End Bal:     -1,059.00


Acct: 8000 Name Salaries - Professional    Beg Bal:    359,700.00
           JE No:    31                                  1,500.00
                                           End Bal:    361,200.00


Acct: 8100 Name Salaries - Clerical        Beg Bal:    125,079.00
                                           End Bal:    125,079.00


Acct: 8200 Name Salaries - Other           Beg Bal:     50,100.00
                                           End Bal:     50,100.00


Acct: 8300 Name Employee Benefits          Beg Bal:     25,100.50
                                           End Bal:     25,100.50


Acct: 8500 Name Expenses: Rent             Beg Bal:     45,000.00
           JE No:    15                                  9,000.00
                                           End Bal:     54,000.00


Acct: 8510 Name Expenses: Utilities        Beg Bal:      5,836.98
                                           End Bal:      5,836.98


Acct: 8700 Name Expenses: Supplies         Beg Bal:      3,000.00
                                           End Bal:      3,000.00


Acct: 8800 Name Expenses: Vehicles         Beg Bal:     15,689.58
                                           End Bal:     15,689.58




   >>>>>  BALANCE IS >>>>>           0.00
```

(screen clears)

```
Processing Successful - Files are now being Renamed

Old files are named:
   Previous Chart of Accounts:    COA.MAY
   Previous Journal Entry Title:  JETITLE.MAY
```

```
      Previous Journal Entry Detail: JEDETAIL.MAY
  PLEASE MAKE COPIES OF THESE FILES FOR HISTORICAL RECORDS
      THEN ERASE THEM FROM THE DISK
Ok
```

· EXERCISES ·

1. Run "ENTERJE.BAS" and enter the two Journal Entries shown in "Program Output for "ENTERJE.BAS" and exit from the program.
   a. Run the program again and enter the following Journal Entry. Number: 20; Date: 051087; Description: Sale of Blue Widgets.

Acct 1001 Cash in Checking Account	1501.75
Acct 7100 Income: Sale of Goods	−1501.75

   b. Make up some Journal Entries of your own and enter them.
   c. Try entering an account number that is not in the Chart of Accounts.
   d. Try writing a Journal Entry that is not in balance.

2. After entering the Journal Entries described in Exercise 1 and any of your own, run the program "POSTJE.BAS". Enter MAY as the posting month. What do you observe about the posting report? Exercise 9 asks you to change this.

3. Currently if an error is made in entering a Journal Entry, the program ENTERJE.BAS requires that the entire Journal Entry be reentered. Modify the program so that after all the detail has been entered for a Journal Entry, the lines are displayed and changes may be made. Design the screen to be as user friendly as possible.

4. (Requires Chapters 11 and 12.) Redesign the screen display for entry in the program ENTERJE.BAS. One possible screen is as follows:

```
      ENTER JOURNAL ENTRIES
JE NO: _____          DATE: __/__/__
DESCRIPTION: _____
      DETAIL LINES
  GL ACCT #: _____   NAME:_____  AMOUNT: _____

  GL ACCT #: _____   NAME:_____  AMOUNT: _____
```
   All messages print on the bottom line of the screen.

5. For audit purposes it is desirable to have a permanent record of all Journal Entries. Therefore, modify ENTERJE.BAS to print each Journal Entry as it is written to disk. Print the description followed by all of the detail lines for that Journal Entry. Design a format of your own or create one similar to the screen layout in Exercise 4.

6. As ENTERJE.BAS is currently written, Journal Entries can be given duplicate numbers. Modify the routine to input the Journal Entry numbers currently in JETITLE into an array at the start of the program. Verify that the new number entered does not duplicate any already entered.

7. a. Write a program that uses just the file JETITLE to print a listing of the Journal Entries. The list shows JE.NO, JE.DATE, and JE.DESC$.

b. Instead of printing the listing in the order found in the file, read the file into an array (maximum 1500), sort by Journal Entry number, and print the report in that sequence. Use the Shell sort.

c. (Requires Chapter 11.) If you wanted to sort by Journal Entry date, how would you do it? Remember that the date was stored as mmddyy.

8. Write a program that uses both JETITLE and JEDETAIL to print a listing of Journal Entries. Print the descriptive data followed by all of the detail lines.

You may assume that both files have been sorted into Journal Entry sequence and that there is at least one transaction per description.

9. a. The posting report printed in the program POSTJE.BAS does not pause for the user to read each screen. Modify the program to halt at the end of each screen until the user presses a key to continue.

b. Change POSTJE.BAS to produce the posting report on the printer. Improve the design of the report to make it more readable.

Using Files and Arrays for Decision Support: Production Scheduling at ABC Widget

Chapters Required: Part I and Part II, Chapters 7 through 11.

This case study demonstrates the use of both files and arrays to solve a production scheduling problem. The user inputs a projected schedule, and the program prints the resulting production report. The program allows the user to enter a variety of alternative schedules and observe the projected results prior to selecting one for implementation.

Problem Specification

Every morning seemed the same after a short while at ABC Widget Manufacturing, thought Jo. At 8 A.M. her job was to find out who's coming in and who's sick, then make out a production schedule for the day. Ideally, the production schedule assigned people to each of the eight production steps in such a way that no backlogs would develop at any station during the day.

In reality some stations always overproduced while others lagged. The result was that station X might have nothing to do, while station Y, next in line, would be swamped with unprocessed widgets. On an average day Jo spent as much of her time bailing out backlogged stations as managing the shop, her main duty.

Then, one day, inspiration struck. Jo realized that their computer could be used, not just for accounting and financial applications, but for production scheduling as well. Jo was also fortunate enough to know a little about programming the IBM PC in BASIC and to have access to a PC at work. She decided to write a production scheduling program.

Jo's first step was to take a fresh look at the production line. The manufacturing of widgets had always seemed obvious to her, but Jo knew that to a computer nothing was obvious. Each step in the scheduling process had to be defined in precise, logical terms.

"Widgets," explained Jo, "are developed in stages, which we call production stations. The first station starts with the core of the widget, purchased from one of our suppliers, and adds the wingnuts. This result goes to the second station, which adds the arms, then sends the result to the third station, which bolts the widget together, and so forth through the eight stations. The last station puts the widget in the package and stocks it for later shipment.

"Suppose we call the stations 1 through 8. The productivity of each station can be measured in terms of widgets per hour (WPH) processed. I know the speed with which each of our employees can work at each of the stations (see Table IV.1). For example, Mary can add wingnuts to 142 widgets per hour, while Fred can do 145. If I assign Mary to the first station, its throughput will be 142 WPH. If I assign Fred, the throughput will be 145 WPH, while if I assign both of them to the first station, throughput will be 287 WPH.

"Obviously, any one station cannot work on widgets it hasn't yet received from the previous station. This means that no more widgets can come out of a station over the course of a day than go into it (see Figure IV.1).

TABLE IV.1 ▪ *Widget per Hour Rating, by Employee and Station*

	STATION							
EMPLOYEE	*1*	*2*	*3*	*4*	*5*	*6*	*7*	*8*
Mary S.	142	29	78	94	164	153	49	159
Jane P.	138	30	82	90	149	156	48	156
Fred R.	145	28	76	95	155	149	49	160
Albert A.	147	31	79	92	153	157	47	158
Murray J.	139	32	81	96	159	151	52	171
Bernice J.	143	28	83	91	158	156	51	171

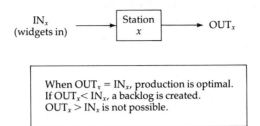

When $OUT_x = IN_x$, production is optimal.
If $OUT_x < IN_x$, a backlog is created.
$OUT_x > IN_x$ is not possible.

Production at a single station

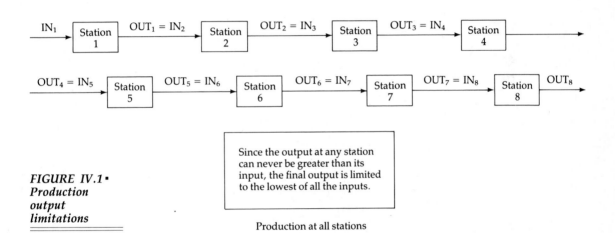

FIGURE IV.1 •
Production
output
limitations

Since the output at any station
can never be greater than its
input, the final output is limited
to the lowest of all the inputs.

Production at all stations

"For the shop as a whole, the output of the last station is the same as the output of the whole shop. Yet the output of the shop as a whole is as slow as the slowest station. Achieving efficient production is a matter of putting the proper workers at the proper station for the proper number of hours.

"I have been filling our a daily assignment sheet of who will work how many hours at each station (see Table IV.2), and from that calculating the productivity at each station (see Table IV.3). When one person is off, I have to rearrange the hours to figure out the most effective schedule, and this takes a considerable amount of time. I should be able to use the computer to do it much more quickly."

To accomplish this on the computer, Jo came up with the following solution.

1. Permanently store in a file on disk the widgets per hour each employee can produce at each station.
2. Each day enter in a projected schedule of the number of hours each employee is to work at each station that day.
3. Have the program use the employee Widgets per Hour file to calculate and print out the projected output for that day. The program also

TABLE IV.2 ▪ *Daily Assignment Sheet, by Employee and Station*

EMPLOYEE	HOURS AT STATION	STATION 1	2	3	4	5	6	7	8	TOTAL HOURS
Mary S.			1			3		4		8
Jane P.			5	1			1	1		8
Fred R.		1			4			2	1	8
Albert A.		2	4				2			8
Murray J.			5		1			2		8
Bernice J.				5				1	2	8

TABLE IV.3 ▪ *Manual Production Report*

EMPLOYEE	STATION 1	2	3	4	5	6	7	8
Mary S.		29			492		196	
Jane P.		150	82			156	48	
Fred R.	145			380			98	160
Albert A.	294	124				314		
Murray J.		160		96			104	
Bernice J.			415				51	342
Totals	439	463	497	476	492	470	497	502

Minimum = 439   Maximum = 502   Variance = 63

indicates the station with the greatest and least output and the variation between the two.

4. If the variation on the projected schedule is too great, revise the schedule and print a new report.

FUNCTIONS TO BE PERFORMED

A. Create file with employee widget per hour rates
   1. This file will be named "WPH.DAT"
   2. The file will consist of the following (see Figure IV.2):
      a. The number of employees
      b. The number of stations
      c. For each employee, the name of the employee followed by his or her productivity at each of the stations

(The program to produce this file is not shown here since it is similar to programs illustrated in earlier chapters.)

B. Program to enter schedule and print production
   1. Input the data from the file WPH.DAT into memory
      a. Place the names in the array EMPLOYEE.NAME$, a one-dimension array with subscript NUM.EMPLOYEES
      b. Place the widget per hour ratings in the array WPH (widgets per hour), a two-dimension array with subscripts NUM.EMPLOYEES and NUM.STATIONS
   2. Enter the projected schedule
      a. Display each name and ask for the hours at each station
      b. Place the hours entered in the array ASSIGN, a two-dimension array with subscripts NUM.EMPLOYEES and NUM.STATIONS
   3. Calculate the throughput
      a. Multiply each element of the array WPH by the corresponding element of the array ASSIGN and store the results in the array PTABLE, a two-dimension array with subscripts NUM.EMPLOYEES and NUM.STATIONS

FIGURE IV.2 ▪
File Layout for
WPH.DAT

Filename: WPH.DAT

First item: Number of Employees (integer)

Second item: Number of Stations (integer)

Followed by the following for each employee:

    Employee Name (string)
    Widgets/hr at Station 1 (integer)

            .
            .

    Widgets/hr at Last Station (integer)

   b. Calculate total produced at each station and store results in the array PRODUCTION, a one-dimension array with the subscript NUM.STATIONS
   c. Calculate the highest number produced, the lowest number produced, the variation, and the variation percent
4. Print the results
   a. Print the projected assignment schedule
   b. Print the production report for this assignment
5. Inquire if another schedule is to be entered
   a. If yes, repeat steps 2 through 5

STRUCTURE CHART

Jo designed the program, drew a structure chart (see Figure IV.3), and then began to write the pseudocode for each module of the structure chart.

DATA DICTIONARY

DATA from File WPH.DAT
Header Record

NUM.EMPLOYEES	Number of employees
NUM.STATIONS	Number of work stations in assembly line

For Each Employee

EMPLOYEE.NAME$()	Employee name, placed in one-dimension array

Followed By, For Each Station

WPH()	Widgets/hour employee can produce at a particular station, placed in two-dimension array

Working Arrays

ASSIGN()	Assignment for the day, two-dimension array
PTABLE()	Calculated production array, two-dimension array
PRODUCTION()	Totals for each station, one-dimension array

Working Variables

HIGH.STATION	Station with the highest production
HIGH.PRODUCED	Largest amount produced

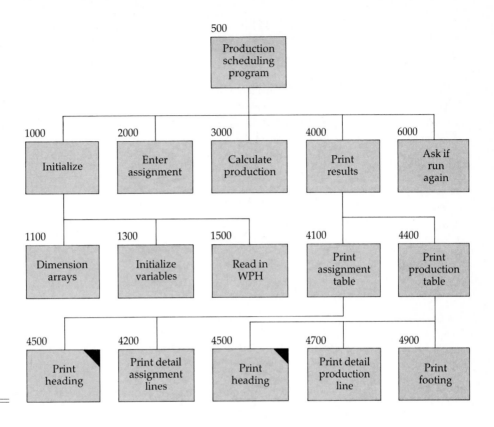

FIGURE IV.3 •
Structure chart
for production
scheduling

LOW.STATION	Station with the lowest production
LOW.PRODUCED	Lowest amount produced
REPORT.NAME$	Heading
VARIATION	Difference between highest and lowest produced
VARIATION.PERCENT	Variation expressed as a percentage

Switches

MORE2DO	True/false variable to control while loop

Constants

TRUE	Initialized to −1
FALSE	Initialized to 0

Counters

I	Subscript — number of employees
J	Subscript — number of stations

Pseudocode

MAIN LINE
    Do INITIALIZE
    WHILE MORE2DO is TRUE
        Do ENTER-ASSIGNMENT-TABLE
        Do CALCULATE-PRODUCTION
        Do PRINT-RESULTS
        Do ASK-IF-WANT-TO-RUN-AGAIN
    WEND

INITIALIZE
    Do DIMENSION-ARRAYS
    Do INITIALIZE-VARIABLES
    Do READ-IN-WPH-TABLE

DIMENSION-ARRAYS
    Define integer variables
    OPEN "WPH.DAT" FOR INPUT
    INPUT number of employees and number of stations
    Dimension as two dimension with subscripts NUM.EMPLOYEES and
        NUM.STATIONS
        WPH (widgets per hour for each employee at each station)
        ASSIGN (hours each employee is assigned to each station)
        PTABLE (calculated production of each employee at each station)
    Dimension as one dimension
        EMPLOYEE.NAME$ (employees' names)—subscript is
            NUM.EMPLOYEES
        PRODUCTION (calculated total production at each station) subscript
            is NUM.STATIONS

In this program, assignments will be for whole hours only. Therefore, the hours and the numbers of widgets will all be integers. The only noninteger will be the percent of variation. The program uses a DEFINT statement to set all numeric variables that begin with the letters A through U or with W to integers.

Storing the number of employees and the number of stations in the file rather than storing them as variables in the program allows this program to be used for different numbers of employees and stations without having to modify the program. Only the data in the file need to be changed. This is called **parameterization.** Notice that these are input into the program before the arrays are dimensioned. Also notice that OPTION BASE 1 is used since we want the arrays to begin with 1 not 0.

```
---------------------------------------------------------
INITIALIZE-VARIABLES
    Set HIGH and LOW station and produced to initial values
    Define TRUE and FALSE
    Set MORE2DO to TRUE
---------------------------------------------------------
READ-IN-WPH-TABLE
    FOR I = 1 to number of employees
        INPUT EMPLOYEE.NAME$
        FOR J = 1 to number of stations
            INPUT WPH (Widgets per Hour)
        NEXT station
    NEXT employee
    CLOSE WPH.DAT
```

As soon as all the data are input from the file, the file is closed since it will not be needed again in the program.

```
---------------------------------------------------------
---------------------------------------------------------
ENTER ASSIGNMENT-TABLE
    Print message to enter hours for each employee at each station
    FOR I = 1 to number of employees
        Print employee's name
        For J = 1 to number of stations
            INPUT hours at each station
        Next station
    Next employee
---------------------------------------------------------
---------------------------------------------------------
CALCULATE-PRODUCTION
    FOR I = 1 to number of employees
        FOR J = 1 to number of stations
            Calculate employee's productivity at this station and store in
                array PTABLE
        Next station
    Next employee
```

To calculate the number of widgets produced by each employee at each station, the element in the array WPH is multiplied by the corresponding element in the array ASSIGN and the result stored in the array PTABLE. Notice that throughout the program I is used as the counter for NUM.EMPLOYEES and J is used as the counter for NUM.STATIONS. This makes the program easier to follow.

```
For J = 1 to number of stations
    Set PRODUCTION for this station to zero
```

```
            FOR I = 1 to number of employees
                    Add this employee's production to PRODUCTION for station
            NEXT employee
            Test for highest and lowest PRODUCTION
      NEXT station
      Calculate VARIATION as difference between highest and lowest PRODUCTION
      IF lowest PRODUCTION is greater than zero
            THEN calculate VARIATION.PERCENT
            ELSE set VARIATION.PERCENT to zero
```

The variation is the difference between the highest and lowest number of widgets produced. To prevent accidental division by zero, LOW.PRODUCED is tested, and the division takes place only if it is greater than zero. Since the DEFINT statement defined only variables beginning with *A* through *U* and *W* as integers, VARIATION and VARIATION.PERCENT will be single precision rather than integers.

```
-------------------------------------------------------
-------------------------------------------------------

PRINT-RESULTS
      Do PRINT-ASSIGNMENT-TABLE
      Do PRINT-PRODUCTION-TABLE
-------------------------------------------------------

PRINT-ASSIGNMENT-TABLE
      Set REPORT.NAME$ to "Work Assignment Table"
      Do PRINT-HEADING
      Do PRINT-DETAIL-ASSIGNMENT-LINES
-------------------------------------------------------

PRINT-PRODUCTION-TABLE
      Set REPORT.NAME$ to "Widget Production Report"
      Do PRINT-HEADING
      Do PRINT-DETAIL-PRODUCTION-LINES
```

Because both of the tables are similar, they can use the same subroutine to print the heading. The only difference will be the value that is assigned to the string REPORT.NAME$.

```
-------------------------------------------------------

PRINT-HEADING
      PRINT REPORT.NAME$
      PRINT "Employee" and on same line,
      FOR J = 1 TO number of stations
            PRINT station number
      NEXT station
      PRINT line under heading
```

We want to print a line under the heading. Rather than print it across the entire screen, we will calculate the number by multiplying the number of stations times the 4 spaces allowed for each value plus the 16 allowed for the employee's name.

PRINT-DETAIL-ASSIGNMENT-LINES
    FOR I = 1 TO number of employees
        PRINT EMPLOYEE.NAME$(I) and on same line,
        FOR J = 1 TO number of stations
            PRINT ASSIGN(I,J) — hours this employee assigned to this station
        NEXT station
        PRINT
    NEXT employee
    PRINT line at end of table

PRINT-DETAIL-PRODUCTION-LINES
    FOR I = 1 TO number of employees
        PRINT EMPLOYEE.NAME$(I) and on same line,
        FOR J = 1 TO number of stations
            PRINT PTABLE(I,J) — Calculated production of this employee at
                this station
        NEXT station
        PRINT
    NEXT employee
    PRINT line at end of table
    PRINT "Totals" and on same line,
    FOR J = 1 TO number of stations
        PRINT PRODUCTION(J) — total production at this station
    NEXT station
    PRINT Highest, Lowest, and Variation

ASK-IF-WANT-TO-RUN-AGAIN
    PRINT inquiry
    INPUT ANS$
    IF ANS$ is not affirmative
        THEN set MORE2TO to FALSE
        ELSE Do INITIALIZE-VARIABLES

The user is asked if another set is to be entered. By using LEFT$ and testing for either an uppercase or lowercase Y, the program will accept Y, y, YES, Yes, or yes as positive answers. Any answer other than one beginning with a y or Y will be considered a negative answer.

The portion of the initialization subroutine that sets the high and low variables is called again from this module so that the variables will be reinitialized for another run.

PROGRAM LISTING

```
100 'Program Name: SCHEDULE.BAS
110 'Written by:   Jo Parness
120 'Date written: August 3, 1988
130 '
140 '
150 '    WIDGET PRODUCTION SCHEDULING
160 '
170 '    Load widget per hr data from file WPH.DAT
180 '    Enter employee assignments and
190 '       Number of hours at each station
200 '    Print Schedule and Production Report
210 '
220 '
500 ' ***********************************
510 ' *******    main  line     ********
520 ' ***********************************
530 GOSUB 1000          'Initialize
540 WHILE MORE2DO        ' MORE2DO will be true until user indicates done
550       GOSUB 2000     'Enter assignment table
560       GOSUB 3000     'Calculate production
570       GOSUB 4000     'Print results
580       GOSUB 6000     'Ask if want to run again
590 WEND
600 END
610 ' ***********************************
620 ' *******  end of processing  ********
630 ' ***********************************
1000 '*******      Initialize      *******
1010 ' -----------------------------------
1020 GOSUB 1100           'Dimension Arrays
1030 GOSUB 1300             'Initialize Variables
1040 GOSUB 1500             'Read in WPH table
1050 RETURN
1060 '
1100 '         Dimension Arrays
1110 '
1120 DEFINT A-U, W
1130 OPEN "WPH.DAT" FOR INPUT AS #1
1140 INPUT #1, NUM.EMPLOYEES     ' input number of employees from file
1150 INPUT #1, NUM.STATIONS      ' input number of stations from file
1160 OPTION BASE 1
1170 DIM WPH(NUM.EMPLOYEES, NUM.STATIONS)          'work per hour array
1180 DIM ASSIGN(NUM.EMPLOYEES,NUM.STATIONS)        'assignment for the day
1190 DIM PTABLE(NUM.EMPLOYEES,NUM.STATIONS)        'calculated production array
1200 DIM EMPLOYEE.NAME$(NUM.EMPLOYEES)             'employee name array
1210 DIM PRODUCTION(NUM.STATIONS)                  'totals for each station
```

```
3140        GOSUB 5000            'accumulate totals
3150 '        subtract number of customers checked out during the period
3160      LET NUM.CUST.CHECKOUT = NUM.CUST.CHECKOUT -
                    INT(NUM.CLERKS * (RATE.HOUR / PERIODS))
3170    NEXT MI
3180 NEXT HOUR
3190 RETURN
3200 '
4000 '#####################################################
4010 '*****                  print results                 *****
4020 PRINT
4030 '
4040 PRINT    "    <------- CUSTOMERS ------->       <--- CLERKS --->"
4050 PRINT    "hr    min    aver    max   actual    high  low  average"
4060 LET F1$="##  #,###   #,###   #,###   #,###       ###   ###  ###.#"
4070 '
4080 '    print averages for each hour
4090 '
4100 FOR HOUR = 1 TO NUM.HOURS
4110     PRINT USING F1$; HOUR, CUST.MIN(HOUR), CUST.AVG(HOUR),
              CUST.MAX(HOUR), CUST.COUNT(HOUR)/NUM.DAYS, CLK.HI(HOUR),
              CLK.LO(HOUR), CLK.TOT(HOUR)/PERIODS/NUM.DAYS
4120 NEXT HOUR
4130 RETURN
4140 '
5000 ' ----------------------------------------------------
5010 '                  accumulate totals
5020 ' ----------------------------------------------------
5030     'get new high, low number of clerks for this hour
5040 IF NUM.CLERKS > CLK.HI(HOUR) THEN LET CLK.HI(HOUR) = NUM.CLERKS
5050 IF NUM.CLERKS < CLK.LO(HOUR) THEN LET CLK.LO(HOUR) = NUM.CLERKS
5060 '  add number of clerks this period to the total
5070 LET CLK.TOT(HOUR) = CLK.TOT(HOUR) + NUM.CLERKS
5080 '  add number of new customers to the customer count
5090 LET CUST.COUNT(HOUR) = CUST.COUNT(HOUR) + NEW.CUST.PERIOD
5100 RETURN
5110 '
5120 '
5130 '  ***** end of program listing  *********
```

PROGRAM OUTPUT

```
Working on Day   1
****
Working on Day   2
****
Working on Day   3
****
```

```
        <------- CUSTOMERS ------->      <--- CLERKS --->
   hr    min    aver    max   actual     high   low   average
    1      90    120     150    120        5      3     3.8
    2     100    150     190    152        6      4     4.9
    3     110    155     180    141        6      4     4.7
    4      80    100     110     97        5      3     3.4
   Ok
```

As we see from the preceding, the simulation suggested to management that they need three clerks all of the time during the beginning and ending hours and a fourth clerk available to check during about half of those hours. For the middle two hours, a minimum of four clerks is needed with a fifth needed for most of that time. Occasionally a sixth will also be needed.

Because the random number generator is not reseeded, this program will yield the same results each time it is run with the same parameters. While writing and testing, you will want to have constant results so that errors can be more easily detected. After the program is thoroughly tested, a statement such as RANDOMIZE TIMER can be added to give more variation in the numbers generated.

· EXERCISES ·

1. Run "SIMULATE.BAS". Your results may differ slightly from those shown in the text because different systems generate different random numbers.
   a. Change the number of days from 3 to 6 and rerun the program. Remember, you will need to change the DATA statement in the program.
   b. Change the number of sampling periods from 15 to 30.
   c. Change the maximum line length from 6 to 3.
   d. Change the checkers rate from 30 per hour to 15.
   e. Which of these changes made the greatest difference in the results?
   f. What changes would you have to make to analyze 6 hours instead of 4?

2. Rewrite the subroutine that simulates arrivals (lines 5000–5070) to use the exponential distribution that assumes that the number of new customers arriving each hour is given by the following formula:

   # of customers $= -1 *$ average per hour $* \log(1 - RND)$

3. Add RANDOMIZE or RANDOMIZE TIMER to the program. Run the program three times. Are the results the same?

4. Change the READ . . . DATA statements to INPUT statements.
   a. First change it so that just the number of days (NUM.DAYS), the number of periods (PERIODS), the maximum line length (MAX.LENGTH), and checker speed (RATE.HOUR) are entered through INPUT statements.
   b. Second, change the program so that the number of consecutive hours to be analyzed and the customer statistics are entered through INPUT statements. (Add a validation test so that no more than 24 hours are entered.)

    c. Organize the program so that

        1) the number of hours and customer data are entered only once at the beginning of the program and,

        2) after the report is printed, the program inquires if the user wishes to try another combination of figures.

        3) if the user responds affirmatively, only the data listed in (a) of this exercise are reentered.

5. If you change the program so the number of hours is entered by the user as described in Exercise 4.b, how could you change the DIM statements so that no more room than necessary is taken by the arrays?

APPENDIX A

ASCII Table

ASCII VALUE	CHARACTER	CONTROL CHARACTER	ASCII VALUE	CHARACTER
000	(null)	NUL	032	(space)
001	☺	SOH	033	!
002	●	STX	034	"
003	♥	ETX	035	#
004	♦	EOT	036	$
005	♣	ENQ	037	%
006	♠	ACK	038	&
007	(beep)	BEL	039	'
008	■ (back space)	BS	040	(
009	(tab)	HT	041	)
010	(line feed)	LF	042	*
011	(home)	VT	043	+
012	(form feed)	FF	044	,
013	(carriage return)	CR	045	–
014	♫	SO	046	.
015	☼	SI	047	/
016	►	DLE	048	0
017	◄	DC1	049	1
018	↕	DC2	050	2
019	!!	DC3	051	3
020	¶	DC4	052	4
021	§	NAK	053	5
022	▬	SYN	054	6
023	↨	ETB	055	7
024	↑	CAN	056	8
025	↓	EM	057	9
026	→	SUB	058	:
027	←	ESC	059	;
028	(cursor right)	FS	060	<
029	(cursor left)	GS	061	=
030	(cursor up)	RS	062	>
031	(cursor down)	US	063	?

ASCII VALUE	CHARACTER	ASCII VALUE	CHARACTER	ASCII VALUE	CHARACTER
064	@	096	`	128	Ç
065	A	097	a	129	ü
066	B	098	b	130	é
067	C	099	c	131	â
068	D	100	d	132	ä
069	E	101	e	133	à
070	F	102	f	134	å
071	G	103	g	135	ç
072	H	104	h	136	ê
073	I	105	i	137	ë
074	J	106	j	138	è
075	K	107	k	139	ï
076	L	108	l	140	î
077	M	109	m	141	ì
078	N	110	n	142	Ä
079	O	111	o	143	Å
080	P	112	p	144	É
081	Q	113	q	145	æ
082	R	114	r	146	Æ
083	S	115	s	147	ô
084	T	116	t	148	ö
085	U	117	u	149	ò
086	V	118	v	150	û
087	W	119	w	151	ù
088	X	120	x	152	ÿ
089	Y	121	y	153	Ö
090	Z	122	z	154	Ü
091	[	123	{	155	¢
092	\	124	¦	156	£
093	]	125	}	157	¥
094	∧	126	~	158	Pt
095	_	127	⌂	159	ƒ

ASCII VALUE	CHARACTER	ASCII VALUE	CHARACTER	ASCII VALUE	CHARACTER
160	á	192	└	224	α
161	í	193	┴	225	β
162	ó	194	┬	226	Γ
163	ú	195	├	227	π
164	ñ	196	─	228	Σ
165	Ñ	197	┼	229	σ
166	a̱	198	╞	230	μ
167	o̱	199	╟	231	τ
168	¿	200	╚	232	Φ
169	⌐	201	╔	233	Θ
170	¬	202	╩	234	Ω
171	½	203	╦	235	δ
172	¼	204	╠	236	∞
173	¡	205	═	237	Ø
174	«	206	╬	238	∈
175	»	207	╧	239	∩
176	░	208	╨	240	≡
177	▒	209	╤	241	±
178	▓	210	╥	242	≥
179	│	211	╙	243	≤
180	┤	212	╘	244	⌠
181	╡	213	╒	245	⌡
182	╢	214	╓	246	÷
183	╖	215	╫	247	≈
184	╕	216	╪	248	°
185	╣	217	┘	249	•
186	║	218	┌	250	·
187	╗	219	█	251	√
188	╝	220	▄	252	ⁿ
189	╜	221	▌	253	²
190	╛	222	▐	254	∎
191	┐	223	▀	255	(blank 'FF')

INDEX

BASIC Reserved Words and Examples

Reserved Word	Type/Example	Explanation
ABS()	Function **PRINT ABS(X)**	Gives the absolute value of the argument
Arithmetic Operators	^ - * / \ MOD + —	exponentiation negation multiplication division integer division integer remainder after integer division addition subtraction
ASC()	Function **PRINT ASC("A")**	Returns the ASCII value of a character
ATN()	Function **PRINT ATN(3)**	Generates the arctangent (in radians) of the argument
AUTO	Command **AUTO** **AUTO 100, 20**	Automatically generates line numbers. Canceled by Ctrl-Break Begins with line 10, increments by 10 Begins with 100, increments by 20
BEEP	Statement **IF AMOUNT < 0 THEN BEEP**	Causes computer to sound a beep. Is equivalent to CHR$(7)
CDBL()	Function **PRINT CDBL(SOME.NUMBER)**	Converts the argument to a double precision number
CHR$()	Function **PRINT CHR$(65)**	Returns a character with specified ASCII value
CINT()	Function **LET INT.VALUE% = CINT(SINGLE.VALUE)**	Converts single or double precision to a rounded integer
CIRCLE	Statement **CIRCLE (5,10), 30, 2, −5, −20** **5,10** coordinate of center of circle **30** radius of circle (in points) **2** color attribute **−5,−20** starting and ending points (radians)	Draws an arc, sector, or circle on the screen
CLOSE	Statement **CLOSE #1, #2**	Removes one or more files from ready status
CLS	Statement **CLS**	Clears the screen
COLOR	Statement **COLOR 9, 4, 14** **COLOR 8,0**	Sets the color for the screen Text mode (foreground, background, border) Medium resolution graphics (background, palette)
CONT	Command **CONT**	Resumes processing after the execution of a STOP statement
COS()	Function **PRINT COS(.79)**	Returns the cosine of the argument (must be in radians)
CSNG()	Function **LET SING.PRES = CSNG(DBL.PRES#)**	Converts a numeric variable to single precision
CSRLIN	Variable **LET HOLD.CURSOR.LINE = CSRLIN**	Contains the line on which the cursor is located

Reserved Word	Type/Example	Explanation
CVI()	Function **LET INTEGER.VALUE% = CVI(A$)**	Returns the integer that was encoded with MKI$
CVS()	Function **LET SINGLE.PRES = CVS(B$)**	Returns the single precision value that was encoded with MKS$
CVD()	Function **LET DBL.PRES# = CVD(C$)**	Returns the double precision value that was encoded with MKD$
DATA	Statement **DATA SAN FRANCISCO, 34503, 45.87**	Stores constants in a program for access by READ statement
DATE$	Variable **PRINT DATE$**	Current date as stored in system
	Statement **DATE$ = "01/01/87"**	Initializes the variable DATE$
DEF FN	Statement **DEF FNCYLIN.VOL(RADIUS, HEIGHT) = .1416 * RADIUS^2 * HEIGHT**	Defines and names a user created function
DEFtype	Statement **DEFINT B** **DEFSNG D–F** **DEFDBL K** **DEFSTR Q**	Defines variable type Defines all variables beginning with B as integers Defines all variables beginning with D, E, or F as single precision Defines all variables beginning with K as double precision Defines all variables beginning with Q as string
DELETE	Command **DELETE** **DELETE 5** **DELETE 50–100**	Erases lines of program in memory Erases entire program Erases line 5 Erases lines 50 through 100
DIM	Statement **DIM ARRAY.NAME(50), TWO.DIMENSION(15,10)**	Allocates storage for one or more arrays
DRAW	Statement **DRAW "U 2"**	Draws a line in direction and distance indicated Draw UP 2 points
EDIT	Command **EDIT 2010**	Displays a line for editing
END	Statement **END**	Terminates execution of program and returns to immediate mode Closes all open files
EOF()	Function **IF EOF(1) THEN GOSUB 9000**	Returns the value of true when the last item of a sequential file has been input
ERASE	Statement **ERASE ARRAY.NAME**	Deletes the specified array(s)
EXP()	Function **PRINT EXP(15)**	Calculates e raised to a power
FIELD	Statement **FIELD #1 10 AS AMOUNT, 15 AS LAST.NAME$, 25 AS ADDRESS$**	Defines a random file buffer
File Names	Up to 8 characters followed by an extension of a period and up to 3 characters Valid characters are letters, numbers, and following special characters **~ ' ! @ # $ % ^ & ( ) – _	\ { } '**	
FILES	Command **FILES "*.BAS"**	Displays names of files, (similar to DIR in DOS) Displays all files ending in .BAS

Reserved Word	Type/Example	Explanation
FIX()	Function	Returns number obtained by truncating decimal portion of argument
	LET NO.DECIMAL = FIX(1234.67)	
FOR . . . NEXT	Statements	Repeats the lines between FOR and NEXT a specified number of times.
	FOR I = X TO Y STEP Z (lines of program) **NEXT**	
GET	Statement	Reads a record from a random access file
	GET #1, 51	Reads 51st record into the buffer
GOSUB	Statement	Passes control to a subroutine. Resumes at line following GOSUB when RETURN is executed
	GOSUB 2000	**' PRINT HEADING**
GOTO	Statement	Branches to a specified line number
	GOTO 9000	**' EXIT ROUTINE**
IF . . . THEN . . . ELSE	Statement	Selects direction of program flow based on conditions
	IF A > 100 THEN LET DISCOUNT = .15 ELSE LET DISCOUNT = .05	
INKEY$	Variable	Accepts 1 character input from the keyboard
	LET CHOICE$ = INKEY$	
INPUT	Statement	Accepts characters from keyboard
	INPUT "MESSAGE"; A	Displays ? and space following the message
	INPUT "MESSAGE", B$	Suppresses ? and space
	INPUT C, D, E	Three variables are to be entered
	INPUT; "MESSAGE", F	Inhibits cursor movement to next line
INPUT #	Statement	Accepts input from a specified file or device
	INPUT #1, A, B, C$	
INPUT$()	Function	Accepts a specified number of characters from keyboard
	LET PASSWORD$ = INPUT$(5)	
INSTR()	Function	Returns the position at which one string begins within another.
	LET COMMA.POS = INSTR(CITY.STATE$, ",")	
INT()	Function	Returns the highest integer less than or equal to the argument
	LET WHOLE.NUMBER = INT(1234.56)	
KEY	Statement	Allows for user definition of the function keys
	KEY 5, "CHARACTERS"	
	KEY OFF	Deactivates display of key definitions
	KEY ON	Activates display of key definitions
KILL	Command	Erases a file
	KILL "OLDFILE.DAT"	
LEFT$()	Function	Returns a specified number of leftmost characters from a string
	LET LEFT.5.CHAR$ = LEFT$(ANY.STRING$, 5)	
LEN()	Function	Returns the length of a string
	IF LEN(LAST.NAME$) > 10 THEN . . .	
LET	Statement	Assigns value to a variable
	LET LAST.NAME$ = "STEVENSON"	

Reserved Word	Type/Example	Explanation
LINE	Statement	Draws a straight line or rectangle
	LINE (5,10) — (25,25), 1, BF	
	5,10 starting point	
	25,25 ending point	
	1 color attribute	
	BF filled box	
LINE INPUT	Statement	Accepts up to 254 characters from keyboard, including punctuation
	LINE INPUT "ENTER THE CITY, STATE, AND ZIP CODE: "; CITY.STATE.ZIP$	
LIST	Command	Displays program currently in memory
	LIST	Displays entire program
	LIST 10	Displays only 10
	LIST 100 – 200	Displays lines 100 through 200
LLIST	Command	Prints current program on printer
	syntax same as LIST	
LOAD	Command	Brings program from disk into memory
	LOAD "FILENAME.EXT"	
LOCATE	Statement	Locates the cursor to a specified row and column position
	LOCATE ROW, COLUMN	
LOG()	Function	Generates the natural log of the argument
	PRINT LOG(5)	
Logical Operators	**AND**	True if both expressions are true
	IF PRICE > 100 AND QUANTITY < 25 THEN . . .	
	NOT	True when condition is false and false when condition is true
	IF NOT A > 100 THEN . . . True when A is 100 or less	
	OR	Is true if either expression is true
	IF A = 50 OR B > 25 THEN . . .	
LPRINT	Statement	Sends a line of output to the printer
	Syntax same as PRINT	
LPRINT USING	Statement	Sends a formatted line of output to the printer
	Syntax same as PRINT USING	
LSET	Statement	Left justifies one character string into another
	LSET RECEIVING.STRING$ = COPIED.STRING$	
MID$	Statement	Copies characters from one string into another
	**MID$(BIG.STRING$, 3, 5) = SMALL.STRING$** copies first five characters of SMALL.STRING$ into BIG.STRING$ starting at the third position	
	Function	Returns characters from within a string
	LET SMALL.STRING$ = MID$(BIG.STRING$, 3, 5) returns five characters from BIG.STRING$ beginning at the third position	
MKI$()	Function	Returns an integer as a 2-byte string
	LET A$ = MKI$(INTEGER.VALUE%)	
MKS$()	Function	Returns a single precision number as a 4-byte string
	LET B$ = MKS$(SINGLE.PRES)	
MKD$	Function	Returns a double precision as an 8-byte string
	LET C$ = MKD$(DBL.PRES#)	
NAME	Command	Changes the name of a file
	NAME "OLDNAME.EXT" AS "NEWNAME.EXT"	
NEW	Command	Clears program and all files currently in memory
	NEW	

Reserved Word	Type/Example	Explanation
ON . . . GOSUB	Statement **ON CHOICE GOSUB 1000, 2000, 3000**	Conditional execution of a subroutine based on value of an expression
ON . . . GOTO	Statement **ON CHOICE GOTO 1000, 2000, 3000**	Conditional branching based on the value of an expression
OPEN	Statement **OPEN "FILENAME.DAT" FOR INPUT AS #** **OPEN "FILENAME.DAT" AS #1 LEN = 50**	Opens a file or device sequential file random access file
OPTION BASE	Statement **OPTION BASE 1**	Causes minimum value of subscript for all arrays to be either 0 or 1
PAINT	Statement **PAINT (X,Y), N** **PAINT (X,Y), TITLE$**	Fills an area with color or pattern Fills area containing X,Y with color Fills area containing X,Y with pattern
POS(0)	Function **LET HOLD.CURSOR.COL = POS(0)**	Returns the column position of the cursor
PRINT	Statement **PRINT PRICE, QUANTITY, TOTAL** **PRINT ACCOUNT.NUMBER; CUSTOMER$; ADDRESS$** **PRINT "HELLO";**	Displays output to the screen Displays variables in print zones Displays variables immediately next to each other Semicolon suppresses movement to next line
PRINT #	Statement **PRINT #1, ACCOUNT.NUM, CUST.NAME$**	Writes data to a sequential file
PRINT USING	Statement **PRINT USING MASK$; A, B, C$**	Displays formatted output to the screen
PRINT # USING	Statement **PRINT #1 USING MASK$; A, B, C$**	Writes formatted data to a sequential file
PUT	Statement **PUT #1, 51**	Writes a record from the buffer to a random access file Writes 51st record to file #1
RANDOMIZE	Statement **RANDOMIZE** **RANDOMIZE 345** **RANDOMIZE TIMER**	Generates a new random number seed Asks user for a number Seeds RND with number 345 Seeds RND using current time
READ	Statement **READ CITY$, ACCOUNT.NUM%, RATE**	Retrieves constants stored by the DATA statement
REM	Statement **REM *** INITIALIZATION *****	Defines a nonexecutable comment line ' may be used in place of REM
RENUM	Command **RENUM 1000, 853, 20**	Renumbers specified lines of code New linenumber, old linenumber, increment
RESTORE	Statement **RESTORE 1000**	Allows next READ to begin at specified DATA statement Next READ will retrieve from DATA statement at line 1000
RETURN	Statement **RETURN**	Resumes processing at line following a GOSUB or ON . . . GOSUB
RIGHT$()	Function **LET RIGHT.5.CHAR$ = RIGHT$(ANY.STRING$, 5)**	Returns a specified number of rightmost characters from a string

Reserved Word	Type/Example	Explanation
RND	Function	Generates a random number between 1 and 0
	RND	Next random number
	RND(X)	Where x is negative, seeds random sequence
RSET	Statement	Right justifies one character string into another
	RSET RECEIVING.STRING$ = COPIED.STRING$	
RUN	Command	Executes a program
	RUN	Executes program currently in memory
	RUN "FILENAME"	Loads program and executes it
SAVE	Command	Writes program currently in memory to disk
	SAVE "FILENAME.EXT"	
SCREEN	Statement	Sets the screen mode
	SCREEN 0,1	Text mode, color enabled
	SCREEN 1,0	Medium-resolution graphics, color enabled
	SCREEN 2	High-resolution graphics (no color)
SGN()	Function	Returns 1, 0, or − 1 based on the sign of the argument
	IF SGN(AMOUNT) = −1 THEN . . .	
SIN()	Function	Returns the sine of the argument (must be in radians)
	PRINT SIN(3)	
SPACE$	Function	Returns a string of spaces
	PRINT SPACE$(10)	
SQR()	Function	Calculates the square root of the argument
	LET DIAGONAL = SQR(A*A + B*B)	
STOP	Statement	Suspends program execution. Displays message "BREAK in line nn"
		Execution may be resumed by entering CONT
	STOP	
STR$()	Function	Returns the string equivalent of the argument
	LET AMOUNT$ = STR$(AMOUNT)	
STRING$()	Function	Returns a string of specified character
	PRINT STRING$(10,"*")	
SWAP	Statement	Exchanges the values of two variables
	SWAP A$, B$	
SYSTEM	Command	Returns to DOS
	SYSTEM	
TAB()	Function	Tabs to a specified position
	PRINT CUST.NAME$ TAB(35) ADDRESS$	
TAN()	Function	Returns the tangent of the argument (must be in radians)
	PRINT TAN(2.5)	
TIME$	Variable	Time stored on the system clock
	PRINT TIME$	
	Statement	Sets the system clock
	TIME$ = "08:15"	
TIMER	Function	Returns number of seconds since system clock was set to 00:00:00
	LET START.TIME = TIMER	
TROFF	Command	Deactivates tracing of program execution
	TROFF	
TRON	Command	Activates tracing of program execution
	TRON	

Reserved Word	Type/Example	Explanation
VAL()	Function **LET AMOUNT = VAL(AMOUNT\$)**	Returns the numeric value of a string
Variable Names	Maximum of 40 characters Must start with a letter Valid characters are letters, numbers, and periods May not be reserved word or start with FN	
VIEW	Statement **VIEW (165,25) — (315,130), 1, 2** **165,25** is upper left physical coordinate **315,130** is lower right physical coordinate **1** fill view port with color attribute 1 **2** draw border in color attribute 2	Defines physical coordinates into which WINDOW contents are mapped
WHILE . . . WEND	Statements **WHILE KEEP.ON.GOING = TRUE** (lines of program) **WEND**	Executes a series of statements as long as the expression is true
WIDTH	Statement **WIDTH 40** **WIDTH 80**	Sets number of characters per row 40 characters per row (med. resolution.) 80 characters per row (hi resolution.)
WINDOW	Statement **WINDOW (−25,−10) — (150,200)** **−25,−10** is lower left coordinate for figure **150,200** is upper right coordinate	Defines coordinates for graphics
WRITE #	Statement **WRITE #1, A, B, C\$**	Writes data to a sequential file